Acclaim for
Becoming the Parent You Want to Be

What the experts are saying:

"This unusually thorough book provides today's parents with rich and abundant insights for discerning and fostering wholeness in their children. This is an enormously helpful resource which sheds light on many issues that are not addressed in other books on parenting."

—POLLY BERRIEN BERENDS, author of *Whole Child, Whole Parent; Gently Lead;* and *Coming to Life*

"Through simple, direct language, touching human stories, and clear messages, the authors reveal sensitivity, understanding, and in-depth knowledge of both children's and parents' development. They know what is required for children and parents to grow and flourish. I think it will become a classic among books for parents."

—BERNICE WEISSBOURD, President, Board of Directors, Family Resource Coalition

"Loving and inspiring, *Becoming the Parent You Want to Be* is a very helpful and hopeful book for the first five years."

—WAYNE DYER, author of *Your Sacred Self*

"I am impressed by this book's thoughtful approach to the underlying issues of childrearing—the continual challenge to be and raise good people in a changing world. The *diversity* of families, children, and cultures in contemporary society is front and center in this book."

—ELIZABETH JONES, Ph.D., Faculty, Human Development, Pacific Oaks College

"This wise guide will help mothers and fathers discover and value their own unique parenting styles. I recommend it highly."

—JAMES A. LEVINE, Ed.D., Director, The Fatherhood Project, Families and Work Institute, New York City

"*Becoming the Parent You Want to Be* is sensitive to the needs of modern parents and offers practical advice for real problems. The real world stories and examples are a treasure-trove for parents looking for help. I'm going to recommend it to my colleagues and patients."

—KATHI J. KEMPER, M.D., M.P.H., author of *The Holistic Pediatrician*

"In addition to being lively, encyclopedic, and reader-friendly, this is a useful guide for parents who want to reclaim their role in the new TV-dominated cultural environment."

—GEORGE GERBNER, Dean Emeritus, The Annenberg School for Communication, Director, The Cultural Indicators Project

"Instead of prescribing a 'right way' to raise children, *Becoming the Parent You Want to Be* offers parents a wealth of ways to experiment, explore, and grow along with their children. I recommend this excellent resource wholeheartedly for parents, teachers, child care workers, foster parents, and anyone exploring their own early childhood."

—CHARLOTTE KASL, Ph.D., author of *Finding Joy* and *A Home for the Heart: Creating Intimacy and Community with Loved Ones, Neighbors, and Friends*

"A masterpiece of wisdom! It's easy to give advice and to treat parents as if they were all alike; but they aren't. It's a challenge to respond to them in all their diversity. The authors have risen to the challenge admirably."

—JANET GONZALES-MENA, author of *Dragon Mom: Confessions of a Child Development Expert*

What parents are saying:

"Love drives this book."

"*Becoming the Parent You Want to Be* is a little like being with a child—thought-provoking, challenging, and enriching; heartfelt, complex, and multifaceted."

"Your book is like a parent support group in print. One that is always available when its 3:00 A.M. and you're tearing your hair out."

"After reading your book I feel so much more at ease dealing with family conflicts and crisis. I can actually smile now whenever I start to hear my children arguing in the background."

"If every parent could read this book, we'd have a much better world."

Becoming the Parent You Want to Be

A Sourcebook of Strategies for the First Five Years

Laura Davis and Janis Keyser

BROADWAY BOOKS
NEW YORK 1997

Dear Reader:

We regret that we are unable to answer individual letters or phone calls. We do read our mail, however, and if you have feedback or responses to this book, we'd be happy to hear from you. Janis offers lectures and workshops for parents as well as training for professionals. If you are interested in bringing her to your area, or if you want to be on our mailing list, send a note to the address below.

Laura Davis and Janis Keyser
P.O. Box 4097
Santa Cruz, CA 95063-4097

For information, address Broadway Books, a division of Bantam Doubleday Dell Publishing Group, Inc.
1540 Broadway, New York, NY 10036.

Broadway Books titles may be purchased for business or promotional use or for special sales. For information, please write to: Special Markets Department, Bantam Doubleday Dell Publishing Group, Inc., 1540 Broadway, New York, NY 10036.

Library of Congress Cataloging-in-Publication Data
Davis, Laura.
Becoming the parent you want to be : a sourcebook of strategies for the first five years / Laura Davis and Janis Keyser. — 1st ed.
p. cm.
Includes index.
ISBN 0-553-06750-8 (pbk.)
1. Parenting. 2. Child rearing. I. Keyser, Janis. II. Title.
HQ755.8.D376 1997
649'.1—DC20 96-12035
CIP

Book design by Claire Naylon Vaccaro

3 5 7 9 10 8 6 4

To my sons,

Bryan Rawles and Eli Bristol Davis,

for walking me down this road

—LAURA DAVIS

To my children,

Lee John, Calvin Lee, and Maya Nell,

for keeping me honest

—JANIS KEYSER

Contents

Part Two: Children's Feelings

Part Three: Children's Bodies

Part Four: Dealing with Difficult Behavior

Part Five: Social Learning and Play

Acknowledgments

This book could not exist without parents. In Janis's classes, in interview groups, and one-on-one, hundreds of parents have shared with us their dilemmas, their struggles, and their joys. Without their collective honesty, commitment, and wisdom, this book would not be possible.

The principles and strategies presented in this book draw upon the research and theories of many visionary thinkers in the areas of child and parent development. Jean Piaget, Erik Erikson, James Hymes, and T. Berry Brazelton have provided much of the basis of the developmental information about children we present in this book. Magda Gerber has contributed specific expertise on infants and toddlers. We have also drawn from research on parents and families by Ellen Galinsky, Virginia Satir, Uri Bronfenbrenner, and Patty Wipfler. We appreciate their contributions to all families.

Together we'd like to thank:

Janet Goldstein, our editor, for supporting and nurturing this seed all the way to fruition.

Betsy Thorpe, for hard work, good cheer, and diplomacy.

The people at Broadway books who transformed our 700-page manuscript into a beautiful book: Claire Vaccaro for the striking design, Umi Kenyon for the elegant cover, and Rebecca Holland for her commitment to excellence in copyediting. We'd also like to thank Trigg Robinson, Maggie Richards, Marysarah Quinn, and everyone else who helped make this book a success.

Charlotte Raymond, our agent, for optimism, unyielding support, and hard work tackling new ground.

Our readers, whose dedication, thoughtfulness, and suggestions improved this book immeasurably: Carmen Alvarez, Mary Ashley, Cecelia Barnes, Karyn Bristol, Nancy k. Brown, Michelle Cooper, Teri and Deb Cosentino, Betty Jane Darling, Abe Davis, Temme Davis, Denny de Harne, Louise Derman-Sparks, Julie Olsen Edwards, Lisa Fitch, Janet Gellman, Janet Gonzalez-Mena, Kate Hill, Eric Hoffman, Jaimee Karroll, Miriam Kent, Vickey LaMotte, Aurora Levins Morales, Tiya Louis, Jennifer Meyer, Irene McGinty, Sharman Murphy, Jeff Norman, Taylar Nuevelle, Nona Olivia, Nop Panitchpakdi, Marta Puga, Kelsey Ramage, Eric Schoeck, Bing Shaw, Shauna Smith, Bill Underwood, Laurel Wanner, Marguerite Whittaker, Sara Woodsmith, and Karen Zelin.

Ellen Bass, for her clarity, insight, humor, and absolute belief in this book. Her incisive feedback and fabulous editing were pivotal.

Karen Zelin, for vision.

Bonnie Aldridge, for her ability to see, nurture, and photograph the beauty in people.

James Hymes, for warmth and wit; also for his careful reading of the chapter "Understanding Difficult Behavior."

Ga Lombard, Kip Nead, Leslie Lawrence-Nead, and Erin Wong, for help choosing children's books.

Monte Burke, George Gerbner, Meri Li, Parker Page, and Annamarie Pluhar, for coming through in the zero hour with research on children and television.

Francis Talamantes and the young women of the Watsonville school-aged parenting and infant development program.

Patrice Vecchione, for inspiring the children's poetry that adds so much to this book.

Janis's children: Lee for helping us get on line, Calvin for his sense of humor, and Maya for helping with names.

Others contributed time, energy, support, and resources: Jamie Allen, Lise Bixler, Kimberly Carter, Martha Chubb, Carolyn Coleman, Linda and Scott Deal, Dana Davis, Paul Davis, Ellen Farmer, Tim Fisher, Denise Fraser, Cliff and Sara Friedlander, Laurie Hammond, Leslie Ingram, Wendy Martyna, Pam McClellan, Matt and Katie McGinty, Jeff Norman, Taylar Nuevelle, Muriel Salmansohn, Jane Scolieri, and Cindy West.

Laura would like to thank:

My parents, Abe and Temme Davis, for teaching me to think for myself, to stand up for what I believe, and to care about the world beyond my doorstep.

Janet Gellman and Nancy de la Pena, Mary O'Neill and Lisa Condon, and Ellen Bass, Janet Bryer, and Max Bryer-Bass, for loving our family and providing Eli with a home away from home.

Denny de Harne, Yosi Kliger, and Tal Kliger, for believing in this book and for all their gifts to our family.

Kathy Caton, John Van De Veer, and Roxie Van De Veer, for so many things, but especially for sharing the ups and downs of daily life.

The parents who've supported our family during Eli's early years: Evelyn Hall, Jim Greiner, Teri Ray, Gene Burke, Patti Tomnitz, Janette Miller, Tracy Brookshier, Kirsten Thomsen, Teri Virostko, Ziesel Saunders, Leslie Ingram, Ellen Farmer, Coleen Douglas, Janet Bryer, Ellen Bass, Marsha Issacson, Gina Van Horn, and Canon Western.

Eli's caregivers: Laurel Wanner, for loving commitment to Eli and to our family; Sue Mayer, Holly Henderson, and the rest of the staff of the Santa Cruz Toddler Care Center, for their vision, skills, and respectful loving care of children; Marty and Kathy Newman, Rosalee Schelstraete, and Katie LaBaron, for continuing to nourish and enjoy Eli at Family Network Preschool.

Maureen Cooper, for clarity and inspiration.

Leon Allen, for smoked chicken and gumbo.

Janis Keyser, my coauthor, for a wonderful collaboration. I love her vision, and the clarity and compassion she brings to it. I appreciate her optimism, her integrity, her hard work, the great lunches she brought, and her wonderful photographs, all of which have enriched this book immeasurably.

Finally, I'd like to thank Karyn Bristol, my partner, for believing in this project, for loving me when I was busy and preoccupied, and for keeping our family going in the final months and weeks of birthing this book.

Janis would like to thank:

Julie Olsen Edwards for inspiration, lighting the path, and creating opportunities for me to do the work that I love.

My past and present colleagues at Cabrillo College who have mentored me and kept things together in my absence and who are deeply committed to the children in their care as well as to all children and families: Nancy k. Brown, Mary Warshaw, Nancy Andreasen, Mary Cardenas, Rosmarie Greiner, Bonnie Aldridge, Vicki Neville Coffis, Eric Hoffman, JoAnn Badeaux, Luz Cardona, Lenore Kenny, Julie Miller, Nancy Spangler, Kim SakamotoSteidl, Margaret Pierce, Gloria Valencia, and Reneta Schreiner.

The Board of Trustees of Cabrillo College and the sabbatical review committee who granted me a sabbatical to complete this book, especially Claire Biancalana, who has personally supported my work and professional growth over the years.

My parents, Betty Darling and Pard Keyser, for caring so much about me and for assuming that I would care so much about the world.

Bill Darling and Cat Keyser-Mary, who have joined my parents in providing my family unflagging physical and emotional support.

Irene McGinty, for friendship, compassion, integrity and humor.

Lise Bixler, Betty Jones, Marilyn Mohr, Barney Wick, and Sara Wood Smith, Kathleen and Michael Capella, Denny de Harne and Yosi Kliger, Miche and Jim Mosher, Stella and Paul Vasquez-James, Cindy and Michael West, Nancy and Mark Wilson, for helping to build a community of caring.

Joe, Josie, Greg, Nit, Stan, Sharon, Eaustachio, and Cheryl for teaching me about family.

Linda, Scott, Nancy and Stu, for sharing the caring.

Laura Davis, my coauthor, for imagining that we could write this book, for commitment to perfection and absolute willingness to work for it, for the ability to listen and negotiate, for honesty, humor, scrumptious cooking, and for doing all the worrying.

My husband, Leon Allen, for his trueness of spirit, poetry, honesty, ease, and love of humankind.

Photo Credits

Bonnie Aldridge, 1 (top right), 10, 81 (bottom right), 95, 105, 124, 127, 133 (top left and bottom left), 148, 151, 155, 176, 177, 184, 218, 277, 280, 285, 291, 293, 309, 326, 333, 381, 405, 413; *Leon Allen*, 30, 51, 98, 162; *Ann Badeaux*, 261; *Karyn Bristol*, 133 (top right), 166; *Laura Davis*, 23, 43, 57, 133 (bottom right), 135, 158, 194, 399; *Denny de Harne*, 174, 200; © 1997 *Mary Kate Denny*, 384; *Charles Foster*, 152; *Debbie Fugate*, 145; *Janis Keyser*, title page, 1 (top left, bottom left), 5, 6, 11, 14, 17, 20, 25, 26, 28, 31, 33, 34, 41, 49, 50, 58, 65, 68, 69, 72, 75, 78, 81 (top left, top right), 84, 85, 86, 89, 92, 96, 100, 107, 109, 112, 117, 119, 121, 156, 169, 173, 179, 180, 185, 188, 189, 190, 191, 192, 195, 199, 207, 209, 211, 212, 214, 215, 220, 224, 226, 229, 235, 237, 242, 244, 247, 251, 256, 262, 268, 271, 272, 279, 280, 281, 284, 289, 302, 307, 314, 318, 319, 323, 324, 327, 328, 331, 337, 353, 356, 357, 359, 361, 363, 364, 371, 375, 380, 388, 393, 395, 397, 402, 409, 412, 415; *Julie Olsen*, 1 (bottom right), 47, 300; *Alison Markiewicz*, 106; *Bryan Rawles*, 81 (bottom left), 91; *Jude Keith Rose*, 306; *Mary Warshaw*, 9, 243.

Preface

Laura Davis: The Parent I Wanted to Be

In March of 1993, when my son Eli was born, my life changed utterly and irrevocably. Before Eli, I'd been a waitress, a car wash attendant, a bartender, a teacher's aide, a reporter, a talk show host, a radio producer, a lecturer, a workshop leader, and a nationally known author. After the publication of my first book, *The Courage to Heal*, I'd spent years traveling around the country helping adults deal with the pain they'd experienced being sexually abused as children. I'd devoted myself to studying what went wrong in families, and in the course of doing that, I realized that what I wanted to do most of all was to come home and create a healthy family.

With my life partner and my teenage stepson, I built a nest and a family, a home I felt happy in. My newfound sense of peace and equilibrium led me to return to one of my most cherished dreams—to have a child of my own.

When Eli was born, we welcomed him into our family with love and no reservations. In those first weeks, I remember watching Eli sleep—his few strands of hair, his thin little arms, and the nursing blister that graced his top lip. I nursed him, slept with him, sang to him, held him. When I wasn't doing those things, I pored over parenting books by the dozen. A precious life had been entrusted to me, and I wanted to do the very best I could. I wanted to be a good parent. Yet I didn't trust my instincts. So I set out to find what the experts had to say. The result was completely confounding.

It was easy enough to find the books. The bookstores were full of them. There were books that told me how to feed my baby, change his diaper, bring down fevers, handle colic, respond to difficult behavior, use positive discipline and build self-esteem. I brought them home by the armful and read for hours in the middle of the night.

But there were major problems with my literary search. For one thing, many of the books contradicted each other. One said to sleep with your baby, that it promoted attachment; another claimed that it was of vital importance that your baby sleep alone. One book encouraged teaching two-year-olds to read. Another warned not to introduce letters to children until they were seven and got their second set of teeth. And each of these books was written by an expert with years of experience in child development. Each presented its message with conviction. As a new parent, I felt vulnerable and uncertain. Although I found nuggets of wisdom in many of these books, they often left me feeling confused, criticized, and, at times, inadequate. I wanted to do it by the book, but which was the right book?

The other problem was that none of these authors knew anything about me, my upbringing, my culture, my values, or whom I had supporting me in my life. None of them acknowledged what was unique about me and my family. None of them asked me to assess the feelings and strengths and vulnerabilities I brought to parenting. Each assumed I was a blank slate, ready to assimilate a new parenting theory and swallow it whole. Yet I wasn't. I came to parenthood with my own strong ideas about what I wanted for myself, my family, and my new son. I needed help realizing my visions, making my dreams for my family manifest, but I knew what those dreams were. And they didn't match up with the books I was reading. In frustration, I found myself asking the question: "Where is the book that is going to help me become the parent *I* want to be?"

When Eli was three months old, I had the good fortune to take an infant development class with Janis Keyser at Cabrillo College in Santa Cruz, California. The first day of class, it became clear that Janis's approach would be different. She told us right away that you can't look at babies and children outside the context of their families and the cultures they come from. So as we watched our babies play and explore, as we talked about their fussiness and their growth spurts, she asked us about our lives at home, our expectations, about what we valued and believed in. Janis wanted to know who we were, what we wanted for our babies. And not being blank slates, we all had something to say.

When the semester was over, a group of us continued to meet with Janis. We still get together once a month. We've discussed diaper rash, biting, teething, television, toys, child care, goodbyes, sibling conflicts, kids who won't eat, gun play, tantrums, taking care of ourselves, intimacy, sex, and, more than once, getting kids to sleep. Janis provides insights, resources, ideas, and perspective on what's happening with our children developmentally.

Janis models her philosophy of respect for children and parents by responding to us thoughtfully and by helping us find our own solutions. I learn something valuable at every meeting—as much from other people's experiences as my own. Janis inspires me to question my assumptions, try new approaches, and see my role as a parent differently, but I never go away feeling ashamed or guilty.

And I've noticed an interesting thing. Time and time again, a parent comes in struggling with a particular dilemma: "Keith isn't eating. What should I do?" And each time, as Janis listens and begins to probe, a more complex set of dynamics emerges: "My husband plays all these airplane games with Keith to try to get him to eat. He doesn't want to waste food, but I don't think it's right to force him."

In her work with each family, the problem at hand rapidly gives way to deeper issues: "What is it I want to teach my son about food and nurturing?" "My husband and I come from such different backgrounds. What should we do when we disagree?" "What does it mean for our kids if I do things one way and my partner does them another?" And sometimes, "It's great to have all these ideals about parenting, but what about when I'm exhausted and I can barely drag through the day, no less be a great parent? When do I get some time for me?"

Again and again, the questions boil down to: What kind of parent do I want to be? And how can I get there from here?

Part of my task in Eli's early years is to build my own perspective, to carve out a point of view that will help me with all the complex and multifaceted choices I'll be faced with throughout his growing-up years. As well as asking "What will fix things in the moment?" Janis has taught me to ask "What is it that I want to teach? What are my hopes for my child in the long run?"

In *Becoming the Parent You Want to Be*, we've tried to create for you the same kind of fertile, supportive environment that exists in Janis's workshops. It is my hope that you find the voices and perspectives in this book as valuable, reassuring, and lively as I do my own parent's support group.

—LAURA DAVIS

They taught me about the unique challenges contemporary families face. Through their willingness to make mistakes, take risks, get back up and try again, they continually impressed me with their commitment, resourcefulness, and courage.

Parents have also taught me how to "find the question." In my early years, I was eager to provide quick solutions, often offering several before parents even had a chance to finish defining what the issue was. But over the years, I've come to see my role as that of a facilitator and a catalyst, rather than as an expert with all the answers.

Janis Keyser: The Teacher I Wanted to Be

I started my work with families as a preschool teacher. I had always been fascinated with children and wanted to work with them in some capacity. However, not long into my work with children, I discovered parents. I loved my time with the children, but I began to relish those special moments at the end of the day when parents came to pick up their children and we got to talk.

Like many a new teacher, I started my work with parents by thinking about what *I* could teach *them*. I knew all these wonderful things about what was good for children and I wanted parents to know them, too. Parents were patient with me and steadily continued to teach me what *they* knew. As a young teacher I had a lot to learn about the love, dedication, and thoughtfulness parents bring to the job of nurturing children.

Over time, I learned to establish reciprocal dialogues with parents. As I taught them about child development, about what motivated their children's behaviors, about ways to define problems and create solutions, they taught me about resilience, struggle, and creativity. As I taught parents about the experiences of children in groups, they taught me what it was like to deal with a child at home, in a family.

I bring twenty-five years of experience as a parent and a teacher to the writing of this book. I've taught preschool and college, led parenting classes, supervised new teachers, directed child care programs, and developed and coordinated programs for parent education. As a member of the Early Childhood Education faculty at Cabrillo College, I have had the opportunity to work with colleagues to develop innovative programs for parents of infants and toddlers and to provide leadership in peace education and anti-bias teaching.

I've had a long, rewarding apprenticeship in parenting under the tutelage of my three children. Eighteen years ago, when I was pregnant with Lee, I was full of excitement about trying out all the child development information I'd learned as a teacher. I wasn't even wise enough to be apprehensive. I was confident that I knew all about children. But nothing I'd learned about babies and children prepared me for being with a newborn twenty-four hours a day. Being a parent was absolutely different from being a teacher. Although I was totally absorbed in and enraptured with Lee, I was also confused and lonely. I began seeking out other parents with new babies and I spent hours just looking at Lee.

Slowly, as I watched Lee develop and as I talked to other parents about their concerns, questions, anxieties, and delights, I began to feel more confident. I relaxed and started to believe that my baby was going to be okay.

Five years later, when Calvin was born, I learned a whole new set of lessons about sibling relationships. Like most second-time parents, I was amazed that my love for this new child only deepened my feelings for my first. And four years after that, when Maya was born, I was awestruck by how much more my heart could open—and by just how unique each child can be.

I've learned more from being a parent than from any other experience. As my most loyal and dedicated instructors, my children drill me repeatedly on each new skill, never giving up until I get it. Each of them has taken me to places the others never took me before. Each has challenged me to grow in a new way. Through my experiences and struggles with my children, I have a heightened sense of respect for all parents.

With my own children, and in my work with parents, there's one phenomenon I've witnessed repeatedly: when parents feel encouraged, they develop a sense of competence and optimism that leads to more enjoyment of parenting and a greater appreciation of their children. Parents who feel supported are more open to learning from their mistakes, more willing to try new strategies when old ones don't work. They're able to think about what they want to teach their kids, and they're better equipped to narrow the gap between that vision and the reality of their daily lives.

I'm committed to building a world where parents have the support they need to build healthy families—families in which children can learn, have fun, play, laugh, and explore; families in which kids can take love, safety, and being fed for granted. I continually work toward creating a community that respects parents for the enormity and importance of their task, a world in which all families are connected to a network of friends, education, and resources. Supporting families is not just crucial for the health of every child; it is crucial for the health of our nation.

When Laura first approached me about writing this book, I was thrilled to have an opportunity to create a family-friendly resource for parents that could begin to meet some of these goals. I envisioned a book that would offer concrete help to parents, answering immediate questions about eating, sleep, discipline, family conflict, tantrums, and hundreds of other concerns that arise in the lives of young children. I wanted to give parents relevant child development information so they could understand why their children were doing what they were doing. But more than anything else, I wanted to present a philosophy of respect for families that helps parents define their goals and develop their own creative solutions.

—JANIS KEYSER

Introduction: The Parenting Journey

When we first become parents, our whole life changes. With the entry of a new human being into the world—and into our lives—priorities are reordered, family relationships shift, our worldview is permanently altered. Values and beliefs we've held for a lifetime are reexamined, and vulnerabilities we didn't know we had come rushing to the surface. At the same time, we feel more love than we ever thought possible.

The first five years of our children's lives are an exciting, wonderful, and challenging time. When we first meet our children, we know remarkably little about each other, yet within a few short years we know each other better than most lifelong friends. Parents and children bring out the best and the worst in each other. We experience our strongest feelings when we are together.

Kids offer us the chance to look at the world through new eyes. They remind us to notice the small things in life—a sow bug, a smile, a song. They help us understand our past and give us a connection to the future. They teach us new meanings for the words "commitment," "love," "frustration," and "persistence."

Children challenge us in myriad ways. As they grow, we're faced with questions and dilemmas we never had to consider before: What should I do when my baby cries and won't stop? When my toddler pulls everything off the shelves? When my preschooler sneaks change out of my wallet to buy candy?

Becoming the Parent You Want to Be can help you answer these and a multitude of other questions. It is full of practical information and advice for parents of children from birth to kindergarten, *and* it presents that information in a way that respects the unique history, values, and perspective each parent brings to the critical job of nurturing children. Throughout this book, we'll help you clarify your own philosophy; at the same time, we'll offer you ours.

Becoming the Parent You Want to Be is based on several assumptions about children. We believe that children are naturally eager, self-motivated, and competent learners who are capable of choosing their own learning tasks. We believe that children aren't blank slates but, instead, actively participate in the construction of their own knowledge. Children come with their own unique personalities, temperaments, and developmental timetables, and we believe that readiness is essential to their capacity to grow and learn. We maintain that almost everything children do is an attempt to learn and that there is always a healthy impulse behind a child's behavior. We assume that children experience and benefit from expressing a full range of feelings and that frustration and struggle accompany joy and triumph as essential parts of learning.

All of the things we believe about children, we also believe about parents: that parents are competent, motivated learners who actively participate in the development of their parenting philosophy. We believe that parents go through certain developmental stages that begin with the anticipation of parenthood and continue after their last child leaves home.

We believe that parents want to learn about parenting and about their children, and that they do the best job they can given their experience, knowledge, and resources. People come to parenting with their own unique temperaments, personalities, histories, and cultures. We believe that parents experience a full range of feelings and benefit from opportunities to express those feelings—and that frustration and struggle are as essential to the parenting journey as triumph and joy.

Finally, we believe that parents are human. We all make mistakes. We all feel uncertain. We all have times when we're confused and don't know what to do, and we all despair sometimes, trying to figure out if we're "doing it right." That's natural. It goes with the territory. Being human, making mistakes, and learning from our mistakes are all parts of effective parenting.

Parents thrive when they have the support, compassion, and wisdom of other parents. To help meet this need, we've included the stories of over a hundred parents throughout the pages of this book. Look at them as people you're conversing with, as people who've been where you are or where you're going, who are struggling and trying to find answers, just as you are.

A wide diversity of parents are represented: mothers, fathers, stepparents, single parents, parents with disabilities, foster parents, gay and lesbian parents, and grandparents. You'll meet men and women who've become parents through birth, adoption, or relationships with their partners' children. You'll meet African American parents, White parents, Asian American parents, Latino parents, Native American parents, and parents in ethnically mixed families. You'll hear from people who came to parenting at different stages of their lives—teen parents and older parents alike. Most of the voices in this book are from parents whose children are still young—because we wanted to capture the freshness and intensity of those particular years—but we've included some older, more experienced voices to reflect a more seasoned perspective.

Although we interviewed parents from a diversity of backgrounds, with a diversity of children, we know we haven't included everyone. Regardless of your particular background or circumstances, we hope that you find at least some stories in this book that resonate with your life experience, your goals as a parent, and the particular challenges you face.

At the core of *Becoming the Parent You Want to Be* are nine principles that deal with issues of time, optimism, struggle, anger, balancing needs, and learning as you go. Reading them will help you clarify what you want to teach your children, whether they are two or five or sixteen. You can find them in Part One of this book, and they lay the groundwork for the practical strategies and information that follow.

Our dream is that *Becoming the Parent You Want to Be* will be a helpful resource and support to parents, offering something thought-provoking, practical, and inspiring. We hope that this book will never sit neatly on the shelf but will be tangled in the bedcovers, dog-eared on the floor, dripping with catsup on the kitchen table, wrapped up with the muddy T-shirts in the diaper bag.

—Laura Davis and Janis Keyser
Santa Cruz, January 1997

• Part One •

A Framework for the Parenting Journey: Nine Principles

Nine Principles for the Parenting Journey

Principle 1: Developing a Vision for Your Family

As parents, it's important that we hold a vision of the kind of parent that we want to be and that we strive to achieve that vision in our daily lives.

Principle 2: Learning About Children

Through learning about our children, and about children in general, we develop a perspective that leads us to be more responsive, effective parents.

Principle 3: Cultivating a Spirit of Optimism About Your Children

Believing in our children and enabling them to find their own answers are two of the greatest gifts we can give them.

Principle 4: Understanding That Parents Are Always Growing

We learn how to be parents as we go along.

Principle 5: Learning to Trust Struggle and Disequilibrium

Periods of disequilibrium—times we feel confused and off-balance—can be essential to our growth as parents.

Principle 6: Working Toward a Balance of Needs

A family rhythm that balances each person's unique needs with the needs of the family as a whole creates mutual respect and harmony.

Principle 7: Teaching Children to Feel Safe, Strong, and Good About Their World

One of the most powerful things parents can give children is an open, optimistic, and safe connection to the world.

Principle 8: Being Human: When You're Not Yet the Parent You Want to Be

All parents get angry and all of us make mistakes. Acknowledging and learning from our mistakes teaches our children invaluable lessons about being human.

Principle 9: Building a Supportive Community

All parents need and deserve a community to support them in the critical work of nurturing and teaching the next generation.

1. Developing a Vision for Your Family

Principle 1: As parents, it's important that we hold a vision of the kind of parent that we want to be and that we strive to achieve that vision in our daily lives.

All of us of us come to parenting with hopes for our children, our families, and ourselves. We imagine the families we want to create. We dream of all that we want for our children. We hold a vision.

Through the experience we gain as parents, this vision is continually reshaped. Our perspective shifts, our values change, and our understanding deepens.

At the beginning of her parenting classes, Janis asks everyone to bring in a list of three of the most important things they want to teach their children. As parents call out their answers, Janis writes them on the board. The resulting list is always a powerful testament to parents' commitment to their children:

- I want my children to always feel cherished and loved, no matter what they do.
- It's important to me to have a close-knit family that always pulls together.
- I want to be the kind of parent my kids can always talk to.
- I want to teach my children to make a difference in the world.
- I want to be able to give my kids a lot of the things I never had.

Creating and holding a vision is critical to us and to the health of our families. When we know what we are striving for, we have a yardstick by which to measure our choices and actions as a parent. We learn to enact our values in the present and project them into the future.

Understanding My Values: What Do I Want to Teach?

As parents, we are our children's first and primary teachers. What we teach and how we teach it has a significant impact on our children. As Jean Illsey Clarke writes in her book, *Self-Esteem: A Family Affair,* "What families have in common the world around is that they are the place where people learn who they are and how to be that way."

Offering values to our children is the thing we do that most clearly defines our family as unique: "The Sanchez family always has the welcome mat out." "The Segals are always out supporting one social cause or another." "You'll be able to find the Wood Smiths out in the backyard with their hands in the dirt."

We acquire values through our family history, our cultural perspective, and our life experiences. Many are absorbed naturally in childhood. In Janis's family, these are called "the values we swallowed whole with our Cheerios." Among these are some values we hold dear, some we are unaware of, and others we no longer believe in but still carry.

Having children also leads us to discover

values that we previously considered unimportant. We find values that we've been carrying but not acting on, or beliefs that we want to make more explicit for our kids. We come to appreciate certain values in relationship to our children that were less obvious to us as single people. It's one of the transformative parts of parenting.

Narrowing the Vision-Action Gap

The dreams we hold for ourselves and our children are impressive. Many of us enter parenthood with ambitious ideas about the kind of parents we are going to be. These hopes were safe and sacred before we had children—the reality of our daily lives didn't challenge or tarnish them. But now we have to struggle to put our principles into practice, and that's often harder than we thought it would be. As Laura once put it, "It's a lot easier to be a parent in theory than in reality."

None of us consistently lives up to our ideals. When we feel criticized, hurried, or stressed, we may not be able to figure out how to implement our values and, instead, may find ourselves making habitual mistakes. Inevitably, there's a gap between our vision and the way we actually live. Even if we think we'd like to approach things differently, we may not have the practical experience or information to implement those changes. Yet the fact that we cannot perfectly embody our vision doesn't make holding that vision any less important.

When Your Values Differ from the Values of Your Partner

Once you become a parent, you not only uncover values you didn't know *you* held, you may also discover values held by partners, family, or friends that you didn't know *they* held. Yoshiko became aware of this in the wee hours of the morning: "Our six-month-old baby had started crying and I was just about to jump out of bed like I always did, when my husband held me back, saying 'Wait, don't go to her, she has got to learn that you can't always fix whatever is wrong. Erin needs to learn independence.' I must not value independence the same way my husband does, because it didn't make any sense to me to leave a six-month-old crying in the middle of the night."

Many parents discover that they have very different ways of doing things from their partner. Thinking about what you really want to teach and discussing the areas where you disagree can be useful. You may discover that you and your partner hold similar values but have different ideas about how to implement them. Or you may discover that you hold different values.

This is not necessarily a problem. Children can benefit from parents who bring different values to the family. When partners are respectful of each other's perspective, children learn that there can be more than one right way to look at things, and they get a chance to choose what is important to them.

It's useful both personally and for the partnership if parents find some time to talk with each other about their current priorities and possible areas of disagreement. This discussion needs to focus on listening and communication rather than on who's right. You may even want to each make a list of your five most important values and share ideas about how you want to pass them on. Or you could answer some of the questions in this chapter together.

Most parents are able to find the areas in which disagreement is acceptable and the areas in which agreement seems crucial—the bottom lines. It is essential that parents figure out how to respect the differences they can tolerate and how to work toward agreement on those that they can't.*

* See "When Partners Disagree" on p. 385 for more on resolving differences between parents.

Our job is to narrow the gap between the vision we hold for ourselves and our daily practice as parents. Here are some ways to bring your vision and your actions into closer alignment:

- **Clarify your own values.** A careful consideration of the values you want to pass on is an essential first step in teaching children what you truly hold important. You can ask yourself: "What are the values I learned in my family?" "In my community?" "What are the five most important values I want to pass on to my children?" "Are there specific ways I've taught those values to my kids?"

- **Look for opportunities to teach values.** There are numerous daily activities through which we teach our children values. A simple trip down the sidewalk, stepping over the caterpillars, can demonstrate the way you value living things. Saving your daughter's half a sandwich for later can show your commitment to avoiding waste. Allowing your son to cry teaches him that you value his feelings.

- **Find parents who support your vision.** Parents who are working to implement values that are similar to yours can support you as you work to put your ideas into practice.

- **Do some thoughtful self-evaluation.** When we regularly reflect on what we have done with our kids in light of what we want to be teaching, we naturally bring our action closer to our vision.

Look at the Bigger Picture

It's easy to get caught up in day-to-day struggles with our kids and forget the long view. When we're dealing with problems, there's a tendency to fall into parenting by objective—defining parenting success by "what works immediately." If your one-year-old son has been biting, you ask yourself what will stop the biting. If your daughter isn't using the potty, you define success by her increased use of the potty. And if your child isn't sleeping as much or as long as you'd like him to, you focus on whatever it takes to get him to sleep through the night. Although these can all be important successes, just solving the immediate problem sometimes overlooks the underlying values you want to teach your child.

When you achieve "what works" by doing what's easiest in the moment, you may manipulate your child or disrespect his feelings along the way. In doing so, you may undermine what you're trying to build with your child. When you're achieving "what works," it's important to ask yourself: "Have I succeeded in getting what I wanted, but lost something more important along the way?"

Rather than focus solely on the narrow end result, it's vital to cultivate an attitude that the process is as important as the outcome. When we succeed in doing this, our kids' behavior doesn't always change immediately, but our relationship with them maintains a critical sense of integrity.

How Do Children Learn Values?

Every interaction with children provides an opportunity to teach values. While no parent tries to make every kiss good night a lesson, it's useful to think about the opportune times for teaching in families:

• **Children learn about our values through daily interactions with us.** When we think about teaching values to kids, we often think about taking them to church or having a talk with them about lying, teaching them about sharing, or encouraging them to give during the holiday season. Yet we teach values every day in our ordinary daily encounters.

• **Children learn through our example.** As one dad, Cully, explains: "My son has seen me pick up trash off the street and he's asked, 'Who dropped that?' I answered, 'I don't know. But it was on my earth. So I picked it up.' "

Leah, who has cared for foster children from troubled families, says, "I do it because I know what I do makes a difference. I can't fix the parents. I can't fix society. But to me, loving one child is enough. The Foster Parents Association motto is 'To touch a life forever.' Even if they're only in my home for twelve hours, they've had twelve hours of seeing that love can make a family work. They've seen people respecting each other. They've learned that it's possible. I also love that it teaches my birth kids values I really care about: flexibility, compassion, and generosity.

"My children are really welcoming of the foster kids. Both of them like to go to the shelter to pick up the new kids with me. Emma, my five-year-old, is my little ambassador. She'll meet the kids at the door and she'll pick up their hand. She'll say, 'You don't have to be scared. It's okay to have feelings here. It's okay to be angry. When we're angry, we run around outside or hit pillows and shout, but we don't hit each other. Nobody will ever hit you here. This is where my room is. This is where you're going to sleep. This is your private place.' "

• **Children learn through the values we strive toward.** While it's true that children learn through what we model, it's *not* true that you need to have mastered a value before you teach it to your children. All of us have some values that are woven into the very fabric of who we are. At the same time, most of us have values we're newly adopting, that we haven't practiced or integrated.

Even if we move toward our values in tiny increments, children will pick up on our intention and commitment, and learn that they, too, can strive toward a vision they haven't yet attained.

• **Children learn values through the way we do things as a family.** Kathleen shares how she teaches the value of family: "Once a week we have an evening where we sit around as a family and talk about the things we like about our family. We play games, sing songs, and do crafts. It's a time when no one has other appointments. I love that time. It tells us that our family is a priority."

• **Children learn values and beliefs through their exposure to the larger world.** Through friends, extended family, books, TV, and the experiences they have in their community, children absorb values and societal norms. Janis recalls, "My three-year-old friend, Melissa, came to me one day with the statement 'All doctors are men.' And I happened to know for a fact that the only doctors Melissa had ever been to had been women. Yet every time she overheard a conversation about doctors, they were referred to as men. Every book she read about doctors showed men. When she came home and told her aunt that she'd gone to the doctor, her aunt said, 'Oh, did *he* give you a shot?' All of a sudden, Melissa's perception, 'I thought my doctor was a woman,' was challenged by the greater authority of her aunt and the accumulated weight of images from the world around her."

• **Children learn values through our explanations of the world.** We can't always control our child's environment. We may have chosen the grocery store, but we don't control all the people who are going to be in the grocery store. Our children sometimes witness or hear things we wish they hadn't seen or heard. But the fact that we are with them or that they can come home and tell us about it gives us a chance to share our perspective on what happened. Even though we didn't choose that experience for them, we get to help them figure it out: "I'm sorry that woman yelled at you for standing in the cart. I think she was worried about your safety. She doesn't know that you can stand safely in the cart and she doesn't know that yelling scares kids."

FOOD FOR THOUGHT: VALUES

• Who are the people I can talk to about my values?

• Where, in my family and community, have I found people who disagree with me in terms of my values? How do I negotiate those differences?

• When did I last have a conflict with another person (my partner, a friend or family member) about how to respond to a child? What values were each of us trying to teach?

• Can I think of a time when my child was exposed to a value that was very different from the values in our family? How did I respond? How did I help my child with that experience?

2. Learning About Children

Principle 2: Through learning about our children, and about children in general, we develop a perspective that leads us to be more responsive, effective parents.

Getting to know your children is one of the pure delights and formidable challenges of being a parent. Children and their parents start as strangers to each other connected by powerful bonds of expectation, instinct, tradition, and love. As we move through the years together, we have an ongoing opportunity to get to know each other intimately.

We learn about our children by watching them, sharing experiences with them, and interacting with them. Our understanding of them deepens as we learn about the nature of childhood. Knowing how children think, develop, and experience the world enables us to gain insight into our individual children.

What Is Child Development and Why Is It Useful?

Child development is the study of childhood. In the last hundred years, child development researchers around the world have built a large body of knowledge about how children grow. This research teaches us:

- **Children go through certain predictable stages of growth.** Children use a nipple before they use a cup; they walk before they skip.

- **Each stage of children's development builds on the success of the previous stage.** Babbling lays the groundwork for later speech. Trust is necessary for later independence. Stages can neither be hurried nor skipped.

- **Each child has her own unique timetable for development, yet there are broad norms that can provide useful benchmarks.** Chelsea might take her first eager step at eight months, while Jack tentatively walks at fifteen months. Conversely, Chelsea might have few words at eighteen months, while Jack begins simple sentences at eleven months. Knowing the wide parameters of normal growth can help parents accept their child's individual developmental clock.

- **Children's development is not linear or even.** Often children take a few steps forward and several back. When a child first learns a new skill, such as using the toilet independently or spending the night away from home, she often "regresses" in other areas, forgetting already established skills.

• **Disequilibrium is part of normal development.** Child development theorist Jean Piaget coined the word "disequilibrium" to describe the out-of-balance times children often go through right before they learn something new. Children who are on the verge of crawling sometimes get fussy or start waking at night. Children who are just about to figure out how to play successfully with other children may become unusually aggressive. Knowing that children's struggles are indicative of their attempts to grow helps parents understand difficult behavior and provide appropriate support.

• **Mistakes are part of normal development.** Children usually make many unsuccessful attempts before mastering a new skill.

• **Children grow in different realms at the same time.** A child who is sitting on the couch reading with his grandfather is simultaneously gaining knowledge in at least four different areas. Cognitively, he is learning about language and the concepts in the book. Emotionally, he is learning that he can trust Grandpa. Socially, he is learning to take turns talking. And physically, he is learning how to make his fingers turn the pages.

• **Learning about child development gives us a framework from which to see and support our children.** When you know that your child's behaviors are normal for his developmental stage, you can respond accordingly, knowing that the resolution of a difficult behavior is often as much a matter of time as it is of teaching. When you understand that mouthing things is part of the healthy development of babies, you can provide a variety of safe things for your infant to suck on and move dangerous things out of her range. Once you know that four-year-olds love to feel skillful, you can provide your son with a sponge to clean the sink or pliers to help put a new bookcase together.

Getting to Know Your Unique Child

While all children share certain common developmental characteristics, each child comes with a distinctive personality. As one great-grandfather, Calvin, put it, "Everybody brings something special to this planet that nobody else brought."

Even from infancy, kids have a knack for letting us know just who they are. Noni, whose daughter's emotions are intense and changeable, explained: "There's been nothing mellow about Sara from the day she was born. She had an intense cry and she let you know what she needed right away. She cried hard and laughed hard, and she's continued to be that way."

Charles, who loves the saxophone, said, "Kids are different, not only in terms of temperament but also in terms of their attributes and talents. You give my son Kenny something

brass and he'll play it—trumpet, trombone, tuba, any brass instrument. And I love reeds. I didn't ever think about a tuba or trumpet. I was amazed when Kenny first brought home a trumpet. How did he get interested in brass growing up in a saxophone household?"

Even if you manage to get the baby you expected the first time around, having a second child—or a third—drastically increases your chances of meeting someone you didn't expect in your family. With one child you can take credit or blame for whoever they are, but when you have another one, you realize that children start out with a lot already going for themselves.

Janis's husband, Leon, recalls: "My first child was a fast mover. He was full of energy. He cried in continual, anxious bursts. My second kid was always cool. He'd cry one long hoarse cry. Then he'd wait for you to do something for him. If we were out of milk, I'd literally have time to go to the store and get the milk and bring it back before he'd cry out again. And the third kid was very different from the first and the second. And so on. None of them were even close to being alike. And I've got eight kids."

Julie remembers fondly, "Neither my first or second kid drew on the walls. I thought, 'It's because of my superior parenting.' Then the third one came along, and I realized I just never had an artist before."

Understanding Your Child's Temperament

Temperament is the term that is often used to describe the distinct characteristics each of us is born with. Our temperament underlies the unique way we respond to people, environments, and circumstances.

In her book *Raising Your Spirited Child*, Mary Sheedy Kurcinka outlines nine characteristics that make up temperament:

1. **Intensity:** the strength of a child's emotional responses
2. **Persistence:** the ease or difficulty a child has stopping or letting go of an activity or idea that is important to her.
3. **Sensitivity:** a child's awareness and sensitivity to tastes, textures, temperature, noise, and emotions
4. **Perceptiveness:** a child's awareness of the colors, people, noises, and objects around her. Perceptiveness determines a child's ability to stay focused.
5. **Adaptability:** a child's ability to adapt to changes in her schedule or routine
6. **Regularity:** a child's regularity or irregularity in terms of her daily rhythms—eating, sleep, and elimination
7. **Energy:** a child's basic energy level—quiet and relaxed or on the move and busy
8. **First reaction:** a child's level of comfort or discomfort in new situations
9. **Mood:** a child's tendency to be happy and content or serious and moody.

Each temperament has its strengths and challenges. Characteristics that are considered "difficult" in children often develop into real assets in adulthood.

One thing that makes a child's temperament easier or harder for parents to deal with is the "match" of the child with the rest of the family. Having a child whose temperament is very different from yours can pose significant challenges.

Bea, the mother of eight-month-old Sean and four-year-old Gabrielle, relates, "I'm kind of easygoing. Gabrielle and I like to be spontaneous, to take off at a moment's notice. She has been that way since she was a baby. But Sean really likes routines. If we're not home during his regular nap times, he can't fall asleep. If I don't nurse him in his familiar chair, he cries. Sean's need to have everything 'just so' has really put a crimp in our style."

Sometimes having a child with a temperament similar to yours can also be a challenge. Barry, the father of five-year-old Elizabeth, says, "Having two of us who are so intense is really hard sometimes. Why can't she be a little more mellow like her mother?"

Although you cannot change a child's temperament, you can play a significant role in helping her learn how to best manage the cards she's been dealt. Janis recalls: "When Maya was five, I finally accepted that transitions were always going to be hard for her. This was not something that she was going to magically grow out of. It became clear to me that my job was not to change her, but rather to help her learn to predict and plan for circumstances that might be hard for her."

Understanding that children have diverse temperaments and strengths can also help us put differences between children in perspective. Temperament gives us clues as to why children behave differently even though they're the same age or are members of the same family.

Learning to Observe

One of the main ways we learn about our children is through observation. When we consciously and thoughtfully watch our children, we gain invaluable insight into who they are and how to best interact with them.

Observation is something parents do naturally. As soon as our babies are born, we find ourselves gazing at them—both when they're asleep and when they're awake. Their every gesture, sound, and random movement keeps us spellbound. There's a reason we find our babies so riveting. It's nature's way of making sure they're protected and cared for.

Parents observe the ways their babies explore, the expressions on their faces, the tenor of their cries, the color of their poops, and the

Magda Gerber on Observation

*Magda Gerber is an infant development specialist who advocates a philosophy of respect for young babies. As the founder of Resources for Infant Educarers (RIE), an organization that offers training for parents and professionals who work with infants and toddlers, she believes children develop best in their own way and at their own pace. One of the primary tools Gerber teaches is observation.**

If we really pay attention when we observe children, we soon learn that everything children do is done with a purpose, that everything children do is 'right'—from their point of view at the time they are doing it.

. . .

"It can be reassuring to see that your child enjoys spending time by himself or herself, and that being alone is something both of you need. Likewise, it is encouraging to see that your child is learning to solve a number of important problems without your help or intervention.

. . .

"When we deal with children, we are not merely one person. We are at least three people: we are parents of our children, we are children of our parents, we are adults with our own interests and needs. Often these 'three people' in us do not agree. Each sees something different when we observe, and each has different ideas about what should or shouldn't be done about it."

* The term "educarer," a combination of the words "educator" and "caregiver," was coined by Magda Gerber to describe the role of people who care for infants and toddlers. For more information on RIE, you can write to: 1550 Murray Circle, Los Angeles, CA 90026.

number of diapers they wet. We notice how long they nap, when they cry the most, and what seems to calm them. It is through this observation, this taking of mental history, that we begin to know our children.

After practicing observation in an infant class, Razel, the mother of eight-month-old twins, remarked, "When I sit back and observe my boys, I learn about the way they each solve problems. They're like little scientists. And the amazing thing is that they each do it so differently."

Most parents rely on observation to learn about their babies in the first year of life. But once children start talking, many parents assume that observation isn't as necessary. Yet there are many things even verbal children can't articulate.

Observing older children—watching their facial expressions, body language, tone of voice, peer interactions, and dramatic play—continues to give parents important insights and knowledge.

What Is Your Child Working On?

At any given moment, children are working on a complex set of things, and if you observe them, you gain insight into what it is they're trying to figure out. At one point your daughter, Kerry, might be working on climbing. She may clear off all the shelves, not because she wants to use the things on that shelf, but because she wants to use those shelves as a climbing structure. She climbs to the top and stands there, loudly declaring herself victorious.

Knowing that Kerry is working on climbing enables you to stop and redirect her with respect for what she's trying to master, rather than just with irritation that you have to put everything back on the shelves.

Sometimes discovering what children are working on requires more subtle observation. A baby, for instance, may be in the stage where he's just discovered all the wonderful little

The Basics of Observation

• **Slow down.** Try to put other concerns and agendas aside and take five or ten minutes just to observe. Get comfortable. Relax.

• **Don't interrupt or distract your child.** Be as unobtrusive as you can. You don't need to interject your own ideas or commentary into your child's activities. This is not a time to get involved in your child's play. Just watch.

• **Cultivate a clear and open mind.** Try to see what your child is doing without judgment or evaluation.

• **Use descriptive rather than evaluative language.** When you think about what your child is doing, try to use language that simply describes the activity: "He's sitting on the rim of the sandbox, his feet are covered with sand, and he's grasping the rim of the bucket in his right fist" rather than more evaluative language: "He's playing so nicely."

things on the floor: bits of paper, shreds of leaves, brown spots, dust balls, fringes of rugs. Having just discovered his pincer grasp, the ability to bring his forefinger and thumb together to pick up an object, he is fascinated with picking up tiny objects.

That was the case with Delrio, a baby Janis observed in an infant development class: "The whole room was full of fun things to climb, foam ramps and balls and bells and brightly colored toys. Delrio's father was saying, 'Oh, look! Here's something you can crawl up! Want to play ball?' He didn't want Delrio to miss out on all the wonderful things that were there. But what Delrio was really interested in was picking tiny little things up off the floor."

Why Observe?

As a busy parent, you may think you don't have time for observation. If you have a limited amount of time to spend with your child, why spend it observing?

Observation can be valuable for a number of reasons:

• **You get to enjoy your child.** Moments of fascination, delight, and pride often accompany observation.

• **You learn about child development.** Jean Piaget formulated his theories about children through the careful observation of his own three kids.

• **You learn what drives and motivates your children.** When you watch children over time, you begin to get an idea of what interests them, how they explore, and what they're trying to learn.

• **Observation enables you to provide children with avenues to further their explorations.** When you know your child is working on pouring, you can supply her with a set of plastic cups in the bathtub.

• **Observation gives you a chance to see your children as they are.** Most parents have some expectations about who they want their children to be. Yet it's also important to balance those expectations by asking kids: And who are you? Observation can help you answer that question.

• **Observation enables you to respond to each child as a unique individual.** Janis notes: "I find I can interact with a child most appropriately once I've observed him. Otherwise I'm coming in ready to interact with all the children his age I've ever been with before, rather than this particular child."

• **When you see what children are working on, you can gain a new perspective on "misbehavior."** This can help you move beyond your own frustration and respond more empathetically to unsuccessful behavior.

• **Observation lets your child know she is important to you.** When children see that we are interested in them and in what they are doing, they feel valued.

FOOD FOR THOUGHT: OBSERVATION

• What are the natural times I observe my children?

• What have I learned about my children through observation? Have I ever been surprised by what I've observed?

• What are the things that get in the way of me observing my children?

3. Cultivating a Spirit of Optimism About Your Children

Principle 3: Believing in our children and enabling them to find their own answers are two of the greatest gifts we can give them.

Through our attitudes and perspective on their growing abilities, we set a tone for our children about who they are. When we believe that our children will successfully master developmental tasks—learn to walk, use the potty, develop empathy, share with others, complete a puzzle—we mirror back to them encouraging and hopeful images of who they are.

Babies and toddlers are naturally driven to achieve developmental milestones. Preschool-age children are similarly motivated, and they also become *aware* of setting goals for themselves. They want to learn to play successfully with their friends, button their coats, and ride big bikes with training wheels, but they don't automatically know they're going to succeed. Sometimes their frustration is intensified by their lack of trust that it's going to happen. Our optimism and confidence in them can go a long way in bridging the gap between their struggle and their ultimate success.

In effect, our job as parents is to hold a vision for our children of the people they are becoming. They're pushing and shoving now, but we believe that, ultimately, they are going to learn to share. It's critical that we strive to keep their potential success in mind rather than defining them as unsuccessful people who haven't yet met our expectations.

Proving Children Wrong

Many of us, despite our best intentions, find ourselves discouraging rather than encouraging our children. Few of us have escaped the commonly held belief that shame and blame are appropriate ways to motivate children. Although employing these techniques can bring momentary changes in behavior, the long-range consequences are detrimental to both self-confidence and real growth.

Especially when we are tired, frustrated, or vulnerable, many parents fall into accusing children instead of encouraging them to recover and learn from their mistakes. Noreen, the mother of four-year-old Connor, described this situation clearly: "Connor and his friend, Alex, were making forts the other day. They worked laboriously all afternoon, moving cardboard boxes, bringing towels and blankets to provide covers, figuring out how to attach the roofs. I reminded them several times that they would need to put their things away when they were finished. They said, 'Yeah, yeah,' and went on. By dinnertime, they had gone off to have snail races on the porch. When I called them in to clean up their forts, they were suddenly 'too tired.'

"Before I knew it, I was berating them with the full weight of my fatigue and disappointment: 'You never clean anything up! What do you think I am? A maid? What's wrong with you anyway?' For an instant, I saw Connor's face fall, and then immediately he became defensive and attacked back, 'Quit yelling at me. I don't have to do any stupid clean-up, dummy! You never help me!' Something clued me in that we were not having a successful communication, but at the time I couldn't figure my way out of it.

"Later that night, when I talked to a friend about what I had said, I realized that my comments were actually telling Connor and Alex 'You're lazy, you can't learn, you never do anything right.' And I wondered how on earth I got so far away from being the encouraging, positive parent I want to be."

Noreen has thoughtfully described a dilemma many parents face.

It is usually our own feelings of frustration and inadequacy that lead us to belittle our children, to try to prove them wrong. In Noreen's case, she felt like she'd done everything she could to facilitate the children's clean-up: she had given them warnings, the freedom to engage in messy, creative play, and lots of time, but they still hadn't been able to put their things away.

It can be unnerving for us as parents when our child isn't responding and we've done the best we know how to do. Many of us have been trained to believe that when situations aren't working out smoothly, it must be somebody's fault. We sometimes make our children "wrong" in order to maintain the "rightness" of our own perspective.

As long as we operate within the closed system that assumes that someone must be right and someone else must be at fault, we won't be able to let go of making either ourselves or our children wrong. When we move past this closed system, however, we can realize that sometimes even though both parents and children are doing their best, there will still be conflict.

"We Never Give Up, Dad": Somchai's Story

Sometimes a particular cultural perspective helps to create a sense of optimism. That was true for one father, Somchai, who grew up in Thailand and moved to the United States when he was a teenager.

I'm from a very traditional Buddhist Thai family. I came to this country when I was sixteen. Although I left behind a lot of the rituals of my childhood, I always draw on my background, on stories that were told to me by my parents about the strength of the Thai people. Thailand is the only country in Southeast Asia that's never been colonized. That's because we've always been able to persevere by adapting to changing times. Those are the parts of my culture I value most.

I want my son to know how to let go of things that have been precious to him, to make do with less, to change with the times.

When I think about transmitting a sense of optimism to my children, one particular incident comes to mind. I was playing with my son at the beach. We were building a sand castle. And the waves were coming in and they were knocking it down. And we kept on building it up. And my son turned to me and he said, "You know, Dad, we never give up, do we?" And I said, "You're right, we never give up." And that's a big part of my native culture that's important to me—the Thai people persevere.

What Are We Actually Saying to Kids?

Let's look at the underlying message we communicate to children when we use shame or blame to prove them wrong:

When we say: "I told you so!"
We might really be communicating: "I'm always right and you're always wrong." "It's not okay to make mistakes." "There's no point in trying to figure things out for yourself!"

When we say: "You *never* put your toys away."
We might really be communicating: "I'm afraid you will never learn this." "I'm worried that I won't be able to teach you." "I've lost hope."

When we say: "Don't try that, you'll fall."
We might really be communicating: "I don't trust your judgment. I don't believe you can figure out what you can climb and what you can't." "It's not safe to be physically active."

When we say: "I've told you a thousand times that you have to put away your toys."
We might really be communicating: "You've failed before and I'm afraid you're going to fail again." "I don't expect you to listen to me."

When we say: "You're lazy (stupid, inconsiderate, selfish)."
We might really be communicating: "There is something inherently flawed about who you are." "I don't respect you." "My love is conditional. It's only available when you do what I want you to do."

What happens when we undermine kids' sense of success and competence? One scenario is that they learn that the only reliable source of decisions is outside themselves, with their parent or someone else. They may become unsure of themselves, unable to make decisions, fearful to try things; they may learn to distrust their own perceptions. Kids who are repeatedly told they make poor decisions often become convinced that those are the only kind of decisions they can make, and then they proceed to fulfill that expectation.

Alternatives to "Proving Kids Wrong"

In the face of children's inevitable mistakes, how can we avoid proving them wrong and, instead, work to prove that they can be right?

• **Appreciate children's efforts even when they don't achieve their goals.** You can say to kids, "I see how hard you tried to climb up that ladder." "You really worked to get your shoes on." Or to babies: "You're working hard to find that thumb to suck on!"

• **Assume that children are putting forth their best effort.** If they aren't being successful, you may need to reexamine your expectations and, together, look for possible solutions.

• **Work with children to solve the problem, rather than blaming them for never being able to get it right.** Starting around age three, you can say to kids: "It seems like it is hard for you to clean up your forts and we really need them to be cleaned up before dinner. How do you think we can solve this problem?"

• **Provide children with information and honor their need to try things for themselves.** Encourage success by trusting your child's competence: "Those apples are really high up in the tree and there are some weak branches up there. When you are climbing, look for sturdy branches. Climb as high as you feel safe, and then come down."[1]

• **Provide safety nets.** Rather than insisting that your child wear a jacket, you can say: "I know you don't feel cold right now, but I'm going to tuck your sweatshirt in your backpack in case you get cold later." Or "I can see you're really trying to balance on top of the couch. I'm going to put this big pillow down here, in case you slip."

• **Support children's courage and persistence.** Notice children's efforts: "You're learning to put your face in the water all by yourself." "It looks like you really want to fit that key into that lock. You've been trying to do that all morning." "You're really trying to figure out how to crawl. You've got your knees up and you're rocking now."

• **Intervene selectively.** Sometimes it's best to let time take its course. As Sherman explains, "A big thing for parents is learning when to stay out of the way. I've learned to ignore some things. Unless they're highly dangerous, I try to stay out of the way."

[1] See "When Children Love to Climb" on p. 254 for more on working with children as they climb.

Paula, the mother of nine, came to a similar conclusion: "My grandmother, who was a really big influence in my life, outlived all of her children. She used to tell me that her regrets had to do with nitpicking about certain little things, like what her children ate. She remembered all the arguments she wished she'd saved for more important things. And that made a really big impression on me. I try to let my kids make their own mistakes."

FOOD FOR THOUGHT: PROVING CHILDREN WRONG

• Growing up, were there times I felt badly about myself? How did the people around me contribute to that feeling?

• Have there been times my children felt badly about themselves in response to something I said?

• Is there another way I could have shared my concerns with my child?

Be Optimistic About Children's Struggles

Struggle is an essential part of learning something new. As Magda Gerber explains, "To struggle and to succeed is one of life's greatest accomplishments."

While many adults aren't comfortable struggling, children accept struggle as a necessary part of life. Babies experience it as they try to lift their heads or reach a shiny cup on the floor. Toddlers struggle to communicate their ideas. Preschoolers labor to dress themselves.

As daycare provider Joan Roemer describes in her book *Two to Four From Nine to Five* (HarperCollins, 1990): "I would have to wait at least twenty minutes while Ana figured out her right and left shoes. She did this entirely by feel. She almost always chose the wrong shoe and so put both shoes on wrong. She'd stand up—I'd think to myself, thank God—start walking, stop and say 'No.'

"Sitting back down, she'd start all over again. Sometimes she'd laboriously take both shoes off, put them on again, and still have them on the wrong feet! But oh her joy, and *mine*, when she got them right!"

Kids repeatedly set their sights on something they can't yet do. Many fuss, cry, and make loud noises while they struggle. Some work for a while, take a break, and come back to the task at hand—until they either succeed or give up. Most persist until they eventually figure out how to accomplish their goals.

Parents play an important role in children's struggles. We can provide the vision and the optimism that struggle does lead to success and offer support while children are trying to learn something on their own.

Yet parents who are uncomfortable with struggle may find themselves wanting to avert their children's frustration. Your ten-month-old daughter is struggling to fit that wide blue plastic letter into the slot of her mailbox, and you feel tempted to help her just a little—to guide her hand, to help her do it faster. For many of us, "successful" parenting includes protecting our child from having a hard time.

Yet ironically, interfering too much can actually make things harder for children in the long run. When we repeatedly intervene, we can take the struggle—and the victory—away from our kids. When we interrupt a child's efforts, his learning is cut short, not just about that particular thing, but also about problem-solving in general. The inadvertent lessons we teach—"You can't figure that out yourself" and "Struggle is to be avoided at all costs"—can negatively impact children's perception of struggle as a natural part of life.

As Keith, the father of two, reflects: "My parents didn't let me struggle. To this day, I want to solve a problem in five seconds or give up."

Jack has also had to learn to allow his two-year-old daughter to struggle: "One of the hardest things for me is to not show people that I always have the answer. So it was really hard for me to let Heidi wrestle with a problem. But it became obvious to me early on that Heidi wasn't going to learn unless she figured things out herself. So I started intervening less. I started observing more. I began to see that there were more subtle things occurring than whatever it was I thought the answer was. Sometimes it was her imagination. Other times it was her way of engineering a solution to a problem. The more carefully I observed her, and the more I got out of the way, the more I was awakened to possibilities that were far more interesting than what I thought the solution was 'supposed' to be."

How and When to Help

Respecting children's right to struggle doesn't mean we should never help them. Rather, it means intervening selectively and consciously, providing assistance that supports their sense of accomplishment. The following guidelines can help children develop a positive relationship with struggle:

- **Maintain safety.** If the child is really scared or there's an actual question of danger, move in quickly.

- **Learn to support the child instead of giving the solution.** Encourage the child who is struggling rather than supplying the solution. Saying, "I can see you're really trying to screw that lid on that jar. It looks hard" is a lot more sup-

portive than reaching over and screwing on the lid for the child.

• **Help in the smallest increment as possible.** If help is necessary, give the smallest amount of help needed for children to solve the problem on their own.

• **Present an optimistic view of the situation to your child.** Try saying, "I'm sure you'll be able to figure that out eventually. I've seen you learn a lot of things." Or "I know you're going to learn to button your shirt. You just need more time and practice."

• **Be a loving supportive presence.** While some children persist in struggling on their own, others appreciate the calm, reassuring presence of a parent nearby.

• **Don't underestimate your child.** Kids can often accomplish things that surprise us, as Laura recalls: "When Eli was eleven months old, he loved crawling under things. The narrower the space, the more he liked to test his body's capacity to squeeze through. One day, he crawled under a chair and got stuck between the rungs. He started to whimper. Karyn started out of her seat. I motioned for her to wait. 'He got in there,' I said. 'Let's see if he can get out.'

"I called to Eli, 'It looks like you're stuck.' His whimpers turned into cries. He sounded frustrated and angry, not hurt. He struggled, trying to move forward, but there was nowhere to go. Then Karyn tried an experiment. She said, 'Eli, I see that you're stuck. You don't know how to get out. But I saw you climb in there. You might have to back out.'

"Eli stopped crying for a moment. He

seemed to be listening, considering what she'd said. ('Of course that can't be true,' I told myself. 'He's only eleven months old.') But as soon as I had that thought, he backed right out! And boy, the look of triumph on his face!"

• **Respect the time it takes to learn new things.** Nothing takes the place of time and persistence.

• **Look at a child's motivation to struggle.** Children are more interested in struggling to bring their own ideas to fruition than in complying with ours. Often when *we* want children to do something or there are time constraints, we may need to provide more help.

• **Assess your child's capacity for struggle.** Some children have a greater capacity for struggle than others. There may also be times when your child is all struggled out. She's had to deal with a whole series of frustrations already. Or you may not have the stamina to support your child in her efforts. At these times, you can make a conscious decision to rescue your child from her dilemma, knowing that she'll have future opportunities to work things out herself.

• **Notice your feelings.** Being aware of your own responses can help you intervene appropriately based on your child's needs rather than your own.

• **Model a positive relationship to struggle yourself.** When parents model competency through struggle, children learn to see the value of persevering. Leah, who uses a wheelchair, remarked: "Because of my disability, there are times I *can't* intervene. I *have* to let them struggle. And my kids are very persistent. In part, that may be because of my disability. So many things are a struggle for me. When my kids see me walk up stairs, when they see me trying to do something that's hard to do, and they see that I don't give up, they learn the value of struggle. I model that for them every day."

When Children Beg You for Help

When children whine or yell, look pleadingly in your direction, scream for help or tug at your pant leg, it can be hard to figure out how to respond. While many of us immediately want to "fix" our children's problems, that might not be what children need. Some children simply struggle louder than others. The grunts, whimpers, or cries that accompany frustration offer children a kind of verbal release. Sometimes begging for help, screaming, and wailing are children's way of asking us to support them rather than a plea to take their struggle away.

Support can include letting children know that we have heard their request for help, coming closer, encouraging them, or acknowledging what they are trying to figure out: "I hear you asking me for help. I see you have your foot on the shelf and your hand on the door. You're really trying to get up. Do you want me to stand near you while you try?"

Listening attentively to your child's frustrations without taking the struggle away teaches children that we believe in their competence and ability to work things through themselves.

FOOD FOR THOUGHT: RESPONDING TO CHILDREN'S STRUGGLES

• What did I learn about struggle as a child growing up in my family?

• Were there times that struggle was an important part of my learning?

• How do I deal with struggles in my adult life? What do I teach my children about struggle through my example?

The Problem with Praise

One of the most important things we do as parents is let children know how special they are. That's our job. There is no one else in the world who is as crazy about our kids as we are. We ooh and aah over them, proclaiming that their wrinkled newborn bodies are the most beautiful things we've ever seen. We cheer them on when they first take on gravity by rolling over that arm that always seems to get stuck underneath. We root for them as they try to hit that ball with that big old plastic bat. The fact that we are excited and proud about the simplest things they do is crucial to children.

Praise is a tool many of us use to let children know that we are excited about their achievements. Many of us work hard to praise our children regularly. Some of us have come from families in which we got very little attention or positive feedback, and it has been a big step to learn to praise our children.

Yet certain kinds of praise convey messages we may not want to give:

• **Praise can imply a judgment.** Words such as "good," "pretty," "nice," and "beautiful" imply a comparison. When you can be "good," there is also the possibility of being "bad." When you're "nice," you could also be "mean" or "selfish." When your painting is "pretty" or "beautiful," it could also be "ugly."

• **Praise is often conditional.** Because children most frequently receive praise for things they "do" or "make" rather than just for being themselves, they can end up wondering if they're okay when they are not "producing" or "achieving."

• **Praise focuses on the end result.** Praise is often reserved for the culmination of the achievement or the "product" rather than for any part of the process. The struggle, the falling down, the mistakes, the hard work leading up to the achievement are not acknowledged nearly as much.

• **Praise is often inaccurate.** Praise that is not descriptive of what the child is actually doing can convey to children that we're really not paying close attention. If your child has lined up all her alphabet blocks, and you respond with "You're such a smart child," she may feel you don't really understand her intent because, in fact, she has just built a train to take all her animals home.

As Francisco recounted: "My daughter had just painted her whole page with dark blue and red. I said to her, 'What a beautiful picture.' She turned to me and said, 'NO, IT'S NOT! IT'S A SCARY PICTURE!' "

• **Praise emphasizes external validation over internal feelings of satisfaction.** Children who have grown accustomed to praise can lose touch with the inherent feelings of accomplishment that come with their achievements. As one father, Keith, recalls: "I was praised too much and ended up feeling like a trained seal. To this day, I want outside acknowledgment for every task, no matter how trivial."

• **Praise can lead to competition.** When children are taught to rely on external validation for their accomplishments, they often become competitive with siblings and peers, in an attempt to win more of the recognition.

Can't I Say Anything Nice to Her?

This perspective on praise can be difficult to hear. Parents often feel confused when they first hear that the kinds of praise they've used

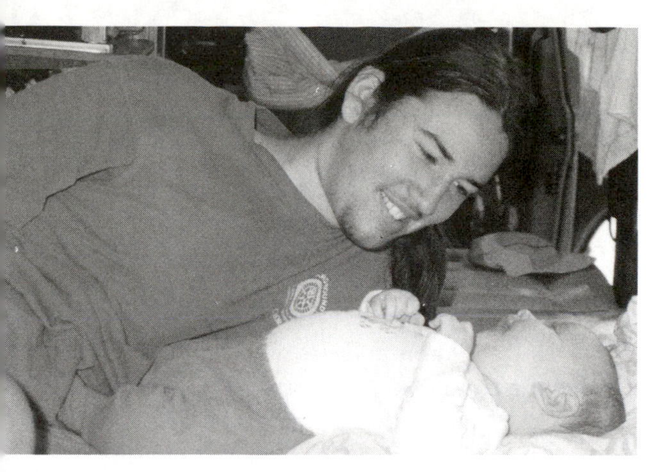

might not be as useful as they thought. These feelings are often expressed in comments such as "Am I just supposed to ignore her accomplishments?" "What about my excitement about her growing and learning?" "Can't I say anything nice to her?"

It can be disturbing to think that the way you have celebrated your child's achievements may need to be reconsidered. But there is an excellent alternative to praise: acknowledgment. Acknowledgment is a way to respond to children that is descriptive and nonjudgmental, yet it lets you convey your feelings. The basics of acknowledgment are:

• **Share your observations.** This can include making observations about what you see children doing all along, instead of just when they're done: "You're smearing that blue paint all over the paper." Or "You're squeezing that play dough so hard it's coming out between your fingers."

• **Use descriptive language.** When you choose words that are descriptive rather than evaluative, you let children know that you're really watching. You teach them vocabulary that relates to what they are doing and open up the conversation for their input. Children are free to respond, "Yeah, my picture is all filled up with the blue ocean." Or "Look, the play dough is even squeezed into my fingernails!"

• **Ask questions.** You can say: "Tell me about your painting." "How did it feel the first time you got up on your skates?" "I see you covering up that box with newspaper. Can you tell me about your project?" Encouraging children to talk about themselves and what they are doing is one of the most powerful kinds of acknowledgment we can give.

• **Use body language.** Body language is a powerful way to show children that we care, are paying attention, and are excited about them. By watching, smiling, or opening our arms to our children, we convey our interest and enthusiasm.

• **Reflect your child's excitement.** Occasionally saying things such as "You seem really excited about finishing that puzzle!" or "You look happy to be sharing that toy with Kwan" can support children's feelings of success.

Acknowledgment vs. Praise

Acknowledgment: "I see you've been painting a long time and your picture has a red line all the way around it."
Praise: "What a pretty picture!"

Acknowledgment: "You gave Josh a turn on the bike! He looks happy."
Praise: "You are such a nice girl."

Acknowledgment: "Thank you for helping to wipe off the table. Now it will be all clean for breakfast."
Praise: "You're such a good boy!"

Acknowledgment: "Wow, you came down by yourself. You've been working on learning to come down that pole for so long, and now you can do it!"
Praise: "You are so brave!"

• **Express your feelings.** Use words that describe your feelings or express your gratitude. "Thank you for . . ." "I love to see you . . ." "It's exciting to see you . . ." "I have fun watching you . . ." "I appreciate it when you . . ." These phrases allow you to express your feelings without labeling children.

FOOD FOR THOUGHT: THE PROBLEM WITH PRAISE

• What kinds of praise or acknowledgment did I receive as a child?

• Were there times when the praise I received didn't match my experience?

• Have there been times when praise or acknowledgment has felt uncomfortable to me?

Finding Your Own Sense of Optimism

Being able to acknowledge our children and celebrate their growth, curiosity, and learning is possible only if we have that same sense of appreciation for ourselves. Feeling optimistic about our own lives has a lot to do with the experiences we've had in life, the culture we come from, the parenting we had, and, to some degree, our temperament. But even if our natural perspective on life tends toward the pessimistic, there are ways to build a spirit of optimism about our kids and ourselves as parents.

• **Strive to focus on the positive aspects of your situation rather than the negative.** Jenny, a twenty-two-year-old mother who's faced a number of hardships because of her age, says: "There are definite advantages to being a young mother. I have lots of energy. I like the fact that when she's sixteen, I'll be thirty-five. It won't be such a stretch for me to look back and remember what being a teenager was like. Even though there might be things I'm missing out on now, I'll get to have them later."

• **Let your children pull you into the future.** Just having children is optimistic. Kids can give us a sense of future that we might never have otherwise. Masai poignantly expressed the difference his son has made in his life: "When I was younger, I never thought I'd get any older. I got stabbed when I was fourteen. I've had people shoot at me. I was in the Black Panther Party when I was sixteen years old. I've been a junkie and a wino. I never, ever thought I would get past twenty or twenty-one. So I never learned how to plan into the future. I could never envision things that were really far away.

"Having my son has changed that for me. I was thirty when he was born. Suddenly I had this kid and I *had* to look into the future. I couldn't just be day to day. I had to know that I was going to have a job next week, that I was going to be able to put food on the table. Now I'm actually thinking about him going to college. That's really an amazing change for me."

• **Pay attention to the things that build your sense of optimism.** Once you have an idea about the kind of situations and activities that help you stay positive about yourself as a parent, you can work to make them happen.

• **Talk to other parents.** When you're new at parenting, talking to other parents whose kids have survived and thrived can help build your confidence.

Ginny grew up in a very strict, controlling family, and she says that peer support has really helped her: "Because of my family history, it's sometimes difficult for me to look at my kids as good people when they're doing normal developmental things—like having tantrums. Sometimes I think 'This'll never end' or 'I'm the only one who has a child who's doing this.' The thing that's helped me regain my optimism more than anything else is talking to other parents. When I hear other parents tell their stories, it helps me realize that I'm not living with pathological demons. I realize that my kids are, in fact, normal."

• **Experience with kids builds optimism.** After you've watched your child learn to sit up, walk, and learn to share, it's easier to believe he'll reach other milestones as well. Rex, the father of two-and-a-half-year-old Eliot, recalls: "All the other kids had words and little sentences long before Eliot uttered his first word. He was grunting and crying and gesturing until he turned two. Then he broke out in five-word sentences. It happened so fast. That really taught me to trust that things will happen in their own time."

Paula reflects: "I've had a kid under ten for the last twenty-four years. I'm finally beginning to see that a lot of the stuff they go through is their way of finding themselves and defining themselves in relationship to their parents. They have fundamental characteristics that remain the same, but they're not going to always be self-centered or inappropriate or eat like that.

"I can't remember the things that used to drive me crazy about my grown kids. At the time, I was sure the selfish ones would be selfish forever, that the obnoxious ones would stay obnoxious. But they didn't. They outgrew almost everything."

Optimism Isn't Blind

Being optimistic about your children doesn't mean that you always think everything is fine, that you will fail to notice a persistent problem or developmental lag that needs to be dealt with. Optimism doesn't say "Marcus is two and he's not walking. If we just wait, it'll happen." Or "Chizu's three years old and she isn't talking. It'll work out fine." If your child is struggling to master a developmental task that most of his or her peers have mastered, it may be time to explore the reasons for the delay.

Having a sense of optimism gives you enough faith in yourself and your child to trust your ability to deal with whatever issues or special needs arise. Rather than being too scared and overwhelmed to face potential problems, optimism gives you a sense that you can deal with whatever comes up.

In her book *Peoplemaking*, Virginia Satir writes, "The parents in a nurturing family realize that problems will come along, simply because life offers them, but they will be alert to creative solutions for each new problem as it appears. Troubled families, on the other hand, put all their energies into the hopeless attempt to keep problems from happening; and when they do happen—and, of course, they always do—these people have no resources left for solving them."

True optimism gives us the courage to ask hard questions and look at tough realities. Optimism in ourselves, our kids, and our families places us on a firmer footing for dealing with life's inevitable challenges.

4. Understanding That Parents Are Always Growing

Principle 4: We learn how to be parents as we go along.

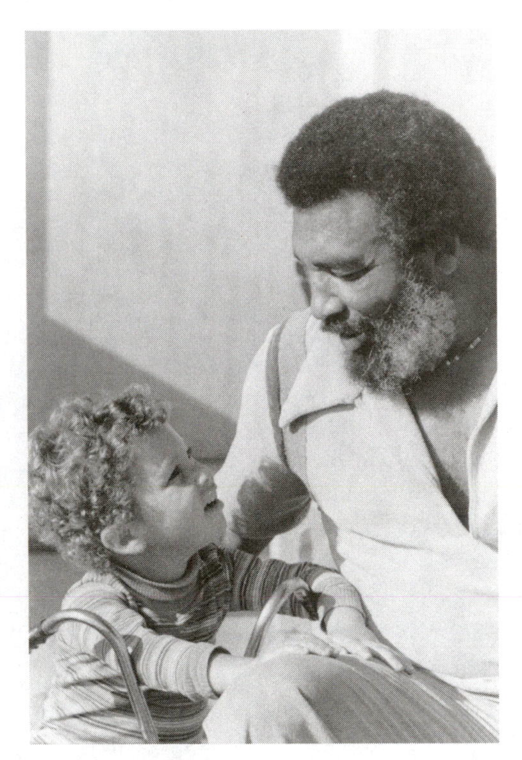

Part of being an effective parent is learning to trust our own evolution, both as individuals and as parents. With information, support, and experience, we can develop a sense of faith that we will be able to handle whatever parenting brings.

Each stage in our children's development brings up new feelings, memories, and challenges. The more kids we have, the more we're led to grow.

Leon is the father of eight, the grandfather of twelve, and the great-grandfather of four. When Laura asked him to describe his experience as a father, he replied, "What do you want to know about? Do you want to know about me as the father of sons? Or of daughters? About me as the father of my first child or my last? My first was born when I was twenty-four; the last the day after my sixty-second birthday. I did a lot of growing in that time. I grew into adulthood and parenthood. Each of my children changed me."

The changes we go through as parents spill over into other parts of our lives and can add a richness and depth to who we are as people as well as to our relationships with partners, families, friends, and work.

Mei expressed it this way: "The great thing about parenting is that I always want to improve myself. If I argue and scream and cry with my husband, I don't think about how I'm hurting him. Screaming at him doesn't have the same impact as screaming at my kids. The kids make me want to stop and change, and that spreads to other parts of my life. It's as if the kids have given me the gift of being a better person. No one else gives me these opportunities. And it's up to me what I do with them."

Bob, who studies Zen Buddhism, put it this way: "If you really focus on anything, it can take you very deep. Parenting is as good a path as any. There's no getting away from it. It's always in your face. You don't have to go to a temple, climb a mountain, or travel to India to find a spiritual teacher. Everything you need is right there in front of you."

Staying Open to Your Children

Many of us begin our lives as parents wanting to figure out what we're going to do ahead of time. Yet there are things children allow us to discover about ourselves that we can't possibly know until they're actually in our lives. The relationship of parent and child is unique.

No matter how much we know about babies, no matter how much we've taken care of other people's kids, no matter how much we know about how children grow and develop, we all move into uncharted territory when we begin to build our own families. We don't get to practice for parenthood.

Faye explains, "Before I had children, I had all these ideas of what parents should 'do.' If a child was acting up, I thought his parents should 'do' something. But once I had a child, I realized a lot of parenting is 'not doing.' A lot of what kids go through are phases, things they work through themselves. Watching my kids, it's clear they're their own people, that I can't take as active a role in managing them as I previously thought. They're not just clay that you mold."

Ginny, the mother of a five-year-old, agreed. "I had all these ideas about parenting, but then my daughter took me down a different path."

As much as we might like to enter parenthood with all our answers, techniques, and strategies in place, doing so would mean building a system that fails to include the input of our children. Our ability to stay open, adaptable, and responsive necessitates that we don't start with all the answers but that we dedicate ourselves to figuring them out along the way.

Being open to our children is a lifelong process, as Maggie explains: "As an adoptive parent, I think I have different expectations than biological parents. I value the uniqueness of each of my children in a special way because I didn't have a preconceived idea that they were going to be like me. It's like going to the nursery and getting an unmarked seed. I nurture it and help it grow and I don't know what kind of tree it's going to be. It's like a surprise package."

What Keeps Us from Being Open?

Although we want to be attentive and responsive to our children, it's not always easy to do so. Sometimes the dreams we hold for our children turn into expectations. Shu Lea explains: "I used to be a dancer. There's a part of me that says 'I never fulfilled my dream of being a real professional dancer. Maybe my children will.' I didn't think that kind of stuff would come up for me. But it did. And neither of my kids seems inclined to take ballet. Now I'm trying to tell myself 'I had a dream. It's time to let it go.' "

It can also be hard to be receptive to children simply because they're so different from us. Gail, the mother of three-year-old Cliff, complained, "My son is obsessed with cars and trucks. I don't mind talking to him about them for a little while, but then I want to do something else. But does he? No way!"

Sometimes it's hard to be open to children because we're uncomfortable with the depth, strength, or direction of their feelings. Social pressure can keep us from listening to children the way we'd like to. Your son starts falling apart in the grocery store and you feel embarrassed. Grandma is asking Holly to hug her good-bye and Holly doesn't want to, but you urge her to for Grandma's sake. In these instances, we sometimes forsake listening to children because we're concerned with what other people might think.

Finally, time pressures can interfere. Listening to children takes time. When we need to get something done, it can be challenging, if not impossible, to take those extra moments to find out what's going on with our child. But being receptive does not require that we always drop everything or change our plans. Being receptive when we're in a hurry may simply mean acknowledging to our child that we don't have the time to listen now, that we want to hear what he or she has to say, and that we will listen later, at the soonest possible opportunity. Like putting a bookmark in a book, we reserve a place for listening and communicating later on.

Growing Alongside Your Kids

Many of us come to parenting with a vision that we're supposed to be a couple of steps ahead of our kids. In truth, most of us are usually a few steps behind. As Rodney puts it, "Being a parent is like being on an obstacle course where you can't see the obstacles. You walk along a little way and 'Oops,' you bump your head. Then a little further, 'Ouch!' you bump your shin."

As parents, we're often asked to teach skills to children that we don't yet have ourselves. Our children draw on parts of us that are undeveloped, unpracticed, and, in some cases, even damaged.

When your son and daughter are fighting with each other, you want them to learn to resolve their differences successfully, but you may have never learned to successfully work through conflicts yourself. Before you can teach your kids to listen, identify the problem, express their feelings, generate solutions, and find common ground, you have to learn those problem-solving skills yourself.

Doing It for Kenji: Maria's Story

Maria is the mother of four-and-a-half-year-old Kenji. Repeatedly throughout his childhood, she has used the support of other parents to help her grow in order to give him what he needs.

One of the things I want to teach Kenji is to stand up for himself, to feel a sense of justice. One day we were sitting at an outdoor performance. Kenji had picked out this little chair that had an umbrella for shade. A man came along with a new baby and the manager asked that we give Kenji's chair to him. And without asking Kenji, I gave his chair away. When he saw that the man was about to sit in his chair, he said, 'Mommy! Mommy! That's *my* chair!' When the manager heard Kenji saying that, she came over and started yelling and shouting at him: 'That is not your chair anymore! I'm the boss and I gave that chair away!' I was shocked. I never talk to Kenji that way. And Kenji looked at me, waiting for me to do something. I was furious, but I didn't have the courage to talk back to her. I wanted to say, 'Don't talk to my child that way!' but I couldn't because I've never learned to say, 'Don't talk to *me* that way.' I couldn't model that for him. I felt terrible and I apologized to him. Since then I've really made an effort to speak up for myself—and for him. I know I have to learn to do it myself before I can give that gift to him.

Fortunately, we can learn right alongside our children. Faye explains how she does that with four-year-old Nico: "Nico was demanding everything and I was trying to get him to ask for things nicely. But then I realized that I wasn't asking very nicely either. I'd be struggling to get the kids out the door and I'd say, 'Just get in the car!' or 'Get your shoes on! Just get 'em on!!'

"So we made this little pact. I said to Nico, 'I haven't been asking for things very nicely. I'll try to remind you to ask nicer and you try to remind me.' Now, when I catch myself not asking for something in a nice way, I say, 'Oh! I didn't say that very nicely. Let me try that again.' Or he says, 'But, Mom, you asked in such a mean voice.' And I remind him, too."

FOOD FOR THOUGHT: PARENTS ARE ALWAYS GROWING

- How did I imagine parenting would be before I became a parent?
- What have I discovered about being a parent since I became one?

Ten Parenting Paradoxes

"Motherhood brings as much joy as ever, but it still brings boredom, exhaustion, and sorrow too. Nothing else will ever make you as happy or as sad, for nothing is quite as hard as helping a person develop his own individuality—especially while you struggle to keep your own."

MARGUERITE KELLY AND ELIA PARSONS,
coauthors of *The Mothers Almanac*

Parenting is full of paradoxes. And paradoxes keep parents growing and flexible. Here are just some of the many paradoxes inherent in parenting. You look at them one way, and they make sense. Then you turn them upside down, and they make sense that way, too:

1. It's useful for parents to have a consistent parenting philosophy but also to be flexible and able to adapt to the uniqueness of any given situation.
2. It's important for parents to pass on family traditions and values but also to allow children to be unique individuals.
3. Encouraging children to express their thoughts and feelings increases the chances that they'll stand up to you.
4. Effective teaching isn't always rewarded by immediate changes in behavior or tidy resolutions.
5. Children move toward independence and dependence at the same time.
6. Parents can be delighted and enthused at the new things their kids can do and simultaneously feel the loss of their child's younger self.
7. When you cultivate independence in your kids, they sometimes become independent in a way that leaves you out.
8. Parents can love parenting one minute and hate it the next.
9. Your biting, hitting, pushing child can actually be evolving into an empathetic, caring individual.
10. We're preparing children to live in a world that we can't possibly imagine.

5. Learning to Value Struggle and Disequilibrium

Principle 5: Periods of disequilibrium—times we feel confused and off balance—can be essential to our growth as parents.

There are rhythms and cycles to being a parent. There are the "successful" or "balanced" times when we feel like we've got it all figured out. Then there are the times we feel confused and inadequate.

Children are not the only ones who experience phases of disequilibrium. Parents do, too. Dalia, the mother of seventeen-month-old Zach, explains: "I had very clear expectations before Zach was born, none of which have come true. I was going to have the right partner. I was going to have a child who slept really well, because I knew how to get kids to sleep. I thought I'd have a well-behaved child. Well, now I'm a single parent, Zach's an incredibly poor sleeper, and he laughs in my face when I tell him what to do."

Classic points of disequilibrium for parents occur because of children's developmental changes: Kids stop sleeping at night, start crying when you leave the room, gain mobility, learn to walk, begin to hold on to their own ideas or start negotiating for what they want. Children go through a change and we're caught unprepared.

Laura went through one such period when Eli was ten months old: "In a one-week period, Eli climbed out of his crib, fell off our bed, and got into a bottle of Woolite. I just wasn't ready for him to become a toddler."

Cooper, the father of three-year-old Austin, expressed his confusion this way: "My picture of him always seems to be who he was a month or two ago."

Disequilibrium occurs when what used to work with your child no longer works; when what used to be a perfect fit doesn't fit anymore. And it's not just shoes that don't fit—it's postures, approaches, and strategies.

One day you're able to say "We've figured out how to get Shantika to sleep at night. We've got this system. Dad gives her a bath. Grandma sings to her, puts her in the crib, rubs her head for a minute, and Shantika goes right to sleep and doesn't wake up until the morning. Then all of a sudden, the system falls apart and we're forced to face the question: How do we figure out what to do when we don't know what to do?"

Some people respond to this loss of control by holding on to the rules more desperately, trying at all costs to get them to work. At times success can feel so elusive that it can be hard to let go of something that was successful in the past, even if it isn't working anymore. As Laura once put it, "What we know, even if it doesn't work, is preferable to a failure we haven't tried yet."

Even when we are flexible enough to try a new way, we may hope that once we figure out the new system, we'll only have to figure it out once: "If Grandma gives you a bottle in the rocking chair before she puts you in bed and *that* works to get you to sleep, we'll just do it for the rest of your life." But children are always changing; our solutions need to change, as well.

Letting Go of the Familiar

Disequilibrium entails letting go of the familiar in order to make room for something unknown. And sometimes it's hard to let go. Ginny was delighted by her baby's growth, but still had reservations: "When Earl was born, I knew he'd be my last baby. It was hard for me when he went from being a baby to a toddler. I wanted him to take babyhood to the max, like maybe not to walk until he was fourteen months old, to just let me carry him around in his sling. Well, it didn't work. Earl walked at nine months and didn't want anything to do with that sling."

Paula agreed. "I felt sad when my kids weren't infants anymore. They went from being such cuddly little balls of need that I could satisfy to having needs that I couldn't always meet so easily."

And Carl, the father of a four-year-old Carl Jr., recalls a recent experience of letting go: "I've always chosen Junior's clothes for him and he's always worn them. But just last week, he absolutely refused to put on the clothes I'd laid out for him. He chose a horribly mismatched outfit instead. He looked ridiculous! I had to stop and ask myself, 'Can I let him go out in the world like this?' And 'What will people think of me?' "

New Parents and Disequilibrium

At no time is disequilibrium more intense than when people become parents for the first time. Joan Roemer expresses this poignantly: "A baby comes into the world, seven and a half pounds, about the size of a large trout, and it changes the way we do everything in our lives. Whether we lock our doors, or wear our seat belts or pay our bills on time or not, we are now vulnerable. A baby changes everything in our lives."

Having a baby changes you from a nonparent to a parent. And that raises all kinds of questions: Who am I now? What does it mean to be a parent? What is my relationship to work now? To friends? To my family? To my partner?

Janis remembers feeling overwhelmed when her first child was born. "Until Lee was six months old, I felt like I was in a fog. Here I was meeting myself as a parent for the first time. I was meeting my husband as a father for the first time. And I was meeting a brand-new person, as well. Those were all totally encompassing tasks."

The Heart of the Matter: Laura's Story

This story talks about the way Laura and her partner, Karyn, each dealt with their sons' vulnerability. At the time this story was written, Eli was six months old and Bryan was sixteen and just learning to drive.

When Eli was a newborn, I came across a quote by Elizabeth Stone that stunned me: "Making the decision to have a child—it's momentous. It is to decide forever to have your heart go walking around outside your body."

I think she got right to the heart of the matter.

When Eli was first born, I'd hold him and feel immobilized by the utter vulnerability of his floppy little neck. His flailing skinny arms and his bony little legs unnerved me. I knew in a place that I could not name that it was impossible to protect him completely. There was SIDS. There were earthquakes. There was spinal meningitis and leukemia. There were kidnappers, the greenhouse effect, and nuclear bombs. There was being in the wrong place at the wrong time, car wrecks, and drownings. I knew I couldn't stop those things, try as I might, and there was a chance that I might be asked to outlive my baby.

I couldn't imagine it. How did those parents do it, I wondered? How did they survive? I listened obsessively to "Tears in Heaven," Eric Clapton's tribute to his dead son, Colin, looking for a clue. I played it over and over, crying into Eli's few strands of hair.

"You have to let it go, Laura," Karyn finally told me one day. I tried to listen. She was experienced. Her son had lasted fifteen and a half years so far. "You do everything you can to protect them, but then you have to let it go. You don't want your fear holding him back."

Weeks later, it was time for Bryan to learn to drive. Karyn wanted nothing to do with it. Bryan's dad, Richard, and I volunteered to take turns teaching him. Sunday afternoons, I took him out to an empty parking lot on the west side of town. No one was there. I stayed cheerful and affirming as we lurched around the parking lot.

Karyn watched these outings with a tight resignation. She knew it was time for Bryan to drive, that it wasn't right to stop him, but she repeatedly lectured him about drunks on the road, never letting anyone have alcohol in the car, and the death rate for teenagers driving after midnight.

"You've got to let it go, Karyn," I told her the day he got his license. "He's a good driver, really. He's going to be okay."

It is hard for us to let our children go, to let them leave the safety of our breasts, our arms, our laps. To cheer on their crawling, walking, and running, even as they move away from us. To send them to school, let them make friends, sleep over, ride in other people's cars, go on weekend trips, fall in love, get hurt, and make their own mistakes.

Forever having our hearts outside of our bodies.

The birth of a first child also shifts the dynamics of your family. Everyone's role gets extended. As Joe explains: "Until I had Tyler, I could fool myself and say 'I'm still a kid.' But now I say to myself, 'My God! I'm now a father. My parents are now grandparents.' We've all moved up. It gives me a sense of the cycles of life. A sense of mortality. I want to make every moment count."

"My Child's Life Depends on Me"

Another reason new parents often feel overwhelmed is that they are suddenly responsible for a new, helpless human being. Such responsibility is daunting and awe-inspiring.

Then we fall in love with our babies, and that falling in love is different from anything else

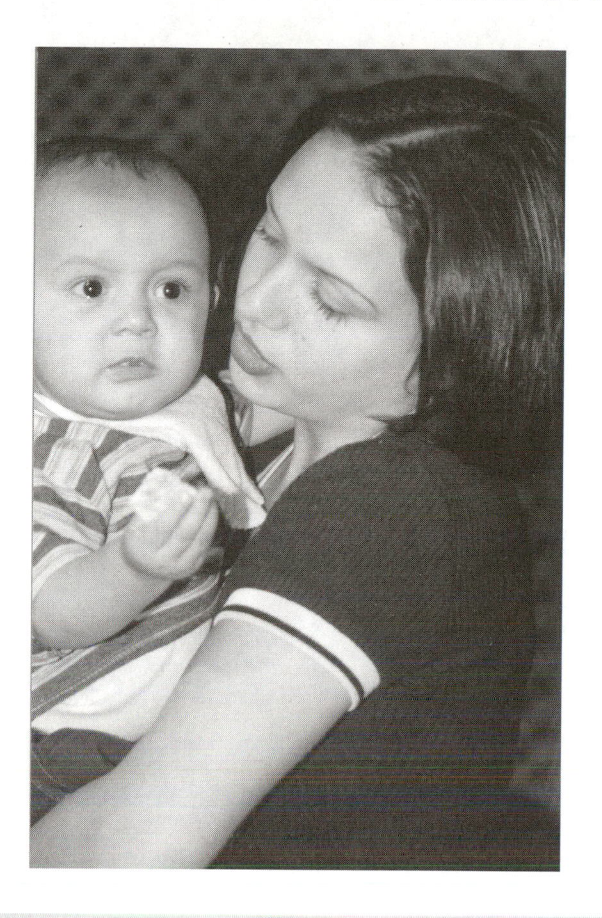

we've ever known. There's no other relationship where the love is so swift and so irrevocable.

Perry, a new father, asked, "How can I feel this deeply about a person I've known for such a short time?"

Laura, too, was surprised by the strength of her feelings when Eli was born. "Before I had Eli, I thought babies were boring. They didn't talk. They didn't communicate. They didn't *do* anything. As my friend Barbara put it, they were basically tubes—you put stuff in one end and it came out the other. I was willing to have a baby only because I really wanted a child.

"I hadn't spent much time with babies. So being me, I expected the worst. I anticipated diarrhea, projectile vomiting, endless crying, and sleepless nights. When Eli was born, I was stunned. What I'd forgotten to expect was love."

In the face of that love—and that responsibility—parents start to worry: Is she okay? What if something terrible happens? I couldn't live without her.

Alejandro says this increased sense of vulnerability dawned on him slowly. "What oc-

The Things I Carried: Sari's Story

Over one shoulder, a diaper bag holding two receiving blankets, three clean diapers, two dirty ones, three pairs of plastic pants, two extra plastic bags, a diaper changing pad, a soiled T-shirt and a pair of poopy pants, one clean outfit, a tube of Desitin, diaper wipes, spit-up rags, a soggy crushed packet of teething crackers, a rattle, a ball, two chewed-up board books, a purple sweatshirt, some socks, a mismatched pair of corduroy booties, a sun hat with flaps, baby sunscreen, a baby thermometer, a water bottle, and the remains of a bottle of infant Tylenol.

Over the other shoulder, a striped baby sling and a lunch bag with a gnawed-on apple and a warm bottle full of lumpy milk.

Around my waist, a fanny pack with checkbook, unpaid bills, wallet, tissues, two grungy squares of chocolate, a pair of sunglasses, and an outdated lottery ticket.

On my back, an empty baby backpack.

On my clothes, mashed yams, patches of drool, and smashed bits of banana. My sweatshirt is on backward and my pants haven't been washed in a week.

In one hand, a plastic basketball hoop and ball just borrowed from a friend, a string of extra large multicolored pop-beads, a dirty plate leftover from a pot luck, a bag containing a quart of milk, some bread and a video of a feature film I missed six months ago.

Tucked under the other arm, the newspaper (never read), the baby's jacket, a blanket, a stuffed duck, and a squiggling eighteen-pound baby.

In between my middle and index fingers, one set of keys (lost and found twice this morning).

Give or take a few things.

curred to me about a year into my son's life was that this relationship was the most profound, important relationship I'd ever had. If this kid were to die, I'd be a basket case for the rest of my life. I've never felt that way about anybody, not even my wife."

As new parents, we sometimes wonder why we've suddenly gotten so pessimistic and gloomy. But brooding—and dreaming—over the terrible things that might happen to our children is a way we explore the depth of the relationship, examine the strength of our connection, and come to accept the extensiveness of our responsibility for another human being. As Janis often tells new parents, "Babies come into our lives as utter miracles. It makes sense that we would worry."

For many parents, this growing vulnerability extends beyond concerns about the safety of their immediate family. Many new parents report that they feel the pain of the world—and of children everywhere—much more keenly. Rebecca, a mother in a postpartum support group, brought up the fact that she'd been unable to read the papers or listen to the news since her baby had been born.

Colleen echoed this sentiment. "I feel the pain of all children more since I've become a parent. I want all children to be warm, to be loved, to not suffer. When I gave birth, I opened emotionally, and I never closed back up."

The Exhaustion New Parents Face

The fatigue new parents experience is another part of their disequilibrium. This exhaustion is not just about lack of sleep. It's also about the incredible amount of attention they're paying to another human being. Getting to know a new person, developing a unique system of communication, and being constantly aware of an infant's needs is exhausting.

New parents often can't believe the intense

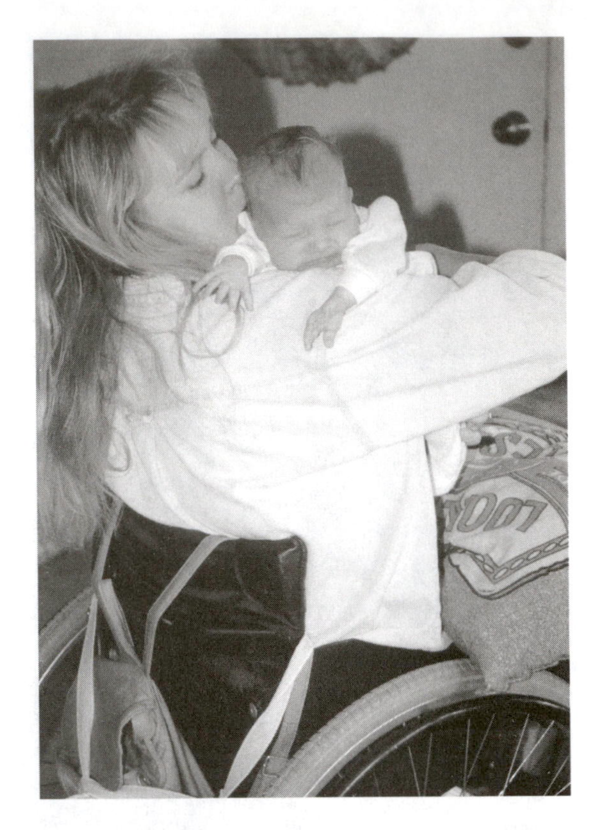

focus and attention a baby requires. They lament, "I'm a mush brain. I can't rub two sentences together." Evelyn, who nursed her boys well into toddlerhood, phrased it this way: "I felt like I was suffering from milk of amnesia."

What parents experience as exhaustion and disequilibrium often signals significant learning. New parents are engrossed in figuring out how to read their child's cries and all the subtle cues of their baby's communication. Parents are learning to discern one whimper from another, to read the subtleties of a baby's nuzzle or look, to engage in rich and complex communication without the benefit of structured language.

Will, the father of twins, explains, "They're six months old and there must be at least eight different ways they cry. Reuben has a whiny cry that means he's tired of sitting and wants to roll around on the floor. When he's really hungry, there's a longer mid-level intensity in his cry. When he has to sleep, he lets out high-pitched

Learning to Value Struggle

"Being an effective parent isn't always graceful. Sometimes it's physical, loud, angry, or a struggle."

—JANIS

As parents, we sometimes labor under the misconception that our job should be easy, that we should be able to smoothly resolve conflicts, quickly fix disputes, and gracefully meet all of our children's needs.

But real parenting is filled with struggle. Every day, parents are forced to call on inner resources they didn't know they had. Janis explains: "My middle son, Calvin, has always been a climber. Once when he was a toddler, I tried to take him to the fabric store. Of course I was interested in the colors and the textures and what would go with what, and he was interested in all the little low shelves and how you climb in between and on top of all those bolts of fabric. When he started pulling down bolts of fabric, I realized that the trip wasn't going to work. So I said to him, 'We're going to go.' He, of course, wanted to continue to explore the lovely low shelves and all the bolts of fabric. They made such perfect climbing structures! I put the bolts of fabric back on the shelf and told him I was going to pick him up and take him out to the car. He started flailing, trying to reach the shelves and jump out of my arms. Carrying a flailing child out of the store wasn't very graceful. I'm sure my face was red with the struggle and I was disappointed and frustrated that I couldn't stay and shop. And yet at the time, I felt successful, not because he said 'Yes, Mama' and walked calmly alongside me, but because I was able to get him out of the store without losing a sense of respect for what he wanted. I was able to do it without blaming him or being mad at him."

Being an effective parent isn't always graceful.

long screams that are more forceful. And David has his own set of cries."

As new parents learn to listen to their babies with all of their senses, they develop a new and sophisticated language. This incredible concentration and focus makes it hard for many new parents to function fully in other areas of their lives.

Disequilibrium During the Toddler and Preschool Years

Just as many parents begin to move past the disequilibrium of infancy and hit their stride, their baby turns into a toddler who has an entirely new agenda: independence and control. Learning to deal with the eruptions of anger and the struggles over power that spring from this push for autonomy throws many parents right back into disequilibrium.

Parenting toddlers brings up a raw vulnerability. There's an opportunity in that—an openness, a freshness. It can also lead to desperation—and desperation's partner, the motivation to really look at things and figure them out.

The vulnerability parents of toddlers feel is partly about who toddlers are and also about what it's like to live with a toddler. Toddlers are incredibly present, full of whatever they're feeling right now. Being with that kind of intensity focuses you and brings you face to face with your most basic beliefs about human nature.

Because toddlers are eagerly trying to learn about feelings, they take every opportunity to explore yours. While most of your friends and family know what makes you angry and carefully step around it, toddlers often will read what's going to make you angry and go right for it. As the parent of a toddler, you'll be questioned and challenged, taken to places that you may have previously avoided.

Patrick, the father of two-year-old Ryan, put it this way: "Their job is to push you as hard as you go to see where you snap, so they can see what happens when you snap."

Preschoolers Present Unfamiliar Challenges Too

Preschoolers are also experts at researching issues of power. Fascinated by their bodies and the importance of language, preschoolers spend lots of time exploring words that make adults cringe, from body and poop talk, to name calling and swearing. Disequilibrium happens for many parents when they realize that they can't fully control what comes out of their four-year-old's mouth.

Children of this age are also engrossed with their ability to make things happen in relationships. In exploring the nature of friendships, they sometimes try out power plays, physical aggression, and exclusionary play. For parents, this means not only struggling to respond to difficult behavior in the moment but also facing disconcerting questions about their child's character.

Preschoolers also become expert negotiators. Mickey, the mother of a child who has just discovered videos, tells this story: "We were driving home and Tim asked if we could stop by the store and rent a video. When I told Tim 'Not today,' he tried, 'I have an idea! How about if we drive into the parking lot, jump out of the car, get a video, and jump back into the car real fast?' When I told him 'no' again he continued to come up with creative negotiations to see if he could hit the magic solution to getting the video he wanted." While most parents want to cultivate the skill of negotiation in their children, working with a preschool negotiator can lead parents to wonder if they've lost control.

Preschool children are in love with their own ideas. Child development theorist Erik Erikson calls this stage of children's development the age of initiative. Children who have no interest in *your* idea of picking up their toys will turn around and spend two hours of hard labor implementing *their* idea of digging a huge reservoir in the sand box. The challenge for parents who want to support children's burgeoning initiative is how to involve children in coming up with ideas for problem-solving, even regarding their own behavior.

The Benefits of Disequilibrium

Until they accumulate experience with these cycles of disorientation, discomfort, and balance, parents often feel vulnerable and overwhelmed when they occur. Few of us go into parenting expecting that we will feel so confused or that we will need to figure out so much. As Kimber, mother of four-year-old Sonya, put it, "It's always seemed to me like parenting should be a whole lot more obvious than it is."

Many parents feel guilty during periods of disequilibrium, wondering if there's something wrong with them or their children. But disequilibrium is a natural, healthy part of any growing relationship.

- **Disequilibrium deepens your empathy for your children.** Knowing what disequilibrium feels like can deepen your empathy for your children, who go through these kinds of changes regularly.

• **Disequilibrium gives you insight into yourself and your children.** Significant learning often emerges from periods of disequilibrium, even if we can't always recognize it right away. Paula explains: "In the moment, I hate struggles with my kids. I often feel 'How can you do this to me with all that I'm doing for you?' But in the long run, struggles always turn out to be fruitful. Through struggle, I've learned who my kids are and what matters to them. I've learned that I'm not right all the time. Sometimes I find myself struggling with a child over something that's also a problem for me in my adult relationships. When I see that, it's a mirror that says 'This is something I need to work on.' "

• **Disequilibrium helps you build and redefine your perspective.** When old strategies no longer work and you're uncertain about what to do, you're motivated to observe and listen to your children, to do some soul-searching about what you want to teach. When you're forced to translate your parenting values into a new set of circumstances, you come to know them more fully.

• **Disequilibrium leads you to develop new strategies.** Every time you're thrown off balance, you're challenged to come up with new solutions, through hashing things out with friends, talking to your partner, reading, seeking out advice, or, most important, testing out different solutions with your child.

• **When you acknowledge and struggle with disequilibrium, you model healthy growth for your children.** Learning to trust—even to welcome—the uncertainty that precedes any new

Helping Children Deal with Change

One of the things we can do for our children is assist them in developing a personal style that helps them deal with change. Here are some general guidelines that can help children cope with everyday changes such as weaning, moving, getting a new bed, or starting preschool.

• **Gradual change is easiest for children.** A child who is being weaned from the breast does better when one nursing is dropped at a time, gradually over a period of weeks or months, rather than all nursing being stopped abruptly.

• **Approach changes with as much clarity as you can.** The clearer your intent, and the more directly you communicate to your child what's about to happen, the easier the change will go.

• **Try different solutions.** Many of us live under the misconception that parents should know what to do automatically. Yet it usually takes a lot of muddling and halfhearted attempts before you find the clarity and conviction to know what you want to do. Responsive parenting means being willing to say "Let's try this. Let's try it and see what happens with our child. Let's see what fits for us."

• **Tell your children what will stay the same.** As you tell your child what will change, also talk about what will stay the same.

• **Accept the fact that change takes time.** Give children time to adjust.

• **Listen to your child's feedback.** If you instigate a change, give it time and consistent follow-through. If it still doesn't seem to be taking, you may need to reevaluate your timetable or your approach.

• **Celebrate change.** Think about a simple ritual or celebration to mark change. Celebrations can be small or large, informal or carefully planned, but marking the occasion can make the change more special and, therefore, easier to assimilate.

growth or discovery is one of the most important perspectives you can hold for yourself and your children.

Sometimes It's a Matter of Time

Moving through disequilibrium is sometimes more a question of time than anything else. You're struggling with a problem—your child is refusing to share, waking up repeatedly at night, or biting other children. It seems like there's never going to be an end to the struggle, and then one day, you hit upon a solution and it works beautifully. You think to yourself "Why didn't I try that sooner?" But in fact, if you'd tried it four months sooner, it might not have worked. Your child might not have been ready or you may not have had the clarity to follow through with the strategy. A variety of factors come together at a given moment to make a particular solution work—which is not something you can anticipate or force.

When we accept that struggle is part of being an effective parent, we no longer have to hold ourselves up to an impossible standard—one in which everything works like clockwork. Instead, we can embrace a more realistic goal—one in which uncertainty appears regularly and is used as a tool for growth and increased understanding. Once we do this, we give ourselves the room to trust ourselves, to try different strategies, and to better evaluate effective solutions.

When Change Comes from the Outside

While some disequilibrium is caused by the ebb and flow of children's development, other times it is caused by forces outside the children. You go on a trip, you move, the time changes, your son gets a new caregiver, a baby sister is born, you and your spouse separate, or someone dies. In some of these instances, it is primarily the child who is experiencing the change, but in others, you also are in turmoil.

When the outside events primarily affect children, it is relatively easy to support them (see box, "Helping Children Deal with Change"), but when you are also affected, it is much more difficult to meet your children's needs.

Faye recalls: "My father died last year. I shared with my kids why I was upset, but I couldn't function as a parent at all. I couldn't answer questions. I couldn't stay focused on their activities and needs. I was almost unsafe to be around. Finally, I realized I had to find other people to take care of my kids."

Deaths and other life crises are hard for all of us to deal with, but when we have young children, our challenge is even greater. Eric asks, "What do you do when the problem is caused by a situation in your life—a major conflict in your relationship, something screwed up at work, somebody dying or really sick—when you're out of control, not because of your kid but because of life? For me, those are the trickiest times in being a parent. How much are you going to say about why you're flipping out or why their mother is crying? When do you let them know that you're not always the rock, that you don't always have the answers? How can you be a responsible parent when you can hardly deal with yourself?"

Helping Children in Times of Crisis

How you deal with children in a crisis will depend a lot on the specific circumstances and your child's age, needs, and ability to understand. But certain basic guidelines apply:

• **Find your own sense of optimism.** In troubled times, children pick up on what we're feeling more than anything else. It's important that we strive to find a way to affirm life for them, even if we can't yet do it for ourselves.

• **Get as much practical help as you can.** Physical support, such as help with moving or meals, can make a difference in a time of crisis. Help, in all its forms, can free your energies to be with your children, to reassure and explain things to them. Often friends are eager—or at least willing—to help, and allowing them to do so strengthens those relationships and builds community.

• **Listen to your child's feelings.** Children often have feelings in response to changes they can't control. It's outside your power to make everything better, but you can give your children the priceless gift of listening.

• **Give your child the necessary information in simple, positive terms.** It is important to give your child information about what's happening. Include possible positive outcomes, as well as difficult information, whenever you can: "I've just lost my job and I'm worried about it. It may take awhile for me to find a new job, but I'll get one eventually." Or "Since Mommy moved out, things have been kind of hard around here. I've been more grumpy and I know that's rough on you sometimes. It's going to take some time, but we'll figure out how to make things work."

• **Tailor your explanations to your child's age and ability to understand.** Children can be confused by elaborate explanations they can't comprehend. Janis explains: "When our friend Wilbur died, Maya was three and I knew she didn't have enough of a concept of time to understand the permanence of death. Yet I wanted to explain to her that Wilbur had died. So I tried to make my explanation as concrete as I could. I told her, 'Wilbur's body doesn't work anymore. He doesn't walk. He can't eat. He can't give hugs. He can't visit us. He can't talk on the phone.' And she asked, 'Why are we going to the funeral?' I answered, 'We're going to the funeral to say good-bye to Wilbur.' And she said, 'But, Mom, you just said he can't talk!' "

• **Share your feelings with children in an age-appropriate way.** It is challenging to figure out how to share painful feelings with children. On the one hand, it's important to be honest with children about our feelings, to give name to the things they can read in our face and our body. They already *know* that we're upset, so it's important that we share some of our pain with them. But it's also important to protect them from the full force of our adult responses to serious situations so we don't overwhelm or scare them.

When you're wondering what to share with your children in a time of trouble, it can help to ask yourself: Is this sharing primarily to meet my needs? Or is to meet the needs of my children? Do I have another place I can let down my guard and express my deeper feelings about this?

Having outside outlets for our feelings can keep us from using our children inappropriately as confidants. Expressing our feelings elsewhere can enable us be more thoughtful about the sharing we do with our children. You can say such things as: "I'm sad about Grandpa dying. I miss him. I think about the way we all picked apples together. After a while, I won't cry so much anymore." This shows your children you're human, reassures them, and also gives them the room to express the things they miss about Grandpa, too.

• **Differentiate your concerns from those of your children.** Adults think differently about life changes than children do. Adults think in broad terms and are able to make long-term projections. Children primarily want to know how the change is going to affect them right now.

• **Reassure your children about what will happen to them.** Children interpret experiences in terms of themselves. They ask questions such as "Will that happen to me?" "Who is going to take care of me?" or "Where will I sleep?" Respond to children's concerns by giving concrete answers: "While Mommy is taking care of Nana, Vivian from next door will take care of you. She will make your meals and read you your stories. She will help you find clean clothes to wear."

• **Use the situation as an opportunity for teaching.** In dealing with inevitable life crises, you have the opportunity to teach your children about the healthy expression of feelings, about the positive aspects of change, and about the human capacity to persevere and continue loving through hard times. Dealing constructively with the disequilibrium caused by changes in the family, even stressful ones, can provide important lessons for children that they can call on throughout their lives.

6. Working Toward a Balance of Needs

Principle 6: A family rhythm that balances each person's unique needs with the needs of the family as a whole creates mutual respect and harmony.

Imagine the following scenario: You have a spouse and two children. It's five-thirty in the afternoon. You're thinking about dinner and trying to make a transition from your busy day. You open the refrigerator and start poking around, seeing what you can come up with. What you'd really like to do is stretch out on the sofa for twenty minutes with the newspaper, but that's never going to happen.

Your four-year-old daughter keeps pulling on your sleeve, asking you to help her get the fingerpaints. She's saying, "Daddy, can Bobbi come over? Please? We'll clean up this time. Really we will." Then she says she's hungry and that she wants to eat the cinnamon red hots you let her buy at the store in a moment of weakness. You tell her you want her to eat dinner first and ask what she wants to eat. "Plain spaghetti," she says, "with cheese on the side."

Your two-year-old-son is hanging on to your left leg. He's saying "Take walk! Take walk! Take walk!" in an unrelenting monotone. You can smell his need for a diaper change. He hasn't had a snack all afternoon and you remember that the only thing he's eaten this week are turkey dogs, cut in quarters the long way, with catsup.

Your partner comes in from work. She wants nothing more than to change her clothes and use the bathroom, but already, both kids are clambering all over her. "Mommy!" "Take walk!" "Can Bobbi come over?"

That's a lot of competing needs to juggle.

What adults and children need in a household often seems diametrically opposed. Family life is an endless series of trade-offs—setting aside the needs of one family member for another. This kind of give and take is useful to children, who as members of families benefit from learning that their needs, as well as the needs of others, will be considered.

Striving Toward Balance

Historically, only adults' needs mattered. Then, for some families, the pendulum swung the other way and kids' needs took precedence. Or, as Janis puts it, "The child wagged the family."

Now we face the dilemma of trying to find a balance of needs. Although such a balance is something that can't be attained permanently, the attempt to find it is full of valuable lessons. When we try to take into account everyone in the family's needs, we teach children that all people should be respected regardless of age, gender, experience, or status. We teach children about problem solving, negotiation, and consensus. We let them know that more than one person can be valued at a time. Balancing needs is an integral part of building reciprocal relationships within a family.[1]

New Parents and Time: Where Did the Time Go?

Our sense of time changes radically when we have our first child. Where we once were able to focus on work, schooling, relationships, and our own interests, we now find our time absorbed by the constant needs of a tiny, dependent infant. No longer free to be spontaneous in our pursuits or pleasures, our relationship to time is permanently altered.

For very young parents who haven't yet been out on their own, there is the additional challenge of taking care of another person when part of you wants to be out exploring the world for yourself. Beatriz reflected on how having a baby has changed her life: "It's hard because my friends go out and have fun with guys and now I don't go. Instead I talk about diapers and what's on sale. And when I'm trying to study and Ultima starts crying, it's really hard. I have to put things aside and feed her. But then I forget what I was reading about and I have to read it all over again. Everything takes more time."

[1] The issue of negotiation between parent and child is dealt with thoroughly in Chapter 21, "Negotiating Conflicts Between Parent and Child" on p. 267.

Dalia rushed into a parent group and blurted out, "Sorry I'm late. Before I had kids I was always five or ten minutes early. I was famous for it. Now I'm never on time anymore, no matter what time it is. If we'd been meeting here an hour or two hours later, it wouldn't have mattered. I still would have been late."

Time can also be a source of conflict between parents, as Eric explains. "The first four or five years of Lauren's life, time was just an enormous issue—the stress of not having enough time to get done what needed to get done. It was really intense—all that scheduling! How do you balance who's working when? Who does what and is it fair? We had big struggles around that."

Time also created problems in Maria's marriage. "When Kenji was young, just being with him, just being able to watch him seemed a lot more important than having the dishes done or folding the laundry. And that caused a lot of problems. There were days my husband came home from work and the house was more of a mess than it had been the day before. He'd say, 'What happened?' He couldn't understand why I 'hadn't gotten anything done.' "

People who haven't had lots of close-up experience with babies sometimes enter parenthood thinking that a baby will fit right in with all their existing plans. Ishmael explains: "I imagined the baby as sort of a package, one more thing to carry as I went about my day. I never thought that it wouldn't work to just take her wherever I went."

Other new parents, who are used to working full time outside the home, sometimes operate under the misconception that being home with a baby will give them a chance to finally get to all those projects they haven't had time for: "Just think, I can clean the cupboards like I've been wanting to." "I can fix the front porch." "I can replant the garden." It's unfathomable how absorbed you can be in just being a parent.

What About My List?

Parents who are used to years of operating independently in the world often find the transition to parenthood—and the inherent loss of control—extremely challenging. Faye explains: "I used to love lists—getting things done and crossing them off. The list was the anchor of my day. Now if I make a list it's way too depressing. The only things that go on my calendar now are doctor's appointments—things I absolutely must remember. But as far as goals for the day—forget it! What am I going to write on there: 'Survive?' When do I get to cross off 'Survive'? At five in the evening? Ten-thirty? Midnight?"

When we think in terms of goals, most of us think about concrete accomplishments, not the kind of repetitive, invisible work parents do with babies. As you anticipate your day, you probably don't say to yourself "I'm going to get some listening done today. I'm going to learn more about how my baby thinks. I'm going to make food and clean it up several times. I'm going to change several diapers. I'm going to put out toys and pick them up and put them out again. We're going to be making clothes dirty at the same time I'm washing them. I'll get my hair combed once and messed up several times. And at the end of day, when my hair is not combed and the toys are all over the floor, I'm going to get to cross all those things off my list and say 'Ah, that was a satisfying day!' "

Why Slow Down to Baby Time?

Janis's friend Rosalie is a real estate agent. Two months after her first baby was born, she had a big real estate meeting. She allowed plenty of time to nurse the baby, to change and dress her, to pack the diaper bag, to dress herself, to get everything together she needed for the meeting. But just as she was getting her

daughter into her car seat, the baby did one of those explosive poops that goes all over everything. "At that moment," Rosalie said, "I realized that I couldn't go on the world's timetable. There was no way I was going to be respectful toward my baby and still make it to that meeting on time."

As infant specialist Magda Gerber puts it, "No matter how slow you're going with babies, go slower."

Why? To begin with, babies' communication is nonverbal, and you can miss a lot if you don't slow down to their pace. If you're moving too fast, you may miss the more subtle communication that's happening with your child.

Children also process things differently than

we do. You may feel done with the scary incident with the big dog in the front yard, but your child may still need more time and attention in order to come to terms with what happened.

But the best part of slowing down for babies is the fact that being truly present is a gift. Being with babies can help us to be fully and wonderfully in the moment. When we're around babies, the rest of the world drops away. You can make yourself a cup of tea, and three hours go by before you get back to it.

As Bryce, the father of four, put it, "Baby time? There's nothing quite like it. A walk around the block can take three days."

Emily, who is home with her children, echoed this sentiment. "Right now I'm really high on all the little profound moments that come up every day—how they can make a rainbow from the water in the hose, the way my two-year-old brings her sister a blanket when she goes to get her own—little things that remind you what's important in life. I really derive a lot of enrichment from seeing them live life right."

Infancy and babyhood are such fleeting moments in children's lives. Cherishing the specialness of what babies and children have to offer is a wonderful reminder of what's important in life.

Balancing Work and Family: Whose Rhythm Do We Follow Today?

With more and more parents working, going to school, or having responsibilities out in the world, the contrast between adults' pace and children's pace is greater than ever.

Often what happens is that work takes up so much of our day that our lives at home, by necessity, have to keep moving at that same pace. Because all of the home activities have been compressed into a narrow slice of time around the edges of outside work, many of us end up hurrying to pick up children at school and day care, running to the grocery store, rushing home, making dinner, getting baths, braiding hair, finding homework, packing lunches, looking for lost keys, and searching for two somewhat similar socks. On top of that, we have to deal with the leaky roof and keep the baby from eating her brother's science project.

In many families, getting out the door in the morning is especially difficult. As Laura explains, "I feel like I have to manipulate Eli to get him out the door on time. I have to wake him up and hurry him along. I have to sidestep his interests. The whole morning I've got these little wheels turning in my mind: 'He doesn't have his shirt on yet.' 'I still haven't changed his diaper.' 'Do we have time for breakfast or not?' 'Is his diaper bag packed?' "

Debbie, who works full time outside the home, explains: "My life is just getting up, getting ready, going to work, getting home, getting ready for bed. There's a lot of preparation at night and then in the morning, we're up by six."

Janis knows just what Debbie is talking about. "I've had days when I got to work and felt like I'd already worked a full day. And it was only eight-thirty in the morning."

This daily drama around time is played out in families more often than any other in terms of balancing needs. In the morning, your child's need might be to open her eyes slowly, to look around the room, to rediscover the toys that she left long ago last night, and then maybe to get hungry for something and mosey on down to explore her Cream of Wheat. And your need is to get out of the house, to get your older children ready for school, to get the baby to child care. The conflict in needs is keen.

When You Have to Juggle Competing Needs

All day long, parents make decisions about whose needs take priority, about who's going to have to wait, about who needs to hurry, about who gets to go at their own pace. When you're juggling needs, here are some things that can help:

• **Go easy on yourself.** It is important to acknowledge that no parent can "do it all." Trimming your expectations to more realistic levels will help you feel more successful. Robin, the mother of an older child and a baby, says she's really felt liberated since she realized that she couldn't possibly do it all—and that she wasn't going to try anymore. "I was thinking about balancing needs and what I decided was that one week I was going to be a great worker at my job and a poor cook and a medium-good parent, and the next week I was going to be a good cook, a mediocre worker, and a great parent."

• **Think about what's really important to you.** Sometimes in the midst of daily pressures, we forget what we really value. Keeping your vision for your family in mind will help you make the best decisions in the long run. As Liane Steele once put it, "Be assured that you'll always have time for things you put first."

Trudy's found that to be true in her family. "Because I've always worked, I had to decide early on that my kids came first. That way each time a real conflict comes up, I don't have to assess it anew. If I have any kind of choice at all, I know I'm going to err on the side of my kids, because that's the value I chose."

• **Set priorities.** Janis explains how she does it: "Those mornings when I feel lucky to get half a bagel down Maya before she goes off to school, when combing her hair is out of the question, I try to remind myself that even though her hair might not be combed and her house might be in disarray, she's been well listened to, emotionally nourished, and cared for in the ways that really matter."

• **Assess the hierarchy of needs.** Balancing needs is often a matter of figuring out whose needs are most critical at any given point in time. Who's in a position to wait? Who can get what they want a little later? Tomorrow? Next week? Is there a way everybody can get some of what they want now? Or that together, you can come up with a mutual solution?

• **Think about the family as a whole.** There are many times in families when children's needs have to take a backseat to the needs of the family as a whole; schedules need to be met, tasks need to get done, or adults need some special time of their own. What's important isn't balance at every moment. Balancing needs in a family happens over time. We just need to make sure that the scale doesn't tip too regularly toward the needs of any one member of the family, leaving the others continuously in the backseat.

When We Need Children to Move at Our Pace

Those times when children's needs come second to our agenda, they may need help doing things they might otherwise be able to accomplish on their own. A child who might be able to tie his own shoes or pour his own milk, for instance, might not be able to do so when he's being hurried out the door.

When we bear in mind that going at our pace is a trial for kids, we can be more understanding. Here are some things that can help when you're in a hurry:

• **Break down tasks.** You can say: "When you get up, you need to eat your toast, get dressed, and put your blankey in your backpack. Which would you like to do first?" Or "We need to clean up your room. Would you like to pick up the dirty clothes or the marking pens first?"

• **Meet your child halfway.** You can tell kids: "If you bring your shoes to me, I will help you get them on." Or "Please get your sister's bottle out of her diaper bag. Then I can help you get dressed." During particularly rushed or resistant times, you may need to do more than half.

• **Explain what's going to happen.** Knowing what to expect in advance helps many children through transitions.

• **Reevaluate and simplify your routines.** Rob explains how he and his daughters figured out a more successful way to start the day. "My three-year-old and my five-year-old and I were having a horrible time getting out of the house in the morning. I was beginning to dread getting up because I knew the struggle that lay ahead. There were fights over breakfast, over getting dressed, over combing hair. Finally, I got fed up enough to look at what was really happening. I realized we were often searching for the right clothes and that I was forcing the kids to eat a big breakfast they weren't hungry for. So I sat down with them and together we came up with some solutions. We now lay their clothes out the night before, they grab a quick bite to eat, and I put a little snack in each of their backpacks in case they get hungry later."

• **Be creative.** We know of more than one family that puts their kids to bed in sweatpants they can wear to school the next day.

• **Make sure your child has some time to go at her own pace.** When children have opportunities to meander, to daydream, to go slow or not at all, it's easier for them to move on our clock when necessary.

"Mom, Is There a Law Against Wasting Time?"

Between kids and stepkids, Paula is a mother nine times over. She is also a professional fund-raiser, writer, and film producer. One afternoon, in a rare moment without children, she talked about the conflicts inherent in having a career and being a mother. Paula mentioned an interchange with her four-year-old son, Sam, which had shifted her perspective irrevocably. "I'd put in the better part of a year working full time on a stressful job that kept my mind filled with deadlines and details and efficiency, not on the daily needs of my kids. One day while I was madly rushing around the house trying to get things done, Sam stopped me and asked, 'Mom, is there a law against wasting time?' That stopped me dead in my tracks. For Sam to ask that question, I knew something was wrong with the way I was living."

Kids need unscheduled time at home when they don't have chores, family expectations, or friends over; when the TV isn't on, when the video games are put away, when they're not being entertained. Kids need open space, free time, time to choose or to flounder, to be faced with, "Gee, I don't have anything to do now. What am I going to do with myself?" If children don't have opportunities to figure that out, they gradually lose touch with their own ideas and imagination. They become more externally motivated and outwardly focused, dependent on others for their amusement. This can hinder their emerging self-reliance and diminish their own creativity.

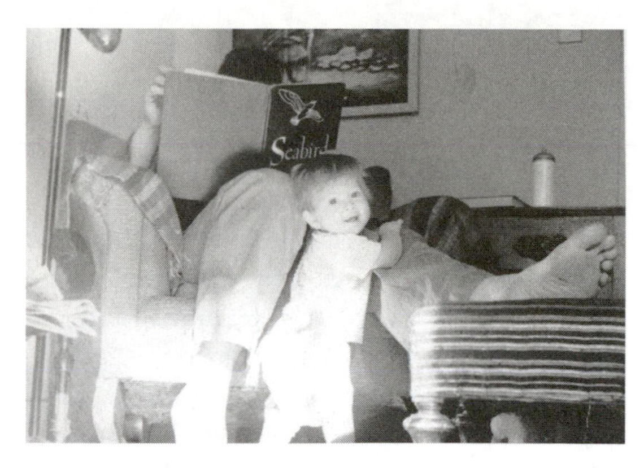

"Dad, I'm Bored": Helping Children Appreciate Free Time

When kids have moved at the world's pace for a long time, they may initially complain and struggle when faced with free time. Older children may come to you and say, "I'm bored." Younger children might hang on your leg, whining. At that point, they may need some support from you in rediscovering the pleasures of free time. The following strategies can help you respond in ways that encourage children to develop their own solutions:

• **Identify what's happening.** Reflect back to your child that it looks like he has some time he could do something with.

• **Be empathetic.** Listen to the feelings of frustration that might come up as your child tries to figure out what to do.

• **Help children reflect on their mood.** Ask older children to think about what they feel like doing and share with younger children what you observe about their energy: "You look like you're full of jumps." "You look like you're ready to curl up on the couch and do something quiet."

• **Help your child think about what to do.** Remind your child about the kinds of things you know she likes to do: "You like to roll in the grass with Spunky." Questions such as "What could you build with your blocks?" or "Where could you do some jumping?" can help start children's creative juices flowing.

• **Help your child get started, if necessary.** If you help your child begin an activity, mention beforehand that you will help her get started, and then you are going to go back to what you were doing.

• **Don't interrupt your child.** Avoid unnecessary interruptions when children become involved in creative, self-directed play. Be as flexible as you can when you need to interrupt: "I need some help feeding the cat. Is now a good time or would you like to do it after dinner?" Also, give warnings about transitions. "In five minutes it's going to be time for all the trains to go back to the station."

• **Create an environment that supports creative play.** Provide age-appropriate, open-ended materials for children's use. Examples include paper, markers, scissors, tape, empty cereal boxes, scraps of material, big refrigerator boxes, small blankets, blocks, sand, water, and dirt. If possible, provide some space that can get messy—a back porch, a corner of the kitchen, a dirt area out back. Children's creative play isn't usually a neat or tidy activity.[2]

• **Slow down, you're moving too fast.** Children learn a lot by watching how we live. When kids see us coming home stressed and preoccupied, day after day, they learn that life doesn't feel very good, that being a grown-up is a grind. So part of the slowing down has to start with us. And it's possible to begin those changes in small, daily ways.

[2] See "What Is Our Role in Children's Play and Learning?" on p. 289 for a more thorough look at what parents can do to encourage imaginative play.

• **Waste a little time with your child today.** When you decide to slow down with your children, you join your child is discovering imagination, spontaneity, fun, and resourcefulness. You get to reexperience simple pleasures: noticing a rainbow, taking a nap, whipping up a batch of brownies, designing a treasure hunt, going for a leisurely stroll. Anyone can do it. You don't have to be an at-home parent to slip a little spontaneity and magic into your moments with your kids. You can be a busy parent and still relax fully and robustly. It doesn't take all day to waste a little bit of time.

• **Take a penny walk.** One mother decided she wanted more open-ended time with her children. So she started taking them on penny walks. She and her kids would go outside with a penny. When they reached the end of their driveway, they flipped it. If it landed heads, they went to the right. If it was tails, they turned left. When they reached a corner, they flipped it again. They kept flipping that penny at every intersection until they got tired and decided to go home. Whatever happened spontaneously on penny walks was okay, but no errands were allowed.

• **Be a role model.** Karyn, who was a single parent when Bryan was three, tells the following story: "One day I was working in the garden and Bryan was hanging on my legs, wanting me to play with him. Exhausted by his constant interruptions, I wanted to pull weeds, to think, to have a few moments alone. I told him, 'I want to be by myself for fifteen minutes. You can still be out here, but I don't want to talk to you or play with you. I need some time for myself. And when the fifteen minutes is up, I'll tell you. Then you can talk to me.' Bryan cried a little. Then he played with his trucks in the mud. I pulled a patch of weeds and went inside. When I came out to find him, he was sitting on a little block of wood at the edge of the patio, looking out at the garden. I said, 'Honey, I'm here now.' And he said, 'Look, I just want five or ten minutes by myself.' 'Okay,' I told him. 'Come to me when you're done.' " By modeling her need for time alone and by respecting her son's request, Karyn taught him to value something that was important to her—the gift of solitude.

Being Real with Your Kids

When parents feel that they don't get enough time with their families, there's a tendency to want to make the time they do have with their children totally kid-oriented. But this can give children a really skewed picture of the world, as Juana, the divorced mother of a seven-year-old, explained: "I share custody of Jaime with my ex-husband. The first few years, I did all my banking, grocery shopping, business, laundry, and socializing on the weeks he was at Silvio's house. That way my time with him was free for us doing things together. I felt so guilty about not being with him all the time, I wanted the time we did have to be really special. But after a while I realized that Jaime was getting a pretty skewed view of life. He saw a mother who never worked, didn't have to balance a checkbook, never dated, and didn't need to see her friends. I realized I wanted him to see me a full person with real-life problems and needs, not as a mother who was always available."

It's important that children see us and our lives as complex and multifaceted. Showing that we can take care of them—and take care of business—gives them a realistic picture of what grown-ups do.

What Is the Quality of Quality Time?

As the parent of young children, it's likely you've heard about the importance of spending "quality time" with your children. Many of us have this image of quality time as this lovely time in which we're absolutely attentive to our kids with nothing else on our minds. There's a romanticized quality to it. Everyone is relaxed, the sun is streaming through the window, and the whole family is engaged in activities that are creative, wholesome, and fun. Yet if we broaden our definition of quality time to include any time a parent and child make a significant human connection, it frees us up to have a much more realistic and dynamic relationship with our children.

Quality time includes times when we focus absolutely on our kids, when we're engaged in a team project as a family, when we're reading books or walking in the rain. But other days, quality time might include peacefully folding the wash while our toddler busily puts his dolly to sleep in the laundry basket.

Quality time also includes sharing work tasks. Doing chores together allows parents and children to make connections with each other in which parents share expertise and children develop feelings of competence. Whether picking up trash from the alley, scrubbing the bathroom sink, helping to repair a broken chair, or pushing buttons on the washing machine, taking the time to allow children to work with us helps them feel skillful, an integral member of the team.

Quality time can mean being with a child who's crying or exhausted, who doesn't know what to do with herself. It can happen when *we're* exhausted and don't know what to do with *ourselves*, but we reach back into some hidden reserves and say "I'm still going to be here. I'm going to hang in here with you."

Quality time includes sitting through a tantrum or resolving a family fight. Both enrich family life by building trust and increasing intimacy.

Finally, quality time can include everyday routines with children—making beds, cooking, taking baths, brushing teeth, or diapering—if those routines are done with full attention.

Paula's grandmother taught her to cherish the little things. "Kids don't have any sense that dressing isn't the real activity and that going to the park is. Whatever is happening in the moment *is* the real activity for them. My grandmother always told me, 'It's not like you're getting ready for something that's going to happen. This is it. All the little things *are* the things that are happening. They *are* your lives. Whether you can do them gently or attentively in the present is what really matters.'"

Both children and their parents learn from and enjoy the intimacy of all these kinds of interactions. Quality time, however, doesn't—nor should it—account for all of the time in families. It is equally significant that children have opportunities to see other kinds of needs being addressed in the family, as well: people working, being quiet, or giving their full attention to another family member.

Food for Thought: Quality Time

• What are some of the best times I've spent with my children? When have we felt the closest?

• What do I want my children to learn about time alone? About time with others?

Memories Happen Now

Juggling all of the myriad tasks that are required to maintain a family can sap our energy and eclipse our focus from the precious moments that happen each day. Laura tells the following story. "Some friends of mine were getting ready to wallpaper their bathroom. In the meantime, they let their kids write whatever they wanted to on the walls. Everyone got gleefully into the act. There were drawings, poems, deep and random thoughts. One day, someone wrote in big block letters: 'Memories happen now.' That really started me thinking."

This is the only childhood our children will ever have. The way we live now, the things we do as a family are the ground from which our children's awareness and expectations are being shaped. Periodically refocusing on what we truly value, and reminding ourselves that family life is not a race to the finish line, can inspire us to make the most of each moment.

7. Teaching Children to Feel Safe, Strong, and Good About Their World

Principle 7: One of the most powerful things parents can give children is an open, optimistic, and safe connection to the world.

With the birth of a child we affirm the cycle of life and invest in the future. As Carl Sandburg has written, "A baby is God's opinion that the world should go on."

Sharing this sense of optimism with our children is critical. Feeling safe and positive about the world—and the people in it—is essential to children's developing sense of trust. As Virginia Satir writes in her book *Peoplemaking*, "In . . . vital and nurturing families . . . the linking to society is open and hopeful." Such a positive linkage to their parents, family, and the larger community enables children to explore confidently, to grow and to thrive.

Yet today, with war in many parts of the world and violence and abuse a reality in our communities, it can be hard to see—and present—a positive image of the world to our children.

Many parents feel ambivalent about letting their children move out into the world. Alejandro explains his fears for his three-year-old son: "I don't want to be overprotective, but the world scares me. Striking a balance between that fear and letting Roscoe grow up is one of the most difficult issues I face as a parent."

Joe feels mixed. "I want to be optimistic, but because of my profession, I'm not. As a city planner, I see more and more people fleeing from problems into gated communities and private schools. Rather than trying to change things, they're removing themselves into their own little worlds where they don't have to deal with people of color or anyone who has a different opinion. It's hard for me to feel optimistic when I see fear and apathy increasing and the gap between the classes widening all the time."

The Man Who Hadn't Learned to Be Kind: Janis's Story

This story about Janis and Maya is a good example of teaching children about difficult realities while simultaneously supporting their sense of optimism.

I took Maya to swimming lessons when she was four. One day, during her lesson, a father grabbed his son and roughly yanked him out of the pool because he hadn't been listening to the teacher. Then the father proceeded to yell at the boy, berating him.

That night, Maya asked me, "Is *that* man going to be at swimming tomorrow?"

I said, "Are you asking about the man who pulled his son out of the pool today?"

She said "Yes," so I went on to describe to her what I had seen: "He was rough with his son. He wasn't being gentle."

Maya asked me back, "Why wasn't he gentle? Why was he yelling like that?"

I reassured her that I wouldn't let anyone hurt her or yell at her like that. Then I started to talk to her about the man. I said, "That's a man who hasn't learned how to be kind."

Maya started crying. Tearfully she asked, "Why hasn't he learned to be kind? Why hasn't he?"

I told her that I didn't know for sure, but that sometimes people aren't kind to children and don't treat them gently, so when those kids grow up to be parents, they still don't know how to be kind.

I could see the wheels turning in Maya's mind. She turned and asked, "Why wasn't anyone kind to him?"

I replied, "Maybe they hadn't learned either. It's sad, isn't it?" Then I went on: "But I can tell you some good news. Lots of people are working to teach people how to be kind. I teach classes to parents to help them learn and there are also groups and books to help people. Maybe that man will find a way to learn, too."

Some people feel scared about the communities their children are growing up in. Beatriz, who lives in a small town struggling with gang violence, is scared for her baby girl. "Everything I see on the street scares me. It gets worse every year—killings, gangs, drive-bys. And it's people you know. It scares me to think my child is going to get to an age where she's gonna do what I did—go out, be on the streets, not care what I think."

Eric, who lives in a middle-class community, is also worried. "I don't even feel safe about my daughter riding her bike up and down our street. When I look back on my own childhood and think about the freedom of movement I had, it brings up a real sense of sadness. I don't know if things really were safer then, but there's certainly more of a perception of danger now."

A Question of Perspective

The view of the world we present to our children depends largely on our perspective. So it's important for us to ask ourselves: "How do I see the world?" "What's the world view I'm passing on to my children?"

Dennis, the father of a young toddler, believes in change. "I don't want to sugar-coat what's out there in the world, but I don't want him to grow up thinking things are hopeless either. I want to give Ricky a sense that he can help to make things better. I want him to be able to say, 'I'm confident change can happen.'"

Trudy, who feels ambivalent about the state of the world, still teaches her children to trust. "Intellectually, I'm not optimistic about the future. But in my emotions and in the way I greet life, I'm always optimistic. I really like people, and as a result, my kids really like people. They feel some basic trust that most people are going to be okay."

Children learn much more from the way we live than from the words we say. If we tell children that there are wonderful opportunities waiting for them out in the world, but we ourselves take a fearful or cynical stance, our kids will assimilate those feelings and attitudes more than any words we say to the contrary.

Examining our own perspective—and where it came from—is the first step in creating a more positive worldview for our children. Noreen explains: "I was sexually abused as a child, and for the first couple of years after I remembered the abuse, I looked at every child and wondered, 'Who's getting to you?' I was convinced that each child I saw was being molested, neglected, or abused. My point of view was a direct outgrowth of what I was focusing on in my own life.

"It took time and energy to shift my perspective. In part, it happened naturally, with healing, but I also made a conscious choice to seek out healthy families so I could see another alternative. Now I no longer see the world through an abuse-colored lens."

Taking the time to examine and work on our own fears can keep us from inadvertently passing them on to our children.

Another significant way to transform feelings of pessimism or fear is to take action. If you're concerned about your children's safety in the world, you can take steps toward making your community safer. And ultimately, improving conditions in the community as a whole is what makes all of us safer.[1]

[1] See "Not Until Every Child Is Safe" on p. 76 for specific ideas about what you can do to improve both your neighborhood and the larger world.

FOOD FOR THOUGHT: OPTIMISM IN THE WORLD

- What do I want to teach my children about the world around them? About human nature? About people they haven't met yet?

- What helps me feel optimistic about the world? What makes it hard to feel optimistic?

- What kind of world do I want for my children?

Scared Kids Are Not Empowered Kids

In the last fifteen years, we've become increasingly aware of the different kinds of hurts that can happen to children. We've been flooded with information about child abuse, and of course, we want our children to be protected from such grievous harm. So we do everything we can to warn them, to prepare them for the dangers they may encounter. But sometimes our warnings leave children feeling scared rather than confident and resourceful.

Sixteen-year-old Mariah, who had extensive exposure to all the dangers that might await her, looks back on the lessons she learned as a preschool child as ones that actually hindered rather than helped her: "By the time I was five or six, I knew everything a child could possibly know about safety. I knew about saying 'no.' I knew about making space between myself and an attacker. I knew that there were bad men in the world who wanted to hurt children.

Still, when I was eight and started riding on the bus alone, I was totally unprepared. Whenever I encountered an uncomfortable or scary situation, I'd freeze up. All I knew was how to be scared."

Ginny, mother of five-year-old Danielle, regrets some of the messages she gave her daughter. "When Danielle was little, I used to tell her, 'You can't run away from me! There are people in the world that might want to take you and you might not see me again.' Now she tells me, 'I saw my girlfriend roller-skating by herself. She doesn't know that someone could steal her.' "

Even though most child abuse happens at home within the family, many parents (and some in-school programs) continue to focus their "safety training" on warning young children about strangers or "bad people" who might try to give them candy, lure them away,

Loud Girls

One night in one of Janis's parent groups, Deborah brought up a problem she was having with her daughter, who'd just turned three. "Mira keeps getting right up into my face and screaming at me 'Mama, you're not doing that right! I said I wanted jelly, not butter on my toast! You're not doing it right.' She's screaming in my face all day long. And I can't stand it. I got yelled at when I was kid. And now I have a kid who just stands there and yells at me! It's pushing all my buttons. I've asked her to use her inside voice. I've told her she can't scream at me. I've tried to respond calmly. I've tried yelling back at her. I don't know what to do. I'm really losing it. How can I get her to stop yelling at me?"

Janis thought for a moment before responding. Then she said, "She's right at the place developmentally where she has a strong sense of what she wants to do, but she can't yet do it for herself. Her capabilities don't match her desires. So she's frustrated much of the time. That's where the yelling comes from. She's voicing her exasperation at all the things she can't do, not at you. And she's using her loud voice with you because you're safe, accessible, and familiar. It's a measure of how close she feels to you."

Janis went on: "I know it's hard, but I don't want her to lose her loud and powerful voice. She's going to need it in the world. There will be instances in the world where her nice voice won't be effective for her.

"It's particularly hard for us to hear girls be loud and to see them be powerful. For years, girls have been told to be ladylike. They haven't had equal access to physical activities and have been deprived of feeling balance and coordination and physical strength in their bodies. And when you don't feel powerful in your body and strong with your voice, you're naturally more vulnerable.

"When Mira yells at you, remind yourself, 'She's not yelling at me. She's yelling in my vicinity.' Try saying to her 'That voice is a loud, powerful voice! You may need that somewhere, but when you're asking me for jelly, I want you to do it in a way that doesn't hurt my ears.' It is important to tell Mira how her yelling affects you and also to set limits about her behavior. Yet even as you teach her other ways to communicate, it's also crucial that she learns that her loud voice might be a useful tool in certain situations."

Janis's words were sobering. There were nods all around the room. All the mothers of daughters were paying particular attention. I wondered how many of us in this room were hurt because we didn't know how to yell and fight back in a loud, unladylike manner. How many of us were taught to do what we were told, never question authority, be nice, compliant, to always say 'yes' and 'thank you' and smile?

We need to remember that loud little girls are learning to be safe little girls. They are the ones who will be able to say, "No, I don't want to," "I have a different idea," "Forget it!" and "Get lost!" when necessary.

and hurt them. This kind of information often just scares kids. Toddlers and preschool children don't have enough experience in the world to take danger and strangers and put them into a larger context. They don't know that being abducted by a stranger is a small probability. They don't know how to sort out the difference between "bad people who might hurt you" and friends they haven't met yet.

It's not that terrible things don't happen to kids. They do. The question is: "What's the best preparation we can give them?"

Teaching Safety Without Fear

As parents, we can do a lot to help children stay safe in the world. Even toddlers can begin to develop the kinds of skills that will ultimately help protect them: the ability to trust their own perceptions, the knowledge that their body has boundaries, the confidence to speak their mind even when they don't agree with an adult.

Here are some suggestions for keeping children safe without scaring them:

• **Supervise your children.** In their early years, children need to know that the world is a safe place that they can explore. It's our job to choose environments and provide supervision that lets them venture out safely. We can make sure we know our neighbors, the families our children meet in day care, and anyone who watches our kids. Formal child care situations also need to be checked out—by getting references, through observation, via daily check-ins with our child's caregivers, and by dropping in from time to time.

• **Don't give children scary information they can't make sense of.** As Trudy explains, "Since trust of people is at the core of my enjoyment of life, I try to teach my kids to be aware of danger without making them feel suspicious of everyone they meet. I don't want to undermine their sense of optimism during their most vulnerable years."

• **Use language that doesn't frighten.** Set limits with children and give information using positive language. When you're concerned about your child running away from you at the mall, you can say, "I want you to stay where I can see you so I can help you stay safe," rather than "Don't run off! Somebody might hurt you!" When your child wants to stay home alone and asks, "Why can't I stay in the house alone? I can take care of myself," you can say, "I want to be there in case you need some help."

• **Respect children's feelings.** Through respecting children's feelings, we help them stay aware of what they're feeling, so when something is uncomfortable to them, they can recognize it. They don't just say, "Oh, this is just how it is with adults. They poke you when they talk to you. You have to kiss them and sit on their laps. Just hold still. It'll be over soon." Rather, they're able to say, "Stop tickling me!" Or "No, I don't want to kiss you."

• **Encourage children to express their thoughts and emotions.** Sometimes what we say in the name of obedience—"Just do it!" "Be polite." "Grown-ups know best." "Keep your voice down!"—doesn't permit precisely the kind of learning that's essential for young children. A big part of creating safety is establishing a family context in which children feel free to bring us their difficult feelings or opposing opinions. Children need to know how to speak their minds, both to us and to strange adults they don't agree with.

• **Teach kids to be in touch with their instincts.** When you're moving through the world with your children, you can ask them how they feel in situations and let them know how you feel, too. You can say, "I felt uncomfortable with that guy. How did you feel about him?" Or "I don't feel safe about that," or "It's not okay for adults to pinch kids like that." That way, children learn to trust their gut feelings and their judgment about situations that might be dangerous.

• **Teach children that their bodies are their own.** Teach your child about personal boundaries by respecting his body and setting limits about your own. Laura explains, "Last week, Eli was intent on sticking his fingers up my nose. Each time, I'd say to him, 'It's my body and I don't want your fingers up my nose. I'm going to stop you. You can touch my cheek or put your fingers up *your* nose, but I don't want your fingers up *my* nose.' "

• **Let children have loud voices.** We can teach kids that there are times it's okay to have a loud voice, to scream, to yell "No!"

• **Present a hopeful picture of the world.** Our culture feeds on sensationalism and violence. There are few front-page stories about kids who are doing significant things in the community, about families building nurturing, supportive networks with each other, about strangers who help people. It's up to us to make sure our kids see examples of human generosity, compassion, and goodwill.

A Delicate Balance

A precious and vulnerable place opens up in us when we have children. That vulnerability can motivate us to take positive steps to keep our children safe and it can be the basis from which we build an optimism that says to our kids, "This world holds some great experiences for you."

As Mitch, the father of one-year-old Mayim, said, "I want him to feel that the world is his home, that he belongs here."

8. Being Human: When You're Not Yet the Parent You Want to Be

Principle 8: All parents get angry and all of us make mistakes. Acknowledging and learning from our mistakes teaches our children invaluable lessons about being human.

As parents, we don't always have the time, energy, or resourcefulness to act in ways that are consistent with our goals and vision. We can't always be the attentive, clear-headed, compassionate parents we want to be. This is not a sign of failure or ineffectiveness. It's simply a sign of being human.

All parents face times of being exhausted, pressured, and stretched too thin. As Vinnie explains, "It's hard to do the right thing when you're dog-tired. You can read about all these wonderful ways to be with kids in all kinds of situations. But most of those books assume that everything in your life is hunky-dory, that you have the time and energy to do what they're telling you to do. I don't know about you, but most of the time, I'm glad just to make it through the day."

"I've Been Surprised by the Extent of My Anger"

There are times when all of us get caught between our own needs, the needs of our children, the demands of our jobs, stress, illness, and financial worries. We can all become angry, short-tempered, and resentful.

There are times when parents get stuck in a vicious cycle: The more angry and resentful we become, the less present we are for our kids, and the less present we are, the more needy they become. In turn, we get angrier and our kids cling and cry and whine more.

When this topic came up in Janis's class one evening, Faye said, "I've made a conscious decision never to hit my kids, but I know it's possible to get to a place where it doesn't matter what you've decided. There have been times

I've wanted to resort to physical violence. I can feel it in my hands. It doesn't even go through my brain; it's cellular. So far, I've been successful in keeping my bargain with myself, but I can really understand the impulse."

Eric talked about a time he was pushed to his limit. "I've never hit Lauren. But one time, when she was two or three, I really lost it. I started screaming at absolute top volume and I saw the moment when I scared the shit out of her. I might as well have been hitting her. For me, that was a horrible, poignant moment—to feel myself raise up and use my size and my power to overpower her. Everybody knows you're going to lose it as a parent. The trick is to be creative about how you lose it."

Dalia, single mother to Zach, has also been surprised by the extent of her anger. "I didn't realize how frustrated I'd get. I'm starting to understand my mother—how it might have felt for her to be alone in the house with three kids. There have been a couple of times I've had to go into the bedroom and shut the door because Zach was just driving me nuts."

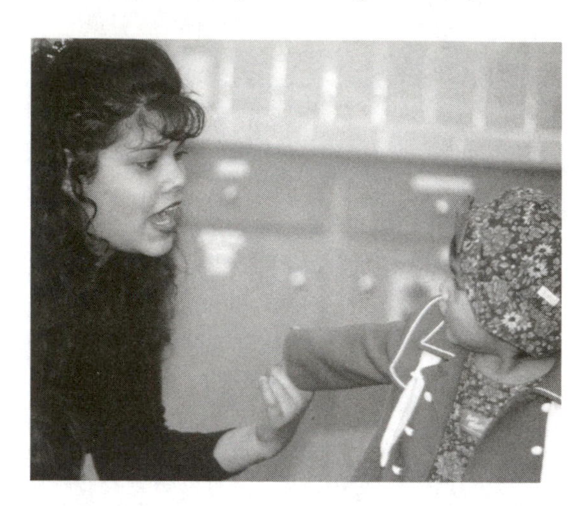

Expressing Anger with Children: A Developmental Look

When we think about expressing anger with children, it is essential to take into consideration how children at various ages might experience expressions of anger. Even preverbal children can read our angry cues: our tone of voice and our body tension. When we are angry with them or when we are angry in their presence, it is important to remember that they can read our feelings even if they can't understand exactly what our anger is about.

Infants and young toddlers see the world from an egocentric perspective. They don't differentiate between their feelings and the feelings of the people who are close to them. It can be very upsetting for babies or young toddlers to be with an adult who is regularly becoming enraged or who is angry for an extended period of time. Not only can this be very frightening for them, but it can also undermine the feelings of safety and trust which are crucial to their growth.

Also, since babies and toddlers don't have a sophisticated sense of time, they don't realize that you can be furious now and not furious later. Young children may think that your present state is permanent. As children mature, their sense of time evolves. At about the age of three, children can begin to understand it when you say, "I'm feeling very mad right now, but I'll feel better in a little while."

Children's development and parents' anger also dovetail around the issue of expectations. Often parents are surprised when they suddenly feel angry about something that hadn't upset them before. Esteban explained, "I expect an eight-month-old to spill her juice, but when my three-year-old does it, I explode." Many of us are not even fully conscious that our expectations of our kids have changed until we find ourselves furious at them about some aspect of their behavior.

It's natural that our expectations about children's behavior change as they grow and become more competent. But often our expectations take a bigger leap than our child is ready to make, and we may need to adjust our expectations in order to reduce our frustration and anger.

Appropriate Expressions of Anger

How can parents appropriately express anger to infants, toddlers,

There are times we all reach our absolute limit, and like this mother, we get to the bottom line: "We won't be doing fancy teaching here. Let's just see how we can keep us both safe without too much guilt on either side."

When Parents Get Angry

Despite our best attempts to be patient, to see where our children are coming from, to keep ourselves nurtured, resourceful, and flexible, inevitably there are times we get angry with our children. Here are some ideas for dealing with that anger constructively:

• **Think about what you want to teach your children about anger.** Children pay close attention when we get mad. In fact, they sometimes provoke us just so that they can see how we handle anger. Awkward as this may seem, it's an opportunity to teach children that we think anger is a healthy emotion, that there are positive ways to express it, and that people can move through it successfully.

• **Give your anger a name.** Even if you never acknowledge your anger, kids see the sweat on your brow, the redness in your cheeks, the tension in your body. If you give them a word for what they are seeing, you let them know that this feeling has a name, and that it's not too scary to talk about: "I feel so angry right now. I had a horrible day at school, I left my bus money on the kitchen table, and now you won't put your shoes on so we can go home."

and preschoolers? For babies and toddlers, expressions should be short and clear, using a serious tone of voice and matching body language: "I don't like it when you bite me. We're going to stop nursing now." Or "I get mad when you throw toys at the door. I'm going to put the hard ones away."

If you feel like you need to yell or hit, put your baby in a safe place (such as a crib) and go into the other room for a few minutes to vent your anger physically without scaring your child. You may also feel the need to talk about your frustration later with a friend. But your infant, one-year-old, or two-year-old is too young to bear the full impact of that kind of anger and frustration.

Preschoolers can handle more information about your anger and some may even be able to deal with your raised voice. "I feel really upset! I don't like it when you dump all of your socks out of the drawer! It took me a long time to fold them and put them in there. I want you to help me put them back in the drawer." Again, remove yourself if you aren't able to control the intensity of your anger. "I'm going to go in the bedroom and shut the door for a couple of minutes. Then I'll be back."

Finding Other Outlets

Expressing anger appropriately with children often necessitates finding other outlets for our feelings. Some parents find these in the moment; others plan regular activities throughout the week that reduce their stress levels.

This topic came up in Janis's class one afternoon. Janis posed the question, "What do you do when you get really angry at your kids?"

Ross shared, "I go upstairs into my room, close the door, roll up a towel, and whack it on the bed for a few minutes. Then I'm ready to go back down and talk to my son."

Elaine added, "Digging in the dirt helps me. I can always tell when I haven't gotten my weekly gardening time in. I'm much more likely to lose it with my kids."

And Vanessa said, "I go in my room, close the door, and yell into a pillow. That way I can yell as loud as I want and the kids don't hear me."

Finding the match between your need for expression and your child's ability to tolerate that expression takes time and practice. But it's important that you work to discover satisfying ways to express anger that communicate feelings and limits to children without overwhelming them. In doing so, you will be providing a model of anger that is clear and honest, without being hurtful.

• **Work to avoid scaring children.** It is important to be honest with children without overwhelming them with the force of our feelings. Janis recalls, "When Lee was eighteen months old, I bravely started a sewing project. He was fascinated with the sewing machine and crawled up and took the thread off. I was really frustrated. I hadn't sewed for months and here he was messing it up. I yelled at him, *'STOP!'* His little face fell and he crumbled in tears. Up until that point, I hadn't had a lot of practice expressing my anger; I'd only learned to stifle it. I realized in that moment that if I was going to express anger to my children, I needed to modulate my voice, so I wouldn't scare the wits out of them."

If you can honestly express your feelings while at the same time keeping your eyes open to see how your children are responding, you will be able to teach respect, even in your angry moments.

• **Work to express anger without blame.** It is inaccurate to tell children that they are responsible for our anger. Certainly they do lots of things that we feel frustrated about, but they are not responsible for our anger. When we say, "You're driving me up the wall," "You make me so furious," or "You are ruining my day," we erroneously give children the message that they control our emotions and behavior.

If, instead, we let children know that we feel angry in *response* to their behavior, we can honestly share our feelings, and their connection to them, without blame. "When you grab me around the neck, I feel scared and mad." We can also share some of the other sources of our frustration (as appropriate) so children understand that their behavior isn't the only thing we're upset about. "I didn't get enough sleep last night, so I'm feeling extra cranky today."

• **Don't hit children.** Hitting hurts and frightens children. It teaches them that violence is an acceptable way to express frustration and solve problems.[1]

• **Find alternatives to screaming.** Yelling and name-calling can be as hurtful as physical violence.[2]

• **Take a break.** Sometimes, in the heat of the moment, we're unable to express anger the way we'd ideally like to. That can be a signal that it's time to take a break. "I'm going to sit on the couch/go to my room/be by myself for a few minutes. I want to talk to you about this mess when we both calm down a little."

• **Observe what triggers your anger.** Most of us have situations that are almost sure to spark our anger. One parent may be triggered by being hit in the face, another by being ignored, and a third by being ordered around. In Janis's family these are called "gorilla buttons." Knowing where your gorilla buttons are can help you anticipate and understand the intensity of your reactions. Also, knowing the things that are likely to trigger your rage enables you to take preventive measures—such as setting clearer limits with your kids in those particular areas.

• **Think about what happens when you get angry.** Each of us has an early warning system that lets us know when our anger is rising. These signs can include tightness in the chest, a change in breathing, or tension in arms or belly. Becoming aware of your body's unique signals can alert you to the fact that anger is near.

[1] For more on spanking, see "The Problem with Spanking," on p. 221.

[2] See "To Yell or Not to Yell?" on p. 222 for more.

• **Pay attention to the emotions that accompany your anger.** Anger is often preceded or accompanied by other emotions. Hurt, fear, frustration, and rejection are often anger's partners. Identifying these feelings and working to resolve them can help you better understand and deal with your anger.

• **Learn to distinguish your own backlog of anger from that which is appropriate to the immediate situation.** Most of us carry around some cumulative frustration. We're worried about money, nervous about an upcoming exam, or upset about a fight with a partner. When we become conscious of the anger we are carrying, it's less likely to get misdirected at our children. Finding appropriate outlets for our own accumulated feelings can help us respond more appropriately to our children's mistakes.

• **Discuss your beliefs about anger with your partner or other adults in your family.** People often come to families with very different ideas about anger and the appropriate ways to express it, depending on their gender, family history, and culture. Through discussion, parents can explore their beliefs with each other and come up with mutually acceptable forms of expression.

• **It's never too late to apologize.** Rare is the parent who hasn't gotten angry with their children in ways they later regret. When this happens, it's important to apologize to your children for scaring or hurting them: "I'm sorry I scared you when I yelled. I got frustrated when you pulled the thread off the machine. I still don't want you to do it, but I didn't mean to scare you. I'll try to tell you in a gentler way next time." Through apologizing, acknowledging the mistake, and learning to express our anger in safer ways, we let our children know that the mistake we made is not what we want to teach.

FOOD FOR THOUGHT: WHEN PARENTS GET ANGRY

• How was anger expressed in my family of origin? Were there different rules for adults and children, for girls and boys?

• What have I learned about anger as an emotion?

• How do I deal with or express my anger now?

• If I wanted to express anger differently, what are my resources to do that? What is a first step that I could take?

Learning from Your Mistakes

Becoming an effective parent entails making a series of educated guesses and seeing what works. In doing so, we inevitably make mistakes. There will be times we're rigid when we should be loose, loose when we should be firm; times we're inconsistent or unfair. All of us will make judgments based on the best knowledge we have at the time, only to find out later that we were wrong. We will say and do things that hurt our children because we were too tired, frustrated, or mad to stop ourselves. At times, we will repeat mistakes that were made by our parents because we haven't come to terms with those particular pockets of history. We all hope that none of the mistakes we make will damage our children by compromising their safety, squashing their self-esteem, or crushing their spirit. Yet whenever we do something we haven't done before, we inevitably make mistakes. It's part of the learning curve.

The Value of Mistakes

"Wrong" answers are at the heart of the scientific discovery process. By discovering what's "wrong," through exploring and examining what doesn't work, we eventually figure out what does work. Mistakes are critical building blocks in the problem-solving process. When a child is learning to walk, falling down is as important as getting up.

Many of us haven't had an opportunity to learn to appreciate mistakes as opportunities for growth. When we make a mistake, we judge ourselves harshly. Mistakes don't fit in with our vision of ourselves as perfect parents. But perfection—even if it was achievable—is not what kids need from us. It's better for kids to have parents who demonstrate how to keep growing despite human frailties.

Modeling a Healthy Response to Mistakes

Children watch us carefully. Through our example, we can teach them that how they deal with their mistakes is more important than the fact that a mistake was made.

• **Acknowledge your mistakes.** Recognizing our mistakes is the first step.

• **Model that mistakes are manageable.** If we make an error and respond by saying "Oh, no! I made a mistake! I'll never try that again!" we teach our children that mistakes are insurmountable. If, on the other hand, we say, "Well, that didn't work. I guess I'll have to figure out a different way," we give our children an incredible statement of optimism. That's significant for a child who's going to learn through making mistakes for a lifetime.

• **Talk to your inner critic.** For many of us, accepting our mistakes requires muzzling an inner critic who tries to convince us that we'll never be able to get it right. We can work to replace that voice with a more constructive one: "That didn't work. I wonder why? What can I try this time instead?"

• **Remember that being able to correct yourself is a real sign of strength.** Admitting mistakes takes courage.

• **Apologize.** "I'm sorry" are two necessary words in every parent's vocabulary.

• **Take steps to avoid the same mistake.** Although it's important to acknowledge mistakes, it's not enough to say "Oops! I blew it. Sorry!" If we stop there, there's nothing to keep us from repeating the same mistake again. If we really want to change, we need to make the critical leap from acknowledging our mistakes to doing something about them.

• **Demonstrate how to learn from mistakes.** Tell your child what you're going to do. "I'm going to go talk to someone who knows a lot about people getting angry so I can stop yelling at you." Or "I'm going to start dinner earlier so I won't be so rushed and crabby in the evenings." Or "I'm going to go to my parent's group and get some new ideas about how we might handle bedtime differently."

• **Include your child in the problem-solving process.** Preschool children love to come up with ideas, and their suggestions can be quite useful. Karyn explains: "From the time he was

Taming the Beast: Mei's Story

Mei is the thirty-four-year-old mother of two children under five. At times, she's lost her temper and been harsh with her children. Through support from parents she's met in classes and her own watchfulness, Mei is learning to express her anger in less hurtful ways. Her story is a model for learning from mistakes, for dealing with ourselves when we don't live up to our ideals.

Parenting brings out the best and worst in me. I didn't know that I could have so much love and patience. On the other hand, I didn't know I could be so cruel. I have a quick temper. I tend to raise my voice. I've seen my children cringe when I yell at them. I've said things to my children that were really mean. I've slapped Eliot on the backside three times, but I decided not to do it again because I felt so bad. I was being impulsive, and right away, I knew it was the wrong thing to do.

There's this beast in me and my children bring it out in me. I don't act that way in any other situation. When I've done something to one of my kids that I don't want to do—like yelling or hitting them—first I feel total remorse. I wait for myself to calm down. I wait for my child to calm down. Then I say, "I would like to be with you." I always apologize. And I've talked to my son about it. I've said, "Mommy has a quick temper and I yell and I can see that scares you." He's talked about how it scares him. I always encourage him to express how he feels.

I've told him, "Mommy's working on this." And I do. I write in my journal. I talk about it with friends and in my parenting group. It's something I have to come to terms with. Inside myself I have to figure out where it's coming from, why it's there, and then work to change it.

young, I always asked Bryan for his feedback: 'What would you have liked me to do?' 'How do you think we should handle that situation?' Over the years, he's come up with a lot of good ideas."

• **Use humor.** Sometimes humor can provide an outlet when we are worrying about all our potential mistakes. Leah came up with a humorous way to assuage her guilt: "I could spend my whole life worrying about all the things I do wrong as a parent: 'I should have listened. I should have done this. I should have done that.' I start worrying: 'I'm not going to protect my children.' 'I'm going to overprotect my children.' 'I'm being too responsive.' 'I'm not being responsive enough.' If I concentrate on those things, I can really put myself into a tailspin. I can't do that and raise my children with joy. I had to find a way to deal with guilt. So I started a therapy fund for my kids. When I make a mistake with my kids, I put a dollar in their therapy fund so they can recover at a later time. It's kind of a joke, but it helps me say to myself 'I can make mistakes and it's not a bad thing.' "

• **Remember that children are durable.** Children are rarely harmed by just one of our mistakes. Children learn more from the consistency of our responses over time than they do from the sporadic times that we "blow it." As Janis always tells parents, "Kids are amazingly durable and forgiving. They give you lots of chances, and they're going to be with you for the long haul."

Learning to Take Care of Yourself

Part of being human is acknowledging that we have needs of our own. While many of us think of ideal parents as those personified on Mother's and Father's Day cards, all parents have times when they cannot be "on" with their kids, when they have to take care of their own needs.

This is important for children in two ways. When parents take time to care for themselves, children get to see that people can take good care of themselves without neglecting the needs of those around them. Specifically, when mothers take care of themselves, children learn that women don't always have to put the needs of others first. Second, as children begin to see that they are not the only ones with needs, the groundwork is laid for developing empathy.

Many of us were never taught to recognize or value our needs. We've been conditioned to nurture others or to provide for our families, and the enormity of these responsibilities has necessitated putting our own feelings aside.

Paula explains: "For the first twenty years I was a parent, everyone else's needs came first. I used to bake the bread to make the sandwiches for their lunches. I used to grow the food. I thought doing everything myself was part of being a really good mother. What I didn't understand was that tending to myself was part of being a really good mother."

Emily, whose daughters are two and five, elaborated: "I didn't start by thinking 'I need an entire day to myself.' I started with taking two minutes for myself because there was no diaper to change at that moment. And slowly, it's grown. I never say to myself 'I can't do anything because I don't have an hour.' I keep lists of very small things to accomplish that otherwise drive me batty—writing a note or sending off a bill. Previously, I felt out of control, that there were just a hundred of those things out there, piling up, blowing up into a crisis. If I get to a few of those a day, it makes me feel a sense of order in my life."

As we look at our different needs, we will discover some that have to wait until our children get a little older and some that can be addressed right away. Starting with the little things we can do for ourselves now builds a habit of self-care that will nourish us throughout our lives as parents.

Then I Go Dancing with My Friends

In Janis's infant observation classes, parents bring their babies to class. A large play area is created for the children in the center of the room. Class is often noisy and frequently interrupted. Babies are being nursed and comforted. Parents observe children and talk with other parents. During one of these loud and friendly mornings, Janis asked parents to talk about how they take care of themselves.

Hector, whose ten-month-old son was leaning against his leg, began the discussion. "Home improvement projects keep me going. They really give me an outlet."

Raneta looked fondly at her son who was struggling to pull himself up. "Twice a month, I take the baby over to my mother's house. Then I go dancing with my friends."

Barbara, the mother of two girls, ages ten and one, smiled at her youngest daughter, Isa: "For me, it's *All My Children*. I watch it every day. For a while I had a job where I could actually have a TV on my desk. At lunchtime, I'd put my feet up, pull out my sandwich and a Coke, and turn on the TV. Everyone knew to leave me alone between twelve o'clock and one o'clock."

Deverick cradled his sleeping child and said, "We play penny-ante poker on Saturday nights. We throw a simple dinner together with friends, and after we eat, one of us gives Shana a bath and puts her to bed. Once she's down for the night, we pull out our cards and coins and play until the wee hours."

Mei spoke next. "I take a dance class three times a week. It's one of the only times in my life no one is on me. I love to cuddle with my kids, but I need my arms to be free once in a while."

Robin, who had listened as everyone else

shared, offered this insight: "What happened for me is that I'd get some time away from Kaya but still feel dissatisfied. Finally, I figured out that I wasn't in touch with what I needed when I got away. Now I realize I actually need five different kinds of time away: time alone at home when I can get things done, time to exercise, time to be listened to, time with friends, and time alone with my partner. I don't get all of those at once, but over time, I can."

Know Your Own Limits

One of the most important skills we can develop as parents is the ability to reach out before we're totally desperate. For most of us, this takes practice. We often don't know where the end of our rope is until we've reached it. But we can learn to recognize our own early warning signs.

If you find yourself repeatedly getting irritable around your child's naptime or begin to recognize that you yell right before dinner, that can be a reminder to take a look at the bigger picture: "Do I need a break?" "Is there something I could do to turn this situation around?"

When I'm Feeling Pushed: Maria's Story

Maria grew up in a violent household. She's had to face her childhood pain repeatedly in order to keep her four-and-a-half-year-old son, Kenji, safe. Maria's story is important because of the clarity with which she's able to differentiate between old feelings from her childhood and what's happening in the present.

There were times Kenji wouldn't listen to me and I wanted to overpower him physically. I remember being really angry and saying "I could easily grab you, shake you, throw you down, and make you do these things!" I felt like I wanted to clobber him. And he had this terrified smile on his face. I'd never seen that look on his face before. I shook him and said, "What are you smiling about? Do you think it's funny?" And he said, "Mommy, I am scared. I am very scared." And that stopped me. Kenji is a very sensitive person. As soon as he said that, I could see how overwhelmed he was. I was glad that he found a way to speak to me even though I was so angry. I decided I didn't want to get to that point again. I've spent a lot of time in classes exploring where those feelings came from. I've learned a lot about how to take care of myself and how to be clear with my son when I get mad. Now when those feelings start building up in my body, I'm able to say to Kenji "Kenji, I'm having strong feelings. I need to put myself in a safe place. I'll be back when I'm feeling better." And I go into my room or into the garage. Or I stick my head under a pile of pillows. And when I'm able to come back to him, he'll say, "Are you feeling better now, Mommy?"

Sometimes it's a really small thing that sets me off. We need to get out the door and he isn't cooperating. I start feeling really pushed. And what I start to feel is not just anger appropriate to the situation, but old feelings I carry from the past. And those feelings belong to me; they having nothing to do with Kenji or the situation. They have come up for me to take a look at them. They are part of me. But they don't belong in my relationship with Kenji. They have to do with me and the person who raised me.

There are times when all of us need help. Although it can be hard to reach out, it's important to push beyond our embarrassment to get the support we need.

Laura explains: "I've called friends saying 'I'm really losing it right now. I need to talk.' And even if it's just for five minutes, they listen. Sometimes Eli's screaming in the background, but I can still feel them nodding and going 'Uh-huh.' Having that voice on the other end of the phone really helps. And no matter how off the wall I think I sound, none of my friends have shunned me afterward. They still tell me they think I'm a great mom."

Maureen, whose family background placed her at risk for hurting her son, related the following story: "I grew up in a violent household. My mom was beaten a lot and she also did a lot of really sadistic things to me. A year after my son was born, his dad left and I became a single mom. I was under a lot of pressure financially and every other way. One day, when Ian was two, he wouldn't stop crying and I found myself shaking him and wanting to throw him down on the bed. I saw what I was doing and I stopped myself. I'd never seen a counselor before, but I knew I needed help. I couldn't afford it, not even remotely, but I flew into therapy."

That was sixteen years ago. Ian is now a thriving young adult. Because she got help, Maureen never hit or abused her son. In recognizing her danger signs, she was able to reach out, build support for herself, and learn better parenting skills, all of which enabled her to pass on a very different legacy to her son.

You don't have to wait until there's a crisis to ask for help. While most of us have been raised with long-standing traditions of pulling ourselves up by our bootstraps, making do, and dealing with problems within the confines of the family, all parents deserve an ongoing network of support. Fortunately, there are lots of models for building supportive communities. The more of us who reach out to participate in them, the stronger and healthier they will be.

9. Building a Supportive Community

Principle 9: All families need and deserve a community to support them in the critical work of nurturing and teaching the next generation.

When we become parents, our social lives, our place in the community, our relationship with our families, friends, and partners all shift dramatically. Whatever social networks we were part of before—whether as single people or as couples without children—may no longer meet the changing needs of our growing family. In addition to our old needs for companionship, validation, fun, and support, a brand-new set of vital interests instantly emerges upon having a child, and those interests immediately take precedence over things that seemed so pressing in our lives just months or even weeks before.

Parents are filled with burning questions and they're often not sure where to turn for answers. "Whom can I talk to when it's 3:00 A.M. and the baby hasn't slept for three nights running?" "Whom can I talk to when my child is covered with spots?" "Whom can I talk to about the fact that I'm doing this alone and I need to connect with a grown-up once in a while?" "Whose shoulder can I cry on after I drop my child off at day care for the first time?"

All sorts of new needs emerge when we have children, and our old network of family and friends may not provide resources to meet them all. For many of us, having children requires that we augment our circle of friends, gradually building a new social matrix that supports us in our role as parents.

Friends Come, Friends Go

For some new parents, friendship networks change substantially. Laura remembers the suddenness with which some of her friendships changed. "I had old friends who'd call me up in the first six months of Eli's life, just to chat, like we always had. And I'd wonder, 'Do you really think I have time to talk on the phone? Don't you know I have a baby over here?' But I'd try. And we'd have these awkward conversations. They'd ask, 'What's new?' And I'd gush about Eli's latest thing. Then they'd say, 'So what else is happening?' And there'd be this dead silence. Nothing else was happening! Eli and I were symbiotic. When he pooped, that was my life! I'd hang up from those phone calls feeling lonely and inadequate. Talking to old friends made me feel as if I was living on another planet. And I guess I was."

Since being a parent is such a big part of our lives, it can become difficult to spend time with people who don't relate to us as parents. As Laird explained, "I feel really offended when people come over to my house when I'm with my kid and they don't acknowledge him. I have some work friends who are very focused on work. The whole issue of children doesn't interest them. They want to relate to me in the same way they always have, and it's no longer possible."

Roger and his partner, Paul, have had a similar experience: "Since Paul and I adopted Brittany, we have a lot more in common with straight parents of toddlers than we do with our gay friends who don't have children."

Another problem for parents is that we live in a society that doesn't welcome children's full participation in community life. Unlike many other cultures, our social lives revolve around activities that aren't family-centered, in which children are left at home so as not to be disruptive. As a society, we've established very few environments for socializing that are friendly and inviting to both children and adults.

Connecting with Other Parents

Although old friends sometimes drop away, having a child also opens the door to new connections. Shu Lea, who stays home with her two children, said, "For me, becoming a mother has been great. Before my first child was born, I was commuting to school and to work, and I didn't know this community at all. But once I got pregnant, I started building a network of other moms. I feel as if I became a member of this community when I became a parent."

Parenthood makes us receptive to relationships in a whole new way. We all need to talk to someone who won't get tired of our obsession with our daughter's cradle cap or our son's adjustment to kindergarten. It's one of those times in life when our need for contact and connection can outweigh any reluctance or shyness we might normally have.

Opportunities for connecting with other parents are all around us. When you have a baby, you suddenly start noticing babies and parents everywhere. Carrying a baby or pushing a stroller invites conversations with people we would previously have considered strangers. Intimacies spring up over swing sets and in the grocery store check-out line.

Groups for parents—exercise groups, postpartum support groups, baby-sitting co-ops, classes for parents, formal and informal playgroups—can all be wonderful places to meet other parents. Some day care centers set up pot-lucks, parent meetings, parent participation work days, or other activities for parents. And parents with computers can even get support on-line.

Karyn recalls the relationships that sustained her through her early years of motherhood. "I was a single mom when Bryan was little. I started exchanging child care with other moms who had babies the same age when he was just a few months old. I did it out of need. There just wasn't any money to pay a sitter.

"When he was a year old, Bryan started going to a wonderful child care center while I worked. He made a couple of really good friends there, and their moms and I traded child care a few times a week. It allowed us to get a break, go on a date, do something for ourselves. The kids got really close, too. We shared car-pooling and meals. We cared about each other's kids. The kids were always sleeping at each other's houses. And that lasted for years."

Mayo, who's been in a father's group for the last five years, said his relationship to other fathers has really sustained him. "Our group gets together monthly, sometimes with the kids, and sometimes alone. The collective wisdom in that group of men is remarkable. I always come away rejuvenated and inspired, with lots of ideas."

Leah has found support and camaraderie meeting other foster parents. "I joined the Foster Parents Association. It was great having other foster parents to bounce things off of. They knew how things worked; they knew the system. Whatever came up for us, someone had already dealt with it."

Not all parents have the same kind of access to these resources. Often this breaks down along gender lines, with men usually having less access to support and information. Single parents, parents with other family commitments, and those who work full time outside the home are challenged to develop creative ways to get support.

Yvonne, a single mom with a full-time job explains: "I have to fit in time with other parents around everyday activities. My son and I have a standing date with our friends Cody, Lisa, and Jeff. Every Wednesday night, our families get together to have dinner at one of our houses. It's never anything fancy, but I sure look forward to it every week."

FOOD FOR THOUGHT: WHO'S IN MY SUPPORT SYSTEM?

- Who in my current group of friends or associates is someone I feel comfortable talking to about my questions, struggles, and joys as a parent?

- Is there someone in my group of acquaintances with whom I'd like to develop such a friendship?

- Are there any places in the community where I might be able to meet parents? Are there parenting support groups that serve parents and kids? If there isn't anything readily available, could I help start something?

Moving Beyond Competition

One thing that can interfere with building strong bonds with other parents is the sense of competition that can creep into those relationships. This topic came up one afternoon in one of Janis's classes. Mei asked the group, "Has anybody else ever caught themselves comparing their kid to someone else? Eliot will be starting kindergarten next year, and I see all these kids around me who are practically reading. They're writing the alphabet and he can barely make an 'A.' And I think, 'Oh, no! He's gonna be behind.' I wonder, 'Should I be working with him on his letters?' Of course what slips in is 'If he doesn't write well, is that a reflection on me as a parent?' I have to work really hard to free myself from all of that."

Tito, a new father, responded right away: "When a friend tells me about something his kid is doing that Ariana isn't doing yet, I get this little clutched feeling inside. I know those competitive feelings are inside of me, as well as all around me."

Clearly, this kind of competition gets in the way of building supportive communities for ourselves and our children. Just how and why does it begin?

Our society is a competitive one. We don't promote the idea that our community benefits from having a large number of diverse, skilled, talented, people in it. Instead we reserve our attention for people who are obviously exceptional in some way. As a result, we naturally want our child to be the best, the most skilled, the most talented, the first to walk, the one who scores highest, jumps farthest, comes in first.

Often it starts early. We go to the playground and the first question we often hear is "How old is your child?" In the best sense, this question comes from a desire to learn more about child development: "What will my child be doing six months from now?" or "What are other twenty-one-month-old babies doing?" But sometimes, the question arises from a place of insecurity. When we ask a father how old his daughter is, we may really be trying to figure out if our child is more or less advanced than other kids her age. Such comparisons create a sort of developmental pecking order that sets one child ahead and another behind. If the results of our informal playground survey show that our child is in fact an early walker, we feel good about ourselves and our child. If, on the other hand, our son is only crawling and the others are all up on their feet, we may feel concerned about his development or even inadequate as a parent.

It's interesting how often we define children according to their perceived deficits: "He's not walking yet." "She's not reading yet."

When we look at children, we frequently assess their development by looking at those skills that are most readily apparent: speech and mobility. In reality, there is a wide range of skills that children are developing. Some, such as fine motor coordination, mechanical ability, and social perceptiveness, are not immediately obvious. And if we feel our children are "lagging behind," it's easy to fall into trying to push or stimulate them so that they catch up with their peers.

There is a way out of this competitive cycle. The following suggestions can help you feel good about your children and clear the way for cooperative relationships with other parents:

• **Remind yourself that children grow at different rates.** Children have their own internal timetable for reaching physical, emotional, and cognitive milestones. Developmental milestones have very little to do with anything we as parents do.

• **Observe your child.** Children are developing and growing all the time. Even though your child may not be walking yet, careful observation will let you know exactly what she is accomplishing.

• **Enjoy what your child is doing right now.** Dianna and Rolf brought their nine-month-old daughter, Jennifer, to an infant observation class. Jennifer was still lying on the floor when all the other babies were rolling over and crawling. As the class observed her, it became

Learning and Teaching by Example: Leah's Story

All of us need people we respect and admire. Nowhere is this more true than in parenting. Many of us are fortunate enough to have inspiring role models in our own families. But some of us have to look elsewhere for our mentors.

Leah grew up in a home where she was abused, and as a result, she spent a lot of time in foster homes. She and her partner now have two kids of their own and do emergency foster care for up to three additional kids at a time. They specialize in working with crack- and alcohol-exposed infants and sexually abused kids. Their house is usually full and bustling with children: birth kids, foster kids, and neighborhood children, some on Leah's lap, others hanging off the back of her wheelchair, or running through the house.

When I was twelve and thirteen I lived with this foster mom named Helen. I acted like I hated her the whole time I was there, but she was always there for me, no matter what I did. She was real constant with her love.

What I'd been taught through the course of my childhood was that kids were a burden. With Helen, I saw how much fun you could have with a kid. I got to see how she was with her own son, Andy, who was four. She really enjoyed him.

My life had taught me it hurt to be a kid. Helen tried to impress on me that things could be different.

Nothing was a big deal to Helen. Andy would spill his milk and she'd say, "Oh, let's clean it up," not "Oh my God! The whole house is going to come apart!" I learned from her to go on with life. An incident happens, you deal with that incident, you keep going. You don't have to go ballistic over everything.

Helen introduced me to music. Before I met her, all I ever listened to was the standard rock and roll. I came home from school one day and there was this really cool music playing and I just had to sit down and listen to it, and I found out later it was Mozart. And I said, "My God! You mean I like classical music?"

Helen came to my school. She talked to my teachers and my counselor. My parents had never come to my school. At the time I thought Helen was being nosy and intrusive, but now I know that's what caring parents do.

Helen talked. And she listened. That was another thing she taught me about parenting. It didn't matter what I had to say, she just listened to it. And because of that, I'm better able to listen to my own kids.

Children come to my house with a lot of baggage. We had one child, who, any time you corrected him at all, even just "Why don't you try the blue block?" would get up, hysterical, and run away. We'd find him in the back bedroom under the crib, sucking his thumb in the fetal position. We've had kids who blasted us with foul language and others who followed us around and couldn't let go of our shirttails. We've had babies in withdrawal; babies we've had to bundle really tightly because if they shake too much, they can feel like they're falling apart. I've had babies I've kept next to my body twenty-four hours a day so they could learn to attach.

Our mandate is to treat these children as our own, and I believe that comes down to love. I can truly say I have loved every child who's come through here. I haven't liked a lot of them, but I have loved them. I think love is a discipline, an attitude, an openness of my heart. I accept these children and what they bring. I think that the basis of parenting is the capacity to love flexibly, to be able to change how you love with the changing personality of different children or the developing personality of one child. Helen was the one who taught me that.

There are times I don't think I'm a very good parent and at those times, I think, "What would a good parent do in this situation?" Very often when I ask myself that question, it's Helen's face that I see. I imagine what she would do, I do that, and most of the time, it works.

clear that Jennifer had an agenda all her own. She would sit or lie on the ground and watch everything and everyone around her. Rolf would mention someone's name and she'd look at that person. She'd figured out who everyone in the room was and what their name was, but she hadn't rolled over yet. By watching her carefully, Dianna and Rolf learned to trust just what it was that Jennifer was doing.

• **Seek out parents who aren't competitive.** Foster relationships with parents who aren't focused on how fast their child is developing.

• **Diffuse competitive remarks.** When someone says, "I can't believe how much Jorge is talking," or "Miranda's still not walking?" respond by saying "It is amazing how different they all are," or "Yes, he talks a lot, and I've noticed that Jeremy really loves to climb."

• **Talk to experienced parents.** Parents who've watched several children grow tend to be a lot more easygoing. Listening to their perspective may help you relax.

Building Support in Your Extended Family

Extended family can offer parents and their children some of the most significant support possible. People in your family are uniquely connected to your child. They share your history and are invested in the future of your family. There is a special familiarity and comfort in many extended families. Mei shares, "When my mom comes to visit, you can feel the stress level in our house just evaporate. I can just run out to the drugstore and pick up something I need, because the kids are with Grandma. We don't have to do all that scheduling. And Les and I are so much happier with each other. The addition of one trustworthy, responsible adult makes all the difference in the world."

Janis agrees. "When my sisters and brothers-in-law are around, we do tag-team with the kids. Leon cooks the dinner. Linda reads the stories. Stu gives the kids their bath. Nancy finds the pajamas, and Scott and I do the

dishes. The kids have such special relationships with their aunts, uncles, and cousins, it's a triple treat for them."

However, as well as being a source of support, extended families can also offer some of the stiffest criticism we face. Natalie remembers the sting of her mother's sharp words. "I'd be on the phone with my mom and Quincy would be pulling all my books out of the bookshelf. I'd say, 'I have to go, Mom. He's destroying the house.' She'd say, 'Why don't you just get a belt and let him know who's boss? That baby is going to rule you and Tom both.' "

Ginny recalls, "My mother-in-law used to say 'If you had more children and you had them closer together, you'd avoid the problem of giving them too much attention,' which apparently is what she thinks I'm doing now. If I had eight or nine, I guess she thinks I'd ignore them a little better."

Such comments can undermine our confidence and make us question our choices and perspective.

One night a group of parents came up with the following list of one-liners they'd heard from parents, siblings, cousins, in-laws and assorted family members:

- "Isn't that child weaned yet?"
- "You're spoiling that child."
- "You're letting her use a pacifier?"
- "You're not going to let her out of the house in *that*, are you?"
- "Oh, you're *still* nursing?"
- "I can't believe you're letting that child throw his food on the floor."
- "Don't be so uptight! A little candy won't hurt him."

Although these comments may feel critical to us, they're usually not coming from a malicious place. The grandmother who says, "Why don't you make him eat those peas?" is letting you know that she cares about your baby and is concerned about what happens to him. But she's also letting you know that she wants to be acknowledged as an experienced mother.

When we do things differently from other family members they sometimes interpret our choices as a rejection of the way they did things. This happened to Maria. "I was raised in a very poor family and emigrated to this country when I was nineteen. Six months after Kenji was born, my mother came to visit from El Salvador. She saw all these books I had for Kenji on the bottom shelf. And she was outraged. 'Books! He hasn't learned to read yet! Wait until he's seven years old. Then you can give him books! He's going to chew on them and ruin them and then when he's seven, he won't have any books.'

"I felt so sad for my mom. I could feel the sense of poverty she carries. I told her it would be okay, that there would be other books for him to read, that it was important for Kenji to have books now so he'd be able to read when he was seven. The next day when I came home from the market, she had put all the books up high out of his reach. She couldn't help it."

How Was It for You, Mom?

Sometimes, even small things can go a long way in strengthening relationships in families. The following suggestions can help create bridges, understanding and mutual support:

- **Ask extended family members about their experiences as parents.** Most parents have devoted large portions of their lives to their children and have generally gotten little acknowledgment or recognition for it. Sometimes giving relatives a chance to talk about their experiences goes a long way in forming a more helpful alliance: "Mom, tell me about when we were kids." "What was it like for you when I was Stevie's age?" Listening to their stories can also be a significant way to maintain family history.

• **Glean what you can from their experience.** Listening to what another generation of parents had to deal with can be both educational and useful.

• **Acknowledge their efforts.** Let them know that you appreciate the care and work they put into their families. Acknowledge that they did their best.

• **Talk about the evolution in child-rearing practices.** Acknowledge that they were parents in a different time with different advice and standards.

• **Describe your philosophy as a parent.** Share your vision for your family. This helps other people understand your choices as a parent.

• **Be flexible and set limits when necessary.** Kids benefit from a diversity of interactions with loving family members. The candy canes from Grandpa and the late nights with Aunt Lizzy are worth the special moments your kids are sharing with their loved ones. However, there may be times when people's behavior goes beyond what you feel is appropriate for your children. At these times clear communication and limits are necessary: "It's not okay for you keep tickling him like that." Or "That teasing is really hurting her feelings. It's time to stop." Or "I don't feel safe letting Evan stay here by himself until that fence is fixed."

• **Nurture your child's relationship with relatives.** Eli's Grandma Temme lives three thousand miles away and gets to see Eli only twice a year. To strengthen their relationship, Laura asked her mother to make Eli a tape of herself singing songs from her own childhood. Eli listened to the tape every night for several weeks before visiting Grandma Temme. When he got off the plane he started chattering to her immediately, as if she were an old friend.

Caring and Criticism from the Community

Beginning with visible signs of pregnancy, new parents suddenly find themselves the focus of a new kind of attention out in the world. Pregnant women experience strangers reaching out to touch their bellies, people smiling broadly in approval (or clucking in disapproval), and folks they never saw before making way for them in bathroom lines.

Rheta recalls, "I was thirty-nine when I got pregnant for the first time. I couldn't believe the attention I received. I met all kinds of people I never would have met otherwise."

Jenny had a very different experience. "I was nine months' pregnant when I was eighteen. I looked really young. People made negative comments to me a lot. I remember one time I was waiting for a bus. My baby was a few days overdue—I was out to *there!* A guy came up to me and said, 'I can't believe you're pregnant and you're only sixteen!' I was floored. Finally I managed to say 'I'm eighteen. And it's none of your business.' And he said, 'You're still too young. What are you going to be able to offer that child?' I felt so hurt by that. He knew nothing about me, nothing about my background, and yet he felt he could tell me that I couldn't be a good parent.' "

Masai, who received a lot of positive attention whenever he was out with his son, had mixed feelings about the attention he received. "People loved seeing my son and I together. People who wouldn't give me the time of day otherwise would talk to me if I had my kid with me. If I saw those same people when I didn't have my kid, it would be like I didn't exist. Then I was just a Black man with dreadlocks, and that made me scary as hell. But when I had my son with me, I was safe. People could see how much I adored him and how much he adored me.

"It was strange. And it kind of pissed me off. Sometimes I'd say to them, 'I'm just a parent. Why are you making such a big deal out of this? How many women do you give this kind of juice to?' And they'd say, 'Men don't usually do this.' And I'd say, 'This one does.' It just didn't feel right to me. This was my kid. Why was everybody congratulating me for doing what I was supposed to do?"

A Dialogue with the World

Once we have children, we enter into a dialogue with the world. People start providing commentary. They say such things as: "What lovely red hair!" "Oh, he's such a little *boy!*" "Where's her hat?" "Be careful, they can choke on hot dogs." Or to the child, "What's that thumb doing in your mouth?"

This collective interest in children is a remnant of the time when the whole community raised the child. It reflects our hopes for the future as well as our human impulse to care for children.

Since most communities don't raise children anymore, and because children spend increasing amounts of time in day care, the larger community has less and less opportunity to interact with children. Therefore, interactions with children are less natural and appropriate, and interest in children sometimes becomes either intrusive or accusatory.

Juju explained: "As a parent, I feel more vulnerable to other people's criticism than I ever did in my life. An innocent remark can really stab me."

Dalia agreed. "Sometimes I'm more distressed about what other people are going to think about my parenting than I am about my son's actual behavior. If Zach is acting out, I usually know where his behavior is coming from: He's tired or hungry or hasn't had any control over his day. But it's still hard for me when he behaves like that in public because people can see it and judge me."

What can we do about this? How can we build on this human impulse to care for children? It is the community at large who votes to fund our schools and build our playgrounds; who decides on parental leave policies and health coverage for families. How can we develop a larger community that serves us as parents and benefits our families?

Most of the time, when the community comes forward, it is to celebrate, to appreciate, to offer something, even if it doesn't quite come out that way. If we can affirm the impulse—"Gee, it looks like you want to say 'Hi' to Sherry," or "It seems as if you really like kids"—we can then go on to share some information with that person about ways they could connect with our particular child. People learn something when we say, "Sherry always turns her head away when she doesn't know somebody. If you stay there for a while, she'll probably turn her head back and look at you." Such a statement says that we value the person's interest in children as well as our child's needs. It also teaches the other person something about how babies communicate.

When Barry, a family friend who doesn't have kids, comes up to us at a social gathering and tries to force our toddler to hug him, our first impulse might be to say "Get your hands off my kid," But such a response may serve only to alienate Barry without enlarging his understanding of the issues.

Although there are times it's appropriate to fiercely protect our kids, there are also ways to give people information while still respecting the feelings of everyone involved. To our child we can say, "This is our wonderful friend Barry. He's a really fun guy that you're going to get a chance to know better. Let's tell him how you like to make friends." And then we can tell Barry, "Tommy usually takes some time getting to know people. If you move slowly and give him some space to approach you, he'll probably come around."

Such an approach respects Tommy's feelings and his right to be in charge of his body, and also encourages Barry to continue to connect with kids and to do it in more appropriate ways. As people learn to relate to children more respectfully, we build a larger, more supportive community for all of our families.

Not Until Every Child Is Safe

There is an underlying premise in this country that individual families are solely responsible for their children. The burden of child rearing falls totally on parents and, in many cases, on only one parent.

Imagine how different our lives would be if we lived in a culture like the one this parent describes. "I heard a man from Africa give a talk recently. He said in his village, which is still an indigenous culture, all the houses are open. There are basically no doors. And at dinnertime, the children go wherever they want to for dinner. So everybody cooks expecting small visitors. And he said children choose their dinner depending on which house smells best. It's such a far cry from what we have here."

In contrast, our society tends to perpetuate the isolation of families. Although we live in one of the richest countries in the world, millions of American families are excluded from necessary nutrition, housing, and health care. Assistance programs for single parents and children have been cut. There's not enough affordable, quality child care. Information and resources for parents are insufficient. These are just some of the ways our society says "You had these children. They're your responsibility."

This generation is the first to live at a lower standard of living, with less financial security, than their parents. In the 1950s, for many families, one income provided a home, a car, and the trappings of middle-class life. But now, two-income families are struggling to maintain, or even approach, the same level of prosperity.

And many families face even more dire circumstances. For middle-class families one paycheck away from disaster, working-class families on the border of poverty, poor families struggling to find work that will sustain their families, the task of parenting can look very different from how it looks for families with more economic stability.

For many families on the edge, neighborhoods have become increasingly perilous. Poor parents are fighting to keep their children away from miserable options such as drugs, early pregnancy, gangs, crime, and incarceration.

Community supports, if available at all, are stretched beyond capacity.

While poverty or economic stressors don't define a person's ability to be a loving, nurturing, responsive parent, worry, fear, shame and day-to-day economic struggles can usurp a parent's time, energy, and optimism. Figuring out how to get kids to child care and yourself to work when your car is broken down, choosing between bread for the family and diapers for the baby when you are down to your last five dollars, and providing jackets and paying

Making the World a Better Place: What Parents Have Done

It is easy to be overwhelmed by the enormity of needs in the world. But we alone do not have to solve all the world's problems. We only have to do our own small part. As it says in the Talmud, "It is not upon you to finish the task, nor are you free not to begin."

Parents have worked small miracles in their schools, in their neighborhoods, and in the greater world. All this work has been accomplished one small step at a time. All it takes is a commitment to do something and the willingness to begin.

Ellen was spurred into activism by the birth of her first child. "Sara's birth was a wake-up call for me about the state of the world. I became very involved in antinuclear work when she was still a baby. I was infused with an urgency to make her world better."

Emily, whose two daughters are under five, says community service projects are a regular part of her family's life. "We've done social projects together, things that affect our immediate community—picking up garbage, giving food to needy people. Once a year, each person in our family gets to choose something the rest of us will do. It could be going to the Boardwalk or something else fun. And my daughter Zoe, who'd just turned four, picked bringing food to a single mother. We were shocked she chose that, but we did it. The girls each took a little grocery cart into the supermarket and they each picked out foods for this family. It was a little heavy on the cookies and chips, but they also picked healthy things. And we took this family a bag of food. Zoe's been talking about it ever since."

Paula also takes conscious steps to expand her children's world. "A lot of people are afraid of people who look a certain way just because they haven't spent any time with them. So I take my kids to places where they're exposed to all different kinds of people. We volunteer at the homeless shelter. We bring down extra hats, socks, and coats. I want my kids to see that everybody gets cold, that everybody needs care. They meet people they might normally be afraid of. I want them to know that just because people look ragged doesn't mean they aren't important."

Some parents use their work as a way to teach activism to their children. Masai is a youth outreach worker. "I see a lot of young people of color losing hope. They don't know who they are or where they're going. They think, 'Things are never gonna get better.' And when individuals have no hope, they do stupid things, like injecting drugs. That scares me.

"My twelve-year-old sees me working for change. He knows I believe that change is possible. He's seen me grieve over the kids I can't save. But he's also seen me persist and finally succeed.

"When I see my son feeling like things are bad and that they aren't going to get better, I talk to him. I tell him that he has to hope. I say, 'Man, if you don't have hope, you don't have anything. And with the hope and the intelligence and the energy you have, you can change a lot of things.' "

For every major social ill, there are people working hard to implement creative, effective solutions. Local community organizing goes a long way to diminish feelings of powerlessness and isolation, and it can have a profound impact on public policy. Getting involved can generate a powerful, contagious sense of optimism.

the heating bill now that the weather has turned cold are a few of the many things that get in the way of the other tasks of parenthood—sharing a book, listening to sad feelings, laughing together, appreciating a child's new skill.

Supporting healthy parenting necessitates that we first look at issues of poverty. As Marion Wright Edelman, of the Children's Defense Fund, writes, "It is morally shameful as well as economically foolish for our rich nation, blessed with one of the highest standards of living in the world, to let children be the poorest group of Americans."

It is our shared responsibility to work for the well-being of all families. It is not only the moral thing to do, it is also practical, for if we live in communities in which children are not well cared for, that community will not be a safe place for any of its members. This is our larger responsibility and opportunity as parents: to join together and create the collective voice that demands that children and families are on the top of this country's political agenda.

Ten Things You Can Do to Make the World Better for All Families

Together, we can work to change the larger consciousness about children and families in this country. As anthropologist Margaret Mead once put it, "Never doubt that a small group of thoughtful committed citizens can change the world. Indeed it is the only thing that ever has."

Here are ten things you can do to make things better for all families:

1. **Broaden your concern from your immediate family.** Think about ways you can support the health of families and children around

you. Some parents routinely send extra money when their child's class takes a field trip, to make sure that all children can go. Others send contributions to homeless shelters, women's crisis support groups, church or synagogue programs for families in need. Families with more limited financial resources can donate time or used clothing.

2. **Greet the kids in your neighborhood.** Marion Wright Edelman reminds us to start with simple steps. She asks us to begin simply, by saying "hi!" to the kids in your neighborhood. You could also take time to talk to them, to show an interest in their lives, but even a simple greeting starts to build the feelings of caring and concern necessary to strong communities.

3. **Encourage and support the parents you know.** Within your resources, you can support the families around you. Parents have organized dinner networks for families with new

babies or in other times of need. Friends have provided transportation or child care. And some families have developed child care exchanges or co-ops.

4. **Volunteer at your child's school.** If your child is in preschool, spend time helping out in the classroom. Even an occasional morning can help you feel more connected to other children, parents, and the larger school community.

5. **Advocate in your workplace.** Whenever the opportunity comes up, you can advocate for family-friendly policies in your workplace. Organize a brown-bag lunch discussion group for parents. In your union or with your boss, talk about the importance of flexible work schedules, family leave or absence policies and benefit packages which make provisions for child care and parent education.

6. **Support parent education in your community.** Investigate the parent education opportunities in your community. Are there any? Are they useful? Culturally relevant? Well used? Do they serve the needs of your community? If your community has the need for more parent education, you can research community groups (YWCA, Planned Parenthood, local colleges or adult education schools, hospitals, or child care centers) that might be willing to sponsor additional classes.

7. **Speak out.** In your local community, you can talk to friends or neighbors and go to school board meetings, city council meetings, or other groups dealing with broader community issues. Whenever opportunities arise, speak up about the importance of providing support for all families. You don't have to use fancy words. It is most meaningful when you use your own voice and speak from your experience.

If you're more comfortable with the written word, you can write letters or send e-mail. By writing to the local newspaper or your local or national legislators, you can keep people aware of the needs of families, respond to proposed legislation, and advocate for specific political action.

8. **Join an advocacy group.** There may be local parent groups you could join, or you may get a group of parents together and start one. Even an organization like the PTA might be open to addressing the larger needs of families. You could volunteer to serve on the board of a family service organization or join a national group, such as the Children's Defense Fund, the Family Resource Coalition, or Children Now.[1]

9. **Open up your home.** Parents have taken in foster kids, "adopted" a teenage mom and her child, become "big brothers" or "big sisters," or done respite care for families in need.

10. **Vote.** Find out candidates' positions on family issues. Be an informed, active voter and talk to other voters.

[1] You can reach the Children's Defense Fund by writing to: 25 E. Street NW, Washington, DC 20001, or by calling (202) 628-8787. The Family Resource Coalition can be reached at 200 S. Michigan Ave, 16th floor, Chicago, IL 60604; (312) 341-0900. Children Now's address is 1212 Broadway, Suite 530, Oakland, CA 94612; (510) 763-2444; e-mail: children@dnai.com

• Part Two •

Children's Feelings

10. Learning About Feelings

"Our feelings are our most genuine paths to knowledge."
AUDRE LORDE

Anyone who's been around children for any length of time knows that their access to feelings is vast and immediate. Children cry, scream, shake, sweat, and laugh readily. They express their emotions easily and authentically in the moment. As Janis once remarked, "Watching children, I sometimes get the idea that people have more feelings than the human language has the words to describe."

During their first five years children experience the most rapid emotional growth of their lives. They go from undifferentiated expressions of feelings to sizable emotional vocabularies. Children learn to recognize and name many of their feelings, and begin learning the socially appropriate ways to express them. They also discover that the same feeling can look different on different people. Through trial and error, children begin to figure out what causes certain feelings and what makes feelings change.

Children readily invite adults into this research. Once they learn that certain feelings are predictable, they begin to test for those feelings—on one hand, trying to make us laugh, and, on the other, deliberately provoking our sadness, frustration, and anger. To parents, this can feel like kids are trying to drive us crazy, but from their perspective, this investigation is perfectly sound.

As parents, we have rich opportunities to assist children in their exploration of feelings. We can teach our kids that feelings are worth listening to, that everyone has them, and that emotions are a vital part of the human experience. In sharing these lessons, we provide children's first schooling in emotional literacy.

Children's Emotional Development: An Overview

Newborns manifest a number of different emotions. Most cry in distress when they are hungry, uncomfortable, or startled. Their faces get red and their bodies tremble with the force of their crying. Babies also smile fleeting little grins in the first few days of life at a pleasant noise or a full stomach. In the first weeks, infants also show wide-eyed interest or surprise. They look intently at faces, lights, or contrasting patterns. Many parents remember the intensity of being locked into the gaze of their newborn.

At about six weeks of age, babies begin to smile socially in response to faces or other people's smiles. In doing so, they discover a way to engage the world. Few people can resist the toothless grin of a passing baby.

By four months old, most babies have begun to laugh when they are pleased. Between the fourth to seventh month, children add anger to their emotional repertoire. You may notice that the tone, pitch, or intensity of this angry cry is different from earlier cries of distress.

For many babies, fears first become evident at about six months. These are usually about something tangible, yet unexpected, in their immediate environment—the sound of garbage cans crashing outside the window, sudden big objects looming toward them, or unfamiliar faces. This is the time when some children start becoming wary of strangers. Sue recalls, "Forest was a friendly baby, smiling easily and often at anyone who greeted him. But at about six months, he developed what I called his 'macho meter.' When certain kinds of gruff men approached him, he would always cry."

Babies begin "reading" the emotional cues of others very early on. Between two and four months of age, a baby may look sad when his parent shows him a sad face, and by eight or nine months that same baby may start to recognize that his parent's feelings are connected to actual events: "It makes my mom smile when I play peek-a-boo with her."

In the second six months of life, babies also start to hear the emotional messages conveyed in language and may begin crying at the sound of a harsh or critical voice. Esteban noticed, "I was training our new puppy and I spoke sternly to her. My ten-month-old daughter, Jasmine, who was playing nearby, burst into tears."

When babies reach a year old, the development of memory affects their emotional growth in a new way: "Because I can remember what happened yesterday, I can predict what might happen today." Your daughter starts becoming excited when she hears the garage door open because she can now remember it signifies Daddy's homecoming.

As children leave babyhood and enter the toddler and preschool years, they develop emotions that reflect an awareness of how others see them: pride, confidence, guilt, empathy, shame, defiance, jealousy, and embarrassment. Norm, the father of three-year-old Julia, shares: "Julia used to just fall down and get right up—sometimes she'd need a hug, but usually not. But recently she has started hiding after she has fallen down. It seems as if she's embarrassed."

As children get older, they become more able to identify, predict, and appropriately express their emotions: "When you and Mommy leave to go to the movie, I am going to feel sad and cry."

As preschool children learn words for their feelings, and as their experiences with feelings broaden, they're better able to express their emotions with words. Rather then hitting and biting, they begin to rely on verbal forms of expression: yelling "no," swearing, name-calling, and eventually "I'm so mad at you." Or "I feel happy."

Feelings and Temperament

While all human beings experience a full range of emotions, the way we experience feelings and the intensity of those feelings depends largely on our temperament. Some children run the gamut from giddy to enraged with the same amount of passion for each feeling. For other children, the continuum of emotions is narrower; it runs between mildly pleased to slightly irritated.

Children's emotional response to events is also affected by temperament. For some, the wrong hairband or an unfamiliar brand of cereal will set off a tirade. For others, the adjustment to a new home in a new city will cause only slight clinginess and a few nights of disturbed sleep.

Learning to anticipate, read, and respond to your children's feelings will be facilitated by your familiarity with their basic emotional temperament.

Exploring Your Perspective on Feelings: Issues for Parents

For many of us, figuring out how to support our children's emotional health is not clear or straightforward. When faced with a screaming baby, an angry toddler, or a frightened child, few of us know what to do. Becoming aware of our relationship to our own feelings enables us to think carefully about the emotional legacy we want to pass on to our children.

Jenny explains: "I've always felt I had to be happy around people. It's hard for me to cry, to break down and say 'I'm sad today. I'm having a really bad day.' And I don't want my daughter to have the same problem."

As children, many of us got the message that adults were uncomfortable, critical, or scared of our feelings as well as their own. In many families, anger, frustration, and sadness were considered "negative" feelings. They weren't viewed as a healthy part of one's experience. Families may have responded to those feelings with punishment, belittling, and name-calling: "Go in your room until you are ready to behave." "Don't be a crybaby." "Scaredy-cat!"

Some of us grew up in families where we absorbed the message that it was best to suppress our feelings because they were too big to deal with and there wouldn't be any resolution for them.

Additionally, many of us learned that certain feelings were acceptable or unacceptable because of gender—girls were expected to feel hurt, sadness, and compassion, while anger was the predominant feeling boys were allowed to have: "Shouting is not ladylike." "Big boys don't cry."

As a result, many of us have several layers of response when we're confronted with the unadulterated expression of a child's feelings, whether it is a newborn's colic, a toddler's tantrum, or a teenager's angry outbursts. We may feel scared that something is inherently wrong with our child, jealous that our children can open up and express their feelings so freely, or inadequate because we have failed to produce a "happy" child.

Drew, the father of a twelve-year-old girl, explained, "One of the hardest things for me as a parent was the night I was sitting on my daughter's bed and she told me that she wished that she was dead. She was feeling lonely and isolated at school, and she was sure it was because she had all the wrong clothes. It was hard for me to just sit there and listen, to let her express her despair."

Many of us have been taught to ignore our children's "negative" feelings. We've been told: "If you give them attention, you will just make things worse." We try to get kids to stop crying or screaming, partly because of discomfort and embarrassment, but also because we've been taught that the crying or yelling is the feeling itself and that if we succeed at making the expression go away, the feeling will also be gone.

Our attempts to quiet children take many forms. We bribe or threaten children (sometimes "successfully") to stop their crying: "C'mon, I'll get you some ice cream." We withdraw our attention: "Don't come back in here until you're done crying." We use distraction to make kids feel "better." We say, "Come on, let's go to the park." Or we pat them and say, 'Shh, shh, there, there, don't cry." But when we respond in these ways, we inadvertently teach children not to trust their own responses and to stop sharing their difficult but important feelings.

As parents, our first task is to come to terms with our own feelings. Learning to understand, accept, and honestly express our emotions lays the groundwork for teaching children that all feelings are valuable. We then have the opportunity to share our children's joy, love, excitement, and delight and the responsibility to show them that they don't have to bear their despair, anger, and pain alone.

FOOD FOR THOUGHT: FEELINGS

- What feelings did I see expressed in my family when I was growing up?
- Were there feelings that were acceptable or unacceptable?
- Were different feelings permissible for boys and for girls? For adults and for children?
- How do I feel when my children express feelings of frustration, anger, sadness or jealousy? Are there emotions that are particularly hard for me to deal with?

Twelve Ways to Support Children's Emotional Literacy

The following strategies can help children acknowledge, identify, and appropriately express their feelings:

1. **Respect children's feelings.** Begin with a premise that children's feelings are important and that all feelings are healthy.

2. **Talk about feelings.** Children are full of feelings they don't have names for. When you acknowledge their feelings and suggest names for them, children learn to recognize them and talk about them, too: "I wonder if you're feeling frustrated?" Or "It looks like you are really pleased."

3. **Share your own feelings.** When we acknowledge and name our own feelings, children's understanding of feelings broadens.

4. **Define and model acceptable forms of expression.** Children take their cues from the way we express our feelings.

5. **Be a witness to your child's feelings.** Stay physically close, as your child shares his happy or difficult feelings, offering touch or holding, as appropriate.

Maintain a listening posture. You don't need to fill up all the space with words but, when appropriate, reflect your child's feelings: "You sound really mad." Or "I can tell you are really upset." Or "You seem so delighted by your new puppy."

6. **Respect nonverbal forms of communication.** When children are crying, we often say to

them "Tell me how you feel," or "What's wrong?" While it is important that we express a willingness to listen, sometimes we demand that children explain their feelings in words before they're ready.

Janis recalls: "Four-year-old Noah shared his wisdom with me one day when I was asking my crying daughter to tell me what happened. He said, 'Don't *talk* to her, she is crying!' And in fact, she couldn't respond with words right then. Her crying was her most appropriate expression. Yet I would have been much more comfortable if she could have used words instead."

7. **Give it time.** Don't rush in to fix things. Full expression of feelings takes time. Although we may feel "done" with children's feelings before they do, children need time to find their own resolution.

Jenny explains: "One day Carly had been crying for a long time and I didn't know why. I said to her, 'Stop crying! Use your words!' I didn't want to tell her not to cry, but I was frustrated; she'd been crying long enough for me. I said, 'I don't know why you're sad. I can't help you until you tell me what's wrong.' She just kept crying. Finally I said, 'Do you want me to hold you?' And Carly said, 'Yes.' She got her blanket and climbed on my lap and sucked her little fingers. Gradually she calmed down and it ended up that the whole thing had something to do with wanting to wear a different pair of shoes. A lot of times she has to be really emotional first. Then she can get to her words later."

8. **Maintain safety, setting limits when necessary.** Sometimes children need your help in keeping themselves and others safe. Excited, happy children may need redirection for their bouncy play. Upset children may need gentle but firm physical holding or moving to a safer environment. These kind of physical limits provide children with a sense of emotional, as well as physical safety.

9. **Differentiate between feelings and behavior.** It's possible to stop a behavior such as kicking or hitting while still respecting the feelings that are being expressed. It is often appropriate to suggest alternative outlets to our children: "If you really feel like throwing something, you can throw this pair of socks at the wall."

10. **Distinguish your feelings from your children's.** Sometimes listening to children's feelings brings up feelings for us. It is important to differentiate your own emotional responses from your child's, so you can continue to give clear attention to your child.

11. **Get support for your own feelings.** Listening to children's feelings is challenging for many parents. Many of us didn't have anyone who listened to our feelings as children, nor do we have anyone who does it for us now. Being adults, we sometimes think we shouldn't need to express sad, frustrated, or angry feelings. We have all kinds of ways to talk ourselves out of expressing our emotions: "It'll just make things worse if I show my feelings," "Maybe if I start crying, I'll never stop," "I have such a great life, I shouldn't feel sad," "I'm a grown-up. I don't need to cry." But people of all ages experience a full range of feelings. Our acknowledgment, acceptance, and expression of all our feelings will allow us to be more responsive to our children's various emotional expressions.

Different people have different ways to work through their emotions. A few people can do it alone, if they have the time and space, but most of us need another person to help, to sit down with us in a relaxed, calm way and just listen. Some of us have friends, partners, or peer counselors who will do this with us. Others can use spiritual leaders or professional counselors. You and your child both deserve the gift of feelings.

12. **Be realistic about what you can do.** There will be times, despite our best intentions, when we will not be available to fully listen to children's feelings. Our own strong feelings may stand in the way. We may be too angry, tired, cranky, or short-tempered. We may be embroiled in a power struggle or unable to step out of the hurt of the moment. We may be in a circumstance where it is not safe or otherwise possible to stop and listen. Or we may just not have the ability that day to stop our own momentum to be available for our child.

At those times when it's hard to listen, there are ways to take breaks from children that don't make them feel wrong for having their feelings. We can say "It seems like you still need to cry. I'm going to give my ears a rest (take a break, go check on your sister). I'll be back to see how you're doing in a few minutes." In this way, we leave children to continue to express their feelings without abandoning them, telling them that their feelings are wrong, or giving them the message that they've driven us away.[1]

[1] For a very clear, straightforward approach to listening to children's feelings, we recommend an excellent series of low-cost pamphlets called "Listening to Children" by Patty Wipfler. Topics include "Crying," "Tantrums and Indignation," "Healing Children's Fears," "Special Time," "Playlistening," and "Reaching for your Angry Child." Wipfler gives special attention to the kind of support parents need in order to listen to children's strong feelings. For information or to order, you can contact: Parents Leadership Institute, PO Box 50492, Palo Alto, CA 94303; (415) 424-8687.

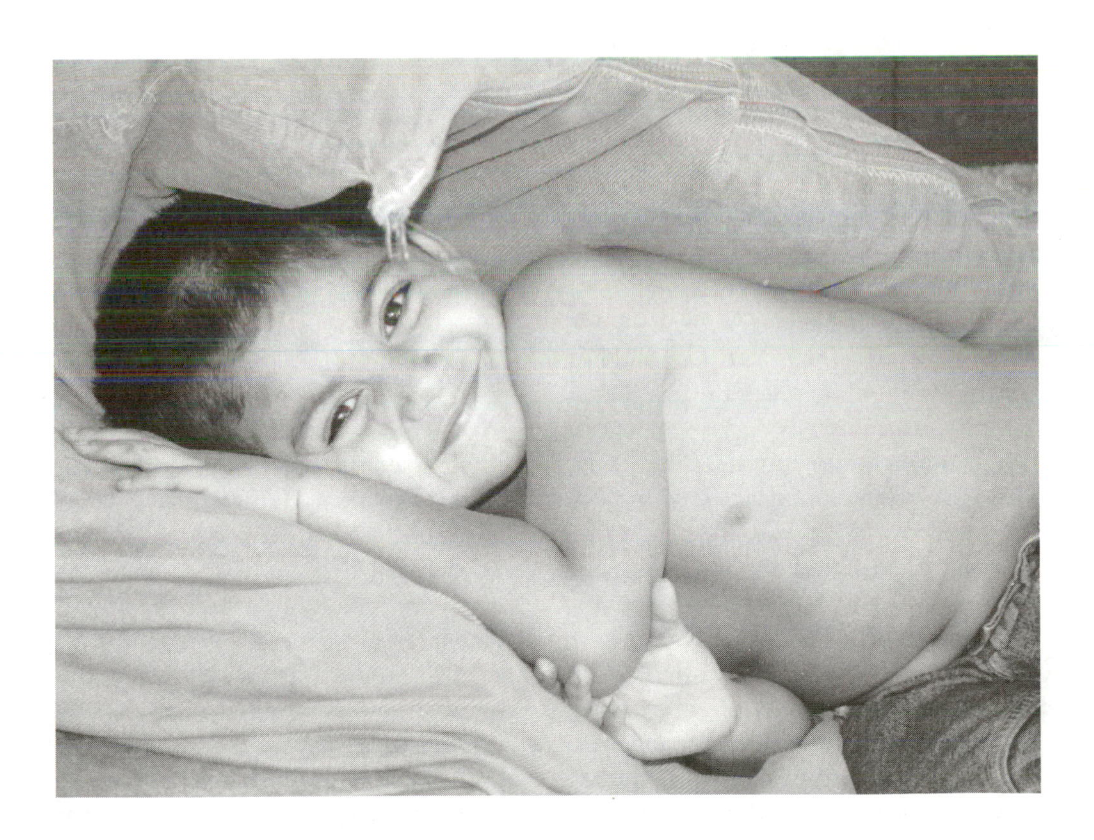

11. Responding to Crying and Tantrums

"Crying happens and it doesn't always need to be fixed. Some feelings just need to be articulated in a cry."

T.J., *father of two boys under two*

"Every time Quincy sprawls out on the ground and starts doing that kicking thing, I want to lie down beside him and do it, too."

NATALIE, *mother of a toddler having frequent tantrums*

Babies cry and parents respond. Through this dance, babies begin to learn the essential lessons of trust. "I can communicate and the world will listen." "I will get my needs met." As challenging, unnerving, and exhausting as crying can be for parents, it is a critical building block of the parent-child relationship.

Similarly, tantrums—explosions of aggravation and anger—are critical to the next stage in children's development, the establishment of autonomy. As toddlers test their limits, try the impossible, and take on the challenge of your authority, they are striving to understand what it means to be a separate person. The by-products of this mission are fatigue, frustration, and rage. While it is critical that we support children's drive for independence, the challenge of dealing with the accompanying tantrums stretches even the most stalwart parent.

Babies and Crying

People of all ages cry. As Somchai, the father of two, put it, "Crying is as natural as breathing." Most people cry to express feelings. Toddlers cry with such frustration and abandon that we call their crying "tantrums." But the crying babies do is different.

Crying is a baby's main form of communication. Through crying they communicate both needs and feelings. It's a baby's job to cry. And it's our job as parents to respond. But how to respond is not always clear. When babies cry, we're faced with certain dilemmas: "What is going on with him when he cries like that?" "What can I do if she doesn't stop crying?" These are major questions that parent and child revisit repeatedly during the first months of life.

Sara Wood Smith, a parent educator, describes two kinds of crying that babies do. The first is crying that the parent can "do something" about. The second kind of crying has less obvious solutions. The first refers to crying that signals a physical need—the baby is wet, hungry, tired, or cold. When you provide a change, food, a place to sleep, or warmth, the baby stops crying. The second kind of crying is more about feelings of frustration, tension, struggle, or overstimulation, and has no discernible remedy. Parents facing it often feel ineffective and at their wits' end.

Although parents through the ages have come up with a myriad of remedies, this kind of crying mostly has to run its course. However, there are significant kinds of support that parents can offer babies who are sobbing in distress.

When we think about responding to this kind of crying, it can be useful to imagine the situation being reversed. What would you want from a loved one if you had difficult feelings you wanted to express? Would you like them to tell you to shush? To say that you had nothing to cry or yell about? To keep trying to feed you or bounce you?

Think about what it would be like if you were crying and someone sat down with you and looked at you with compassion and love and said, "I'll be here with you while you cry. I'll listen as long as you want." How would it feel if that person didn't get tense or panicked, but instead gave you their full attention?

It can be more difficult to do this as a parent of the baby than it is as a friend. As a parent, you are responsible for the care of your baby, and it can be difficult to determine when the crying is the kind that you can "do something" about and when it's the kind that you just need to be there and listen to. Even when you have run out of "solutions" and the baby continues to cry, there is still something you can do—you can stay, listen empathetically, and reflect on what might be happening with your child. Even if your listening doesn't "stop" the crying, it is an effective way to support and teach your baby.

Will has learned a lot about crying from his six-month-old sons: "I stayed home the first two months after Reuben and David were born, and I remember holding them for days while they cried in distress. Reuben would cry rhythmically. His mouth would be open and his tongue would be flapping, and it was difficult for him to get any relief. Sometimes it felt like he just needed to cry. At those times, I'd tell him, 'I'm with you. I love you.' I'd try to clear my mind, to just accept his crying. Whenever I started feeling worried, I'd tell myself, 'It's okay for him to cry.' I had to remind myself of that again and again.

"Often, when the boys were crying, I'd be struggling between two things. On one hand, I felt like the provider, that it was my job to alleviate their distress. On the other, I didn't want to control what might be a bodily need to cry. Sometimes it was a struggle to differentiate between the two, but it got to the point where I could often tell."

Through supportive listening, babies learn that their feelings aren't something to be afraid of. They learn that you're available to them during times of struggle. They begin to learn that their feelings are their own and not yours. And they continue to honestly express their feelings.

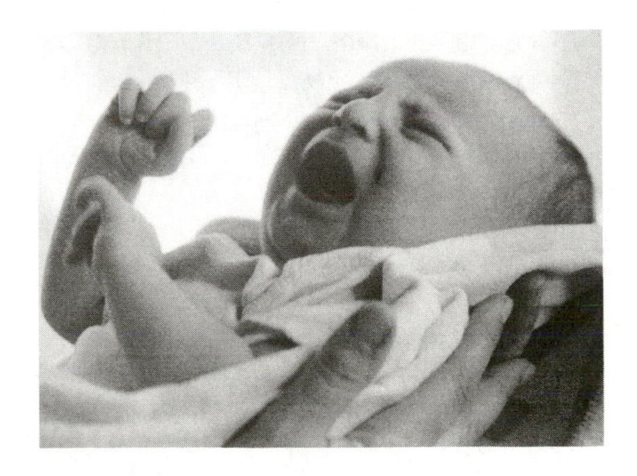

What Exactly Is a Tantrum?

The terms "tantrum" or "temper tantrum" have been loosely used to describe much of children's anger. Children's anger can emerge as early as the second half of the first year. At this point, children's memory has developed to the point where they can begin to hold on to their ideas in a new way. Angie noticed this happening with her daughter Lena, who, at eight months old, began to cry fiercely when Angie turned off the water she was playing with in the kitchen sink. While this kind of anger has a different quality to it from earlier crying, it is generally not until sometime between twelve and eighteen months of age that children start having the intense emotional outbursts we call "tantrums."

A tantrum is an uncontrollable release of anger, lasting more than a few minutes, in which the child is doing one or more of the following: yelling, screaming, crying, kicking, biting, hitting, throwing, name-calling, or head-banging. Tantrums are loud, sweaty, and physical.

Children's tantrums vary, yet anyone who's ever witnessed one can testify as to their intensity and inevitability. Although tantrums can sometimes be averted or prevented, once a child is fully in the throes of one, the tantrum generally needs to run its course until the rage and frustration have been fully released.

Tantrums are normal during the toddler years, although some children cruise through their twos easily and don't start having tantrums until three. A few children never have tantrums at all. Others continue having tantrums beyond three or four, but the tantrums generally diminish in frequency.

Temperament has a lot to do with whether, and how often, children have tantrums. Some children's expressions of frustration are so subtle that they are perceptible only to the people who know them best. At the other end of the continuum are children who have frequent, loud, prolonged outbursts that can be heard by everyone on the block. Although children at the more expressive end of the continuum may be more challenging for parents to deal with, frequent tantrums are not necessarily indicative of anything other than a lively disposition.

Toddler Tantrums

Tantrums make perfect sense in light of toddler development. Understanding why young children are prone to such fierce and powerful outbursts can help us respond to them effectively and with compassion.

Toddlerhood is a unique, challenging time in human development. Toddlers are beginning to get a sense that the world may be bigger than their own bodies and their immediate experience. They are starting the process of separating themselves from the important people in their world. As Janis often tells parents, "Toddlers are going to fight us like heck and that's their job. It's a healthy part of their growth and maturation."

At the same time, toddlers are beginning to develop a sense of memory, of a past and a future, and that enables them to remember what they want. Toddlers are famous for holding on to their ideas tenaciously, and that can lead to repeated disappointments when their desires are thwarted.

Let's take a simple example. Marguerite eats her first cookie. She likes it and asks for

Eli's Thunderstorm: Laura's Story

Many of us are stunned the first time our child has a major tantrum. That was certainly the case for Laura when Eli erupted in rage shortly before he turned two. Initially, Laura was shaken. But after being confronted with many more tantrums, she found an image that really helped her: "I tell myself, 'This is like a summer thunderstorm. It's intense, but it will pass.' "

We'd been having a quiet afternoon. We were playing with some play-dough on the table and I told Eli it was almost time for me to change his diaper and for us to get ready to go over to Max's house for his weekly visit. Every Wednesday night, Max's family takes care of Eli.

Eli started crying "No! No!" and throwing play-dough on the floor. I told him I was going to put it away if he kept throwing it. He kept throwing it. Then I said, "It seemed like you really got upset when I said it was time to go to Max's house."

His crying increased, "I don't want to go. Stay home! Stay HOME!!" He was wailing and kicking at the chair. I helped him down to the ground and he ran away from me, screaming and crying. The tantrum was building. I followed him from room to room, not getting too close, but staying close enough to keep him safe. His fury kept mounting, his nose was dripping with snot, and every time I came within reach, he tried to kick me. I was shocked at the strength and depth of his feelings. Moments passed and I watched him. He was immersed in his "no." I was both fascinated and horrified. How could such rage come from my little boy?

"You're telling me you really don't want to go," I said to him, making every effort to mirror his feelings. "You're telling me that you really want to stay home."

His wailing increased. "STAY HOME!!!!!"

"It must be hard, Eli," I said to him. "There are so many times you don't get to decide whether you stay home or not."

He nodded and sobbed some more. "Stay HOME! Stay HOME!"

I felt scared and shaky inside. Was I handling this right? Was it really okay for me to let Eli express such strong feelings? Or was I just egging him on, encouraging him to rage more?

I went back in my mind and tried to remember what Janis had said about tantrums in class. I stayed close to him, as close as he seemed comfortable, and breathed. I tried to listen, to just be with him, to stop trying to fix it, to stop myself from trying to make his feelings go away.

Finally, we ended up in the kitchen. He started pushing me and I pretended to let him push me down to the floor. I fell in an exaggerated manner. Whenever I tried to lift up my arm or my foot or my head, he pushed me back down. He towered over me, all three feet of him. "You're really powerful, Eli. Look what you made me do!" I lay on the floor and waited to see what he would do next.*

The tantrum was starting to wind down. Eli stood there, not knowing what to do either. Then he lay down on the floor, curled up, and laid his head on my chest. I stroked his hair. We both lay there, recovering. Finally, I said, "In a minute, it's going to be time to get up and get ready to go." And when the minute was over, he got up willingly and calmly lay down for his diaper change. He talked about playing with Max's blocks. Clearly, he'd made the transition and was ready to go. It was amazing for me to see the theory in practice—by being with him, by giving him the full expression of his feelings, the storm had passed.

For Eli, it was over as quickly as it had come. But for several hours afterward, I continued to feel ragged. Finally, I realized that my upset was more about me than it was about him. I felt scared and uncertain, as if I were breaking every rule about letting children "run wild" or "be out of control." Letting Eli have his feelings, accepting his rage as well as his delight, felt dangerous, as if I were crossing over into uncharted waters.

* Under many circumstances, letting children push you down might be frightening or confusing to them. However, done carefully, in certain interactions, "play pushing" might help the child regain a sense of humor and power. See "Physical Play and Roughhousing with Children" on p. 192 for specific guidelines on how to gauge the appropriateness of "fighting" with children.

more. You give her one more, maybe two. The next morning Marguerite wakes up and thinks "Cookie!" So she asks for one. Marguerite hasn't yet learned that some times are cookie times and some aren't, but she does remember that she likes cookies. So thirty times that day, she asks, "Cookie?" And each time you tell her "No," she experiences a fresh wave of frustration.

This frustration is compounded by the fact that toddlers naturally want to do more and more for themselves. But their aspirations and desires far outstrip their physical capabilities. Your son wants to put on his own shirt, fasten his own shoes, or buckle his own car seat, but he isn't yet capable of doing those things. He tries and he fails. He struggles and may not be able to do it without help, and his sense of frustration continues to grow.

Because they're beginning to gain an awareness of themselves as individuals, toddlers are also beginning to see possibilities for themselves that they hadn't previously considered: "*I* could make decisions! *I* could take my own clothes off. *I* could refuse my diaper change. *I* could turn on the dishwasher. Maybe I could make *all* of the decisions!" Toddlers don't want to just try *some* of the decisions; they want to try *all* of them. And it's not enough for toddlers to try out decisions once; they need to try them repeatedly.

Although it may be frustrating for us, it is ultimately useful for toddlers to have such grandiose goals. It is precisely what helps them grow so effectively. Without aspiring to big things, toddlers wouldn't be able to meet the huge obstacles of overcoming gravity in order to walk or decoding the mysteries of communication. Their boundless aspirations are, however, yet another setup for enormous frustration.

Take a moment to think about how a toddler agenda is put together. Before she's even had breakfast, your daughter has struggled to fit her oversize teddy into her undersize dump truck. She's reached for the cat's tail and been hissed at in return. She's had to argue with her dad about getting her diaper changed, fight with her sister about who's going to sit in the red chair, struggle with Grandma about turning on the TV, and reprimand big brother for pouring her juice into the wrong cup.

Families on the other end of these struggles often feel victimized by the constant challenges to their authority. It is helpful to remember that your toddler didn't choose her agenda, it *chose* her. If she were choosing it, clearly she would implement it in more manageable stages. No doubt she'd choose a peaceful waking and breakfast, then work on autonomy for a couple of hours before taking a break for lunch and nap and play in the afternoon. But when an autonomy agenda has a hold of a child, it drives her constantly and frustration is sure to follow.

The Straw That Breaks the Camel's Back

Sometimes when a child erupts in tears or screams, we could have predicted it would happen. We've tried one too many errands, our son has missed his nap or is starting to get sick. In fact, because we know that certain situations are too stressful for children, we do our best to avoid them. Then there are the situations we know will be stressful but that cannot be avoided, and when the tantrum comes, it is not a surprise.

Other times, anger bursts forth and catches us unsuspecting. We lovingly take off our daughter's socks, cut her sandwich, open the door for her, and she breaks into a million pieces because we have done it wrong. Our initial response may be "That's nothing to cry about," or we may quickly try to right our wrong, only to have the screaming escalate.

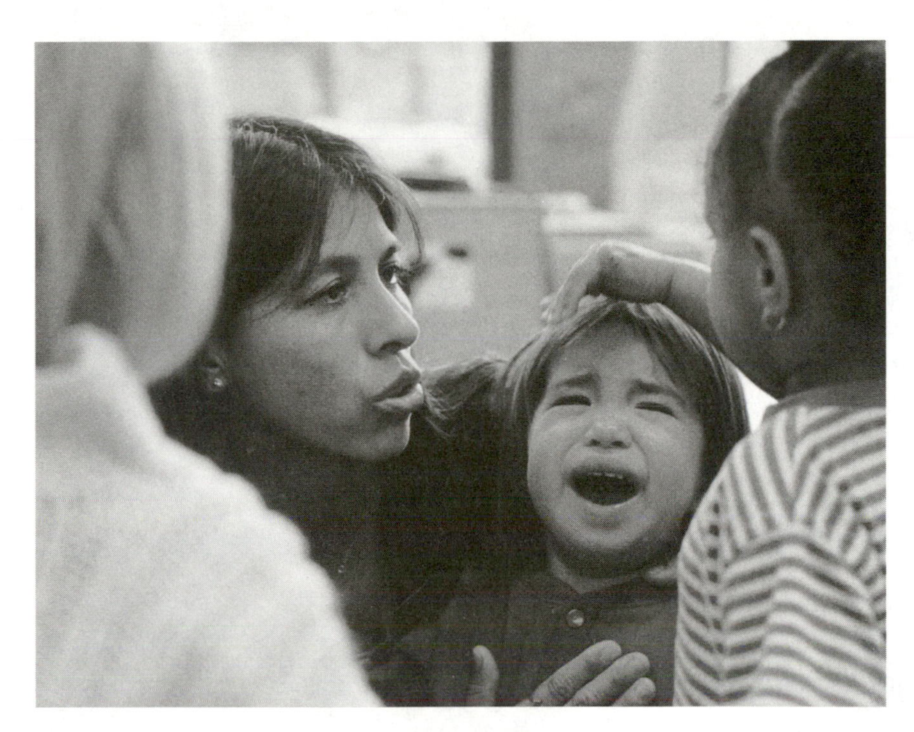

teenth time things didn't go their way. And whatever that final straw is, it reminds them of all the other parts of their life they don't get to control.

It is helpful for us to know that children have tantrums because of real frustration, sadness, rejection, and anger. Even if we can't see the "reason" for the tantrum, we can still value that it is reasonable from the child's perspective.

When confronted with such seemingly irrational behavior, it's natural to wonder "What's going on? Why such a fuss over a crooked seam in her sock?"

Toddlers accumulate little frustrations all day long. Most of these frustrations are invisible to us. Your daughter picks up your keys and confidently says, "Park," and you respond, "No, dear we aren't going to the park right now." Your daughter thinks to herself, "Every time Mom picks up the keys and says 'We're going to the park,' we go to the park. Why isn't it working for me?" Later that same day, she marches over to the TV, turns it on and says "*Sesame Street*," and it isn't *Sesame Street*! Yet every time Dad says "*Sesame Street*" and turns on the TV, it *is Sesame Street*. Frustration builds.

Children don't explode every time a little frustration happens; they save them up, until they reach the last straw. Perhaps it's the thirty-fifth decision they didn't get to make that day, the twentieth thing they tried to do by themselves that they couldn't accomplish, the fif-

The First "No" of the Day

In Janis's class one night, Marsha was expressing exasperation over her daughter's tantrums and refusal to obey. One-year-old Jojo was repeatedly running toward the hot furnace, ignoring her mother's warnings and insistence that she stop. Marsha explained, "When I tell Jojo 'no,' I *know* she understands it, but then she cries and throws herself on the floor and acts like I've hurt her desperately. I want her to be able to understand 'no' without having a tantrum every time. Why can't Jojo just obey me?"

Janis replied: "Let's start by looking at it from Jojo's perspective. Imagine that you've saved all your money and your favorite movie has come to town. You've gotten child care and you're out with your best friend. You walk into the theater, there's plenty of seats, but then they say, 'No! You can't come in here.' So you decide, 'Maybe I'll do my favorite sport instead.' So you get all your gear and make all the arrangements. You imagine how wonderful you're going to feel, and just when you're about to play, someone says to you 'No, you can't play!'

"How would you feel if that happened to you? My sense is that Jojo has that feeling every time you tell her 'no.' She's crushed. And her tantrums are coming from the fact that from her perspective, you are being totally arbitrary. She doesn't yet understand the concepts of 'safety' or 'danger.' "

Marsha responded: "But she has a tantrum on the first 'no' of the day!"

And Janis replied: "And Jojo can't believe you said 'no' the very first time she tried to do something fun. It's got to be frustrating for you that she'd be falling apart over such a little thing, but from her point of view, it makes perfect sense."

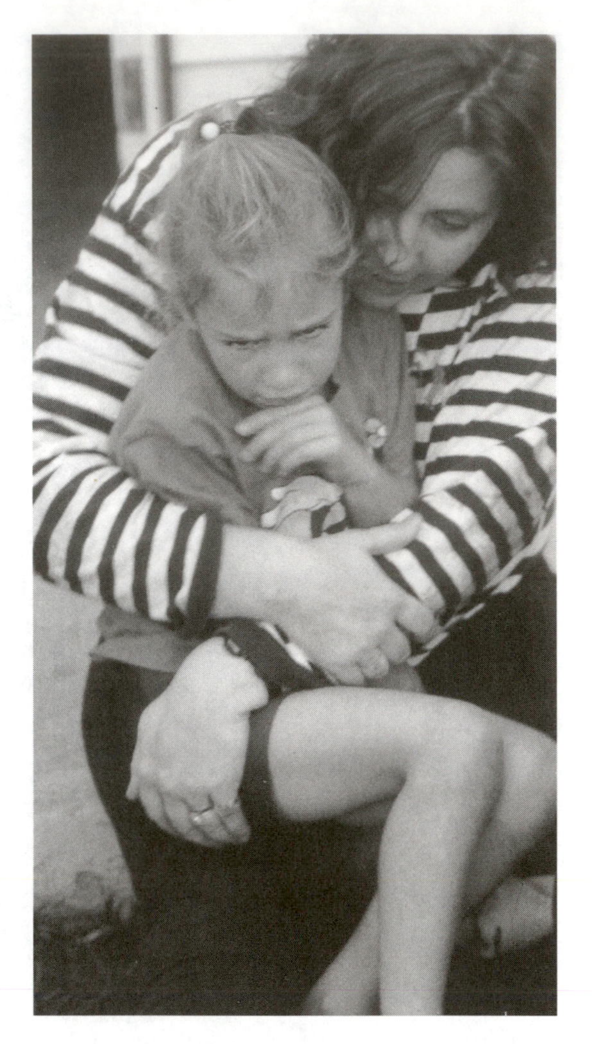

Dealing with Tantrums: Issues for Parents

Parents are often mystified and upset by their children's tantrums. It can be shocking to have a previously cooperative baby turn into a raging toddler. As Catherine, the mother of two, put it, "Adam is twenty months old and he's having tantrums every day. It can be over anything—the wrong blanket, the wrong bowl—anything. Then he's just inconsolable. What happened to my little boy who used to be so mellow?"

Jenny remarked in confusion, "A tantrum can be over something as small as the wrong pair of underwear: 'I wanted to wear Lion King underwear! And you gave me Beauty and the Beast!' "

And Ginny said, "I keep thinking if I was a better mom, he wouldn't be having these tantrums. I feel responsible for his anger."

Tantrums rarely occur at a convenient time or location. Parents often feel frustrated, embarrassed, scared, and helpless when their children break down in front of them and, often, in full view of others. In exasperation, Faye said, "By the time the tantrum is over and the aftermath of the tantrum is over, suddenly this one little limit I set has taken an hour and a half. And we were supposed to be somewhere an hour ago."

Even experienced parents can be at a loss when it comes to dealing with tantrums. Paula explains: "I never had a kid who had temper tantrums before Sam. He screamed for his first three years, pretty much. I can't remember sitting down to a meal that wasn't drastically interrupted. Sam was always demanding something, and the way he did it alienated everyone in the family.

"I'd raised a lot of kids before Sam and all of them had responded to my authority. I raised my voice a little bit and they responded. I'd never spanked any of them. I thought their obedience had to do with my technique as a parent. But with Sam, nothing I'd tried before worked. It completely blew my mind. Having Sam was the first time in twenty years of parenting that I considered using physical force."

Sometimes children's tantrums lead parents to take extraordinary measures. Janis explains: "My friend Cleo was desperate one time because she had flushed one of Stevie's first toilet poops before he was ready. Stevie was screaming and having a very hard time. How many times do we wish we could reverse our action, roll back the cameras, and try it again? Well, Cleo got an idea. She snuck one of the poops from the cat box into the toilet. Stevie was delighted to have his poop back so he could flush it all by himself."

Although this mother showed great ingenuity, it is not necessary for us to always try to fix the "cause" of the tantrum. Since most tantrums are cumulative expressions of frustration, the event that "triggered" them is usually just a convenient excuse to let off steam.

Five Strategies for Preventing Tantrums

Although there are many tantrums we can't prevent, there are ways to reduce the frustrations that lead to tantrums:

1. **Make sure children are fed and rested.** A skipped nap, a late night out, or no snack are at the root of many a tantrum.

2. **Know your child's threshold for stimulation.** Children have different levels of tolerance for change, crowds, or new situations. Some circumstances (lots of unfamiliar people, too many errands, a big store with lots of shiny things he can't touch) may be impossible for certain children at certain ages. Knowing your child can help you avoid situations that are likely to overwhelm him, thus preventing some of the tantrums that are more predictable.[1]

3. **Learn your child's early warning signs.** When your child starts getting cranky, clingy, and irritable, it may be time to modify your plans, cancel her afternoon play date, or skip your trip to the hardware store.

4. **Choose your battles carefully.** When children are experiencing periods of frustration and having lots of tantrums, there may be times we decide to step around a particular conflict. It may be worth it to give your daughter the bottle of milk she wants or to let her stay in the bathtub for five more minutes. At the same time, it is crucial not to fall into the trap of always giving children what they want. It is better to set clear limits and deal with a resulting tantrum than it is to feel as if you have to tiptoe around your child for fear that she might explode.[2]

5. **Change gears if the tantrum is inevitable.** No matter how careful you are, there will probably be numerous instances in which a tantrum is inevitable. Once children are engaged in a full-blown tantrum, you will need to switch to a different set of strategies—those that allow you to listen, to keep your children safe, to be a protected harbor in the storm.

[1] See "Lousy Local Conditions" on p. 215 for more on environmental causes for difficult behavior.

[2] See "Gracefully Bowing Out of a Conflict" on p. 277 and "Why It's Important Not to Give in to Kids All the Time" on p. 279 for more on this important idea.

Responding to Tantrums

Although every situation, every child, and every parent is different, here are some basic guidelines for dealing with tantrums in a clear and empathetic way:

• **Keep it safe.** Don't let your child hurt herself or anyone else. You don't need to get slapped, hit, or bitten in the name of your child's self-expression. Also, gently keep your child from damaging her own or anyone else's possessions.

• **If necessary, restrain your child with gentle firmness.** Sometimes it's necessary to restrain a child who is having a tantrum. Many of us equate physical restraint with violence and anger. But it is possible to physically hold a struggling child with gentleness and compassion. When you firmly hold a child who's angry in a gentle and supportive way, that child eventually moves from anger and lashing out to sobbing. But if you hold that same child in an angry way, she will continue to resist you longer, and it will be much harder for her to get to the sadness that's often underneath the rage.[3]

• **Consider your environment.** You may need to move your child if the tantrum is happening in a place that isn't safe—such as in the middle of a parking lot. You may also choose to carry your child from a public place to a more private one, such as from the Laundromat to the backseat of your car. Your decision here may depend on a number of factors—your level of comfort or embarrassment, your child's needs, the intensity of your child's struggles, your physical capacity to lift a flailing child, and what you consider to be socially appropriate.

• **Stay close.** A child in the middle of a tantrum feels out of control and doesn't know how to rein himself in. Your solid physical presence can help give your child the grounding he needs. He may want to be held or he may be definite that he doesn't want to be held—but that doesn't mean he wants you to go far away or leave entirely. Even if he says, "Leave!" or "Go away!" it's usually part of an ambivalent feeling, the other half of which says, "Stay!"

• **Practice listening.** Children need to know that we care about their strong, powerful, and sometimes scary feelings. Listening can go a long way toward helping children find resolution.

• **Talk about what you see.** Let your child know you see what's happening: "It looks like you're really mad right now." "It looks like you're really feeling frustrated. You really wanted to eat eggs for breakfast and Papa made oatmeal." At times you won't know why your child is upset. In that case, you can simply say to your screaming child, "You seem really upset."

• **Don't rush in to comfort the child prematurely.** When we hug children and say, "It's

[3] See "Learning to Value Struggle" on p. 35 and "Physical Limit Setting: When You Need to Restrain a Child" on p. 232 for a more thorough exploration of this idea.

okay, Mama's here," we may be giving them the message that we can take away all their frustrations and pain when, in reality, we can't. Sometimes our attempts to comfort children are aimed at stopping their crying before they've fully expressed their feelings. This is often indicative of our own discomfort, and it can stifle the child's expression rather than supporting it.

• **Don't try to distract your child out of it.** Let your child cry until she's done. Tantrums have an ebb and flow, and they do come to a natural end. Often when children have released a big pent-up load of frustration, there's a kind of clarity and lightness at the other end. Sometimes kids are exhausted and sleep longer or more deeply than usual. If we interrupt that process, we take away an opportunity for them to explore the extent of their feelings and find resolution.

• **Explore alternatives to isolation.** Although there may be times it's impossible to stay with a child who's having a tantrum, regularly sending children away until they "pull themselves together" can teach them that they can't have strong feelings around other people. Many of us have learned to express our deepest feelings only in isolation; it's important that we ask ourselves if that's the message we want to pass on to our kids.

• **Remind yourself that tantrums are a measure of intimacy.** Children usually reserve their tantrums for the most trusted, safe, and consistent people in their lives—their parents. The next time your child is having a tantrum, remind yourself you're being chosen because your child feels close to you.

• **Don't take it personally.** It can be particularly hard to continue listening when your child's expression of frustration and rage is directed at you, when your child is screaming "Go away!" "I don't like you!" "I hate you!" or "You did it wrong!" Children's accusations often intensify our own feelings of inadequacy, so it's important to remember that children's outbursts have more to do with their hurt and frustration than with us.

It doesn't serve you or your child to take their accusations personally. As much as you can, reflect the feelings your child is expressing: "You're feeling so mad right now, you really want me to go away." "It's really frustrating to you when I don't tie your shoe the way you want me to." "I know you're feeling really angry right now, but I'm going to stay with you."

• **You can be compassionate and still hold your ground.** Supporting your child through a tantrum doesn't mean you have to "give in" or let her have her way. While it's important to be flexible, to listen to children's ideas, and at times, to change your mind, it's also essential that you don't "give in" every time your child expresses strong feelings about what she wants.

• **Think about what you want to teach.** Every family will have its own ideas about acceptable expressions of anger. Clarifying your family's beliefs is an important first step in teaching your children how to handle their anger. Masai, who's comfortable being loud, said, "Me and my kid made an agreement that he's allowed to shout when he's really upset. Most parents, it's like 'Don't you dare holler at me!' But if he's pissed, he's pissed as much as a big person, and if he needs to shout, he shouts. I tell him, 'You can't call me names. You can't cuss at me. But other than that, you can yell all you want.' "

• **Redirect the child by providing safe outlets.** Children often need to express big feelings physically. Parents have "redirected" children from hitting and biting people to punching and biting stuffed animals. Children have learned to throw soft things instead of breakable ones. Some parents have suggested that their child scream into a pillow or into an open closet instead of right in someone's ear. Older children have been given powerful words, such as "furious," "enraged," "irate," and "exasperated," as a substitute for name-calling or swearing in anger.

• **Consider the circumstantial evidence.** Although it's generally a good idea to let tantrums wind down on their own accord, there are times that other factors get in the way of children finding resolution. Your son is exhausted. Your daughter didn't eat lunch and it's four in the afternoon. When children are exhausted and hungry, it can be appropriate to say, "You haven't eaten for a really long time. I think part of what's going on is that you're really hungry." Or "You seem really tired. I think you could use a nap. I'll help you find a comfy place to lie down."

• **Learn from the experience.** When your child has a tantrum and finally falls asleep in a heap on the bedroom floor, you can often learn from the experience: "Oh, this happened before when he skipped his nap. Maybe I need to make sure he gets a rest earlier." Or "I was afraid four errands were too many." Reviewing what's happened can help you develop more effective strategies for the future.

• **Develop resources for yourself.** All of the above strategies ask for a lot of emotional strength and clarity on your part. You're not a failure if you don't immediately have those resources or if you don't have them on a particular day. Taking small steps to build your own network of support can help you develop the resources you need to stay supportive during your child's tantrums.

Preschoolers and Tantrums: What Parents Can Do

While tantrums are classically associated with the toddler years, they still occur as children reach three, four, and five years old. While less frequent, preschool tantrums happen for some of the same reasons that toddler tantrums do. Frustration, the inability to control things, and thwarted expectations are all "just" cause for explosions during the preschool years. While preschool children's experience allows them to more realistically predict events and manage their responses, there are still times when fatigue, repeated stretching for out-of-reach goals, and trying to control unresponsive parents and friends can push the preschool child past her ability to cope.

Dealing with the tantrums of three-, four-, and five-year-olds is similar to dealing with those of younger children. However, there are some additional things you can do when re-

A Tantrum in the Mall: Ginny's Story

Tantrums can be brought on by developmental factors or other stresses in a child's life. Ginny's five-year-old daughter, whose tantrums had waned, started having them again shortly after her little brother was born.

Ginny's story is important not only in the particulars, but also because it demonstrates an effective problem-solving process. Initially Ginny responded without thinking. Then she learned from her mistake and went on to try out a different strategy.

Danielle has had some really intense tantrums lately. And she has them in public. Because I feel embarrassed, it's hard for me to do the right thing—to validate her anger, not to shut her up. This latest time we were at the mall and she wanted to go into a store and I said no. So she started hitting me and spitting at me. At first, I just wanted to shut her up, so I smacked her. I had just had it. I said, "You stop having this tantrum *right now!*" She was quiet for a second, but then she started up again with renewed vigor. I thought, "Oh, great, that really helped!" She kept right on having the tantrum, and I took that as a cue that she was giving me the opportunity to try again and to get it right.

Dragging her to the car was out of the question. She was too big for me to carry her when she was struggling like that. And for me, it would have been a lot more embarrassing to drag a screaming child out to the car than to just deal with it right where I was.

I rose to the occasion. I said to myself, "She's having a hard time here. She needs some extra attention from me right now and I'm willing to give it to her."

And so I asked myself, "What am I supposed to do?" I remembered everything I'd learned in parenting classes, everything other parents had told me.

I got down on the floor with her to make her safe. I had her sitting between my legs and I held her so that she couldn't scratch me or hit me or spit on me. But she was still raging and screaming and saying "I want to scratch you! I hate you! You're the worst Mommy ever!" And there I was, sitting on the floor in the mall thinking "Oh, great, this is really fun!"

But I kept sitting there with her, saying "You're mad enough to hit Mama. You're mad enough to want to spit on me. I'm going to hold you and keep you safe so you can't hurt me and you can't hurt yourself. You're so mad. You really wanted to go into that store and I wouldn't let you." She was struggling and I was red trying to hold her, but I wasn't angry. I was staying centered and letting her have her anger. And all of a sudden, she just went limp.

Then she said, "I want to sit over on that bench." And so we went over to that bench and sat down. And all of a sudden she put her hand in mine and said, "Let's go. I'm ready." It was over. The whole thing took maybe five minutes, but it felt like five hours.

sponding to older kids. Preschool children have more language and experience dealing with their feelings and an increased ability to think about the past and future. This gives you the opportunity to:

- talk with your child about what happened
- think about the roles both you and your child played before and during the tantrum
- think about factors that led up to the explosion
- come up with ways for your child to deal more effectively with those stresses that can be anticipated
- talk about things your child would like you to do to help
- invite your child to help come up with effective ways to respond to future tantrums

Children are usually more responsive to this kind of discussion when they've gotten a little distance from the actual tantrum. Later that evening or the next day you can initiate a talk: "Boy, we really had a hard time after we went sledding this afternoon. You really didn't want to go home. Can you tell me more about what was going on with you?" After some sharing from your child, you could continue, "I also realized that you didn't get a chance to eat your full lunch before we went sledding. That may have been a mistake. I wonder if you were feeling too hungry after sledding." Or "I notice that sometimes it's really hard for you to stop doing your favorite things. I wonder if there is a way we could make that easier for you. Do you have any ideas?" Any ideas for solutions generated from these talks need to be agreed on by both of you before you try them. After you've tried them, you can assess together how they worked.

Parents and their preschoolers have the opportunity to use tantrums and emotional outbursts to further their learning about themselves, their feelings, and their relationship. By dealing effectively with our children's tantrums, we have the chance to send them out into the world emotionally literate—and maybe we'll learn a few things along the way, too.

FOOD FOR THOUGHT: TANTRUMS

- What do I believe about tantrums? What was I taught about them as a child?

- What feelings come up for me when my child is having a tantrum? How do I deal with those feelings?

- Are there people close to me and my child who have different ideas about how to handle tantrums? What are we doing to deal with those differences?

12. Helping Your Children Deal with Fear

"You gain strength, courage and confidence by every experience in which you really stop to look fear in the face."
ELEANOR ROOSEVELT

Fear is an inevitable, important part of the human experience. When we feel afraid, our body is giving us valuable information. Fear warns us of danger. It helps to keep us safe and can guide us in making wise and sometimes critical decisions.

For children, the opportunity to have a fear, to face it, and to work through it builds feelings of resourcefulness and confidence. In the process, kids learn that they can be afraid and still respond effectively.

When our children are afraid, we're asked to comfort them, to be with them, and, ultimately, to help them develop their own skills for dealing with fear. Responding effectively to our children's fears requires that we look at our own beliefs and experiences, that we think about what it is we want to teach our children, and that we form a basic understanding of how childhood fears arise.

Why Fears Emerge: A Developmental Overview

Children don't have consistent levels of fear in their first five years. There are times fears become more intense and times fears are less intense. These are often related to developmental cycles as well as to temperament.[1]

The fears of infants are immediate and reflexive. Babies will startle to a loud noise, such

[1] While most fears are part of children's normal developmental learning and should be dealt with as such, it is important that special consideration be given to those that arise from a traumatic event. Fears that result from trauma, such as a serious accident, death of an immediate family member, or childhood abuse, require a different level of response. In addition to the suggestions in this chapter, children who've experienced trauma need professional counseling and support.

Mice, Foghorns, and Woolly Mammoths: Janis's Story

Whenever children have to adapt to changing perceptions, a larger world view, or altered circumstances, they are particularly vulnerable to new fears. Fears are often signs of increasing intelligence and sophistication. Whenever cognition explodes, feelings of fear and vulnerability explode, too.

During these times, "windows of vulnerability" appear, and the child may identify a startling image or a new idea as the thing he or she fears. But often, the feared thing is only a symbol for all of the ways the child feels vulnerable, as Janis learned by observing her children.

My first son, at about two, was startled by a mouse that popped out of a vacuum cleaner he was examining. For several months, whenever he was feeling vulnerable, he would say "Mouse scares you, Mama," which was his two-year-old way of saying that the mouse scared him.

At first I tried to work with Lee directly on his fear of mice, but over time, I came to understand that the mouse was symbolic of bigger and less tangible fears. It seemed that whenever Lee started feeling "The world is bigger than I am" or "There are things out there I can't predict or control," he would start talking about "the mouse."

My second child, Calvin, did much the same thing with "foghorns." Like many parents, I tried to convince Calvin that the thing he feared wasn't really scary. I drew elaborate pictures of foghorns keeping boats safe. I talked to him extensively about foghorns. I wanted him to accept my explanation that foghorns were useful and, therefore, not something to be scared of. Calvin watched my efforts with patient interest, but clearly he was not convinced.

I think there were two reasons why. First, I couldn't accurately portray "his" foghorn; my drawing didn't look like the image he associated with his fear. And second, because "foghorns" symbolized a greater vulnerability, he wasn't going to be able give up his fear until he matured developmentally.

But still, I continued to work with Calvin on his fear. And at the same time, Calvin and his seven-year-old brother, Lee, started playing foghorn games. They took turns becoming the foghorn. While one would sound the foghorn signal, the other one would "pretend" to be afraid. Then they would switch. Each got turns to be "scary" and each got turns to

as a cough or a door banging. They will blink when something comes toward them rapidly. During the second six months of life, most babies develop a wariness of people they don't know, an aversion to loud, unusual sounds, and a fear of new or unpredictable animals.

Older babies may experience some of these scary images while they are dreaming. Parents have remarked that their babies have awakened crying fearfully, as if from a bad dream.[2]

Young babies, however, aren't afraid of the dark. Some parents who have worried about this being an issue for their child smugly proclaim, "I just turn off the light and my eight-month-old plays happily in his crib." Several months later, however, the same child who blithely played in the dark won't step foot in the dark hallway alone and cries in terror when his parents reach to turn off his light. What happened to that trusting baby?

What happened is that trusting baby got smarter. When the light went off before, everything disappeared for him. He didn't see it, so it was gone. But near the age of one, children's perceptions of the world undergo a critical shift. They develop an increased understanding of "object permanence"—the idea that things exist even if they can't immediately see or touch them. For the baby, where there once was only

[2] We don't deal specifically with nightmares in this chapter, but rather in our chapter on sleep. See "Helping Children Who Are Having Nightmares" on p. 149.

be "scared." I was impressed with their ingenuity and with the effectiveness of their therapy.

My third child, Maya, taught me one more thing about fear—that children will strive repeatedly, with great persistence, to work through their fears.

When she was two years old, we took her to visit a museum, and Maya was brought face to face with a mechanically moving woolly mammoth. It was totally different from any creature she'd ever seen. She leaped four feet up into my arms and demanded that I hold her six-year-old brother, too, because she was afraid that the woolly mammoth would "get him." After a couple of unsuccessful attempts at explaining the "unrealness" of this bigger-than-life creature to her, I suggested that we say good-bye to the mammoth and move on. But every time we got more than a few feet away, Maya would "drive" me back from her perch around my neck to see the woolly mammoth again. Each time she stayed petrified, yet glued to the exhibit. And each time I faithfully tried to convince her that it wasn't real and couldn't hurt her.

But my words were inadequate to the task. There was no common language between us with which I could adequately address her fear. I couldn't tell her that the mammoth was mechanical or battery-operated; she didn't have the experience to apply those concepts. I couldn't tell her that woolly mammoths were extinct; she knew life only from the perspective of a toddler, not a paleontologist.

But finally, on the fourth trip back, I accidentally hit upon a piece of information that she could use to help her make sense of her experience. I said to her, "You know, Maya, the woolly mammoth can't walk." She looked at me in awe and repeated, "It can't walk?"

Shortly after that, Maya climbed down from my arms and, keeping a careful distance, continued to observe her moving, but not walking, monster. A few minutes later I was finally able to convince her that it was time to go (but not without stopping at the gift shop to purchase a take-home, hand-size, woolly mammoth).

Watching Maya's tenacious struggle to gain mastery over her fear was inspiring. As she was affixed to my body, I could feel the fear pulsing through her, and my impulse was to remove her from the thing that was so scary for her. But she was driven by a force as powerful as her fear to confront it.

darkness, there is now the possibility of new and terrifying things hiding in the dark.

As babies grow into toddlers, their perception of the world shifts in another crucial way. Time and space open up for them. Suddenly, there is more than just the present place and moment—there's the memory of yesterday and the possibility of tomorrow. The swings at the park exist even when they're not swinging on them. Grandma exists even though she's not here right now. And so does the big yellow dog that barks down the street.

These cognitive leaps open up all kinds of wonderful and exciting possibilities for toddlers, but they also make the world a more uncertain and scary place. Toddlers start to see themselves more realistically: "The world is very big, and I, by comparison, am very small." As a result of this realization, new levels of fear may emerge. Typical toddler fears include fear of

Halloween Can Be Scary for Kids

When Halloween approaches, many of the places we go are filled with scary masks and costumes, pictures of ghosts and other ghouls. As adults we may be amused or even excited by this. But for young children, especially toddlers, Halloween can be an altogether different and very frightening experience.

For young babies, Halloween either goes unnoticed or is something of a lark. They are still working on their definition of "normal." So, if they can find eyes and a mouth on a face, they may very well grin at it. They may be delighted by a giant rabbit.

Toddlers, on the other hand, know enough to know that the weird faces and costumes at Halloween are unusual and, therefore, scary. Even a benign "giant bunny" has been known to scare toddlers, because they have enough experience to know that bunny creatures don't come in that size and, therefore, that something must be wrong (especially if the bunny tries to talk to them).

Most toddlers will not be able to be "taught" not to be scared, because it is their own "intelligence" that is telling them what is scary. Many people try to show a child that it is "just a mask" by taking it on and off, but often children are just not ready to "get it."

So what can parents do to minimize children's fears around Halloween? Here are some suggestions for making Halloween more fun, and less scary for kids:

• **Take your clues from your child.** No two kids are at the exact same stage of development. What may scare one won't necessarily scare another, and you may not be able to predict what will be scary. If you can stay flexible in your expectations, it will help keep things relaxed.

• **Get into pumpkins.** Going to the pumpkin patch and finding one just the right size to carry home can be quite a wonderful achievement for a toddler. Remember that toddlers may have their own ideas about their pumpkin and should be consulted before you carve it. They may want it whole, just as it is. Also, since toddlers and preschoolers are not able to use sharp knives safely, carving is basically an adult-centered activity, although some children delight in drawing on their pumpkin and having you cut out the design.

Experiencing the seeds and goop inside can be a terrific toddler activity, although some children might want nothing to do with the sticky seeds. Others might enjoy gluing tissue paper on the outside or coloring on their pumpkin with magic markers. Others may be happy taking their pumpkin everywhere with them, including to bed.

• **Forgo elaborate costumes.** As parents, many of us look forward to the opportunity to dress up our children for Halloween. Some children love fantasy clothes and enjoy putting on funny hats, bunny or kitty ears, purses, neckpieces, shirts, vests. Problems may arise when parents spend many hours or dollars creating a costume that their child doesn't want to wear. It's important to separate what is important to you and what is important to your child, knowing your child may change her mind at any time.

As Janis points out, "Sometimes adults go to great lengths to make the most darling costumes—or the cutest or the scariest—and oftentimes children are very interested in them all the way up to the moment that they're supposed to put them on and wear them. Parents put all this time and energy into this costume and their child has a whole other idea about it: 'I want to wear it every single day before Halloween,' or 'I only want to wear it before Halloween comes,' or 'I never want to put it on,' or 'I only want to put in on in December when I've had a chance to really get used to it.' So thinking about our expectations is really important."

Toddlers are less likely to be scared if costumes don't cover faces. Preschool children may enjoy experimenting with face paint or with paper-plate masks that they can decorate and hold up to their face.

• **Hold off on trick-or-treating or do so in a very controlled environment.** Trick-or-treating can also be confusing and scary for young children. Going to unknown houses at night, passing unexpected scary creatures, and then getting more candy than you're allowed to eat may be overwhelming. If you've succeeded in agreeing on a costume and you want to introduce the concept of trick-or-treating, you can go to one or two familiar neighbors' houses while it is still light.

Several groups of families we know trick-or-treat inside somebody's home. Children knock on different doors in a hallway, and then someone opens the door and gives them a box of raisins, a plastic spider, some stickers, a pair of plastic sunglasses, a piece of fruit leather, or some other healthy treat.

• **Offer support to your child.** Even if you avoid trick-or-treating, it is likely that your child will see people around town or coming to your door in costume. It is helpful to have someone who doesn't have to answer the door available to be with your child, so she can keep as much distance as she wants between herself and the goblins. If children do see scary creatures, you can ask the creatures to take off their masks while they're near your child.

• **Continue to assess children's needs as they get older.** Many preschool children continue to be scared by ghouls and goblins and surprises in the night. Using simple costumes, visiting familiar homes, and sticking to predark activities can benefit many three-, four-, and five-year-olds. Other preschoolers are thrilled to be out after dark and may even enjoy being "scared" in manageable doses. Knowing your individual child can help you assess what's appropriate.

Books to Help Kids Deal with Fears

Books help children deal with fears in several ways. Some are reassuring and comforting, giving children a sense of safety and predictability in the world. These books are especially useful for one-, two-, and three-year-olds, although many four- and five-year-olds will enjoy an occasional trip back to the safety of *The Runaway Bunny*.

Other books show scary things in a funny light. If the child is old enough to "get" the joke and to laugh at the fearsome thing, these books can be reassuring and wonderful. Children who are too young, however, may not "get" the joke and may simply be scared by the weird pictures.

Last, books can help children with fears by presenting scary images and then showing the main character overcoming them. These books can be very useful for older four- and five-year-olds who have mastered two particular concepts. The first is a developed sense of time and sequence that enables the child to hold on for the resolution of the story. The second is that the child needs to be able to clearly distinguish between the pictures on the page and real life. If children don't yet have these levels of understanding, they can get stuck in the scary images and not be able to get past them. Likewise, these books may actually introduce new scary images to younger children. For these reasons, it's important to use the utmost care in deciding when to present these books.

Books That Reassure and Comfort*

The Runaway Bunny, Margaret Wise Brown, HarperCollins.

A little bunny tries to run away from his mother, but wherever he goes, she always finds him. Ages 1 and up.

You Go Away, Dorothy Carey, Albert Whitman and Company.

Simple text and pictures explore separations from simple to complex in the life of a number of toddlers. Ages 1 and up.

Books That Use Humor

Dog Donovan, Diane Hendry, illustrated by Margaret Chamberlain, Candlewick Press.

A whole family of frightened people learns how to overcome fears when a scared dog joins their family. Ages 2 and up.

Franklin in the Dark, Paulette Bourgeois and Brenda Clark, Scholastic Books.

Franklin the turtle is scared of small, dark places so he won't go in his shell. Instead he carries it behind him on a rope. Franklin goes on a search for help dealing with his fear and discovers that everyone is afraid of something. By the end of the book, Franklin comes up with his own solution to his fear of the dark. Ages 3 and up.

A Halloween Mask for Monster, Virginia Mueller, illustrated by Lynn Munsinger, Puffin Books.

On Halloween, a baby monster tries on a girl mask, a boy mask, a cat mask, and a dog mask, and decides they're all too scary. So he goes out as himself in his regular old green monster face. Ages 3 and up.

Books in Which Fears Are Overcome

Beast, Susan Meddaugh, Houghton Mifflin Company.

The simple story of a girl who takes on a creature the whole family is afraid of. Ages 2 and up.

Can't You Sleep, Little Bear? Martin Waddell and Barbara Firth, Candlewick Press.

Little Bear is frightened by the "dark all around us." Father Bear brings him a little lantern, but Little Bear is still scared. So Father Bear brings him a bigger lantern, but Little Bear is still scared. So finally, Father Bear takes Little Bear outside to see the biggest light of all—the moon. Lovely nurturing between a father and a son. Appro-

* For other books in this category, see our list of recommended bedtime books on p. 150. For general guidelines on reading to kids, see "Sharing Books with Children" on p. 300.

priate for children who are scared of the dark. Ages 3 & up.

Brave Irene, William Steig, Farrar, Straus and Giroux.

A contemporary fairy tale about Irene, who must bring the dress her mother sewed to the palace over the mountain in the middle of a terrible snowstorm. She gets there before the ball and we experience her triumph and courage. Ages 3 and up.

Thunder Cake, Patricia Polacco, Philomel Books.

This book effectively and lovingly deals with a common childhood fear of thunder and lightning. A caring, wise grandmother, Babushka, helps her frightened granddaughter by helping her bake a real Thunder Cake on her Michigan farm. The illustrations are heartwarming and the text reveals both the intimacy and the power of the approaching storm. Ages 4 and up.

The Nightmare in My Closet, Mercer Mayer, Dial Press.

A young boy who is scared of a nightmare in his closet decides to get rid of his nightmare "once and for all." Once he confronts the nightmare (a rather scary-looking monster), his nightmare starts to cry and won't stop crying until the boy invites the monster to join him in bed. Ages 4 and up.

The Little Old Lady Who Was Not Afraid of Anything, Linda Williams, illustrated by Megan Lloyd, Crowell Books.

The little old lady who was not afraid of anything goes out for a walk in the woods at night and finds a pair of shoes that clomped, a pair of pants that wiggled, a shirt that shook, two gloves that clapped, a hat that nodded, and a head that went "Boo!" These were scary. So what did the old woman do? Her solution shows both her ingenuity and her mastery over her fears. Ages 4 and up.

Where the Wild Things Are, Maurice Sendak, HarperTrophy.

Max, who is feeling very wild, takes a nighttime trip to the land of the wild things. Max becomes the king of the wild things and has lots of adventures before returning to the safety of home and his warm dinner. Ages 4 and up.

Storm in the Night, Mary Stolz, illustrated by Pat Cummings, HarperCollins.

A beautiful story of a grandfather and his grandson on a stormy night. Lots of text. Ages 5 and up.

Do Not Open, Brinton Turkle, Dutton.

An old woman and her cat live together in a cottage. As they scavenge and collect things from the beach after a storm, they find a mysterious bottle containing a very scary monster. Undaunted, she and her cat figure out how to get rid of the monster. Ages 5 and up.

Sofia and the Heartmender, Marie Olofsdotter, Free Spirit Publishing Company (400 First Avenue North, Suite 616, Minneapolis, MN 55401. 612-338-2068).

Sofia is afraid of the shadow-monsters and no one is helping her deal with her fears. Her heart breaks. A special dog takes her to a magical clearing in the woods where she visits the heartmender and discovers how to fix her broken heart. This book is full of magic and wonder, and has concepts that might be frightening for younger children. Ages 6 and up.

vacuum cleaners, doctors, blow-dryers, masks, Santa Claus, Halloween, firefighters, and the dark.

For some children, three is a time of consolidation and equilibrium. Many children who've been fearful as toddlers show a lessening of fears during this time. But then, around the age of four, children's perceptions take another giant leap. Their world once again becomes larger, and simultaneously many children develop an awareness of "magic" and "supernatural powers." This provides them with intellectual challenges and fuels their pretend play. You will often see four- and five-year-old children putting on magic costumes, mixing powerful potions, designing secret weapons, and pretending to be superheroes. This kind of play can help children regain a sense of mastery, yet they are often just as fearful as they are fascinated by these powers.

Rita, the mother of four-year-old Mitchell, remarked, "I've noticed that the times when Mitch seems the most fearful are the times that I can't even get his Batman cape off him to wash it. He's pretending to be a big bad actor, but inside, he is clearly very afraid."

Common preschool fears include monsters, superheroes, villains, robbers, separation, and once again, the dark.

Helping Children Deal with Fears: Issues for Parents

Many of us are shaken when fear first encroaches on the calm waters of our child's security. When we witness our child trembling or crying out in fear, many of us experience a sense of powerlessness, a disappointment that we were unable to hold fear at bay. When that initial response fades, many of us feel unqualified for the job of reassuring our children and responding effectively.

Children's fears can also resonate with unresolved fears of our own. Most of us still remember our childhood fears. If we successfully overcame them, we may remember them with a chuckle. If we didn't, we may still carry a lingering sense of vulnerability.

Unresolved fears can also get passed on to our children, either consciously or unconsciously. A father who's had a terrifying experience with a dog may feel the need to teach his child to be afraid of dogs. Even if he decides he doesn't want to pass that message on, his body may still convey his terror whenever a dog is around. Recognizing and working on our own fears can help us avoid passing them on to our children.

Some of us also need to work through stereotypical messages we learned about fear based on gender. Girls, generally, are expected to be fearful and aren't given tools to deal with their fears. Instead, they are taught to rely on adults and males for their sense of safety. Boys, on the other hand, are generally discouraged from feeling fear. The credo "Be Brave" has forced many a boy to suffer his scary feelings alone. In order to allow all children to have an honest and effective response to fear, we need to recognize and rethink those messages.

Whether our own experiences have prepared us to deal with our children's fears or not, thoughtful consideration, observation, and practice will help us develop a posture from which we can support children's healthy responses to their fears.

Strategies for Helping Children Deal with Fear

Children naturally move through many of their fears as they come to a more balanced or sophisticated understanding of the world. But that takes time. What can we do in the meantime? How can we help our children when they're in a period of accentuated fears?

Although there are no remedies that will work in every situation, here are some ideas for helping your fearful child:

• **Know your child.** Children's fears, their timing, and their expression, are unique to each child. Observations of your child and knowledge of his temperament will give you important clues about where his fears are coming from and how best to respond to them.

• **Avoid scary situations.** When possible, avoid exposing your child to things that terrify him. Often things that seem quite harmless to an adult can be very upsetting to children. Check out books, TV shows, movies, or excursions ahead of time if you suspect that something particularly scary awaits.

• **Take your child's fears seriously.** Even if a little bug or stuffed bunny rabbit isn't scary to you, it may be very frightening to your child. When you belittle your child's fears, you give your child the message that something's wrong with her perceptions of the world. Fears are often based on the very best thinking your child can do at the time. Respecting your child's fears is a way of respecting her natural growth and intelligence.

• **Respect the fear but don't reinforce it.** There is a fine line between acknowledging your child's fears ("I can see you're really scared of the monster") and validating the reality of those fears ("Those *are* scary monsters!"). Joining your child in her fears can make her feel confused and more frightened.

• **Don't try to talk children out of being afraid.** Logic, bribery, and cajoling won't eliminate children's fears. If kids get the message that it's not okay to be afraid, their fears will just go underground. Even though they might stop talking about them, the fears will still be there. And as many of us know from personal experience, it's much harder to face fears alone.

• **Don't try to fix it.** Parents are often tempted to jump in with "I'll scare the monster away for you." Rather than just "getting rid" of the monsters in the bedroom, help your child figure out what she needs in order to feel safe. This gives her the message you think she's capable of dealing with her fears.

• **Talk with children about their fears.** Sometimes parents think it's best to tiptoe around children's fears, as if not mentioning them might somehow keep them at bay. In reality, the opposite is true. Fears become less obscure and generally diminish in size as children address and define them.

Asking children questions enables you to get information you can use to help them. "Tell me about your monster." "What does it look like?" "Does it make a sound?" "Do you know where it lives or what it likes to eat?"

Once you have an idea about the content of their fear, you can sometimes provide information which may help children put their fear in perspective. "The only kind of lions we'll ever have in this house are stuffed lions and they don't have real teeth." Or "That kind of bug can't hurt people. If it got on you, it would just tickle."

When children are too afraid or uncomfortable to talk, respect their feelings, but keep the doors open for future conversations. "It looks like you don't want to talk right now. I'll check with you again this evening."

• **Expect children to dwell on their fears.** Your child may need to talk about the scary thing repeatedly. Often this will be far past the point that you want to hear about it. You might find yourself thinking "Aren't you over that yet?" wondering if talking about it is keeping the fear alive. But talking about fear with a supportive person is a crucial part of overcoming it.

Cherise explains: "Sometimes when Kizzy is going on and on about something that's scaring her, I get annoyed with her level of obsession. But the times I ignore her, brush her off, or listen with only half an ear, her need always seems to escalate. It's only when I'm able to find the presence of mind to focus on what she needs to tell me that she seems able to work through her fears and find a sense of peace."

• **Invite children to action.** Since children feel helpless in the face of fear, it is useful to help them think about what they can do: "What do you want to tell that monster?" "What could we do to help you feel safe?"

Janis describes how Maya was finally able to resolve a persistent fear by taking action: "One day a police officer visited Maya's preschool. Something he did startled and scared Maya, and from that moment on, she developed a fear of people in uniforms who had attachments on their belts—things like beepers, walkie-talkies, and guns. After almost a year of dealing with her fear, I began to wonder whether she'd ever get to the other side of it.

"I remember so clearly the day she decided to write a letter to the police officer to ask him about his gun. He wrote her back a lovely note full of colorful drawings, answering her questions about his job and about guns. She was delighted with his response and her fear diminished almost completely."

• **Help your child make a book.** If your child is old enough to draw representationally (even if it doesn't look representational to you), you can have him draw pictures or tell a story (that you then write down) about the thing that is scary. By stapling a couple of these pages together, you can help your child create *The Fire Engine Book* or *The Scary Dog Book*. Reading

and rereading *The Scary Dog Book* can be a safe way for your child to revisit the fear and start gaining mastery over it.

• **Let children know what to expect when entering a potentially scary situation.** Some scary situations are unavoidable. Many toddlers, for instance, develop a fear of going to the doctor. Parents have found an array of creative ways to prepare their children for these visits. They've taken their children to see the office ahead of time, read them books about going to the doctor, taken photos of the doctor, or acted out what was going to happen ahead of time.

Laura recalls: "When Eli turned one, he became terrified of going to the doctor. From the moment we walked in her door, he wailed in terror and outrage. I tried to explain to him what was going to happen, to talk him through it, to comfort him, but to no avail. I had to hold him screaming to get through the exam, I felt like I was torturing my son.

"Two months before his two-year checkup, Karyn bought Eli a doctor kit and we started talking about seeing Dr. Baskerville. We went over the whole thing in great detail. He was very interested and asked for the story dozens of times. If we missed any details or got them wrong, he corrected us. We even made up a song about going to the doctor; Eli asked for it every day.

"When the big day arrived, I didn't know what to expect, but Eli was open, curious, and engaged. It was a dramatic turnaround."

For some children, getting used to scary situations takes a long time, but we can still support their growth by providing thoughtful preparation.

• **Help children face the fear in increments.** Think about the least scary kinds of steps your child can take. If your child is afraid of dogs, you might want to look at a picture of a dog together. You might want to read a book about a dog. You might want to make a tape recording of dogs barking so that your child can listen to the sound when he wants to—and stop it at will. If you're going to visit a dog, you might start with a small, quiet, nonjumpy dog.

If your child is afraid of vacuum cleaners because of the loud sound they make, you can bring out the vacuum cleaner and say, "I'm not going to plug it in, so it won't make any noise. Would you like to practice turning the switch on and off?" Or "Would you like to help me hook the hose and the brush together?" "Would you like to help me change the bag?" Allowing the child to approach the feared object in small, manageable steps may eventually lead her to be ready to turn it on so it makes "the noise."

• **Don't force anything.** When encouraging a child to approach a scary situation, don't push. When your child cringes and runs away or says, "No want to see Betsy's dog," "Betsy's dog go away," respect those feelings. But always leave the door open to trying again. You can say to your child, "Okay, we'll leave now. But maybe we can try another day." In doing so, you give your children the message that fears are not static and that their relationship to a fear can change over time.

• **Find the manageable distance.** Rather than remove children entirely from the things that scare them, work to find the closest distance at which they can feel safe enough to confront the thing they fear. When children are consumed with terror, they can't open their eyes and look at the thing that is scaring them. Help them move farther away. Your child's manageable distance might be ten feet, across the street, through a fence, or safely at home retelling the story of the scary incident. Always observe your child for signs that he wants to move closer and is ready to take the next step.

The Orange, the Bee, and the Flowers: Laura's Story

Most of the techniques presented in this chapter apply equally to younger and older children. However, there are some special things to take into consideration when dealing with children who haven't begun or are just beginning to talk. The following story demonstrates some ways to effectively help a young child who has beginning verbal skills deal with a scary situation.

One day when Eli was a year and a half old, he was hanging out with his Aunt Janet on our back porch and she cut up an orange for him. Soon his mouth and shirt were smeared with juice. It was late August and several yellow jackets started to fly around him. Janet was worried that he might get stung so she said to him in a loud, strong voice, "Eli, we have to go inside!" And she got him inside as quickly as possible. Then she washed him up and got the orange juice off his face. The urgency in her voice and actions alerted Eli to the fact that something scary had gone on. From then on, Eli needed to talk about what had happened again and again.

When I got home half an hour later, Eli and Janet were sitting together on the front porch. I sat down quietly and watched their interaction. Eli was standing between Janet's legs, leaning back on her chest. They were talking about the bees. He said, "Orange. Bee. In." And Janet replied, "Yes, Eli, you were eating an orange and the bees came and started flying around you. They liked the sweet juice you had on your face. I wanted to make sure that you were safe, so we went inside. There are no bees inside the house. Bees are only outside." Eli had a look of complete concentration on his face. He looked at her and said, "Home," and then he wrinkled up his nose and sniffed. "Yes, Eli," Janet replied, "the bees flew home to their flowers." He sniffed again, smelling an imaginary flower. "Yes, they flew home and went to their flowers. That's where bees live."

Then Eli looked fearful and said, "In," and motioned to go in. And Janet said, "Eli, there are no bees here now. And I'm going to make sure you stay safe. I want you to look around. Do you see any bees in the tree? Do you see any bees by the gate? Do you see any bees on the steps?" Dutifully he looked around, and then he visibly relaxed against her chest. Then he looked at me and began all over again: "Orange. Bee. In." Clearly he wanted to make sure I heard the whole story, too.

I listened while they went through the whole sequence half a dozen more times. Janet said, "We've done this at least twenty times." And after several more tellings, it seemed like Eli was done. He brought it up a couple more times before bed and over the next few days, and I reiterated the story about the bees and the orange and the flowers. After that, he stopped talking about it. It seemed that he'd worked the experience through for the time being.

As A.J. relates, the distance at which children will be comfortable is ever-changing: "When Nathan was a young toddler, he loved trains. He always wore a striped conductor's hat and was constantly hooking things together to make trains. There was a big black engine at a park near where we lived, and he loved nothing more than to climb all over it. We lived near a railroad line, and whenever we'd hear a train, we'd run to see it.

"Then one day, when he was two, we heard a train and ran to see it. When we got close, Nathan became hysterical. It was as if he'd suddenly realized just how huge and powerful and fast trains really were.

"For the next year, he was scared of trains but still fascinated. He still wanted to watch them, but from a distance. And then one day, Nathan said he wanted to ride the train. So we did. The fear had passed."

• **When in the scary situation, offer physical support at the child's level.** We're often tempted to swoop down and lift our children away from the object of their fear. In some situations this may be appropriate (as when a big dog is about to knock the child over or when the child makes it clear it's what *he* wants), but often, offering physical support on the ground, from the child's perspective, can help to bolster the child's confidence. When we come down to their level and squat behind them or beside them, we give children the message that we're there, that we'll protect them, but that we don't think they need to be rescued.

• **Find other ways to support children's competence.** When children are experiencing a lot of fear, they're usually feeling scared and powerless in the world at large. You can help them feel more competent in the world by supporting their developing sense of mastery.[3]

• **Let children know that everyone gets scared sometimes.** Kids benefit from the information that fears are a normal part of life. Knowing that the adults around them have successfully dealt with fears can be reassuring for kids. Share a story about a fear you successfully dealt with as a child. But make sure the "fear" and the "story" are appropriate for your child and not something that will add to her fear.

• **Try to see the bigger picture.** Dealing effectively with your child's fears doesn't necessarily mean those fears will go away. Usually eliminating a fear takes time and maturity. But that doesn't mean that our efforts are ineffective or that our teaching isn't relevant. Children learn tools and postures for dealing with fear even if they aren't ready to overcome the fear that is immediately before them.

[3] For specific suggestions on how to do this, see "Inviting Children's Initiative" on p. 238 and "Create an Environment That Encourages Mastery" on p. 246.

In Their Own Way, in Their Own Time

Children have their own timetable for successfully working through fear. Because overcoming fears is a complex interface between intellectual and emotional development, one can never predict the timing of the process. It is useful to remember that even though children are sometimes quite undone by their fears, they have enormous potential for learning as they work through them. Once a child has successfully dealt with something that has frightened her, she'll be equipped to deal with fears that come up later in life.

FOOD FOR THOUGHT: DEALING WITH FEAR

• What kinds of things was I scared of as a child?

• Did adults support me in resolving my fears? Are there ways that support could have been more effective?

• What kind of fears do I have today? How do I deal with those fears?

• What would I like to teach my child about dealing with fear?

13. The Dance of Separation

Sadness, sadness tears streaming
down my eyes.
ISIS SIEN, *"A Poem of Sadness," grade 1*

Saying good-bye to your kids can be really hard—and at times, it can be as hard for you as it is for them. Most parents have been faced with leaving their children at times they wished they didn't have to and have asked themselves, "Will she be safe without me?" "Am I neglecting my duties as a parent if I leave her for two hours?" "Will she be mad at me for leaving?" "Will she remember who I am when I come back?" Most of us have felt torn when faced with a child who was reaching for us and begging us not to go. Yet separation is an inevitable part of life.

There's a natural ebb and flow to relationships that encompasses being together and being apart, being close and being independent, exploring the world and then coming back to our family, our home base. Good-byes and reunions are an integral part of family life. We go away and we come back. Learning to deal with these separations is a skill that evolves throughout our lives.

Children's experiences of separation vary widely during their early years. In some families, children are left only with family members. In others, children are cared for by a community of trusted caregivers.[1] Some children are in child care starting shortly after they are born. Others are not cared for by anyone besides their parents until they go off to kindergarten. Ideas about acceptable separations vary widely among child development experts as well as among families and cultures. It is important to consider both your child's developmental readiness and your family's needs and beliefs when making decisions about separations.

Why It's Hard for Children to Say Good-bye: A Developmental Perspective

In the first five years of life, children go from being merged with their primary caregiver to developing a completely separate, autonomous

[1] We're choosing to use the word "caregiver" instead of the more familiar terms "baby-sitter" and "nanny" to describe people who care for children, including child care center teachers, in-home child care providers, family day care home staff, and family or friends. We believe the term "caregiver" most accurately and respectfully reflects the valuable work done by these people.

identity. In the course of this evolution, children go through periods of "separation anxiety" in which they fear being away from the people they are closest to.

Very young babies are generally happy for short periods with anyone who holds them securely and lovingly, even though they can differentiate a familiar face, voice, touch, or smell from those that are unfamiliar. Babies whose temperament makes them more highly sensitive to touch or changes sometimes balk at a new caregiver, crying because that person feels different. It's important to remember that all babies need time to gradually accustom themselves to anyone new who takes care of them.

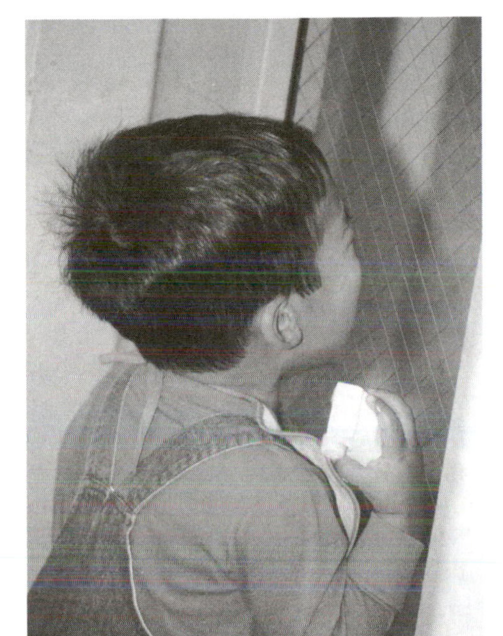

In the second half of the first year, children's increasing mobility coincides with their discovery of separateness. When children first become mobile, they often eagerly crawl off across the room only to look back and find that you have "moved" and are suddenly far away. For many children this experience introduces the idea that they are really physically separate from their anchor person. Increased anxiety about a parent's whereabouts often accompanies this discovery. Babies in this developmental stage frequently whine when you walk into the other room or cry when you leave them in someone else's care.

Toward the end of the first year, two other discoveries add to children's fears of separation. One is the development of "object permanence," the understanding that objects or persons may still exist even though the child can't see them. Babies begin to grasp the fact that when you leave you are somewhere else. Given that knowledge, they want you to stay with them.

Second, one-year-olds begin to use their previous experience to predict events in the future. They learn that when you pick up your keys, it means you are going to be leaving, and that when you leave, they're going to be without you.

Although their memory has increased, older babies and young toddlers still don't have a linear conception of time. Their experience when you leave is often "You're going away and I don't know if or when you're coming back!"

Often what looks like regressive behavior when you leave—clinging, crying, wanting to be held all the time—is actually a sign of a more sophisticated awareness on the part of the child.

Toddlers also go through periods of difficult separations because of their rapid growth. Any time a child is having a developmental spurt or going through a period of increased fears, she may want to stay closer to her family. As toddlers push for autonomy, the natural counterbalance is clinginess: "I want to be out climbing, throwing, jumping, making my own decisions, playing with the kids, and I want to be on your lap, all at the same time."

Although there are big individual differences as to when children experience difficulties with separation, it's important to know that a child who's previously been comfortable with separation may all of a sudden start crying when you leave. Although any dramatic shift in your child's behavior needs to be looked at carefully, a change in your child's response to being left doesn't necessarily mean that anything is "wrong." It may just mean that he's reached a new level of understanding about being away from you.

Separation may also be more challenging depending on children's temperament. Kids who are very sensitive and have developed a relationship with a parent in which the parent helps to buffer the world for them may have a more difficult time separating. Children who are late talkers and who rely on a unique communication system with their parents often find separations more challenging. And children who tend to be observers, who like to "take a lot of notes" before they move out into the world, may also find that comfortable separations take longer to develop.

In the preschool years, many children experience an easing of separation anxiety. By the time they reach three or four, most children who've had the opportunity to experience some predictable separations adjust more easily to the idea of "good-byes." As children move out of the toddler years, they become more certain of their relationship with you and start to have a more sophisticated sense of time that allows them to "remember" that if you aren't here now, you will still return. However, there may still be times, due to developmental changes or other stresses, when children go through temporary tears or clinginess and need renewed support around separation.

Why It's Hard for Parents to Say Good-bye

While children are learning to deal with separation, their parents are often having their own complex, ambivalent feelings: "I desperately need some time to work, be by myself, and get things done *and* I can't stand the thought of leaving you."

With both men and women under increasing pressure at work and at home, more and more parents feel torn, as if they're aren't doing any of their jobs well. As Golda Meir once said, "At work you think of the children you have left at home. At home you think of the work you've left unfinished. Such a struggle is unleashed within yourself. Your heart is rent."

These feelings of inadequacy often surface when parents begin their transition back to work after a child is born. Many parents experience guilt, anxiety, and self-doubt when they first leave their child. They worry about whether they can find a trusted person to care for their child and wonder if their child will be okay without them. As Faviola recalls, "I would kiss my daughter and wave good-bye, then make a dash for my car and bawl my eyes out."

When children are also having a hard time saying good-bye, parents' feelings of distress over leaving often increase. Sari recalls: "After Lola had been caring for Jordan for a number of months, he entered that stage where he couldn't bear for me to leave him. Whenever it was time for me go, I felt wracked inside. How could I leave my son when he was holding up his arms, sobbing his heart out, crying 'Mama! Mama!'? If I went to work, would I damage him forever?"

These doubts and worries are natural. They are a barometer of the depth of love we feel for our children, a testimony to both our connection and our sense of responsibility. It is not easy to go from being the "primary" caregiver for our baby to sharing our baby's care with someone else.

Our feelings about separation continually lead us to clarify our priorities as a parent. Sorting through these feelings, dealing with those that just need to run their course, and responding to those that are clues to a need for change is an ongoing process in our lives as parents.

FOOD FOR THOUGHT: SEPARATIONS

- What do I remember about separations as a child?

- How have separations been with my own children?

- When is it easier for my child to say good-bye to me? Harder?

- When is it easier for me to say good-bye to my child? Harder?

Daily Separations

Daily separations have some degree of regularity to them—every Sunday afternoon your son goes to Uncle Phil's house; on Monday, Wednesday, and Friday mornings, your daughter goes to preschool; every morning at seven-thirty, you kiss your kids good-bye and go off to work. Daily separations have a quality of predictability and sameness that, over time, children can learn to anticipate and grow used to. This consistency helps make separations easier for children. But even regular separations may be difficult at first—or even later, after they have already been successfully established. A child's difficulty saying good-bye is often related to changes, development, stress, or temperament—factors over which parents may not have control.

Changes such as a new child care situation often cause tearful good-byes. This is a normal response. Children need time to become comfortable in new surroundings. Some children go off happily the first several days, never seeming to notice that Dad is gone, and, all of a sudden, on the fifth day, they break down in a sobbing good-bye. It is not unusual for a child to be fascinated by the new setting for a few days—"This looks like an interesting party. I don't mind being here for a while"—but then to respond differently when he realizes that it's a permanent situation.

Stress can also cause difficult separations. If Mom has the flu for a few days, the child's equilibrium may be thrown off. He may feel, "My mom has been different for a few days. I wonder if she is okay. I wonder if she is still my same mom. It's hard to leave her when I have all these questions." If there is a move, a divorce, or other changes at home, a child may also experience increased difficulty with separation.[2]

As well as sometimes being difficult, daily separations can also be valuable and worthwhile for children. They help children establish trust ("You go away and then you come back") and give them opportunities to build significant connections with other caring adults. The security that comes from those relationships—and from experiencing day in and day out that you always do come back—ultimately makes separation easier.

Strategies for Dealing with Daily Separations

Consistency, clarity, and confidence can all help ease daily separations between you and your child.

• **Make your comings and goings as regular as possible.** You can't say to a baby, "I'll be back at a quarter of two," and have her reply, "Okay, I'll keep an eye on the clock and pace myself till you get back." The only way babies can anticipate that you're going to come back is through practice. And if you leave at predictable times, it's easier for them to get used to the schedule. You drop your daughter off at day care right after breakfast and you always pick her up after lunch. You return for your son every day after his nap. If you come back at a predictable time, your child's internal clock begins to expect it, and that helps him deal with the separation. But if your work schedule is such that you work six hours on one day and an hour and a half on another day, maybe two days a week, maybe six days a week, it will probably take longer for your young child to adjust.

[2] See "When Parents Separate: Making It Work for the Children" on p. 390 for more on separations after a divorce.

• **Always say good-bye.** In Janis's toddler development class one night, Stanley, the father of three-year-old Amir, confessed, "It's just too hard when I drop Amir off and he cries, so I just sort of vaporize." Stanley told the class that he'd wait until Amir was involved in something, then he'd slip out of the room without saying he was leaving.

When children are struggling with separation, it can be tempting to slip away unnoticed. Yet often kids whose parents leave without telling them feel they have to be constantly vigilant: "I can't really get involved in anything because somebody I care about might slip away.' " Even when you have to interrupt your child, saying good-bye is important.

• **Have confidence in your child's capacity to make a successful transition.** When you take the time to tell children good-bye, you let them know, "I'm leaving. I'm going to come back. I trust that you're going to be okay while I'm gone and that you can handle this separation."

• **Develop a predictable good-bye routine.** For some children, leave-taking rituals make separations easier—standing at the window with the caregiver, blowing three kisses, walking you to the elevator, looking you in the eye and saying "Good-bye." Sometimes the caregiver can sing a special song of good-bye or welcoming. Such rituals reassure children.

• **Leave a token of yourself behind.** Leaving something with your child can help—for babies, a familiar shirt or nightgown that has your smell on it; for older children, a plastic-covered photograph they can slip in and out of their pocket. Give the item to the child and say, "Will you hold this for me while I'm gone?" Then they can keep the cherished article in their cubby, in a special hiding place, or in the bed where they nap. Touching it and looking at it throughout the day can help bring back the tangible memory of you.

Cap, a day care worker, explained, "One child was having a hard time coming to the center so her dad started putting a note in the pocket of her overalls that said 'I love you.' She'd walk around all morning, showing that to people."

• **Respond to your child's needs for reassurance.** During those times when kids are more clingy and they seem to need you more, it's useful to be more available if at all possible. But even when your children are struggling with your absences, it's still helpful to keep up some of the separation you've already established. Even when it's hard, separation teaches valuable lessons. When kids are nurtured and well cared for by someone else, they learn to trust other people, to see the world as a safe and friendly place.

• **Stick with familiar caregivers.** When children are having particular problems with separation, try to avoid introducing new caregivers.

• **Try for a daytime date.** If you're leaving your child so you can go to work or school, you probably have a set routine that can't be changed. But if you're going out to see friends, to get a few moments alone, or to reconnect with your partner, you have more flexibility. Although concerts and movies, dinner and dancing all happen at night, that's often the hardest time for children to be separated from you. In the evening, kids are tired and want their familiar routine; they have fewer resources for dealing with things that are different. So it can be helpful to try "going out" earlier in the day, at a time when your child is refreshed.

• **Make the child's activities away from you special.** You can leave a treat or suggest a favorite activity for your child and caregiver to do while you are gone. In Mimi's family, the kids all look forward to playing nerfball tag with Marcy, who comes over from next door to take care of them.

Part of making the time special for your child is the way you introduce the idea. Laura explains: "Whenever Eli's Aunt Janet is going to watch him, we talk about the fact that we're going out on a date and that Eli is going to have his own date with her. Even if his 'date' is still hours away, he starts strutting around the house yelling, 'Date! Janet! Ready!' He's not just being baby-sat. He has something special that he's doing, too."

Strategies for Coming Home at the End of the Day

At the end of every separation is a homecoming. For those of us who work, go to school, or have other responsibilities outside the home, reuniting with our families at the end of the day can present challenges as well as delights. Moving from the world's pace into our lives at home requires that we slow down, clear our minds, change our rhythm, and leave the day behind.

For Shinta, the transition between work and home is the hardest part of her day: "I'm always happy to see Momo and to hold her, but sometimes when I'm sitting on the floor reading her a book, my mind is still racing with the work of the day. If I could just learn to be in the moment with her, and at work when I'm at work, everything would be easier."

Homecomings can be hard for kids, as well. Children often fall apart when they're picked up at day care or just as we're trying to get dinner on the table. The reuniting time, which we've looked forward to all day, is often a setup for short tempers and trouble.

Every family will develop its own strategies for reuniting after the day's separation, but here are some ideas that have worked well in many families:

Coming Home: Paula's Story

Paula has almost always worked outside of the home, and the transition between her work life and the needs of her family has been a constant challenge she's had to deal with. After twenty-plus years of coming home from work, she's learned a few things, but she still hasn't worked it all out.

Coming home from work to my family has always been horrendous for me. Everybody needed me the minute I came home. Somebody had a spelling test the next day, someone had a report due, someone had an emotional experience, someone just tried out for a sports team. My littlest kid had a ton of needs. Each person had a real need of me when I walked in the door.

I used to stop the car and sit in it for ten minutes and prepare to go from intellectual, cohesive thinking to absolute chaotic frenzy. In my mind, I finished any loose ends from the day. I wrote myself notes about things I needed to follow through on. Then I let go of the day as completely as I could so I could walk in the door with a clean slate. I needed to do that because my grumpiest time was always when I still had something I wanted to do for work, when what was needed was to give my absolute attention to my kids.

Basically, I have to come in with no needs of my own, ready to see and acknowledge each kid. I'm a firm believer that a little bit of attention, eye contact, and physical closeness can make children feel acknowledged in a way that they then won't act out. And if they don't get that, they will.

It's really helped me to think "I just have to spend five minutes with each kid right now" instead of "The need is overwhelming. I think I won't look. There's too many kids. I can't deal with them. I'm just going to shut everybody out and deal with this one who has the most pressing need."

Actually, my very best scenario was the one time I had a car phone and I commuted. I had five kids at the time. I'd call home ahead of time and talk to my big kids, and they'd tell me what happened at school that day. So by the time I walked in the door, I could tend to my youngest, and the big kids felt okay because they'd already told me the highlights of their day. Then I'd get the little one to bed and go back and follow up with the big kids. That worked out the best.

• **Take time to clear your mind before you arrive home.** Some people do this before they leave work; others while commuting home. Some make a quick stop at the YMCA, take a short walk, or go for a run around the block.

• **Check in.** Take ten or fifteen minutes to check in with the people you haven't seen all day. You can talk, sing, read a book, or play "horse-y" before you begin the tasks for the evening. Some parents have found it necessary to focus this time on the children and leave most of their adult check-ins until later.

• **Connect physically.** Many families have hugging, cuddling, back rubs, wrestling, or playing ball built into their days. These can be wonderful opportunities for physical contact, immediate connections, and play.[3]

• **Find out about your child's time away from you.** If you're picking up your son or daughter at child care, ask your child's caregiver about what your child's day was like. Having some knowledge enables you to ask specific questions: "Tell me about the dinosaur cave you made out of blocks." "Tell me about the fire truck you saw."

• **Talk about your day.** If you find that it's hard for your children to answer questions about their day, start by sharing stories about your day—about running for the bus and almost having the door close, about seeing a whole bunch of yellow and red flowers on your way to work. This gives children a chance to see what "sharing stories about your day" looks like.

• **Simplify the things you need to do when you get home.** Think about what's really important for you to do and let go of the rest. Janis explains, "When my kids were young, I worked full time outside the home. One thing I did was simplify the things I did outside of work. Housework went way down on my list of priorities. So my house is a total disaster. It's been a disaster for years. Part of what I do when I come home from work is step over all the clutter—piles of newspapers, clothes, toys, and dirty dishes—and go spend time with my kids. Every couple of weeks or so, I do a big blitz and clear things up, but in between, it can turn into a hurricane. If effect, I'm saying to my family 'I'm away from you for this period of time that I'm working, and when I'm home, you're my priority.' "

• **Involve children in homecoming routines.** You can say to your kids: "Come help me bring in the newspaper." "Help me open the mail." "Let's water our plants." Babies can watch the activities in the kitchen from a safe vantage point. Toddlers like to wipe tables and cupboards with sponges, scrub potatoes in the sink, or wash vegetables in a low dishpan. And preschoolers like to cut zucchini, tear lettuce, or pass out the dishes for dinner.[4]

• **Share the responsibilities.** In families where there is more than one adult, divide up the tasks: "It's your night to cook and my night to be with the kids." "It's your night to do the bedtime routine and my night to read the paper."

• **Make space for regular family time.** During family time, turn off the TV and video games, and put away newspapers and books, so that the family gets a chance to be together.

[3] See "Physical Play and Roughhousing with Children" on p. 192 for safety guidelines regarding this kind of play.

[4] See "Cooking with Children" on p. 172 for other ideas on including children in the evening preparations for dinner.

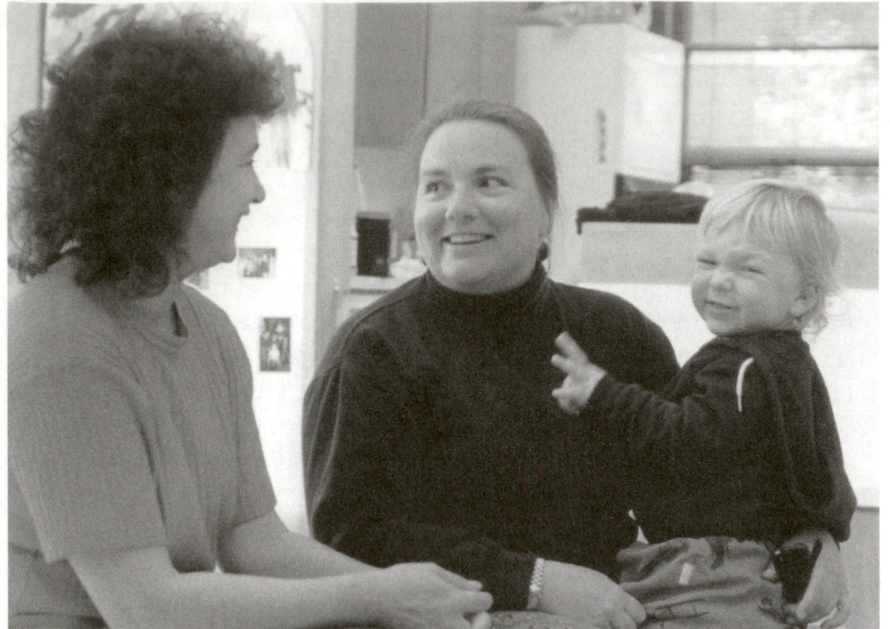

Longer Separations and Reunions

When you leave your child in a way that differs from your usual routine, a whole new set of dynamics comes into play. The separation doesn't have to be long for it to be significant; the important factor is how different it is from what your child is used to. Separations in this category include time in which your school or work responsibilities demand more of you, time spent dealing with illness or family emergencies, time spent traveling for work, trips you take without your children, as well as time your children spend away from you—when they're visiting relatives, sleeping at someone else's house, or staying with their other parent in a different home.

Generally, this type of separation is harder for children to deal with than normal, daily separations. As such, it requires more careful forethought and planning. When you're considering a different or more extensive separation than your child is used to, here are some things that can make it easier:

- **Tell kids your schedule and reassure them that you're coming back.** Let children know when you're going, where you're going, and when you'll be back.

- **Choose a caregiver and location the child is used to.** It's easiest for your child to stay with someone she knows in her own home or in familiar surroundings.

- **Help the child acclimate to new surroundings.** If your child isn't being cared for at home, help her become familiar with the place she will be staying. Look at where she'll eat, sleep, and play. If distance or circumstances preclude visiting, see if you can get a photo or make a little book called *Visiting Grandma* so your child can begin to get used to the place where she'll be.

- **Send familiar things along.** Pack so your daughter can sleep with her favorite blanket, cuddle with her favorite stuffed clown, drink from her favorite cup, or read a well-loved book.

- **Prepare your child ahead of time.** Your ability to do this will depend on your child's understanding of time. Young toddlers can't imagine the future, three-year-olds will benefit from a couple of day's notice, and five-year-olds can imagine an upcoming event two weeks away.

Let your child know what to expect while

you're away: "I won't be here in the morning when you wake up, but Dhira will make oatmeal for you and be with you all day. And then after dinner, right about time for your bath, I'll be back."

• **Start small and build up from there.** If you're planning to have your two-year-old daughter stay overnight at Aunt Toni's house, start by having her go over for an evening or by taking an afternoon nap there. As she demonstrates she's comfortable with these small steps, consider taking a bigger one.

Of course, emergencies come up and there are times we're all forced to leave our children in circumstances that are less than ideal. Even in these situations, do what you can ahead of time to make the experience a positive one for your child. If you have neighbors, friends, or relatives with whom your child has already built relationships, things will be easier if they're the ones called upon to provide emergency backup care.

• **Consider your child's developmental readiness when planning extended time away.** Parents often long for the intimacy and freedom that they had before their children were born. Some consider taking long vacations away from their kids to recapture some of the spontaneity and closeness they've lost. While this might be beneficial to the parents' relationship, it can be hard on the children. If you're considering taking such a trip, it's important that you factor in your children's temperament, past experience, developmental stage as well as their comfort and familiarity with their caregiver.

From the standpoint of babies and many young toddlers, separations of more than a night or two are very difficult. After several days or a week, some young children may even begin to give up the idea that their parents are coming back. The potential for this kind of emotional stress can be significantly reduced if the child stays in her own home with someone she is familiar and well attached to.

By the time children are three or four, most can tolerate longer separations more easily. Children who understand time may enjoy such activities as marking the days off a calendar until you return.

Some parents have found that taking a couple of overnight or weekend trips helps them to have the time they need without putting as much stress on their children. On longer trips, others have taken along a caregiver or another family member to help with child care. There are families who routinely take trips with other families who have children of similar or complementary ages, an arrangement that allows for both adult time and child time.

Things You and Your Caregiver Can Do While You're Away

When you're leaving your child for a period of time that is longer or different from usual, you can use many of the same strategies we recommended for daily separations. You can also:

• **Encourage the caregiver to talk about you.** Sometimes caregivers think it's better not to mention you when you're gone, because they don't want to "make Julian sad." But actually, talking about you helps Julian remember you and gives him a chance to express whatever feelings he's already carrying.

Your child's caregiver can casually mention you a couple of times in the course of the day. In the morning, he could say "Hey, Julian, I wonder what your mom is having for breakfast. Do you think she's eating eggs or French toast?"

Julian may cry when you're mentioned. Inevitably, he will have some sadness and confusion about you being gone. But it's beneficial if he can express some of that while you're gone, instead of saving it all for your return.

• **The telephone has its limitations.** When you call three-year-old Omi, she may be delighted to hear from you. But she may also burst into tears or not want to talk to you. The moment you call may not be the exact same moment Omi was missing you. Older children sometimes talk readily on the telephone, but one-, two-, and three-year-olds are often confused or frustrated by hearing your voice on the telephone—they don't understand why they can hear your voice but not see you or climb up on your lap.

• **Make a tape of your voice.** Use a tape recorder to make a special tape for your child. Talk to him, read him books, tell him stories, sing some of his favorite songs. Having a tape he can turn on and off can be preferable to the telephone because the child can listen to the tape whenever he wants to hear it. Since he doesn't have control over when you leave or when you come back, it's helpful for him to have control over a small piece of you while you're gone.

• **Caregivers can prepare children for your return.** Caregivers can reassure children about your return and tell them when to expect it. They can help children "write" a story about their day, buy some apples, or pick some leaves to share with you when you get back. Doing something with you in mind helps children feel connected and prepares them for your homecoming.

Things to Be Aware of When You Come Back

Reunions from longer or unusual separations can be difficult for children. Here are some of the more common responses you may see upon your return:

• **Hanging back.** You may come home with the expectation that your daughter is going to rush headlong into your arms and hold on to you for all she's worth. But that may not be what she does at all. Some children run straight into your arms and sit there for a day. Others, after they notice you've come in, turn away and go back to what they were doing. They stay aloof and distant. They may cry, tell you to "Go away!" or even ignore you.

This can feel devastating to parents. You may jump to the conclusion that your daughter is mad at you, when that's not what's happening—or when it's only a small part of what's happening. Most likely she's simply taking the time she needs to make the adjustment to being back together with you. Her sense of time is different from yours.

What happens is this: You go away for the weekend. As an adult, you know what Friday to Monday looks like. You can feel how long it's going to be until you hold your daughter again. When you start driving into your town, when you reach your neighborhood, when you head down your street, you warm up to being with her. But your two-year-old doesn't have the capacity to do that. She has to start warming up after you arrive.

Janis remembers arriving home after being away for two nights: "Maya was three at the time. When I walked in, she was at the sink washing dishes. She said 'Hi, Mom' and went back to washing dishes. I was left standing there thinking "She's really absorbed in what she's doing. She's not ready to connect with me yet. She's making the transition from being a girl in the world with her brothers and her father. She's remembering how to be with me; she's figuring out how to depend on me again." About forty-five minutes later, she was all over me. She was like white on rice. But it took her that long to warm up."

Give your child the time she needs to warm up without getting your feelings hurt, "rejecting" her back, or assuming "She's mad at me." Be available, but let her move at her own pace.

• **Ambivalent feelings.** When you come back after being away, children are often full of ambivalent emotions: "I'm not used to being with you. So you should go away! But I missed you horribly so you should come close!" That can be confusing for both of you when you don't understand where it's coming from.

• **Testing.** Often kids want to find out if you've changed, to see if you'll react in the same ways you did before you left. They may test you by immediately doing something they know you'll have to stop. It's as if they're saying, "You haven't been here. So I need you to show me in a very physical way that you're still my mom."

If you can recognize that this is what's happening, you can respond to testing with more compassion. "I see you're throwing your food. Let's move your food away for a minute. Do you want to come over here and sit with me?"

• **Clinging.** Your child may need to be attached to you for several days after you come back. He is going to want to reconnect with you in some real, tangible ways. If possible, clear your schedule so you have at least one day you can really devote to being with your child.

• **Preference for the other parent (or caregiver).** When you get home after being away, your daughter may repeatedly insist, "No, Daddy do it." Your daughter has grown accustomed to Daddy doing everything. That doesn't mean she doesn't like you, it just means she's more used to Daddy and she wants to choose. Give her some time to change gears and get used to you again.[5]

[5] See "When Children Prefer One Parent over the Other" on p. 382 for more on dealing with this situation.

Building a Bridge to Child Care

The issue of child care comes up very tangibly when we think about leaving our children. There are three main components of building a strong bridge to child care: making a good initial choice, supporting your child's transition, and nurturing your family's relationship with your child's caregiver over time.

Choosing a Caregiver

Finding the person who will care for your child is a highly personal decision. Here are some important considerations in making your choice:

• **Think about what you value most in a caregiver.** Clarifying your values is an important first step in making the right choice. Sometimes the process of meeting several caregivers will help you clarify what you really want.

• **Think about what you need to trust a caregiver.** Assessing what you need to build trust is at the core of finding the right person for your family.

Finding Quality Child Care Programs

What is quality care? How does it differ from unsafe, inadequate, or mediocre care? What does it take for children to be well nurtured in a setting away from their families?*

Some determinants of quality care are low staff turnover, well-paid, well-trained caregivers, a low child-adult ratio, and good communication between staff members and between parents and caregivers.

There are several ways to evaluate a child care situation. You can begin by interviewing caregivers, the director, and other parents who are familiar with the program. Initial screening questions might include:

Staffing

- Do staff members have early childhood training? Are they involved in ongoing education and training?
- Is the staff paid a living wage?
- What's the frequency of staff turnover? Are staff members usually here long enough to establish long-term bonds with children?
- Do children have consistent caregivers to provide the safety and trust they need?

Group Size and Ratio

- What's the ratio of adults to children? (For infants, we recommend a 3:1 ratio; for toddlers, 4:1; and for preschoolers, at least 6:1.)
- Is the group size small enough to prevent overstimulation, to ensure that children will be well cared for? To provide good supervision, attentive care, and personal relationships between children and caregivers?

Licensing and Accreditation

- What kind of a license does this daycare home or program have?
- Is the program accredited by the National Association for the Education of Young Children?

Health and Safety

- What are the health and safety policies and procedures?
- Are caregivers trained in first aid and CPR?

Once you've gathered this basic information, it is important to visit. If at all possible, go a few times during different parts of the day. Although it is important to visit with your child, it can be useful to visit on your own, as well, so you can observe the center without having to pay attention to your child. Through observing and talking to staff, you can address the following questions:

Philosophy

- Most centers have a written philosophy statement that reflects the values and goals of the program. Does this statement reflect your values?
- Is the philosophy evident in the environment?
- Is it consistent with the day-to-day interactions between caregivers and children?

Environment

- Is the environment safe, clean, attractive, well cared for, child-centered?
- Are there places for large physical play, quiet play, group play, individual play, pretend play, messy play, sand play, reading, art, science, block building?

Respect for Children

- Are interactions between children and caregivers respectful?
- Are children's feelings respected?
- Are children's needs for free choice considered in the schedule?
- Are their needs for flexibility, predictability, stability, for quiet as well as active times, taken into account?
- Is there adequate time for transitions?

* The National Association for the Education of Young Children has brochures to help parents recognize quality child care. It also has national lists of accredited programs. For information or a catalogue of resources, write to NAEYC, Information Services Department, 1509 16th Street NW, Washington, D.C. 20036-1426; call (800) 424-2460; e-mail: aauj82d@prodigy.com

CHILDREN'S AUTONOMY

- Is the environment set up so that children can get the toys and materials they need by themselves?
- Do the toys encourage creative play?
- Are both girls and boys playing with a diversity of toys?

PROBLEM-SOLVING

- Are children supported in solving their own conflicts?
- Are children who are testing limits responded to safely, respectfully, and without punishment?

PARENT INVOLVEMENT

- Are parents invited to participate in the program?
- Are there places for parents to meet, to talk with other parents?
- Are there places for parents to talk to caregivers?
- Are resources available for parents?
- Are parents free to drop in and visit anytime?

DIVERSITY

- Does the group of children include diversity in terms of ethnicity, income levels, culture, physical ability, and family structure? Is that diversity valued and acknowledged in the program—through books, stories, pictures, caregiver's language, and parent information forms?
- Are children of both genders equally respected?

MEALS

- If the center provides snacks or meals, are they nutritious and wholesome?
- Are children invited to participate in serving and feeding themselves and in making choices about what they eat?

You may want to bring up other questions to address your particular concerns. It's also important to remember that no one program will meet all of your criteria. Knowing what is most important to you will help you choose the program that's best for your family.

Many excellent programs have long waiting lists. Even if you're not sure when you need care or exactly where you want your child to go, putting your child on the waiting lists at several places you might consider in the future can be helpful so that an opening is available when you need it.

• **Get referrals.** When friends, other parents, or coworkers suggest caregivers, ask specific questions, such as "What especially do you like about Gretchen?" "What does your child enjoy about her?" "Have there been any problems or things you dislike?" "How have you and Gretchen dealt with these differences?" "Would you recommend her wholeheartedly?"

• **Check references.** Knowing how a caregiver has worked with other families can help you assess a potential good fit with your family.

• **Screen over the phone.** You can save a lot of time by doing your initial screening by phone. Ask about basics such as cost, availability, hours, training, and experience. Then ask about the issues that most clearly reflect your values. You may know that you want a caregiver who speaks Spanish, helps kids with conflict resolution, or who's had experience with special needs. Conversely, if you find out that a caregiver smokes, doesn't respect your religion, or has the TV on all day, you may know right away that she's not a match for your family.

• **Interview caregivers.** After your initial screening, set up a mutually convenient time to talk in person. Interviews will be somewhat different for in-home caregivers than they will for staff at a child care program.

For initial interviews, kids don't need to be present. Spend a little time getting to know each caregiver. Have them talk about their interests, what they enjoy about children, their work history, and their skills. You can also ask hypothetical questions, such as: "What would you do if Jake refused to put on his shoes?" "How would you respond if Lucy kept trying to bite you?" "What would you do if Lucy and Jake were pulling on the same toy and screaming?" "How do you imagine a morning with Jake might go?" "What would you do if you and I felt differently about handling a situation?" You may also want to ask what the caregiver thinks would make for a good relationship between the two of you.

No one caregiver will ever answer every question exactly the way you hope for. That's why it's essential to know which answers are most important to you. Would a negative answer on any particular question disqualify this person? Or are there certain differences you can live with? It's important to know which issues carry more weight, which are negotiable, and which aren't.

• **Pay attention to how you feel.** While it's important to listen to what caregivers say, it's also crucial to pay attention to how you feel when you are with them. Not everyone can articulate who they are with words. Sometimes the way people are with you, the way you feel when you're with them, is more descriptive of who they are than anything they say.

• **Observe the caregiver with your child.** Once you've narrowed down your choices, set up an informal time for you, your child, and the caregiver to get together. The way the caregiver initiates contact, interacts, and responds to your child can give you important information about her style and skills. Even if your child is cool or standoffish, you'll have an opportunity to see whether the caregiver can read his signals.

• **Consider how a caregiver deals with your child's feelings.** When children are having trouble saying good-bye, it's important that they have help dealing with their feelings. Since children's good-byes often include crying, it's valuable to know how a prospective caregiver will respond to crying: "What will you do if my baby cries?" "What if she keeps crying?" If you want a caregiver who will be accepting and comfortable with your child's feelings, you may not choose someone who responds only by providing distraction: "Well, I'll bounce her up and down," "I'll just find something fun to do."

For caregivers, working through tearful good-byes can be an important part of their relationship with children. As Sue, a full-time caregiver, put it, "I can tell the level of bonding I have with a child by the sad times we spend together."

• **Trust your intuition.** Intuition plays an important role in making a good choice. Patti, who was putting her son, Kevin, in group care, said, "I visited one center. The children were clean. The room was bright and cheerful. The activities seemed appropriate and the teachers were okay with the kids, but there was something that just didn't feel right about it. I couldn't put my finger on it, but I knew I couldn't choose that center for Kevin. He ended up in a center that was a little less well ordered and a little less well scrubbed, but there was something about the way the adults were with the kids that felt just right to me."

Supporting Your Child's Transition to Child Care

How children begin care can foster their successful experience of separation. Here are a few suggestions for a smoother start:

• **Arrange some time when you, your child, and the new caregiver can be together.** Such time can create a meaningful bridge. The caregiver gets to see you with your child, and you get to see the caregiver with your child. Your child also gets to explore the new person (or environment) with you there. Once you know that your caregiver understands your child's cues and communication system, you can leave feeling more confident. And when your child and your caregiver have some sense of knowing each other, neither one of them is left with a stranger.

• **Ease your child in gradually.** Visiting a child care program with your child, either once or on several occasions, can ease the transition, as can leaving your child for a short time the first day, then gradually building up from there.

Some child care centers have a policy of doing a "home visit," either before or shortly after children begin care. Home visits enable caregivers to learn about a child's family and culture and gives the child an opportunity to integrate both of her worlds.

• **Value crying as a form of communication.** Even when children are well prepared for child care, they may still be upset when you leave them. For many children, crying is part of the good-bye, a reasonable way to make the transition from you to a caregiver. If your child quickly recovers, spends the rest of the time exploring, and is relatively happy, you can assume that the crying is just how your child says good-bye. If, however, your child cries the whole two hours, several days in a row, it may be time to reassess what you're doing: "Is this the right caregiver for us? The right schedule? The right situation?"

If you're clear that these are right, look at ways to help your child ease in more gradually. You can ask yourself: "What can I do to make the separation more comfortable, familiar, and predictable for my child?"

• **Regularly evaluate how things are going.** Effective indicators of a good child care match are the child's overall demeanor (not just his behavior during good-byes and hellos), his relationship to the caregiver, the reports the caregiver gives you about the child's day, and your own observations. You can also ask yourself: "Am I continuing in a comfortable relationship with the caregiver?" And if your child

Changing Child Care

Children are often in the position of changing caregivers or moving from one center to another. Such transitions are significant in children's lives, and kids need support making them.

• **Take the change seriously.** When your child is about to say good-bye to an important person in her life, you have the opportunity to think about what you want your child to learn about transitions, rituals, and good-byes. Early experiences such as these teach children important lessons about permanence and change in relationships.

• **Talk about it.** Prepare your child for the forthcoming change. Depending on the age of the child (two weeks is usually adequate preparation time for a two- or three-year-old), you will have to decide when to talk about the move from one child care setting to the new one, but do talk about it. Give a simple explanation of why the change is being made.

• **Help your child say good-bye.** Help your child find a channel for expressing his appreciation of the caregiver he is leaving. This can be helping to roll up spring rolls or bake muffins as a gift to bring to school, narrating a simple story the parent can write down, drawing a picture, giving a gift, or scribbling on a piece of paper with a photo of the child pasted on it. This helps your child realize that the last day is a different kind of day and also helps him learn about expressing appreciation to his important people.

• **Make a book.** You can make a simple book to help the child remember the situation she is leaving behind. Such a book could also be a lovely going-away gift for your caregiver as well. (For guidance on making such books, see "Making Books for Your Kids" on p. 298.)

is struggling with the separation: "Is the caregiver continuing to support me and my child through this difficult adjustment period?"

Building a Relationship with Your Child's Caregiver

One of the most critical aspects of a successful relationship between a child and a caregiver is the bond we, as parents, form with the caregiver. The more connected we feel, the more of a sense we have that we're on the same team, pulling together for our child, the more successful that caregiver can be with our child. Here are some keys to forming a strong connection with your child's caregiver:

• **Communicate.** Good two-way communication is essential to a positive parent-caregiver relationship. Both of you should feel free to bring up concerns, problems, or issues as well as joys and accomplishments. Each of you should feel that your perspective is being understood and valued. Having a chance to talk to your child's caregiver at the beginning and end of each day is extremely beneficial. For those situations in which this is not possible, communication can happen through notes or regular check-ins by phone. Individual "parent conferences," time set aside for parents and caregivers to talk without other distractions or responsibilities, also offer important opportunities for communication. These should happen at least twice a year.

• **Take care of your caregiver.** One obvious way to take care of your caregiver is by paying as much as you can afford, but money alone is not enough to compensate caregivers for what they provide to our families. Acknowledging and appreciating your caregiver's work, caring about her life, and valuing her point of view are important elements in building a mutually respectful relationship.

• **Let them love the one they're with.** Children need to know that we feel good about the people we're leaving them with: "This is someone my family has embraced. This is someone they say can be trusted." Parents need to let children know that it's okay for them to bond with their caregivers, to depend on them, to enjoy them, and, ultimately, to love them. Ironically, part of establishing a successful child care arrangement is getting out of the way.

Yet some parents find it extremely difficult to let their child love someone else. They feel threatened when their child cares deeply for someone outside of the family, as if that love might in some way diminish their own relationship with their child. But teaching children that the world is full of nurturing people, that there are safe harbors on many shores, is an important part of opening up the world for them.[6]

The Dance of Separation

In their lives together, parents and children experience many leave-takings and many reunions. The bonds of attachment are stretched for moments as a child crawls into the other room, for hours as children skip off to child care, for days as parents leave for a weekend, and finally for months or years as children mature into young adults and move out into the world. In a lifetime of comings and goings, we explore our separateness, discover the depth of our connections, and learn to trust our love.

My mom is inside of me everywhere I go,
even when I'm not there.
My mom is always in me,
mostly in my heart.
My mom is always with me.

—ZACK MATTHEWS, GRADE 1

[6] For more on this idea, see "Mothers As Gatekeepers" on p. 379.

• Part Three •

Children's Bodies

14.
Helping Children Sleep

"People who say they sleep like a baby usually don't have one."
LEO BURKE

Laura attended a postpartum yoga class with Eli the first months after he was born. One morning, Carolyn, a new mother, was sharing her frustration about her lack of sleep. "Brooke's up around the clock. We never get any sleep." Three-month-old Brooke was lying innocently in her lap, asleep. "Really," Carolyn insisted. "This is the only time she does this."

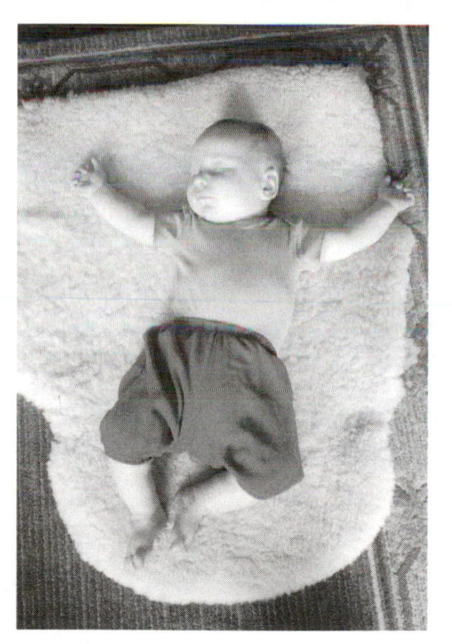

Bing, the instructor, asked a few questions about when Brooke slept. With great compassion she asked, "Does she nap?"

Silence. No answer. All of us held our breath, thinking it was a pretty easy question. We looked from Bing to Carolyn, wondering if Carolyn had heard the question or if she was just too tired to form a reply. She said nothing. The silence grew. Everything was in slow motion. Carolyn looked as if she was pondering one of the great questions of the world. "I don't know," she finally managed, her face quizzical. "Is ten minutes a nap?"

Sleep is a core issue in parenting. It is one of the first areas where we grapple with the reality that there are things about our children that we cannot control. As parents, we can set the stage for relaxation, but we cannot force children to sleep. For many of us, this fact comes as a surprising realization.

There's a range of roles that parents play in getting their children to sleep—on one hand, rocking children, singing to children, cuddling or nursing them until they fall asleep, and on the other, establishing a good-night ritual and then leaving children to find sleep themselves. In most families, there's a gradual shift between parents easing children into sleep and children learning to do it on their own sometime during a child's first five years of life. When that transition occurs and where parents are on the continuum of participation has a lot to do with parents' needs and expectations, their availability, the pressures they're under, their particular child, their perspective on children's independence, and the eventual goals they're working toward.

Sorting out these things is not an easy task, especially in the middle of the night when your thinking may be dulled by a lack of sleep. Even in the light of day, figuring out solutions to sleep problems is not always a clear-cut proposition. Parents don't always agree and families' needs vary. Finding comfortable sleep routines and determining the right level of adult participation in children's sleep is an ever-changing process.

What is important for your family's success is that you do what is comfortable for you and what works for your children, not that you use one particular system or another. In some families, getting children to sleep through the night in their own bed holds a very high priority. Other parents enjoy an extended nighttime ritual with their child as well as check-ins in the middle of the night. This works as long as both parents and children feel comfortable with the system and are getting the rest they need.

However, even if your family comes up with a sleep solution that works for you, one system probably won't last through your child's whole childhood. What parents are willing to do when their child is three months old, they may feel less willing to do when the child is one or two years old. As the balance of needs shifts in the family, new solutions need to be found.

Families find themselves looking again and again at where children sleep, when they sleep, how they get to sleep, and what to do when children wake up. When your child is sick or has nightmares, when you travel, or when a new sibling is born, sleep patterns change, and you will be faced with these questions anew.

Sleep: A Developmental Overview

During the first five years of life, children's relationship to sleep gradually evolves. They go from dropping off to sleep whenever they are tired to becoming aware of their need for sleep. They go from several naps a day to none; from frequent periods of waking at night to sleeping through the night. Often they move through a series of beds. Starting with a very different sleep schedule from their families, most children move to one that resembles the norm in their family.

For all young children sleep is related to issues of trust and safety as well as to physical rejuvenation. Children need to feel a sense of security in their world in order to let themselves fall asleep. Because of the vulnerability that children feel as they are moving into sleep, bedtime is often a prime time for fears and concerns about separation to emerge. Also, since sleep is a time for processing the day, children often revisit their daily experiences, accomplishments, upsets, and frustrations during the night.

Babies and Sleep

New babies generally have an "around-the-clock" sleep rhythm. Many don't distinguish between day and night. Slowly, in the first several weeks of life, babies learn to adjust to sleeping more at night and being awake more during the day. Newborns sleep an average of sixteen hours a day, and babies up to six months of age sleep between ten and eighteen hours a day. For most newborns, sleep comes without much fanfare. They aren't yet struggling or resisting sleep.

As babies get a little older, some start to have a fussy period when they are tired. They may be overstimulated, colicky, or seem like they need to let off steam before they are ready to go to sleep. They may not yet know how to let their bodies relax, to go from being awake to being asleep.

For the first several months of life, most babies need to eat at night. After that, some continue to wake out of habit at their usual feeding times. Some parents enjoy the closeness and quiet of nighttime feedings and continue them past the point when the baby "needs" to eat around the clock. Others want to end nighttime feedings as soon as the baby can safely tolerate it. Determining when your baby no longer needs to eat at night will involve checking with your child's doctor and observing your child.

Some breast-fed babies, who've nursed primarily during the day, begin to wake more often for night feedings at six or seven months of age because they've become distracted during the day and nursing is easier when it is dark and quiet.

Young babies may wake because of heat or cold, wetness, loud noise, teething or other pain. Some babies also wake during important developmental phases. Growth spurts don't stop just because it is nighttime. Babies who've just learned to pull up, crawl, or walk often wake several times a night during the lighter period of their sleep cycle. It's not clear whether they bolt themselves awake, as if to say "Wait a minute! I need to be crawling!" or whether they start crawling in their sleep and wake themselves up with their movements.

Toddlers and Sleep

For some toddlers napping, going to sleep at night, sleeping through the night, and waking up cheerfully are an easy, natural part of their day. However, for many, the toddler years bring struggle, testing, and resistance around sleep.

Young toddlers begin resisting sleep for several reasons. Sometimes they are just too busy: "Hey, I just learned to jump off the bed. How could you expect me to go to sleep now?" Other times, toddlers resist sleep as a way to maintain and explore control: "When I was a baby sleep just happened to me. But what if I just keep my eyes open and keep playing? Could I avoid sleep indefinitely?" This kind of testing extends also into relationships with parents: "If my mom says I need to go to sleep, or stay in my bed, that's my cue to say 'NO!' "

Toddlers also fight going to sleep because of separation anxiety. With their newfound understanding of separateness, they realize that going to sleep is a way of saying good-bye and that being asleep is a kind of separation.

Like babies, toddlers sometimes wake during the night for physical reasons, such as noise, sickness, or discomfort. Children will also wake if they are working on a developmental milestone, or for emotional reasons such as fears or nightmares, adjusting to a move or other changes: a new bed, a new sibling, or a new child care situation.

Preschoolers and Sleep

By the age of three, many regularly occurring sleep problems will have found some resolution. Many children will be either sleeping through the night or putting themselves back to sleep if they do waken.

By age five, there may still be some issues about how much time children spend in their parents' bed, when children go to bed, and when children get up, but most children will have moved from sleeping easily as newborns, to resisting sleep as toddlers, back to a easier entry into sleep.

During the preschool years, children often "play" with the idea of sleep in order to understand it better. They pretend to go to sleep and pretend to put their dollies, animals, and the grown-ups around them to sleep: "You go to sleep now, Daddy. It's night-night time."

Preschool children also begin to recognize the body's signals of fatigue. Even though many continue to resist bedtime or sleep, most can tell when they're tired.

Most preschool children don't yet have a clear idea that anything goes on in the world or that time passes while they are sleeping. However, some three-, four-, and five-year-olds start talking about their dreams.

Issues with fear may continue to affect children's going-to-sleep routines as well as their dreams. One preschool boy, Philipe, began lamenting at bedtime, "I'm worried that the scary thing is going to come." Some children will insist on a light on in their room, others, even those who have never slept in a parent's bed, will show up in their parent's doorway because of nightmares.

The Role of Temperament in Children's Sleep

Within these broad developmental norms, children's sleep patterns vary widely. Some sleep long hours and sleep deeply; there could be a rock concert in the next room and they wouldn't budge. Other children are light sleepers, easily disturbed and hard to settle back down. And some can be both, depending on the circumstances. Shauna, whose son Nicholas prefers to sleep next to her, nursing through the night, explained: "My fifteen-month-old can sleep through anything as long as he's in my arms. But if I put him down, even the buzzer from the dryer a flight of stairs away wakes him."

Some children need thirteen or fourteen hours of sleep; other function well with a lot less. Some children nap until they're five and others give up their naps at a year old. There are children who are up with the sun every day of the week, and there are others who, given their own choice, would play happily into the wee hours of the night. Some children wake up instantly cheerful, bouncing and ready for the day, while others strongly resist coming awake and frequently emerge from bed cranky and out of sorts. Temperament, physical needs, body rhythms, and metabolism all play a role in children's sleep patterns. There is no one standard that fits for all children, as any parent in a large family can attest.

Julie explains: "My middle child almost always falls asleep in the vicinity of other people, on the couch where we're talking or snuggled in my bed. He goes to bed earlier than the other kids, and no matter when he falls asleep, he always wakes up bright and early the next morning. My oldest son likes to sleep in his own room. He's a sound sleeper, and no matter when he goes to bed, he doesn't get up until he has to. And my youngest loves to make little nests around the house to sleep in. Like her oldest brother, she loves to stay up late and sleep in."

Problems can occur in families when children's rhythms and needs around sleep conflict with those of their parents. As children get older and become more self-sufficient in putting themselves to bed, making their own breakfasts, and getting ready in the morning, these individual differences become more manageable. But in children's early years, parents are continually faced with balancing their own needs with their children's sleep patterns.

Sleep in Families: Issues for Parents

Coming to terms with our role in helping children sleep poses a variety of challenges for parents. Once we recover from the daunting discovery that we can't control our child's sleep, we embark on the long process of clarifying, testing, and evaluating just what our role *is* in children's sleep. To this discussion, we bring our history and expectations, our partner's history and expectations, as well as our family's current sleep habits, level of exhaustion, and needs.

In the Middle of the Night: Laura's Story

In the middle of the night.

Eli is three weeks old. I haven't had a dream since he was born. He is in bed with us; he is still nursing every hour or hour and a half. Once he slept for three and a half hours in a row; I was ecstatic. I felt rested the next day.

When he's asleep, I lie awake in bed, wondering if he is breathing. I often touch his chest to check. I always wake up just before he cries, the sheets soaked with milk. We still feel like one body.

Eli is three months old. I sit with him at my breast in the rocking chair. It is silent in the house. His body is warm and delicious in my arms. He has just finished nursing and his heavy head rises and falls on my chest. I have my nose buried in his scalp. I take great whiffs and am intoxicated. We sit like that for a long time. I could put him back down in the bassinet, which sits beside our bed, but I don't want to. I am savoring the moment; I cannot believe I am holding my baby in my arms. After so many years of waiting and wishing and hoping, I feel like I am the luckiest person in the world.

Eli is six months old. His crib is in the corner of our room. It's one in the morning; I brought him into bed with me to nurse. Now he is sitting up between us, wide awake, wanting to play. We pretend we are dead and very, very boring. We make our breathing thick and slow, like we are asleep. Eli chatters to himself for a long time and finally goes back to sleep.

Eli is ten months old. He's been waking up a lot at night. At first it was once a night, but that once grew into twice, then three times, now every hour and a half. It is like having a newborn all over again. When he cries, we lie there frozen with dread, waiting to see if the other one gets up. We have been taking turns: I get up and nurse him once, then Karyn gets up and pats him or rocks him. It helps a little, but we are both exhausted, dragging through our days.

He was up just an hour ago. Now he's crying again. Karyn whispers to me, "I can't believe this. I have to get some sleep." She sighs in exasperation, gets up, and walks over to the crib. She pats Eli. He keeps crying. She says, "Eli, go to sleep." He keeps crying. She says, "I'm not going to pick you up, Eli. It's nighttime and TIME FOR SLEEPING! GO TO SLEEP!"

I remember the times Karyn has gently saved me when I was losing it. I go over and touch her softly on the back. She returns to bed. I pick up Eli and nurse him. Fifteen minutes later, we are all asleep.

Eli is eleven months old. We are letting him cry in the night in hopes that he will go back to sleep on his own. We lie next to each other, listening to his sobs. He is angry, furious at us for not picking him up. He is standing in his crib, peering out at us through the darkness. We call out to him, "We're here, Eli. But we're not going to pick you up. It's night-night time. Go to sleep." I feel impotent, cruel, and determined. I know we must sleep.

Karyn and I lie in bed, afraid to turn over, to whisper, to make any sound at all. If he hears us, his cries increase. We lie next to each other, still and miserable.

After ten minutes of angry crying—and then pausing—and then crying, Karyn says, "Eli, lie down, baby. It's night-night time." We hear a thunk in the crib. He's dropped down on his belly. His sobs subside, but his breathing is ragged for a long time. I feel like I've been through a war. He is finally still and quiet at 4:15 A.M. Karyn's alarm goes off forty-five minutes later.

Eli is thirteen months old. He's been sleeping through the night, more or less. We have just moved him into his own room down the hall. This is his first night in there alone. I feel giddy with freedom. We have our room back!

I am worried that we won't hear him in the night. Karyn assures me we will. She says she'll go in if he wakes up; we don't want to reinforce the idea that he can nurse in the middle of the night. We discuss this in a normal tone of voice, the first time we haven't whispered at night in over a year. I'm feeling op-

(Continued on next page)

timistic. Maybe neither of us will have to go in. People say that babies often sleep better on their own. I imagine a long, solid, private night of sleep, feeling rested and cheerful in the morning.

At a quarter to two, he awakens crying. Karyn goes to him. She is gone a long time. Finally I hear his cries stop. She comes back to bed. The moment she lifts the covers, the crying starts again. It grows frantic in seconds; he sounds scared. Karyn flings back the covers, stands and mutters, "This is going to be a great start to my week." It is Sunday night. She has to work a fourteen-hour day tomorrow. Why did we start this on a Sunday night? Because in the afternoon it seemed like a good idea.

I listen to her soothing him, but he continues sobbing: "Mama! Mama! Mama!" Ten minutes go by. Fifteen. I think to myself, "Why did I think I'd sleep better with him in another room?" She is the one who got up, but I am just as awake as she is, waiting, hoping, praying for silence.

Karyn calls out to me, "Laura, he really needs you."

I put on a robe and meet her in the hall. She hands him over to me. I take him back into his room and nurse him. He gets drowsy and I put him back in his crib. He starts crying immediately. I say, "Eli, I'm going to sit here in the chair until you fall asleep. Settle down." I go back and sit in the chair. His breathing begins to even out. I stand up. The floorboards creak. He cries out again. "Eli," I say, "go to sleep." He calms to the sound of my voice. I go back and sit in the chair. It is 3:00 A.M. I am wide awake. At a quarter to four, I creep out of his room. I head out to my office to write. I know there will be no more sleeping tonight.

In the middle of the night.

Concerns of Parents with Babies and Toddlers

For most new parents, the fact that they are up day and night tending to an infant does not come as a surprise. But as babies get older, exhaustion mounts, and parents begin to look for ways to get their babies to sleep in patterns more closely aligned with the rest of the family.

Sleep deprivation is a major stress in the lives of many parents of babies and toddlers. When we don't get enough sleep, we lose our perspective, our clarity, and sometimes our tempers. It becomes hard to concentrate, to feel good, and eventually to feel much at all.

Dalia, whose seventeen-month-old son, Zach, was waking up five times every night, said, "I never feel well rested. There's not one day since Zach's been born that I've felt well rested. It makes me depressed to be this tired. I feel like my life is a mess and that everything is going wrong. And if someone says to me 'You feel this way because you're really tired. You need to get some sleep,' I know they're right, but I can't identify it myself because I'm too tired to remember that's what the problem is."

As DeeAnna, the exhausted mother of a toddler, remarked with great longing, "I know if I could sleep till seven, my life would be completely different."

Crystal, the mother of two kids under two, put it this way: "My definition of 'sleep through the night' has certainly changed."

In the face of such exhaustion, parents are challenged to figure out how to get the sleep they need. You can follow a formula in a book, but a book doesn't know what you want to teach your child about dependence, independence, or struggle. A book can't respond to your personal perspective on sleep and how it was shaped—who slept with you as a child, how you were or weren't comforted, what happened when you cried, or how bedtime was handled in your family.

Frequently parents are involved in a sleep system that isn't really working for them, even though it may still be working for their child. While rocking, nursing, or driving their child around the neighborhood may have worked at one time for the parents, the system now feels too costly. And if they keep up the same pattern of response, exhaustion and frustration set in.

Janis likes to cite the story from *The World of Pooh* where Pooh is coming down the stairs, bouncing his head on every step: "It is, as far as he knows, the only way of coming downstairs, but sometimes he feels that there really is another way, if only he could stop bumping for a moment and think of it."

Issues for Parents of Older Toddlers and Preschoolers

For parents of older toddlers and preschoolers, much of the raw fatigue of the first two years has waned, yet new challenges rise to fill the void. Parents of older toddlers and preschoolers are faced with their children's pushes for autonomy and initiative. Children want to have more say about when they go to bed, about who helps them, about what they wear, and about whether they brush their teeth.

Kids who've discovered the magic powers of language and negotiation often use bedtime to practice their new skills: "Just one more story, pleeeeeez?" "But I'm thirrrrrrsty. I need a glass of water." Parents are pushed to figure out nightly how much they are willing to negotiate and when to hold the line. And since parents' expectations about time for themselves often increase as children get older, extended bedtime routines may become grounds for growing resentment.

Many children in this age range are giving up their naps, and that transition can be hard on parents. When children nap later, they often aren't tired for bed at night, yet when they skip their naps entirely, they're prone to fall apart in the evenings or not make it through dinner.

As children's fears grow more sophisticated in the preschool years, parents may be again called upon to rescue, reassure, and respond to scared children.

During the preschool years, parents may also feel the need to make changes about where children sleep, for increased privacy, because a new baby has joined the family, or because children have outgrown cribs or small beds. Parents may also want to change the timing of children's sleep, so that children go to bed earlier, get up earlier for child care, or sleep later on weekends.

Most parents of toddlers and preschoolers enjoy some sense of predictability and familiarity around their children's sleep patterns, yet because both children and families are always changing, new sleep strategies may continue to be necessary, well into children's fifth year and beyond.

What Families Have Done: Sleeping Arrangements

There are a myriad of sleeping arrangements in families. Some children sleep with their parents. If things start to feel crowded, parents have put two mattresses together on the floor or have gotten a bigger bed. At some point, either the children or the parents decide they want to sleep separately, and gradually the child learns to sleep somewhere else, sometimes moving first to a pallet on the floor or a bed across the room, and finally to a bed in another room, either alone or with a sibling.

Jessica, the mother of two-year-old Heidi, recalls, "Sleeping with Heidi has always been delightful. I've always loved it. I love hearing her breathe, I love her smell, the feel of her feet pressing against me. Sometimes I hear her talking when she's dreaming. It's a little window into her experience. And it's really fun waking up next to her.

"When my friends complain about their babies waking up, about being so exhausted, I can't relate to it. I feel bad that they're struggling, but I've always enjoyed those times in the middle of the night when Heidi wants to nurse and cuddle. I never really wake up fully and I go back to sleep easily. It's such an intimate connection, and it felt even more important to me once I went back to work."

In other families, parents and children sleep separately, either right from the start or in the first few months of life. In these families, children may sleep in their own bed (cradle, bassinet, or crib) in the parents' room or they may start right away sleeping in a separate room. In some families, parents and children get their cuddling time on their way in or out of sleep; kids come into the "big bed" at five or six in the morning to enjoy that dreamy, sweet morning time together, or everyone piles in one bed in the evening for stories. In other families, physical closeness happens during the day, with hugs, snuggling on the couch, or working on a project together, but not around bedtime or sleep. People go to sleep, wake up, and get up on their own.

Teddy explains how it works in his family: "Teddy Jr. has always slept in his own bed. He loves it in there. I remember when he was a little baby, we'd put him in his crib and he would do this little wiggle, like he was burrowing down a rabbit hole. He is still like that. 'Give me my bed, I'm going to wrap myself up in a little cocoon.' I always go in and look at him before I go to sleep. I love to see his sweet face all wrapped up in his blankets."

Still other families do a little of both. Some play musical beds: Who's sleeping where, and with whom, shifts during the course of the night.

Figuring Out What Works in Your Family

In order to decide what sleeping arrangements work best for their family, parents have to look at their needs for sleep and privacy, what fits in their living space, what's best for their adult relationships, and what actually works.

Before her son was born, Carla decided she

Children Learn Independence in Many Ways

People have very strong opinions about where children should sleep and what parents' role in children's sleep should be. No matter how you do it in your family, there are going to be people who strongly disagree with you.

The experts contradict each other, as well. Some say it's critical that children sleep with you, that a "family bed" builds the security children need to foster later independence. Other experts say it's crucial for children to learn to put themselves to sleep and to sleep alone—that the development of autonomy depends on it.

In reality, there are benefits and drawbacks to each system. Children who sleep independently are often proud of having their "own" bed and frequently learn self-soothing skills earlier. Parents of children who sleep separately gain privacy and time alone to nurture their adult relationships.

On the other hand, children who sleep in a family bed often have fewer bedtime struggles and benefit from the security and closeness of having their parents nearby.

Parents who choose to have a family bed often feel criticized for not giving their children a chance to learn independence. However, children who sleep with their parents have lots of chances to accomplish autonomy at other times during the day.

While most parents living in this country will be influenced by the larger societal push for early independence, it's important to remember that each family also holds its own personal and cultural beliefs about independence, which will greatly influence its decisions around children's sleep.

wanted him to sleep with her. But it didn't work out that way. "Sleeping with Joaquin was like sleeping with a helicopter blade. He kicked me all night long. There was no way I could keep that up."

Michelle and Maceo, who started with Mara sleeping separately, discovered that Mara nursed a lot at night, and that having Michelle get out of bed six times every night was taxing on the whole family. Their solution was to have Mara sleep next to Michelle in bed. When Mara woke up to nurse, Michelle didn't have to wake up all the way, and everyone slept better.

These solutions didn't necessarily fit the parents' original vision, but through trial and error they figured out what worked for their family.

Often parents' beliefs or wishes around sleep conflict with their actual needs; they want to be available to their children throughout the night, but they need to get up in the morning rested enough to be safe and conscious the next day.

Parents use a variety of methods to get their children to sleep independently. One such strategy includes sharing a good-night ritual and putting the child in his own bed while he is still awake. When he cries, the parent comes in to offer quick verbal reassurance but does not pick him up. The parent continues to check-in with the child, at first every five minutes, and then at increasing intervals of time until the child falls asleep on his own. Parents do this for between three days and a week until the child learns to put himself to sleep.

Dalia used this system with Zach. "When he was a year and a half old, I decided that Zach couldn't keep waking up five times a night. I wouldn't care if he woke up once at night, but he didn't wake up once—he was sleeping with me and he was still waking up five times every night. I'm a single mom and I work. I had had it. I couldn't function at all. So I moved him to a crib in his own room and I let him cry himself to sleep.

"I had one really horrible night where he screamed for two hours and threw up twice. I went in every five minutes to reassure him, but he kept screaming. I called my friend at three in the morning and said, 'I don't know if he's ever going to sleep. What am I going to do if he screams for two more hours?' She said, 'Do you want me to come over?' I said, 'No, just talking to you helps.'

"I know it sounds horrible, but I'm glad I did it. The next night Zach slept from nine to five. It's not that he's slept through the night every night since then. In fact, after we moved, I had to do it all over again.

"It was the worst thing I've had to do as a parent, but my experience was that it was much more traumatic for me than it was for him. He was in a great mood the next morning—loving, affectionate, not clingy or irritable. And I was a wreck. It's real hard to listen to your baby scream like that. But in my family, it was the only thing that worked."

FOOD FOR THOUGHT: SLEEP

- What helps me go to sleep? What helps my children go to sleep?

- What are my child's needs for sleep? My own? When either of us doesn't get enough sleep, what does that mean for our family?

- What role do I think adults should play in helping children sleep? How much should children do independently? At six months? A year? Two? Three? Five?

- (For parents with partners) Am I in agreement with my partner about how sleep should be handled in our family? If not, how do our perspectives differ? How do we deal with those differences?

When You Want to Make a Change

Here are some general guidelines for making changes regarding your child's sleep—moving her to a new bed, establishing a new bedtime routine, helping her fall asleep more independently, shifting the time for going to bed or waking, eliminating or shortening a nap, or intervening less in the middle of the night:

• **Approach changes with as much clarity as you can find.** Watching your child struggle brings to the surface any ambivalence you might have about the change you're trying to make. For that reason, it is useful to have as much clarity as possible about changes before you implement them.

Sometimes, because of desperation or past experience, you know that you have the clarity necessary to weather the struggle of change. Other times, parents try a new sleep regime and the first or second night, or fifteen minutes into the first crying spell, they realize "We're not ready to do this yet."

• **Think about the ways this change will be useful for your child as well as for you.** Many parents want to make changes in their children's sleeping habits because the current system is too hard on the adults in the family. This is a vital element in the decision to make a change, but it's also important to think about what your child stands to gain. As kids grow more independent, their sense of competence increases. Also, cutting down on fatigue as well as struggles around sleep is bound to cut down on parental stress. When parents are rested, they are more responsive and better able to meet their children's needs.

• **Make sure that you feel you have given enough of yourself.** Almost all parents feel at one time or another that they haven't given enough to their child. It's the nature of our contemporary parent job description—guilt. There is always more time, energy, attention, listening, watching, playing you could be doing with your child. This feeling of imbalance becomes obvious at times when your child is physically holding on to you and asking for more. It's very hard to say "no" to a child at night when you feel you haven't spent enough time together during the day. If bedtime has been an important connecting time and you are thinking of limiting it, finding other time during the day that you can spend together will be helpful.[1] Then at night you can say 'You've had enough of me and I've had enough time with you. Now I'm going to let you do this part on your own.' "

• **You don't have to make all of the changes at once.** It may feel like too big a task to get all the way from A to Z. It might be more realistic to start with a plan to get from A to B. As Charmaine relates, "Eventually, I would like Simon to sleep *all* the way through the night, but for now I would be happy if I could just get him down from five wakings to three."

Often parents find a temporary solution, even as they work toward a different outcome. You may not want to sleep separately from your partner for the next eighteen years, but it may be the best solution the week in which your son has an ear infection or during the month your daughter is being weaned at night.

• **You don't have to use a rigid formula.** If you learn about a particular strategy for getting children to sleep independently, and you decide you don't like a certain part of the advice, you can still use the parts that make sense to you. It's okay to modify someone else's sytem,to combine a lot of different ideas to come up with what makes sense for you.

[1] See "What Is the Quality of Quality Time?" on p. 49 for specific ideas on creating this kind of time in families.

• **Be creative.** Kirsten and Gil, parents of four-year-old Kyle, three-year-old Tory, and eighteen-month-old Phoebe, felt concerned because Gil always came home from work too late to spend any time with the children. Gil was a "weekend dad," and both he and Kirsten wanted to figure out a way he could have more family time during the week. Their solution was an unusual one—Kirsten started putting the kids to bed at six in the evening, so they'd be asleep by seven. Some nights she went to bed with them; other nights she waited up until Gil got home at ten. Before she went to sleep, Kirsten set the table for a simple breakfast. In the morning, the whole family got up by five-thirty and had a leisurely morning sharing a meal, catching up on the day before, and playing together. Gil took Kyle to preschool on his way to work, much happier for having had time with his kids. Although not all children or family schedules are this flexible, Kirsten and Gil's story can inspire us to look at solutions we might never have considered before.

• **Help prepare children for changes.** Children are best able to make changes when they know what to expect. "I want you to learn to be able to go to sleep by yourself, so tonight after I sing you the 'night-night' song and give you seven kisses and hugs, I will sit in the chair by your bed until you go to sleep, but I won't hold you, and we won't talk or cuddle any more until morning."

• **Make changes gradually, if possible.** Often, by the time parents decide to "do something," they feel desperate to make a change immediately. Yet it is still better to introduce change in small steps rather than all at once. If you have been rocking your child until she falls asleep every night and at naptime, you could start by holding your child until she is almost asleep, then putting her in bed to fall asleep herself. If you have been lying down with your son until he is completely asleep, you could sit on the floor close to him and hold his hand. Making changes gradually allows children to have some time to adjust and develop new skills.

• **Expect resistance.** Most changes that are somebody else's idea involve some degree of struggle for children.

• **Set some parameters for trying new strategies.** When you're trying a new sleep strategy with your child, things often get worse before they get better. Therefore, it is helpful to think beforehand about how long you plan to give the new system to work. As your child is crying and you're getting less sleep than ever, you are likely to say to yourself: "What am I doing this for? I don't want to live like this for the rest of my life." It is important to remember that the struggle you are going through is part of a "change mode" and is not indicative of the way things will be once the change is established.

Most commonly, children begin to learn a new behavior or strategy in three to seven days. This is not to say that the change will be miraculous or complete, but in that amount of time you should see some change or adaptation. If you set up a specific time frame beforehand—say four or five or six nights—you're likely to have more energy and clarity to implement your plan. It helps to know that you're not going to let your daughter cry her eyes out for the next six months.

• **Reevaluate your strategy.** At the end of the designated time, ask yourself: "Have we seen enough progress to continue what we're doing?" "Do we need to come up with another idea or modify this one?" Ironically, it's often just at the point parents decide to give up that something starts to shift.

• **Be flexible.** There will be times you'll choose to be available to kids at night, even when they're older or have already established an independent sleeping pattern. When they're sick, sleeping in a strange place, or are otherwise dealing with new challenges, children may temporarily need more of your support, comfort, and reassurance at night. You can make an exception to your family's regular routine and still go back to the way you usually do things, although some children may need to "relearn" independent sleeping once things are back to normal.

Babies and Sleep: What Parents Can Do

Families with young babies are always working to find a balance of needs. Newborns require round-the-clock attention, but as babies get older they are able to do more and more on their own. Here are things you can do in the first year to ease your baby toward sleeping on her own:

• **Set the stage for success.** Babies benefit from predictable routines and surroundings when they are preparing for sleep. Some babies have more of a need for a consistent schedule than others. Observing your baby will give you valuable information about what helps her sleep, how she relaxes, and what makes it hard for her to sleep.

• **Encourage children to find ways to soothe themselves.** Many babies learn to suck their thumbs or to find other ways to relax or calm themselves. Self-comforting skills are necessary in putting yourself to sleep and also in putting yourself back to sleep once you have awakened.

• **Ease babies into change.** During the first year, parents may want to stop nursing children to sleep or giving them a bottle to fall asleep with. This can also be done by gradually lengthening the amount of time between the end of the nursing or bottle and the baby's falling asleep.

• **Adaptations go both ways.** Parents with babies often find that they need to make significant changes in their lives to deal with a baby's sleep patterns. Some parents have the ability to simplify other aspects of their lives. As Enrico, the father of two young children, put it, "I know from experience that the dust will still be waiting for me in six months."

Other parents find that they need to share responsibilities more equally with their partners or that they need outside help. When this topic came up in Janis's infant development class one night, Veronica, the mother of six-month-old Tasha, explained her family's system: "Al always takes the first shift from bedtime until 2 A.M. and I take the second shift from 2 A.M. until morning."

Don, the father of two young boys under three, shared what works in his family. "Each week, either Miriam or I gets a night to sleep on the couch with earplugs, undisturbed, while the other one takes care of the children's nighttime needs. Knowing we're going to get that one full night of sleep really makes a difference."

And Ingrid, single mother of eight-month-old Caitlin, said, "This class is the only time I'm ever away from Caitlin in the evenings. My best friend, Tia, comes over, feeds Caitlin, gives her a bath, and puts her to sleep. It's such a treat to get home from class, all excited, and not to have to put the baby to bed. Then Tia and I sit up and talk. I'm always tired on Thursdays, but it's worth it."

Toddlers and Preschoolers: When You Want to Move Children Toward Independent Sleep

As children get older, most parents want them to sleep more independently. Here are some ideas for encouraging greater self-sufficiency at bedtime:

• **Set up a consistent bedtime routine.** A routine offers children a predictable series of things that help them begin preparing their bodies to relax. This routine can include quiet play, a bath, a snack, reading stories, singing songs, teeth-brushing, talking about the day, or other activities that help the child wind down. Some families enjoy being close physically before going to sleep: cuddling, lying down together, sharing massages.

In some families variable schedules and personal styles don't lend themselves to a consistent routine, and the stresses involved in

Special Stories at Bedtime

For many children, the time when they start to relax, just before they go to sleep, is a time to reflect on and integrate the experiences of the day. If you can allow time for talking about the day, this may be one of your best opportunities. With nonverbal children, you can be the one to talk about their day. But even children who can talk sometimes don't know how to start, and it's useful for you to offer a small story that they can relate to about your day: "This morning, I was all ready to eat my Shredded Wheat for breakfast and I went to the cupboard, pulled out the box, turned it upside down and NOTHING came out. It was empty. I was disappointed. Guess what I did?" Soon children begin to chime in with stories of their own. When you include feelings and struggles in your stories, children get the message that this is appropriate and may begin to include them in their stories as well.

Sometimes these stories of the day expand into family history stories. One father and son developed stories about experiences they had that they would tell together. Each one of them had their part of the familiar tale. This father also wrote them down and made a book that they could share of their stories. You can also develop shared stories by telling the same story again, and again, periodically stopping to say ". . . and then what do you think happened?"

Children love stories about themselves and their families. It is important when you are picking stories to tell that you choose stories that are respectful and loving. Although children love humor, they can be very sensitive if they feel that they are being made fun of.

Some parents are natural storytellers, finding that they can make up and weave tales from one night to the next, building characters, adding fantasy and adventures as they go. Some of these stories contain dilemmas (that might look a lot like the child's own struggles of the day) for which children can help discover solutions: "When Gabriella the Goat got up one morning, her dad told her, 'We are going to the park today. What will you wear?' Gabriella didn't want to get dressed. Her pajamas were all warm and comfortable and so she told her dad, 'I'm not getting dressed!' What do you think her dad did?' or 'If you were Gabriella's dad, what would you do?' "

Since these tales, stories, and recaps of the day are always evolving and changing, it's fun to periodically record them on tape, so that you not only have a record of your child's voice and vocabulary at an early age, but also some favorite stories to play back. Unless your child is very comfortable with the tape recorder, you may want to put it out of sight while you are recording. If the child is focused on the fact that you are recording, his participation may change and the activity may turn into exploring the machine.

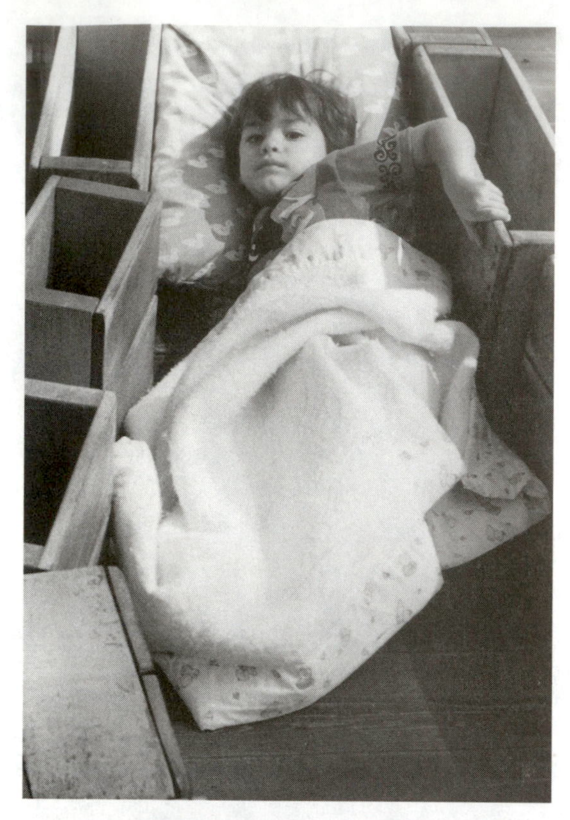

setting up a routine in this situation would outweigh the benefits. Sometimes in these families parents are willing to provide more support for helping children go to sleep, and that becomes the consistency. Other families have a kind of loose routine or a set of possible things they might do during the bedtime ritual, which becomes what's predictable for that family.

• **Give children choices about their bedtime ritual.** Because so much resistance over bedtime has to do with children's needs for autonomy, it is useful to give them a chance to make some limited choices: "Would you like to pick out two or three stories for bedtime?" "Shall we sing our new funny song or would you like a different one?" "Do you want to brush your teeth before or after you put on pajamas?" Older children may be able to handle more open choices: "What would you like us to do together before you go to bed tonight?"

• **Try to keep other struggles out of the bedtime ritual.** If brushing teeth is a struggle, try doing it earlier or at a different time of day.

• **Observe what helps your child relax and provide it.** Young children haven't yet figured out just how their bodies work, so it can be useful for parents to observe what seems to help or hinder their sleep. Certain TV shows, video games, or roughhousing may make it hard for children to relax and go to sleep, so you might choose to limit these activities in the time right before bed. You may also notice that cuddling, reading, listening to music, bathing, or having some time alone helps your child get ready for sleep, or that some active play outside in the afternoon precedes an easier transition to bed. Some parents discover that if their child takes too long a nap, she can't settle down at night. Alternately, other parents observe the somewhat ironic fact that their child is more able to calm down for sleep if he has had a nap and less able to if he hasn't.

• **Ask your child five minutes before you leave if there is anything else he or she needs.** Upon being left to their own devices to fall asleep, most children will systematically go through the list of things they know you won't be able to ignore. These may include hunger, thirst, toileting, kisses, and fear. If you have checked out their needs beforehand, it will be easier for you to let them know that you will help them with these in the morning—or that they can help themselves.

• **Help your child learn ways to relax.** At about the same time your child starts to actively use her imagination, you can begin talking to her about relaxing things as she falls asleep: "Think about being on the back of a big gentle horse, rocking and rocking you to sleep." You can ask her to pretend that she is in her favorite place: "Can you imagine that you are floating on a stream and little bits of sunlight are coming down all around you?" With four- and five-year-olds, you may suggest that they think about what they want to dream about.

When children complain that they can't sleep, you can teach them that they don't have to. When Ellen's son Max says "I can't go to sleep," she tells him, "You don't have to. Just rest and sleep will come to you."

• **Be clear about where your jurisdiction ends.** While many of us would like to have it otherwise, we can't make children go to sleep. All we can do is set the stage for it to happen. We can require that children spend time alone in their rooms or sleeping spaces, but as Ellen Galinsky and Judy David make clear in their book *The Preschool Years*, "It is the *parent's* responsibility to put the child to bed; it's the *child's* responsibility to fall asleep."

Some of the largest struggles families have about sleep arise because of confusion about these roles. Ironically, the goal of falling sleep sometimes becomes impossible because of the tension we create trying to make it happen.

In her book *Whole Parent, Whole Child*, Polly Berends reminds us, "The baby needs peace more than sleep. Believe it or not, so do you. So don't struggle over sleep; just learn to be peaceful together." If we, as parents, can come to terms with what we really get to control, bedtime struggles will diminish.

• **Be a human fence.** Many of us decide that we want our children to be more independent sleepers after they are capable of climbing out of their beds or cribs. Without environmental limits, there are complications when we try to leave and children don't want us to—for instance, they can follow us.

If this is happening in your family, you need to decide how you want to enforce the limit of "staying in your bed" or "staying in your room." Some people figure out an environmental solution, such as a gate, but most people have to do "the human fence." The human fence, quietly, gently, and without fanfare, lecture, reminders, or anger, takes the child back, each of the seven, thirty-nine, fifty-five, or one hundred times she gets out of bed.

If you give your child those little reminders—"Now, you know you are supposed to be in bed," "It's night-night time. You're supposed to be in your room"—it may be worth her while to keep getting up just to hear what you will say next. If you get angry, as most of us are apt to do in that situation, that also becomes an interesting and worthwhile interaction. You will be able to avoid anger more easily if you understand that it is healthy for her to want to push this limit as far as it goes *and* if you have a place for yourself to talk about how hard it is to stay consistent, clear, and firm. The good news is that if you are clear and consistent for several nights, your child will eventually get the message and the testing will most likely subside.

Helping Children Who Are Having Nightmares

In the last half of the first year, when babies start having tangible fears during the day, they may also experience those same images at night and wake up afraid. In the second year of life, children's nightmares can move beyond just a startling image to a more developed sequence that is frightening.

Often children can't talk about or explain what was scary. Sometimes they have night terrors where they don't even seem to wake up, even though their eyes are open. But even if you can't figure out what the nightmare is about, you can still support your child by letting him express his feelings and listening carefully to what he tells you.

Recommended Bedtime Books

Bedtime is a traditional time for reading to children. Even babies under a year might enjoy chewing over a good book before bed. With older children, books can become a special part of the nightly routine.* Along with some standard bedtime classics, we've included some lesser well-known favorites:

Books for Babies

Goodnight Moon, Margaret Wise Brown, illustrated by Clement Hurd, HarperCollins.

First published in 1947, this book is a favorite in many households. The simple rhyming text and ritual of saying good night to all favorite things is a comfort to many young children. Ages 1 and up.

In the Tall, Tall Grass, Denise Fleming, Henry Holt & Company.

A colorful book about what happens in the tall, tall grass throughout the day and into the night. Simple rhyming text. Ages 18 months and up.

Time for Bed, Mem Fox and Jane Dyer, Harcourt, Brace and Co.

Exquisitely illustrated poem begins "It's time for bed, little mouse, little mouse, Darkness is falling all over the house." Shows various baby animals with a parent, each saying a special good-night reassurance. Some animals sleep with a parent, some sleep independently. Ages 18 months and up.

On Mother's Lap, Ann Herbert Scott, Clarion Books.

A wonderfully illustrated book about a young Inuit boy who's sure there isn't room on his mother's lap for him, his boat, his puppy, his dolly, his reindeer blanket, *and* his baby sister. The mother's calm reassuring voice saying "There's always room on Mother's lap" makes this book especially important for older siblings. But all parents and children can thoroughly enjoy it for its simple clarity and beauty. Ages 18 months to adult.

Ten, Nine, Eight, Molly Bang, Mulberry Books.

An African American father puts his daughter to bed in this delightful countdown bedtime book. Ages 18 months to 3.

More, More, More, Said the Baby, Vera B. Williams, Greenwillow Books.

Beautiful paintings illustrate this delightful story of three children who always want "more" of whatever game is going on! A very wonderful book for the youngest child. Shows ethnic diversity and fathers as nurturers. Ages: 18 months and up.

Books for Twos

Tucking Mommy In, Morag Loh, Orchard Books.

A lovely story about a very tired Southeast Asian American mother who falls asleep while trying to tuck her daughters into bed, so the daughters reverse roles and tuck Mommy in. This book shows the girls as both competent and nurturing, and their father comes home from work at the end of the book and helps tuck them in. We love that the house shows some real-life mess. Ages: 2 and up.

The Midnight Farm, Reeve Lindbergh and Susan Jeffers, Dial Books.

An Anglo mother and son take a poetic counting journey through their farm to see what farm animals do at night. Age 2 and up.

Grandfather Twilight, Barbara Berger, Philomel Books.

Soft illustrations and a simple, well-paced text follow the twilight-colored grandfather through the forest to the seashore where he nightly launches his pearl that is to become the moon to the "silence above the sea." Ages 2 and up.

The Napping House, Audrey and Don Wood, Harcourt Brace Jovanovich.

A humorous look at an extended family bed. Everyone—the fly, the cat, the snoring grandma—

* See "Sharing Books with Children" on p. 300 for guidelines on choosing books and reading to kids.

ends up in one bed in this book, until something happens! Anglo family. Ages 2 and up.

Pigs in Hiding, Arlene Dubanevich, Four Winds Press.

A very funny book about a game of hide-and-seek in which one pig fails to see hundreds of other obviously hidden pigs. Children who have discovered hiding games love finding the pigs. The humor only grows as children's awareness of "hiding" increases. Ages 2 and up.

Night Is Coming, W. Nikola-Lisa and Jamichael Henterly, Scholastic Books.

A beautifully poetic story of night setting on a farm. This book has a lovely peaceful quality to it and features a grandfather. Young children will enjoy the photos; older children will appreciate the poetry, as well. Ages 2 and up.

Close Your Eyes, Jean Marzollo, illustrated by Susan Jeffers, Dial Books.

A dreamy book that tells children they can be anything they want to be—and go anywhere they want to go—once they fall asleep. Shows an Anglo father putting his child to bed with a fair amount of realistic struggle. Ages 2 and up.

Mama, Do You Love Me? Barbara M. Josse and Barbara Lavalle, Chronicle Books.

A captivating story set in the Arctic about a young girl testing the limits of her mother's love—and finding it unconditional. Powerful and heartwarming with beautiful illustrations. Ages 2 and up.

Books for Three and Up

On the Day You Were Born, Debra Frasier, Harcourt, Brace and Co.

Beautifully illustrated book that poetically describes how on the day you were born, the world was waiting just for you; the migrating animals, the burning sun, the quiet moon, the ocean, the wind, and the rain. Ages 3 and up.

The Salamander Room, Anne Mazer and Steve Johnson, Dragonfly Books.

Richly illustrated story about an Anglo boy who brings home a salamander. In making an appropriate habitat for it, he slowly turns his room into a forest until his bed is under the stars with owls hooting and crickets singing. Ages 3 and up.

Owl Moon, Jane Yolen and John Schoenherr, Scholastic Books.

Beautifully written peaceful story about an Anglo father who takes his daughter out "owling" in the deep, cold winter night. Ages 3 and up.

In the Middle of the Night, Kathy Henderson and Jennifer Eachus, Macmillan.

In the middle of the night, the baby and the city are asleep—or are they? Astronomers are watching the night sky, people are sorting mail on the night train, a baby wakes and is comforted. In the hospital, someone very old dies and someone long awaited is born. Beautiful realistic illustrations accompany the poetic text. Ethnic diversity. Ages 4 and up.

If we think about dreams as our mind's way of processing things that happened to us when we were awake, we can look at nightmares as tools for the exploration and expression of fears. If your child is having nightmares, it can be useful to think about what he is grappling with. If you can figure out what is scaring him, you might be able to help him work on it during the day.

When children can begin to talk about their dreams (usually around four or five), there are a few things you can do to help:

• **Ask children about their dreams** (nightmares and otherwise). If you use open-ended questions, you're more likely to get a response from your child. "Tell me about your dream." "And then what happened?" "What did she look like?" "Is there more?" You can also repeat your child's words back to encourage him and let him know you are listening: "She was bigger than the sky?"

• **Practice "rewriting" nightmares with children.** Help children "rewrite" or add on to nightmares. "You didn't like it when the big scary fish was climbing in the boat. Where did you want that big scary fish to go instead?" This helps children begin to understand that they can affect the content of their dreams and puts nightmares in the same categories as other stories you can change.

• **Suggest to children that they can have some choice in their dreams.** Ask, "What would you like to dream about tonight? Maybe we could tell the story about the big scary fish who learned how to be friendly."

• **Ask children if they'd like to illustrate or tell the story of their dreams.** The more children are able to talk about and explore their nightmares, the less scary they seem. Ask them if they'd like to draw a picture from their dream. (Even children who aren't yet drawing representationally may want to draw some significant scribbles and tell you the story that goes along with them.) You can write down their story and read it back to them.

• **Use books when appropriate.** Four and five-year-olds can sometimes benefit from books that address the topic of nightmares. (See "Books to Help Kids Deal with Fears" on p. 108.)

• **Suggest to children that they could wake themselves up.** Older children may be receptive to the information "This is a dream and you could choose to wake up and not have it any more." People vary in their ability to do this. Janis still can't do it, but her seven-year-old, Maya, can.

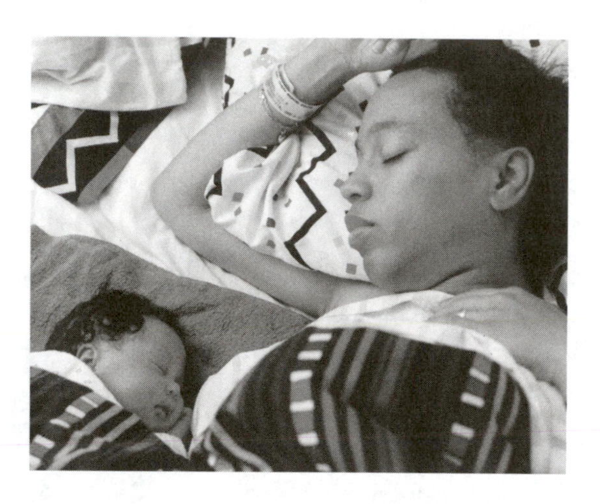

Eventually We All Find Sleep

In families where sleep is uncertain, elusive, and seemingly unobtainable, achieving successful sleep for children and parents can feel miraculous. Often figuring it out takes more energy and resourcefulness than parents ever imagined they had. Yet, over and over again, families figure it out—not always gracefully, smoothly or rapidly, but almost always with increased insight and understanding about themselves and their children.

15. Children and Eating: Building a Healthy Relationship to Food

"It tastes like frosting for fruit." —Bonnie
"It gives you a pink face." —Alice
"Mine tastes like flowers." —Amelia
"This tastes so good, I'm going to take a long time eating it." —Bonnie

KIDS COMMENTING ON THE FRUIT DIP THEY JUST MADE[1]

Providing food for our children can be one of the most satisfying and delightful aspects of our parenting. Feeding children is a tangible way we nurture, nourish, and care for them. Experiencing your body's amazing capacity to manufacture milk, carefully preparing your daughter's first bottle, and watching your son's face the first time he licks a banana are just the beginnings of your relationship with your child around food.

Watching your children develop eating skills can also provide special, sometimes humorous moments. We chuckle observing Ginger as she learns to drink, carefully bringing her cup to her lips and just as carefully pouring her juice down her shirt. We hold our breath watching Carlo capture a bit of applesauce on the end of his spoon, just to have it slither off as it approaches his mouth. We cringe as Sasha delicately picks up his bowl of soup and turns it over onto his head, saying "hat?" As we watch the miracle of children learning to feed themselves successfully, we may also reflect back on some of our early experiences with eating.

Food is one of the ways we share childhood memories with our children. Delighting in early-morning hot chocolate together, sharing a picnic in the park, or teaching your child how to roll out tortilla dough can be opportunities to pass on significant traditions from one generation to the next.

Most of us, however, also experience challenges as we try to provide for our children's nutritional needs. As parents, we have lots of information to sort through. We've all read conflicting reports about the best kind of formula, the effect of sugar on children, the dangers of cholesterol, and whether butter or margarine is better.

Parents are also faced with providing food for people who have ever-changing nutritional needs and desires. Once you've finally figured out how many nursings will suffice or which formula to use, you're faced with introducing solids. Once you've firmly established a sugar-free diet for your child, Uncle Eddie comes

[1] Mollie Katzen, and Ann Henderson, *Pretend Soup and Other Real Recipes: A Cookbook for Preschoolers & Up* (Berkeley: Tricycle Press, 1994), p. 90.

In Our Family, We Always . . .

How we eat, what we eat, and what we teach our children about food are all strongly tied to our own family history and cultural traditions. In some families, food is utilitarian—a necessary fuel to make your body go. Food is prepared simply, with little fuss, and eating is not a big focus or center of activity. In other homes, food preparation, presentation, and mealtime hold great importance, and food is much more than simply a source of nourishment.

In many families, food is a vehicle of communication and family togetherness. Mauro recalls, "You couldn't visit anyone in my family without being sat down to a meal. It didn't matter if you were hungry or not, you had to eat. Feeding people was the main way people showed that they cared."

Laura recalls, "I still have my mother's recipes for ruggelach, stuffed cabbage, chopped liver, and brisket. One of the most pleasurable parts of our relationship are the times I'm in the kitchen, preparing for a big holiday, when I call her long distance, three thousand miles away, to ask for some critical detail of one of her recipes. It's an intimacy we both savor."

Food can also hold a vital place in the maintenance of health, with certain foods designated to provide specific health benefits and others as designated cures for illness. Velma recalls, "Mama always fed the pot liquor from the collard greens to the baby when he wasn't feeling well."

Isabel remembers, "My mother always made vitamina, a kind of Brazilian smoothie full of bananas, oranges, apples, and mango."

Food also plays a role in the emotional health of many families and is frequently used to provide comfort or show affection. Aida remembers, "Lumpia. I still dream of my mother's lumpia. No one can make it the way she did."

Albert recalls, "Macaroni and cheese is great when you are feeling low, but you have to serve it with Campbell's Tomato Soup."

In most families and cultures, food goes along with family gatherings, celebrations, and rites of passage. Gloria remarks, "Mama Mamie's Christmas cake was a red, green, white layer coconut cake, but Aunt Lena always made the best sweet potato pies."

Ophelia recalls, "Every New Year's, you could find my daughter and me in the kitchen, mixing the masa, cooking the chicken, and making the tamales. It was a lot of work, but how could we have New Year's without tamales?"

And Sari remembers, "As a child I always loved chopping the apples, walnuts, and cinnamon for charoses in the big wooden bowl that belonged to my grandmother. Passover was the only time of the whole year we brought that bowl down."

Family events and trips are often occasions for other kinds of special food. Pete recalls, "My grandmother used to make a big pot of adobo for our three-day fishing trips. I remember watching her tie it down in the boat."

Leon remembers, "When we took a car trip, we brought along hard-fried chicken because it didn't need refrigeration."

And Sally relates, "We always stop for fast food when we are on a long trip—no other time, just when we are driving for a long time in the car."

In our daily lives, how and when we eat also says a lot about our family and cultural traditions. Aurora recalls fondly, "There was always a pot of something on the stove, black beans and rice and platanos, slowly cooking. We didn't really sit down for meals, we just picked a lot from the big pot."

Dafna remembers, "In our family, rice was omnipresent. Between Brazilian and Chinese traditions, if you didn't eat rice, you didn't really eat. If I ate dinner at a friend's house and they didn't have rice, I'd always come home and eat a second dinner."

And Janis muses, "In my kitchen there is always some evidence of food: dirty dishes, someone cooking or eating, leftovers around, or bags of groceries to be put away. I'm always a little surprised when I go to my cousin Roy's house. I have never seen any trace of food in that kitchen. I know they must eat, but the kitchen is always immaculate with nothing on the counters."

over and gives her a tub of gummy worms. Many of us also have to negotiate with a partner who has different ideas about food and eating than we do.

Building family patterns around food is an evolving process, and teaching our children good eating habits is an important goal. Fortunately, every day our families need to eat, and every day we get to develop and refine our perspective and practices around food.

You Provide the Food, Your Child Decides What to Eat

What is our goal in feeding children? On the most obvious level, it is to see that they are well nourished. But it's also important for parents to take their job a step further—*to help their children build a healthy relationship to their appetites and to food*.

What does this mean? Ideally, having a healthy relationship to food means being able to recognize your hunger, identify what you need to eat, enjoy your food, and stop eating when you've had enough.

Critical to parents' helping children develop these skills are three things: clarity about our role in feeding children, a respect for children's hunger and fullness, and avoidance of power struggles around food.

A groundbreaking study done in the 1930s by physician Clara Marie Davis made the discovery that babies would choose a balanced diet for themselves when offered a variety of healthy foods "prepared as simply as possible without the addition of salt or other seasoning and served . . . each in its own dish." [2] For the study, the seven- to thirty-month-old babies sat at low tables, were given their own spoons, and were attended by a nurse who sat by quietly with another spoon and helped only if the baby pointed to a certain food. The babies were allowed to eat as much as they wanted of the foods they chose, "without comment on, or correction of, their manners or their choices." [3]

Despite varying preferences and occasional food jags (like the baby who ate nine eggs for dinner one night), the babies thrived and consistently chose a diet that included all the nutrients necessary for healthy growth and development. Davis concluded two things from

[2] The foods offered to the babies included meats (muscle cuts): beef, lamb, and chicken; glandular organs: liver, kidney, brains, sweetbreads; seafood: haddock; cereals: whole wheat (unprocessed), oatmeal, barley, corn and rye; eggs; raw milk and lactic (sour) milk; fruits: apples, oranges, bananas, peaches, pineapples; vegetables: lettuce, cabbage, spinach, cauliflower, peas, beets, carrots; and sea salt.

[3] Descriptions of this study have been taken from two articles: "Can Babies Choose Their Food?" by Clara Marie Davis in *The Parents' Magazine*, January 1930, pp. 22–23, 42–43, and "Do Young Children Know Instinctively What to Eat: The Studies of Clara Davis Revisited" by Mary Story and Judith Brown in the January 8, 1987, issue of *The New England Journal of Medicine*.

her research: first, that children should be offered only those foods that have the highest nutritional values, and second, that children's appetites are a reliable indicator of the amount and type of food they should eat.

Davis's studies were revolutionary in her day (and perhaps in ours, as well) and have formed the basis of much medical and nutritional advice for the last sixty years. Her research teaches us that given a choice of fresh, unprocessed foods in an open, no-pressure atmosphere, children will select a balanced diet for themselves, not necessarily in any one day, but over a period of time.

These findings have often been misinterpreted to imply that kids will be able to choose a balanced diet given *any choice of foods*. Yet a critical variable in Davis's research was that children were not offered any of the highly salted, sweetened, processed, or convenience foods that are a regular part of so many families' diets today. While it is important to trust children's inner wisdom about food, it is also essential that we do our part—giving them healthy choices to choose from.

Ellyn Satter, a contemporary nutritionist who's worked extensively with children with eating disorders, has further defined the roles parents and children should play in ensuring that children eat well. In her book *Child of Mine: Feeding with Love and Good Sense*, she outlines a "division of responsibility in feeding." She writes, "To be successful in feeding your child, you have to be able to share responsibility with him: You, the parent, are responsible for what he is offered to eat. But *he* is responsible for how much of it he eats." [4]

More specifically, she writes, parents are responsible for "selecting and buying food, making and presenting meals, regulating the timing of meals and snacks, presenting foods in a form the child can handle, allowing eating methods a child can master, making family mealtimes pleasant, helping the child participate in family meals, helping the child focus on his eating, and maintaining standards of behavior at the table." They are not, however, responsible for "how much a child eats, whether he eats or how his body turns out." [5]

Trusting Children's Food Choices: Issues for Parents

Despite this research, it's challenging for many parents to give their children the freedom to choose their food and how much they want to eat. Many of us, who were schooled in the four food groups and the importance of a balanced

[4] Ellyn Satter, *Child of Mine: Feeding with Love and Good Sense* (Palo Alto: Bull Publishing Company, 1983, 1991), p. 406.

[5] Ibid., p. 424.

diet, may find it difficult to give up the idea that it's our job to make sure children eat the right combination of foods at each and every meal.

Additionally, many of us feel that there's a direct link between what our children eat and our competence as nurturers. Not only are we supposed to prepare the food, we're also supposed to make sure it gets in our kid's mouth.

Julie remembers, "I steamed squash out of the garden for Randy when he was seven months old. He ate it with relish and I thought, 'Oh, he loves my cooking!' Later that same afternoon, I took him to the beach and he was eating handfuls of sand with as much enthusiasm as he'd eaten my specially steamed garden-fresh zucchini. I was crushed."

The Fallacy of One More Bite

A common parental myth is that "one more bite" is better. At one time or another, most parents have airplaned food into babies' mouths or pushed spoons of baby peas into the faces of children who were turning away and holding their lips tight. We have thought we were supposed to cajole, trick, or otherwise pressure children into eating.

Jenny explains: "On a theoretical level, I believe that Carly knows her body and what she needs to eat better than I do. There's been evidence of that—days she's come and asked me for carrots. Some days she won't even touch broccoli, and then the next day she eats more broccoli than I've ever seen her eat before. So I try to relax, set a meal in front of her, and let her eats what she eats.

"But Carly is really tiny and she hardly eats anything. Sometimes when she's not eating, I think to myself, 'She's never going to grow! She *has* to eat.'

"As a result of my own fears, I've gotten involved in some of the same power struggles I got into over food with my own mother. If I didn't finish a meal, it showed up a few hours later when snack time rolled around. I don't do that to Carly, but I have caught myself saying 'Mommy's not going to let you eat your cookie until you have two more bites of your dinner.' Then I stop and ask myself, 'Why is it better if she takes two more bites? Do I really want to teach her to ignore the fact that she's full?'

"Whenever I start to get uptight about what Carly is eating, I remind myself that she has tons of energy, that she runs around all the time, that she's healthy and clearly thriving. When I really look at my daughter, it's clear I have nothing to worry about."

"But He Eats More Than a Truck Driver"

Some children put away enormous quantities of food, and the parents of these children may worry as much as the parents of light eaters. If these big eaters have round little bodies, their parents may even feel more concerned. Parents of these children may be tempted to limit their child's food intake, but when we stop children from eating before they feel full, we fail to respect their bodies and their appetites. Most kids who eat large quantities of food do so because that is what their bodies need. Our job remains to offer a variety of healthy food, to make sure that food is not being offered as "comfort" or "reward," and, if necessary, to remind friends and family not to tease children because of their size.

Parents also struggle to accept children's appetites when kids are sick or teething. Just when we're most concerned about their health, they refuse to eat. Our children are small in size (relative to us), and even a slight weight loss can frighten us.

As parents we are asked to walk a delicate balance as we monitor our child's physical health for signs of illness or other problems. On the one hand, we do this by using our adult wisdom and experience, consulting medical professionals and talking to experienced parents. On the other, we do it by trusting our observations and intuition and the wisdom of our child, especially around his own bodily functions. We need all of these elements to make informed decisions about our child's health. Each factor needs to be looked at, weighed, and put in balance with the others to provide the basis for the best decisions possible.

Infants, Young Babies, and Food: A Developmental Overview

Healthy babies are born with reflexes that ensure that they will be nourished. They cry when they are hungry. They automatically know how to suck and will "root" or turn toward a nipple that touches their cheek.

Babies can thrive on breast milk or formula for at least six months. At that point, most are ready to venture into the world of solid foods. Many babies begin to show an interest in eating solids as early as four or five months old, watching intently as the people around them make things disappear into their mouths.

There are several challenges for babies when they first begin to eat solids: They have to become accustomed to new flavors and textures, learn to "chew" or swallow in a new way, and figure out how to get a spoon into their mouths.

Babies have different responses to their first experiences with solid food. Some gobble it down ravenously as if to say "Where have you been keeping this great stuff?" Others have less enthusiastic responses, sometimes frowning or shuddering. Charlotte recalls, "The first time Wesley tried sweet potatoes he was seven months old. He made the most incredible grimace and stuck his tongue—and a little glob of sweet potatoes—right back out again."

These are natural responses to new flavors as well as to new textures. Food may also be ejected out of your baby's mouth because he hasn't yet learned how to use his tongue to work his food back. Instead he uses the same motion he used to suck, which thrusts the food out of his mouth.

Food is a sensory experience for babies. They smear it, lick it, pat it, rub it in their hair, and sometimes get it in their mouths. Babies explore food as a way to get to know it. Since most food shows up on their tray as a stranger, they want to make friends with it before they put it in their mouths. Because they are tactile learners, babies don't really learn about bananas or applesauce or milk *until* they've squished them through their fingers.

Ralph was amazed watching eight-month-old Leota eat. "I was holding the container of yogurt and offering her small spoonfuls. First, she grabbed the spoon with her fist, next she took a fistful of yogurt and applied it to her hair, then she reached for the whole yogurt container."

Foods for Your Baby's First Year*

The following is a recommended guideline for when to start feeding foods other than breast milk or formula.

AGE	WHAT FOODS TO START	COMMENTS
Birth to 4–6 months	Breast milk and/or formula only	No solid foods, although this can vary with particular child and situation.
4–6 months	Infant cereal	Start with iron-enriched rice, oats, or barley by spoon once a day. You can buy boxes of infant cereal and mix it with breast milk or formula, or grind your own uncooked brown rice in the blender. Cook it, 1 part rice to 4 parts boiling water. Do not use sweeteners.
6–8 months	Strained or mashed yellow or green vegetables Strained or mashed fruits Can sip from a cup you help hold	Do not give corn, tomatoes, citrus fruits, pineapples, or berries until 12 months. Offer two meals a day.
8–9 months	Cottage cheese** Plain yogurt** Strained baby food meats Mashed fruits/vegetables Finger foods: —toast squares** —strips or slices of cooked vegetables —peeled, soft or steamed fruit slices	Begin changing consistency of foods and offering finger foods. Offer small amounts of juice, water, or formula from cup. Offer three meals a day.
9–10 months	Eggs yolks Small, tender pieces of meat Fish, beans, tofu	Do not give the egg whites yet.
10–12 months	Food from family table Child can do lots of self-feeding: —vegetables and fruits —cereal, bread** —beans, fish, meats, tofu —potatoes, rice, noodles —cheese**	Some babies do not like seasoned foods.
One year	Can add: —whole milk, whole egg —citrus products, tomatoes —peanut butter —berries and pineapple	Can eat regular family meals, unless baby has shown some allergic symptoms. Cut up or grind food depending on her number of teeth.

* Thanks to pediatric nurse practitioner Suzanne Shaw for permission to use this food chart.
** These foods are common allergens. Watch for possible allergic reactions.

(Continued on next page)

Important Guidelines

1. The most common foods to which babies have an allergic reaction are milk, egg white, wheat, citrus, pineapples, berries, tomatoes, corn, nuts (including peanut butter), and chocolate. It is best to avoid these foods in the first year of life, especially if you have allergies in your family. Common allergic symptoms include chronic congestion, upset stomach, diarrhea, constipation, skin rashes, and vomiting.
2. *Do not give honey in the first year.* Infants can develop botulism from honey.
3. Do not give your baby small, hard foods that he can choke on such as nuts, peanuts, seeds, popcorn, raw apples, raw carrots, and the like. Hot dogs and uncut grapes are also choking hazards.
4. Hold your baby while feeding her a bottle. Propping a bottle in a baby's mouth may cause problems, especially if she is prone to ear infections.
5. Offer small amounts at first and gradually increase the amount offered. Start with a couple of teaspoons and increase slowly to a couple of tablespoons. Two to four tablespoons is an average serving of food for a nine- to twelve-month-old.
6. Your baby is the best judge of how much to eat. Never force your baby to finish a bottle or serving of food.
7. Do not add salt or sugar to homemade baby foods.
8. Desserts are not recommended since they provide few, if any, nutrients. Also watch for "hidden" sugars in yogurt, Jell-O, and fruit drinks.

In the first year of life, babies who sit in high chairs also discover the joys of gravity, the thrill of dropping beans, crackers, Cheerios, or cereal over the edge of their chair. Parents usually tire of this game after a few minutes, but babies generally enjoy it for several weeks or more.

Older babies and young toddlers often continue to spit out food. This is normal and is their way of saying, "I don't recognize this flavor or texture." Or "I'm full." Even though it can be frustrating or unappetizing for parents to see the food come back out, it is an important part of the self-regulating that young children do.

Infants and Young Babies: Developing a Healthy Relationship to Food

Even with newborns, parents can help children build healthy eating habits as well as providing nourishment. Here are some ways:

• **Feed babies when they're hungry.** It is important to a baby's physical and emotional health that they are fed when they are hungry. Asking infants to "wait" more than a few minutes to be fed creates anxiety and frustration for them.

• **Establish two-way communication with your baby.** Through a set of complex communications, you and your baby will work out which of her cries signify hunger. There will be some trial and error when you try to feed her and she lets you know she's not hungry or when she has to intensify her cry to get you to understand, but eventually you'll smooth out the kinks in your system. Likewise, a baby may use "body language" to tell you she is full. Turning her head away, pulling away from the nipple, and keeping her mouth closed can all signal "I've had enough."

• **Make loving contact with babies as you feed them.** Feeding babies provides opportunities to nurture and love them. Holding them, making eye contact, talking, and listening all let babies know that we cherish them.

• **Feed solids with a spoon, not in a bottle.** Babies can better regulate their intake of cereal when they are eating off a spoon rather than sucking it from a bottle. Babies need to learn how to eat and swallow using a spoon; if a baby is not ready to eat from a spoon, he is probably not ready for solid foods.

• **Introduce new foods gradually.** Adding new foods one at a time, and waiting a few days in between, allows you to see how your baby responds to each new food. If your son has eaten several different new foods at once and later breaks out in a rash, you won't know which food was the culprit.

• **As much as possible, feed babies the same food as the rest of the family.** The more children are included in the family diet early on, the more readily they will eat what everybody else eats later on. While we can't let babies and young toddlers have everything that they see us eating, if children are excluded from the family eating pattern for long enough, they often begin to exclude themselves. The family food will feel strange to them and they will continue to demand specially prepared food.

Many of us have expended enormous effort to prepare or buy special foods for our babies well into their second year, thinking that they wouldn't be able to eat what the rest of the family was eating. In fact, there are probably several things in most meals that can be mashed for babies to eat: the carrots, potatoes, and broth from the soup; the rice, squash, and tofu from the stir fry; plain noodles, mashed-up collard greens, cornbread, or rice. As Janis recalls, "In our family we used to wash Leon's spicy sauce off the beans, mash them up, and the kids loved them." (See "The Trap of Special Meals" on p. 169 for more on this idea.)

• **Take preventive measures for the inevitable messes.** You'll be better able to relax with your baby's eating if you aren't worried about the mess. If you set up an eating environment that's easy to clean, it allows you to focus on your child and the meal rather than on "keeping things tidy." Parents have rolled up rugs, laid out an old shower curtain, lined the area around the baby's chair with newspaper, worn big aprons, or fed the baby outside, weather permitting.

There are also all kinds of bibs for babies, some quite elaborate. For a couple of years, Eli used a plastic bib with a trough he proceeded to fill with food at every meal. Sometimes the best bib is not having a shirt on at all. As Leticia notes, "Skin is the most washable. My kids used to get popped in the kitchen sink for a quick bath or wash-up after meals."

Weaning from the Breast or the Bottle

Weaning is often an area of controversy in this culture.[6] Even if parents and children find agreement, there's likely to be conflicting ideas from extended family, friends, or the medical profession. Opinions about when weaning should happen range from six months to the worldwide average of 4.2 years.[7]

[6] We deal here with weaning, without going into detail about the mechanics of nursing or bottle-feeding children. Resources for parents who want to nurse include: La Leche League, hospital nursing counselors, and the Nursing Mother's Council, all of which should be listed locally in your area. We also recommend *The Nursing Mother's Companion* by Kathleen Huggins, The Harvard Common Press (535 Albany Street, Boston, MA 02118), 1990, an excellent practical guide. For information on bottle feeding, contact your pediatrician or a local public health nurse.

[7] This statistic comes from La Leche League International.

Parents begin to think about weaning because of their own as well as their children's needs. Children may show they're ready by refusing to nurse or by becoming disinterested in the bottle. Parents may decide to wean because they're worried about their children's diet or teeth. Parents also feel concerned when children are using the bottle or breast as their primary source of comfort.

Other reasons for weaning from the breast include a nursing mother's tiredness or illness, readiness to have her body back, a desire to get more sleep or a return to work. Nursing mothers also wean because they're experiencing a diminished sex drive or are pregnant again; because nursing has started to hurt or their child is persisting in biting.

Some mothers wean because of pressure from the outside. Their partner is complaining or feeling left out. A friend, someone in their extended family, or a doctor has decided that their child has reached the right age for weaning. And that age can be surprisingly young.

Mei remembers: "A good friend came by when Eliot was four months old. I mentioned that he was still nursing twice at night. She was aghast. She stopped dead in her tracks and said, 'You're fostering a habit,' as if I was doing him some dreadful harm."

Despite this kind of criticism, it's important that parents make the decision they feel is the most appropriate for their child and family, rather than the one they're being pressured to make.

Weaning Strategies

• **Get clear.** One thing that makes weaning successful is clarity on the part of the parent. But that clarity is not so easy to come by. Many of us would like to be able to just make the decision "I will wean her at ten months," but often, at ten months, either you or the baby—or both—have a different idea about it.

Often parents feel ambivalent about the decision to wean. Even if you are absolutely sure that now is the right time to wean, there are often feelings of sadness. For mothers who are weaning from the breast, there is also a hormonal shift that can intensify feelings of loss.

• **Recognize your child's individual needs.** Children have different needs for sucking. A few can wean from the breast to a cup by eleven months, and others are still nursing well after two years. As well as being aware of your child's nutrition and teeth, it's also important to respect her emotional needs.

• **Take advantage of times your child's interest wanes.** When children start crawling and get more engaged in the world around them, some lose interest in nursing. Some nursing mothers take advantage of these periods to initiate weaning. Others continue to nurse, and the child regains interest. However, some children never lose interest in nursing or bottles, no matter what's happening with them developmentally.

• **Wean gradually.** Gradual weaning gives the child a chance to get used to sucking less and to slowly substitute other forms of nourishment and comfort. Gradual weaning can take several weeks or even months.

Janis did what she calls the "weaning dialogue" with each of her kids. "I initiated weaning slowly. Each of my children resisted heartily the first time I brought it up, so I backed off for a few weeks, and then began

The Importance of Self-Feeding

It's important for children to learn to feed themselves at an early age. When you feed yourself, you get to choose exactly what and how much you want to eat. Self-feeding also promotes feelings of competence in children. It gives them a chance to develop and practice fine motor skills and develop coordination. When children are feeding themselves, they feel less dependent and more grown-up.

It's sometimes hard for parents to give up feeding children. Parents fear that their kids won't eat enough if they're in charge of getting the food to their own mouths. Yet most children go through a period in which they really want to feed themselves, and it's useful from an early age to give them the chance to practice.

THE EVOLUTION OF SELF-FEEDING

The groundwork for self-feeding can begin in infancy. When a newborn baby feels the nipple on her cheek, she can turn to it and initiate taking it into her mouth. This provides her an early opportunity to participate in her own feeding. Throughout the time that babies use the bottle or breast, it is important for parents to be aware of offering the nipple, rather than sticking it or forcing it into babies' mouths. In this way, babies learn that we trust their ability to read and respond to their own hungry feelings.

Once spoon-feeding begins, parents can make sure the baby sees the food on the spoon before they bring it to the baby's mouth. Then the baby can open his mouth, showing his readiness. From the very beginning, this creates a sense of "I want you to see it and choose to open your mouth because you want the spoon to go in" rather than "I'm going to trick this spoon into your mouth when your mouth accidentally opens."

When a child starts reaching for the spoon, you can encourage her to hold it with you. Most babies will be happy with this for a short while but will soon want one (or several) of their own. Janis calls this period "musical spoons." The baby has a couple, the floor has a couple, and you have a couple. Among all those spoons, some food gets in the child's mouth, and the child gets to participate.

During this time, children begin to enjoy finger foods. (Some children will only eat finger foods and will refuse anything from the spoon.) Finger foods provide children the up-close sensory relationship with food that many of them love. It also allows many children to feed themselves sooner. "Sucking rice cereal off my fingers is so much easier than trying to balance it on that precarious spoon that keeps tipping over."

Finger foods need to be squishy enough for children with few teeth but firm enough for them to be able to grasp and get into their mouths. Squash, apples, potatoes, carrots, greens, and other foods that are steamed until they are very soft but still hold their shape provide children with a chance to see food in a more natural form than puree.

Certain kinds of mashed or ground food hold together well enough for babies to pick up. Examples of these are mashed beans, potatoes, or yams. An inexpensive hand grinder will grind many foods to a tacky consistency that babies can hold. Rice, millet, and oatmeal or other grains, ground alone or with other foods, make wonderful little self-feeding clumps (which may dry to a concretelike substance on your baby's chair, the wall, and the floor, unless you wipe them up fairly soon). If you use rice to hold the mixture together, you can grind up and serve meat, vegetables, fruit, or other foods your child would normally have to eat off a spoon.

Gradually, after the first year, children may begin to get interested in silverware again, at least for some of their feedings. Children at this age are getting more skilled with their hands, and managing a fork or a spoon is no longer such a monumental task. Some children, however, still prefer eating primarily with their hands. Each family decides how long it feels comfortable with that and at what point the child really seems ready to successfully master silverware.

again. By the third or fourth time I initiated it, either their resistance had dwindled or my conviction had increased, and we weaned successfully over the next few weeks."

A first step in weaning could be to determine a set number of times that she can nurse every day. It is helpful for children if these times are consistent, so they can learn what to expect—for instance, nursing when they first wake up, after lunch, or before a bath.

If your child has had free access to her bottle, a gradual step could be to limit her to using it in a certain area. "You can have your bottle while you are sitting on the couch."

Once you have made an initial change, it is important to give your child some time to adjust. Let a couple of weeks go by before you make the next step, which might be cutting down on the number of bottles or nursings. In the case of a toddler, gradually diluting the bottles with water can lessen their appeal.

Some parents decide to wean first at night. This can also be done gradually. Cutting back slowly will give your child the chance to increase her eating during the day.

To wean at night, some parents rock, walk, or hold their child while she cries. Others leave their crying child in bed and check in periodically to let her know that they are listening to her. Some families have the nonnursing parent stay with the child while she struggles. Children who are sleeping with their parents might sleep next to the nonnursing parent.

In those few instances in which weaning has to be abrupt—a mother has to take an unexpected trip, becomes ill, or has suddenly decided that she can't keep nursing for another minute—children will figure out a way to cope but may need lots of extra support while they adjust to the sudden change.

• **Offer children support and alternatives during weaning.** Breast- and bottle-feeding usually provide comfort and closeness as well as nourishment. Provide alternatives for those times your child expects to nurse or have a bottle. "Simon, we are not going to nurse right now. If you are thirsty, we can get you some juice or water in a cup. If you want to cuddle, we could read a book on the couch."

For toddlers, this is an especially useful time to give them the chance to make choices and practice new skills. "You could have milk or chamomile tea in your cup." "Can you open the spout on your new cup?" "Would you like to push the buttons on the blender while we make your smoothie?"

Children who are in the process of weaning often show stress in other areas. Anita recalls, "I remember Luis went along with weaning fairly easily, but then I noticed that he'd gotten more fearful of strange noises all of a sudden."

Many children have lots of feelings to share during their weaning process. Your willingness to listen to your child will demonstrate the range of resources that are available in your relationship with him.

Toddlers, Preschoolers, and Food: A Developmental Overview

As children become more mobile, their appetites frequently decrease. This usually coincides with a slowing down in their growth rates. Also, since toddlers are always on the move, they have a harder time sitting still to eat. Many sit for a few bites and then want to be off exploring the world again. For this reason, most toddlers need a number of small meals or nutritious snacks a day.

Children of this age are also inconsistent in their appetites and fickle in their tastes. Foods that they have previously loved can be rejected overnight. Children often leave toddlerhood eating fewer foods than they did when they entered it.

Toddlers can also put away giant portions of food one day and hardly eat the next. They sometimes binge on particular foods. Jessica, mother of two-year-old Heidi, recalls, "The other night Heidi helped me pick ten plums in our backyard and we put them out on a plate. The next time I turned around there were ten pits on the plate. She wasn't hungry for dinner after that."

Young children also don't share our sense of timing. They don't know that pancakes are supposed to be for breakfast, that sandwiches are usually for lunch, or that dessert belongs at the end of the meal. Sari observed her one-year-old son, Jordan, at a local "all-you-can-eat" salad bar restaurant: "As we go through the line, I put a variety of foods on his plate. He'll eat a dozen raisins, suck on a pickle, maul an ear of corn, and then move on to kidney beans and peas. Next he'll suck on a lemon—grimace—pick it up and suck on it again. Then he'll bury his nose, mouth, and cheeks in a vanilla frozen yogurt cone. Afterward he'll ask for pasta and eat half a serving of tortellini with red sauce. It's clear he doesn't share my sense of sequence."

As children move into the preschool years, they begin to use their initiative in many ways around eating. They love to choose what they are going to eat and to serve themselves. As three- to five-year-olds develop clearer ideas of what they like and don't like, it may be harder to persuade them to "take a bite," because they can remember that they don't like peas, and they would rather be right than expand their list of acceptable foods.

Preschool-age children are generally more proficient at using silverware than toddlers are. They make fewer spills and less mess. Most don't test as much around food as toddlers do.

The Role of Temperament and Metabolism in Children's Eating

Each child has her own rhythms and needs around eating. Metabolism and temperament affect the quantity and frequency of a child's eating as well as the variety of foods she enjoys.

Children's willingness to try new foods has a lot to do with their temperament. Some children jump right into new foods. Other children with a different level of sensitivity are more careful and hesitant about trying new tastes and textures.

Janis recalls, "Maya has incredibly sensitive taste buds. She can distinguish between two different brands of bottled water. And she is a very particular eater. Often something she eats one day won't taste right to her the next. When she was three, there were a lot of things she just wouldn't eat or even try. By the time she was five, she was more open to trying new things, but still cautious. She'd start by smelling the new food and looking at it. Then she'd carefully stick her tongue out to taste it, and then she would decide if it could go in her mouth. Once she got it in, she still sometimes changed her mind. But at least she was trying. The other day she actually said to me, 'Mom, I wish I liked more foods.' "

Metabolism also plays a major role in how much children eat, and because of metabolism, the quantity of food that children eat isn't always reflected in their body size. In Janis's class one day, two parents looked at their respective toddlers at the snack table and marveled. Soft, round Brianna was picking at her food as she usually did, and thin, wiry Jocelyn was on her third serving of mashed potatoes and going strong.

Metabolism also regulates how often people need to eat. Most young children need to eat at least five times a day. While some are able to grow into a three-meal-a-day pattern, many people, even as adults, find that "grazing" works best for them because of their metabolism.

Toddlers and Preschoolers: Encouraging a Healthy Relationship to Food

As children move into the toddler and preschool years, their emerging independence and separateness raises new issues around food. These strategies can help you deal with some of their special mealtime needs:

• **Don't make food a battleground.** Next to good nutrition, avoiding mealtime battles is the most important factor in children's eating. When we fight with children over food, the fight often becomes the focus rather than the food. Sometimes children refuse food they really want to eat because we've engaged them in a battle of wills and their need for autonomy overrides their appetite.

If there are times you and your child have different ideas about what she should eat, there are ways to keep it from escalating into a full-blown struggle. If Alisha only wants to eat yogurt and strawberries, for instance, you could give her some and then say, "Now we're going to have our dinner. If you're still hungry for yogurt and strawberries afterward, then you can have some more." That way you're not demanding that she eat a set amount of dinner, and you ensure that she comes to dinner with at least a little appetite. And if she still wants her preferred food after dinner, she's free to have it.

• **Don't use food as a reward or punishment.** All children deserve to be fed; food shouldn't be a privilege they need to earn—or one that can be taken away. Linking food to behavior rather than to hunger teaches children to ignore their bodies' signals. When food is withheld as a punishment, it can undermine children's trust in you and their feelings of safety in the world.

• **Feed children when they're hungry.** Sometimes in our eagerness about food or in our focus on adult schedules, we put food in front of children when they're not hungry. When we do this, they're less likely to put it in their mouths and more likely to explore it in other ways. While it may challenge the family schedule, providing a reasonable amount of flexibility around children's eating schedules helps them eat when they're hungry versus when they're "supposed to."

• **Offer regular snacks.** Provide nutritious snacks for children who like to nibble throughout the day. Jack, who calls himself "the food guy in the house," shares his snack strategy: "Heidi's timing is not adult timing. When she's hungry, she's not interested in waiting. Having healthy snacks is what works for us. That way, if she's not interested in eating at mealtime, it's no big deal."

In some families, healthy snacks are available at certain predictable times. The parent puts out the food and children sit and eat. Other families have found that self-serve snacks better fit their style. Finger food is set out within children's reach and children help themselves. In some families, children take this snack back wherever they were playing. However, to prevent the danger of choking, it's important to make sure that children don't run or do active play while they are eating.

Healthful snacks for children include fruits and vegetables (raw or steamed), raisins or dried fruit, whole-grain crackers, low-salt pretzels, whole grain bread, cheese, yogurt, peanut butter, humus and other healthy spreads, beans, tofu, and bits of roasted meat. Many more traditional snack foods are high in salt, fat, and sugar. Foods such as chips, cheese puffs, "Goldfish," candy, fruit drinks, soda, cupcakes, and cookies provide empty calories and little or no nutrition, and should therefore be limited.

• **Offer foods that appeal to a toddler's sensibilities.** Toddlers love finger foods, foods they can dip, and sandwiches cut up in bite-size pieces.

• **Give children small amounts of food at a time.** This cuts down on waste, allows children to ask for more when they're still hungry, and also gives them less food to play with once they're full. Many children also prefer each food to be separate on their plates, instead of in mixtures or casseroles.

• **Monitor children's consumption of milk and juice.** Some children fill up on milk or juice, especially if they are drinking lots of bottles. This can inhibit their appetite for solid food. If your child tends to get full on liquids, try giving him bottles after meals, instead of during or before. Also, if toddlers are asking for a bottle or to nurse when they're hungry, offer them food first, and then top it off with the milk if they still want it.

It's also important to offer children water regularly. Children sometimes ask for milk or juice when water would more adequately quench their thirst.

• **Encourage children to try new foods.** While smelling, touching, and looking at new food all help children become more familiar with it, a study by Leann Birch and D. W. Marlin found that children were more likely to finally accept a new food if they'd had several opportunities to taste it. Interestingly, in order to get their two-year-old subjects to "taste" the foods, they had to reassure them that it was okay to spit the food out if they didn't like it.[8]

While it's important never to force your child to take a bite, you can offer new foods in a low-key manner. "Maybe if you taste a little today and a little next time, you might start getting used to it." Or "Maybe your eyes have one idea, but your mouth might have another."

Janis recalls, "I think Lee spit out tomatoes the first five occasions he tried them. On the sixth, he ate them with gusto. It seemed like it took him that long to get used to them."

• **Help children concentrate on their food.** Eliminate distractions such as TV, video games, and toys at the table.

• **Set clear limits around acceptable mealtime behavior.** When your child starts playing with her food at the table, you can say clearly, "Can you stop squishing your potatoes or shall I put them away?" Or "If you throw your food again, your meal is going to be over."

[8] L. L. Birch and D. W. Marlin, " 'I Don't Like It; I Never Tried It': Effects of Exposure to Food on Two-year-old Children's Food Preferences," *Appetite* 4 (1982): 353–360.

Rather than just reprimanding your child for playing with her food, give her an alternative. If she's squishing her potatoes, make sure she has other substances she can squish later on—dirt, sand, water, play dough. After dinner, or in the morning, set her up outside with a dishpan, an inch of dirt, and a little pitcher of water. Or visit your local sandbox with spoons and containers for mixing and pouring.

• **End meals when children show signs of being full.** Signs of being full include not eating, playing with food, throwing food, or trying to climb up on the table. If you take the food away from toddlers as soon as they start tossing it and say, "Looks like you're done," they will eventually learn not to throw food when they're hungry. You can also teach children other ways to signal that they're full. "When you're done, you can push your plate away, hand it to me, or tell me 'I'm done!' "

• **Engage children in clean-up activities.** You can say, "Looks like you're done. I'll take your food. Here's a sponge you can use to wipe up your tray." Or "Here's a warm cloth. You can wash your hands and face." This provides a transition and gives kids another way to feel competent.

• **Encourage independence at the table.** Other ways to respect children's autonomy include letting them climb in and out of their high chairs (when they're ready and interested) and having them join in family meals as soon as possible. This might mean taking off the tray and pushing your son's high chair right up against the main table or getting rid of the high chair entirely and introducing a booster seat. Set a place for your child at the table, just like everyone else. Such measures help the child feel included and may encourage him to learn the family rules around meals and eating.

You will get a sense of when your child is ready for this—and then you can give it a try and see if you were right. If it's too much of a struggle or if your child insists on climbing up on the table, you can move him back to his high chair and try again later.

By the time most children are two and a half, they are capable of serving themselves and passing things to other people at the table, two additional ways they can participate as full-fledged family members.

• **Cook with children.** In the toddler and preschool years, children love to be involved in food preparation. And they're much more likely to eat things if they've been involved in preparing them. (See "Cooking with Children" on p. 172.)

• **Model the eating habits you'd eventually like your children to develop.** Children imitate all of our habits, even our bad ones. Don't expect your child to eat his oatmeal plain when you heap yours with butter and brown sugar. As Paula put it, "I eat healthy food in front of my kids all the time, and I think that's the most critical thing. If I come home first thing and make a salad, they'll think it looks good. But if I say 'It's really good to eat salad' while I'm eating a cookie, they'll go right for the cookies."

• **Develop realistic expectations about family mealtime.** The dream many of us hold that our family will have intimate time together over an evening meal may come crashing down when we have young children. Aside from not always being hungry at "mealtimes," children aren't interested in sitting as long as we are for a meal, have little interest in anyone's conversation but their own, and usually want to sprawl in the middle of your lap, making relaxed eating next to impossible. Many families have reported toddlers who screamed through entire meals.

It can work better to have your "family time" before or after dinner or at another time of the day. You can also ask gradual cooperation from your toddler. "We'd like you to sit with us for a few minutes and then you can get up and play," or "I have three more bites. You're welcome to stand next to me, but I'm not going to hold you. I'll be done soon and then I'll come be with you." And many preschoolers can be told "We're going to have family conversation now. You can start with anything you would like to say, then Mom and Grandma are going to talk, and then you can have another turn to talk."

FOOD FOR THOUGHT: FOOD AND EATING

- How were mealtimes handled in my family when I was a child?
- What kind of relationship do I have to food now?
- What do I want my child to learn about food, eating, and nutrition? How can I teach those values and/or skills?

The Trap of Special Meals

An interesting paradox presents itself when we think about children's eating. On one hand, we want to encourage children to learn to read—and heed—their body's messages about what they want to eat and when they want to eat it. But on the other hand, providing children with unlimited food choices is not possible.

Families run the gamut when it comes to this paradox. Some provide everyone in the family the exact same food, insisting that they

eat it. As Leon describes it, his mother had some success with this system. "The first four times I came in from play and said I was hungry, Mama offered me black-eyed peas. When I told her I didn't like black-eyed peas, she sent me back out to play. The fifth time I came in, I decided I loved black-eyed peas. Mama taught me that hunger was the best seasoning."

Other families cook several different things at mealtimes and offer other choices throughout the day, as well, to ensure that everyone gets exactly what they want to eat.

Most families try to find a middle ground—providing children with a reasonable amount of flexibility without becoming resentful of the effort it takes. Saul said, "If Melissa and Matt don't want what we're eating, then they need to get themselves something that they can fix: cereal, yogurt, bagels and cream cheese, or some fruit. I don't want to make a big deal out of them having to eat the family meal, but I sure don't want to be jumping all over the kitchen saying 'Do you want this? Should I fix you that?' If they end up eating only a little I don't panic. I figure they won't starve before the next meal."

Joan tries to provide alternatives at each meal and a safety net afterward: "If I know there is a vegetable or particular food that somebody usually doesn't like, I provide an alternative in the meal. I often make two vegetables. And if the kids don't eat a good dinner, I usually fix a nutritious snack later in the evening."

Periodically, parents need to reevaluate eating and mealtime patterns to make sure they're meeting the needs of everyone in the family. Ideally, each family will find a comfortable system that meets the nutritional needs of children without creating overworked, resentful parents. Within such a system, children can learn to enjoy a variety of foods, gain cooking skills, and experience the pleasures of sharing food in a family setting.

What About Sweets?

There's a great old Indian story. A woman has been waiting for months for an audience before the great master. When it is finally her turn, she stands before him and says, "My son here won't stop eating sugar. It's ruining his teeth. They're falling out of his head. What should I do?"

"Come back in two weeks," the master says.

Two weeks later, the woman comes back with her son. They stand before the master again. "Stop eating sugar," he tells the boy.

"That's it?" the woman asks. "Why couldn't you say that two weeks ago?"

"Because," the master replies, "two weeks ago I was still eating sugar."

For many children, an important determiner of how many sweets they eat is what they see modeled in their families. If desserts and sweets are a big part of your family diet, no matter what you serve children and what rules you set up, kids are likely to grow up eating lots of sweets.

Metabolism also plays an important role. Some children are less interested in sweets than others. Daryl shares, "Vera will almost always choose something like toast over candy." Other children seem to constantly ask for sugar. While this craving can sometimes represent a nutritional deficit, other times it simply points to a child who loves sweets.

Some children eat sweets and still eat nutritious food. Others eat sweets and then refuse healthier food. Leila remembers: "My first kid could eat dessert at the beginning of the meal or in the middle of the meal, and he would go back and eat the nutritious food that was on his plate. My last child, on the other hand, tends to eat more of the sweets and doesn't necessarily go back and eat the rest." It is important to take each child's eating style into consideration when deciding if and when to offer sweets.

Sweets are used in lots of ways out in the world—to celebrate and reward, to show affection and appreciation. In light of these larger influences, it's important to think about the role we want sweets to play in our children's lives.

Some families have substituted other kinds of "treats" on occasions where sweets might have been used before. Piñatas have been filled with little toys. Trick-or-treaters have gotten stickers. Parties and holidays have focused more on games and activities and less on cake and ice cream.

Many of us have been given food or sweets as a reward for desirable behavior or achievement. While occasionally this can be fun, if we consistently do this with our children, we may be setting up a pattern in which children feel that every time they do something well, they deserve or need to eat sweets.

Helping Children Develop a Healthy Relationship to Sweets

Parents deal with children's consumption of sweets in many ways. Some families allow no sweets or only offer sweets on special occasions. Parents using these systems report a range of outcomes. Some say their kids grow up basically disinterested in sweets. Others report children who are obsessed with the sweets they've been forbidden.

At the other end of the continuum are families in which sweets are in ample supply and are not regulated or monitored in any way. In some of these families, children self-regulate and in others, children eat a lot of sweets, frequently experiencing the effects of poor health: cavities, low energy, and sickness.

Families fall at many places along this continuum, with varying degrees of comfort, struggle, and success. If children have a basically healthy diet, there is no one answer to the question of how many sweets they should have. However, an important thing all parents can do is educate children about sweets and give them a chance to practice making decisions about what they eat.

• **Give information.** Often children think we are making arbitrary decisions about what they can or can't eat. Sharing basic nutritional information gives them the tools to be able to eventually make their own decisions: "The eggs and meat you ate today are both protein. Your body still hasn't had any vegetables or bread or noodles today."

Janis has taught Maya about junk food since she was a toddler. "I've told her that junk food tricks her body into actually thinking she's had food. Then she's not hungry for the food that's going to help her muscles grow and help her jump and climb—the food that's going to keep her healthy."

• **Give choices.** Figure out the rules for your household and offer choices that fit. "I'd like you to have some vegetables if you're going to have that ice cream bar. You can look in the vegetable drawer and pick the ones you want." "If you want something sweet you can have dried fruit or yogurt." "You can have one of your candies today. Would you like to eat it after lunch or after dinner?"

Such choices, of course, need to be limited, not only by what's healthy but also by what's on hand, the time available, and your willingness to help your children prepare the food they choose.

Susanna and her five-year-old son, Sky, worked out a system where they went to the store and he was allowed to choose a set amount of sweets. These went into a special tin that only he could open. They were the only sweets he was going to get that week, and it was up to him when he ate them. He could eat them all at once or he could stretch them out over time. Once this solution was instituted, fights over sweets declined dramatically.

• **Limit the sweets you keep on hand.** It is much easier for children to focus on nutritious choices if there aren't bags of cookies or candy around.

• **Include children in the problem-solving.** As early as three or four, kids may be able to help come up with some of their own solutions, as Janis explains: "One day, Maya fell apart at the end of the day, and I realized that she'd gotten ice cream from her dad and candy from me. So I said to her, 'I'm wondering if part of the reason you're feeling so cranky now is that you've had a lot of sweets and not too much nutritious food. Let's see if we can put together a nutritious dinner.'

"By the time I said 'no' to her first dinner choices—McDonald's, Burger King, and Taco Bell, she was able to help me plan a fairly nutritious meal. She chose homemade pizza, broccoli, and carrots. She felt good about that food, because she chose it, shopped for it, and helped to make it. The nourishment of the food felt good to her, but so did being a participant in the process."

Cooking with Children

From a young age, most children are interested in the processes surrounding food. Beginning in toddlerhood, children like to pluck green strawberries from the garden, pull bunches of bananas off the counter at the store, pour their own juice, wipe up their own spills, and squash their individual peas with a finger.

Children who participate in cooking experiences have the opportunity to develop their sense of competence as well as their physical and cognitive skills. They have a chance to learn about foods and the scientific transformations that take place as flour turns into dough and dough turns into bread. They can learn about numbers, counting, and measuring, and they can develop positive relationships with different foods. It's also a lot more fun to eat something you've helped to prepare.

Here are some ways to involve children in food preparation from an early age.

• **Think simple.** Cooking processes that we do so fast we almost take them for granted can be fascinating for children. The following activities are appropriate for toddlers, as well as for older children.

Putting produce in the bag at the market is very interesting for young children. So is helping to lift and place items on the checkout stand. Some stores even go so far as offering child-size shopping carts for children to shop alongside you. Grocery stores are also a great place to initiate other activities, such as naming, identifying colors, and counting.

Picking fruits and vegetables allows children to see where food comes from. Visiting a small farm or garden with your child, either to pick or just to see food growing, can be both a magical and an educational experience. Anyone who's seen a child in a field of berries knows how much small children love to harvest food.

Carrying a small bag of groceries into the house, taking the potatoes out of the basket, lifting bread out of the bread box, or getting the measuring cups out of the drawer all give children a chance to show off their strength and their knowledge of where things are kept in the kitchen. These kinds of tasks also give them a chance to experience the pleasure of helping, of playing an important role in food preparation for the whole family.

Putting things in the pot or bowl. Children can put the cut-up kale in the pot or the vegetables in the bowl for the salad.

Shucking corn. If you set children up with a dishpan or other large container, they can pull the husks and corn silk off corn on the cob and put the ears in a pot.

Shelling peas. Children are fascinated and delighted to find the little peas hidden inside the shells! (Younger children may need help opening the shells.)

Washing vegetables (potatoes, carrots, celery, squash, lettuce, greens), like any form of water play, is very fun for children. If you use a limited amount of water in the sink or wash tub, splashing will be slightly minimized. Children can also enjoy tearing lettuce to put in the salad. If you're brave, you can invite them to "toss" the salad in an oversize bowl.

Pouring their own drinks from a little pitcher into their cup can be exciting for children. (Start with a little bit in the pitcher so spills are easy to clean up; and try water first—it's less sticky than juice.) Children can also pour premeasured ingredients into the mixing bowl.

Stirring and mixing pancake or muffin batter or scrambled eggs gives children an opportunity to see some of the transformations of cooking: The dry cornmeal and flour turns into sticky batter, the gooey eggs turn yellow and thick. If you use oversize flat-bottomed bowls, children's early attempts to stir won't result in so much splashing and spilling.

Sifting and greasing. Children can also enjoy sifting flour, baking powder, and salt as well as greasing cookie sheets and muffin tins.

Spreading soft butter, peanut butter, or cream cheese on toast can build feelings of competence and make snacks fun.

Cutting soft things with dull butter knives is a safe way for children to start using cutting tools. Soft things include sandwiches, muffins, mushrooms, zucchini squash, tofu, avocado, bananas, dumplings, and cooked potatoes.

Using small appliances is something children love. With constant adult supervision, children can successfully help to hold small hand mixers, push buttons on the blender or food processor, or participate in making toast.

Cleanup. Children love sponges, wiping, and working in the sink. Some people have children wash plastics and nonbreakables in one side of the sink or in a nearby dishpan while they wash the rest of the dishes in the other sink. Children may also be able to put rinsed dishes in the dishwasher or help unload the cooled dishes when the cycle is done.

As children get a little older, you can add egg cracking (some people do it with toddlers), kneading and rolling out dough, making cookies, cracking nuts, squeezing fresh citrus fruit for juice, setting the table, and cutting with paring knives. If you enjoy cooking and want to share it with children, there are lots of wonderful ways you can include them.

• **Keep it safe.** Children need to be supervised at all times when they are cooking. If you need to leave the room, make sure you move anything dangerous out of the way or take your child with you until you come back.

Set the stage for success. Move sharp knives and breakable things out of children's reach. If you feel safe enough to have your child up at counter height, it is important to think ahead of time about what that gives them access to, so you can move anything that might be dangerous. If children are using knives, it is important that they have had practice with less sharp knives, are stable (not likely to lose their balance), and are cutting on a flat surface. It also helps to give them flat, not round, things to cut—you can slice the zucchini, mushroom, apple, or other food lengthwise so it can lie flat on the cutting board.

The other thing to watch for in the kitchen is heat. Anything on the stove is potentially dangerous, as is anything that has just come from the oven, even though it's sitting innocently on the counter looking like people could help themselves. Anything that is hanging off the counter (cords to appliances, towels under hot or heavy containers, knife handles) could be pulled off by a child. As we said earlier, any time they are using small appliances, children need constant supervision.

• **Keep it low.** It is easier for some people to create a low work space in their kitchen than it is to have their child up to the counter. Low work spaces may be a small table, an overturned box or crate, or a piano bench. People who don't have a low work space can have children work on their high chair tray or devise another safe way to get their child up to the counter.

• **Prepare ahead of time.** Assembling all the things you will need ahead of time cuts down on some of the running back and forth and allows you to stay with your child while he or she is cooking. Remember to put out towels and sponges for spills.

• **Go slow.** It takes a lot more time to cook when you include children. It helps to think of it as your "special time" with your child for the day. Otherwise, the slow pace of your child's work may be frustrating to you.

• **Choose an appropriate time.** Since cooking with children takes extra time and energy on your part, it's important to think about how relaxed you are before you begin. If you feel rushed or exhausted, it's best to postpone your cooking activities to another time. If you feel frustrated with the process, it won't be fun for anyone.

Sometimes it is much easier to cook with children when you're not under pressure to get a meal on the table. You could make the cornbread

for dinner early in the afternoon, or you could make muffins for the morning the evening before. Since cooking takes a considerable investment of time, you may need to trade it for another activity you usually do. "Instead of going to the park today or instead of reading stories before bed, we are going to cook together."

• **Anticipate a mess.** There will be a mess when you include children in cooking. They can be included in the cleanup, but that will probably be a mess, too. There are some things you can do to prepare for the mess, minimize the cleanup, and limit your frustration. Some people do simple cooking projects outside or on a deck where things can be hosed off. Inside, you can put down newspaper, an old shower curtain, or a splat mat if the activity is likely to entail a lot of spilling on the floor. Janis tries to do cooking projects with kids before she mops the floor, so that she is more relaxed about spills. If children are washing or working in the sink or with water, it helps to put old towels down on the floor to keep it less slippery and help with cleanup.

• **Enjoy yourself.** Cooking with children can be a pleasure, a way to share meaningful, special time together that you can cherish for years to come. If you enjoy the kitchen yourself, sharing your enthusiasm with your child is a wonderful way to pass on special family traditions or to develop some new ones.[9]

[9] Molly Katzen and Ann Henderson have written a wonderful cookbook for preschool children, *Pretend Soup* (Berkeley: Tricycle Press, 1994). Each recipe includes written instructions for grownups and step-by-step picture illustrations for kids. The recipes, which are simple, healthful, and will appeal to a child's palate, include Bagel Faces, Green Spaghetti, Number Salad, Hide and Seek Muffins, and Pizza.

FOOD FOR THOUGHT: FAMILY MEALTIME

• What makes mealtimes successful in my present family?

• What makes mealtimes difficult?

• Are there ways I would like to include my children more in meal planning, shopping, or cooking?

Our Daily Bread

From the time they are infants, we teach our children important lessons about nourishment, making healthy choices, participating in family mealtimes, and being part of a larger family and cultural tradition around food. Our answers to many of the basic questions around eating will be unique to our individual family, but all of us have the opportunity to give our children these gifts—a healthy respect for hunger and fullness, an awareness of the foods their bodies need, and a comfortable, enjoyable relationship to food.

16. From Toilet Training to Toilet Learning

"The most significant help we can give children as they are learning to use the toilet is our faith that it will happen."

JANIS

Many of us who have confidence in our children as learners in every other area feel nervous and unsure when it comes to their use of the toilet. If we are dealing with our first child, successfully we may never have seen a child make the transition from diapers to the toilet and may wonder how it's ever going to happen. Yet there is no reason that process should be different from other developmental tasks children master.

Many parents have erroneously been taught that it's their job to "toilet train" children, that they are the ones who should be in charge of this important transition in children's lives. However, since most children give up their diapers during their toddler years—a time when they are programmed to balk at our ideas—it can be helpful, both for us and for our children, if we shift our thinking from "toilet training" in which children are passive participants to "toilet learning" in which children are the ones taking the lead.[1]

Being a facilitator rather than a "trainer" means setting the stage for the learning to happen and providing the necessary information and resources, but leaving the timing and rhythm up to the child. This approach provides our children with needed autonomy and independence, eliminates unnecessary toileting battles, and clears the way for their eventual mastery.

[1] Alison Mack coined this phrase in her wonderful book, *Toilet Learning* (Boston: Little Brown, 1978). We appreciate and draw on the perspective she brought to children's toileting.

Readiness for Toilet Learning: A Developmental Overview

Learning to use the toilet is an ongoing process that begins with finding out about your body and how it works. Children start becoming aware of their bodies while they are still in diapers. Well before children reach their second birthday, many can tell you if their diaper is wet or poopy. Children at this age are often interested in what you find in their diaper, and many become aware that their poop or pee is something that they made. Many children have revealing expressions on their faces or body language that lets you know they are pooping. Others say "pee-pee" or "poop" while they are actually doing it in their diapers. Some toddlers will seek out "private" places to poop—standing behind a door, squatting under the table, or simply turning their back on you. All of these behaviors show that children are becoming aware of their body processes.

During this same period, many children become fascinated with the toilet: first, because it's full of water and, later, because they can make it flush. Toilet paper is another delightful discovery for toddlers. You pull it and it just keeps coming.

Many young toddlers "practice" with their potty chair, as well, sitting on it with or without clothes, putting their doll or teddy bear on it, carrying it around the house, using it as a chair or storing toys in it.

All of these steps show that a child is preparing to use the toilet on her own. However, often many weeks and months of early interest go by before a child really makes up her mind that she wants to sit on the potty *and* is capable of letting go of her pee and poop.

Between one and a half and two and a half, most children try out the potty, although these early attempts are usually sporadic. Over time, children become more interested and use the potty more consistently, though there still may be times in which they lose interest. Even after weeks or months of "success," many children refuse to use the toilet or start having lots of "accidents." Although this regression may be tied to an emotional upset, more often it is a natural part of the learning process. Toddlers eagerly begin to use the potty, mustering the energy necessary to be successful, and then decide that they aren't really ready to take it on full time. ("It was a nice place to visit, but I don't want to live there yet.")

Sometimes children discover that using the potty just takes too much energy and focus that they need to be putting toward other developmental tasks. Laura recalls: "Eli first climbed on the big toilet to poop when he was fifteen months old. It was summertime and he was toddling around naked a lot of time, but still, we were shocked. We'd never encouraged him. We'd never talked about it. He did it on his own. And he was just tickled with himself. For the next six months, Eli loved pooping in the potty, dangerously sloshing his potty bowl on his way to the toilet to dump it out and flush it away. I remember thinking 'Boy, we've got it made on this one.' But then a couple of months before his second birthday, he stopped using the potty entirely. He wanted diapers all the time, so that's what we did. It wasn't until many months later that he began showing an interest in using the potty again. And he continued wearing diapers on and off until he was almost three."

For most children, the normal process of toilet learning involves lots of practice, "accidents,"

Toilet Learning Begins with Diapering

From the beginning, babies can be included in their diapering and dressing activities. Such participation lays the best foundation for independent toileting later on. It teaches children, from an early age, "This is a process that involves you, and at some point, you're going to be in charge of it."

Often adults take all of the responsibility for diapering and dressing children until it is time for them to learn to use the toilet. For their first two and a half years, we wipe their bottoms, lift them on to the change table, fasten and unfasten their diapers, and pull up their pants, then all of a sudden, we expect them to start doing it themselves.

In the first years of life, when caregiving is such a large part of being with our children, it's easy to look at repetitive caregiving activities such as diapering as routines to get through as quickly as possible. Yet many valuable opportunities for teaching, communication, and learning are missed when we hurry our children through diapering or view the task with disdain.

One of the cornerstones of parent educator Magda Gerber's philosophy is the premise that diapering—as well as other daily caregiving activities—can be interactions that fully engage both caregiver and baby. Gerber suggests that parents and caregivers focus their attention to make diaper changes fully human interactions. The goal is to change the baby's diapers while paying full attention—not talking on the phone, chatting, or thinking about what you're going to do as soon as the diapering is over—and allowing the baby to participate to the greatest extent possible.

Gerber discourages distracting your baby as you change her, but instead suggests making eye contact and letting her know what's going to happen each step of the way. The youngest, of course, can't fully understand the words "I'm going to change your diaper now. Here's some nice, warm water on your bottom," but they can sense the difference between a distracted, hurried parent and a relaxed, focused one. It feels different to have your arms jammed into the sleeves of a shirt than it is to have them slowly and gently helped inside.

When young babies are changed in a relaxed manner, diapering can be an opportunity for them to make loving eye contact with their parents, to freely move their arms and legs, to discover their bodies, and to feel the air on their skin without the constraint of diapers and clothes.

All children can participate in diapering. For a two-month-old, that involvement has a lot to do with pacing. Before you pick up your infant son, you can look at him and say "I'm going to lift you up and change your diaper." If you then wait a few seconds, it gives him a chance to hear your words, watch your face, and possibly respond. Throughout the diapering, describing what you are doing and moving at a deliberate pace gives the baby a chance to respond and to feel respected and included. An eight-month-old child may be able to hold the dry diaper, pull off the wet one, or admire the poop before you flush it.

Toddlers can participate even more. They can bring the clean diaper, choose where they want to be diapered, pull off their pants, lift their bottoms, unfasten the old diaper, hold the diaper cream, help wipe themselves, choose the color of diaper covers they want to wear, help to pull up their own pants, and wash their hands afterward.*

Diapering like this is a time ripe for learning. Repetitive encounters provide children rich opportunities because they can learn to predict what will happen. They hear the same language over and over: "Where are those little toes hiding?" "Here's a washcloth. Now I'm going to wash your vulva." Even the youngest babies learn that their bodies are to be respected, that their bodies (and the substances they produce) are not shameful. They learn that they will be listened to and that their pace will be taken into consideration. Older babies can learn about sequencing ("First we pick up the diaper, then we get the washcloth, now it's time to take your old diapers off"), colors ("Do you want the red diaper cover or the blue one?"), and much more.

Children who have had these experiences don't come to independent toileting as strangers to the concept of self-care. They have already had the opportunity to develop some knowledge about their bodies and their pee and poop. And they expect to be active participants in their own toileting.

* It's important to point out that toddlers love to test around familiar routines—and at some point during the infant and toddler years, your experience of diapering your child may change from a cooperative, relaxed venture to one that is full of struggle. This does not mean that anything is wrong with you or your child. (See "From One to Five: Why Are Children Always Testing?" on p. 240.) If diapering is a place of conflict for you and your child, if you're feeling stressed and challenged by getting one diaper off and the next one on, see "Physical Limit Setting: When You Need to Restrain a Child" on p. 232 for tips on diapering a struggling child.

and regression. It's not until somewhere between two and three and a half that most children give up their diapers and consistently use the toilet. And frequently, night dryness comes much later than daytime control. (See "Bedwetting and Nighttime Dryness, Page 187.)

The Three Areas of Readiness

In order for children to make the successful transition from diapers to "independent toileting," they need to be "ready" in at least three different areas. Children need to be *physically* ready. This means that they can hold their pee and poop and also release it at will. As children approach this stage, their diapers will stay dry for longer periods of time, indicating that they are learning to hold their pee. Letting go, however, takes more time.

Janis explains: "I've watched so many children patiently and expectantly sit on the toilet only to finally get up and have the pee dribble down their legs to the floor. It wasn't for lack of wanting that the pee didn't come while they were on the toilet. They just hadn't learned to 'let it go' when they wanted to."

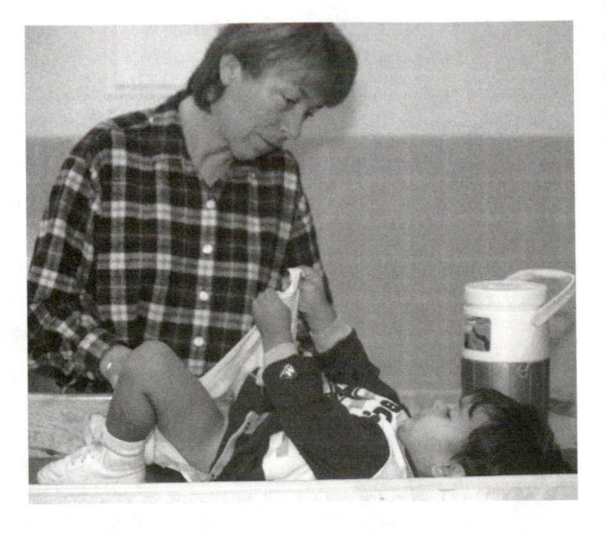

Other areas of physical readiness include being able to take down and pull up one's pants and being able to get oneself onto the toilet and hold on securely.

Another area of readiness is *cognitive*. Children need to be able to understand where the pee and poop should go. Children learn this by watching the people around them use the toilet.

In order to consistently use the potty, children also need to keep the status and condition of their bladder and bowels in their awareness *all* the time. Being able to keep two ideas in your mind at the same time is a specific developmental stage of cognition, and this is the area of readiness that stumps many children: "While I'm riding my trike, painting a picture, digging in the sand, watching the bear at the zoo, I have to be always ready to pay attention to the call of my bladder. It's a big job and I'm not sure I can do it."

Since this ability to keep two ideas going at once is developmental, there is really no way to teach it, but you may see signs that your child is approaching this level of understanding when she starts broadcasting to you that she is "pooping" in her diaper, or when she stops what she is doing to announce "The pee-pee is coming, Daddy."

The third area of readiness is *emotional*. When children are emotionally ready to learn to use the toilet, they *want* to. This is the area of readiness that really distinguishes "toilet training" from "toilet learning." In toilet training, the adult is the one (and maybe the only one) who wants it to happen. In toilet learning, the child chooses the task.

A toddler's "wanting to" use the toilet is actually quite complex. Because two-year-olds are working on issues of autonomy and are driven to make their own decisions, beginning to use the toilet *has* to be their decision. If we are continually coming up with the idea ("It's time to use the potty." "Would you like to try to sit on the potty?" "You have to sit on the toilet until you make pee-pee."), our child's only independent alternative is to refuse: "No, I don't want to." It's not until they discover the idea on their own that most toddlers truly get excited about using the potty.

For some children, "wanting" also involves a willingness to let go of their familiar, safe diapers, to take a step into being "grown-up." As much as children strive to be grown-up, when it comes down to it, most have real ambivalence about leaving babyhood behind. Sometimes children who are quite "sophisticated" in other areas will be hesitant to give up their diapers, their last stronghold on that familiar babyhood.

Three Steps Forward, Two Steps Back

Growth is not always even. These areas of readiness don't necessarily come together in an orderly fashion. Often one or two of them is in place, but not the third. A child may be emotionally and physically ready but have lots of accidents, especially in new and interesting settings where there is not enough presence of mind to take in all the new and stimulating information *and* remember to pay attention to his bladder. Sometimes children are cognitively and physically ready but not emotionally ready. They can hold and release their pee or poop and they can remember, but they choose not to give up their diaper. Children who need to be "reminded" all the time may be ready in the physical and emotional realms but not in the cognitive.

Often children who have learned to pee in the toilet still ask for a diaper when they need to poop. This is quite common; some children go several months using the diaper to poop, until they become comfortable with the idea of putting their poop in the potty. Parents can gently suggest and can encourage the child to shake the poop off the diaper into the toilet and flush it, but ultimately, it is the child who will decide. Inevitably, in a few weeks or months, she will be ready to poop in the potty, as well.

Food for Thought: Toilet Learning

- What are my expectations about my child learning to use the toilet?

- What kinds of explorations, experimentation, and accidents am I comfortable with?

- Do I have any worries about my child learning to use the toilet? What are they? How can I begin to deal with those concerns?

Children's Toilet Learning: Issues for Parents

Toilet learning, while natural to children, is often quite challenging for parents. Books, articles, and experts of all kinds give parents the message that they could ruin their children for life by the errors they make in toilet training. Because of these pressures, it can be difficult for many parents to approach this natural learning process in a relaxed, confident way.

Janis remembers one mother, Mariah, coming to her in anguish over the fact that her thirty-month-old, Reeve, still hadn't learned to use the toilet: "Some well-meaning parent educator had said to her, 'When your child is ready, it will be easy.' And that comment was true in a very narrow sense. But it didn't take into account the dynamics in her family, the pressures Mariah and her husband experienced from outside, or the struggles that came up for them around Reeve's transition out of diapers."

Mariah had learned that "toilet training" was mostly the parent's job and had worked very hard trying to do everything she thought she was supposed to do to help her son learn to use the toilet. Reeve, being a healthy toddler, was systematically refusing to cooperate, and in response, Mariah felt inadequate and escalated her efforts. He, then, predictably, increased his resistance.

This is not an uncommon cycle in families. Parents often get messages from the larger society that they need to push, prod, remind, and manipulate their children into using the potty. Toddlers, who are just entering the age of "Me do it!" are programmed to resist most of our ideas, especially the ones we continually remind them about.

Voices from the Past, Pressures in the Present

Our society holds many cultural perspectives that influence our thinking about toileting. There are issues around privacy, nudity, and bodily functions.[2] There are strong beliefs about when and how children should learn to use the toilet. Some of these cultural beliefs and practices are useful guides for us and others create pressure, uncertainty, and feelings of guilt.

Sue remembers: "My grandmother trained me with M&M's while my parents were away on a trip. I still need to eat chocolate every day."

And Justin recalls: "I remember my cousin being forced to sit on his potty chair in front of the TV, eating Cheerios, for what seemed like hours."

Many parents have to deal not only with questionable legacies but also with conflicting opinions in their immediate or extended family. Taylor explained: "My mother swears that each of her children was trained by the time

[2] See "Learning About Bodies" on p. 190 for more on these topics.

they were ten months old. She thinks I've created a monster with my twenty-six-month-old who is still in diapers."

Maureen, a single mom who works full time outside the home, remembers the pressure she felt to train her son by a certain date. "Ian was in a toddler care program where diapering was an integral part of the program. But he could only go there until he was two and a half. Then he had to switch to a preschool which insisted that children be potty-trained. I tried, but Ian just wasn't interested.

"I had to have the child care, so I lied. I said he was potty-trained. His first week at the new center, he pooped in the sand box every day. The teachers were upset. But some time during his first two weeks there, another boy said to him, 'Ian, why don't you just use the toilet like we do?' Well, that was it. Ian started pooping in the toilet that day, and he never had a problem after that."

Coping with external pressures, sorting through what we have learned in our families and through the often contradictory advice of the experts can challenge the most resourceful parent.

FOOD FOR THOUGHT: TOILET LEARNING

- What does my family believe about children and toileting?
- How was the transition from diapers to independent toileting handled in my family? Was there an expectation that children be out of diapers by a certain age?
- Are there any external factors pressuring me to get my child out of diapers?

Big Boy Underwear?

Often parents are encouraged to emphasize the "big girl" or "big boy" aspect of learning to use the toilet. We may label the new underpants "big girl pants," and promise that when you learn to use the toilet, you will be a "big girl." We do this in hopes that it will inspire the child to use the toilet because he or she wants to be "big." While this approach may come from our desire to encourage our child's growth, it can present certain dilemmas for the child.

One problem is that even if the child accepts the "big girls use the toilet" concept, she may not be physically and cognitively ready to use the toilet, so no matter how hard she tries, she's unable to live up to her own and her parents' dream of being a "big girl."

Another problem with the threshold concept of "big boy" (one day you are a baby and the next day you are a "big boy") is that this is not how growth happens, nor is it how most children are comfortable with it happening. Most toddlers have a lot of ambivalence about growing up. Parts of them are working desperately on being big and parts of them are holding firmly to being a baby. To ask them to give up all of their familiar babyhood as they learn to use the toilet may actually backfire and cause them to resist using the toilet. Instead, focus on the learning process and let your child know that mastering new things takes time.

What Is the Adult Role in Toilet Learning?

Even though children need to take the lead in toilet learning, there are ways parents can support them on the road to independent toileting. These strategies fall into three major categories, which we call *ready*, *set*, and *go*.

Ready: Building a Foundation

Before your child actually begins using the potty, you can set the stage for future learning:

• **Involve your child in diapering.** This can begin in infancy. (See the box "Toilet Learning Begins with Diapering" on p. 178.)

• **Give children appropriate language.** Although the specific language used in families varies, give your child words for "pee," "poop," and other aspects of toileting. Since children think of their pee and poop as parts of themselves, it's important to avoid negative words such as "filthy," "nasty," and "stinky." Instead, use simple statements of fact: "After we wash the poop off, we can put on your dry diaper." It's also helpful for children to have clear language for their body parts, "This is my penis." "This is my vulva." "My poop comes out of my anus."[3]

• **Provide information.** Provide information about how your child's body works: "When you are wearing your diaper, the poop comes out of your bottom and goes into your diaper. When you sit on the potty, the poop comes out of your bottom and goes in the potty." Providing this kind of information to children is consistent with the idea that toileting is something they need to learn about, instead of just be trained to do.

• **Give children room to explore.** Children often want to study what you have created after sitting on the toilet or will sit for a second themselves, then get up and flush furiously, unroll yards of paper to stash in the toilet, or wash their hands for as long as you will let them. These are all normal explorations that help children warm up to the idea and the tools of toileting. However, children don't need to be allowed to do them endlessly. You get to decide how much of this play you're comfortable with on any given day.

• **Provide role models.** As we've already said, it is useful for children to see others using the toilet. If you are comfortable having visitors in the bathroom, kids can benefit from watching you.

Some preschools have established an open bathroom tradition in which the toilets are in an area in which other children can casually observe. This can give children access to useful information and models.

While many families have an open-door policy in the bathroom, it's important to remember that children also successfully learn to use the toilet in families where modesty and privacy are the norm. It's important that families use the bathroom in ways that are comfortable to them.

• **Look for signs of readiness.** Parents can provide support by observing and listening to their child. You will probably be the first one to notice your child's beginning clues that he is ready and interested in using the potty.

Once you have collected several clues, you can mention the fact that one day he will learn to put his pee or poop in the toilet. Depending on your child's response, you could offer to get him some of the tools of the trade.

[3] See "Body Language: Talking to Children About Sex" on p. 203 for more on giving children appropriate language for body parts and body functions.

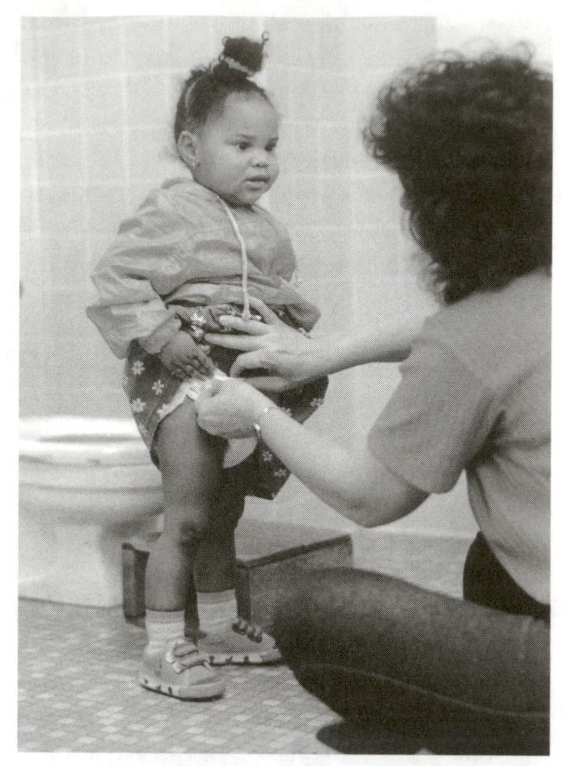

Every time you initiate something new, wait for your child to make the next move before you offer more assistance.

Set: When Children Start Using the Potty

When your child first starts using the potty, you can provide necessary props and encouragement:

• **Let your child take the lead.** As much as you can, set your anxiety aside, avoid pushing, and let your child set the pace.

• **Provide the props.** Provide your child with the tools he or she might need. These include some easy-off underwear or loose elastic shorts (without diapers underneath). During this time, tight pants, button pants, or overalls should be avoided since they could seriously slow down a child with limited lead time. Snug training pants or pull-ups can also be difficult for children to get off themselves. Also, feeling the pee can be part of the learning process for kids. When kids wear superabsorbent pull-ups or underpants, they might not feel the wetness and may miss out on the information that signals that something has happened.

Many children also appreciate a potty chair or a small step up to the toilet and a seat to fit over the toilet, so that they feel more secure. Other children will be adept at hopping up on the adult seat.

Remember that introducing these tools is one of the first steps in learning to use the toilet, and as such, they should always be offered as choices.

• **Set up the environment for success.** Put a potty chair near where the child plays, bring the potty along on outings where there aren't quickly accessible toilets. Roll up your expensive rugs, gate off your white wall-to-wall carpet, spend lots of time outside, and provide accessible towels for children's help in wiping up. These steps may help parents relax enough so that "accidents" turn into learning opportunities when children are in the "got it–lost it" phase.

• **Let your child move freely without diapers as much as possible.** Being naked is one of the best ways for children to learn to associate their body signals with the arrival of pee and poop. When children are naked, they don't have to struggle to get everything off; they only have to get to the potty. In many families children run around naked after their bath or before getting dressed. If you have a warm outdoor area or an easy-to-clean indoor area, you may feel com fortable letting children roam freely without diapers. If, however, you are uncomfortable with pee and poop on the floor, it will be easier for you and your child to help him keep his diapers or training pants on.

• **Offer choices.** The really important choices for children are whether and when they want to use the toilet and whether they want to wear diapers or underpants on a given day. It's not unusual for children to want to go back and forth between the two for quite some time in the early stages of learning. When possible, it's valuable for children to be able to choose. The important thing is that parents don't feel as if they or the child has failed when the child chooses diapers.

There will, of course, be times when it's not practical for a child to choose. Jesse has worked out a compromise with his daughter, Nicoya. She gets to choose at home, and Jesse chooses when they go out. "Right now, Nicoya doesn't want to wear diapers or pull-ups. She either wants to be naked or 'just wear shorts.' However, her use of the potty is quite sporadic, so she usually ends up peeing on the floor or soaking her shorts. As far as I'm concerned, this is fine when we're at home, but when we are going out, I insist that she wear diapers."

• **Use books, as appropriate.** There are a number of "toileting books" for children on the market. Many provide useful pictures and ideas that can support a child's learning. Preview these books before you share them with your child. Some reinforce messages about toileting that you may not want to perpetuate. ("Now you're a big boy!" Or "Once you use the toilet, of course you're going to use it *every* time.") Since toddlers aren't reading these books themselves, feel free to use the illustrations and alter the story line to fit what you want to teach.

Recommended Books About Poop

These two books differ from the usual toileting books in that they focus more on the poop itself and less on getting children to the potty. Although some adults find them distasteful, children are universally delighted.

Everyone Poops, by Taro Gomi, Kane/Miller Book Publishers.

This wonderfully matter-of-fact Japanese book was finally translated into English. All kinds of creatures, including younger and older humans (unfortunately all male), are shown with their poop. The concluding spread shows a whole lineup of animals eating, and the caption reads "All living things eat, so . . ." Then you turn the page, and they're all pooping. And the caption concludes "Everyone poops."

The Story of the Little Mole Who Went in Search of Whodunit, Werner Holzwarth and Wolf Erlbruch, Stewart, Tabori & Change.

Children are fascinated with everything to do with poop, and this German picture book appeals to their interest in how different animals do it as well as their sense of justice. Little Mole pokes his head out of his hole and plop, someone poops right on his head. "Who dared to drop that on my head?" shouts Little Mole angrily. Thus begins Mole's hysterical search for the animal who did it. Children from two on up will delight in this story, although younger children will miss some of the more sophisticated humor.

Go: Supporting Independent Toileting

As children use the potty more consistently, here are ways you can support their success:

• **Share your observations and give feedback.** Feedback helps children learn. You may notice that your child, who wakes up with dry diapers nearly every morning, pees in them almost immediately. You can say to him: "I've noticed that you hold your pee all night long and that you pee when you first wake up." Or to a child who's just learning to go out in the world without diapers: "Last time, when we went to the store you had to pee and it was hard to find a toilet. Would you like to pee before you go or wear a diaper this time?"

• **Keep your excitement in line with theirs.** The old-school belief about toileting was that you had to make a big deal about it or children wouldn't want to do it. But learning to use the toilet *is* exciting for children. Too big a response on our part can actually overshadow our child's achievement. Celebrate children's successes with them, but let their feelings and excitement hold the primary position.

• **Rewards can be distracting.** It's tempting to use rewards to "motivate" children to do things we want them to do, and in fact, rewards do sometimes change behavior. There are, however, drawbacks to using rewards. When we "reward" children for their natural learning process, we may inadvertently detract from their internal sense of accomplishment. We may also communicate a lack of confidence in their own timing or motivation. Finally, children who are regularly "rewarded" may begin to expect external rewards and refuse to do anything unless a prize is offered.

Rather than using rewards, simple acknowledgment and appreciation of their learning lets children know that they are important to us and that we are paying attention to what they are doing: "I noticed that you went into the bathroom and went pee in the potty all by yourself!" "It's fun to see you learning new things."[4]

• **Perceive accidents as opportunities.** When you discover the inevitable puddle or poopy pants, your response can support or discourage your child. Statements such as "I can't believe this!" or "Won't you ever learn not to have accidents?" may shame the child or tell her that she is unable to learn.

If you see "accidents" as learning opportunities, you can talk about what happened in ways your child can learn from. "Oh, the peepee is on the porch. You must have been standing there when it came out." "Oh, there's poop in your pants. Let's change them and you can decide if you want to try pants again or a diaper this time."

When children do make puddles or piles on the ground or the floor, they can help to clean them up (not punitively, but rather "Oh! you made pee, let's get a cloth and you can wipe it up"). Few children will resist wiping with you (making the pee disappear!), but a child should not be forced to clean it up.

• **Cultivate a spirit of optimism in your child's ability to succeed.** Probably the most significant help we can give children as they are learning to use the toilet is our faith that it will happen. "Everybody learns to use the toilet and you will learn, too, when you are ready." This calm sense of assurance may not be easy to muster when you're surrounded by messages about how hard it is and about how many ways you can mess it up. But if you can look around

[4] See "The Problem with Praise," on p. 22 for a thorough discussion of this idea.

Bedwetting and Nighttime Dryness

Most children achieve daytime bladder and bowel control before they do at night. For some children, it is a matter of weeks or months before they have control both day and night. For others, it may be years before they are dry at night. Here are several ways to support children in the meantime:

• **Help children understand that their toileting timetable is normal for them.** Children don't know how or when toilet learning should happen. You can provide the information and set the tone: "Everyone learns to be dry at night when they are ready. It happens at different times for different people." You may also give examples of people in the family who've learned it at different times.

• **It is normal for there to be disparity between day and night control.** There are a number of children who are still learning night control up to twelve years old. While this won't be the case for most children, it's important to remember that many children won't achieve night dryness in their toddler years.

• **Night control involves a complex set of factors and isn't just a matter of the child "wanting" to be dry at night.** Physical and developmental readiness are also important factors in night dryness. For some children, the size of their bladder and the quality of their sleep make it more difficult for them to stay dry all night. Many people are never able to go all night without urinating. They just have to learn how to wake themselves up to go to the bathroom. Supporting children's success at night may involve putting a potty chair by their bed, waking them up to take them to the bathroom before you go to bed, setting an alarm for them if they are older, and periodically trying a night without diapers (if the child wants to) to see if she is ready.

If children are going to try a night without diapers, it is important that it be done from an experimental base, with no failure or disappointment involved. "Let's see if you are ready." "It looks like you are not quite ready. We'll try it again later."

• **Children need to be protected from ridicule either from inside or outside the family.** Children learn better and quicker the more competent they feel about themselves. Parents, siblings, extended family, and friends should be asked not to tease or make fun of someone who "wets the bed."

Often people tease from their own sense of fear or inadequacy, so it will be useful for everyone to hear "People learn things when they are ready. Everybody has a different time that is right for them. Maybe you have already learned to be dry at night, and now you are working on learning to skate. Jasmine is still learning to be dry at night, but she has already learned how to ride a bike." Some people may need clearer limits if they continue to tease. "That's not something we tease about in our family. I can't allow you to tease Jasmine about it."

Spending an overnight with friends may be a time when children become uncomfortable with wearing diapers at night. It will help your child if you can talk with the other parent beforehand to make sure that they will be supportive of your child's needs.

• **As with daytime toilet learning, it is important for the family to be comfortable with the "accidents" that are a natural part of the learning.** As well as understanding that learning night control may be a long process, it is also important to set up the environment so that "accidents" are easy to deal with and are not a cause for anger or shame. Diapers are usually available in all sizes, and a rubberized flannel sheet can protect the mattress.

you at all the people who have learned to do it successfully, you may be able to take the leap of faith that it, too, will happen for your child.

Once you develop that trust, it is easier to convey your confidence to children. Their timetable seems more tolerable, accidents seem less devastating. Children will be able to look to your confidence and take their cues from it.

Foibles of Newly Independent Toileters

Children who have recently achieved success with toileting have several typical characteristics. It is not uncommon for children who've put a lot of energy into learning to use the toilet to regress or become inflexible in other areas. Soledad recalls, "Juan Carlos learned to use the toilet quickly. It seemed as if it happened overnight. But almost immediately I noticed that he became demanding and controlling with the family. He started trying to boss me around, telling me where I could sit, when *I* could use the toilet. He also started waking up at night. He became clingy and wouldn't let me leave him with his baby-sitter. After a while he was back to his old self, but it was rough for a while."

Once children discover the joy of toilets, many begin their own personal research project. Cara describes an impossible shopping trip. "We went to the mall one day right after my daughter, Stephanie, had learned to use the toilet and it was like she was obsessed. Every new store we went into, she said she had to pee. Often we would get into the bathroom and she would change her mind. It drove me crazy, but I think it was her way of finding out if there were going to be potties for her out in the world. She'd never considered whether there were potties in these places, but all of a sudden, it was relevant."

Other children have an opposite response, refusing to use any new toilet. Scott recalls: "We were at a gas station and I took Brent into the bathroom and he looked at the toilet with this shocked look on his face and yelled 'No!' I think it actually surprised him that it wasn't the same toilet we had at home. He refused to go in it and we finally compromised on the bushes outside. After that, we began to carry his potty with us."

Some children discover power in their newfound skill and vocabulary. At times when there is no other ploy that will get their parents' attention, children are almost certain to get a response by announcing "peepee!" Janis's seven-year-old daughter, Maya, loves to hear Janis tell this story about when she was a toddler: "We were driving back from visiting family in Los Angeles. Maya had just learned to use the toilet consistently, and this coincided with a time that she also hated being in her car seat. We had planned to do most of our driving at night, but she was still awake for the first leg of the trip. We hadn't gotten too far along when Maya proclaimed from her car seat, 'PEE-PEEEE!' So we pulled the car over to the side of the road (as was our custom), took her out of her car seat, walked her over to the bushes, helped her get her pants down, and she announced, 'NO PEE-PEE!' We got back into the car, struggled to get her into her car seat, and drove for another five minutes or so when she said again, 'PEE-PEEEE!' We stopped, got her out, pulled down her pants, and she said, 'NO PEE-PEE!' Being slow learners, and also wondering if she finally would need to go, we stopped about eight more times for the same drama, before she announced 'PEE-PEEE!' once more and I turned around to her and said, 'If you need to go pee, you can go in your pants in your car seat. That's fine with me.' We didn't stop any more and amazingly, she was still dry by the time we pulled into our driveway seven hours later."

Toileting As a Metaphor for Learning

Helping children learn to use the toilet is one of the first ventures into "teaching" that many parents take. Toilet learning provides parents with an opportunity not only to help children get out of diapers, but also to begin to figure out how "teaching-learning" relationships work with their children.

As you support your child in learning this new skill, you have the opportunity to demonstrate trust in her healthy drive to learn new things in her own time, which enhances her sense of confidence. Your child has the opportunity to learn about how her body works. You have the chance to demonstrate your availability and creativity as a resource person, and you will, no doubt, get to show your child that you, as a parent, are still learning and growing, too. Most important, learning to use the toilet provides lots of chances to teach the usefulness of making mistakes. It's likely that both parents and children will have the opportunity to practice this.

17. Learning About Bodies

"We need a flashlight, can we have a flashlight?" Meredith said excitedly as she came out of the bathroom . . . "Do you have a flashlight?"
"Yes," I said. "In the bottom drawer. What are you looking for that you need a light?"
"We're looking for Mary's penis."

CONVERSATION BETWEEN A FOUR-YEAR-OLD AND HER DAY CARE PROVIDER[1]

For children, the process of getting to know their bodies—what they look like, how they feel, how they work, how they change—is like exploring a foreign country without a map. Children are eager explorers on this journey, equipped with their senses, their curiosity, their persistence, and their ingenuity.

For parents, the job of helping children learn about their bodies presents a unique set of questions and challenges. We help our children identify and acknowledge the bodily sensations that tell them they are hungry or tired; we help them figure out if they are feeling fear, sadness, pleasure, joy, anger, or excitement.

We are also called upon to respond to our children's sexual curiosity, which is inextricably tied to their interest in their bodies in general. This particular curiosity, however, may raise new questions for us: "How can I talk to my child about her body and about sex?" "What kind of sexual exploration is okay with me?" "How can I set limits without making my child feel ashamed?" In clarifying these issues for ourselves, we begin to teach children what's appropriate and safe. We pass on values around nudity, privacy, personal boundaries, and touch.

Parents are also the mirrors who let children know that their bodies are beautiful, that it's okay to explore the world with confidence, that it's safe to move freely and vigorously.

All of this is part of the physical legacy we pass on to children.

[1] Joan Roemer, *Two to Four from 9 to 5*, p. 203.

Children Are Naturally Curious About Their Bodies: A Developmental View

Newborn babies don't know that they have bodies. Figuring this out is one of their first tasks. As they begin to watch and experience the world, babies begin to recognize some familiar things in their environment. Three-month-old Gaby notices that one particular thing sometimes feels good to suck on. She discovers that she can make this thing appear and disappear, and learns that this wonderful thing is actually attached to her. She discovers that it's her hand and that it can come from either side of her body!

Babies and young toddlers learn about their bodies by moving and trying them out. They bounce up and down with their legs. They try out the muscles in their arms to see if they can hold themselves up. As soon as they can stand, they begin walking, running, and climbing, exploring the outer limits of their balance, strength and coordination. In doing so, they explore the questions: "How does my body work?" "What kinds of things can it do?" "How strong are my arms and legs?"

Preschoolers define and refine their physical skills even further, jumping, running around obstacles, hanging upside down from their knees, balancing on one foot, mastering tricycles, and learning to hop.

Children are also developing their smaller muscles during these years. Babies learn how to use their thumb and finger to pick up tiny things that they previously used their whole fist to grasp. Toddlers can pick things up, manipulate them in their hands, and fit them into a container. Preschoolers can button, lace, and screw lids on jars.

During these same years, children go from moving their hands without conscious control to being able to use their eyes and their hands in unison to perform millions of small tasks. Ultimately, they learn to do things with their hands—roll a ball of clay, pick their noses, or pull up their pants—without even looking.

Young children also explore their voices, testing the range of sounds they can make, using their tongues, lips, throats, and listening to the results with their ears. Toddlers and preschoolers also experiment with volume—practicing how loudly they can scream—trying their voices out into a blanket, a cup, or in a hallway, the park, the garage, or the car.

In the first five years of life, children are also figuring out where their bodies begin and end. They learn about their size in relationship to other things in the world. Babies sometimes bump their heads against the wall behind them to find out: "What's back there anyway?" "How far does my head stick out?" You can observe toddlers trying to fit themselves into impossibly small spaces or ducking their heads much lower than a particular tunnel requires. Young preschoolers have been afraid that they would go

Physical Play and Roughhousing with Children

Many parents have traditionally played with their children through wrestling, tickling, or "chase and catch" games. In most families, these have been fun ways to play and show affection. However, wrestling, tickling, and chasing can become scary for young children.

Because adults are bigger and stronger than children, they can easily slip into "overpowering" children with wrestling, tickling, or chasing, while convincing themselves that children are enjoying it because they are still "laughing." However, laughter does not always indicate that children are having fun. Sometimes children laugh hysterically, but the tone of their laughter and the tension in their voices indicate underlying feelings of panic or fear. Because of this, parents should pay close attention to the quality of their child's laughter. It's also important that games not be competitive, that adults take care not to overpower or pin children. (Children do, however, enjoy "pinning" the adult and, when wrestling, should have opportunities to do so.)

In many families, the only physical contact males have been allowed to have with children is through tickling, so fathers and uncles and brothers may be left with the frustration of trying to demonstrate all of their affection for kids in that way. While short, gentle tickling can be enjoyable for both parent and child, long, extended, can't-breathe-anymore episodes of tickling can be horrible experiences for children.

In "chase" games, there is a fine line between the enjoyable thrill of the chase and actually being scared. Young children, still unsophisticated about possible transformations, can slip into believing that the loving parent roaring behind them is really a dangerous lion. There is a subtle but important distinction between your child's squeal of delight and his scream of terror. Sometimes children will not ask adults to stop or will beg them to continue these games, even though they're uncomfortable, because they still want the adult's attention. In these circumstances, it is our job to read our child's verbal and nonverbal signals and to stop or alter the game before she becomes frightened.

Successful physical play with children involves stopping the play periodically to see if the child wants to continue. You can do this by asking children directly or by simply backing off or collapsing on the ground, then waiting to see if they reinitiate the play or shift to another game. It's important that kids have lots of other ways they can be with you, that they get to initiate or lead parts of the play, and also that they get a chance to be the tickler or the chaser. It's also important for grown-ups to let children "win"—which allows children to increase their sense of mastery.

Through this kind of responsive physical play, children learn that they have personal boundaries that will be respected. They learn that they have the right to say "no" and that their "no" will be listened to. They learn that they can change an interaction that is uncomfortable without losing their connection with that person. They experience the pleasure of mutual, reciprocal, physical closeness and play.

down the bathroom drain. By the time they reach five, children develop a much more realistic picture of their body and its size.

At no other time does physical development happen as rapidly as if does in the first five years. Nowhere is the drive to be physical more compelling. Children are bursting with energy to discover everything they can about their bodies.

Helping Children Feel Comfortable and Confident in Their Bodies

There are some basic things parents can do during children's early years to encourage children to feel relaxed, confident, safe, and "at home" in their bodies:

• **Provide for children's basic physical needs and encourage children's self-help skills.** Meeting children's physical needs and allowing for their participation in self-care (feeding, dressing, washing, grooming) teaches them about their bodies as well as health and safety.

• **Treat your child's body respectfully and lovingly.** Parents have the opportunity to teach appropriate ways of demonstrating affection. Children who are snuggled, nuzzled, and cuddled experience the pleasure of touch and the delight of sharing physical contact with a loved one.

Children use this information to create successful relationships, both with their peers and later in life. When children's bodies are treated lovingly, they learn that they deserve that same kind of respect in all of their relationships.

• **Help children learn to read their body's signals.** You can help children gain this awareness by talking to them: "You're rooting all around for that nipple. You look hungry." Or "I notice you're rubbing your eyes and yawning. That's your body's way of telling you it's time for a nap."

• **Teach children about basic body functions.** Children need simple, correct information about how their bodies work. You can gradually say more as they show an interest: "When you go all day without a nap, you get tired earlier." Or "You were running really hard. Your heart is beating fast." Or "After your body is all done using the food that you eat, the rest comes out as poop."

Children may also become curious about adult body parts and functions, especially visible ones such as body hair, pregnancy, and menstruation. Having simple answers to their questions can cut down on children's later feelings of fear, discomfort, and embarrassment. (See "Body Language" on p. 203 for specific ideas on answering children's questions.)

• **Encourage freedom of movement and provide opportunities for physical play.** Children love to dance, climb, jump, and move to their own inner rhythms and drives. In order for children to develop physical competence and a comfortable relationship with their bodies, they need to have opportunities to move freely. Through verbal and nonverbal cues, parents let children know whether it's okay to engage in active, physical play. By trusting their explorations and allowing them to try new things, you demonstrate your confidence in children's emerging physical abilities.

Parents can encourage physical exploration by providing both boys and girls with easily washable clothes that allow freedom of movement. You can also create opportunities for jumping, climbing, and other physical play by regularly taking children to playgrounds. Children also really enjoy the physical challenges available to them in nature: in the forest, by a creek, in an open field, at the park, or in someone's backyard.

• **Respect your child's curiosity.** Honor your child's interest in her own body: "Seems like you're really curious about your body. Bodies are really interesting and they do lots of things."

• **Develop a vision.** Both consciously and subconsciously, parents carry ideas and expectations about the kind of relationship they want their children to have with their bodies. Parents may hope that their children are healthy, coordinated, active, athletic, strong, or cuddly. Most parents want their children to feel good about their bodies, to grow into adults who feel comfortable with their sexuality.

Many parents want things for their children that they missed out on. Felicia has forged a new vision: "The people in my family have never been satisfied with their looks. They complained about the size and shape of their noses, butts, bellies . . . even their knees. It took me most of my adult life to finally learn to appreciate my physical beauty, and I am definitely going to pass that idea on to my kids, 'You are beautiful just the way you are.' "

Some parents find that their vision doesn't match who their child naturally is. Ken explains, "Growing up, all the kids in my family were strong and active. I just assumed that my two girls would be the same. And my first daughter was. From the very start, Oona looked like she was ready for the baby Olympics. But Lydia, my second daughter, loves to draw and spends most of her time indoors. I've had to adjust my expectations in order to enjoy and cherish the kind of child she is."

• **Provide healthy models for children.** Children pay attention to how you feel about your body and how you treat it. One mother, Eileen, found her two-and-a-half-year-old looking in the mirror, pinching her thighs and saying "Fat! Fat! Fat!" Eileen realized immediately that her daughter had learned that behavior from her and had to quickly make some changes.

When we tell children that their bodies are beautiful but don't demonstrate that same appreciation for ourselves, kids become confused. When we tell them that they need to take good care of themselves and yet *we* don't get enough sleep, exercise, and good food, children become skeptical. Although none of us has "arrived," working toward a healthy relationship with our own body is essential modeling for our children.

Children's Sexual Explorations: A Developmental View[2]

Even before children are fully aware of the parameters of their bodies, many reach down and discover their genitals. In the first year of life, many babies experience that touching their penises or vulvas feels good. Babies and young toddlers often stick their hands down their diapers for comfort, as well.

Children's curiosity about their genitals

[2] Using the word "sexuality" in conjunction with children can be misleading because children's experience of sexuality is very different from what adults experience. Yet early childhood experiences of love, safety, trust, relationship, and body pleasure do lay the groundwork for later relationships and adult sexuality. As we talk about children's sexual explorations and sex play here, it's critical to remember that we're talking about *children's* feelings, experiences, and perceptions, not *adult* sexuality.

usually ebbs and flows. Some time between a year and a half and three, many children start more active investigation of their genitals. Children involved in this kind of exploration are answering the basic questions: "What does it look like?" "How does it work?" "What's the shape of it?" and "How does it feel?"

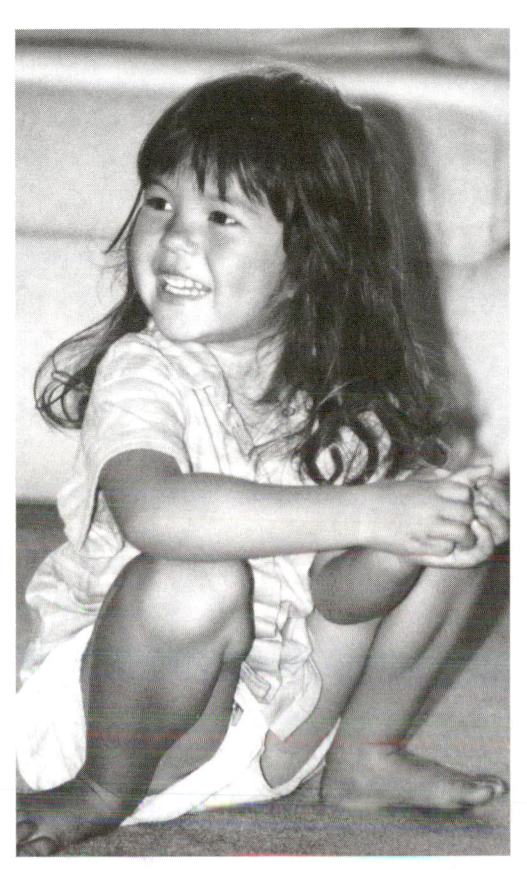

Little boys get erections regularly from infancy on, and their primary response is not just one of pleasure but also one of surprise, interest, fascination, and, at times, even fear: "What's happening to me?" "What's my body doing?" Since young children don't know what's going to change and what's going to stay the same, a little boy can become fearful when his penis becomes bigger and sticks out. He may be concerned that it won't change back to the familiar penis that he's grown to know and love. Once boys begin to observe that their penis changes, they may begin to test to see what makes it stiff and what makes it relaxed.

Children's natural curiosity often moves from exploration of their own bodies to exploration with other children. By the age of three or four, many children have had the chance to see other children naked: in the bath, getting dressed, or playing in warm weather. For these children, seeing another person with his clothes off is not a brand-new experience.

Because of their emerging ability to categorize, to figure out similarities and differences, preschool children often become fascinated by the differences between girls' and boys' bodies, between men's and women's bodies, between childrens' and adults' bodies. As they become sophisticated enough to see that there are differences, they often want to explore those differences.

One of the ways children do this is through language. Keith told the following story: "My daughter went through a period where she was fascinated by penises and vaginas. She'd look at her little brother and say, 'Nicky has a penis. Daddy has a penis. Mommy has a pagina. I have a pagina.' She'd name all the people she knew and say whether they had a penis or a pagina. It was particularly embarrassing one night at McDonald's. She was holding her Barbie doll and she said in a really loud voice, 'Mommy, does Barbie have a pagina?' We quietly told her, 'Yes, Barbie *does* have a pagina.' "

Children often try to make sense of how bodies work in terms of experiences that are familiar to them. One mother, Lexie, recalls, "When Darla was four and a half, she came in one day and said to me, 'Mom, remember when I was borned out of you? If I had been a letter, then your vagina would have been a mailbox."

Another way children explore gender differences is by looking at or touching another child's genitals. Sometimes this happens when kids take baths with siblings, cousins, or friends. For some kids, the exploration stops there. They move on to another activity, like trying to see if they can put their faces underwater.

Other children go on to further kinds of exploration. Sometimes sex play happens in one particular relationship, or it may become a common game among a group of friends. This research can go on between girls and boys or between children of the same gender. Mostly it's all part of children's healthy curiosity.

Children's sex play evolves as they get older. Three-year-olds and young four-year-olds may touch each other a little, giggle, and say, 'Pee-pee, pee-pee!" As children get to be older fours or fives, they sometimes get into a more extended kind of exploration. Depending on what they've seen or the information they have, children may begin getting under the covers together, rocking on each other's bodies, or playing elaborate doctor games.

Sometimes children use dramatic play to help them work through real events in their lives. Bethany explained, "Isabel was four when her sister, Sofia, was born. For weeks before the birth, Isabel went to preschool and talked about fallopian tubes and uteruses. She was at Sofia's birth, and soon afterward, she was out on the playground orchestrating this whole scene in which one of her playmates was lying fully clothed on the ground, spread-eagled, and another one was lying on the floor in the fetal position between her legs. Isabel was the midwife. As she would say, 'Push,' the one in the fetal position would come wiggling out from in between the other girl's legs."

Toddlers and preschool children are also busy exploring social rules. What starts as curiosity about bodies often moves into social research as children begin to get feedback from their parents and the world. Children quickly learn that people have different degrees of comfort talking about bodies and that "grown-ups sometimes respond differently when I touch my knee than they do when I touch my vulva."

Kids explore such questions as: "Why is my mother blushing?" "What does it mean that I can do this at home in the bathtub, but not at church?" "Why did my dad say I couldn't play with Jenn anymore?" For parents, it's useful to remember that even though children sometimes push against the rules we set, they are pushing because they are very interested in knowing what those rules are.

The Continuum of Curiosity

Within the range of normal development, children's interest in their bodies and their genitals varies greatly. Some children move through their early years hardly seeming to notice their genitals, rarely touching them and never asking questions. Esme, mother of three-year-old Guillermo and five-year-old Raul, says that she has never seen her children exploring their genitals: "As far as I know, they just don't do it."

Wendy, mother of five-year-old Kristen, agreed, "I was all prepared to talk to Kristen about bodies and sex, but she's almost in kindergarten and she still hasn't shown any interest."

Some children, who have little or no interest in genitals during their early years, become more aware and interested as they get older. For others, it's not until their adolescent years that an awareness of sexuality develops.

At the other end of the continuum are toddlers and preschoolers who are actively curious about their bodies and explore every part of them thoroughly. Jessica describes one of her two-year-old's favorite activities: "Heidi loves to look in the mirror, bend way over, and open her labia to peer into her vagina. She must do that two or three times a day."

Maury remembers: "Anders loved his penis.

At four years old, he loved to have an erection and gallop around the house, watching it bounce. He had a long robe he wore to bed and he was fascinated with making his penis poke out the opening."

Sometimes children's natural curiosity leads them to explore in unsafe ways. Kylie, mother of two-year-old, Joy, shared: "One day Joy was in the yard and I noticed that she was putting little pebbles in her vagina. I was stunned. I had to hold her still on the grass and gently take them out. I've felt like I have to watch her every minute since then. It was interesting, though, that same week she put shrimp in her ear and yogurt up her nose. It was like she was determined to explore all of her orifices."

Children's curiosity falls all along this continum, depending on their individual personalities and temperaments as well as their experiences. It's important to note that the degree of a child's natural curiosity isn't always indicative of later sexual behavior. People who show a strong interest and curiosity in sexual exploration as young children don't necessarily grow up to be sexually precocious teenagers or sexually preoccupied adults. Likewise, children who show little interest in their early years may be quite sexually active and interested as adults.

Children's Sexual Explorations: Issues for Parents

Families have widely diverging perspectives on issues related to sexuality, nudity, and children's sexual explorations with friends. Some parents are comfortable with their children's curiosity. Others don't want their children engaging in any kind of sexual play. Still others want to be more comfortable than they are. Most parents, at times, have felt awkward or confused about how to respond when faced with children's explorations.

Our society leaves little room to develop a healthy, integrated attitude toward sexuality. We're surrounded by powerful sexual images in which sex is used to sell products or gain an advantage. In such an environment, it can be hard for parents to be clear about what healthy sexual development is.

Family history also plays a big role in our comfort or discomfort around bodies. Some of us grew up with a sense of openness and comfort about our sexuality. Others have been able to develop a much healthier relationship to our sexuality than our own parents had. Many of us, however, carry a legacy of shame, silence, and disapproval about sex. Dorrie explains: "I grew up in a really conservative, fundamentalist family. We were absolutely forbidden to explore our genitals. But I did it anyway—with my siblings and with the neighbor kids. I always walked around feeling guilty, scared that we'd be found out.

"One time word got out that I'd been doing sex play with my five-year-old friend Frankie. My mother chose to confront me at bedtime prayer in front of the whole family. She asked me, 'Did you show Frankie your panties?' Although I understood that lying to a parent was a very grave sin, I also knew that I hadn't shown Frankie my panties—I'd shown him my genitals. So in all sincerity, I said, 'No.' My mother believed me and let it go. I knew I'd gotten away with something I would have been severely punished for."

Janis also remembers a ban on any kind of sex play in her family: "My father's mother used to call his penis his 'uh-uh toy.' "

Many of us grew up with silence around sex. Ginny recalls, "There was never any talk about body parts in my family. I remember being five and lying on the bed watching my mom get dressed. I'd never seen her naked before. She took off her pajamas, and before she put her bra and clothes on, I became aware of her breasts for the first time. So I said, 'Mom, what are those?' And she said, 'Skin.' Even at five, I *knew* that she wasn't telling me the whole truth. I knew there was something special about them, that they weren't just skin, but that for some reason, she wasn't giving me the word for them."

A history of childhood abuse can also create confusion about sex. Leah, who's an incest survivor, says: "Because I was sexually abused, I tend to have a lot of confusion about boundaries. I'm always afraid I'm going to cross the line. If I get the slightest indication that somebody doesn't want to be touched, I won't. Touch isn't something I can be casual about."

Most of us don't want to transmit feelings of confusion, discomfort, or shame to children regarding their bodies, yet sexuality is often the one area in which what we want to teach is furthest away from where we are in our own lives.

Figuring out how to teach a healthy attitude about bodies and sexuality requires a lot of learning, thinking, and practice. For some of us, this means working on our fears, confusions, and hurts around sex. In the process of helping our children learn about their bodies, we often grow, learn, and find new clarity ourselves.[3]

[3] Many of us growing up in this society carry a lot of pain and hurt about our sexuality. Thinking about these issues as parents is likely to bring up any unresolved issues and feelings you may still be carrying. It's important to know that there a lot of resources and support available for both men and women who were hurt sexually as children and that it is never too late to resolve and heal from such hurts or abuse. You can begin the process now. In doing so, you will be giving both yourself and your child a valuable gift of healing. For a comprehensive and supportive resource you could refer to *The Courage to Heal* by Ellen Bass and Laura Davis (HarperCollins, 1988).We also recommend *The Sexual Healing Journey* by Wendy Maltz (HarperCollins, 1991) for further reading.

FOOD FOR THOUGHT: LEARNING ABOUT BODIES

- What messages did I get about my body when I was growing up?
- Were those messages different for boys and girls?
- Were bodies, genitals, and sexuality talked about in my family? How and by whom? Were there unspoken messages, as well?

Responding When Kids Touch Their Genitals

When adults see children touching themselves, they often think about a level of sexuality that's beyond what most young children experience; they think of masturbation to a climax. This is generally not what children are doing when they touch themselves. Most children rub their genitals simply because it feels good. Some do it in stressful situations as a way to relax. As one mother, Jacqueline, explained, "Sucking his thumb and playing with his penis usually go hand in hand."

As you try to figure out what's appropriate around this self-exploration, it's useful to ask: "Where and when is my child touching his genitals?" "How does that fit in terms of what's comfortable in our family?" "In the larger community?"

Some parents tell children they can touch their genitals only in their bedrooms, only when they're at home or in the backyard, only when they're alone and not with friends, or never around Aunt Judi.

A lot depends on a parent's level of comfort. Ginny explains: "The first few times I found Danielle touching herself, I just wanted to scream 'Don't do that!' But I kept my mouth shut and went to my parents' group to talk about it. I really needed help figuring out what to say. It bothered me that she was getting pleasure from her body."

Neil remembers, "I ignored it until my kids got to be around two and a half. At that point, I figured they were ready to learn about the importance of privacy."

Alison set limits when her son was older. "Jason loves to play with his penis. I think I would, too, if I had one. His first few years, we basically ignored it. When he was four, we decided it was time to teach him a few social restraints. We told him it was fine to play with his penis, but only when he was at home. At seven, we set a few more limits. We told him it was something you did alone, not around other people."

How Can I Know If It's Really Okay?

Once children discover the pleasures of touching their genitals, it's not unusual for them to spend some pretty focused time doing it. Occasionally, when children spend an enormous amount of time touching their genitals, something besides healthy exploration may be going on. When touching themselves is their major activity for more than a few days, it may be indicative of unmet emotional needs, inappropriate exposure to sex, or some kind of sexual abuse that the child is trying to make sense of.[4]

In most cases, however, children's exploration of their genitals is a healthy, normal part of their development. Genital touch feels good. Although it may be harder for most of us to welcome our child's self-stimulation with the same enthusiasm we greet their other physical accomplishments, it's important that we strive to keep our responses as shame-free as possible.

[4] If you feel concerned about your child's sex play or what seems to you a sudden inappropriate knowledge of sex for your child's age, it's important to explore what's going on. Talk to your child. Look for other changes in your child's behavior—pronounced fears, especially of certain people or places, nightmares, abrupt emotional or behavioral changes, unexplained redness or swelling around the genitals. These *can* be signs of sexual abuse, but most of them may also be indicative of other problems or developmental issues your child is struggling with.

Although it's important not to jump to conclusions, it's equally important not to ignore such symptoms. If you feel concerned about possible abuse, take your child to the doctor for a thorough physical exam. It's important to note that if your doctor suspects abuse, she is mandated by law to report her findings to the local child protection agency, which will then investigate.

You can call the National Child Abuse Hotline at (800) 4-A-CHILD for information and referrals. There are also some good books for parents dealing with child sexual abuse: *When Your Child Has Been Molested* by Kathleen Hagan and Joyce Case (New York: Free Press, 1988) and *The Mother's Book: How to Survive the Incest of Your Child* by Carolyn Byerly (Dubuque, Iowa: Kendall/Hunt Publishing), 1985.

"But They're Touching Each Other": Responding to Mutual Sex Play

Parents are often at a loss when they walk in and find their child playing doctor or engaging in sex play with another child. Many parents freeze or panic. They immediately think of adult sex or molestation, making it difficult for them to recognize what children are actually trying to explore.

Parents' experiences, perspective, and values all influence how they feel about children's sex play. In some families, such explorations are accepted openly. Lisa explains, "My son, Louie, has a best friend, Trina, who's a year

"I Never Ran Up the Stairs So Fast in My Life": Faye's Story

In families where some mutual sex play is allowed, the parents' role is to provide clear parameters and ensure safety. In the following story, Faye demonstrates the basic strategies we outline here, and, when things went too far, she set limits, consulted with the other parent, and sought out the source of the children's behavior.

My son, Nico, is five and his best friend, Celine, is a little girl the same age. One day, about a year ago, they were playing up in his bedroom. I was cooking down in the kitchen, and it just so happened that my daughter's baby monitor was turned on in that room, so I could hear everything that was going on. I was listening to their play, not really paying too much attention. All of a sudden I heard Celine say, "Let's trade underwear. Then I'll be a boy and you can be a girl." That caught my attention, but it sounded innocent enough. When they started talking about touching penises and vaginas, I listened a little more carefully, but it sounded like there was mutual consent for what they were doing. No one was being forced to do anything and no one was getting hurt. I figured that meant the play was okay.

Then I started to wonder how Celine's mother was going to feel. I had a responsibility to her, and I was also concerned about how she might feel about me for letting it continue. Right about then I heard in the monitor, "Now you put your mouth on my penis and I'll put my mouth on your vagina."

I never ran up the stairs so fast in my life. I was giggling because I was so nervous and embarrassed. I stood in the doorway, thinking "Now what do I say?" Then I told them, "I think you should put on your underwear now." So they did. Then I went into the next room to calm down about the whole thing.

Later I asked them, "Where did you get that idea about putting your mouths on penises and vaginas?" They said, "Nowhere." I really wanted to know where that idea came from. I called and talked to Celine's mother about it. We figured out the information probably came from Celine's teenage sister.

Nico and Celine continued to play together, and they kept doing sex play for a while after that incident. But we monitored them carefully. Things never went that far again. And a couple of months later, they dropped that kind of play and were on to other things.

younger. Trina lives next door and the kids have played together all their lives. For years, Trina would hold her labia open and they'd both look at her vagina. Then they'd giggle. They played that game a lot and it mostly involved a lot of giggling. There never seemed to be much exploration of his penis.

"It seemed innocent. We kept an eye on what they were doing, but basically we left it alone. Eventually they stopped doing it on their own."

In other families, sex play between children is not allowed. Regina explains, "Our family is very big on privacy. I always told my kids that their bodies were private, that they alone were allowed to touch them. I let them know that they weren't supposed to show their private parts to other people until they grew up and got married. I wanted my children to know that their bodies were very special and that they shouldn't just show them to anyone."

Guidelines for Responding to Mutual Sex Play

When dealing with children's explorations with friends, there are four basic goals to keep in mind. First, children need to learn about safety. Second, children need to know how to set clear limits about touch. Third, children's curiosity needs to be respected. And last, children need to learn about our rules and what's socially appropriate.

The following guidelines can help you achieve these goals:

• **Let children know that their curiosity is okay with you.** Regardless of whether you allow the play or not, you can make it clear to kids that you respect their curiosity. "Looks like you're interested in each other's bottoms, but I'd like you to put your pants on now." Or "Seems like you're curious about what your vulvas look like. It's okay with me for you to look, if it's okay with each of you."

• **It's okay to buy yourself some time.** If you don't trust your first response or if you're not sure what you want to do, you can say to children (in a nonpunitive way), "I'd like you to get dressed and find something else to play." After you've had a chance to think about it and maybe explore your thoughts about it with another adult, go back and talk to the children.

• **Find out more about what the children are actually doing.** You can do this by asking questions: "Looks like you're really curious about each other's bodies. What have you found out?" Or "I see you're under the blanket. Is this a special game you're playing? Tell me about it."

• **Establish open lines of communication.** If you keep communication open with your children, most likely they'll bring their ideas to you. You'll learn about their thinking, their questions, and their play. You'll be able to share your ideas and beliefs and also keep track of the information they're getting.

If you feel children have been privy to inappropriate information, it's useful to ask, "Where did you hear that idea? Were you talking to someone about that?" or "That's an interesting idea. Can you tell me more about it?"

When children know that they can talk to us, we're better able to help them if they're struggling with confusing information or a hurtful situation.

• **Establish some limits and safeguards.** Tell children what is and isn't allowed: "You can only *look* at your friend's body," or "You can only explore your body with *your* hands. No one else is allowed to do that."

Rules should also deal with basic safety issues: "You don't stick anything but fingers up any of the holes in your body—ears, noses, vaginas, anuses, or mouths." "It's important to wash your hands after you poop or touch your anus."

• **Teach children to ask permission.** Introduce the concept of asking permission: "Your friend has to ask you before he touches any part of your body." Or, "Anyone gets to say 'no' to any part of the play they don't like."

• **Work with kids on saying "no."** If you think kids might have trouble setting limits, help them practice. Say, "It looks like this game is okay with you now. If Roberto wanted to do something and you didn't want to, what would you do?" Or, "How would you tell Sandra if you didn't want to play this game any more?"

Sometimes children won't say "no" because they want to keep playing with a particular friend. If this is the case, give them the option of changing the game: "Roberto, is this a game you still want to play, or would you like to play something else instead?"

If you have a feeling that the children aren't comfortable answering honestly in front of each other, stop the play and take them aside privately.

• **Know the children who are involved.** Sex play can become problematic if one of the children has been sexually hurt or had an unhealthy experience. This may lead them to bring a different level of knowledge or emotional intensity to the play. Children who've been hurt around sex often try to come to terms with that hurt through play. They might try out some things with another child that are unsafe or inappropriate.

When you're dealing with sexual exploration between children, it's important to know the other child and her family and to find out a little about her history. Another thing that is crucial to consider is the other family's level of comfort. Sex play is an area that families are very sensitive about. It's important that parents communicate with each other about what is happening and work together to set up consistency about what is allowed.

If you're not sure how the other family feels, stop the play until you find out. You could say, "It looks like you're interested in each other's bodies. I'm going to ask you to stop and play something else for now. I want to talk to Darcy's parents and see what their ideas are about this kind of play."

• **Be on the lookout for any kind of power imbalance.** Watch for the same dynamics you'd look for in other kinds of play. See if the children are comfortable, and make sure there's not an imbalance of power between them. That's where sex exploration between children can become problematic.

Younger children sometimes do things they're uncomfortable with just because they're fascinated with an older child. Power imbalances can also occur because of gender differences, family roles, or dynamics in the friendship. A child might "go along" because he's afraid of losing the friendship.

Consider each child in turn and ask yourself: "Can this child say 'no' in other aspects of his relationship with this child?"

If children have been playing together for some time, sex play would probably not be the first time you'd see this kind of imbalance. It's a dynamic that would most likely show up in other areas first. It's important to help children with these kinds of inequities in all aspects of their play.[5]

• **Give children other play options.** Sometimes children will get into a pattern of "doctor play," "marriage play," or some other kind of sex play with a particular friend. If you're concerned about children being stuck in that kind

[5] See "Children's Friendships: Cooperation and Conflict" on p. 304 for specific ideas on how to do this.

of play, structure some other activities when those children get together, so they have a chance to broaden the kinds of things they know how to do together as friends.

• **If you're not comfortable with children's sex play, provide alternative means of learning.** If you've asked children to stop what they're doing, help them find another way to satisfy with their curiosity. Help them get access to the information they need about bodies. Provide anatomically correct dolls, share age-appropriate books about bodies, and honestly answer their questions.

Body Language: Talking to Children About Sex

Despite all the available resources and information, the increasingly graphic images in the media, and all the sexual liberation that's supposedly taken place, talking to children about sex is still a challenge for many parents.

Many parents are taken by surprise. When we think about talking to kids about sex, many of us think that, *maybe*, the topic might come up as early as the preteen years. When it comes up with our two-, three-, or four-year-olds, many of us don't know how to respond.

The Milk's All Gone: Laura's Story

In the following story, Eli demonstrates the way young children gain knowledge about how bodies work—and shows his two-year-old attempt to apply that knowledge to himself. Through listening to Eli, Laura learns what he does and doesn't understand about bodies and is able to give him information in a way that he can understand. Eli doesn't yet know the basic difference between adults and children, between males and females, nor is it important that he learn that right now. But he is beginning to perceive the similarity—and the differences—between his body and his mother's.

Soon after he weaned himself, Eli and I were lying in my big bed one evening. I was trying to do some reading and I'd told Eli he could lie there if he was quiet. It was a hot night and I had my shirt off. My chest was showing above the sheet. Eli reached over and pushed my nipple in. When it popped out, he said delightedly, "It popped out." Then he reached over and tried the other side. I kept trying to read. I felt slightly annoyed. Then he did it again. And he said, "There used to be milk in there. Talk about it."

I put my book down and turned to him. "When you were growing in my womb, my body started making milk for you. Babies need milk. You didn't have teeth then, so all you did was nurse. You looked like this." I pursed my lips together and made sucking sounds.

Eli giggled. "Again! Tell me about when I nursed when I was a little, tiny baby again!"

"It wasn't really that long ago, Eli," I said. "You just stopped nursing a little while ago."

"There's no more milk. It's all gone," he concluded.

"Yes, when you stopped nursing, my body stopped making milk. Now it's all gone."

Eli thought for a moment. Then he pulled up his own shirt and looked down at his own nipples. "They used to have milk for Zev and Kobi, but they drank it all up." (Zev and Kobi are six-month-old friends who are twins.)

I smiled. "Oh, you nursed Zev and Kobi?"

"Yeah," Eli said with a big smile. "But they used up all the milk." Then he paused and looked over at my breasts. He smiled and held up his shirt again. "When I'm a big boy, my breasts will get big."

"Eli, when you get big, your chest will grow just like the rest of you. But your breasts will never grow like mine. Only women grow breasts like mine. Yours will stay flat."

"Mine will stay flat," he repeated, trying to take it in. "My breasts will always stay flat." Then he seemed finished with the conversation and pulled down his shirt again.

Talking to Children About Where Babies Come From

Many children under five, particularly those whose families add younger siblings, have questions about how babies are made and born. Here are some ideas for simple and gradual explanations. As you take cues from your child, you will develop other appropriate ways to respond, as well.

If your child asks "How did the baby start growing?" or "How do you get a baby?" your answer could be: "A woman has something special in her body called ovum and a man has something special in his body called sperm. When you put ovum and sperm together a baby starts growing," or "A man puts some sperm in a woman's body and if that sperm finds her ovum, then a baby starts growing." Amazingly, many children won't ask more at this point. Others will. "How does he give it to her?" At that point, you could say "He uses his penis to give it to her in her vagina," or "A man and a woman have a special way to get together that helps the sperm go into her body. They get close and hug and when he puts his penis in her vagina, the sperm comes out."

When your child asks "How does the baby get out?" you could say "From a special opening between the mother's legs," or "Through the mother's vagina," or "The mother pushes and pushes. Then her vagina slowly opens so the baby can come out," or "After the baby is done growing inside the mother, she gets a special signal called labor. During labor she pushes the baby out of her special opening."

Families in which conception has happened differently can come up with equally simple, developmentally relevant explanations. Adoptive parents, parents who've used in vitro fertilization or surrogacy, and parents who've used donor insemination will be called upon to respond to their child's question "Where did I come from?" with their own personalized conception and birth stories.

Yeseñia, a Mexican American mother with a strong Catholic background, explains: "My husband and I are both educated. We both have master's degrees. But when it comes to talking about sex with my kids, it's been a real struggle for me. My mother never, ever told me anything about sex. If it wasn't for the movie we saw in fifth grade, I wouldn't even have known about getting my period. I would have thought I was dying.

"Because I never had that from my mother, I can't talk to my kids about it. I know I should. I know what I'm supposed to say. I know I'm not supposed to be like my mother, but simple questions like 'Where do babies come from?' totally throw me.

"My son was three when his sister was born and he asked me where babies came from. I told him, 'In my stomach,' which wasn't really accurate. Then he asked, 'Well, how did it get out?' And I couldn't answer.

"This went on for some time until finally he said to me, 'You're not going to tell me. You avoid the question every time. I'm going to ask Daddy.'

"My husband went into this real technical explanation about hormones. He talked way over my little boy's head. So he wasn't much better.

"I don't want my kids to get married and to be afraid and ignorant like I was. I know I'm going to have to figure out how to talk about it, but it's just not part of my vocabulary. I know the technical words, but how to open up and tell them? My brain tells me to talk, but my heart and stomach won't let me."

If your mind wants to talk, but your heart and stomach say no, what can you do to break the ice and talk to your children about sex?

When Answering Children's Questions Is Difficult for You

• **Talk about your discomfort.** Find someone you trust and talk honestly about what's scaring you. What are you afraid might happen if you talked about sex with your children? What's the worst thing that could happen? Exploring your fears with a supportive person can be a first step in alleviating them.

• **It's okay if it doesn't come easily.** Feeling awkward around children's sexual questions is common. Don't worry if you can't respond easily or smoothly.

• **It's okay to share your discomfort with children.** When you're going through the motions of using the right words but you're feeling embarrassed, nervous, and flustered, kids sense your anxiety. You can mitigate this somewhat with some honest sharing. "When I was little, we didn't talk about these things in my family, so I get nervous talking about them now. I don't always know how to answer your questions, but I'm glad you're asking them." Or "When I was a kid, we weren't allowed to play like that. People thought it was wrong. I don't think it's wrong, but it's still embarrassing to me." Such explanations help kids make sense of the feelings they are picking up from you.

• **Practice what you want to say.** Try bouncing ideas off your partner, a friend, or a more experienced parent. Role-play prospective conversations and practice answering questions your child might have.

• **Find alternate resources.** If you still feel too uncomfortable to answer your child's questions, find another trusted adult who could talk to your child with you.

General Guidelines for Talking to Kids About Sex

• **Give children language for their body parts.** Through a combination of family words and correct anatomical terms, children develop a vocabulary to talk about their bodies. Babies learn to find their "eyes," "toes," and "noses." Later, children learn names for "elbows," "chins," "vulvas," and "penises."

As a society, we are generally more familiar with words for boys' genitals than we are words for girls'. Historically, boys had penises and girls "didn't." One thing we can do is make sure that boys and girls both have language for all of their body parts. We can tell girls about their vulvas, vaginas, labias, and clitorises. We can let boys know about their penises, testicles, and scrotum.

Some of us, having rarely heard these words, may feel uncomfortable saying them. Practice. Eventually, you'll stumble over them less.

• **Talk about genitals just like you'd talk about any other part of the body.** You can do this, beginning in infancy, as you bathe children or change their diapers: "I'm going to put this warm cloth on your vulva now," or "I have to wipe the pee off your penis."

Sometimes giving children accurate language about their bodies requires a little creativity. Laura tells the following story. "From the time he was a year old, Eli loved this big naming book that had pictures of everyday things with the names printed underneath. On the first page were two naked children, a boy and a girl, with labels such as 'mouth,' 'fingers,' 'hair,' 'belly,' and 'eyebrows' connected by thin black lines to the appropriate parts. Both children, however, were sitting in such a way that their genitals didn't show. By the time Eli was two, we'd name all the body parts together, and then I'd say, 'And look, that's boy's penis is hid-

Talking to Children About Menstruation

In some families, menstruation is never talked about. In others, girls learn about menstruation, but boys don't. Yet it's important for both boys and girls to know about how men's and women's bodies work. Having access to such knowledge cuts down on children's later fear, discomfort, and embarrassment.

How might a conversation about menstruation go with a preschool child? Let's say a four-year-old walks into the bathroom just as Mom is changing her tampon. The child sees blood on the toilet paper and a red swirl in the toilet bowl. The child asks, "Why are you bleeding?"

The mother could initially say "This is called a period. It happens to women's bodies and it doesn't hurt. It's what our bodies are supposed to do."

At this point she could wait and see if her child has more questions, or she could go on if her child still seems interested: "Inside women, there's a special place called a uterus that fills up with this red fluid. Every month, it empties out and starts filling up again."

Again, if the mother wants to go on, or if her child asks for more, she could continue: "If the woman wants to have a baby, it grows inside her uterus. Every once in a while her body gets ready, just in case she decides to have a baby grow. To get ready, the uterus fills with this special stuff to help the baby grow. It looks like blood, but it's partly blood and partly other stuff. If a woman isn't growing a baby, it comes out of her body and that's what's happening here."

ing!' or 'Where's that girl's vulva?' And he'd delightedly respond, 'It's hiding right there between her legs!' "

• **Ask the question back.** Often we try to answer children's questions without really knowing what they are asking. We make assumptions that children have the same definition for words that we have. When a child asks, "Where do babies come from?" and we ask back, "Where do you think they come from?" we give her a chance to tell us what she knows and to more clearly direct us to the information she wants. In this way, we may be able to pinpoint the real question she is asking.

• **Pace your answers to your child's developmental level.** When parents consider talking about sex, they often think of talking about all of it at once. It can be hard to figure out the developmentally appropriate information for your child. A three-year-old doesn't need to learn about intercourse, embryos, or orgasms.

• **Keep it simple.** Children often ask a simple question and get bombarded with information that is far beyond their interest or ability to comprehend. Answer the child's question simply, then wait to see if she's satisfied or wants more.

• **Expect it to come up again.** Sometimes in their anxiety, parents talk to kids about body parts, sex, or how babies are made and then breathe a sigh of relief: "Whew, I'm glad that's over with!" Yet it's important to give children information about body functions and sex throughout their childhoods. Children's ability to understand and assimilate what you're saying increases with age.

• **It's worth it.** Even though talking to kids openly about sex and their bodies can be challenging, accurate information from us is better than the sketchy, erroneous version they may get from friends. Children *will* seek information, so it's important that parents choose whether they or someone else will teach their children.

Clothes On, Clothes Off

Long before we tell children whether it's appropriate for them to run around naked, they get a lot of information by watching us: "What are all the different times my mom is naked?" "Is she naked outside?" "In the bathroom?" "In the kitchen?" Depending on what's okay in the family and what Mom's comfortable with, the answers to these questions can vary widely.

Regardless of the messages young children get about family nudity, they generally like to do some experimenting themselves. Many love to spend long hours with their clothes off.

Denise explained, "When they were little, my kids always liked to be naked. I was always running after them, trying to put on an article of clothing."

Odell agreed. "My son loves to run around naked. It's his favorite thing to do, next to ice cream."

Because our culture associates nudity with sexuality, parents sometimes worry that children's desire to run around naked means that they're obsessed with their genitals or with sex. But, in fact, that is not the case. For many kids, being naked just feels wonderful.

In some families, parents are comfortable letting children run around naked. In others, it's acceptable for children to take off their clothes only when they're using the toilet, changing, or taking a bath. It's possible for children in families all along this continuum to feel comfortable about who they are and good about their bodies.

Parental Nudity

There is a lot of controversy about parental nudity and there's a wide variation in what parents actually do. In some families, parents cover up and get undressed only behind closed doors. In others, nudity occurs casually while parents bathe or walk through the living room to sort through piles of clean clothes for something to wear.

Sometimes parental nudity is determined by factors beyond simple choice. Leah, who has MS, explains: "I don't get to do many things in private. When the nurse comes to bathe me and dress me, my five-year-old daughter comes in and likes to help."

Some parents' practices around nudity shift as their children get older. Keith explains: "I've always been more comfortable with nudity than my wife. When our daughter was a baby, it was fine with Nadine for Ali to bathe with me. But when Ali turned two, Nadine said she was no longer comfortable. It still felt okay to me, so we talked about it and decided it was okay to continue. But then when Ali turned three, she started wanting to touch my penis. That's when I stopped taking baths with her—or put my bathing suit on."

There is no magic age at which parents should cover up in front of their kids. Many parents take cues from their kids—when the kids begin covering up and asking for privacy, the parents follow suit. In other families, casual nudity continues to be the norm.

The most important thing regarding nudity in families is that everyone in the family is comfortable with the nudity and privacy that takes place. It's not so important whether families keep open or closed doors as it is that children see adults who are comfortable with their bodies.

"This Is What a Real Woman's Body Looks Like"

A benefit of being around family members as they dress, shower, and bathe is that children learn natural lessons in anatomy, gaining a realistic perspective on what men's and women's bodies look like.

Tina explains: "I was getting dressed when my ten-year-old son walked in. Jon had seen me naked all his life. I casually continued changing. Jon was just starting to gain a different level of awareness about women's bodies, and he asked me why I didn't look like the women on MTV and in the magazine ads. I looked down at my round, full belly lined with stretch marks, my drooping breasts which had nursed two babies, and my soft, dimpled arms which had rocked and carried my children, and I said to him, 'Jon, *this* is what a real woman's body looks like.' "

What If Children Ask to Touch You?

Some children express an interest in touching their parents' genitals. Parents who have tried to be open with their children may feel confused about what to do in this situation. While this can be a normal extension of children's curiosity, it is important to set limits with children in this area. Since adults don't allow people to touch their genitals unless that person is a sexual partner, letting children touch them would send a confusing message to the children as well as create an awkward situation for the adult.

Setting limits around your body with children sends them the message that people have interpersonal boundaries and models ways to set those boundaries. You can say to children: "No, I don't want you to touch my vulva, that doesn't feel comfortable to me. If you are curious about how vulvas look, we could find a book that has some pictures for you to look at." Or "I see you are curious about my penis, but I'm not going to let you touch it. It's private and I usually don't let other people touch it."

If you're not sure what to do, it's best to set a limit. If you are feeling confused or aroused in any way, it's critical that you don't let your child touch you and that you don't touch your child. This is an area in which it's essential that parents set clear limits, both to teach clear boundaries and to maintain safety.

Learning About Bodies Together

Helping children learn about themselves and their bodies can be the sweetest and most personal of all parental teachings. It can also be one of the most challenging and confusing areas of parenting, the area in which parents have the farthest to grow and in which they have the least societal support.

Parents have the responsibility to help children as they go from babies who don't know the parameters or capabilities of their own bodies to five-year-olds who have learned where their bodies begin and end, how their bodies work, and thousands of neat things they can do. Ultimately, we get to help our kids blossom into young adults who feel good about who they are and comfortable in their bodies. We are also called upon to help children learn how to keep their bodies safe and comfortable and to pass on standards around privacy and touch.

As parents travel this road, it is hoped that they will find opportunities to communicate with their children around significant areas of learning and self-awareness, to pass on a healthy, shame-free legacy to their children, to find humor in some of their experiences, and to have a chance to do some growing themselves.

• Part Four •

Dealing with Difficult Behavior

18. Understanding Difficult Behavior

"Parenthood is the art of bringing children up without putting them down."
ANONYMOUS

As parents of young children, we all encounter frustrating, exasperating, difficult behavior. Children bite, refuse to get dressed, run away from us, yell "no" at everything we suggest, throw food, dart into the street, push other children down, scream at the top of their voices, refuse to go to bed, whine, and delight in using profanities, just to name a few.

Children's difficult behavior can provide us with important information. It can give us clues about how our children think, what their questions are, and what's hard for them. In figuring out the causes of children's misbehavior, we gain a deeper understanding of them as people.

If our primary goal with children is to help them grow rather than just to "stop the difficult behavior," it becomes important to address the causes of their behavior as well as its manifestation. When we take the time to explore the reasons, we're more apt to reduce our own sense of anger, frustration, and victimization and better able to respond to our children effectively.

In the next four chapters, we thoroughly explore the topic of difficult behavior. In this chapter, we examine the four main reasons children "misbehave."

In "Moving Beyond Punishment" we look at the challenges parents face in dealing with difficult behavior and explore how parents develop their ideas about discipline. We share our perspective on spanking, yelling, and time-outs. Then we present a new cooperative model of limit setting, which involves twelve strategies that gradually teach children internal controls so they can learn to discipline themselves.

"Putting It All Together" takes these perspectives, tools, and strategies and applies them to a range of difficult behaviors that come up with young children: testing, hair pulling, saying "no," biting, spitting, climbing, whining, nagging, being ignored, swearing, lying, and stealing. We look at the underlying causes of these difficult behaviors and give clear examples of how to respond to each.

"Negotiating Conflicts Between Parent and Child" looks at the question of how power is divided between parents and kids in families, at how decisions get made, and at who makes them. We present age-appropriate ways to gradually include children in decision making without tipping the balance of power in the family. Finally, we talk about teaching kids manners, helping them learn to wait, and present a new approach toward family chores.

Reasons for Difficult Behavior

Child development theorist James Hymes explains that there are four different sources of difficult behavior: developmental, unmet emotional needs, lousy local conditions, and "hasn't been taught yet." His model is a valuable tool for exploring the reasons behind our children's most challenging behaviors.[1]

Developmental Reasons

According to Hymes, the first explanation to consider is whether the difficult behavior is developmental. Much of what we find challenging in our children's behavior can be attributed to the necessary, somewhat predictable stages children go through in the course of healthy growth and development.

Babies mouthing everything they can get their hands on is developmental, toddlers saying "no" is developmental, four-year-olds using swear words is developmental. These behaviors can be explained by the growth issues of children at each of these ages.

Sometimes a certain behavior is appropriate at different ages for different developmental reasons. A young toddler throws his food to see what happens to it and how you will respond. A four-year-old might revisit throwing food to see if she can make her friends laugh.

When we are challenged by children's difficult developmentally based behavior, it's helpful to remind ourselves that the learning tasks children are working on during these stages, no matter how frustrating they are to us, are important and necessary for their growth.

Got It, Lost It

One of the confusing things about looking at behavior developmentally is that children rarely develop in a steady progression. They take three steps forward and two steps back. They make a giant leap toward independence, and the next day it's "Hold me like a little baby," "Feed me," "No Eva can do it. Daddy do it."

Toddlers, in particular, can often do something perfectly well one day and appear incapable of doing it the next. As parents, we may feel tempted to say "I know you can pull up your pants (put on your shoes, stay away from electric outlets, feed yourself, carry your own bowl to the sink). You already did it. Why won't you do it now?"

There are two main reasons for these seeming lapses in abilities. The first is that development encompasses physical, social, emotional, and intellectual growth. Sometimes a child is physically capable of doing something, but isn't

[1] We'd like to thank James Hymes for the wisdom and insight he has brought to generations of parents and teachers, and also for his generous contribution to this chapter. A revised edition of his most helpful book for parents, *The Child Under Six*, long out of print, was republished by Consortium Publishing in West Greenwich, Rhode Island, in 1994.

ready emotionally or intellectually. As we discuss in Chapter 16, "From Toilet Training to Toilet Learning," one place this typically comes up is in learning to use the toilet.

Other times needs conflict with each other. Your two-year-old daughter usually remembers that it's not safe to run in the street, but at a particular moment, her developmental need to make her own decisions is so strong that it overrides her awareness that the street can be dangerous. Therefore, when you tell her to stop, she looks at you, smiles gleefully, and bolts right for the curb.

Sometimes a child who is physically capable of doing something can't do it because strong emotions supersede her abilities. Roxanne, the mother of five-year-old Polly, explained: "I was with Polly at an indoor rock climbing gym, and I knew that she could scale the wall. She'd done it before, but she'd gotten scared and didn't feel safe enough to make the climb. It took a long time before she made it up to the top again."

Another reason children sometimes seem to lose abilities they had yesterday is what Janis calls "Got it, lost it." In one of Janis's classes, Ruth, the mother of eleven-month-old Hayden, brought in a dilemma that typified this response. Hayden was biting Ruth whenever he nursed. She had been working with him to stop his biting, and as she explains, she was exhausted, angry, and desperate. "After weeks of telling Hayden 'You can't bite Mommy. You can bite other things,' he picked up his shovel and bit it. So it was clear to me that he understood that he could bite other things. But then the next time we nursed, he bit me again. What's going on?"

Janis replied, "At the moment when Hayden doesn't have your breast in his mouth, when it's covered up, and when there's a shovel close by, he can remember 'I can bite other things.' But at the moment he has your breast in his mouth and his teeth are hurting—or whatever it is that happens when he bites you—he can't stop and think 'The other day she told me to bite other things. That means I shouldn't bite her breast. I should let go and go find a shovel.' Just because he can do it under some circumstances doesn't mean he can do it under all circumstances or that he'll do it predictably."

Responding to Developmentally Driven Behavior

There are two main ways to respond to problematic behavior that is developmental in nature. The first is to find another outlet for the behavior. This technique is known as redirection. You say to the child: "Since you want to kick like a Power Ranger, let's find a safe place for you to do it." Or "It looks like you want to draw. Let's go outside with a piece of chalk where you can make all the marks you want." Redirection helps you provide safe, appropriate opportunities for your child's successful expression of developmental impulses.[2]

The second thing you can do with developmentally driven behavior is wait it out. We can give children information and alternatives, but ultimately, developmental stages need to run their course. The child who is pulling your hair at eighteen months may do it for a few months but is unlikely to do it when she's three. The child who is pushing other children and grabbing toys away will probably outgrow it in six months or a year. And it can be reassuring to know that your child won't be biting people for the rest of her life.

Unmet Emotional Needs

If development does not seem to be the cause of a child's difficult behavior, Hymes suggests thinking of a second possibility: unmet

[2] See "Twelve Strategies for Cooperative Limit Setting" on p. 226 for more on this technique.

emotional needs. This refers to behaviors that are calls for help, stemming from a child's unmet needs. Sometimes these are caused by temporary stresses such as moving, traveling, starting a new school, having to share their house with relatives who are looking for a place to live, a death in the family, a new baby, or a parent who is absent temporarily. More serious situations such as ongoing stress, neglect, and abuse can also cause difficult behavior.

Every family, at one time or another, experiences stress, and most children have temporary unmet emotional needs at some time. This is normal, yet it is important for parents to respond to their child's special needs during these times.

Sometimes kids need an extra dose of special time with a parent, an evening where the child gets to set the pace, a weekend where spending time with kids is at the top of the agenda. The focus of these times should be on being together rather than going lots of places. Each family will find its own special activities: indoor picnics, building dinosaur houses in back of the couch, cuddling, talking, singing, making paper-bag puppets, recording voices on the tape recorder, or telling stories.

When dealing with temporary stresses, familiarity and consistency are stabilizing forces. When you take your child on a trip, pack familiar things, continue the same bedtime ritual, bring along favorite foods. If a new baby is coming into your household, maintain as much of the older child's routine as possible. Reassure the child by your presence and your affection.[3]

When your child is upset by a change in the family, listen to his feelings. Let him talk about what it's like to have a new baby. Let him express his fears about living in a new place. And understand that change is not easy for children.

In these situations, time and supportive attention are the major curative forces. The child becomes familiar with her new home or reestablishes security in her changing family.

With long-term or continuous unmet emotional needs, it is essential to work toward alleviating the source of the problem. When a child is living in a dangerous, hurtful, or continually stressful situation, it is imperative to find resources that can help address the source rather than just the manifestation of the problem.

In all of these circumstances, children need emotional support. This support should be available both when the difficult behaviors occur and also on an ongoing basis. Children need to have their feelings acknowledged through listening and other creative outlets. Often children who are in emotional distress find pretend play and sensory materials such as sand, water, dirt, paint, play-dough, or clay useful mediums for emotional expression.

When a child has been hurt emotionally,

[3] See "Introducing New Siblings" on p. 397 for an in-depth look at introducing a new baby.

it's important to create safe places for the child to talk about or express his feelings. Difficult experiences create one level of stress and pain for the child; not being able to express the feelings around those difficult experiences creates another. Being heard by someone who cares is a big part of the healing process for children.[4]

Lousy Local Conditions

If neither developmental reasons nor unmet emotional needs seems to be the likely explanation for children's difficult behavior, Hymes suggests considering "lousy local conditions." This refers to an immediate environment that is stressful or a situation that is set up so that if children engage in normal play and exploration, they will be breaking the rules. A lousy local condition is the home of a friend who collects expensive crystal and displays it at your toddler's level. For a toddler who is programmed to explore, touch, and maybe throw everything that catches her eye, your friend's house is an environment that is likely to produce trouble and frustration.

Many parents have discovered that doing too many errands with a young child is a "lousy local condition." (Janis calls this "Four errands, no nap.") The child needs to run and play freely, yet he is forced to get in and out of his car seat and walk around in stores where he is not supposed to touch things. We've all seen the child who has had one too many errands dissolve in the grocery store aisle. (At certain ages and for particular children, even *one* errand may lead to a tantrum.)

Janis says this happened to her when her kids were toddlers: "I found K Mart to be a lousy local condition for my kids when they were very young. Everything on the shelf says 'Grab me! Pull me off! Put me in your shopping cart!' That's what the adults are doing. Yet what we say to our children is, 'No, no, no! We're not going to put that in our cart. Put that back on the shelf.' And the child thinks, 'You put all that other stuff in the shopping cart. Why can't I?' Such stores are a real set-up for a child who is wanting to imitate adult behavior."

Too many kids and not enough adults is another example of a lousy local condition. So is a rainy day, which sometimes causes crankiness, bickering, and restlessness for children who love to be outside, engaged in active play. Cleaning supplies stored in a low, unlocked cabinet in homes with young children is a lousy local condition, since children are naturally curious about cupboards and their contents and can be expected to go exploring. A child care program that is too crowded is a lousy local condition in which children might begin to push other children, jump over furniture, or leave the classroom without permission.

Public places that demand quiet are also impossible at certain stages in children's development. Gino, who had to leave the theater early, said, "I tried to take my fifteen-month-old son to the movies with me. I figured maybe he'd sleep through it. Boy, was that ever a mistake."

Responding to Lousy Local Conditions

There are three basic ways to deal with lousy local conditions. The first, which is not always possible, is to get out of the situation. Instead of saying, "Don't pull that off the shelves. Don't touch that!" leave the store,

[4] For more on supporting children emotionally, see Part Two "Children's Feelings" on p. 81.

walk away with your child (or carry her if she's already past the point of no return). Basically you say to your child "We're going to leave this environment because it's too hard for you to be here right now." When dealing with lousy local conditions, it is usually too much to expect that children will be able to change their behavior without the situation or environment being changed.

Which brings us to the second strategy—altering the circumstances so they are more conducive to your child's success: put up the cleaning supplies your mother keeps under her kitchen sink, give your daughter a nap before you run errands, take along some of your son's toys. A rainy-day solution might be to bundle up and go jump in mud puddles, to clear a space for tumbling, or to put on dancing music inside. At your friend's house, the fragile crystal can be put up out of your daughter's way and an assortment of plastic containers can be arranged within her reach so she still has a chance to explore her environment.

If you're in a situation where you need to take something away from your child for safety reasons, you can still acknowledge her fascination with the items that had to be put up. "I know you love those shiny crystals, but they are breakable, so I will put these things out for you to play with instead."

The last option for dealing with lousy local conditions is toughing it out. We do this when it isn't possible to leave or alter the environment. In this instance, there isn't much hope that children will suddenly "behave." But even when we're stuck in a terrible situation and our child is acting like someone we wish we didn't know, we can remind ourselves that there's a reason she can't pull it together. We can listen to our child's frustration, hold her while she flails or cries, and gently remind her of the limits while acknowledging how difficult those limits are for her. As we describe in Chapter 11, "Responding to Crying and Tantrums," understanding that our child's behavior is reasonable under the circumstances can help us respond in a more compassionate, nonpunitive way.

When a Child Hasn't Been Taught Yet

If none of the explanations discussed thus far seem to explain the difficult behavior, Hymes suggests a final possibility, that the child hasn't yet learned the appropriate way to behave. A five-year-old who has never played with other children may not automatically know how to listen to someone else's viewpoint or share toys. He is old enough to understand many of the elements of friendship and sharing, yet he hasn't had the chance to practice or learn those skills. Given the opportunity, he will probably learn the skills readily.

Children who "haven't been taught yet" can be taught by being given positive limits, information, and redirection, ideas that are thoroughly explored in the next two chapters. Positive limits focus on what you want the child to do rather than on what you want him *not* to do. You can say "The water needs to stay in the sink" instead of "Don't spill water on the floor." Or "I want you to keep the bunny safe in his cage" instead of "Don't kick the bunny's cage."

The child who is developmentally ready to learn but hasn't been taught yet can also benefit from information: "Water makes the floor slippery and unsafe." "The bunny gets scared when you kick his cage."

Last, it is also useful to ask the child for her ideas about other ways to safely or successfully do what she is trying to do: "Can you think of a safe place to play with the water?" "Can you think of a safe way to play with the bunny or a safe thing to kick?" And if the child is too young or is otherwise unable to come up with workable ideas, you can suggest alternatives: "Let's set up the hose and the bucket outside on the grass where it can't get slippery." Or "You can touch the bunny's back gently. And if you still feel like kicking, you can kick those red balls outside."

Sometimes problem behavior is attributed to "hasn't been taught," but it actually comes from another source. Hymes warns, "Because this final explanation is so simple and appealing, many parents leap to it first as their favorite." At times, patiently and persistently helping a child learn *is* the answer. If you give the child appropriate direction, exposure, information, and encouragement, and the child learns the behavior quickly, the chances are that you have put your finger on the right cause. But if the child does not respond relatively quickly, you may need to go back to look at other possible explanations.

So Which One Is It?

It's not always easy to categorize behavior into one of Hymes's four categories. You can't always say, "Oh, that's a classic developmental behavior!" or, "That's an unmet emotional need." Children's difficult behavior is often caused by a variety of factors and it may take some time to sort them out.

There are certain cues to look for. If your four-year-old is still consistently mouthing toys or if your five-year-old is biting, these behaviors would no longer be considered developmental and other reasons should be considered.

Some behaviors that are developmental might also reflect unmet emotional needs. A toddler who is experiencing normal separation fears in a new child care setting might be having emotional needs because he's adjusting to his parent's new work schedule, as well.

Through careful observation and by trying different responses, you usually will be able to determine what the underlying issue—or issues —are.

A Pair of Paradoxes

Even when we correctly identify the source of problem behavior and respond appropriately, it doesn't necessarily mean that the behavior will stop. As parents we often feel, "If I say the right words, if I do the right thing, my kids will do what I want them to do." Or we get exasperated: "I'm trying so hard. I should be getting some results here!"

But it doesn't always work that way. As early childhood educator Vicki Neville-Coffis makes clear, "You may be doing exactly what you want to be doing and teaching exactly what you want to be teaching, and your child's behavior may still not prove you right—at least not immediately."

This reality can be very frustrating, which leads us to the second paradox: Even though we understand where our children's' difficult behavior is coming from, it doesn't mean we won't feel irritated, angry, or inadequate. But even though our buttons get pushed and we get frustrated sometimes, children still benefit from our thoughtfulness about their behavior.

19. Moving Beyond Punishment

"Punishment backfires because the child isn't learning to solve the problem. She's only learning how to react to the force of the disciplinarian."
JACK, *father of two-year-old Heidi*

Many people automatically associate discipline with punishment. This approach to discipline is tied to an underlying (though often unexplored) assumption that children won't learn unless "they're made to," that they won't cooperate unless they are threatened with unpleasant consequences, and that fear of punishment is an effective and useful modifier of behavior.

We make different assumptions about children. We see them as highly motivated learners who, despite their needs for testing and autonomy, are eagerly taking in information about how the world responds to their actions. We believe that children can do this critical learning more effectively if they aren't feeling attacked, belittled, manipulated, or scared.

The goal of discipline, as we present it here, is for children to learn how to act in situations because they know how to think about them. When children have been helped to make decisions based on empathy, understanding, and their own critical thinking skills rather than on just what the "rule" says, they have a skill they can use in a multitude of different situations and carry with them for the rest of their lives.

Finding a Disciplinary Strategy: Issues for Parents

One of the reasons dealing with difficult behavior is so challenging for parents is that it forces us to continually reevaluate the balance of needs in our family and our teaching goals. Every time we are confronted with a new behavior or with wanting our children to change what they are doing, we have to think about how we want to respond.

Mallory, the mother of two-and-a-half-year-old Nola, recalls, "When we first started coming to play group, I remember always wanting Nola to share whatever she was playing with. When another child wanted what she had, I always told her to give the toy up. Often Nola would cry, refuse, or just hold on. I started thinking one day, 'What am I teaching her here?' I do want her to learn to share, but I also want her to know that her feelings and needs are important.' "

Control is a major factor in discipline. When our children don't do what we want them to do, we're faced with a number of questions: "Am I being too strict?" "Too lax?" "How much should I control my kids' behavior?" "When and how should I enforce limits?"

Personal history also plays a powerful role in shaping our views on discipline. The way we were disciplined has a direct impact on what we do with our own kids. When we're in a stressful, challenging situation with our children, our first impulse may be to respond the way our parents did.

For some of us, this natural impulse will be a welcome guide. Paula explains: "My mother always encouraged us. She took a lot of pride in mothering and had a lot of respect for it. When I became a mother, I found that I could rely on the instincts I learned as a child being mothered. There are times I find myself saying kind and supportive things without really consciously deciding to. One friend told me that I say 'yes' instinctively more than any other mother she knows. And it's true. I am more inclined to say 'yes' than to say 'no.' I give my children a lot of room, just like my mother did."

Not all parents have such positive models to draw from. For those of us who don't want to perpetuate the way we were treated, our first impulse may be a red flag—an indication of what we *don't* want to do. And it takes conscious effort to do something different.

Alejandro explained: "In my family growing up, authority was immediate and uncontested. There was always the threat of physical punishment. I've rejected that almost entirely, but the model is still there. I've internalized it. I have to deal with it every time a difficult situation comes up.

"I want to get out the door and Roscoe's not getting ready to go. In dealing with that situation, I have to deal with the fact that in my family, if my father needed me to get ready, he was going to *make* me get ready. Am I willing to do that to my child? And if not, what are my alternatives?"

Culture is another factor in the way we think about discipline, though each culture has wide variations in the kinds of discipline that are used. Leon shares the different approaches he experienced within his extended family. "My mother believed in physical punishment. She would pull out her strap to deal with any number of my transgressions. I remember one time I had done something that Mama had a taboo against. She went to the drawer to get the strap to whip me. I told her that whipping me might make her feel better, but it wasn't going to stop me from doing what I wanted to do. She folded the strap back up, put it in the drawer, and I never saw it again.

"My father's sisters had a totally different approach. They never used intimidation as a means of discipline. They didn't believe in it.

When I did something wrong at Sister Nellie's, she lifted an eyebrow or told me she thought my behavior was wrong, and I always listened. Sister Nellie didn't need to use punishment with me because I *wanted* to please her. Her smile was the greatest reward that I could ever get."

Our beliefs about human nature also influence the discipline we use. Do we believe, like Leon's mother did, that beating is the best way to "keep children in line"? Or like Nellie, that children, with love and clear guidance, naturally develop into healthy adults? Our perspective on what causes difficult behavior is intrinsically connected to how we respond.

Our expectations play a role in discipline, too. While a parent may be tolerant or understanding of a one-year-old grabbing his friend's toys, that same parent may feel embarrassed and upset when his five-year-old does the same thing. As children get older, our expectations for socially appropriate behavior, private time, uninterrupted conversations, and peaceful meals increase. As parental expectations change, so do disciplinary goals.

Finally, we make disciplinary decisions based on our values and the energy and attention we have in the moment. We may aspire to treat our kids one way, but, under stress, we fall back on methods we wish we'd left behind. Our range of choices reflects the support and resources we do or don't have.

Important questions come up when we look at the personal resources we bring to discipline: "How can I deal with the hurt feelings that are coming up for me in this situation?" "How can I deal with all the anger I'm feeling right now?" "How can I get in shape for the kind of limit-setting I want to do?" "How can I nourish myself so I can treat my child the ways I really want to?" These questions are critical to the whole question of discipline. They're intrinsic to our ability to discipline effectively.

FOOD FOR THOUGHT: DISCIPLINE AND DIFFICULT BEHAVIOR

- What is the purpose of discipline? What am I trying to teach my kids when I discipline them?

- What methods of discipline were used with me when I was growing up? Which of those methods would I like to use with my kids?

- How do I discipline my children now? What, if anything, would I like to do differently?

The Problem with Spanking

Libby and Sterling's five-year-old son, Trevor, had been waking at night for some time. There had been several changes in the family: the sudden death of an uncle, absences of parents dealing with that death, and a transition to a new school. Trevor had begun waking several times at night, going into his parents' room, needing reassurance and considerable attention before he could go back to sleep. Libby and Sterling were exhausted and emotionally spent, both from dealing with the family crisis and from their run of interrupted nights. Finally, in exasperation one evening, Sterling told Trevor, "If you come into our room one more time, you are going to get a spanking." Later that night, they heard footsteps and a small voice at their door, "Can I just get a little spanking?"

Parents spank their children for a variety of reasons. Some believe that spanking is an effective primary means of discipline, and they use it frequently. Others use spanking only occasionally, when they want to make a really strong statement to their child about something that isn't safe. Still others resort to spanking because they don't know what else to do and they've never had the opportunity to learn other alternatives. And last, there are parents who don't really want to spank but who lose control in the heat of the moment—usually out of exhaustion, exasperation, or anger. Gaining a perspective on spanking means looking at each of these reasons individually.

We take issue with the idea that spanking is good for children, although spanking can seem effective in the short run. Children who are hit often stop doing the thing you want them to quit doing. They may be more obedient and less prone to expressing dissenting opinions (at least while the disciplinarian—or the threat of the disciplinarian—is present). So in the most immediate sense, you might say "spanking works." But these results are deceptive.

When children are hit, they feel scared and defensive, neither of which is conducive to learning. The most useful kinds of discipline sets a child up so she can learn something.

Children who "behave" because of the threat of force aren't learning internal controls. They are only learning to "act right" out of fear. They don't learn to assess their own behavior, to weigh alternatives, or to make appropriate choices because they understand the situation, but only because they want to stay out of the way of Daddy's belt.

Spanking doesn't enable children to think about why they're pushing their sister, screaming in the restaurant, or jumping on the couch. It doesn't help them assess danger, gauge social appropriateness, or make choices based on compassion for what someone else feels. Nor does spanking—or any punitive form of discipline—lead them to understand the impulse that led them to "misbehave" in the first place.

So even though spanking may work in the short run, it teaches children things that we may not really want them to learn in the long run—to be afraid of their parents, to distrust themselves, to look to the outside for what would be the wise decision in every situation. Perhaps most critically, spanking teaches children that *it's okay to hit and it's okay to be hit.*

Children learn a tremendous amount through our example. They watch us carefully. If we consistently model spanking as part of the problem solving, they will carry that on, both as the giver and as the receiver: "This is the way you teach." "This is how you show your concern." "This is an appropriate way to express anger and frustration." When children are hit repeatedly, it increases the chances that they'll become involved in future relationships where hitting is the norm.

To Yell or Not to Yell?

Many of us understand that hitting or spanking a child is a hurtful way to express our feelings. Yet we may be less clear about the impact of yelling.

When we discuss yelling, it is important to remember that each family has its own communication style. Some families are robust and loud in all of their interactions. Others hardly speak above a whisper. Part of what children learn at home includes "how people communicate in our family."

There are several different kinds of yelling. There is shouting with the goal of changing your child's behavior, which includes raising your voice to get her attention, to scare her or shame her into doing what you want.

Blaming and name-calling fall into this category: "You're stupid. You never understand what I tell you!" That kind of yelling often "just comes out" when we feel overwhelmed, and it usually arises from our own hurts, present or past.

Berating another person, no matter what our goal, is hurtful behavior. Children can be as hurt emotionally by this as they are by being hit.

Some yelling helps us get out our feelings. Parents yell in frustration; they yell to let off steam. This kind of yelling ranges from the familiar ranting and raving: "This family is driving me CRAZY!!" to the more positive "I" messages: "I get so furious when you leave the door open and let the flies in!"

There is also screaming in the vicinity of our children, but not directly at them: "I hate it when this house is such a mess!" Or we yell at our spouse within our child's earshot: "I'm so sick of it! You never take out the trash without being reminded!"

Yelling at children about our feelings, without making them responsible for those feelings, can be tolerable for specific children at certain ages. Children who aren't terrified by loud voices can learn to hear the content of our message without being overwhelmed.

Likewise, if the yelling is directed at another person or toward the world in general, and does not contain hurtful language, some children will be able to tolerate it in their vicinity. However, if fights in front of children become hurtful or too intense, they can be very scary for children.*

Children's ability to deal with yelling is related to their age and temperament as well as the norms in their family. The younger the child, the more possible it is that he will be startled or frightened by a raised voice. However, even older children who are especially sensitive may react strongly to yelling.

Finding New Ways to Express Your Frustration

While yelling at children is rarely the most useful form of communication, many of us find ourselves doing it regularly. Even when we recognize that yelling distresses our children, most of us won't be able to change our behavior immediately. Developing a new communication style can be especially challenging for those of us who are used to expressing ourselves loudly or who grew up in families where yelling was the norm.

In order to make a change, we first need to think about all of the different ways we could express our anger satisfactorily without scaring our children. (For ideas on how to do this, see "Expressing Anger with Children" on p. 58.) Then we need to pay close attention to the response of our particular child when we express anger. This kind of observation can yield important clues about the kind of expressions that are appropriate with each of our children.

Figuring out expressions of anger that are satisfying to us and that also meet the needs of our children will, no doubt, be a project we work on over time.

*For more on this, see "Fighting in Front of the Children," on p. 389.

The parent who hits occasionally—and purposefully—around safety issues, such as not running into the street—is probably thinking: "I need to teach something here that's very important and I need really strong measures to do it. If I make a deep impression on him this time, he'll remember it forever. Smacking him on the butt is the best way to make sure he won't run out in the street again."

However, there are many ways to convey to children that you are serious about a limit. A serious, clear voice, with genuine emotion and concern, makes an impression on children, as does gentle, but firm, physical restraint.

In this situation, spanking, once again, puts kids' attention more on fear than on learning. Your child might run into the street looking over his shoulder to see if you're coming to spank him rather than looking to see if there are any cars. Instead of developing self-discipline, he focuses on the punishment.

The third scenario—the parent who hasn't learned a different way—is very common. Spanking and authoritarian discipline are widely used and accepted, and many parents haven't seen other methods modeled. When parents haven't been exposed to other options or ideas, their only recourse is to continue to hit their children and to ignore any feelings of discomfort that come up when they do.

Yet many parents who were spanked as children have learned to discipline in different ways. Through information, example, and support, it's possible for parents to develop new ways to respond to their children.[1]

These changes are challenging, particularly if you're going against the beliefs of the rest of your family. Emily explains: "My mother believes in spanking. She believes in discipline through fear, and she thinks my children are out of control and spoiled. She criticizes me constantly for what I'm doing with them. At first, her criticism would send me into a total tailspin: 'I'm doing it all wrong.' I'd doubt myself as a parent.

"Now I'm able to step back, check in with myself about what I'm doing with the kids, and then come back and respond to her. But it's painful. When I see the things she wants me to do to my girls, I remember things she did to me. I'm grieving a lot for myself as a little girl. And I'm sad for her—I know she didn't enjoy parenting at all."

The last circumstance in which parents spank their kids is the one that reflects the simple fact that we're all human: We don't want to hit our kids, but we're pushed beyond our limits, and in the moment, we can't come up with any other alternatives. So we reach back to what is familiar to us—we hit. Or we're in a situation in which we feel embarrassed and pressured to "do something" to control our children—and for many of us, spanking is a clear way to demonstrate we're "doing something."

If this kind of lapse is something that happens only occasionally, children don't necessarily absorb the idea that we think spanking is right. Jenny explains: "When I had Carly, I knew I didn't want to hit her the way I was hit. Instead of punishment, I want to give her the reasons she shouldn't do things. A lot of the time I succeed at that. Yet if I'm tired or stressed and Carly is throwing a huge fit over something that I think is little, it's easy for me to stop thinking logically and to start yelling: 'Would you just *stop* that!' My mom was a big yeller, and it's easy for me to fall back into that. Just like that—boom—I fall back into how I was raised.

"Once I got so frustrated, I said to Carly, 'Mommy's going to give you a *spanking!*' Carly didn't even know what a spanking was. She'd never been hit before. But I lost control and hit her. I did it out of anger. Carly turned right around and said, 'Don't do that!' And she hit me back, right on my thigh.

[1] For examples of this, see Chapter 8, "Being Human: When You're Not Yet the Parent You Want to Be," on p. 57.

"I felt really bad. I had to walk away and cool down. I remember thinking 'I can't believe I just hit my child. This is something I swore I would never do.' I cried. Then I had to take the time to sit down and think, 'What am *I* doing wrong? She's just being three. I'm the one with a problem.' When I looked at the situation, I could see how stressed out I was. I had school *and* I had work. And she was being a three-year-old.

"Then I thought about what I had done. I'd given my daughter the message that when you're angry, it's okay to hit. So I went back to her and said, 'I'm sorry I hit you. That's not right. When we're angry, we shouldn't hit.

"Then I asked her, 'How did that make you feel?' And she said, 'Sad.' And I said, 'Yeah, I felt sad that I did that to you. I was feeling very frustrated. I have a really big paper at school and lots of work to do. But I still shouldn't have hit you. I'm sorry.'

"That incident had a big effect on both of us. I think she really got the message that it was something I felt bad about; that I think it's unacceptable."

If, as Jenny did, we acknowledge to our children that we don't believe in spanking and that we're going to work not to do it again, kids can learn that spanking isn't right but that their parents are human and made a mistake.

What About Time-outs?

Many parents who have decided they don't want to hit their kids use time-outs as an alternative. Basically a time-out means that you move a child out of the problematic situation, sometimes isolating her for a limited amount of time (usually a very short one), so she can "think about what happened" or bring her behavior under control. At that point, she is allowed to go back to the situation (or to find a more appropriate one).

When Are Time-outs Most Effective?

Time-outs can be used to set a clear limit with a preschool-age child. Used carefully, they can sometimes calm down an escalating situation or make a clear statement to a child about unacceptable behavior.

Time-outs can also be used to give parents a break. As Jim put it, "Sometimes I need a breather more than Chris needs one. I'm the one who needs the time-out."

Mei agrees. "Sometimes I just have to say to my kids, 'Mommy is too angry to deal with this right now. Mommy needs to take a time-out.' My children know not to push me beyond that point. They'll go read a book or do something on their own for a while. They know that I need to calm down and they respect that."

When you do this, it's important to tell kids that you are taking a break, to let them know when you're coming back, and to make sure they're in a safe place.

When used occasionally with children three and over, time-outs are far preferable to spanking and can give both parents and kids a needed break. However, time-outs do have some limitations:

- **Time-outs can be scary for children who don't understand time.** Most children under two and a half can only understand "now." A five-minute time-out, or even a two-minute time-out, can seem to them like an eternity.

- **Time-outs deal only with behavior, not with the reasons behind the behavior.** Time-outs focus on what the child is doing, not on what the child is trying to figure out.

- **Time-outs often remove the child from a situation he still has a lot to learn from.** Children can learn from situations in which they've made mistakes or in which they've been unsuccessful. Learning to turn circumstances around, to try new approaches, and to communicate more effectively are all valuable lessons for young children.

Rather than isolate the child, it may be preferable to help him find a new solution or environment. For instance, if Andrew, who's banging his harmonica on big brother's keyboard, has not been able to stop after your initial intervention, he may need to be told, "Let's find something you can bang safely." "Let's find another way for you to explore the keyboard." "It seems like you can't stop yourself right now, so I'm going to help you move." In other words, "While you're learning to control those impulses, I'm going to help you be successful." That's a much less punitive approach than, "You did something wrong so you lose your chance to keep trying. Now you have to sit here and think about it."

Likewise, when dealing with conflicts between children, it can be much more useful for children to stay in the interaction and work through it successfully than to be removed. Supporting children in resolving their conflicts allows them to leave the interaction feeling positive, competent, and successful.[2]

Time-out Guidelines

- **Time-outs should never be longer than a few minutes.** You can use the child's age as a guide—no more than three minutes for a three-year-old, four minutes for a four-year-old, or five minutes for a five-year-old.

- **Your child should know what to expect.** You can say: "I'm going to take a five-minute break in my room, then I'll come back." "I want you to sit on this pillow for three minutes, then you can get up." "When you feel like you can be safe with your sister, you can come back in."

- **Time-outs should not be overused.** If you want children to understand the seriousness of time-outs, use them sparingly.

- **Whenever possible, include children in setting up their own time-outs.** If you involve the child in thinking about how a "break" might help her calm down and include her in determining when she will be ready to rejoin the activity, eventually she can learn how to create safe outlets for herself.

- **Discuss solutions.** Just interrupting the behavior isn't enough. It's also important to explore acceptable alternatives to the behavior you want changed.

[2] For detailed guidance helping children resolve conflicts, see Chapter 23, "Children's Friendships: Cooperation and Conflict" on p. 304 and "Working with Children Who Bite" on p. 249.

Creating Discipline Together

We sometimes think about discipline as a special system of rules that we impose on children from the outside. We act as enforcers and our children are the recipients.

For many of us, discipline is something separate from the rest of what we do with our children, but actually how we teach discipline is integral to all aspects of our relationship with our kids. If we have a strong, communicative relationship with our children, discipline isn't something we have to impose from the outside. Rather it's something we create, figure out, and modify together.

From the time our children are babies, we begin to establish how discipline fits into our relationship. "I want you to touch my hair gently." "I am going to keep my glasses on my face." As our relationship grows and develops, we are challenged to expand our limit-setting so it will meet our family's changing needs while still making sense in the context of our whole relationship with our children.

In this chapter, we present twelve strategies for problem solving with kids. They represent different avenues through which you can guide and support your children in developing critical thinking skills, and in learning to respond to situations with clarity and empathy. In short, they lay the groundwork for teaching your children to ultimately discipline themselves.

It's important to remember that you won't always have the time, energy, or presence of mind to use these strategies. But keeping them in mind and striving to use them whenever possible will create a respectful climate between you and your children that will teach many valuable lessons and also balance the times you have to take a more rushed approach.

Twelve Strategies for Cooperative Limit Setting

The following strategies are building blocks that can be used to respond to a whole range of difficult behaviors. While most of these techniques can be used with children from babyhood to five years of age and beyond, some are more suited to nonverbal children and others work best with verbal children.

Not every situation will call for all of these techniques, and there may be times you need to repeat a step several times in the course of an interaction. Also, the order in which they're presented doesn't reflect a particular sequence for you to follow.

Some of these strategies will probably be familiar to you; others may be new. As you read through them, take the opportunity to think about what you want to teach in your family through discipline, how you are already doing that, and which of these new ideas might be helpful to you.

1. Honoring the Impulse

Whether we're comfortable with children's behavior or not, whether it's safe for the child or appropriate out in the world, it is driven by an impulse we can appreciate. In the midst of children's' challenging, difficult behavior, it is worthwhile to ask: "What's the impulse that's behind this behavior?" "Is there something my child is working on that I can support, even as I help her adjust or change her behavior?"

In order to answer these questions, you have to know your individual child and understand something about child development, so you can make educated guesses about what your child might be doing. "Looks like you want to say 'hi' to Davey." "Looks like you want Juanita to move." "Looks like you want to touch the baby." "Looks like you want to tell Ronnie that you're angry."

The reason we say "looks like" in all of these instances is that unless the child tells us, we can't really be sure that we're right, and we don't want to give children the message that we know more about their feelings than they do.

We can explore this idea of honoring the impulse by examining a common problem that comes up with babies and young toddlers—throwing food on the floor. Often this activity begins as an exploration of gravity. Children aren't born knowing how gravity pulls liquids out of containers. When you hand a young toddler a cup and a pitcher, he'll frequently place the cup on top of the pitcher. He has the basic idea that the water should go in the cup, but he doesn't have a clear idea how it gets there. So pouring juice out of cups or toys out of baskets is often an exploration of gravity: "Does it really work?" "Will it really work again?" "Does it work with this container?" "How about with this one?" "Do I have to tip it a lot or just a little?" "What happens if I tip it fast?" "If I tip it slowly?"

Once children begin their gravity exploration, whole new areas of inquiry emerge—like the sound things make when they hit the floor. New levels of physical exploration open up before children, like dominoes, and they're drawn to explore each one of them.

In the case of pouring juice, physical exploration very quickly leads to social exploration. As soon as children start dumping things on the floor, they learn that other people have strong feelings about it. You get your cup taken away and you don't get any more juice. Or you get your cup back the first six times and then you get it taken away. If you're lucky, you're given a cloth, lowered down to the floor in the vicinity of the spill, and when you put the cloth on the juice, the juice magically disappears! That's pretty interesting, too! It's a whole metamorphosis: The juice is in the cup. Then it's on the floor. And now it's gone!

There are levels of social exploration, too: "What does Dad do when I pour my juice on the floor?" "What does Grandma do?" "What does big sister do?" "How does my teacher react?" "How does it feel to pour the juice on my friend's head?" A whole world of unanswered questions arise for our curious explorer.

Does this mean we should let children pour juice on the floor unimpeded? Not at all. Learning social rules is an important part of children's development. But once we understand the impulse, we can set limits in such a way that we respect the child's need to explore at the same time we say "no."

What might this look like? In the scenario where your eighteen-month-old is pouring juice on the floor, your response might go something like this:

"It looks like you're really interested in pouring your juice." *(You begin by honoring the impulse.)* "When you pour juice on the floor, someone has to wipe it up." *(You give the child information.)* If the child is about to dump her juice yet again, you gently take the cup and say, "I don't want you to dump juice on the floor. I'm going to take your cup." *(You set a verbal limit and you back it up with a physical one.)*

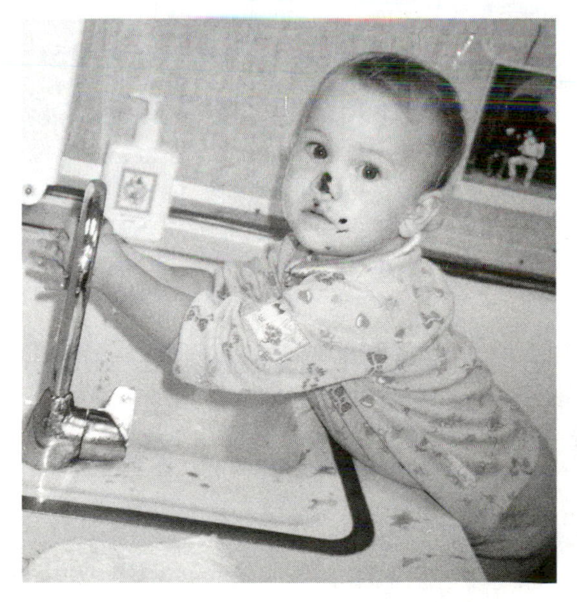

"When you pour your juice on the floor, it's all gone. There's nothing left for you to drink." *(You let the child know the natural consequences of her actions.)*

Or you can take a slightly different approach, giving the child information in a technique we call *"sportscasting":* "I see you poured your juice out. Now it's on the floor." You let her participate in the solution: "Let's get a cloth and wipe it up." And ultimately, you can use the tool of *redirection:* "Let's make a bath and we'll find lots of cups you can pour from."

When we recognize the impulse behind children's actions, we show them that we value their ideas. We demonstrate respect for what it is they're trying to learn. We let children know that we believe they're acting on valid interests and not simply being "bad." We're able to respond to situations more effectively and are less likely to get caught up in just the difficult behavior.

Faye explains: "When I understand what my daughter is working on, when I can see what she's trying to accomplish, I begin to understand her perspective. Seeing her perspective helps me get over the feeling that she's just trying to manipulate me and drive me crazy."

In some cases, it may be more difficult to see the healthy impulse behind the behavior. When children are biting, pulling hair, or knocking other kids down, it can be harder to recognize the positive motivation behind their actions, but as you will see in the examples in Chapter 20, "Putting It All Together," there is almost always a positive impulse you can respond to.

What Am I Interfering With?: Leon's Story

Janis's husband Leon, who's been a parent for just under half a century, shared his evolving perspective on discipline.

I started out being a disciplinarian like my mother. As I've grown older, I've learned what my father always knew—that you just have to allow people to be, that you have to encourage the expression of differences.

Whenever I have the urge to discipline one of my kids, I ask myself, "What am I interfering with?" I always ask that question because discipline is always interference of some kind. I'm stopping the child from disciplining himself. I'm not giving that child a chance to use his own brakes, accelerator, and steering wheel. I'm stopping him from exploring something. Children are in a constant process of exploration, and we need to support that whenever possible. Yet we often cut that process short in the name of discipline. We don't stop to find out what our child is exploring; we don't stop to look at what we're responding to.

Often discipline is attached to parental fears, or we're embarrassed by what our kid is doing. So we have to ask ourselves, "How much is this need to keep my kid in line attached to my fears? To my sense of embarrassment? To my anger? To old hurts I carry?"

What we call discipline is most often punishment in one form or another. We think, erroneously, that punishment controls. And the culture tells us we should have control over our children. We want that power, yet when we discipline without thinking, we rob ourselves of something and we rob the child of something. So when I start to feel that need to clamp down on one of my kids, I always ask myself, "What am I interfering with?" And when I don't know, I ask my kids, "What are you trying to do?"

I'm not saying "Don't discipline." I'm saying "Ask yourself the question." What it means is that sometimes I go back to a child later and say, "I interrupted you earlier because I felt anxious. I felt like I didn't have enough time."

I've been a father for almost fifty years, and in that time, I've become more relaxed. I no longer get caught up in trying to control my kids. Now I just try to control me. And if I can do that, that's real good.

2. Active Listening

Active listening is the tool that allows us to mirror back to children what they're feeling or doing. Active listening is another way to honor the impulse: "Looks like you're really frustrated." "Looks like you want to climb up there." "Looks like you want that toy."

Basically you repeat back to the child what she is saying or expressing: "You really don't want me to change your diaper." "You really don't want to leave Jorge's house." "I hear you telling me you're not ready." "You're saying 'No!' and you're saying it really loud. It sounds like you really don't want me to put your coat on right now."

With preverbal children (or with verbal ones who are too upset to be clear), we can use observation, combined with our previous experience with our child, to give us clues about what's happening. With older children, we get to mirror back what they're telling us directly: "You'd really like to dig a great big hole in the backyard. And you're really excited about it right now!"

Active listening is valuable because it reinforces the idea that the process of communication is useful. It gives children tools for verbalizing an idea. It shows kids that we think they're valuable people who deserve to be listened to. And it teaches children that they can expect to have their ideas heard, even if we can't let them carry them out. Active listening is also the first step in negotiating, in learning to balance needs, and in problem solving.

Let's take the example of four-year-old Darlene, who desperately wants to buy a fancy red truck at the toy store. You know you're not going to buy Darlene the truck, and in your exasperation at her insistence, you might end up preventing her from having her idea as well as the truck: "Oh, you don't really want that truck. You just got a brand-new cement mixer last week." Or "Quit asking me! You're not going to get it. I said 'no' and I mean 'no.' " Conversely, if we're feeling particularly worn down that day, we might even give in and buy the truck, only to feel resentful about it later on.

But through active listening, it is possible to acknowledge what Darlene wants even though you're not going to buy it for her: "I know you really want that red truck. It looks like you're really mad right now because I won't buy it. You *really* want that truck." You can even help her extend her idea: "What did you want to do with that truck?" "What do you especially like about that one?" Such approaches don't necessarily mean Darlene will stop asking for the truck, but they do acknowledge her feelings and ideas.

3. Sportscasting

Sportscasting looks a lot like active listening, but it's more focused on the events that are taking place than on the feelings of the people involved. You talk to the child about what you see, in a kind of running commentary: "I see you holding on to that toy tightly." "I see that Boo just dumped over your sand container." "You got pushed off the slide." By describing what you see, you help the child figure out why he's upset.

Sportscasting is especially useful when you're dealing with a conflict between two younger children. When you step in and describe what's happening with both children in a nonjudgmental way, each child gets to see what he's doing and what the other child is doing. Both children get the message that their point is valid, and they're also reminded that someone else is involved who holds an equally valid perspective. Starting from a base of sportscasting, children often can be helped to find their own solution to the problem.

4. Facilitation

As children get older and gain more verbal skills, facilitation can be used in addition to sportscasting when dealing with conflicts. When we facilitate children's conflicts, we ask questions and give kids information that helps them find their own resolution.

Facilitation helps children express their ideas and feelings to the other person: "Lizzie, I see you grabbing Nayim's toy. Is there another way you can ask for it?"

Facilitation also involves describing the problem and inviting children's problem solving: "Looks like you both want to go down the slide at the same time, and there's only room for one person. Can either of you think of an idea that might solve this problem?"

Preschool-age children are also ready to learn basic tools in brainstorming solutions. You can ask: "Marc, can you think of a solution that Jenina might like?" Marc might say, "I'll go down the slide and Jenina can watch." The next step might be, "Jenina, is that okay with you?"

Facilitation checks to make sure kids are listening to each other: "Jenina, did you hear Marc's idea?" And then: "Marc, Jenina didn't hear you. Could you tell her again?" In doing so, you encourage children to tell each other their ideas, to listen, to come to a mutual solution.

As the facilitator, you go back and forth between the kids, asking them to express their feelings and listen, helping them reframe attacks or unclear communication, asking them to come up with solutions, to check out those solutions with the other person who's involved, to see if they can come up with a mutually acceptable resolution.

Using Your Voice As a Teaching Tool

There's a lot more to communication than just the words we use. Through our body language, our tone, and the way we use our voices, we communicate a tremendous amount. Learning how to use our voices effectively is an important aspect of communicating our feelings and responses to children.

Laura recalls: "I remember one time when Eli was a year old I was telling him 'No,' that he couldn't bite me. He ignored me and kept biting. Eli's Aunt Janet remarked that I told him 'no' in the same sweet, understanding voice I always used when I talked to him and that I had to make my voice serious if I wanted him to know that this was really important to me. I realized she was right. My voice only had one intonation with Eli, and I needed to learn to use it differently in order to really communicate with him."

With practice and forethought, you can learn to use your voice consciously. You can use a strong, powerful voice to indicate danger, a quieter, calming voice when you're walking into a loud conflict between children. When you're able to do this, your voice becomes a teaching tool that communicates far more than the actual words that you say.

Facilitation is time-consuming and exacting and it requires a clear mind, an ability to deal with uncertainty, and compassion for both of the kids involved in the struggle. At times, it can seem easier (or necessary) to step in with a ready-made solution when children fight, but if we are able to take that extra step toward facilitating children's conflicts rather than patching things up ourselves, we teach children valuable skills in communication, listening, brainstorming, and consensus building. We give children a crucial vote of confidence: "I think you can learn the skills you need to solve this."[3]

5. Using "I" Messages

"I" messages give us an opportunity to share our response to children's behavior without negatively labeling or judging them. An "I" message includes a description of the behavior or situation and our feelings about it. "I" statements allow us to replace "You're making me mad again! Why can't you just obey me?" with "When I ask you to come inside and I give you warnings and you're still not coming, I feel really frustrated." Or "When you ask for one more book and say you'll get dressed after that, and then you keep fighting me, I get really mad." When we make "I" statements, the bottom line is, "This is a feeling I'm having. It's not something you've done to me."

"I" statements are useful in communicating with children of all ages as well as with adults. "I" statements tell people that we're responsible for our own feelings and, by extension, that they're responsible for theirs. Learning to identify and articulate feelings is an important communication skill. By using "I" statements, we model this for kids. Also, "I" messages place less blame on children, thereby keeping them in a frame of mind in which learning is possible.

[3] The concepts of sportscasting and facilitation are explored thoroughly in Chapter 23, "Children's Friendships: Cooperation and Conflict" on p. 304 and in Chapter 28, "Building Strong Sibling Relationships" on p. 395.

6. Positive Limit Setting

Children thrive on clear limits. Even though they repeatedly push against the limits we set, knowing that we are keeping them safe is essential to their sense of security. Through limits, we teach children several things: "When you can't keep yourself safe, I'll keep you safe," "I'm going to teach you about the kinds of behaviors that work in our family," and "I'm going to stop you from hurting other people." Clear limits are reassuring for kids. Knowing what the boundaries are gives children the freedom to explore.

Limit setting can be verbal or physical, or a combination of the two. Often we think that our words alone should be enough to stop children. Especially with very verbal children, we may assume that they understand and therefore should respond to what we say to them. So if the first set of words we use doesn't work, we move on to louder and stronger words, sometimes getting mad in the process.

It's important to understand that words alone are frequently not enough. Just because children understand what we're saying doesn't mean they're capable of stopping themselves. At that moment, in those circumstances, self-control may be impossible for them.

As a result, children often need to have verbal limits backed up by physical ones. If we intervene before we get angry, we can do this in a nonpunitive way. We can gently hold the child's wrist and say "I'm not going to let you hit Jody." We can restrain our toddler gently and firmly around the waist and say in a serious voice "I'm not going to let you run into the street."

Generally, the need for this kind of physical follow-through decreases as children get older. Toddlers frequently need physical limits; by the time most children reach five, they've developed more inner controls and are more capable of responding to your voice alone.

When setting limits, it's important to do so in a way that still honors the impulse and allows for

Physical Limit Setting: When You Need to Restrain a Child

Sometimes being effective as a parent requires that we physically hold children or make them to do something they don't want to do. You need to change your child's soaking wet diaper and he refuses, screaming 'No, on! On! On!" Your eighteen-month-old is repeatedly darting into the street. Your two-year-old is having a tantrum and in danger of hurting her head on the hard wooden floor. Your feverish baby is flailing and refusing to take any medicine.

In a culture that associates physical force with violence, it can be hard to feel okay about ever using our superior strength and size to physically restrain a child. It's easy to become confused about the use of force; difficult to differentiate between physical abuse and necessary loving restraint. When we have to physically restrain a child, it's easy to assume that we must be hurting him or taking his power away.

But there are ways to hold children that don't hurt them or take their power away, that say to them "I know you can't do this right now. One day you're going to be able to cooperate. But for the time that you're not able to, I'm going to help you."

Ivan, whose one-year-old son, Doug, hates to be buckled in the car seat, told the following story. "It's very different to angrily shove Doug into the car seat than it is to say 'I know you don't want to get in the car seat now, but you need to be in it to be safe. You can get yourself in or I can help you get in.' And when Doug still refuses to get in and screams, 'OUT! OUT! OUT!' I say calmly, 'Okay, then I'm going to help you get in.' And sometimes it requires real physical strength to do it. He's like a little rigid board. I have to physically bend him in the middle and force him in. But it's very different for me to do that from a place of compassion for what he's feeling than it is for me to do it from a place of rage."

As Ivan says, the critical thing to look at when you're considering physical intervention is what you're feeling at the time. If the struggle you're involved in has pushed you over the edge, if you're feeling enraged or out of control, or if you're wanting to overpower or punish your child, it's not a good time to be physical with him. It's better to back off and get some help if you possibly can. But if you can approach your struggling, straining child from a place of compassion—"I know you really don't

active listening: "It looks like you're really interested in Mama's sewing box. But there are a lot of sharp things in there, and it's not safe for you to dig around in there when I'm not with you."

Part of setting limits in a positive way has to do with the language we use. Rather than saying "Don't do this! Stop doing that," you can state limits positively: "It hurts when you hit kids. You need to be safe with your friends." "Bikes stay outside when you're at day care." "Feet stay on the floor." "Touch the kitty softly." "Food stays on the table." "Sand in the sandbox stays low."

It's also useful to pair each "no" with a "yes." "You can't dig up these flowers, but you could dig up these weeds over here."

7. Giving a Choice

Giving choices whenever possible is an essential part of honoring children's autonomy. This is especially important with preschoolers, who are fascinated with their own ideas, and with toddlers, who want to have a say in everything that happens to them. As Shimon, want to take this medicine, but you need to have it to get well"—physical holding can come from a place of love and caring. And it can be effective parenting under the circumstances.

Janis learned this in a very visceral way when her middle child, Calvin, refused to be diapered. "I started off by giving Calvin a choice: 'Do you want me to change your diaper on the bed or while you're standing on the floor?' He screamed 'No!' to both. So I took a deep breath and said, 'If you can't make a decision, I'll make one for you.' I knew I didn't have to let him get diaper rash in the name of self-esteem. And again he refused to choose.

"So I was faced with physically holding Calvin down to change his diaper. And that felt really challenging to me. I hadn't grown up in an abusive family, but I'd assimilated the cultural message that physical restraint had to be punitive. And in the past, I'd always waited until I was mad, and then the holding did have a punitive quality.

"But that day, before I got angry at him, it was clear to me that he *couldn't* lie still himself. Once I realized that, I was able to move in and hold him physically from a loving place. Instead of saying 'You can't hold still? Well, I'm just going to pin you down!' I was able to hold my leg across his midsection and say 'Looks like you can't hold still. I know you don't want your diaper changed, but I'm going to help you hold still.' The fact he couldn't do it himself wasn't a sign of my failure or his failure. And what Calvin got from the interaction was 'She's helping me because I don't know how to do it yet' rather than 'I'm bad. I failed. I'm being punished.'

"What clicked for me that day was the understanding that Calvin was doing exactly what he should be doing. It was his job *not* to want to get his diaper changed. Diaper changes didn't make sense to Calvin. He was thinking 'Why shouldn't I be able to run around with my poop? Why should I have to stop in the middle of what I'm doing and lie still? That's Mom's idea. It's not my idea.'

"When I looked at him from his perspective, it was perfectly reasonable that he wouldn't want to stop his play. He had a really big list of things he wanted to be doing. I was coming along and interrupting his agenda, which didn't make any sense to him. And knowing that he felt that way really liberated me from being angry that he couldn't cooperate. It enabled me to be physical with him in a nonpunitive, nonhurtful way."

father of a two-year-old Tal, put it, "Toddlers don't know what they want, but they certainly want to be the one to make the decision."

Choices for toddlers can be simple and specific: "Do you want the blue bib or the red bib?" "Do you want water or milk in your cup?"

Older toddlers and preschoolers can handle more open-ended choices: "What shall we take with us to play with in the park?" "What shall we do together when I pick you up from child care?"

Children three and older can deal with more creative choices: "Do you want to hop up the stairs or do you want to slither up the stairs like a snake?" "Do you want to play with your blocks or help me put the silverware in the drawer?"

Choices can also be used when a clear limit is being set: "Can you hold still while I change your diaper or should I help you?" "Can you walk to the car or should I carry you?"

Even when children are unable to pick from the choices you've given them (and this will happen frequently), presenting them with options teaches them that they're entitled to have opinions and make decisions about what happens to them. In giving them choices, you increase their feelings of power and control in the world. And you give children a vote of confidence—you let them know that at some time, you expect them to be competent decision makers.

Let's look at an example in which a child wasn't capable of making a choice but still came out of the interaction feeling respected. Beth gave her twenty-month-old daughter Ruby the car keys to hold. When it came time for Beth to start the car, Ruby refused to relinquish the keys. So Beth presented her with a choice: "Do you want to give me the keys or should I take them?" And Ruby continued clutching the keys tight. So Beth said, "I can see you really want to keep those keys. But it's time for us to go and I need those keys to drive." Then she repeated the choice: "Can you give them to me or should I take them?"

When Ruby clutched them even tighter, Beth started prying her fingers away, saying: "It looks like I need to take them away from you. It's really hard for you to let go." By this time, Ruby was screaming and crying, and Beth really had to struggle to free the keys. But she managed to say to Ruby, "You really wanted to hold on to the keys. But I needed to take them. It looks like you're feeling really upset that you don't have them anymore."

In this example, Beth was able to set a clear limit, give Ruby a choice, listen to Ruby's feelings, and honor Ruby's impulse.

When we offer children choices, it's important to offer realistic ones. In our exasperation, we sometimes give choices that aren't really choices but are actually threats in disguise. When four-year-old Arnoldo refuses to come in from playing outside, you may ask in frustration "Are you going to come in now or shall I leave you outside all night?" When Arnoldo still doesn't come in, you might yell "Can you come in by yourself or are you going to *make me* come get you?"

In this situation, our anger may come from believing Arnoldo should be able to come in the first time we call him, without complaint or resistance: "Oh, thanks for reminding me. I'll just gather up my things and come in with you." We have the vision that if we do it right, things should go easily, and that if our child resists us, we've failed. But in reality, his resistance may actually be a healthy thing.

Sometimes it seems kids want to play for the next month straight without bothering to come home. That's absolutely normal. Moving out into the world, forming social relationships, and not clinging to his family are signs of healthy growth. Keeping that in perspective can help you understand why Arnoldo isn't coming when you call him. At that point, you can offer choices that are a lot less loaded: "Can you walk in yourself or shall I help you?" In this case, you give Arnoldo two real options, neither of which makes him bad or wrong.

If understanding why Arnoldo doesn't want to come in doesn't stave off your anger, then it's not the time to offer him choices. Choices offered between clenched teeth don't give children any real freedom to choose.

8. Giving Information

In the process of dealing with children's difficult behavior, one of the things we can do is give them information about the impact of what they're doing: "Cecelia feels sad when she gets pushed on the slide." "Shovels are for digging. If you swing it around like that, someone might get hurt." "When paint gets all over the table, it takes a long time to clean it up." "When you keep banging your fork on the table, the sound hurts my ears."

We give children information to teach them social rules: "It's not okay to hit Corbin." "You need to be gentle with Lila."

We also use information to teach children about safety: "When you hold the baby, you need to use two hands and put one under her head, like this." "Don't touch the oven. It's hot and it could hurt you."

Giving information tells children, "You're worthy of an explanation." When we don't give them information, when we say, "You have to stop because I told you to stop," "Because I'm the boss," or "Because I said so," we basically communicate to them, "You have to always have me—or some other person in authority around, because you're not going to be able to figure this out for yourself."

Giving children information tells them that we expect them to be capable of making independent decisions someday, to gauge what's dangerous and what isn't. We expect them to learn to assess whether the stove is hot and if it's safe to lean against. Ultimately, we expect they'll be able to make significant life decisions, as well.

It is important that we gear our explanation to our children's level of understanding and not overwhelm them with words. However, there are times it's appropriate to give kids information before they're able to understand it fully: "I want you to turn off the hose now, so we don't waste water." Even if your three-year-old doesn't fully understand the principles of water conservation, offering her information lets her know that we value her thinking.

9. Natural Consequences

Helping children understand the natural consequences of their actions gives them another kind of information. Since children learn best through direct experience, allowing them to experience the impact of their actions can provide them with important feedback. This kind of cause-and-effect learning becomes increasingly important as children get older, but even young children can benefit from experiencing the natural consequences of their behavior. Eleven-month-old Sal carefully empties his cup of applesauce onto his tray and experiences that his applesauce is "all gone." Three-year-old Danny resists brushing his teeth for so long that there's time for only one

story before bed. Four-year-old Lulu doesn't put her toys away for a week and soon can't find her favorite dinosaur amid the clutter. Experiencing these natural outcomes of behavior allows children to receive information necessary for their growth and learning.

Natural consequences vary. There are those that occur between the child and his environment: Five-year-old Jared leaves his favorite truck outside in the rain and it gets rusty. Then there are those that occur between children and their peers: When Rudy hits Tiffany, she turns and pushes him down. Finally there are natural consequences that are structured and set up by parents: "If you don't put your shoes on, we won't be able to go for a walk."

When parents are the ones setting up consequences for children, it's important to take into account three things: the child's age and developmental level, the suitability of the consequence for the child, and the negative impact the consequence could have on you.

While it would be age-appropriate to ask a two-and-a-half-year-old to pick up a few toys before he got out the musical instruments, it wouldn't be appropriate to make him clean up the entire room before he could play with anything else. A three-year-old could help spray and scrub the crayon off the wall but shouldn't be expected to clean all four walls himself. A four-year-old could learn from being without her balls for a day, after she teasingly threw them over into the neighbor's yard for the third time, but losing them for a week would be too costly to be a useful learning experience.

It's also inappropriate to use natural consequences when they are too obscure for a child to understand, or too dangerous. One-year-old Elena has just discovered the joys of flinging sand. We can tell her that throwing sand is dangerous, but she can't yet understand the seriousness of someone getting sand in their eyes. Two-year-old Soon Yung delights in the sound of her ceramic bowl on the table in the kitchen. She doesn't have enough experience to predict what could happen, and we can't allow her to find out. In these situations, positive limit setting, information, and redirection would be more effective strategies.

Finally, there may be many situations in which we don't choose to let children experience the natural consequences because of the impact on us. If you have been looking forward all morning to visiting Theo and her dad, you probably won't want to let your daughter's continuing refusal to get dressed result in a canceled visit.

Moving from Enforcer to Ally

In many circumstances, following through with clear limits and allowing children to experience their own natural consequences is all kids need in order to figure out how to be more successful the next time. But other times, children may need help in figuring out what went wrong and support in coming up with alternative strategies for the future.

Riva shared her struggles with her five-year-old son, Slater, who is always losing things: "He leaves his backpack, his sweatshirt, anything that's not attached to him, wherever he is. I've said to him 'So now you don't have a backpack and a lunch box.' I've cut off his TV privileges. But Slater's continued to lose things."

In this situation, it became clear that the natural consequences of being without his backpack and even the more contrived consequence of not getting to watch TV weren't sufficient to help Slater keep track of his things. Riva realized he needed a different kind of help, so she started asking Slater questions and providing him with some feedback: "I've noticed you seem to have a harder time remembering your things when you are out on the playground. What have you noticed about when you forget things? Do you lose things more at a certain time of day?" Another time

she asked him, "When do you find it easiest to remember your things? Can you think of anything that might help you remember?"

This approach goes beyond just leaving a child with his consequences to figure things out on his own. While it still lets him experience the natural consequences of his actions, it also puts parent and child on the same "team" to define and figure out solutions to the problem together.

10. Redirection

Redirection is the natural extension of acknowledging and honoring the impulse. When you understand the impulse behind a child's actions, you can stop her and then redirect her to a more appropriate way of expressing that same impulse: "Looks like you're really wanting to kick. Go get your ball. We can take it outside and you can kick it really far!" "If you want to touch your sister, you can do it gently, like this. Let's see if that's all right with her." "Looks like you really want Marta to move. You can tell her 'Move, Marta!' "

Redirection is frequently confused with distraction, which has a very different result. Distraction changes the child's focus and pulls him away from his inner direction: "Oh, look at that airplane up in the sky." "Would you like a cookie?" "Want to read a book with me?" In other words, "You shouldn't be interested in what you're interested in. It's really not important, so let's go and find something else that will grab your attention." Rather than encouraging them to be self-initiated learners, distraction gives children the message that adults always have a better idea what they should be doing.

Redirection, on the other hand, says "What you're working on is important. Even though I will stop you from biting or shoving, I can still value your desire to communicate with your friends." When we redirect children, we help them find an alternative way to express their impulses and lay the groundwork for them someday being able to choose those ways on their own.

We won't always be able to find an appropriate redirection for every impulse our child demonstrates, but the fact that we try, and sometimes succeed, makes it clear to children that who they are and what they want to learn is really important to us.

11. Inviting Children's Initiative

Much of young children's difficult behavior originates from the healthy developmental drive we call "initiative." This is the term child developmental theorist Erik Erikson used to describe the major growth task of children between their third and fifth years.

Children's thinking at this stage goes something like this: "I *have* my own ideas that are different from those of the people around me. When I get to use my ideas, I feel powerful and competent." Children of this age are driven to actualize their ideas, because otherwise, their ideas don't seem real to them. Preschool children are also compelled to explore "When my idea doesn't agree with yours, whose takes precedence? And how exactly is that decision made?"

It's natural for there to be considerable testing and frustration during this time, but if we work with children's initiative, rather than against it, things will go easier for all of us. We lessen children's need to test limits and "act out" by providing them with a variety of outlets for their burgeoning initiative.

One way to do this is to help children expand their interests. If your daughter is really interested in bugs, you can help her find recycled jars she can collect bugs in. Take her to the library to get bug books. Go on an insect walk with her in your neighborhood.

You can also help children expand their abilities. Preschool children are fascinated with developing new abilities such as hammering, building, lacing, weaving, and using small tools and appliances.

Opportunities in which children have open-ended time, space, and materials encourage them to come up with their own ideas and use their creativity.[4]

You can also celebrate children's creative thinking: "Wow, you figured out a whole new way to build that tunnel."

Preschool-age kids can also be asked to solve their own and other people's problems: "You really want to spray water and I really don't want water sprayed inside the house. What can we do about that?" "Your sister has been crying all morning; do you have any idea what she might be telling us?"

Finally, you can offer children appropriate choices, not only about their own destiny but about wider family decisions: "What vegetable would you like us to have tonight?"

There are many ways to creatively engage children's growing sense of initiative. With a little creativity and open-mindedness, it's possible to channel much of your child's exuberance and abundance of ideas into avenues that work for everyone in the family.

12. Setting the Stage for Future Success

An important way to deal with difficult behavior is through prevention. Drawing on your experience, you strive to set up circumstances that minimize the stresses that typically cause difficult behavior. Each time a challenging situation comes up with your child, you have the opportunity to figure out what the contributing factors might have been.

Maurice explained: "After several days of carrying a sleepy, wailing, half-dressed child out of the house to go to child care, it dawned on me that LaShana needed a different routine in the morning. So we began to do a slower waking-up routine, with several gentle wake-

[4] See "What Is Our Role in Children's Play and Learning?" on p. 289 for more on setting up these kind of environments.

up calls, accompanied by her favorite music tape. Just those few small changes led to more successful mornings."

Looking at difficult situations with a problem-solving approach allows you to think creatively about setting the stage for future success.

Developing a Disciplinary Strategy That Works for You

Many of the strategies in this chapter probably are already a part of your repertoire as a parent. Some may be new to you. Bear in mind that these strategies are not meant to be a rigid list of "how-tos" but, instead, a list to refer to, to stimulate your thinking. In deciding which of these ideas work for you, it is important to refer back to what you want to teach and the style of discipline that best fits your family.

Most of us find that even if many or all of these strategies match up with what we want to teach, there are numerous instances where time, resources, or our own energy doesn't allow us to use them. It's valuable to remember that "perfection" is not the goal of parenting; children who are listened to and respected on a regular basis can handle the times when life does not allow us to live up to our highest ideals.

20.

Putting It All Together: When Children Test Limits

"Our daughter has a real flare for drama. At two and a half she learned to say, "YOU DAMN IT POOPOO SHIT!' Ava would point her finger and say it really loud in public places like the meat counter at the grocery store. She'd say it with so much intensity. Everyone would stop and look and I would just want to die."

VIVIAN, *mother of Ava*

For parents, coming face to face with a biting, whining, swearing child is a real-life opportunity to put our disciplinary ideas into practice. In this chapter, we look at a number of challenging behaviors parents face in the infant, toddler and preschool years. By providing developmental information about each behavior and applying the strategies presented in the last chapter, "Moving Beyond Punishment," we offer you a disciplinary framework you can build from and use in a wide variety of situations.

From One to Five: Why Are Children Always Testing?

Testing is a young child's job. In the first five years of life, children push against every limit we set. They test to find out about the world and to learn social rules. They test to find out about us and the parameters of our tolerance. In the course of this testing, they exhibit the difficult behaviors so typical of early childhood.

Babies first test their physical world. They poke at eyes, grab hair, crawl off the diaper table, and pull the dog's ears. This testing gives them valuable information about the people and the things in their environment.

Toddlers go on to discover that there are decisions to be made in life—and they become very interested in making them. Testing is their way of discovering how decisions get made and which decisions they get to make. Toddlers want to answer the questions "What do my ideas look like in the world?" "What happens when I do something different than what you say?" They test repetitively because they need to verify their results.

It's typical for toddlers to test the things that are most familiar to them—and to do their testing with the people closest to them. They feel comfortable enough getting in their car seat or putting on a bib that they think, "Wait a minute! What if I *don't* get in the car seat?"

This is the exciting stage in which children begin to become autonomous. Yet they aren't particularly graceful about it. Instead of saying, "Maybe I'll try just five decisions today," they're compelled to try to make every single decision that comes along.

When toddlers first begin to test, the pleasure of the activity seems to be in just making something happen: "I'll pull on the lamp cord—then you'll come and stop me!" From the child's vantage point, his job is to test, and your job is to stop him. That's why children often call attention to what they're doing when they break the rules: They call "Momma!" as if to say, "Here I am, Mom, swishing my hand in the toilet!" Or "Hey, Dad, look! I'm getting close to the radiator. You better come stop me!"

One of the things that's frustrating for parents is the fact that limits often have to be set again and again: One-year-old Arturo is going toward the electrical outlet, and you say "No, it's not safe" and you move him away. The next minute he's back at it again. Again you peel him away and set the limit. He screams in protest and heads back toward the outlet again. And you ask yourself "Why can't he just obey me?"

To begin with, children don't understand danger, mortality, or electricity. To them, you're just setting an arbitrary limit. And even when children begin to understand the word "no," their drive to explore the outlet may override their capacity to listen to what you're saying.

Often we see young toddlers going toward something dangerous, saying "No, no, no!" the whole time they approach it. Clearly they have "no" associated with the activity, but in their minds, that doesn't have anything to do with stopping themselves. As far as the child is concerned, that's your job. And that can be exasperating for us.

It can help to remember that your toddler didn't write that job description. He woke up one morning and there it was: "You have to test every decision today." It's exhausting for him, too. Kids get tired and frustrated and whiny because it's a big job to contradict their parents at every turn.

You may feel like you're the victim, because all of a sudden your limit-setting system is being challenged. But when you think about it, your child is at the mercy of his developmental drives, too.

Sometimes toddlers test out of what Micah called "outlaw delight." Her twenty-month-old son, Ethan, had just figured out the whole category of things she didn't want him to do. "Yesterday Ethan was into the pure thrill of being an outlaw. He climbed on the table. He banged on the glass. He bit my toes. He pulled on the blinds. He was a having a celebration of lawbreaking. He was joyous. And he was so happy, I couldn't help but be happy."

Is This an Irritating Noise to You?

Preschoolers elaborate on this theme of testing, adding more complex variations. Three-, four-, and five-year-olds love to push the boundaries of language, often to the extreme: "What is the power of language?" "Which words are powerful words? What happens when I say them?"

Having fully established separateness from adults, preschoolers are also grappling with the issue of who's in charge. They're driven to explore the lines of power and control in any given situation, so they may need to test each new adult: "My experience has shown me that adults respond differently to what I'm doing. Show me what you're going to do."

This happened at Faye's house during a visit by her son's three-year-old friend. "Quinn was eating over one evening and we were letting him stand up in his chair. After a while when I hadn't said anything, Quinn asked, 'Is it okay for me to stand on the chair in this house?' After dinner Quinn started making this noise over and over again. I was tuning it out and he asked, 'Is this an irritating noise to you?' And later, when Quinn was petting my dog, he asked, 'Should I be gentle with this dog?' It was really clear that he was doing research—trying to figure out if the same rules applied at my house as they did at his."

Children's exploration of limits is rarely subtle. Alejandro, father of a three-and-a-half-year-old Roscoe, said his son's testing is so obvious, it's sometimes funny. "Just yesterday, Roscoe was taking the cereal boxes and dropping them on the floor and I told him not to do it. So he took them and dropped them on the table. It was like, 'Well, that was four-and-a-half feet. This is just a foot and a half. Is that okay?' "

Toke, the mother of two-year-old Nils, agreed. "Nils takes his toy telephone and he bangs it against the television. Then he looks at me. Then he does it again. He's just begging me to react."

Laura says Eli's ongoing research into how decisions get made has gotten more and more refined. "We don't let Eli put his feet on the table. He's tried that repeatedly and we always say, 'Eli, feet belong on your high chair,' and he takes them off. One night, after he took his feet off the table, he gave me this impish smile and put his feet right against the edge of the table. I had to laugh. "Well, Eli. I guess that's okay. It isn't on top of the table, it's on the side."

When a child tests repeatedly, he's trying to figure out "If I do this often enough, can I talk you into letting it happen?" "If not, how do you go about stopping me?" And when he's putting his feet on the side of the table, he's testing to find the exact parameters of the limit: "Is this considered 'on' the table or not?"

Testing As a Way to Show Us They've Changed

Testing is one way children show us that they've grown, that old rules may no longer be appropriate. When children continually push on certain limits, it may be a signal that it's time to reevaluate what we're going to let them do. Let's say you've never let two-and-a-half-year-old Josie use a knife. But now she keeps grabbing for the knife, saying "I do it!" She's telling you that she thinks she's ready to use a knife. After fifteen times of saying "No! Knives aren't safe," you might start thinking to yourself, "She's really interested in using a knife. Is there a way I could help her use a knife safely?" "Is there a knife I feel okay about Josie using?" "Would it be okay if she used a table knife to spread mayonnaise?" "Could she cut her own banana?" "At what point am I going to start teaching her about how to use a knife safely?"

While you are figuring out your revised knife policy, Josie is probably going to continue to push the limit. That's completely healthy. She's exploring a new frontier. And so are you.

Trish, whose son, Paco, was nearing two, found this process of revising limits troublesome but worthwhile. "I get irritated whenever Paco is testing something I thought had already been decided. We'd already decided that these cupboard doors were going to stay closed! Whenever I get irritated, I have to check in with myself and ask if I'm holding on to a limit that was right for another time but no longer applies to what Paco's capable of today."

It's good that children continually explore their parameters, climbing to places they haven't climbed before, opening cupboard doors they haven't opened before, yearning to cut their own bananas. They find great things on the other side of these limits, and we should encourage them. We want our children to grow, to become independent, to increase their competence. We don't want them to go along blindly with what everyone else tells them to do. When we look at testing in that light, we can see it not just as a time of frustration and irritation but also as a time of reevaluation and positive change.

Testing As a Way to Explore Safety

Testing is also a way that children make sure they're safe in the world. Kids know they can't always keep themselves safe. They know that their behavior gets out of control sometimes, that they're small in a big world, and that they need help making decisions and staying safe. One of the reasons kids test limits repeatedly is to reassure themselves that you'll stop them. Reasonable limits are comforting to kids.

When kids feel they're getting away with something, they often feel scared. So if you're going to let your child do something that hasn't been permitted before, let him know the limit is being changed. If you don't do that, if you just try to ignore what he's doing, he'll often escalate to doing something more severe so that you'll step in and stop him: "I'm going to try this . . . and this . . . because I want my dad to come and stop me."

Why Do Kids Always Seem to Test the Most When We're Having a Bad Day?

When we're preoccupied, stressed, or angry, it often seems that kids escalate their testing. Some of this may just be our perception, but it's not unusual for kids to bounce off the walls when we're feeling cranky. Why do they do this? Is it to manipulate us? To drive us crazy? Or is there another reason?

It may be that children feel the tension in the air or that they sense we're in a different mood and they want to check us out. In essence, they're asking, "Are you still my same mom?" "My same dad?" "Even though you're different right now, will you *still* be able to keep me safe?"

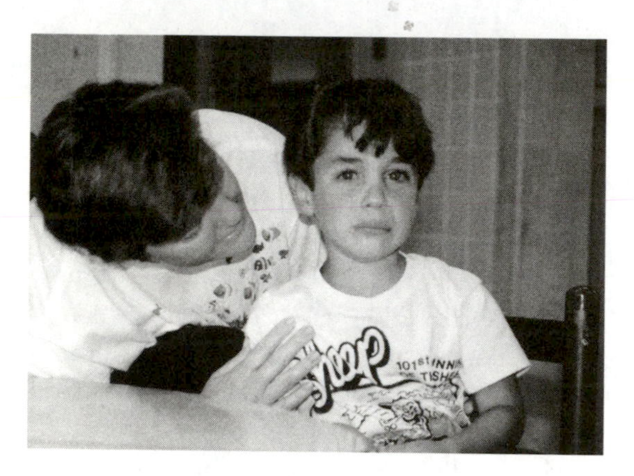

It's also helpful to remember that children have bad days, too. Sometimes they need to fall apart and express a load of built-up frustration. Two-year-old Tate "paints himself into a corner" by testing over and over again, in effect saying, "I need to cry, so I'm going to pick a fight with my mom. I know! I'll use my drum sticks on the window—that always gets her!" So you stop Tate and he has a giant tantrum over the limit you've set. That enables him to cry the way he needs to, and afterward, he feels much better.[1]

Responding to a Child Who Is Testing

• **Honor the impulse.** Respect your child's drive toward autonomy, her necessary exploration of decision making.

• **Use active listening.** "It looks like you have a different idea," or "It looks like you're curious about what happens when you bang your hammer on the TV."

• **Set limits and give information.** "I know you really want to be out of your car seat. But your car seat helps keep you safe, so you need to stay in it."

• **Redirect.** "I see you want to hit the window. I can't let you do that because the window is breakable, but you can bang on the couch all you want."

• **Invite their initiative.** As kids get a little older, you can say, "It's not safe to hit the window. What could you hit safely?" Or "Can you think of another way to touch the window?" When children are given the chance to come up with their own alternatives, they learn important problem-solving skills that can help them manage their own behavior eventually.

• **Cultivate an attitude of acceptance.** Testing is an inevitable and important part of children's growth and development. Cultivating an attitude of acceptance for what our children are trying to do while respectfully setting limits

[1] For more on this kind of emotional release, see "Responding to Crying and Tantrums" on p. 90.

can help us get through this stage in their lives with less frustration.

Hair-Pulling

Hair-pulling is an annoying behavior that babies and young toddlers engage in. It starts as a sensory exploration: "This hair is so graspable and feels so good in my hand." Then it shifts to a social exploration. "Make that funny face again, Dad!"

It goes something like this: You're trying to hold or rock or feed your baby, and all of a sudden—yank!—your little pumpkin has a wad of your hair in his chubby little fingers, and he's not letting go. A shooting pain races across your head and you say sternly, "NO! That hurts Mommy!" And your child laughs in your face, delighted. Then he tries to do it again. You feel angry and confused. What's going on? Does your son really want to hurt you?

The answer to that question is no. Your son doesn't know that you're feeling pain or that he's hurt you. All he knows is that when he pulls your hair, you make a very interesting face and talk in a different kind of voice. He's made something happen and that's fascinating to him. He's delighted by the strength and predictability of your response. So he says to himself, "I don't get to see that face very often. How can I make it come? Will it happen again if I pull your hair?"

And your son learns that every time he pulls your hair, he immediately gets your full attention.

A slightly older child might be pulling hair to explore what your pained face is about. While children experience emotions, they don't fully understand them. They don't know why they start crying. Nor do they know that we have feelings. But once they discover that we have them, they will do everything they can to elicit them. They'll pinch us on the cheek or pull our hair, and wait to see what happens next. "What happens when she gets sad? When she gets mad? What will she do?"

Responding to Hair-Pulling

When responding to hair-pulling, you can *honor the impulse*, *set a limit*, *give information*, and *redirect the child*. Depending on the age of the child, you may need to physically stop him, prying his fingers away from your hair if necessary. Gently hold his hand if it looks as if he's going to try to grab your hair again. Say to him: "I see you're interested in my hair." Then tell him, "It hurts when you pull my hair. I'm going to stop you. I'm going to put up my hair (move you off my lap, take your hand away)." Then you can redirect him: "Touch my hair gently." Or "You can grab and pull this toy." While you say that to him, gently stroke his hair or hand him the toy.

Since hair-pulling is often done by young babies, it's unrealistic to expect them to be able to stop themselves or even to understand exactly what you're saying to them. (Though eventually, they will get it.) So the best defense, at least for a while, is probably environmental. Arrange the environment so the hair-pulling is less likely to happen again. Keep your hair pinned up or pulled back, your beard shaved, or your baby out of the backpack until the fascination wears off.

Children and Defiance: Why Are They So Demanding and Why Do They Always Say "No"?

Saying "no" is a necessary part of children's development in their second and third years. It is universal. The "nos" cannot be avoided. As Janis explains, "I know one family that never used the word 'no' with their child on the premise that the child wouldn't learn the word. It didn't work."

When toddlers begin to discover the word "no," they see how powerful it is. They see that "no" makes things happen, and they want to make things happen. So they begin saying "no" all the time. It's not an exploration most children enter into delicately. They're *driven* to say "no."

Sari had an experience with Jordan right before his second birthday that epitomized this obsession. "We were driving down the road and I said to Jordan, 'It looks like the sun is coming out.' And he said with great vehemence, 'No out! Sun back in! No sun out! Back in! Back in!' He was insistent. And I said, 'Honey, not even mommies can tell the sun what to do. The sun does just what it wants to do.' But he was undeterred. He kept orchestrating the world from his car seat. 'No out! No sun! Sun back in!' It was kind of the ultimate in trying to control things."

Ty remarked, "Chantal is saying 'no' to everything right now. Even in her sleep, she's moaning 'No! No! No! No!' "

Laura also had some extreme moments with Eli when he was going through this period. "If I say up, he says down. If I say down, he says up. If I arrange to take him to his favorite playground, he says he wants to go, and a minute later he cries, 'No, stay home! Stay home!' Once we're in the car, he says, 'Walk! Walk!' and I have to explain that we need to drive to get to the playground. When we're almost there, he starts yelling 'Different playground. Different playground.' Once we get there, he plays happily. But then after my ten- and five- and one-minute warnings, when we have to leave, he cries all the way home, 'More playground! More playground!' He yells at the red lights to turn green. And when he's drop-dead tired, the last thing he cries out is, 'Eli awake! Eli awake!' right before he drops into a deep slumber. It's gotten so extreme, it's almost funny. But I try not to laugh. I know he's really working on something that's serious for him."

When children are in this stage, they *can't* be agreeable. Even if you offer a child ice cream or something else he really loves, he may still say "No!" because at that moment, being able to make his own decision is more important than the outcome—even if it's eating ice cream.

Coping with the "Nos"

Here are some specific strategies that can help increase children's feelings of autonomy and power, thereby lessening their need to say "no":

• **Don't expect children to always be agreeable.** They're not saying "no" as a personal affront to you. Respect their agenda even if you can't go along with it.

• **Give choices.** When children feel they have some control over what happens to them, they have less need to be defiant. Jenny explained: "I ask Carly 'Do you want to put your jacket on or do you want me to help you do it?' I try to be as courteous to her as I would want someone to be with me. I like people to ask me if I need help, not just be right in my face, helping me. I give Carly as many choices as I think she can handle."

• **Create an environment that encourages mastery.** Set up your child's environment so she can be as independent as possible. Hang pegs for clothes at her level. Supply clothes that are easy to put on and take off. Have bowls and cereal and spoons where your child can reach them. Keep toys and books on a shelf that's easily reached.

Children resent the fact that they still need our help just when they want to be doing everything for themselves. It frustrates them that we're the ones who pick the cup, choose the flavor of juice, and pour it. So it's preferable to say, "There's a pitcher of juice (a small one with just a little juice on the bottom). You can pour it when you're ready."

Sometimes parents hesitate to let their children do things independently because they invariably take longer and create more messes. It's true, when your one- or two-year-old is learning to pour, there will be spills. Part of your son's budding autonomy can be learning to clean up his own messes. (Although he's more likely to follow through if you do it with him.)

The more children can accomplish for themselves, the less they're reminded of how dependent they are on you. That can take some of the wallop out of needing you so desperately and resenting it so much that they do.

• **Set up opportunities for children to really help you.** Children like to make real contributions to the family. They love to imitate whatever it is we're doing. When you're folding laundry, let your son fold the washcloths. Let your daughter search for matching socks.

When kids help, don't criticize their efforts. Paula remarked, "From the time they were really little, I've always had my kids help, even if it was to pull the diaper bucket in closer to where we're doing the diapering. I let the kids help in a way that makes them feel they're making a genuine contribution. I never fix their work in front of them. When you're teaching a kid to mop floors, you have to understand that you're not really going to have clean floors. But I never go over their work or point out all the ways it's inadequate. They mop the floor and we put everything back in place. Maybe later, after they're in bed, I might take a rag and wipe it up a little better. I think it's important for them to feel a sense of accomplishment and completion with what they did, to know I'm actually counting on them to help out."[2]

• **Give your children opportunities for independence which will be safe and successful.** When you're going to begin to let kids make some of their own decisions, ask yourself: "Is there a safety net? Or is this a circumstance in which making a mistake could have dire consequences?" It's important when we're helping our children develop independence that we do it in situations where there aren't dangerous consequences.

"But I Want It NOW!"

In Janis's class one night, Debbie was talking about some struggles she was having with her two-year-old daughter, Ana. Ana was objecting to absolutely everything Debbie did, making all kinds of unreasonable demands, and it was driving Debbie crazy. "Even when I'm coming through for her, somehow I'm do-

[2] See "But He Won't Clean Up His Room," on p. 272 for more on encouraging children to do chores.

The Five Power Words Babies and Toddlers Love the Most

In the course of learning about language, communication, and social rules, children inevitably hit upon certain words that are both fascinating and powerful. These words make things happen, and children love doing things that generate a predictable, strong, or unusual response. "No" is an obvious choice for this list, as is "now." Here are some of the other more frequently used words in the one- to three-year-old set:

• **Hi.** This is one of the first great power words that babies discover. When you say 'hi' everyone smiles at you and says 'hi' back. Other baby power words include "bye-bye," "mama," "papa" as well as the names of other family members and pets.

• **More.** Alternately known as "mo," "moah," and "again," this word resonates deeply with young children's love of repetitive activities. And when they say it, things often do happen again!

Many children develop their own unique versions of this, as Eli did when he was two. Laura explains: "Whenever we were doing something he really loved, Eli would hold up his little index finger and say, 'Just *one* more time.' After we did it again, he'd repeat the gesture and say, 'Just *one* more time.' He'd do it as many times as he could get away with, until we finally alerted him, 'Eli, this is the *last* time.' Even then, he'd test to see if he could get 'just *one* more time' out of us."

• **Mine.** "I own, therefore I am." This basic tenet of toddlerhood is expressed most concretely in the frequent, often loud, repetition of this word. "Mine" is frequently coupled with an unyielding grip on the object in question. Variations on "mine" include: "MY truck," "MY bear," "MY dolly," "MY DADDY!"

• **Why?** Children want to get information about the world, and "why" is the perfect way to get it. When you ask "why" about the same thing repeatedly, you usually get an answer that's slightly different from what you were told before. Parents get bored saying the same thing over and over, so they vary their answers; that's fascinating to children.

Also, there are many times when kids don't really understand what adults have said, and asking "Why?" can be a way to say, "I didn't quite get that. Run that by me again. Maybe I'll be able to understand it this time."

The popularity of "Why?" and other variations, such as "Talk about it!" also arise from the delight children take in the fact that they can keep conversations going indefinitely through the use of a single word or phrase.

Parents have different levels of tolerance for answering "why?" at different times of day. Generally, we all hit a limit, whether it's after fifty-five responses or three responses, at which time we say, "You can keep on asking, I'm glad you're curious, but I'm not going to talk about that anymore."

• **Peepee.** When children say this word (or one of its variations—pee, potty, wee-wee, hungry, thirsty, tired—meaning "I have a bodily function that needs attending to") parents come running, drop what they're doing, and immediately come to see what they need.

ing it wrong. She'll be happily singing one minute, and the next she's screaming 'Pasta! Pasta! PASTA!' So I say, 'Okay, I'll get it for you, honey,' and she screams 'NO!' I tell her what I need to do to make the pasta and Ana screams, 'NOW! Pasta now! NOW!!' What's going on?"

Janis replied: "There are a few different

things going on. For one, she doesn't know how long it takes to cook pasta. Second, she has to keep talking about pasta because she hasn't stopped wanting it and it's her way of holding on to her idea. The other thing is that she's learned two very powerful words: 'no' and 'now.' When kids first get 'now' they think if they say it, it will make things happen right away. She may understand part of the sequence to making pasta: you get it out of the bag, you boil water, you put it in, you wait, wait, wait, then you drain it, let it cool, and eat it, but once she has the word 'now,' she may think it overrides what she already knows about how long it takes to make pasta. And if 'now' doesn't work at first, she thinks if she just says it a little louder or more often, it will work. When she says 'Now' and nothing happens, she gets disappointed: 'Wait a minute! I thought this word was going to change everything!' And her frustration has very little to do with you and a lot to do with her own exploration of the power of language.

"There are two ways you can deal with it. You can remind her of the process: 'First I have to do this, then I have to do that.' Then involve her as much as you can: 'I'm going to get the pasta. Here's the bag. Can you pour the pasta into this bowl? Can you hold the spoon while I pour the oil in it?' If she's involved, she doesn't just have to sit there and wait while you do everything. She'll have much more of a grasp on the fact that the pasta is really coming. She'll feel less critical of you and will be more able to wait.

"There will be times, however, when no matter what you do, she'll be frustrated and exasperated and will yell. At those times, try to remember that she's not yelling at you, she's yelling about her powerlessness in the world. She feels comfortable enough with you to let it out."

FOOD FOR THOUGHT: COPING WITH THE "NOS"

- Were children allowed to say "no" when I was young?
- Were there names for "demanding" children?
- What is useful about children who know how to say "no"?
- How can I teach the social skills I want to teach without discouraging assertiveness and independence?

Working with Children Who Bite

Although this section deals specifically with biting, most of the principles apply equally to hitting, pushing, grabbing, kicking, and other forms of aggressive behavior in both toddlers and preschoolers.

Biting is a normal developmental behavior for babies and toddlers, although sometimes biting is caused or intensified by other factors. Not all children do it and some do it for longer than others, but it is very common for young children to go through a phase in which they bite.

Whether your child bites or not is not a reflection of your parenting, as Janis explains. "Those of us who happen to have children who don't bite may be tempted to feel somewhat virtuous: 'If those parents were only more like me, their child wouldn't bite.' But that's not the way it works. It's usually just the luck of the draw."

Because it hurts, and because biting is socially unpopular, biting is a particularly challenging behavior for parents to deal with. As grown-ups, it can be hard for us to understand why kids bite. But there are a variety of developmental impulses that cause the behavior:

- **Anger:** "I'm angry." "You're in my way."

- **Frustration:** "I'm frustrated." "Things are out of my control." "Nothing is going the way I want it to."

- **Frustration coupled with limited vocabulary:** "I have an idea and I can't get it out." "I wish I could talk but I can't."

- **Communication:** "Move!" "I didn't like that." "I want that."

- **Physical needs:** "I'm really hungry." "I'm so sleepy."

- **Teething pain:** "My gums feel funny. I'm trying to relieve them so I can feel better."

- **Imitation:** "I saw Rudy bite Eliot and it seemed like an interesting interaction. So now I'm going to try it and see what happens."

- **Exploration:** "Someone did this to me and I'm trying to figure out what it feels like to bite someone."

- **Experimentation:** "What happens when I do this?"

- **Social exploration:** "I'm asking for some social rules." "How do people keep me from doing this?" "I wonder what Mommy will do when I bite?" "How does Grandma feel about it?" "Is biting kids different than biting grown-ups?"

- **Release of tension:** "It feels good when I bite. When I do it, I feel a little bit better."

- **To get attention:** "You've been talking on the phone for a long time, Dad."

- **Being powerful:** "All kinds of big things happen when I bite!" "Look at me! I can make things happen."

- **Sensory pleasure:** Even adults like to bite sometimes.

- **Initiating Play or Affection:** "I want you to be my friend. Do you feel like playing together?" Or "Hi, you look interesting. I think I'll bite you."

This may seem farfetched, but babies and young toddlers don't understand that biting hurts people. They know that their mouths are a very important part of who they are and so their thinking may go something like this: "What could be more loving than putting my mouth on you? It's a lot like kissing. People always kiss me when they want to tell me they love me. So I'm coming toward you with my mouth open. Now I'm sinking my teeth into you because it feels so good! It must feel good to you, too. So why are you crying?"

- **Accidentally:** "I didn't really mean to bite you. My mouth just happened to be near your arm, and I just kind of slipped."

Often we think that toddlers bite in a premeditated way to hurt someone, but as Janis explains, "I've seen kids start to bite someone, and when that person moves out of their way, the child goes on to bite the table. It's kind of like 'I've got this bite here and I need to put it someplace. It's not really that I want to hurt somebody, I just have to do this with my mouth.' "

Responding to Children Who Bite

In each of the reasons for biting just listed, there is an impulse we can support. Of course we don't want children to achieve these things through biting, but addressing the source of the behavior is at the basis of an appropriate response.

How you intervene in a biting situation depends on the status of the bite: Is the child going after someone with his mouth open, ready to bite? Has the bite already happened? Is there another person (besides you) involved?

• **Set a limit.** When a bite is about to happen, physical and verbal limit setting often come first. You hold the child's mouth away from the intended target and say, "I'm not going to let you bite Tyrone." Or "I will help you stop biting." You can do this by gently cupping your hand over the child's mouth. If you stay calm, you will avoid raising the tension level of the interaction.

• **Honor the impulse.** Through observation and by knowing the child (that he gets stressed in big crowds, that he tends to bite when he's tired), you can make an educated guess about why the child is biting. Then you can check it out with the child: "It looks like you want to say 'hi' to Joshua." "I wonder if you're trying to tell Pablo to move." "I'm wondering if your mouth is hurting." Then watch for the child's reaction. If the child relaxes or cries, that may be a sign that you've hit on the right reason.

• **Give social information:** "Biting hurts. I won't let you bite people."

• **Redirect.** Redirect the child either to bite something else or to channel his initial impulse into a behavior that is more acceptable. If you think the child is biting because his teeth are hurting, you can say: "Looks like you need something to chew on. You can bite on this washcloth (soft toy, plastic ring, sock)." Then place the object within reach of the child's mouth.

If you think the child is biting because he's angry, you can say, "It looks like you're really mad! You can roar like a lion." Or "It looks like you want Mohammed to stop pushing you. You can tell him 'Stop!'"

If you think the bite is a social gesture, you can say, "It looks like you want to say 'hi' to Georgia. You can say 'hi.' You can hand her a toy. You can sit in the sand box with her."

Redirection is a technique that can be used not just by adults but by kids, too, as Janis relates. "My older son Lee, was playing with his younger brother, Calvin, who was two. Calvin was biting a lot at that time. They were on the couch together and Lee had his little brother in his arms. Calvin was coming at Lee with his mouth open. It looked like he was ready to bite, and Lee kept saying, 'Kisses! Kisses! Kisses!' By the time Calvin's mouth reached Lee, it was a kiss. Lee made it clear to Calvin what was okay to do with his mouth."

• **Don't bite them back.** There's a school of thought that says, "Bite children back so they'll see that it hurts." But there are several problems with this line of thinking. First, biting hurts kids. Second, babies and toddlers aren't capable of real empathy, so the fact that their arm hurts won't necessarily be taken as evidence that someone else's arm hurts. Third, if we bite them back, we essentially tell them, "Biting is an okay thing to do." They learn the rule "If you're bigger or stronger or older, biting is something you can do." It's challenging, but crucial, that we set limits for kids in ways that model behavior we want to see back from them.

• **It's crucial not to stigmatize a child who bites.** Calling a child a "biter" or a "piranha" can reinforce the behavior. The child thinks to herself, "Oh, I'm a biter. I guess that's what I do in the world."

Biting: Facilitating Resolution Between Children

When one child bites another child, your first impulse may be to separate them. But often the moments that follow the injury are full of valuable lessons for both children. When we remove the child who bites and only comfort the other child, neither child is allowed to complete the interaction.

If, however, we facilitate a resolution between the children, we have the opportunity to teach several things: how to communicate safely, how to respond to being hurt, and how not to bite.

Let's look at a typical example. Your two-year-old son, Tadashi, is playing with his best friend, Jake, who's just turned three. The boys are in the living room playing peacefully and you've just stepped into the kitchen to make lunch. All of a sudden, you hear Tadashi crying, "No bite me!" You rush into the room. Tadashi has a big wet red mark on his cheek and Jake is looking upset. What should you do?

You can begin by acknowledging what happened. "Tadashi, it looks like you got bit." Then you can turn to Jake and say, "Tadashi's crying. It hurt him when you bit his cheek." That's important information for Jake, who hasn't fully grasped the fact that someone else might feel pain.

You can then ask Jake, "What were you trying to tell Tadashi?" Once you've helped Jake figure out a safe way he could have shared his ideas, you can say to him, "I'm going to get some ice for Tadashi's cheek. Do you want to come with me or do you have another idea of how to help Tadashi?" Then Jake can either go with you to get the ice or he can get Tadashi his blanket, a toy, or offer a hug. (In this circumstance, it's important to make sure that Tadashi is open to Jake's overture.)

When Jake is able to pay attention to Tadashi, it enables him to leave the interaction not as the "biter," not as someone who hurts other kids, but as someone who made a mistake and helped to fix it. Jake learns that he can make mistakes in relationships and that they don't necessarily fall apart. Additionally, he learns that his ideas will be valued even if his expression of those ideas is imperfect.

Working with Tadashi is equally important. When you get bit, two things happen: You experience physical pain and you get "done to."

Your power is taken away. When people have been "done to," they often respond by being fearful, cringing, or shrinking from contact, all of which may invite continued aggression.

It's important for Tadashi to get his power back, to feel that he can stand up for himself and respond effectively. Victims may need support to express their ideas. Let Tadashi know he can speak up for himself: "You can say 'No!' 'Stop!' 'I don't like it!' 'Go away!' "

Learning to stand up for yourself when you've been hurt is significant, as Janis relates in the following story. "When he was two, Lee had a best friend, Lamar, who bit him all the time. There were times he had bite marks up and down his arm. I remember saying to my husband, 'Maybe we shouldn't let them play together any more.' And Leon said to me, 'This might be the most important thing Lee ever learns to deal with.'

"Leon began to tell Lee, 'Don't let Lamar bite you. You can make him stop.' And Lee learned how to stop Lamar without hurting him and without running away. He learned to move, to yell 'Stop!' to pull his arm out of the way.

"Now Lee is a teenager, and it's clear that he is a person who feels confident that he can deal with whatever comes at him in the world. I can't help but think that learning to deal successfully with Lamar all those years ago had something to do with who he is today."

Spitting

Spitting is another behavior that toddlers and preschoolers love to explore, a behavior for which parents have little tolerance. After years of only knowing how to put things *into* their mouths, it is quite a discovery for toddlers and preschoolers to learn that they can purposefully make things come *out* of their mouths. The physical coordination required to gather enough saliva, locate it in the right place in your mouth, and propel it out into the world is admirable. Disappointingly, though, most adults are not ready to cheer on their children's accomplishment.

Children learn to spit through exploration, practice, and by watching others. They learn social rules about spitting through observation, as well. The child who imitates her favorite baseball player and spits on the ground before picking up her bat will probably expect no reaction. The child who spits because he has been spat *at* by an older child may already have some idea that spitting is an offensive or hurtful act.

If you are distressed by spitting, it is important to tell children about your concern and to *give information:* "I get *really* upset about spitting. It can hurt people's feelings." Or "I don't like spitting. You could give your friend your cold by spitting on her." At the same time you express your displeasure, it is also important to *honor the impulse:* "It looks like you figured out how to spit!" "I wonder if you are practicing what you saw that baseball player do." "I heard that some kids at your school have been spitting. It looks like you're trying it out."

Then you can *set limits* and *redirect the behavior:* "I don't want you to spit at your friend, but if you want to experiment with spitting, you can do it outside, away from people." "You can do it in the bathroom sink when you brush your teeth." Or "We don't allow spitting in our house. If you are angry, you can tell me 'I'm mad!' "

Responding to Spitting: Things to Consider

Babies and toddlers put lots of things in their mouths that they shouldn't eat, and it's crucial for them to learn to spit dangerous or inappropriate things out. They also need to be able to spit out food if it doesn't taste right to

When Children Love to Climb

"For a while we didn't have to watch him so much, but now he's scaling everything and balancing on the ends of things, and throwing himself backward. It's great, but it's really labor-intensive. I wonder where the line is between keeping him safe and allowing him to explore."

—TRISH, *mother of twenty-one month-old Sonny*

Although climbing is a healthy form of exploration that young children engage in, it can often be nerve-wracking for parents. While it doesn't exactly fall into the category of difficult behaviors, having a child who loves to climb can be challenging and scary for parents. Here are some basic guidelines for reassuring yourself and helping your young explorer stay safe:

• **Honor the impulse.** Climbing is an integral part of healthy physical development. It's natural for kids to want to test their abilities in increasingly challenging locations.

• **Be there.** If your child is in a climbing spurt, your best strategy is to be close by when she is experimenting with heights. That way you can see what she's doing and make sure she stays safe.

• **Make sure the equipment is stable.** Your child's job is to climb. Your job is to make sure the equipment is stable. You can talk to your child about that: "Let's see if this stool is stable before you climb on it. Do you think it's stable enough?" Introduce that word into her vocabulary.

• **Assess the groundcover.** When you're at a playground, what does the groundcover look like? What will your child be falling on if he fell?

• **Spot your child.** Be there if your child needs help, but don't wait nervously. Rick, who worked professionally as a climbing instructor, called this "loitering with intent." He said, "I'm controlling the climbing site and being vigilant, but the climber doesn't know it. I'm hanging out in a relaxed kind of way, but I can get to him if he actually gets in any kind of trouble."

• **Use pillows.** If your child is into testing her balance on the back edge of the couch, make sure there are lots of soft things for her to land on if she falls. Janis recalls running around her house with big pillows, placing them strategically under her climbing baby.

• **Don't touch your child unnecessarily.** When we touch children while they climb, they often stop climbing, reach for us, let go, or fall into our arms. When we don't touch climbing children unnecessarily, they become much more competent climbers.

• **Help children learn to climb safely.** You can talk your child through a difficult climb. "Does that look like a safe place to put your feet?" "I've noticed that that pole is

them or if they have already eaten enough. We don't want to discourage babies and young toddlers from this survival strategy. On the other hand, older toddlers and preschoolers are beginning to be old enough to learn what is socially appropriate. While we don't want to teach them that whatever goes in their mouths has to stay, no matter what, we can begin to show them how to spit things out in the appropriate places: into napkins, the trash, or the sink.

Because it can be such an accomplishment and because people often have such a strong reaction to it, spitting may persist for a while. But if children are acknowledged, given information and alternative ways of expressing themselves, they usually move out of spitting or learn the "socially acceptable" ways and places to do it.

kind of wet from the rain, and that might make it slippery."

• **Encourage barefoot climbing.** Surface and weather permitting, bare feet provide the best traction. Sneakers and rubber-soled shoes come next. Boots, sandals, and dress-up shoes are a lot more slippery.

• **Help your child stay focused.** When kids get distracted by something or someone else, there's more chance of falling.

• **Redirect your child when necessary.** If you don't want your daughter climbing up the shelves in the refrigerator, make sure she's got places that are okay for her to climb instead. Take her to a playground with climbing structures that challenge her current abilities. Although this won't stop her from scaling things at home, it may quench some of her thirst to climb.

• **Don't lift your child into places she can't get to on her own.** Children are less likely to get hurt or stuck when they're only climbing in places they can get to themselves. If your child is frustrated that she can't reach the high slide, you can listen to her frustration and acknowledge her effort: "It's frustrating not to be able to get up there. I saw how hard you tried to stretch your foot up. Someday you'll be able to make it up there."

• **Intervene as little as possible when children fall.** You don't need to rush in and scoop up your child every time he falls. If he isn't seriously hurt, let him get up and recover from the fall on his own. Sometimes simply reflecting back what happened is enough: "Gee, it looks like you fell." "You were up on your stool and your foot slipped." Other times children will want a hug, a Band-Aid, or kisses for their boo-boos. Give them the reassurance and physical support they ask for, but don't make the fall bigger than it really was.

• **Work on your own fears.** Your own level of fear or confidence has a direct relationship on your child's physical abilities, as Janis relates: "Twenty-month-old Maura came into the toddler program with her mother, Dana. Dana, who was always two inches away from Maura when she climbed, believed that children were prone to have accidents. Dana believed that it was her job to keep Maura from falling, and Maura fell a lot when her mom was there. Maura's dad, Mac, on the other hand, believed that people are basically coordinated, that they have a natural sense of balance and can figure out how to climb. He gave Maura a lot of freedom in her climbing, and when Mac was around, Maura fell a lot less and she fell more skillfully."

• **Expand your own physical abilities.** Often our fears for our children's safety derive from a lack of confidence in our own physical abilities. Finding a way to challenge yourself physically can remind you of the satisfaction involved in physical exertion and accomplishment.

Whining and Nagging

Although toddlers and preschoolers often cry or scream when they're upset, they sometimes communicate their feelings indirectly through whining, nagging, or aggressive behavior. Janis remembers watching three-year-old Russ storm through a block area, growling, knocking down everything in sight. "At first glance, you might look at Russ and think 'He's so aggressive.' But what Russ really needed were subtitles. He needed a script running along the bottom of his screen that said, 'I'm feeling scared and small so I need to growl. I want to play with these blocks, but I don't know how.' "

Children who whine also need subtitles. When your son is clinging to your leg and whining, he really needs subtitles that say "I'm feeling fussy. I don't know if you're going to be here or if Dad's going to be here. I'm confused."

Children don't intentionally mean to be hard to read. They are doing the best they can to express themselves with the tools they have available, but they often don't have words or a clear understanding of their feelings.

Our job, in these circumstances, is not just to stop or redirect the behavior but also to help the child understand what it is he is really feeling or trying to say. Once we do that, we can respond to our children's underlying feelings and help them develop clearer ways to communicate.

When Children Whine: What Parents Can Do

Whining is a particularly difficult behavior for many parents because of what Janis calls "the hook." Whining has a hook because it's hard to listen to and also because we believe we need to do something about it. Often the more irritating the behavior is for us, the more difficult it is to step outside of our first reaction and see what our child is really telling us.

Many parents, consciously or unconsciously, feel that if they were better parents, their child wouldn't whine. Yet if we can "unhook" ourselves from whining, we can begin to read the subtitles and help our children think about what they're actually trying to express.

Your four-year-old says, "But I wannnnnna go to Benji's house nooooow!" If you respond from the "hooked" place, you're likely to be defensive and attacking: "Look! I told you already that we are not going to Benji's house and that's final, so quit your whining!"

If, on the other hand, you're able to respond from the "unhooked" place, your response might sound like this: "You really want to go to Benji's. I hear in your voice how strongly you feel about it. I'm sorry you can't go right now."

Another whining dialogue might start with a three-year-old saying "Get me my juuuuice."

The hooked response might be "I'm *getting* it as fast as I can. If you don't quit using that baby voice, I won't get it at all!" The unhooked response might be "I hear you asking for your juice. When I hear you use that voice, it sounds like you're telling me it's hard to wait."

If we can respond to our child's feelings rather than just trying to stop the whining, often the need for whining decreases. Also, taking time to listen *before* children escalate into whining can prevent them from relying on whining as the only sure way to get our attention.

Sometimes the simplest and most effective response to whining is just to stop what you're doing and say, "Let's just be here together for a while."

For most parents, a whiny voice is unacceptable. If that's true for you, it's important to let your children know you are uncomfortable with whining. "It's hard for me to listen to that voice. It sounds like you're having some strong feelings. Is there another way you could tell me what you're feeling?"

Since whining is so pervasive with young children, it's useful to think about the purpose it serves. Whining provides a unique form of emotional expression that is different from crying, screaming, or talking. Viewing it and responding to it as an emotional expression rather than as a demand for action takes some of the "hook" out of it. This, in turn, allows both children and parents to focus on effective listening and communication. As children feel listened to, the need for whining decreases.

Making Successful Transitions

In the routines of our daily lives, there are many times we ask our children to change from one activity to another: to stop playing and get in the car, to finish eating and get washed up, to stop playing video games and come to dinner. Any change that is not a child's own idea is often met with resistance. This can throw a wrench in your schedule and create conflict.

Transitions are hard for kids because they don't see time in a continuum. They can't look ahead or project into the future: "I'm going to walk out to the car. I'm going to have this nice car ride home. I'm going to go home and play and have a warm bath and get in bed." They can't think through to the next activity, so when they get pulled away from one activity, they may feel like they're being thrust into a void.

The way children handle transitions is an interplay between development and temperament. Some children have an easier time with transitions all along. Others have a longer period in which transitions are difficult. Many children are still struggling with transitions during their preschool years.

If you look at your child's temperament, you can tell where your child might fall on that continuum. If you have a child who asks for routines, predictability, and consistency, she is likely to have a hard time with transitions, especially unexpected ones. On the other hand, if you have a child who's a good traveler, who's flexible, he's probably going to have an easier time with transitions.

Here are some basic strategies for making transitions easier with all children:

- **Give warnings.** Alerting children to upcoming transitions can help: "In two minutes, it's going to be time to go. So I want you to finish playing with your trains." "In a few minutes, we're going to change your diaper."

- **Let your child know what's going to happen ahead of time.** On the way to the store, you can tell your toddler: "We're going to the store. You're going to ride in the cart and I'll buy you some strawberries." For some toddlers and preschoolers, this will be helpful. However, younger babies won't be able to imagine ahead.

- **Before making a transition, set up a structure for what will happen afterward.** Try telling your child, "When we get home from the park, we could read a book. Which one would you like to read?" Or "Let's take bear along to wait in the car while you're playing at Mimi's. Then bear can ride home with you."

- **Offer your child a strategic role in the transition.** Ask, "Can you unlock the car doors for us?" "Would you be the one to carry the umbrella?"

- **Use transitional objects to help the child bridge from one activity to the next.** You could say, "Would you like to take this pinecone home to show Aunt Lucy?" Or "We could take this rock home and put it in your choo-choo train."

- **Use good-bye rituals.** Sometimes saying good-bye to all your favorite activities in the park helps: "Good-bye, swing. Good-bye, big tree. Good-bye, slide." The children's book *Goodnight Moon* isn't a classic for nothing.

When Children Ignore You

One thing that makes parents irate quicker than almost anything is being ignored. You have an agenda, you're being clear about it, and your kids act as if you haven't said anything! That can be infuriating.

It can help to bear in mind that when children ignore us, they are choosing to pay attention to something else that's more important to them at that moment. Your four-year-old daughter is continuing to dig in the flower bed even though you've asked her to stop. She's choosing to explore what plant roots look like; she's consumed with mastering the use of a shovel. At that moment, those things are more important to her than responding to you. It's even possible that she'd like to obey you, but right now, her own agenda takes precedence. It's not that she's not listening to you. It's more like, "I heard what you said. However, it's not that relevant."

This conflict comes up frequently when we want toddlers and preschoolers to get dressed. We have ideas about when they should get their pants and socks on, and they have other ideas that are just as important to them—like whether they can fit the Lego car they just made into their shoe. This is much more compelling to them than getting dressed. By four, most kids have mastered dressing themselves, and doing it for the three hundredth time isn't very interesting to them.

Sometimes kids don't respond to our requests to "Stop digging in the flower bed" or "Get your shoes on" because they're testing us to see exactly how we're going to stop them. Four- and five-year-olds may also be engaged in an exploration of the power of language: "You told me with your words. Do your words really have the power to make me stop?" And the child discovers, "Words can't make me stop. I can keep digging." And so the next question becomes, "What's your next trick? What are you going to do now that your words haven't worked?"

What You Can Do When You're Being Ignored

Your response to a child who is ignoring you will vary depending on the age of the child and the reasons her attention is focused elsewhere. But here are some general strategies for working with kids who aren't responding to you:

• **Honor the impulse.** Take a moment to orient yourself toward what the child is trying to do, either through observation or by asking. Even though your wishes may need to take precedence, your child's interests are as relevant to her as what you need her to do. Remember, even staring off into space can be a valid agenda for a child whose life has been busy.

• **Move in closer, get on your child's level, and make eye contact.** If you're standing on the porch asking your daughter to stop digging in the flower bed, walk down the steps to where she is. Squat down so you can make eye contact. Talking to her from a closer vantage point will help you see what she's trying to do, and it may make it easier for her to listen to what you're saying.

• **Active listening.** You can say to your daughter "It seems like you'd really rather be digging in the garden than getting ready to pick up your sister."

• **Use "I" statements.** Let your child know how you feel: "When I ask you to stop digging in the flower bed and you don't look at me or answer, I feel mad."

• **Set a limit.** Say "We have to leave to pick up your sister in five minutes. You can dig for a few more minutes, but then it's going to be time to get dressed."

• **Give a choice.** Offer alternatives: "Do you want to leave the shovel here or put it in the shed?" "Can you stop digging with the shovel, or should I come and help you put it away?"

• **Negotiate a solution that gives both of you some of what you want.** This requires listening and compromise on both your parts: "Sounds like you want to make sure you get another chance to dig today. We'll have some time before supper."

• **Invite your child's initiative.** You can invite a preschool child into this problem-solving process: "You want to keep digging and we need to pick up your sister. Do you have any ideas of what we can do?" After the situation has been resolved, you can ask your child, "Do you have any ideas about how I could have gotten your attention? Let's think about how we could do it the next time."

• **Reinforce verbal limits with physical ones if necessary.** When children can't choose, stop themselves, or listen to your words, you may have to help them or stop them physically. They may need a lift out of the garden. "It looks like you can't get yourself inside, so I'll help you." "I see that you're not dressed yet and we need to go now. So I'm going to help you put your clothes on."

Swearing: When Kids Love to Say the Words We Hate to Hear

Preschoolers love name-calling. Favorite "curses" among young preschoolers include dummy, dumbo, butthead, poo-poo head, peepee head, and stupid. When children use these names, they are exploring the power and significance of words. They're exploring social rules and are testing to see how children and adults respond.

Generally, young children respond strongly to name-calling that talks about their characteristics because they don't yet understand the power of words. They may think the words "poo-poo head" have the power to turn them into a "poo-poo head." So these kind of epithets draw a strong response. Kids also use these words to explore relationships: "If I call you dummy and you crumble, I must be really important to you."

Older preschoolers often move from "dummy" to more serious "official curse words," such as shit, fucker, and asshole. These are important words that generally garner a very big reaction. With just one exposure to an official swear word, children may pick it up and begin to use it, because hearing it even once lets them know, in no uncertain terms, that it's an important word that expresses strong feelings.

It's fascinating for children to think, "If I talk about the 'ditch' I'm building, everyone is very interested in what I'm saying. But if I say, 'bitch' suddenly I get a whole different reaction! And those two words sure sound alike to me!"

Children use "official curse words" for many of the same reasons they use "dummy" and "butthead." But the exploration of these words goes further because four-letter-words hold a certain mysterious power. When a four-year-old says "butt," he generally knows what a "butt" is, but when he says "fuck," he generally doesn't know what the word really means. The only way for him to figure out exactly why the word is so special is to use it again and again, in as many circumstances as possible.

Cursing is an exploration into issues of power. Despite all the attempts parents make to get their kids to stop using these words, they ultimately can't control what comes out of their kids' mouths. Children find that very compelling; they want to explore what their parents will do to try to stop them and to see what happens when they can't.

Responding to Swearing

• **Honor the impulse.** Knowing why your normally sweet child is now cursing a blue streak can help you cope with this behavior. If your daughter is cursing because she's angry and frustrated, you can help her find another way to get her anger out. If she heard the curse words at school and is bringing them home to try them out on you, she's probably asking, "What's an appropriate response to this word? How does this word affect people? I want to see how my family deals with it."

• **Provide social information.** Give children information about the word and how people respond to it, without making them feel bad about themselves. "That's a word that sometimes hurts people's feelings." "Lots of people feel those are hurtful words." "Many people in the grocery store would be uncomfortable if they heard you using that word." "Those aren't words we use in our family. We find other ways to tell people we're mad."

• **Explore the child's exposure to the words.** It can be valuable to get information from the child, as well. "Who do you know who uses these words? How do you feel when they use them?"

• **Respond honestly, but don't overreact.** Be honest and informative. Bear in mind that the stronger your response, the more children may be compelled to explore your intensity by using the words again.

• **Set limits.** You can say, "I feel really upset when I hear you say those words. They are unkind words. I don't want you to use them around me." Or "If you feel like you really need to use those words, you need to do it in the other room."

If you're not personally upset by the language your child is using, you can say "It looks like you're really interested in words that have to do with your body, like poo-poo and butt. However, I'd like you to save those words for home because Grandma is uncomfortable with them."

• **Redirect.** "If you're mad, you can stomp all over this big pillow." Or "If you're trying to get my attention, you could say 'Mom, I really need you.'"

• **Give children other powerful words they can use.** Teaching a child to say "I'm irate!" "I'm furious!" "I'm befuddled!" "I'm exasperated!" "I'm so mad I could knock down a tree!" can give them interesting, articulate alternatives to standard curses. It can be fun, as well, as Janis relates. "My daughter, Maya, came home from preschool with the words 'fucking asshole bitch.' Her brothers worked with her to come up with creative alternatives that were all food oriented: 'spaghetti head,' 'banana ears,' 'cauliflower breath,' 'salad head,' and 'pizza belly.' She went around using them with great pride and expressiveness."

• **Help children explore language in other ways.** Part of the appeal of swear words is that they allow children to play with language. Introducing silly songs, limericks, rhyming words, nonsense words, stories that children can complete, or songs in which they can make up verses can channel some of their desire to explore language in new and exciting ways.

• **Model the language you want your child to use.** Children learn a lot through imitation, as the following story makes clear. A teacher was having a hard time with a student who was constantly cursing. Every other word out of this child's mouth was "fuck this" and "fuck that." When it came time for parent-teacher conferences, this boy's father came in, walked right up to the teacher, and said: "So, how's the little fucker doing?"

• **Don't just ignore it.** The idea that you should ignore children when they curse operates on the belief that the more energy you give it, the more energy kids will have for it. But this approach fails to give children input and social information, and can also fail to help them find alternative ways to communicate. When you ignore your child's communication, no matter how crass or distasteful, you inadvertently give the message that you're not interested in what he has to say.

However, if you have given children information, provided redirection, and listened to their ideas, and they continue to curse, ignoring it sometimes can be a useful technique.

• **Give it time.** Like other challenging behaviors that are developmentally based, it takes time for many children to move beyond their fascination with curse words. Even when you use all of your best strategies, kids are still likely to explore words you'd rather not have them use. Yet given appropriate modeling, clear information, and viable alternatives, your child will eventually find words that are more appropriate.

Lying and Stealing

Sometime around the ages of four or five, many parents are confronted for the first time with their child "lying" to them. It can be unnerving to hear your child speaking bold untruths and frightening to wonder if you are ever going to be able to trust his word again.

Penny recalls, "I remember distinctly when Oren realized that he didn't have to tell the

truth. He was four or five, and it suddenly dawned on him. He never told really big lies, but he'd lie about the little daily things of life he'd rather not do. I'd say, 'Oren, did you brush your teeth?' and he'd say 'Yes,' when he hadn't. It took me awhile to catch on. He'd never lied to me before. When I realized what was going on, I really freaked out. I thought, 'My God! My son's a liar!' I remember going down to the bookstore and buying books on the moral development of children. I didn't realize it was a normal thing."

Until the age of five, children lie primarily for developmental reasons and occasionally for emotional reasons. Developmental needs include experimenting with the power of language, researching their parent's omnipotence, engaging in wishful thinking, and being confused about the line between fantasy and reality. Emotional reasons include needing extra attention, wanting to be recognized, or needing to feel important.

Young children are driven to explore the nuances and meanings of language. At around four or five years old, children generally begin to test the power of words to affect certain events. Children at this age often wonder if words have the power to make things happen. We see children trying out expressions, such as: "*Please*, I *need* to go to the toy store."

This curiosity extends both into the future and into the past. The child thinks, "Maybe something will have happened if I just say it did." Their first attempts at changing reality are often quite charming, because they don't yet have a developed sense of probability: "Dad, I went to Disneyland today." "My mom bought me a new truck that I can really drive." "There was a dinosaur at my school today." These fabrications are a manifestation of children's wishful thinking: "If I just imagine it to be, maybe I can make it happen."

Children also wonder about what their parents know. From a young child's perspective, parents seem to know everything. We pick our children up from their cousin's house and ask, "Did you have fun making cookies?" We call into the other room asking "Are you done building with blocks?" When we're driving in the car we suddenly say (as if out of the blue), "We're going to go to get pizza." How did we know what food was going to appear? To our children, it looks like we magically hold all the information in the world.

But around ages of four or five, children begin to get an inkling that their parents might not know everything and, specifically, that their parents might not know all of the same things that *they* know. So, like good little scientists, they begin to experiment. Janis recalls, "When Maya was almost five, she came out of the bathroom where I had asked her to clean up all the cups, bottles, and towels she had been playing with. She carefully shut the door behind her and said to me, 'I cleaned everything up, but you can't go in there.' Maya was beginning to figure out that I might not always know what went on if I didn't directly see it and that she might be able to use her words to convince me of a different reality. She might even have believed that if she closed the door and said that it was clean, it might really happen."

This kind of lying also has to do with a child's new ability to predict another person's response. Maya was now able to predict that Janis wasn't going to be happy if the bathroom wasn't clean, and she was trying to avoid her mother's unhappiness. Finding a way to avoid Mom getting mad at you seems like a great solution to kids.

Other fabrications occur because of children's newfound creativity with ideas and language. Children at this age weave the most fanciful tales, using fantasy and reality interchangeably, not always being sure themselves which is which.

Children also make things up because of a kind of imitation. Children see people around them talking about all kinds of things they don't understand and can't see. From a child's view, it may look like adults are weaving great tales that, as far as the child knows, are not grounded in real events: "Aunt Marjorie told us a great story about how she went on an airplane and then she saw some kangaroos with babies in their pockets! I bet I could tell a terrific story, too!"

Putting It All Together: Lying and Stealing

What does it really sound like to talk to young children about lying and stealing? Here are some sample dialogues:

Child: Mom, there were fairies and fireworks at my school today. I know, I saw them!

Mother: Wow, that's amazing. Tell me more about them.

Child: Well, the fairies rode little scooters and brought us cookies and candy and cupcakes and cotton candy and licorice and milkshakes and gummy bears for snack!

Mother: You have such a creative imagination. I'd love to hear more of your great story.

. . .

Child: Dad, I brushed my teeth already.

Father: Hmm, I didn't see you go into the bathroom and I still see some food on your teeth.

Child: But I *did* brush them.

Father: It sounds like you wish you had already brushed them. I know it's hard for you to interrupt your play to brush sometimes.

Child: But, *Dad,* I did brush them.

Father: Well, it seems like you and I have different ideas about this. I will go in with you to brush, because your teeth still have some food on them and I don't want you to go to bed like that.

Sometimes you will be asked to respond to lying and stealing together, as in the following example of a five-year-old:

Child: Mama, look at my new racing car.

Mother: It looks like it goes really fast. Where did you get it?

Child: Uh . . . My friend Matty gave it to me.

Mother: How'd he do that? You haven't seen Matty in over a month.

Child: I mean my friend Lucy gave it to me.

Mother: You haven't seen Lucy in a really long time either. That car looks like the one you were looking at in the toy store yesterday.

Child: No, it's not that car, Mom. I found this car in our backyard.

Mother: I know how much you wanted that car in the store yesterday and how disappointed you were when we couldn't buy it, but it's really important that you don't take things without paying for them.

Child: But, Mom, I didn't take it.

Mother: I can understand that you wanted it and that it's hard to tell me what happened, but it's important that you tell me how you got it and that we figure out together what to do next.

Child: But you never get me what I want!

Mother: I know that is frustrating to you, but right now we need to do two things. We need to figure out what you can do when you want something very much and you can't get it right away, and we need to figure out what to do with this car. If everyone just took toys out of the store without paying for them, then the store owner wouldn't have any money to buy new toys for her store.

Child: How can I get one, then?

Mother: Let's make a plan to take this one back and tell the store owner what happened first. Then we can work on a plan for you to do some extra chores so you could earn the money to buy one. Do you want to practice what you will say to the owner?

Finally, when children lie for emotional reasons, it is important to pay attention to the requests for attention or help that they are making. When a child who has a new sibling lies about hiding the baby's bottle, it's more important to respond to the child's need for special attention than to her "mistruth" about the bottle.

Stealing

Just about the same time children start experimenting with lying, they often try taking things that aren't theirs. For children under five, stealing comes from many of the same healthy impulses as lying.

Young children are beginning to figure out the systems people use to acquire goods. They often become fascinated with money, which seems magical to them. Being unsophisticated about numbers and quantity, young children are often just as excited about a quarter as they are about a dollar. Being unknowledgeable about the ins and outs of economics, exactly how people get money seems fairly arbitrary to them. They think that adults can get money whenever they want to: "My mom just goes to the cash machine at the bank and gets her money there!" "My grandma just shows the people this little card, draws her name on a piece of paper, and she can have all the toys she wants."

Everywhere children look, people are putting things into shopping carts and taking them home. Kids would also like to collect things and take them home, yet they get turned down for 90 percent of what they ask for, even on a good day.

Children who watch TV are also the targets of multimillion-dollar advertising campaigns. Bo explains: "My son asks for stuff he's seen on TV and he doesn't even know what it really is, but when he sees it on TV, he wants it. I must say 'no' to him two hundred times a day!"

We live in a consumer-driven society. Given children's interest in acquiring new things, the fact that they are surrounded with people who seem to be able to get what they want, and their inability to understand the more complicated aspects of economics, it makes sense that children would try to figure out a creative system to get what they want on their own.

Karyn remembers the lengths to which Bryan once went to get something he desperately wanted. "When Bryan was five years old, he really wanted He-Man action figures. Money was really tight and Bryan rarely got to buy toys. One day he came to me holding a ten-dollar bill. He said he'd found it in the street. I said, 'Oh, someone must have dropped it when they opened their car door.' I thought about asking the neighbors if they'd lost a ten, but then I just thought, 'He just got lucky.' So I told him, 'Gee, you were really lucky. I guess the money's yours. What do you want to do with it?' Well, we drove right down to the toy store and Bryan bought an action figure.

"By golly, the next day, he found twenty dollars in the mailbox! It was in an envelope with his first name written on it in childlike letters. There was no address and no stamp. Bryan told me his friend had sent it to him and asked if we could go to the toy store. It was obvious what he had done. Also, I was sure of every cent I had in those days, so I was positive he'd taken the money from my wallet. Then I started thinking about the first ten. It had never occurred to me that he could have taken it. I was dumbfounded."

Responding to Children When They Lie and Steal

Traditionally, lying and stealing have evoked some of the strongest, most punitive responses from parents who want to make a very clear statement that such behavior is unacceptable. Many parents worry that the behavior will escalate and their child will get into really big trouble if they don't punish him right away. However, punishments such as spanking serve to make children fearful, defensive, and secretive. Shaming responses tell children that because of one mistake or experiment, they are no good.

Karyn recalls, "When my brother was really young, he once took some money from a relative's purse at a family gathering. He was never forgiven. He had humiliated my mother and he was seen as a thief in the eyes of the family forever afterward. He was dealt with in the worst possible way. When Bryan starting 'finding money,' I knew I didn't want to do that to him. I wanted to use the incident as an opportunity to do good parenting.

"I saw Bryan as a child who was trying to get what he wanted rather than as a thief. I took the money back and asked him, 'Bryan, did you take this money out of my wallet and put it in the mailbox so you could find it?' He said no. I asked him again. He never admitted it. I could tell he was really confused. I felt for him. He really thought if you found money you could keep it.

"So I sat him down and said, 'I know you really want those things. But we don't have much money and I can't worry about you taking money out of my purse.' I explained that the money he had found wasn't extra money, that we needed it to buy food. I left it at that. And it never happened again."

It is important for adults to remember that just because lying and stealing make sense to children at four or five doesn't necessarily mean they will make sense to them at seven or ten or fifteen. Most children naturally grow out of their propensity for telling "lies" and "stealing." Knowing this can ease some parental worry, yet your responses are crucial to helping children move through these stages successfully. Here are some suggestions for helping your child learn from the experience without feeling badly about himself:

• **Honor the impulse.** Look at what children are doing from their perspective. Sarah recalls, "After Gena's dad left us, she kept telling lies about all the special things they did together. I sat down with her and said, 'I can tell you really miss your dad. I bet you really wish he was doing all those things with you.' "

• **Actively listen and give information.** You can say to children, "It sounds like you wish you could keep that puppy, but I heard your Uncle Raymond say that you wouldn't be able to keep it." Or "I know that you really wanted to buy that candy, but the money you used to buy it didn't belong to you."

• **Redirect the behavior.** You can ask, "Would you like me to write down that wonderful story? Then you could draw pictures to go with it and we could read your story to your brother when he gets home." Or "If you really want that candy, I will help you work on a way to earn some money so you can buy some."

• **Help children acknowledge what really happened without cornering or labeling them.** At the point that you are clear that children are not telling you the truth, be careful not to berate them, trap them, or call them "liars." Cornering children makes it hard for them to tell the truth. It's important that kids be able to save face. Sometimes, given a little space, children can come up with the truth voluntarily. You can say to your child "I don't think that's what really happened. I know sometimes it's scary to tell me something you think I might be mad about, but what's really important to me is that you tell me the truth. Can you tell me again what happened?" The shorthand version of this, with humor, might be: "Oops, try telling me again what happened. See if you can remember it any differently this time."

On the other hand, it's important to let children know that what we recognize as truth is different from what they are telling us: "To me, it seems like it happened differently than what you are saying. I saw you eating some candy and I also noticed that the candy in the drawer is gone." "I have a different idea about how you got that scarf. I saw Sol wearing it in school yesterday."

• **Help your child with follow-through.** If your child has succeeded in obtaining goods that don't belong to her or in giving someone misleading information that will cause problems, it's important that she gets an opportunity to put things back to rights. This may be very uncomfortable for children, so it's important that we let the consequences speak for themselves and don't add punishment or shame to them. In fact, children need our support, empathy, and optimism as well as our firm commitment that they will follow through. "Jackie, we need to take that racing car back to the store and tell the clerk what happened. I'll go with you and we can explain that children sometimes make mistakes." "Lila, you need to give that scarf back to Sol. He's probably wondering where it is. Would you like me to go with you or do you want to do it by yourself?" "We need to tell your friend Joshua that there really isn't a stegosaurus in your bedroom. He's too scared to come over."

• **Children will tell you as much truth as you allow.** After children's initial experimentation with the power of lies, most will want to settle down to a life of truthfulness, unless they have discovered that the consequences of telling the truth are too painful. We can encourage children to tell the truth by appreciating them for doing it even if they have told us something that makes us mad: "I'm glad you told me that you hit your brother. I feel angry when you do that, but now we have a chance to figure out how to help you learn to stop hitting him."

• **Model honesty.** At first glance, modeling honesty seems fairly easy, but children notice even the small ways that we are dishonest: "Tell her I can't come to the phone right now. I'm not home." "Let's not tell Mommy that we had ice cream, she always gets so mad." "No, Brent, you can't watch TV, because it's broken." If we work at being honest in all of our relationships, children will come to assume that being honest is the only way to be.

• **Share your family beliefs about truthfulness and honesty.** When children start experimenting with lying and stealing, it is an opportune time to teach them how much we value honesty. Janis has a little speech that she has developed to let her children know how important it is to her: "One of the things I know I can count on with my friends is that they will always tell me the truth. I never have to guess or wonder, 'Did that really happen? You are a very, very special friend of mine, and I want you to know that I will always tell you the truth and it's important to me that you do, too."

• **Be alert to clues that your child needs outside help.** For most children lying and stealing naturally wear themselves out in a period of a few weeks or even a few months. If you observe that your child seems to be using lying as her major form of communication, or if lying or stealing persists for more than a few months, you may want to consider talking with an outside resource such as a preschool teacher, a child therapist, or a child development specialist.

FOOD FOR THOUGHT: PUTTING IT ALL TOGETHER

• Which of the difficult behaviors typical of young children are hardest for me?

• What do I want to teach my child in these instances?

• How can I respond in a way that respects both how I'm feeling and my child's needs?

21. Negotiating Conflicts Between Parent and Child

"The course of true anything never does run smooth."

SAMUEL BUTLER

Some of the most challenging behaviors parents have to deal with stem from conflicts within the family. As we discussed in Chapter 6, "Working Toward a Balance of Needs," family life is an endless series of trade-offs, some of which result in conflict. There are conflicts of needs: Baby Rosey needs to be held and Daddy needs to cook dinner. There are conflicts of ideas: Toddler Bren wants to play in the fish tank and Auntie wants the fish undisturbed.

There are conflicts regarding time: How much time do we spend reading stories? How long do we spend visiting our favorite cousins? What time do kids go to bed?

There are conflicts about clothes. "But I don't want to take off my pajamas." "Why can't I wear my Rosh Hashanah dress to play in Ora's sand box?"

And inevitably, there are conflicts about food. "But I don't liiiike cheese on my spaghetti." "But I want my cupcake nooow."

Other conflicts revolve around behavi or. Parents want children to share, to listen, to do what they're told, to learn patience, and to stop whining. They want children to learn manners, to say "please" and "thank you," to respond when spoken to.

All of these conflicts afford parents the chance to learn where their bottom lines are, to clarify appropriate limits, and to teach children problem-solving skills.

In this chapter, we introduce the tool of negotiation, which parents can use to resolve conflicts, balance needs, and come up with mutually beneficial solutions. Negotiation involves you and your child listening to each other's feelings, wants, and point of view, and then, together, trying to find a solution that works for both of you. Sometimes this happens easily. Other times, because of time pressures, fatigue, or crankiness, neither of you has the resources or presence of mind to come up with a cooperative solution. But even then, both of you still can have the benefit of having been heard and respected.

Through negotiation, children learn that we want to listen to them, that their ideas have value, and that they can make things happen in the world. Negotiation builds their ability to express their ideas and feelings clearly, and gives them practice taking another person's feelings and perspective into account. In the long run, children come to understand that solutions that give everyone some of what they want are preferable to ones in which only one person comes out on top. Those are lessons that will be valuable through a lifetime of relationships.

Although every conflict that happens provides an opportunity to teach children problem-solving tools, it's important to remember that no parent has the time, resources, or energy to deal creatively with every single conflict that comes along. Children don't need us to demonstrate these tools every time; they will master them through regular, but not continuous, demonstration and practice.

Negotiating Conflicts: A Developmental Overview

In the early days of the parenting relationship, most conflicts involve balancing needs. While parents of babies do have to figure out creative ways to meet the needs of all the people in the family, they still have a certain illusion of control. For the most part, babies are portable, they stay where you put them, and you still get to choose what they eat and wear. While some babies are very demanding in terms of their needs for sleep, food, and attention, parents still control most of the larger decisions.

When children enter toddlerhood, all that changes. As toddlers discover their separateness, they are driven to challenge the control of their parents. Both verbally and physically, they branch out on their own, discovering areas of conflict with parents all along the way. Struggles arise over who gets to push the stroller, how many sticks to bring home from the park, or how many bottles the child drinks in a day.

In the preschool years, conflicts between parents and children take on new dimensions. As kids get older, parents' expectations increase, and conflicts may increase accordingly. Parents expect preschoolers to dress themselves, to get out of the house on time, to clean up their toys, and to help with chores. Children, on the other hand, only occasionally want to dress themselves, rarely get ready on your schedule, don't see clean-up as a necessary activity, and want to be helpful only if it involves spray bottles, knives, or hammers.

At the same time, three- to five-year-olds have learned to state their point of view, come up with new ideas, to bargain and negotiate. Yet

their ability to listen to someone else's point of view is still sketchy, at best. Because they are in love with their own ideas and have a limited ability to include anyone else's, preschoolers often don't take "losing" very gracefully.

Resolving Conflicts with Children: Issues for Parents

Our perspective on how to resolve conflicts with kids has a lot to do with our immediate needs, our particular children, and our own ideas about who should "be in charge." Some of us came from families in which all decisions were made by one person and almost nobody could move without this person's permission. In other families, lines of power weren't so clear. While one parent may have been a "figurehead," in actual day-to-day decisions, the other parent ran the show. Some families may have been influenced by decision making from the extended family: "When Big Mama speaks, everyone listens." And in some families, children were consulted and included in the decision-making process.

Now more families are interested in including children in at least some decisions. But parents approaching this particular threshold must look at some complex and confusing questions: "What does it mean to 'share power' with a child?" "Will it lead to confusion? Will my child be overindulged?" Or "My kids don't have the same experience I do. How can I trust them to make wise decisions?" And finally: "Which are the decisions I should make on my own? Which can my children help to make?"

Including children in problem solving can challenge long-held beliefs. Karl, the father of five-year-old Danielle, explains: "A child who is in touch with her feelings, who knows what she wants and how to ask for it, is not always an obedient child. Even though we've raised Danielle to express her opinions, it can be hard for me sometimes. I was raised to value obedience above all else."

As a parent who allows kids to participate in family decisions, you may also have to deal with other people's opinions: "You're giving in to that child too much!" "You're spoiling that boy."

Choosing a path of negotiation means being up against the question "Is this something I want to negotiate or not?" many times each day. Kids learn through trying things out repeatedly. When they're taught that they will have a say in decision making, often they try to negotiate in every conceivable situation. "My dad will listen to me, so I'm going to try him on *this* one." Since we're the ones who set the boundaries, we decide whether to negotiate or not. "This is a decision I'm going to be in charge of." Or "I'm willing to talk about this one."

Including children in decision making also takes time that many of us, as busy parents, are hard-pressed to find. When we choose negotiation rather than an authoritarian path, conflicts are not always tied up quickly in a neat solution.

Despite these challenges, many parents are committed to teaching their children the skills of negotiation and the basis of thoughtful decision making.

Which Decisions Are Up for Grabs?

When parents consider giving children a say in family decision making, they often imagine a system in which children control everything, chaos reigns, and parents lose all of their authority. Some mistakenly believe they have to let kids do whatever they want in order to give them an active role in the family, yet valuing children's input and always doing what they want are not synonymous.

Kids need limits. They need parental help. Many of the decisions that get made in families are not appropriately made by young children: where the family lives, when parents go to work, how space is shared in the household, whether it's okay to play with the cleaning solutions under the sink, when kids go to day care. It is the job of parents to carefully choose and orchestrate which decisions children get to participate in. Yet even in some of the decisions in which parents have the ultimate say-so, kids can still be allowed and encouraged to express their feelings and ideas: "We're trying to decide where to put the red sofa. What is your vote—

Learning to Wait

Taking other people's needs into account is something children can start learning early. Even very young children can delay gratification for a very short time in order to allow someone else to get what they need. We can ask babies for tiny bits of time: "We can nurse as soon as I unbutton my shirt." The amount of time can gradually be extended for toddlers: "I'll be with you in a minute, as soon as I'm off the phone." Or "I'll lift you up as soon as I put these groceries down and take off my shoes."

At first, young toddlers may be able to wait only about five seconds, but with practice they can learn to wait longer. However, the process of teaching them to wait isn't always enjoyable, as Laura recalls: "When Eli was eighteen months old, working toward a balance of needs meant Eli clutching my leg, plaintively crying 'Up! Up! Up!' after he'd finished his dinner and climbed down from his high chair. I'd have my chair tucked tightly into the table, and I'd be saying to him, 'Eli, I'm going to finish eating my dinner. I know it's hard for you to wait. You can build with blocks or find something else to play with until I'm done. Or you can stand there and keep crying. But I'm going to finish eating. When I'm done, I'll come and be with you.' Then I'd wolf down the rest of my food while I listened to him wail. I couldn't really call what I was doing 'eating,' but getting through the meal seemed really important to me."

Children's ability to wait may vary depending on our activity. When we are animated and engaged with another person—checking in with our partner at the end of the day, talking on the phone, or visiting with a friend—our children are more likely to feel left out. In these situations, it can be useful to keep it short, to let children know when we will be done, to hold them, or to find something they can do while they are waiting.

As children get a little older we can also teach them that adult's *and* children's needs can get met. One way to do this is to use what Janis calls "the sandwich approach": "I need to talk to your mother about my day. If you would like to tell us about your day first, we'd love to listen. Then after I'm done talking to mom, you could have another turn if you want." Or "I am going to sit down with a cup of tea and the newspaper. If you would like, I can read a book with you first. And after I'm done with the paper, I'll help you with your bath."

With young children, our level of success at getting them to wait will depend on our clarity about what they need and what we need, how much time we've already spent with them as well as our child's temperament and level of fatigue. A few children are capable of postponing gratification at a very early age; others won't be able to do it until they're older.

in the basement or in the hall?" By valuing children's input, even as we make the final decision, we encourage kids to become responsible members of the decision-making team.

The seeds for making responsible, well-thought-out decisions can be planted early. Every day, there are numerous decisions that young children can participate in—whether to go for a walk or read a story, what to eat of the food that is offered, which toys to play with. When you take a few moments to figure out with your child whether she's going to take her bath in the morning or after dinner, she begins to learn the basics of negotiation. She learns that everyone in the family, no matter how young, has a voice worth listening to. She begins to learn about the consequences of her decisions: "If I take my bath in the morning, I have more time to play with my kitty at night."

The capacity to participate in family or personal decisions increases with age. Young children can be overwhelmed by being asked to participate in too many decisions, yet even a two-year-old can appropriately decide which shirt to wear or whether to swing or slide at the park. As they grow older, children can gradually be entrusted with bigger and more complex decisions. A five-year-old could be in charge of deciding whether the family goes on a hike or for a swim. An eight-year-old could decide whether she wants to play T-ball or not. And a ten-year-old could play a vital role in a family decision about whether money should go toward a family trip or a VCR.

Each family will have different ideas about which decisions are open for discussion and which aren't. Parents will have widely diverging answers to the questions: "Who decides when a child goes to bed?" "Who decides what children wear?" "Who decides what children watch on TV or whether they watch TV?" "Who chooses the child's playmates, and until what age?"

Answering these questions is a trial-and-error process. Sometimes parents assume too much control of the decision making themselves or give too much of it away before they find a balance that feels right.

Ultimately, many parents end up with a system in which children make decisions within certain limits. As Laura puts it, "Eli gets to have up to two apple juice popsicles in a row. After that, I get to decide."

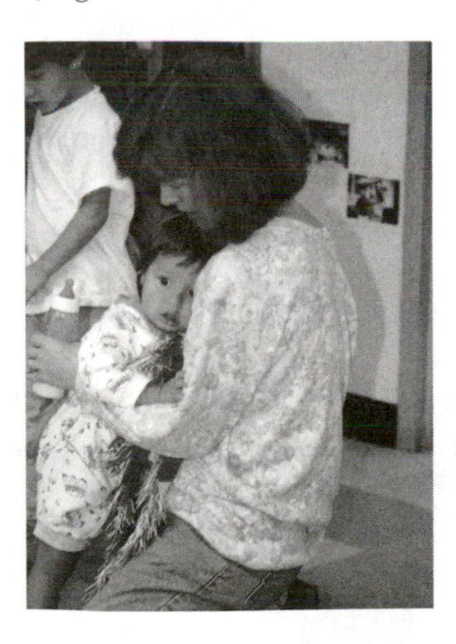

Strategies for Resolving Conflicts Between Parents and Children

Many of these specific strategies are designed for older toddlers and preschoolers, who are competent in their verbal skills. However, several of these ideas can be applied to conflicts with younger children, as well.

• **Assess the situation.** Deciding on the kind of solution most appropriate to a particular conflict involves assessing your immediate circumstances: where you are, the time pressures you're under, the resources and energy you bring to the situation, and how exhausted or receptive your child might be. In looking at all of these factors, you choose: "Is this a good time for negotiation, or is it a time for an adult-generated solution and a firm, nonnegotiable limit?"

• **Communicate to your child whether you are willing to negotiate.** Once you figure out whether or not you're in a negotiable situation, let your child know. With practice, you'll learn how to give clear signals as to whether you are or aren't open to negotiation: "Okay, let's talk about this." "No, Kelly, the decision is made. You are not going to ride the little pony today."

• **Find your bottom line.** Sometimes we enter into a disagreement with our child knowing where the clear limit is. Other times the process of negotiation helps us clarify what is really important to us.

Janis explains: "I may start a dialogue with Maya insisting that she wear her coat to gymnastics, but when she fiercely resists, saying that her coat is scratchy, I may have to clarify what my goal *really* is. I soon discover that my real bottom line isn't that she wears her coat,

But He Won't Clean Up His Room

One evening, Toke came to Janis's group with a question about encouraging her two-year-old son, Nils, to pick up his toys. "I'd like Nils to pick up his toys in the afternoon before dinner. I'd like to be able to say, 'Now it's time to pick up your toys,' but he refuses and just walks away. Should I ignore it when he does that? Or should I say 'I'll help you clean up, but at least you have to stand there and watch me?' Or would it be better for me to just wait a couple of months and see if he's ready?"

Janis asked, "What do you want him to learn by picking up his toys?"

Toke responded, "That's a good question, because it doesn't really take me all that long to pick them up myself. I guess I want him to get the idea that he should pick up after himself. I don't like him just throwing everything around and then walking away."

Janis asked another question: "So there's some aspect of teaching him about respecting and taking care of his things? About being a helpful member of the family who helps create a space you can all live in together?"

Toke nodded her head. "Yes, exactly."

Gail jumped in. "Sometimes John gets Tanya to pick up her toys. He makes it really fun for her. He'll say, 'The stuffed animals need help getting ready for night-night time. Let's help them get ready for bed," or "Let's see how fast we can get these toys in the basket.' He does it with her. He makes it into a game. It's never a heavy thing. He's not uptight about it, and they both seem to enjoy it."

Janis agreed, "Traditionally clean-up has signaled the end of play, and that's been the big problem with it: 'Okay, now the fun stuff is over. Now we have to do the icky stuff.' In a lot of our minds, clean-up is drudgery, and we inadvertently pass that on to our kids. Instead, if you can make it playful, you can

it's that she stay warm, and that her real bottom line isn't that she won't wear any outer clothing, just that she doesn't want to wear her jacket. Knowing that frees us up to work together toward a mutually satisfactory solution to the problem of her being cold."

• **Listen.** Whether you decide to negotiate a given conflict or not, it's still important to listen to your child's idea. If you are not compromising, you can still appreciate your child's ideas. If you *are* negotiating, listening is crucial to coming up with mutual solutions.

• **State your needs or the problem.** "I need to have the living room cleaned up because we are having company over." "You want to stay and roll in the leaves and I am getting hungry." "You still want to play with your friends and I want us to have some special family time."

• **Brainstorm solutions that meet both people's needs.** Once you state your bottom line and define the problem, you and your child can then think of possible solutions. With preverbal children, you provide the options: "It looks like you don't want me to put you down, but I need teach kids that cleaning up isn't so bad; that it can be fun, that it can be interesting.

"Another reason clean-up isn't interesting to kids is that it's not their idea. We know they can physically do it. They have willingly hauled all of those blocks and dolls and trucks off the shelf all day long. But they have done it on their own initiative as part of the game that *they* were playing. And they have done it one block, one doll, one toy at a time. When they look at cleaning-up the whole huge mess, it's hard for them to conceptualize that they could really do it precisely because it's *not* the one thing they took at a time. Breaking it down into smaller parts can really help: "Can you pick up all the red blocks? I'll pick up the yellow ones," or "If you hand me all the trucks, I'll stack them on the shelf."

Janis turned to Toke and continued, "The reason I asked what you wanted to teach Nils was that sometimes when we ask kids to clean up their stuff, we forget that we are really asking them to be responsible members of the family. We forget that that's our goal and instead think that picking up *this* toy is our goal. Often children are very willing to help. They *want* to put the lettuce in the vegetable drawer. They *want* to spray the front of the oven and wipe until it's clean. If what you want is for them to feel helpful, to enjoy work, to enjoy cleaning up, and to enjoy being a part of the people that make your household run, you can often come up with a choice: 'Would you like to put your blocks away or would you like to help me in the kitchen?'

"When we say to kids, 'I want you to do this. It's *your* room. It's your responsibility,' we're likely to end up in an entrenched battle. If we say instead, 'Which job would, you like to do? Do you want to wash potatoes or put your trains on the shelf?' we end up with a much broader spectrum of successful outcomes.

"If we say, 'You did it, so you clean it up' instead of 'We all work together for the good of our family,' kids may come back to us later and say 'I didn't do that! It's not my mess so I don't have to clean it up.' "

We need to make a switch in our thinking to accept that young children's contributions may not actually be as useful as we'd like them to be. What many of us want is some *real* help, and that's probably not what we're going to get, at least not with children under five. But if we encourage kids to feel that they're part of the responsible people who get to clean up, eventually, as their skills increase, they will turn into significant contributors. They may even turn into people who clean up because they see the importance of their participation rather than doing it because they "have to."

to start dinner soon. Would you like to be in the backpack, or would you rather sit up here in your high chair so you can see what I'm doing?"

Verbal children can state their own ideas. When you ask kids for suggestions, remind them of the problem and ask them to think of remedies. "I want you to stay warm. How could you do that?" Or "You don't feel cold now, but what could we do in case you start feeling cold later?" When kids come up with impossible or unacceptable solutions, you can say, "That's an interesting idea. What other ideas can you think of?" Or "If you wear my coat, then I'll be cold. Let's see if we can come up with a different idea."

You can also model what possible solutions might look like, using humor when appropriate to loosen up your child's thought process: "Well, you could wear your blue sweater or we could just bring your bed along in the car—you're always warm in your bed!"

By four or five, children frequently will be able to come up with solutions that meet both their own and another person's needs.

Doug explains: "There was a period in

Shopping with Maya: Janis's Story

This story focuses on the struggles Janis went through in shopping for clothes with her daughter, Maya. What is valuable in this story is not Janis's particular point of view but the way she and Maya went about negotiating a solution that worked for both of them.

Being a child in this culture, Maya was enormously attracted to clothing with pictures of cartoons, superheroes, and all kinds of commercial symbols on them. I was unwilling to buy them, to have her wearing those images. There were times early on where she'd want something really desperately and it would be a matter of carrying her out of the store kicking and screaming. One time it was over a *Beauty and the Beast* shirt. Other times we'd struggle over things I wanted to get for her that she didn't want to wear.

I wanted Maya to participate in decisions about how she looked and what she wore. When she was four, we made an agreement that we wouldn't buy anything that she didn't like and we wouldn't buy anything that I didn't like.

I've had to stretch a lot, because the things she likes don't necessarily fit my idea of how she should dress. I remember the day she fell in love with red patent leather shoes, the kind with little bows on them. At the time, I remember thinking, "All she needs is tennis shoes." But since then, I've seen how important it is to her and I've bought her a pair of leather flats.

It's been a long process with a lot of struggle and negotiation involved. Now I'd say we've gotten to the place where we have faith that we'll be able to find a solution that will be pleasing to both of us. Spontaneously, she often reminds me, "We won't buy it unless *you* like it and *I* like it."

which Jayce only wanted to wear pants with pockets. She had a drawer full of wonderful pants, but she insisted on wearing only her one pair of pants that had pockets. I was irritated because I felt like she was wasting her other clothes and also because her pants with pockets often looked grungy. I didn't want to be doing laundry all the time, and I didn't have the money to go out and buy her a whole new set of pants with pockets. I told her all of that. And she said, 'Dad, I've got an idea. How about if we sew some pockets on some of my other pants?' And so that's what we did."

When we allow children to become part of the problem-solving team, they use creative thinking to come up with solutions they can really feel invested in.

• **Decide on a solution.** After the two of you have come up with ideas, choose one to try. While often you'll be able to decide on a mutual solution, there may be times when your child is still resistant. At that point, you can shift gears and give your child a limited choice and follow-through as necessary: "Do you want to wear your soft blue sweatshirt or tie it around your waist for later?"

Strategies in Action: The Art of Parent-Child Negotiation

Let's look at a couple of examples of what negotiation with a child looks like. In the first scenario, Jamil needs to go to the grocery store to get food for dinner and his three-year-old daughter, Ramey, wants to go to the park. Their dialogue goes something like this:

Jamil: C'mon. We're going to the grocery store now.

Ramey: No! I want to go to the park.

Jamil: Oh, you want to go to the park. *(He actively listens.)*

Ramey: Yes!

Jamil: What do you want to do at the park? *(He invites her to share her idea.)*

Ramey: I want to slide and go on the horseys.

Jamil: Oh, I remember you had fun on that horsey the last time. *(He extends her idea.)*

Ramey: Yes! That bouncy horsey.

Jamil: I'll tell you my idea. What I want to do is go to the store so that we can have some food for dinner. *(He shares his idea.)*

Ramey: But I want to go ride the bouncy horse.

Jamil: So you still really want to go to the park and play on the horse. And I want to go to the grocery store. That sounds like a problem. How can we solve our problem? *(He actively listens, defines the problem, and invites her initiative.)*

Ramey: I want to go to the park!

Jamil: You really want to go to the park because you want to slide and ride the horseys. And I want to go to the store and get something for dinner. Do you want to help me think about what to have for dinner? I was thinking we could get black-eyed peas and cornbread, or we could have chicken. What would you like to have? *(He invites her into helping with his idea by offering a choice.)*

Ramey: Chicken.

Jamil: So you're hungry for chicken. How about if we go to the store, get some chicken, and then go home and start it cooking. And then we can go to the park for a little while. *(He suggests a solution that includes both of their ideas.)*

Ramey: Yeah! We're going to cook chicken *and* ride horseys.

In this situation, Jamil had time to include both of their ideas. If there hadn't been time to go to the park, Jamil could have just done the active listening and offered to go to the park another day.

In this second example, four-year-old Christopher is talking to his mother, Becky at the toy store:

Christopher: I want that remote control car! My friend Ralph has one and it goes really fast.

Becky: Wow, it sounds like you are really eager for a car. But, you know, this isn't a toy-buying trip. We're just here to return some things. We're just looking today. *(She actively listens and gives information and a limit.)*

Christopher: But I waaant a car. I need one! Pleeeease!

Becky: It's really disappointing that you can't have the toy you want. What do you especially like about that car? *(She actively listens and helps him extend his idea.)*

Christopher: It can go on its own, you don't even have to touch it.

Becky: That's amazing. How does it do that? *(She appreciates his idea.)*

Christopher: It has batteries inside and a special control unit that makes it go zoom, zoom.

Becky: Well, we don't have any cars that do that at our house. But I wonder if we could build a road that had some special places on it where your cars could go fast without you touching them. *(She gives information, suggests an alternative, and invites his initiative.)*

Christopher: How could we do that?

Becky: Do you have any ideas? *(She invites his initiative.)*

Christopher: We could build some ramps. Can we do it right now?

Becky: I have to finish shopping and make lunch, then I can help you.

Of course, many conflicts are not tied up so neatly. There will also be times you have to set a limit without taking the time to negotiate a mutual solution. Conflicts come up dozens of times a day, and you can't spend all day negotiating with your children. But kids don't need to negotiate with us all the time. If we do it some of the time, on a consistent basis, kids get the idea that their ideas are valued. They learn the basics of negotiation, and pretty soon they start initiating the problem-solving process themselves.

Teaching Manners

One of the areas of behavior that parents and children struggle over is manners. It doesn't readily occur to young children to think about how their behavior affects other people. So aside from wanting to imitate, they don't have much inherent drive to learn "manners."

Parents, on the other hand, want their children to be friendly and sociable, to be likable, and to demonstrate to the world that they are being "well brought up" by "good" parents.

The social graces around greeting people often elude young children. Children at different developmental stages are reluctant to greet or respond to people for various reasons. As babies, they may be experiencing fear of strangers. As toddlers and preschoolers, they may be absorbed in another activity, wrapped up in their own thoughts, or wanting to exert their own initiative. When strangers approach at temple, your baby may turn her head away. When the bakery clerk greets your toddler, he may shout "No!" And when your neighbor asks your preschooler how she is doing, your daughter may act as if she didn't even hear her.

Saying "please" and "thank you" can also cause conflict in families. While most children go through phases where they use these words profusely, many don't use them predictably or consistently. Because of the way kids think, most don't really see the usefulness or necessity of these words on a regular basis.

Difficulties with saying thank you have to do with three things: a child's limited ability to predict future pleasure, her undeveloped sense of empathy, and her inability to talk about her feelings. When adults receive presents, we are able to anticipate the enjoyment that lies ahead. But a three-year-old who gets a book doesn't know how to be grateful right then because she hasn't had any experience with the present. Nor does it occur to her how the "giver" might feel. Older preschool children may even have some expectations about what is in the box and may be disappointed if their prediction is wrong.

Kids don't verbally reflect on their feelings—they just enjoy the present. Often a child will be utterly charmed with something that has been given to him, yet it doesn't occur to him to put those feelings into words.

Teaching children manners in the first five years is rarely a straightforward process. Here are some ideas for helping children develop manners in a developmentally appropriate way:

• **Talk about family customs.** You can tell your children what you value. "I really like it when you say 'please.' " "In our family, we always say 'hello' when a new person comes into the room." "I'd like you to look me in the eye when you say 'good-bye.' " " 'Thank yous' are very important to your grandparents."

• **Model the skills you want to teach.** The way you treat others and the way you treat your children are the most significant teaching tools you have. It's where you really get to demonstrate what you think is important: "Thanks, Uncle Vinney. I really appreciate your giving Sasha that wonderful trike."

• **Give your child information.** You can tell children: "Bubbie spent a lot of time finding just the right book for you." "It would make Poppa glad to hear how much you like the overalls he sent you." "When someone says 'Hi' to you, they would like you to say 'Hi,' too." "Evelyn is asking you how you are doing. I'd like you to answer her." "I feel more like getting you milk when you say 'please.' "

• **Make your expectations clear.** You can say to children "I want you to figure out a way to say 'good-bye' to your friend." "We need to find a way to help Sonya feel better."

• **Give your child choices.** With a toddler, you might say "You could wave or blow kisses to your friend." Or "Would you like to get Sonya her blanket or some ice?"

With preschool children, you can ask for their ideas. Geneva, mother of five-year-old Grace, explained: "I was starting to nag Grace about the fact that she hadn't thanked her grandma for the birthday present she'd sent. Finally I caught myself nagging and instead said, 'Grandma sent you a backpack in the mail and I would like her to know you're pleased you got it. How do you want to do that? Would you like to call? Do you want to draw a picture? Should we make her a tape?' Once I made room for her input, Grace got pretty excited about deciding what she was going to do."

• **Support the development of empathy.** Manners are meaningful when they are indicative of caring, appreciation, compassion, and empathy. When teaching manners, it is important to keep these human values in focus. Teaching manners without teaching the underlying values will train children to "behave properly" in certain situations without teaching them to be truly responsive.*

*Helping children develop empathy is a consistent theme throughout this book. For more, see "Working with Children Who Bite" on p. 249, "Children's Friendships: Cooperation and Conflict," on p. 304, "What Enables Children to Share?" on p. 320, and "Working Against Stereotypes and Predjudice: An Anti-bias Approach " on p. 358.

Gracefully Bowing Out of a Conflict

Whenever a conflict is escalating and your child is expressing very strong feelings about something—such as not wearing a bib—it's a good idea to ask yourself "Is this worth it or not?" "How strongly do I feel about this?" Sometimes the answer will be "It's not as important to me as it is to him. If he doesn't wear his bib, and his shirt gets all dirty, I can just wash it. It's not really a big deal. I can let this one go." Other times, you'll check in with yourself and say "It really is a big deal. I really don't want him to ruin that shirt, and he's about to eat spaghetti with tomato sauce." So you come back to him and say, "It's very important to me that you don't get spaghetti sauce on your new shirt. You can either take it off or wear your bib. Which would you like to do?"

Those times that you do change your mind, when you decide you really don't care about the bib, it's important to tell kids: "I changed my mind about that." If you give up grudgingly and say, "Okay, just be that way! Don't wear your bib!" it's like you're not on the same team, and you give your child the message, "You've gotten away with something. I can't get you to do what I want."

"But I Want Chips!"

What does it mean to back down gracefully when you change your mind? Let's take the example of two-year-old Finn, who's crying for chips in the store. Irene, his mother, says, "We're not going to buy chips today." Finn continues whining and crying "Chips! Chips! Chips!" Irene repeats, "No, we're not going to buy chips." Finn continues screaming for chips. Irene may not want to buy chips, but by this time, she may realize, "No nap, a strange caregiver at school this morning, third errand. Maybe I don't want to add this particular stress." So she turns to Finn and says, "You know, I'm going to change my mind. All these errands have been my idea. I'd like you to get a chance to choose something too. Come on, you can pick out some chips."

Giving your child a clue as to why you're changing your mind and letting him know that this change isn't arbitrary is very useful. It's also helpful, if you are going to change your mind, to do so early in the interaction. If you change your mind only after children have screamed and cried, children will learn to rely on these techniques to negotiate with you.

On the other hand, whining and crying may be your young child's best way to tell you that something is really important to him. Recognizing that, you may decide to change your mind. The critical thing is to change your mind because you respect the strength of his conviction *and* because it seems reasonable to change your mind, not simply because you want to quell the racket. On those occasions when Irene decides not to buy Finn the chips, she can say, "No, I'm not going to change my mind this time." And she can still respect his idea by saying, "I hear how much you want those chips. Those are your favorite chips. But we're not going to buy them today."

Wanting to Be Right

Even in circumstances in which changing our minds would be the wisest thing to do, many of us find it hard to shift gears. We want to be right or are afraid of looking weak to our children.

Joe explains: "It happens all the time. I get into a power struggle with one of my kids and halfway through it I realize, 'Gee, I'm being stupid. I don't really care about this.' At that point, I can either be macho and say, 'I said this and this is the way it's gonna be,' or I can gracefully try to bow out of the situation and leave with some dignity. The first few years I was a parent, I often took the macho route. Now I just try to say, 'You know what? I was wrong about that. I don't really care if you have another popsicle.' And what becomes significant in that interchange isn't the popsicle, it's the fact that my kids learn that their father can make mistakes."

Leah has also had to learn to back down. "I'm like a pitbull. I just cannot change my mind. For a long time, I didn't know how to look at something midstream and reassess it. I thought if I told my child 'No,' it had to be 'no.' And the first word out of my mouth, just because of who I am, is 'no.' 'Mama, can I go over to Renee's house?' 'No!' And five minutes later, I think, 'Why don't I want her to go over to Renee's? There's no reason for her not to go to Renee's.' So I'm learning to turn back to my child and say, 'Sorry. I made a mistake. Go to Renee's.' I'm learning to say 'I'm sorry. I was wrong.'

"Part of it has to do with respect. I want my children to respect the fact that if I say 'no' it means 'no.' But I also want to hear what my kids have to say. They have a right to tell me if they disagree, and why. I thought about that a lot as my five-year-old was starting to argue with me more. I realized it doesn't do a whole lot of good for me to say it's okay for her to disagree with me, if I'm not willing to listen, to actually hear it with my heart, and maybe to change my mind.

"The thing that amazes me is that they still respect my authority. I thought that they wouldn't respect my authority unless I was always consistent. But now I understand that they need to know that I will always be consistent with my love and my respect and my values, but that I am a changing person. I am capable of changing my mind about things. I am learning flexibility."

Why It's Important Not to Give in to Kids All the Time

Even though it's important to be flexible, it's equally important not to back down too much. The balance of power in a family can get out of whack when parents cater to their children's desires to the exclusion of everyone else's. As we discussed in Chapter 11, "Responding to Crying and Tantrums," this sometimes happens when parents are uncomfortable with children's tantrums. Every time a child looks like he's going to be upset about a decision, the parent backs down to avoid the situation coming to a head.

You see your twenty-month-old begin to erupt into firestorms and you get scared. You do whatever you can to stop the tantrum from coming. Often that means giving in on whatever the issue is. It's okay if this happens occasionally, but when it happens consistently, children can get the message that their feelings are too big and scary for adults. At the same time, children learn to get what they want by threatening adults with an explosion. They start wielding a kind of power that is unhealthy for the family.

In this situation, the parents have made a decision—conscious or not—to keep their son from expressing strong, powerful feelings. In the process, they short-circuit their son's healthy relationship to his feelings. Because he doesn't have to deal with the needs of anyone else in the family, he also misses out on valuable lessons in empathy and give-and-take. In the meantime, parents start to feel as if they've lost control, that their child is manipulating them.

Another way parents avoid conflict is through diversion: spending most of their time with their children doing things with an entertainment focus (TV, movies, video games, shopping, amusement parks, family fun centers). In these activities, parents and children can miss out on opportunities to interact, to check in with each other, and to work through the inevitable conflicts that arise in families.

It's critical that children learn to resolve conflicts with their parents. When parents and children lose the ability to fight and work things out, to disagree, to have strong feelings around each other, the intimacy of the relationship is lost. The relationship gets stuck and doesn't get to deepen in the ways relationships do when conflicts have been successfully weathered.

Putting things back in balance requires that parents reintroduce relaxed, everyday activities into their relationship and that they make room for the angry, disappointed feelings that inevitably arise when they set clear limits with their children.

FOOD FOR THOUGHT: FAMILY CONFLICTS

- What decisions in my family need to be made by adults?
- Which decisions can children participate in?
- What would I like my children to learn about making decisions? About being listened to?

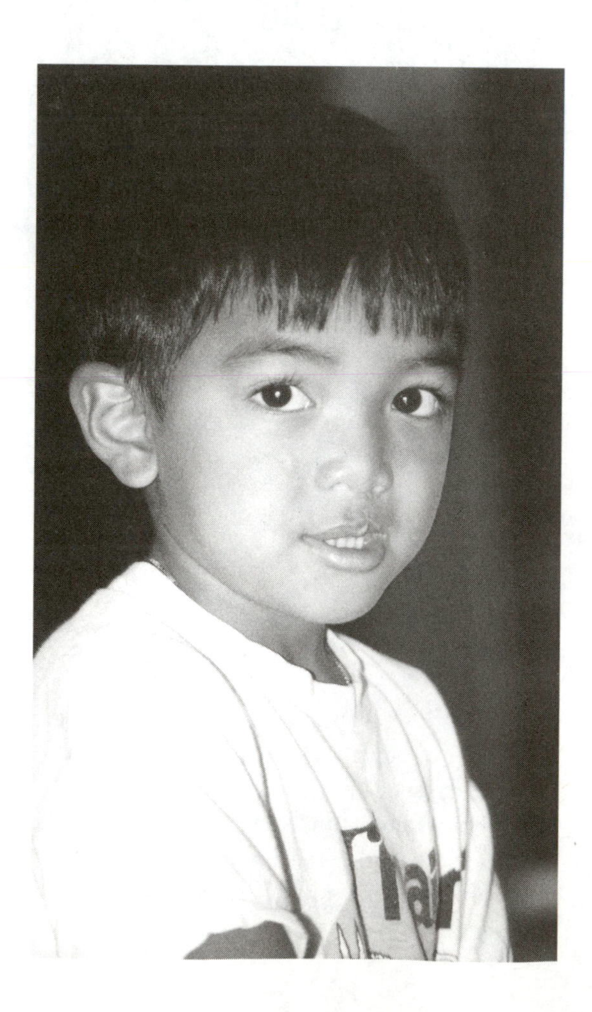

• Part Five •

Social Learning and Play

22. Supporting Children's Play and Learning

"When a child plays, he is the manipulator; he makes do with whatever is at hand. His imagination transforms the commonplace into the priceless. A wooden clothespin, rescued from under the kitchen table and wrapped in a dishcloth, becomes a baby; a penny thrust under a cushion becomes a buried treasure."

EDA J. LESHAN

Play is at the core of children's learning. Through play, kids develop and practice their skills, learn how the world works, and build their knowledge and understanding. They interact with the world on their own terms: they explore, create, make choices and mistakes, experience cause and effect, and have fun.

To be considered "play," children's activities need to be self-chosen and self-directed. Kids who are experienced and competent at play are creative, confident, self-motivated learners.[1]

Children's play *is* their work. As Milo, the father of three-year-old Kiki, put it, "Kiki's concentration, her focus, and her determination when she is playing are phenomenal. She punches the clock the minute she wakes up and you practically have to force her to close her eyes at the end of the day."

[1] This book includes many additional references to children's play. In particular, see " 'Dad, I'm Bored': Helping Children Appreciate Free Time" on p. 47 and "But Girls Can't Do That: Helping Children Move Beyond Limiting Gender Roles" on p. 329.

Sometimes we think of learning as the process of soaking up knowledge. However, children don't just absorb information. Unlike sponges, they need to work with information, apply it to what they already know, and reinvent it until it makes sense to them. As child development theorist Jean Piaget said, "For children, to invent is to understand."

Learning Through Their Senses: Play and Development

Young children gather information through their whole bodies: their feet, their cheeks, their arms, their hands, their mouths. By moving freely, children take in important information about texture, temperature, density, and shape. For young babies, moving from hard, smooth, cold linoleum to fuzzy, warm, bumpy carpet with bare hands and knees is a rich tactile experience. For toddlers, jumping in a mud puddle and feeling the squishy, wet mud on the bottom of their boots and the big, wet splashes on their legs is an important sensory exploration.

Babies and toddlers also do lots of exploration with their mouths. At first glance, we might think they are interested in "tasting" things, and sometimes they are. But much of the mouthing young children do has more to do with their sense of touch: "How does this feel on my tongue?" "How does it fit in my mouth?"

Children use as many senses as possible in each investigation. Let's look at nine-month-old Tatiana playing with a zucchini for the first time. "Ah, let's check out this zucchini. It looks green and long. Can I get my hand around it? Ah, yes . . . hmm, it's heavy. It's a little fuzzy in my hand, let's see in my mouth, hmmm, fuzzy, smooth, ridges . . . oops, it broke. Hmmm, now there's a smell. Now there's a zucchini in each hand. What happens if I bang them on the table? *Thud, thud.* Hmmm, they make a noise. Let's try the mouth again." Giving adult words to this baby's exploration shows us what she might be perceiving as she uses all of her senses to explore a new object.

Kids on the Go: Physical Play

When children engage in physical play, they are learning how their bodies work; they are strengthening and developing their muscles and coordination. As we discussed in Chapter 17, "Learning About Bodies," children develop small motor skills when they use their hands to pick up peas, put sticks in a cup, tear the pages in a magazine, turn the pieces of a puzzle to make them fit, draw, paint, or use scissors. When they roll over, crawl, pull up, climb, walk, hop, run, drum, dance, wrestle, build with big blocks, or kick a ball, they are

developing large motor skills. As children engage in physical play, they simultaneously engage in other kinds of learning, as well.

"Me Do It": Emotional Learning Through Play

Throughout their play, children develop emotional skills. Spontaneous play for babies often addresses the issue of "trust," the emotional task for the first year of life. "Peek-a-boo," while challenging children's understanding of "object permanence," reminds babies again and again that they can trust that their loved ones will reappear. "Chase the baby" also reassures babies that their parent will always be there to find them.

One- and two-year-olds, working on the theme of "autonomy," are willing to play almost anything, as long as they get to choose. Young toddlers' play often imitates the big people around them: "I can water the plants, take off my clothes, and carry my backpack, all by myself."

Older toddlers begin to use pretend play to practice making decisions about themes from their daily lives: making and eating food, driving the truck, taking care of the baby, going to work, and coming back home again. This play helps them make sense of their world and the people in it.

Toddlers also love to do "work" as their play. Real tasks such as cooking, cleaning, building, gardening, dusting, and polishing offer children a feeling of competence as well as autonomy.

Preschool children, who are working on the emotional task of "initiative," are bursting with their own ideas, plans, and schemes. "Here's my idea." "How about if we did it like this?"

During the preschool years, children need lots of chances to design and define their own play. Play materials which allow for children to build, create, pretend, and use their own ideas all support their emerging sense of initiative.

Children's Make-Believe: Creativity and Pretend Play

Most toddlers begin engaging in pretend play shortly after their second birthday. This kind of play grows in complexity and duration throughout the preschool years. By playing out familiar themes and ideas, young children reconstruct and create their own version of life. In pretend play, children can be whoever they want to be.

When children pretend to be different people, animals, or characters, they are challenged to take another's perspective as they create the "role" of that person. This affords not only an intellectual and creative challenge but also a chance to develop feelings of empathy. Dramatic play offers children a chance to literally "walk in someone else's shoes." A child who becomes a "cat" has to figure out how a cat looks, moves, sounds, and eats.

Children use dramatic play to make sense of their experience. A child who's been upset about doctor visits may choose to spend a considerable amount of time playing "doctor's office." This allows him to think about what happens at the doctor's, to create his own story about it, and to play it out repeatedly at his own pace. The control he experiences as he plays helps him master the experience: "I have gotten more comfortable with stethoscopes and shots because I have pretended to use them myself."

Children also use dramatic play to practice relationship skills. Figuring out who is going to wear the black boots and who is going to wear the red, where the fire station should be located, and what will be used for fire hoses are just a few of the decisions in which children get to practice communication, balancing power and control, negotiation, and conflict resolution. Often working on these skills becomes even more important than actually putting out the fire.[2]

[2] These kinds of negotiations can cause frustration and conflict and may require some adult facilitation. See Chapter 23, "Children's Friendships: Cooperation and Conflict" on p. 304 for more on supporting children's play relationships.

Young children take pretend play very seriously, often not making clear distinctions between reality and fantasy. Unless someone is in danger of getting hurt emotionally or physically by the play, parents do not need to step in with clarifications about what is real and what is pretend. Children will eventually figure out most of that on their own naturally, through their direct experience or through conversations at other times.

Understanding My World: Intellectual Learning and Play

As kids move, experiment, explore, and practice their skills in the world, they use their existing knowledge and simultaneously develop new understandings. As new experiences come in, children often have to extend their current thinking to accommodate the new information. Often what children figure out in this process is "inaccurate" from our perspective, yet it makes perfect sense given their level of experience and their best thinking.

Eight-month-old Erica, who has just learned how to pull up on the couch, crawls eagerly over to the rocking chair and reaches up to grab the seat just as she's done with the couch. When she starts to pull up, the rocking chair moves, and Erica plops down on her bottom. She tries it two more times with the same result before she crawls back to the couch.

Yesterday Latisha, three years old, asked her grandmother for a glass of juice. Her grandmother told her that she could have it if she said "please." She said, "Please, I want juice," and her grandmother gave it to her. Today, when she asked her father if she could drive the car and he told her "no," she added "*Please?*" She was devastated when the answer was still "no."

Both Erica and Latisha had recently acquired knowledge that they tried to apply to new but similar situations. Erica knew a little bit about "things you could pull up on," and she learned a little bit more when she tried the rocking chair. Latisha tried her newly acquired "all-powerful" word to get what she wanted but discovered that it wouldn't work in every situation.

Children make dozens of intellectual discoveries about the physical world through their experiences and their play. As three-year-old J.T. pours the sand from the big bucket into the small cup for the sixth time, he begins to understand something about volume, weight, density, and gravity. He begins to realize that the bucket is bigger than the cup and that it holds "bigger sand." Eventually he may understand that the bucket will *always* be bigger than the cup and that it will overflow every time. He also learns about the physical properties of sand as it forms a neat little peak at the top of his overflowing cup.

Janis recalls an incident from an infant play group: "I was observing ten-month-old Hannah, who'd picked up a lime in one hand and a lemon in the other. In that moment, she had the beginnings of one-to-one correspondence—one hand, one piece of fruit. Then she spotted an orange. Here she was, two hands, three pieces of fruit. Now what? At that point, she understood in her body something about 'more than' and something about 'too much,' something about 'twoness' and something about 'threeness,' something about having two hands and three pieces of fruit."

The amazing thing is that much of children's learning takes the form of knowledge that they don't yet have the language to talk about. J.T. knows lots about the physics of the sand box, but he has only a few words to describe his discoveries. Hannah was figuring out some crucial math concepts with her fruit, but she probably couldn't say the word "two."[3]

[3]Children also develop social skills through play. For information on social learning, see Chapter 23, "Children's Friendships: Cooperation and Conflict" and Chapter 24, "What Enables Children to Share?"

Kids and Computers

It is estimated that 60 percent of the homes in the United States have computers and at least half of those households have children. More and more children are gaining access to computers either at home or in their preschools. Software programs and CD-ROMs are being marketed for toddlers and preschoolers.

Parents who want to support their children's learning often wonder how and when to introduce their kids to computers. It's important to think about how educational and appropriate computers are for young children.

A lot of what children learn from computers is not what the software is intending to teach. Computers enable children to practice fine motor skills and eye-hand coordination. If used in age-appropriate ways, they can also promote thinking skills. It is important to remember, however, that none of these lessons is unique to computers. Each can be accomplished through more open-ended activities.

Most software for kids contains drill and practice exercises. A computer will tell a child if her answer is right or if it is wrong, but it will rarely tell her what is wrong about her answer. When a child types an "F" instead of an "E," there is no one to say "Wow, look how similar those letters are. Can you find the difference?" Given that children's wrong answers are critical to their learning, being "bleeped" for a wrong answer does nothing to encourage a child's creative thinking or problem-solving ability. As with television, children may learn to "memorize" certain words through using a computer without really understanding the concepts behind them.

Some programs encourage children's problem solving, but the "right" answers still fall within a narrow range. Others enable children to "choose" their own ending to a story or to click on an image and make something happen. Although there is no such thing as a "wrong answer" in these open-ended interactive programs, they still cannot fully take children's own ideas, thinking, or creativity into account.

There are also painting or drawing programs for kids, yet even these reduce creativity to moving a mouse on a pad. Harriet Cuffaro, a Bank Street educator, critiques one of these programs: "The experience is reduced and limited by eliminating the fluid, liquid nature of paint. There are no drips to control or spills to mop up. Neither are there opportunities to become involved in the process of learning how to create shades of color [or] . . . the effects achieved by rotating the brush and varying the pressure."*

The specific things young children *can* learn from computers is how to turn them on, how to move and click the mouse, how to use the arrows, the space bar, and the return key, and how to get from one screen to another. Through practice, kids can develop a certain comfort and competence with technology, growing to understand the logic of it. While this is important learning for children in a technological society, computers are not the only way for children to learn about technology and early childhood is not the most appropriate time for extensive computer experience.

The kind of active, hands-on, messy, three-dimensional, self-directed, creative, physical, and social experiences that children need in order to learn during these years are not, for the most part, what computers offer. Remember that most of the people who are building the information superhighway didn't have computers as toddlers and preschoolers—they had blocks, mud, sand, dolls, cars, play-dough, and friends.

On the other hand, many young children enjoy exploring computers. If a child has plenty of other opportunities for creative play and learning, if the software is understandable, if a relaxed adult is available to help explore what she is interested in, and if there are no expectations about what a child should be "learning" or "accomplishing," occasionally playing on the computer can be fun and worthwhile.

* Cited in Ellen and Judy David Galinsky, *The Preschool Years* (New York: Ballantine, 1988), p. 92.

Issues for Parents: What About Baby Flash Cards?

People often talk about the need to motivate children. When Swiss child development specialist Jean Piaget lectured in the United States, he always got what he called "the American Question": "Yes, yes, these stages are fine. But how do we speed children through them?"

Many parents feel pressured to stimulate their babies, to get flash cards for their toddlers, to buy computer programs for their preschoolers, or to place their children in academic preschools. Parents wonder how to best support their children's learning. We've all been told that young children have an incredible capacity to learn, and we don't want to miss out on the opportunity to develop that potential.

Yet children's natural thirst for knowledge and new experiences is insatiable. Infants put everything in their mouths, toddlers are obsessively on the move, preschoolers constantly ask "Why?" As one father put it, "Curiosity is a better motivator than any parent. And it's built-in."

However, many of us have been taught that "learning" looks a certain way: being able to recite the alphabet or identify all of the colors. We picture children who read at three or four. We think of learning as something kids need to sit still to do. We narrow learning to include only a few intellectual tasks and assume that play is the frivolous or relaxing thing you get to do *after* you've done your "real" learning. Given this false dichotomy, many of us experience frustration trying to get our children to learn something they are not ready for.

Sue remembers trying to drill her son, Forest, when he was three: "Forest could count to fifteen, but he always left out seven and thirteen. For the longest time, I tried to teach him to include those numbers, but most of the time he just left them out. Now he is four and a half and about a month ago, he began including them all of the time."

Robert remembers feeling pressured when Bobby Jr. was two and a half: "His best friend, Monique, who is two weeks younger than Bobby, could say the names of all the dinosaurs in her book. I tried to sit Bobby down and teach him those names, but he was more interested in skating across the floor with the book under his foot than he was in learning about pterodactyls."

Even though children aren't always exploring the things we want them to explore, they are learning faster in their early years than they will at any other point in their lives. To hurry them along is unnecessary and redundant. Pushing them into premath, reading, and other kinds of structured activities can increase their sense of frustration and interfere with the very experiences that provide the best underpinnings for later learning.

Everything babies and young children are doing—whether they're building blocks, doing puzzles, or working with containers—is full of rich, vital lessons. Children learn about sequencing, categorizing, logical thinking, physical relationships, cause and effect, and recognizing differences and similarities. All of these are prereading and premath activities. Recognizing the difference between a grapefruit and a lemon is the first step in recognizing the difference between a big O and a little o. Children's hands-on interactive learning is the best foundation for academic learning.

Our role as parents is not to "motivate" our young learners but to nurture and support their natural motivation. Jack, father of a two-year-old Heidi, explained: "We don't have a plan for 'educating' Heidi. We try to get her outside as much as possible. We have a variety of toys for her. We make sure that she has free play that stimulates all of her senses—play that includes sight, sound, smell, touch and taste. And we talk about what we are doing.

"We beat out rhythms on signposts and

fences and anything else that makes noise. We make sure she has exposure to other children so she gets to learn socially. Our only curriculum is making her world as large as we possibly can. I have complete faith that she'll learn about numbers and letters through the random exposure she gets being a child excited by the world."

Jenny, the mother of three-and-a-half-year-old Carly, agreed: "Carly's still trying to understand the way paint feels on her skin, the way the crayon feels between her fingers. She's exploring the medium itself. Why should I be encouraging her to draw a picture of the sun?"

One of the most critical things young children can learn is that they are competent learners, that their own internal direction is valuable and worthwhile, that their impulse to learn is a strong, purposeful force. Such confidence prepares children for a lifetime of learning.

As Spencer Kagan, a pioneer in the cooperative education movement, writes, "Eighty percent of the information we're teaching children today will be obsolete in twenty years. The best education we can give children is to teach them how to learn."[4]

FOOD FOR THOUGHT: PLAY AND LEARNING

- What were my best experiences playing as a child? What made my play successful (time, space, friends, toys)? What was my family's view on play?

- What kinds of play does my child like to do? What kinds of learning have I observed during that play?

- Have there been times I've been tempted to "push" my child?

[4] Spencer Kagan, *Co-operative Learning Resources for Teachers* (San Juan Capistrano: Resources for Teachers, 1989).

What Is Our Role in Children's Play and Learning?

Parents are children's first and primary teachers. Our role is not to define the learning or the play but to observe our child to see what her goal is and to provide safety, information, and necessary materials as well as time and space.

- **Respect the importance of choice in children's play.** Children need ample opportunities each day for unstructured play, play in which they get to choose what they want to play, what they want to play with, for how long, and with whom.

- **Create environments that are conducive to children's play and learning.** Parents generally define, create, and equip children's play spaces. Whether children play in the common areas of the home, in playrooms or bedrooms, or outside, parents provide parameters for where and with what children can play. While children don't need large areas that are defined as "just theirs," they do need some space that allows for their play.

Children don't need elaborate furniture or equipment in their play spaces; the most important thing they need is some open space. In smaller living spaces, parents and children get creative finding play spaces: kids might play on the bedroom floor, under the kitchen table, or in an available corner. Pillows and a small rug can provide some softness for children on the floor. Kids are often happy to play with and around the family's belongings, creating climbing structures and forts out of couches and trampolines out of any beds or cushions they're allowed to jump on.

Children who are drawing, building, or playing with clay might need a smooth surface to work on. Small tables and chairs can be useful for children between eighteen and thirty months of age, but many prefer to do their writing, drawing, building, and reading on the floor. A cutting board or a small piece of plywood can provide a work surface in carpeted areas.

Outside play space provides different opportunities. Some families have yards, porches, decks, or sidewalks that provide room for outside play. It is important that any play space is safe (fenced, if necessary) and free from dangerous things. If your home doesn't have any outside access, your child can benefit from regular outings to parks, forests, open spaces—or just plain walks. It is helpful if children's outside play allows them to interact with the world. A botanical garden might not provide places for children to dig, pick, throw, climb, and run as they like to do outside, but an open field would.

One of the advantages of outside play is that children can make messes and not have to be so careful about clean-up. The rearranged leaves, dirt, and snails in the backyard can be left in their new locations. The play-dough, water, or paint they spill outside can be hosed off.

Regardless of where children play, there are ways we can equip and set up areas to support their play and learning. Toys should be stored close to children's play areas. Kids are best able to choose what they want to play with if their things are visible, perhaps arranged on a low, open shelf or in a cardboard box turned on its side.

Deep toy boxes or overloaded toy baskets are hard to see into, and toys are more likely to get lost or broken stored this way. Small separate baskets are useful for sorting sets of play things—all the dinosaurs in one; the bells, shakers, and maracas in another; building blocks in a third; leaves, rocks, and shells collected from neighborhood walks in a fourth.

It is useful to store and display children's toys in consistent locations. Even though children are masters at carting toys from one location to another, if we work together to put toys away in the same locations, children will be better able to find them. They will also begin to learn a sense of order. Some people even "label" the location with pictures or toy names on masking tape.

• **Provide a variety of open-ended, multiuse materials and toys.** As far as children's play goes, the more toys do, the less creative children are, and the less toys do, the more creative children are. This information can be hard to put into practice amid the barrage of mechanized and computerized toys lining the shelves of toy stores and advertised on TV.

Multiuse toys allow children to shape, move, form, and use them in an endless variety of creative ways. A baby's rolling toy can become a tower for a three-year-old engaged in fantasy play. By providing open-ended toys, we invite children's evolving ideas and initiative.

For older one- and two-year-olds, open-ended toys include water; sand; assorted containers; boxes; safe kitchen equipment; play-dough and clay; crayons; big chalk and paint (provided children aren't still eating everything); milk carton blocks; nesting containers; shape sorters (all of which can be homemade); big building toys for small hands; small blankets; dolls and stuffed animals; dress-up hats, vests, and other easy-on clothes; boxes of all sizes including large appliance boxes; soft balls; hand-size vehicles (not battery-powered); push toys and carts; small wagons; dirt, leaves, and other natural materials.

For preschoolers, you can add wooden blocks; small play people figures (not just specific characters, but generic people of different ages, genders, and ethnicities); other more complex building-type toys; dress-up clothes and other simple dramatic play props; child-size pieces of fabric of different textures, including

some long pieces for creating endless variations on costumes or sets; a variety of balls; a tricycle or a bike; "art caddies" that include a number of art materials including small scissors, nontoxic markers, colored pencils, tape, different sizes and textures of paper, cardboard, glue, and junk (buttons, cloth, bottle caps, popsicle sticks, shells, and acorns) for collages.

Less open-ended but equally wonderful toys include children's books, puzzles, picture-matching games, and tools for carpentry, gardening, cooking, and sewing.

Multiuse toys that allow children to do something besides push buttons and watch encourage creativity in a way that "single-use" toys, such as blasthammer guns, "Mighty Max Ax Man," or "Fabulous Hair Friends" dolls do not.

It's interesting to note, however, that if children don't have an ever-fresh supply of single-purpose toys, they will eventually develop creative ways to play with the ones they do have. Children are more apt to do creative play with these toys if they are not constantly barraged (even though they may beg for more, more, more) with the newest movie character doll or the latest action figures.

• **Provide a variety of toys and play opportunities to both boys and girls.** Many of us have ideas about appropriate toys for girls and appropriate toys for boys. By providing a diverse selection of play materials for all children, both boys and girls will get a chance to explore their full potential.[5]

• **Provide a manageable number of toys that rotate regularly.** Many children own more toys than they could ever possibly play with at any one time. Sometimes in our attempts to give children a "choice," we put *all* of their toys out. Yet too many choices can be overwhelming to children and can actually inhibit their creativity. Through watching children play, assessing how many toys you and your child are capable of picking up, and trial and error, you will be able to figure out an appropriate number of toys to keep out at any given time. Your child still will be able to

[5] This idea is explored thoroughly in Chapter 25, "'But Girls Can't Do That': Helping Children Move Beyond Limiting Gender Roles" on p. 329.

have access to her other toys if you rotate a *few* new ones (not a whole new set) in every few weeks from the ones you've put away and take out some of the lesser used ones.

• **Provide "nontoy" things to play with.** Some of us have watched in dismay as our child has sped by all of their specially purchased educational toys just to spend several hours engrossed in the kitchen cupboard or taking apart our purse or camera bag. Often a trip to Woolworth's or the secondhand store will provide more interesting things for children to explore than specially designed toys. Toddlers love all kinds of recycled plastic containers, canning lids and rings, clean, empty cans with the rough edges covered or smoothed, pots and pans, old hats and purses. Not only can such toys generate hours of creative play, they can also help teach children the value of recycling and simple things. (It's important to be aware of safety when children are playing with household or "nontoy" items. Careful cleaning, inspection, and testing of items as well as close supervision will help maintain your child's safety.)

• **Don't interrupt children unnecessarily.** Often we assume that just because they are kids, they don't have an important agenda and that we can talk to them, hug them, tickle them, or pick them up whenever we want to. Children who aren't interrupted unnecessarily feel comfortable getting really engrossed in their project or investigation. In order to respect children's work, we need to first observe what they are doing before we jump in with our words or actions.

• **Let children create from their own imagination.** Often children ask us to do things for them in their play—for instance, to draw or build something. While our adult skills can be useful in making some of the props for children's play, it's important to let the child be the main creator. Specifically, when we draw pictures or build things for children, they sometimes lose touch with their own creativity and ideas, become discouraged with their own work, only want to imitate what we made, or refuse to draw or build.

Brent, the father of four-year-old Amanda, shares: "I love blocks. I loved them as a kid; I used to build whole cities and fortresses with them. So I was eager to get Amanda her first set of blocks at three. At first we'd build and she'd knock them down, but slowly I noticed she was doing less building and more wanting me to build: 'Build a house, Daddy. Build a horsey, Daddy.' And when I suggested that she build, she told me, 'No! You do it.' So I had to go back to the beginning and start slow. I'd put out one block and then say 'What should go next? How should it go? Help me get it on there.' Slowly she started building again, but I had to back way off and make the space for her ideas and ingenuity."

Lydia, the mother of three-year-old Danny, has figured out how to support her son, but not too much: "Danny has a chalkboard and chalk. He likes to draw on it, but a lot of times, he begs me to draw something for him. I tell him I won't do it for him but that I will 'help' him. I get a wet rag and wash the board down for him carefully and sit next to him attentively. Then I ask, 'What color do you want to start with?' If I give him that much support, he's usually fine doing the drawing himself. It doesn't look like the bus I would have drawn—it's more like a bunch of squiggly lines, but it's his bus."[6]

• **Playing with children.** Each of us brings our own individual expectations to our play relationship with our child. Many parents jump at the chance to revisit childhood pastimes once

[6] See "How and When to Help" on p. 19 for more on parents' role in children's learning struggles.

they become parents. Others are less enthusiastic about spending long hours talking on toy telephones or building towers.

There are several things to note about parents playing with children. First, you don't have to be your child's main playmate. Your job is to provide the space and materials, and, sometimes, to arrange for friends to visit.

If you do enjoy playing with your child, it's important that you share leadership with him. Often parents have great ideas about how the pretend play should go or love to spend hours swinging children around. In this kind of play, children can become props rather than designers and instigators of the play. It's important to let children initiate and control play whenever possible. Let your son assign the roles and the direction of the game. Let your daughter create the design for the bus and decide where it's headed.

Also, it's important to recognize children's need to repeat the same game over and over.

Finally, if your child does spend lots of time playing with adults, it is useful to make sure that he also gets to play with people his own age. The play dynamic is different when children play with each other, and children learn many valuable things from playing with their peers.

Homemade Toys

In Janis's toddler development classes, parents are asked to bring in a homemade toy or book for their final project. Janis gives some basic guidelines and brings in some samples of toys parents have made other years, and then parents come up with all kinds of creative toys, usually made simply with objects that are readily found in most homes—empty cans with plastic lids, milk cartons, empty toilet paper rolls, old oatmeal containers.

Often, through watching what children naturally play with, parents figure out how to design some of their children's favorite playthings. Here are some suggestions that parents, children, and teachers have come up with:

• **Sorting boxes.** Using a coffee can with a plastic lid, a well-cleaned detergent box with a hinged lid or other container, you can cut a hole or several differently shaped holes that children can put things into. For older babies, you just need one fairly big hole that will fit a variety of spools, plastic curlers, or small blocks. For toddlers, you can make a hole for round things and a slot for frozen orange juice lids, playing cards, or other flat things. The container can be covered with colored Con Tact paper or pictures and clear ConTact paper or left plain.

• **Cardboard blocks.** Big, lightweight blocks can be made out of cardboard milk cartons. Wash thoroughly, open the top, stuff with newspaper, fold the top in flat so that the block is a rectangle (instead of pointed like a milk carton top), and tape the top shut. If you use pint, quart, and half-gallon sizes, children will have different size blocks to build with. For a sturdier block, take two cartons of the same size, open the tops, fill one with newspaper, and with the open ends facing each other, push one carton inside the other. Cover blocks with colored ConTact paper, if desired.

• **Stacking or nesting toys.** Graduated containers of the same shape allow children to experiment with size, nesting, and building. A half-pint, a pint, and a quart yogurt container or graduated-size metal cans (with the edges taped over), covered in ConTact paper, could either be nestled inside of each other or turned over to stack.

• **Pull toys.** Newly accomplished walkers love to drag something behind them. Any small open box (slightly weighted or reinforced on the bottom with extra cardboard, if needed) can be a vehicle that you attach a two-foot-long cotton cord to. Knot both ends of the cord and the child can pull the box around and even load it up with treasures. Another pull toy can be constructed using a metal can open at both ends (make sure the edges are smooth or covered with tape). Tie a two- to three-foot cord in a circle that goes through the can. When you pull the rope, the can becomes a wheel. (Always supervise children carefully when they are using long lengths of string, cord, or rope.)

• **Boxes.** Boxes of all sizes make good toys. (When using boxes, inspect them thoroughly before children use them. Many have big staples, plastic liner bags, Styrofoam, or other materials that need to be removed before they are safe for children.) A large waist-high box can be stuffed with newspaper and some sand or other weight, taped shut, covered with ConTact paper, and used for babies to pull up on or to push around. Big refrigerator or furniture boxes make wonderful forts or houses for young children. Either one or a few taped together with matching doors or connecting hallways will provide weeks of fun. Doors can be cut (adults or older children will have to do this part) so that they are hinged on the side or the top. Windows of different shapes and designs can be created. Houses can be painted or decorated with markers. (Older toddlers and preschoolers can help with this—or do it all themselves.) Fabric can be taped over window openings. Have fun using your own creative ideas.

Other boxes, open at the top or with flaps that close, big enough for one child to sit in, carry around, or hide under can be incorporated into all kinds of creative play. Children have lined such boxes up to make trains, added soft blankets to make doll beds and houses, and turned them on their sides to make shelves for a playhouse.

• **Shaker toys.** Children love toys that make a sound. Clear plastic drinking water or soda bottles, or gallon plastic milk cartons, partially filled with colored water or a small handful of rice or beans make wonderful shakers. Take the paper off the bottle and avoid putting dangerous things such as coins inside. Fasten the lids securely with glue or tape, inspect the toys regularly for holes or leaks, and supervise children while they are using them to ensure safety.

• **Play-dough and other wonderful things.** Children love stuff they can sink their hands into. You can simply set up containers (dishpans or flat-bottom bowls) with a little sand or cornmeal for children to explore. You can add a small pitcher of water or include two different materials in one tub. You can also make play-dough and other sensory materials (with the help of children, as appropriate). These materials are easy to make and store and provide hours of fun for kids:

Uncooked Play-dough

1 cup water (with several drops of food coloring, if desired)
1 tablespoon oil
1 cup salt
2 cups flour—more if dough is sticky

Mix together and knead all ingredients. Store in a zip-lock bag or covered plastic container. Lasts longer if refrigerated.

Cooked Play-dough

4 cups flour
2 cups salt
4 tablespoons cream of tartar
4 cups water (with several drops of food coloring, if desired)
2 tablespoons oil

Mix together all ingredients in a saucepan. Cook over medium heat, stirring constantly until stiff. It will be very lumpy at first. Let cool and knead. Store in a zip-lock bag or plastic container. This dough is especially long-lasting.

Ooblick

Ooblick is a wonderful substance to play with. It has the qualities of both a solid and a liquid. It is runnier than play-dough, so it needs a bowl or tub to hold it. It is easy to mix up and can be refrigerated between uses for repeated play. (Throw it out when it becomes moldy or smelly.) It is nontoxic, washes out of clothing easily, or can simply be brushed off when dry.

1 box cornstarch
1–2 cups water (enough to make a thick but runny consistency)

Combine ingredients in a large container, preferably a tub or flat-bottomed bowl. You can add a little more of either ingredient to get the right consistency—like runny yogurt. Children love to help mix this with their hands. You also can add food coloring.

Glootch

Glootch is a non-food-based play material that's appropriate for preschool children. It should not be used by children who are likely to eat it. Glootch has some of the properties of play-dough but is slicker and less sticky. It does not need refrigeration and should be kept in an airtight plastic container.

1 1/2 cups water
1–2 tsp. 20-Mule-Team borax
2 cups of Elmer's glue
food coloring

Mix together 1/3 cup of water and a teaspoon of borax. Dissolve any lumps with your fingers. In a separate plastic container, combine glue, remaining water and food coloring. Gradually add the borax mixture to the glue mixture, stirring with a plastic spoon, until it congeals. If necessary, add the second teaspoon of borax dissolved in a little more water. (It's okay if there's some liquid glue mixture left at the bottom of the container.) Roll the glob of glootch gently in your hands until it stops sticking.

FOOD FOR THOUGHT: TOYS AND PLAY

- What nontoy things does my child like to play with?
- How does my child demonstrate creativity in play?
- How do I see my role in my children's play?
- Is there anything else I want to do to support my child's play?

Supporting Children's Language Development

Even the youngest of babies communicate with their parents. In the first few months of life, each baby and set of parents develop their own system of communication, which includes cries, whimpers, coos, giggles, and gurgles. This system also involves nonverbal cues, such as touching, looking, body postures, and facial expressions. In establishing this wordless communication system, the groundwork is laid for language development. Children get sold on the wonders of communication. They experience being listened to and they begin to hear and understand language.

Diana, whose fourteen-month-old son, Luke, isn't using words yet, remarked, "His communication is so rich and clear and complex without words that I can't imagine that words will really add very much."

Long before children can use language of their own, they begin developing "receptive language," the ability to understand what's said to them. Louise recalls, "I was muttering to myself about trying to find my shoes the other day and Tanisha pulled one out from under the bed. I better watch what I say! She only says a few words, but it seems like she's starting to understand everything."

Each child has his or her own timetable for learning language, and there is no evidence that the age at which children begin speaking has anything to do with their level of intelligence. Some children have several words before their first birthday and others are just beginning to blossom with language at two and a half. Often children who begin speaking later are busy in another area of development. Janis recalls, "I have watched more than one twenty-five-month-old tearing around the yard, climbing everything in sight, building complicated towers of blocks, carefully lining up the cars and trucks, from smallest to largest, putting together puzzles, but hardly speaking a word."

Children Have Their Own Styles of Learning Language

There are two main styles of learning language. Some children focus mostly on individual words, carefully naming single objects: dog, cup, ball, wa-wa, blankey. Other children practice the cadence, rhythm, and intonation of language without using many understandable words. These children will tell long stories, with lots of expression, clearly speaking a familiar language, but you will be able to decipher only a few, if any, specific words. Most children use some combination of these styles. All are equally effective ways to learn language.

Children who are just beginning to use language sometimes use "telegraphic speech." They use one or two words combined with gestures or intonation to communicate a whole thought. A child might say "Me go!" This could mean "I went to the store," "I want to go to the park," "I want to go with you," or "I'm going to hide behind the couch."

Children will also use one word to describe different things that they see as the same. These are called "holophrases." Many children use the term "uh-oh" to mean a variety of things: "The cup fell down." "The egg broke." "I hit somebody." "My hat is lost." Or they use the word "hot" to describe any kind of danger.

Janis's four-year-old niece, Monica, from Michigan always calls the ocean a "lake" when she comes to visit California. It's her phrase for a big body of water that you get to swim in. Many children generalize certain kinds of animals with just one name before they have learned about the specific differences. "Goggy" is a common word for any fuzzy, four-legged creature with a tail.

It's also important to remember that children have concepts that they don't have words for and words they don't know the meanings of. Most children can differentiate between triangles and circles long before they have the word for each. They also learn words that they have only partial or minimal definitions for. As one dad, Terry, explains, "The other day Jeremy said to me, 'Did you know that dinosaurs are extinct? Let's go find one!!" It's always important to take children seriously, but not necessarily literally, when they talk.

How Do Parents "Teach" Language?

It is said that if we could teach reading as naturally as we teach oral language, there would be no illiteracy. For the most part, parents teach

Learning Two Languages

Some children are fortunate enough to have access to more than one language. Families in which two languages are spoken sometimes divide up the languages so that one parent speaks only one language when speaking directly to the children and the other parent uses only the other. In other families, one language is spoken in the home and another language is spoken out in the world.

It is important for children who are learning two languages to hear them separately and not all mixed together in one sentence or conversation. From a very young age, children learn to keep the languages separate and distinct. One of the Spanish/English bilingual toddlers Janis knows coined the word "shoepatos," which is a combination of *shoe* and *zapatos*. But by the time most children are five years old, they will know exactly which words go with which language and with which people.

Children who are learning two languages sometimes begin to speak later than children who are learning one language. This is a natural response to a more complex learning task.

Unfortunately, most non-English languages in this country are not well represented or valued. Unless families live in communities or extended families where their home language is used, valued, and represented in a variety of different settings, they may need to create other language supports for their child.

Families have joined groups or cultivated friendships with people who speak their language. Some children attend child care or schools where their primary language is spoken, and some families take children to spend time in their country of origin where they will be surrounded by their primary language.

Making Books for Your Kids

One of the most treasured gifts you can give your child is a handmade book. Parents have delighted their children with small, child-size books about simple, everyday topics: "Maria Ventura Is Two Years Old!" "My Kitty Book," "A Day In the Life of Eric," "People I Love," or "Grandma's Visit." (What better way to keep a faraway relative in a child's thoughts?)

With simple, readily available materials and a little time and creativity, you can make a book for your child that will quickly become a cherished possession. You don't have to be an artist, a photographer or a writer to make one. Here are some basic ideas for getting started:

• **Keep it simple.** Even a parent with very little time can put together something a child will love.

• **Get some basic supplies.** A drugstore, stationery store, office supply store, or art store can provide you with poster board, markers, individual loose-leaf binder rings, and glue. Parents have also made books using small photo albums or have used single sheets of plastic to encase some special pictures.

• **Take some pictures.** You can use single photos or cut them up for a collage. You can have the pictures speak for themselves, or you can generate a simple story line. When taking pictures, get close to your subject. You can fill the whole frame with the kitty rather than having a tiny cat on a big rug.

• **Protect your original photos.** It's a good idea not to use your only copy of a precious photo for your child's book. You can make an extra copy from the negative or try color photocopying.

• **Make it child-friendly.** A sturdy book that fits easily in a child's hands, that has pages that are easy to turn, makes your books something a child can "read" on his own. Laminating pages or covering them with plastic or clear ConTact paper can protect photos from spills, drool, and tooth marks. If you're binding your book, use notebook rings or another method that can't hurt children. If you staple your book together, cover the sharp staple ends with tape.

• **Make special books to help children deal with new or scary situations.** Parents have made special-interest books: "Jasper Duggan Goes to the Westside Child Care Center" for a child starting day care, "Bik's Visit to the Dentist" for a child who feared the dentist, and "When I Had to Get Stitches," which retroactively documented a trip to the hospital. Such books help children work through those experiences.

• **Consider giving books as gifts.** Grandparents and other relatives love these books. They're a wonderful way to keep family members who are far away in touch with your family. And what better way to chronicle a special visit?

language so naturally they aren't even aware of "teaching." But there are things we can do to consciously support our children's developing language skills:

• **Talk to children.** Although young babies don't understand the full content of what we're saying, talking to them brings language into their lives and gives them the message that one day they will be full participants in the magical world of communication. It is through hearing language in context that children begin to derive meaning.

• **Talk about what you are doing.** As we move through our daily lives, there are innumerable opportunities to teach language: "I'm going into the other room to get my sweater, because I'm cold. I'm back now." "I'd like to pick you up to change your diaper, so you can be warm, too. Are you ready?" Describing daily routines, especially the ones that involve our children, not only provides rich language modeling, it also lets them know that we want them to be included in what is going on.

• **Talk about what children are doing.** In Chapter 19, "Moving Beyond Punishment" we introduced the idea of "sportscasting." Talking to children about what you see them doing gives them words for their experience. While it is important not to fill up all of the empty air space with words, providing vocabulary in context "teaches" words and communicates to kids that we are interested in what they are doing.

• **Don't limit yourself to baby talk.** While it can be fun to use baby talk with young children, it's important to use everyday speech with them, as well. While babies enjoy hearing silly words and their own sounds repeated back, they learn language most effectively when we model for them language used correctly.

• **Respond to children's communication.** When children first begin to talk, parents often have a seemingly uncanny ability to understand their utterances. The fact that parents and children share a history and develop their own vocabulary and signals also plays a part. Janis's son Lee used to say "Wa-lilla." Only people who had read his favorite book, *Little Gorilla,* with him knew that he was talking about the baby gorilla.

But sometimes the period in which children switch over from gestures and sounds to using words can be frustrating for both parent and child. Miguel, the father of eighteen-month-old Toni, explained: "Toni is beginning to tell me things with her 'words.' I know they are words because she says the same ones over and over, emphatically. I only understand about half of what she's saying, and that's frustrating for both of us. Sometimes I'll say 'Show me,' and she can point or take me to something, but lots of times I stand there listening, looking attentive, wracking my brain for meaning—but not understanding."

Even if we don't always understand them, it is significant to children that we are listening, paying attention, and trying to understand.

• **Extend children's language.** One of the most natural communication tools parents use with children is extending children's own words and utterances. When the child says, "Uh, mama car," we respond with "Mama went to work in her new red car." When the child says "Geeeuice!" We respond with "It sounds like you want some juice to drink."[7]

• **Teach language through modeling.** It is not necessary to correct children's language on the spot, make them repeat themselves, or wait until they get it perfectly right before we respond. If we repeat back to them what they said with correct grammar or use the correct form in our answer to them, over time, children will naturally begin to self-correct.

• **Create a language-rich environment.** Through speaking, singing, reading, telling stories, making up silly words and rhymes, children have lots of chances to develop a love of language and a proficiency with the spoken word.

• **Preserve your child's language.** While this isn't a necessary strategy to help your child learn language, it is wonderful to have language samples preserved from your child's early years. Some people have a big calendar on the wall where they record new words or the funny, endearing, innovative things their

[7] For an example of a young toddler's language being extended, see "The Orange, the Bee, and the Flowers" on p. 114.

children say. Others keep a language journal. Parents also use various recording devices to preserve their child's voice. You can use a tape recorder to record your baby's coos, cries, and gurgles, your toddler's early words, your child's conversations, or the sounds of your child's play. If your child is old enough to be interested in machines, you may need to keep the tape recorder out of sight. (Although pushing buttons, making recordings, and listening to themselves can be a fun activity for kids, too.) Some families use a video recorder to record language and action.

Often ordinary days are richer resources for this kind of documentation than holidays and birthdays. Since many families historically have used cameras only to record special events, some of us may have to remind ourselves to bring them out to record daily life.

Sharing Books with Children

I like it when you read to
me. You read with such force
that the pages turn without
you laying your fingers on the book.
You have read so many stories to
me they could fill up a swimming
pool. Pa, I like it when you read
to me.

Miles Grobman,
"My Dad," grade 4

Study after study has shown that children whose families regularly read to them become the most successful readers later on. There's something significant that happens as an adult and a child make contact over a book. A love of books is a wonderful legacy to pass on to children.

Reading is fascinating to kids. Before they know how to read, the fact that the same story comes out of the book every time delights children. As time goes on, kids discover that there's something about that page that gives you those same words every time, and as children memorize parts of stories, they start to see themselves as readers. These are important prereading activities.

Even before they can talk fluently, children who've been regularly exposed to books begin to learn the structure of reading. They hold books, turn pages, and talk in gibberish and intonations over the pictures, all behavior that shows that they understand "This is how people read. I can take part in this, too."

Books are also a way that new ideas and new words can be introduced into children's lives. As you tell your child that the horse is big, that it whinnies (and then you both make the sound); as you explain that horses eat lots of hay and like apples, you elaborate on the story and teach the child new ideas. When the child points to the horse and says "Doggy," and you say "Yes, it's a lot like a doggy, but it's even bigger. It's a horse," the child learns from your interaction. Books are a way to extend children's usable language.

Selecting Books for Children

When you walk into the library or your local bookstore, you may have a tremendous number of children's books to choose from. If you're not familiar with children's literature or if you don't have time to sit and read a bunch of books (like when you have your kids in tow), how can you decide what's best for your child?

The following criteria can help:

• **Does the subject matter interest me and my child?** If your child is interested in bugs or trucks or pictures of other children, those are good books to start with. Choose books that reflect your own interests as well as your child's. Books are a way to share the things we love.

• **Is this book aesthetically pleasing?** Is the artwork interesting? Inspiring? Beautiful? Pleasing to the eye?

Children love rich paintings, drawing, and photography. They love real art in their books. That art doesn't have to be restricted to bright colors, either. Some very special children's books feature simple black-and-white line drawings. When choosing books for children, try to include variety in the illustrations: photographs, watercolors, line drawings, collage, and paintings.

• **Does this book promote creativity and open-ended play?** Many of the children's books that are widely available feature commercial characters from TV or movies. While some of these books deal with useful subject matter, expose children to reading, and feature familiar characters, generally they don't inspire children's creative thinking. Because the characters are everywhere in the media, children are less likely to make up their own stories or to create new play themes after reading these books. Moving beyond books that present "cute" or commercial images can expand your child's thinking and world view.

• **Is the language rich and beautiful?** Language doesn't have to be overly simplified for children, yet it has to have enough accessible words that children can hang on to the familiar ones while they learn the new ones. Even very young children can enjoy poetry, verses, rhymes, and evocative language.

• **What are the values portrayed?** Books convey values in myriad ways. They set norms and give social information. When choosing books for kids, it's important to ask yourself: "What does this book say about life?" "About the nature and durability of friendship?" "About family ties?" "About our relationship with nature and the earth?" "About work and play?" (For more on this, see "Children's Books and Bias" on p. 343.)

• **Do the books promote peace and cooperation?** Books can teach powerful lessons about peace and cooperation. Choosing books with peaceful themes can help offset some of the violent images in children's media.

The Rosmarie Greiner Children's Peace Education Library exemplifies high-quality children's books. The library houses a wonderful collection of books for children from two and a half to six that support children's growth as peacemakers. In choosing books for the library, Rosmarie identified seven elements she saw as the fundamentals of peace education for the very young: sense of self, awareness of others, joy in diversity, love of nature, imagination, creative conflict resolution, and global awareness. These seven characteristics are good ones to look for in books if you want to encourage children's capacity for peace.[8]

[8] For an extensive bibliography and guide to choosing children's books from the Rosmarie Greiner Children's Peace Library, send $6.00 to: Peace Library, Early Childhood Education Department, Cabrillo College, 6500 Soquel Drive, Aptos, CA 95003.

• **What about the public library?** The public library is a wonderful resource in selecting children's books. You can check out a number of books, take them home, and get a sense of what both you and your child like. Tell the librarian how old your child is and what kinds of things she is interested in, and ask for a selection of books to choose from.

• **What about mail order?** For hard-to-find books, we suggest several mail-order services that specialize in quality children's books. You can call or write *Seeds of Change Bookstore*, 417 Capitola Avenue, Capitola, CA 95010; (408) 464-1601), or *Chinaberry Books*, (800) 776-2242), to receive a free catalogue. A good source of multiethnic children's titles is The Heritage Key, 6102 E. Mescal, Scottsdale, AZ 85254, (602) 483-3313.

Tips for Reading with Children

Reading with children can become a joyful, relaxed part of your daily routine. Here are some ideas for building a strong reading relationship with your child:

• **Make book sharing an intimate time.** Children ask for books for all kinds of reasons. Sometimes they want to hear a particular story. Other times they simply want to sit close and snuggle with you—and what better way than by sharing a book? You can keep reading times special by limiting interruptions. You don't have to limit yourself to the more traditional bedtime reading, either. How about a wake-up book? A before-bath book? A nothing's-working-today-let's-try-a-book book?

• **Go at your child's pace.** As adults, many of us are conditioned to read all the words on one page and then turn the page. Children, on the other hand, may want to dwell on one picture, image, or idea. They may not want to read books from start to finish. They may want to read only the beginning of a book or a favorite page in the middle. Allow your child to enjoy books at his own pace.

You also don't have to read all (or any) of the words. Children's capacity for length and number of words varies greatly. Some two-year-olds can sit for books with a lot of words; others will sit only for one or two words before they are up and gone.

• **Let your fingers do the walking.** Children love to have things pointed out to them in stories, and they love to point. Use your fingers to highlight different illustrations: "Oh, look, here's the hippo taking a bath." "Here's the baby lamb going night-night." Encourage children to do the same: "Where's that baby's nose?" Even very young children will delightedly thump on the baby's nose. And early on, children will try to lift the grapes right off from the page to eat them.

• **Books are interactive.** Talking about what's happening in books is a critical part of children's appreciation and learning. Each book has two story lines—the author's story line and the one you develop with your child. Be open to children's questions and digressions. Encourage your child's participation by asking questions as you go along: "Where do you think that monkey is hiding?" "Can you find the keys?" "What do you think is all wrapped up in that little white bag?" "What do you think Little Sal is going to do with those blueberries?" You can also can stop at a suspenseful point in the story and wait expectantly, giving your child the exciting opportunity to fill in the missing words.

• **Shape the story to suit your values.** When you're reading to children, you can read selectively. If there's a book you've always loved that you're not entirely comfortable with, you can take poetic license.

Ginny explained, "When I read fairy tales, I always change things around. When the book says the woman is beautiful, I take out the physical characteristic and say instead 'She's smart' or 'She's courageous.' If I know someone else is going to read her the stories, I actually change the words in the book itself. Now that she's almost six, I've started to talk to her about why I've made those changes. I say, 'I changed this word because I don't believe in it.' "

• **Be prepared to read the same stories again and again.** Children adore repetition. They will want the same books over and over. For that reason, it's a good idea to choose books that are pleasing to both you and your child.

• **Encourage your child to grow with his or her books.** Children appreciate books on a variety of levels. Some books, which are designed for older children, can be enjoyed by much younger children if you do some selective editing of the text. The illustrations of a beautiful alphabet book or counting book can be enjoyed by young children who aren't interested in numbers or letters yet.

You don't have to use a book solely as it was intended. You can summarize the story line, spin off your own story, or forget the words and focus on the pictures instead. Younger children may appreciate the images in a book and love naming familiar objects, while older children may be more interested in the story line, the theme, or the relationships between characters.

• **Children should have free access to at least some of their books.** Books that are placed on low shelves, that are as accessible as toys, benefit children. Displaying books in a way that children can see the covers, and not just the bindings, encourages them to choose and interact with books.

• **Physical exploration is part of how children become familiar with books.** In their earliest forays into the world of books, many children begin by touching, biting, chewing on, rearranging, piling, and dropping books. Children often love to practice turning pages, and this exercise in manual dexterity may or may not coincide with an interest in the story. Physical exploration is an integral part of getting comfortable with books. Fortunately, many wonderful sturdy board books are constructed specifically with young toddlers in mind. These books are made to withstand all kinds of innovative handling.

If you give your child a chance to thoroughly explore some books, you can also have some special books that the grown-ups help hold. One family called these "clean-hands" books. Truly precious (or fragile) books are best saved until a little later. With time, children will learn to respect books and care for them, if it's something that's modeled by the rest of the family.

• **Enjoy books yourself.** When children see everyone else in the family reading, they are naturally drawn to books themselves.

23. Children's Friendships: Cooperation and Conflict

"Now that Billy's a year old, he's getting into social conflicts. Kids are yelling and toys are being grabbed back and forth. I'm thinking, 'I've been a provider, a supporter, a diaper changer, a shoulder to cry on, but I've never been a mediator. How do I put on this new hat?' "

WAYNE, *first-time father*

The social impulses young children bring into relationships are spontaneous, energetic, and playful. Babies squeal with delight when they spot another child in the grocery store. Toddlers lay wet kisses on the cheeks of their buddies, and preschoolers beg to see their friends.

Yet these same social impulses can be hurtful and unpredictable. Imagine the following scene: You bundle up your fifteen-month-old daughter, Angie, and equip her with a red plastic pail and a bright yellow shovel and take her to the neighborhood park. When you arrive, you spot a friend of yours and his son, Robbie, playing on the swings. When Robbie bounces over and picks up Angie's shovel, she screams, "NOOOOOO! Mine! MINE!!!" and grabs it out of Robbie's hands. Everything Robbie touches evokes the same response from Angie. You try to intercede, but Angie's screaming only escalates. You smile apologetically at the other dad, but your gut is churning. You feel ashamed and embarrassed, angry and ineffectual. You want Angie to "behave," to "share," to "be friendly and nice" to the other child, but what's actually happening is that she's hysterically defending her turf. Soon both children, you, and the other father are miserable. Your park visit ends a lot sooner than anticipated, and you're pretty sure it will be a long time before that dad and child will want to visit with you again.

Afterward, you feel frustrated and confused. And you're left with some pretty big concerns: "Is Angie going to be able to get along with other kids? Will she have friends? Is there something wrong with her? With me? Is she spoiled? Selfish? Why can't she share?"

It is hardly fair that parents who haven't had advanced classes in conflict resolution are called upon to mediate high-level human interactions with people of limited language ability and experience, under the serious scrutiny of their peers. Yet that is precisely the situation parents of young children find themselves in every day.

Parents are often surprised at the amount of time they spend mediating conflicts between children. Yet children's conflicts are a natural, inevitable part of their social learning. How we respond to them determines, to a large degree, the lessons our children learn from their disagreements, fights, and squabbles. Teaching children the social skills of communication and conflict resolution is an essential part of parenting.

The challenge for many of us is that we're being asked to help children figure out solutions using tools we may not have learned ourselves and, furthermore, didn't anticipate would be needed. The good news is that we can learn right alongside our children. And the opportunities for practice are plentiful.

When we support children in resolving their own conflicts, the resolution of those conflicts may take longer and be noisier, but we will be helping our children learn about cause and effect, listening, feelings, self-expression, empathy, effective power sharing, and problem solving.

Children who are taught conflict-resolution skills develop self-assurance and a willingness to deal with differences constructively. Not only does this process give them tools they'll be able to use in future conflicts, it also respects that they are on their way to being creative, resourceful, and caring social participants.

The Evolution of Social Play

Children start on the road to social play as babies, by *watching* other children play. This kind of observation is the first step in learning to play socially.

Older babies and young toddlers start to enjoy playing in the same vicinity as other children. They don't necessarily play with the same materials or talk to each other, although they may be singing, talking, or babbling to themselves. Sometimes it seems that children don't even notice the others who are playing nearby, but their play is often more animated, busy, or long-lasting when it is done in the presence of other children.

In the next stage, toddlers or preschoolers play alongside each other, using the same kinds of props or toys, but each with his own separate fantasy or idea. They might speak to each other, alternate using the same toy, or incorporate ideas from the other child's play into their own, but their play themes stay separate. Lyle and Annalise, both three years old, were playing in the playhouse. Lyle was making birthday cake, carefully counting out the candles: "One, free, foar, six." Annalise was making waffles, pizza, burritos, and milkshakes, moving dishes around, arranging food, serving all the dolls and occasionally asking Lyle "You want thum buweetos?"

The most developed form of play that preschoolers engage in is called "cooperative play." Here, children share a common theme or idea. They work together to negotiate the rules and roles of the play. They say, "Let's play mail truck. You write the letters and I'll come and pick them up." "I know, you can be the big furry dog and I'll be the little baby dog." This kind of social play, which involves sophisticated verbal negotiation, usually doesn't happen until children are four or five.

Children progress through these stages as they go from babyhood to kindergarten, but like all growth, it doesn't happen in a straight line. Often, in new situations, children will return to a less sophisticated kind of play until they feel comfortable enough to engage in the more fully developed social play they are capable of.

Making Friends: An Overview of Social Development

Children aren't born knowing how to play with each other, but during their first five years, they develop skills that build a strong foundation for successful play and cooperative social interactions. Through social play, children gain important information about themselves and others.

Babies use social interactions with their peers to explore their own and each other's boundaries. They reach for faces, poke eyes, bite toes, and crawl over each other. As a ten-month-old reaches out to get a handful of his friend's ear, he begins to learn that touching his friend is different from touching himself.

Having figured out the boundaries of their own bodies, toddlers begin exerting control over the space and things around them. They bite, hit, shove, and kick their friends. They wonder "If I'm inside the playhouse and you come in, can I push you back out and keep the house for myself?" They seem incapable of sharing, and often they *are*. (As we explain in Chapter 24, "What Enables Children to Share?" certain developmental milestones have to be attained *before* children can share.)

Preschool-age children push the boundaries of control into the interpersonal realm. They continue with some toddler behaviors and go on to test the power of language as a means of making other children do what they want: "You be the daddy. But you *have* to be the daddy! If you won't be the daddy, I won't like you anymore." They also discover name-calling and exclusionary play: "You're a poo-poo head. You can't play with us!"

Children also use social play as a way to practice communication. A baby reaching for the fluffball of her friend's hair may be saying "I'm interested in you." A toddler who hits another child over the head with a plastic bat may be saying "I don't want you to stand there. You're too close to me." Or "Hey, you, let's play!" A preschooler who wants to invite a friend to play chase might bounce over in his direction yelling "You're a dummy, you're a dummy!" Lacking the words or experience to clearly communicate their ideas, children often try to begin social interactions using physical gestures or misleading words.

Children *want* to learn how to play with other kids, and these very missteps, which can distress parents, are a crucial part of learning. The amazing thing is that children keep coming back to try again, even if they weren't "successful" the first time. Thankfully, the urges that bring children into conflicts are often the same urges that can help them stay and resolve them—the urge to communicate, to connect, to have fun, and to figure things out about each other and with each other. Learning how to harness those urges toward problem solving is an essential part of building successful relationships.

Making Friends: How Does It Happen?

Initially young children make "friends" with children their parents know. "Friendship" is based on familiarity: "Heather is my friend because our moms visit and we lie on the blanket next to each other." Some of these early relationships grow into significant connections for children. If older babies and toddlers have regular and consistent opportunities to get together, a special friendship often develops.

Lorraine shares, "Kip and Kendra have been seeing each other twice a week since they were babies. When they turned eighteen months old, Miranda and I started taking turns watching them. They are at her house on Wednesday mornings and at mine on Fridays. They are twenty-six months old now. There are still plenty of fights, but they have a great time together and ask about each other every day."

Older toddlers and preschoolers often begin to choose their own friends from a larger group of children in their neighborhood, preschool, or child care center. At this point, children may be drawn to certain kids and may spend much of their time playing with a particular child. Parents can still support these friendships by meeting the other child's parents and arranging for some "one-on-one" play time. Since children play very differently in a group setting from how they play with just one other child, having individual children to your home to play on a regular basis

allows children to explore and deepen these friendships.

Temperament and Friendship: A Wide Range

Children's temperaments affect the ways they play with others, the kinds of friendships they make, the time it takes to develop a friendship, and the particular children they choose for friends. Some children are very social. Even as babies, they crawl over all the toys in the room to mouth the baby sitting in the corner. They smile readily at people they don't know. They may enjoy large and busy gatherings. As toddlers, they may be the ones who greet each new toddler they meet by grabbing their toy or hugging them until they fall down. As preschoolers, they prefer spending time with friends over any other activity. These children do well in groups and may have a harder time playing alone.

Parents may need to help these children learn how to approach other children without bowling them over. They may also need to support these children in learning to play alone.

At the other end of the continuum are children who are less gregarious, take more time to warm up, and enjoy smaller, familiar groups. As babies, they may look away or cry when they are approached by unfamiliar people and may be less comfortable being held by people they don't know. As toddlers and preschoolers, they may prefer playing with one or two special friends rather than a wide variety of children. These children are often very perceptive socially and can develop significant and trusting relationships.

Parents of these children can help them get comfortable by giving them time to warm up and by providing familiar, small, low-key child care or social gatherings. Parents can also help the world to understand these children: "No, she's not shy, she is very interested in what is going on. She just likes to take her time to get comfortable before she starts to play."

Children at both ends of this continuum sometimes get stuck with labels: "She is so aggressive." "He is the bashful one." Yet social styles all along this continuum are healthy. While it's important to acknowledge each child's individual temperament, it's equally important not to pigeonhole him.

Helping Children Make Friends: Issues for Parents

Parents want their children to be kind, well liked, and friendly. If we have a child who makes friends easily, who is outgoing and gregarious, we may feel particularly fortunate, but if our child hangs back, is hesitant around new people, or doesn't make friends readily, we may worry, wondering why we have an "unpopular" child.

It can be particularly difficult if the social style of our child is opposite to our own. An outgoing parent may have unrealistic expectations of a more reticent child. And a quieter, more introverted parent may be challenged by an extroverted child who makes friends with everyone at the bus stop.

Dealing with Children's Conflicts

Most of us have been trained to avoid conflicts, not to welcome them as learning opportunities. When we see our two-year-old head straight for the shiny new toy held by a child in the sand box, we cringe; when we watch our four-year-old scream at her best friend and bring her to tears, we feel terrible.

Because few of us have had training or experience in successful conflict resolution, many of us come to children's conflicts with prepared scripts or expectations that may, in fact, hinder our ability to facilitate a rich learning experience. Examples of such scripts are: "Whoever had it first gets it," "Whoever started it is wrong," "The older child has to give in to the needs of the younger," and "Children should always share."

Early in her parenting, Janis operated out of the script "the faster the better." She recalls: "I did whatever was necessary to get everyone quiet as soon as possible. In the process, I often manipulated children, encouraged them to ignore their feelings, prevented them from discovering their own solutions, and generally communicated that adults were the only ones capable of resolving disputes. I gave them the message that conflicts were bad and that they should be avoided whenever possible."

Another dilemma parents face in responding to children's conflicts is finding agreement with the other child's parent. Parents have different levels of comfort with children's struggles, and not all believe that children should be helped to find their own solutions. Finding common ground while children are screaming at each other can be daunting.

José recalls, "My daughter Leti and I were visiting my sister's family. Shortly after we arrived, Leti and her cousin Bennie both started pulling on this big stuffed brontosaurus. They were holding on for dear life, screaming. I went over and began talking to them about it. My sister Renee came over, snatched the dinosaur away, and put it up on a shelf. She said, 'You kids find something else to do.' I know she was trying to be helpful, but I really wanted to help the kids work it out."

Other issues for parents include discomfort with the strong expression of feelings, dismay over physical aggression, feeling pulled in several directions because of competing priorities and needs, as well as feelings of inadequacy, fatigue, anger, or frustration. Yet despite these obstacles, it's possible for parents to develop the

skills, perspective, and knowledge they need to successfully mediate children's conflicts.

Assumptions for Successful Conflict Resolution

Five basic assumptions about people in conflicts are at the root of our model for successful intervention in children's conflicts:

- **Behind every behavior is an impulse or an attempt to communicate that can be supported.** Even "hostile" gestures can come from a basic desire to communicate.[1]

- **People hurt others only as much as they themselves are hurting.** When children hurt other children, it is often because they are feeling hurt, mad, or scared themselves. A child

[1] For an in-depth look at this idea, see "Honoring the Impulse" on p. 226.

who pushes another child out of the toy car may be feeling crowded and scared. A child who walks up and hits another child may have just been called a "dummy" by somebody else.

When a child is hurting other children, it can be hard to remember that he's feeling vulnerable or scared himself. But if you merely punish him, you load more hurt on to the existing hurt and, in the long run, perpetuate the cycle of hurtful behavior. If instead you take into account his circumstances and motivation, you can approach conflict resolution from a less punitive perspective than "Let's punish the wrongdoer."

• **People in a conflict are best served by a mutual solution.** When conflicts are resolved in such a way that somebody "wins" and somebody "loses," there are always scores to be settled later on. Mutual solutions are far more satisfying to everyone in the long run.[2]

• **Everyone deserves to be listened to.** Really listening to another person's point of view, while being able to clearly state your own, is at the core of effective problem solving. Listening helps people grow. Even when people's opposing desires, needs, and wants make it impossible to come up with a mutual solution, people who feel their ideas have been heard and valued experience a lot less disappointment and anger when they don't get what they want.

• **Conflicts are resolved only when each person involved in the conflict is finished with the interaction.** As long as someone in the conflict still has unresolved feelings or ideas about the conflict, the conflict isn't over. All parties need to participate in the resolution of the conflict until it's resolved from everyone's point of view. Some children will need a break before they're ready to talk, but coming back and discussing what happened is important for a sense of real resolution.

The Basics of Conflict Resolution

The basic skills you need for effective conflict resolution are active listening, sportscasting, and negotiation. These were introduced in Chapter 19, "Moving Beyond Punishment."

In all conflicts between children, your role is to keep children safe and to help them learn problem-solving tools. With babies and young toddlers, your main role will be describing what you see, reflecting feelings, and demonstrating appropriate behavior. With older toddlers and preschoolers, you can facilitate their interaction by listening and by asking strategic questions that help them discover mutual solutions.

• **Think about what you want to teach.** As always, it's important to think about the values and ideas you want to teach children. This is at the core of any facilitation you provide.

• **Assess the situation.** It's important to take a quick look at your own energy and the energy of the kids who are struggling. Dozens of potential conflicts can come up in a day, and no parent is going to have the time or energy to go through a thorough facilitation process each time. You do it when you have the resources and the time. You try to make it consistent enough that kids learn enough skills to begin to resolve simple conflicts on their own.

In your role as mediator, you get to choose. When a fight breaks out, take a quick inventory: "How much energy do *I* have to help them right now?" and "Do *they* have the energy to learn from this?" There are times it's more realistic to give children a couple of limited

[2] For more on what happens when solutions are one-sided and for more on conflicts between siblings, see "What Is the Parents' Role in Children's Conflicts?" on p. 411.

choices or to provide an adult-initiated solution than it is to involve them in coming up with their own solutions.

• **Calm yourself.** The more calmness, confidence, and clarity you bring to children's fights, the more useful your facilitation will be. When children are screaming and yelling and hitting each other, it's easy to get caught up in their emotions, to become agitated and anxious. Whenever possible, take a moment to find a place of stillness before you approach two struggling children.

• **Keep both parties safe.** If one child is hurting another child, get down to the children's level, step in, and stop the interaction. Firmly and gently hold back the child who is about to hit, bite, shove, push, or slap. Set clear limits both in words and physically: "I'm not going to let you hit Ahmed. Hitting hurts."

• **Model what you want to teach.** With babies, this might mean gently stroking a child's hair and saying "Gentle" after he's pulled another child's hair. With a toddler, you could say, "Tell Ahmed 'Move back!' " in a strong voice to model an alternative to hitting. With preschoolers, you could demonstrate what it looks like to brainstorm solutions to a problem. With all children, you can model effective listening.

• **Focus on the children rather than the toy they're fighting over.** When children are grabbing toys from each other, a common solution is to find one of the children something else to play with: "Oh, here's another ball." However, if you always just supply toys, you're not putting the same value on human relationships as you are on objects. When you focus instead on helping kids work things out, you give them the message "The fact that you learn how to communicate is more important than who gets the ball."

• **Help children communicate.** When children are engaged in conflict, the adult's job is to help them figure out what they're trying to communicate and to help them find a safe, successful way to get their message across. In order to do this, you may need to keep the children together to "talk."

If one child still has something to say and the other child has walked away, this might mean walking over to that child and saying "Ahmed has something to say to you. Come over here so we can talk." Or you might say to Ahmed, who's been left standing there, "Do you still have something to say to Gina? Do you want me to go over with you to talk to her?" Some of the time, all Ahmed may be able to "say" is more crying, but being listened to teaches Ahmed that his feelings and perspective are important.

• **Support effective communication.** When Ahmed is standing there crying, you could offer a suggestion based on your observation: "Are you telling Gina that you still want the rake?" "Are you trying to see if Gina will play with you?" A preschool child might be able to respond to the question "Adam, what's your idea?" "What are you telling Mikey?" Or "Mikey, what are you trying to say?"

• **Encourage both parties to listen to each other.** You can say "Gina, do you see that Ahmed is still crying? He's still feeling upset that you took the rake." With preschool children, you can ask for more acknowledgment: "Adam, did you hear Mikey's idea?" "Can you tell me what Mikey's idea is?"

If there's an object that's being fought over, and the child who has grabbed it is engrossed in playing with it, he's not going to be motivated to listen to the other child. You may need to say to him "I want you to bring that rake over here while you talk to Gina." Or "I'm going to hold the rake while we figure out what to do."

• **Clarify communication by reframing name-calling and other hurtful language.** With three-, four-, and five-year-olds, you can model accurate and appropriate language. When Adam yells, "You poo-poo head!" you can say, "Adam, it sounds like you're really mad at Mikey." When Mikey yells, "He's a stupid dummy!" you can say, "Mikey, it sounds like you really don't like Adam's idea." You can also help children move from negative to positive information: "Adam, I heard you tell Mikey 'Don't take my shoe!' What would you like Mikey to do?"

• **Encourage problem solving.** Preschoolers may be capable of generating some of their own

Why It Doesn't Work to Make Kids Say They're Sorry

It happens every day. Our child hurts another child by snatching a toy, hitting, shoving, or calling names, and we step in and say, "Tell him you're sorry." We ask children to apologize because we want them to learn important lessons, to be socially appropriate, to be accountable for their actions, to show respect, to get along, to have and keep friends. We also experience pressure from other parents who expect us to make our kids say "I'm sorry." It's the response we've seen modeled most often.

"I'm sorry" can also come from our sense of discomfort and embarrassment at what our children have done. We want to hurry on to the completion of the painful episode, and in our mind, we hope "I'm sorry" ends it. But does it?

We often ask kids to say they're sorry before the children figure out what actually happened. Two-year-old Jody hits her friend Amy, and Amy starts to cry. Jody is surprised and upset by Amy's tears, but has no idea that Amy was hurt or that she had anything to do with that hurt. Because Jody doesn't understand this basic progression of events, she has no basis on which to *feel* sorry. Making her say "I'm sorry" doesn't give her any useful information about what happened.

It's more useful to bring Amy and Jody together and to go over the situation with them: "You were playing together and you hit Amy and now Amy is crying. Let's figure out what you were trying to tell Amy and see if we can do something to help her feel better."

When you insist on "I'm sorry," you may actually interfere with a real resolution of the problem and keep children from figuring out their own compassionate response.

Children who are given the opportunity to participate in helping the other child feel better often do amazing things: bring their blanket (or the other child's), get ice, or volunteer a hug. When children aren't pressured into making a pat response, they watch intently, learn about the other child's hurt, and, if given the opportunity, in their own time, find ways to express their caring and concern.

While apologizing can sometimes help a child get out of a situation, kids don't learn compassion by saying "I'm sorry." They do, however, learn sequencing fairly readily, and *can* learn that saying "I'm sorry" goes with certain actions. They can kick another child, say "Sorry," and go on to another activity. This may mislead kids into thinking the interaction is done, that saying the words "I'm sorry" resolves the situation. However, it's the feelings behind the words and the child's ability to alter his behavior that we're really interested in.

Ultimately, we make rules about conduct because we want our children to be compassionate, and we're not sure that compassion evolves naturally. But with support, it does. By bringing children together to talk and listen to each other, and by modeling respect for people's feelings, we give them the message that we eventually expect them to be able to care about other people. In doing so, we assist them in becoming responsive, empathetic people.

solutions. You can encourage this by saying, "It looks like you're both still holding on to that shovel. You both really want it. Can either of you think of a way to solve this problem?" Or "Mikey, can you think of a solution that both you and Adam might like?" Or "Adam, can you think of a solution that Mikey might also like?"

• **Look for a mutual solution.** Once children have come up with possible solutions, check each one out with the other child: "Mikey, do you like that idea?" If Mikey doesn't, ask him, "Can you think of another idea?" Keep working until you find a solution both kids accept. Sometimes one child will go get the other child another toy. Sometimes one child will hand over the sought-after object. Other times they'll both do something else together or one child will walk away. The solution works if both children seem at peace with it even if it doesn't fit adult notions of "fairness."

Conflict Resolution in Action: Toddlers

Let's look at an example of this kind of conflict resolution in action. Eli has a best friend named Roxie. They've been spending time together since they were infants. For many months, all was peaceful, but when they reached toddlerhood, the inevitable conflicts broke out.

A typical conflict occurred when both kids were a year-and-a-half old. Roxie's mom, Kathy, and Laura were watching them play on the back porch. Eli was pushing Roxie down at every possible opportunity. As Laura later recounted to Janis, "It's one thing to understand these things in theory, but in practice, it's a lot harder. When Eli is shoving Roxie, I feel bad inside. I wonder why I have such an aggressive child. I wonder if Kathy will want Roxie to play with Eli any more. I think about the fact that he's a boy and he's shoving a girl to the ground. In the midst of all that static in my head, it's hard for me to stay in touch with all the important things both kids could be learning from this interaction."

Janis asked, "So what happened?"

Laura replied: "I said to Eli, 'I'm not going to let you push Roxie,' and I physically restrained him so he couldn't do it again. Kathy and I stayed close by and had both kids face each other. I said to Eli, 'When you push Roxie down, it hurts her and now she's crying.'

Janis nodded, smiling. "That's teaching empathy and unconditional love. You're telling Eli 'I'm not going to let you push Roxie, but I still love you. You're not a bad kid. And eventually I want you to understand what Roxie's feeling."

Laura went on: "Then Kathy said to Roxie, 'You don't want Eli to push you! You can tell Eli 'NO!' " And Roxie vehemently shook her head back and forth and repeated 'NO!' "

Janis interjected, "Roxie was learning to recognize and express her feelings. She was learning about effective communication. Kathy was saying to her 'I believe you can state your idea and I believe other people will listen to you." By helping Roxie respond effectively to Eli, Kathy was also teaching her daughter to be assertive—that she didn't have to be a victim."

Laura continued: "Then I let Eli go and he went to push Roxie again. I stopped him and said, 'It looks like you're frustrated at having Roxie so close to you. Do you want Roxie to move?' His body language affirmed my guess. So I told him, "You can tell her 'Move!' Then he said to her 'Move!' And Roxie moved back really fast!"

Janis said, "You helped him identify his feelings. You helped him be more articulate, more safe and effective in his communication. You modeled a strong, powerful voice. And when Roxie moved back, he saw how effective communication could work in the context of relationships."

Laura added, "But then he kept trying to push her and I kept having to stop him. I got really worn out. I just wished he'd stop pushing her."

Janis responded, "Sometimes children are too tired, hungry, or overstimulated to successfully resolve a conflict. They're stuck. They can't figure out how to be together successfully. Sometimes they need time apart. When one child has consistently been pushed down or had everything grabbed out of her hands, it may be time to end the visit or to intervene more actively, saying 'Roxie's been playing with that. I'm going to stop you from taking it.' Or 'Right now, I'm going to help Roxie hold on to it.'

"But a lot of times, kids are able and willing to struggle with the conflict. They're screaming at the top of their lungs, but five minutes later, they're ready to play again. Often it's the parents have too much discomfort with the volume and intensity of the feelings to help kids work through their conflict."

Laura interjected, "Sometimes I feel ashamed I don't have a nice child. It's hard to see my not-nice child out in the world."

Janis replied, "It's important that you want Eli to stop pushing and grabbing, but that awareness needs to be in balance with the appreciation of him as an evolving person who is working on building empathy but doesn't fully have it yet."

"I Want the Wagon! I Had It First!": Preschoolers and Conflict Resolution

As children get older, their ability to solve conflicts increases. Preschool-age children are capable of incorporating more complicated negotiation skills into the basic skills of listening, stating their ideas, and working on empathy.

Let's take a conflict between four-year-old Ellie and five-year-old Mariel in a preschool setting. Both girls are fighting over a wagon. When their teacher, Mark, comes on the scene, the conflict has escalated. Both girls are holding tight to the handle of the wagon and pulling with all their might. They are yelling and screaming at each other, hurling insults, and asking Mark to take their side in the dispute. An effective facilitation on Mark's part might go something like this:

Mariel: NOOOO! I want to pull it!
Ellie: No, I want to pull it! Let go!
Mariel: I had it first! Let go of my wagon!
Ellie: But she's had it all morning!
Mark: *(stabilizing the wagon with his hand)* It sounds like you both really want that wagon. I see that you're both holding on to the handle and pulling really hard. *(Mark maintains safety, uses active listening and sportscasting.)* It looks like there's only one

wagon and two people who want to pull. *(Mark outlines the problem.)*

Mariel: I had it first! She's a dummy!

Mark: *(to Mariel)* It sounds like you're really feeling mad. You really want the wagon. *(He reframes name-calling and validates Mariel's feelings.)*

Mark: *(to Ellie)* How does it feel when you're called a dummy?

Ellie: I don't like it.

Mark: You can tell Mariel you don't like it. *(He listens to the child who's been hurt and encourages her to state her feeling.)*

Ellie: *(to Mariel)* I don't like it! Don't say that to me!

Mark: *(to Mariel)*: Calling someone a dummy can hurt her feelings. You can tell her instead "I'm mad. I want the wagon!" *(He provides social information and an alternative means of expression.)*

Mariel: I'm mad! I want the wagon.

Mark: You're both feeling pretty mad right now.

Ellie: I want it. I want the wagon.

Mark: *(to Ellie)* Ellie, what's your idea? What do you want to do with the wagon? *(He encourages each child to state her perspective and idea.)*

Ellie: I want to pull the wagon over to the fence.

Mark: *(to Mariel)* Mariel, what's your idea? What do you want to do with the wagon?

Mariel: I want to pull it really fast so I can go get the dolls that are caught in the tree.

Mark: *(to Ellie)* So, Ellie, what do you think Mariel wants? *(He builds empathy by getting each child to state the other's point of view.)*

Ellie: I don't know!

Mark: *(to Mariel)* Mariel, could you tell Ellie what your idea is?

Mariel: I want to pull the wagon over to the tree to rescue the dolls.

Mark: *(to Ellie)* So, Ellie. Now do you know what Mariel wants?

Ellie: But I don't want her to pull the wagon!

Mark: *(to Ellie)* So you heard Mariel say she wanted to pull the wagon. *(And to Mariel)* And do you remember what Ellie said she wanted to do?

Mariel: She wants to pull it fast.

Mark: Okay, so we have two children who both want to pull the wagon. You both have different ideas about what to do with it. And we only have one wagon. *(He validates each person's perspective and restates the problem.)*

Mark: Ellie, do you have an idea that Mariel might also like? *(He helps the girls generate ideas that might solve the problem.)*

Ellie: I get to pull it first.

Mark: Mariel, is that okay with you? *(He checks out the potential solution and builds consensus.)*

Mariel: No! I get to pull it first.

Mark: Mariel, do you have an idea that Ellie might like?

Mariel: We could pull it really fast to rescue the dolls.

Mark: Ellie, what do you think about that?

Ellie: I want to rescue the dolls. I want to!

Mark: So you'd like to go with Mariel to get the dolls?

Ellie: Yes, I want to.

Mark: Is that okay with you, Mariel?

Mariel: Yes.

(And both girls take off together with the wagon.)

Although specific responses may vary (most conflicts wouldn't require all of these techniques), this kind of intervention often leads children to find their own mutually satisfying solutions.

Often a solution is generated right away. Sometimes it takes longer. When children are unable to come up with a solution on the first try, the adult can wait it out, repeating the negotiating steps outlined above, asking "Mariel, do you have another idea we can try?" or offer an idea of his own. Another thing you can do is call over Stu, who's riding a tricycle nearby, and describe the situation to him: "Both of these girls want to pull the wagon. Do you have an idea of what they could do?"

Many times Stu, as an outsider to the conflict, will be able to come up with a workable solution. He may reiterate a solution both girls have already considered and rejected (which they now suddenly accept), he may mention that there's another wagon available, or he may come up with a third alternative they haven't thought of but that satisfies them both. Even if Stu doesn't come up with a viable solution, inviting him into the problem solving teaches the children about the value of community—that just because two people are having a problem doesn't mean they have to solve it all by themselves.

FOOD FOR THOUGHT: CHILDREN'S CONFLICTS

- How were fights between children settled when I was a child? What did that teach me?

- What expectations do I bring with me when I walk into a conflict situation?

- What would I like to teach my children about resolving conflicts?

"You Can't Play with Us": Exclusionary Play

At four and five, a new dynamic emerges in children's play. Two kids who are digging a tunnel in the sand box shut out a third child: "You can't play with us. We don't want you here. Go away!"

When parents first hear their child reject another child, or when their child is rejected, they're often devastated. Parents worry whether their child is becoming a bully or whether their child is always going to be picked on or excluded. It's unnerving to see your child actively hurting other people's feelings or being hurt. But knowing where exclusionary play comes from can help parents move through these initial reactions toward an effective, appropriate response.

Why Exclusionary Play? A Developmental Look

In order to understand exclusionary play, we have to revisit the evolution of play. When children begin to play together as toddlers, they mostly bump into each other and play with the same materials in the same areas. At times, they may have loosely defined play where they are mommies, cooks, or firefighters, but usually there aren't a lot of agreements made between the kids.

In this stage, children aren't at all sure what it is that makes their play work. Often two children just stumble on something that engages both of them. They may not know how to make it happen again. Even as they near four, children aren't sure that they can hold their play together. When another child comes and wants to play, there may be some fear that their play will be lost if they let another child join. So the first two children exclude the third child because they're reluctant to upset the delicate success they've achieved. In this scenario, exclusionary play comes from a fairly innocent place: "I can't figure out how to include another person and I'm scared we'll lose this play if you join us."

Children of this age also understand that they play differently with different friends. It can be a stretch for them to be with their block-building friend, Darla, when they're already playing with Tracy, their doll-playing buddy. They don't know how to be simultaneously the person who plays with blocks *and* the person who plays with dolls.

At three or four, as children begin to engage in cooperative play—play in which one theme or idea governs the play of two or more children—the question arises: Who gets to make the decisions about how the play is going to go? In trying to answer that question, a lot of negotiating and testing goes on. Children experiment with different methods of having control over the play.

Those methods may include threats: "If you won't be the puppy, then you can't play with us." "If you don't wear this hat, I won't be your friend." "If you won't give me that shovel, you can't come to my birthday party." Children investigate the role pressure and power plays in relationships.

Kids also use exclusionary play to explore other children's feelings: "What happens when I say that you can't play here? Does it make you cry?"

Children also don't understand the parameters of friendship. They often assume that playing with a child makes them "friends," and conversely, that *not* playing together means they're "not friends." So if Jasper wants to play with his friend Nona in the sand box, and he doesn't want anyone else to join in, he might say to Scott, who wants to join them "You're not my friend anymore" rather than "You can't play with us right now."

Exclusionary play can also be used as a way for two children to bond: "We're friends if we can agree on something and, right now, the thing we can agree on is that we don't want to play with Lynette." Children who are engaging in this kind of exclusion may actually follow Lynette around, taunting "We don't want to play with you. We don't like you." It's almost as if Lynette becomes an integral part of the play by being the odd person out.

Finally, exclusionary play can arise from a particular turn in cognitive development that takes place during the preschool years. Children begin to think in terms of categories: They realize that fish are different from birds, that there are people inside their family and people outside their family. When children discover that there are some people who are like them and some who are different, they may use those categories as ways to exclude other children: "Only girls can play here!" "We don't want any boys!" "Only people with ponytails can play."

Responding to Exclusionary Play

Parents often respond to exclusionary play by overriding children's wishes. They insist that children include the child who's being pushed out, saying "You have to let Jenny play ambulance with you." They tell children, "You're not being nice. Let Peter be a pirate, too." While these strategies can sometimes be successful, they don't help kids resolve the conflict themselves.

Here are some ways to include children in the problem solving:

• **Acknowledge the play that is already going on.** Because children are often worried about loss of control or a loss of their play, acknowledging what they're playing can reassure them. You can say to Aaron and Donnie, "It looks like you're digging a deep tunnel in the sand box." Or "It looks like you're getting dressed up to go out. Are you two headed to the grocery store again?"

Once you get the children who are doing the excluding talking about their play, there's often much less resistance to having someone else join in because they feel more confident that their play is going to be valued and not overrun.

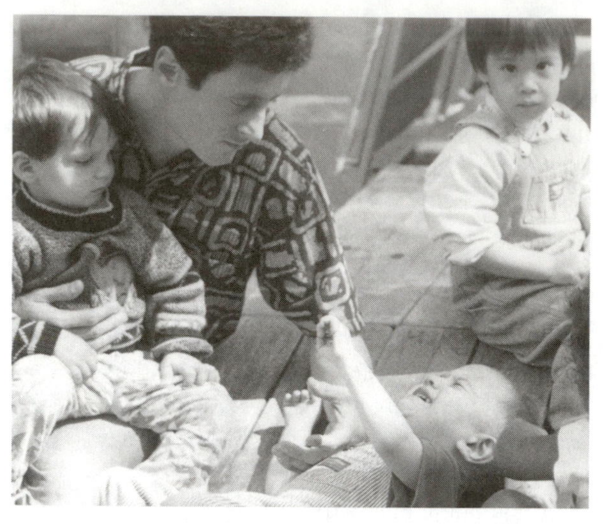

• **Invite children's initiative.** Use specific or open-ended questions to help children think of ways their play might be extended to make room for another child: "Is there a way that Cheung could help you with that tunnel?" "Do you need someone to bring over the wheelbarrow to help you move that dirt?" "Do you need someone to load your groceries?" Frequently, when you acknowledge children's play and suggest ways to integrate another child into the existing play, they find a way to open their play to the third child.

• **Make sure the child who's being excluded has a voice.** Intervening adults often speak for the child who is being excluded, inadvertently setting that child up in a passive role. It's important to check with the child: "How do you feel about that?" "What would you like to play?" "Is that idea okay with you?" "How is it for you when kids talk to you like that?" "Was there anything else you wanted to say?" As in all conflict situations, if the excluded child still has feelings or wants to talk about what happened, the others need to listen to what he has to say. Ultimately, whether excluded children get into the play is not as important as being allowed to express their feelings, state their ideas, and be heard.

• **Respect children's right to choose.** Sometimes two children are really involved in their play with each other. They've just discovered their special connection or are exploring the idea of "privacy." Preschoolers are capable of establishing strong friendships, and that should be respected.

In a situation where the excluded child will have no one else to play with, an activity that includes everybody needs to be negotiated. However, in a larger group, when two children want to play alone, you can teach them to help the third child find something else to do: "Misha, we want to play alone right now, but maybe you could go play fire chief with Troy." In setting those kind of parameters, you give children the message that it's okay to exclude someone from their play but not from their caring.

• **Keep some play areas open for all children.** When you're dealing with a group of children, you can set up a rule that particular children can't monopolize a whole play area: "If you're in the sand box, you can't keep other children out of the sand box. The sand box is for everybody." In other words, you may decide not to include Tyler in your immediate game, but he still gets to play in the sand.

• **Establish safety limits to prevent children from being physically or emotionally hurt.** You can set ground rules: "It's not okay to use those kinds of names with kids. Those are hurtful words. Let's figure out another way to say what you're trying to say." Or "It's not okay to tell anyone that they're ugly. Those words hurt Carla, and I'm not going to let you hurt anyone's feelings." Or "I wonder if you're trying to tell Carla 'I just want to play with Gwen. I want it to be just the two of us.' "

In the scenario in which two children were chasing a third to tell her she couldn't play with them, you could intervene and say: "It looks like you really want to play with Lynette. You're chasing her all over the yard. Is there another game you could play with her?"

• **Find ways to challenge exclusions based on categorical thinking.** Working with categories is developmentally appropriate thinking for preschoolers, but we still don't want to allow children to treat somebody differently based on their membership in a particular group.[3] As well as letting children know that they aren't permitted to exclude someone because she or he is a "girl" or a "boy" or has "curly hair," it is also important to challenge children's categorical thinking.

You can do this by asking "So what do you need to be able to do to play here?" Kids may answer, "You need to be really strong so you can dig deep." "You need to be able to build." "You need to have a cape." Once they've delineated the necessary skills, you can turn to the child who's being excluded and say, "Do you know how to build?" "Do you have strong muscles that can dig?" "Shall we find you a cape?" More often than not, that child will say "Yes," and then she has a ticket in because she's got the necessary qualifications. That kind of gentle challenge can help kids break down stereotypes.

In cases where children set up skills that are beyond the abilities of another child, you can help them identify the particular skills that child could bring to the play: "You're right, Henry can't stomp in the puddle with rain boots, but he could use his wheelchair to bring wood over for a bridge. What do you think, Henry? What would you like to do?"

In cases where kids can't get past a categorical rule such as "Girls can't play here!" you may have to step in and make a clear statement: "You can't stop someone from playing just because she's a girl. And we also don't stop boys from playing anywhere just because they're boys."

• **Set the stage for success.** If you find that having two of your son's buddies over at the same time usually ends up with one being excluded, you may want to stick to having just one friend for awhile.

[3] For more on this idea, see "Helping Children Learn About Unfairness" on p. 364.

24. What Enables Children to Share?

"I knew a woman who was teaching sports to kids in Africa. And she decided to teach them how to run a race. After explaining the basics, she lined them up, showed them the finish line, and said, 'Ready, set, go!' And all the children joined hands and ran together until they crossed the finish line. Their culture had such an emphasis on sharing and community that competing against each other never even entered their minds!"
JESSICA, *mother of Heidi*

Most parents want their children to be sharing, empathetic people. They want them to get along with their peers, to form loving, close friendships, to experience the give and take of caring. That desire to have children be gracious, generous, and gregarious runs smack into a developmental wall: Most children (in this society at least) go through a stage where real sharing is impossible.

In order to understand what makes it possible for children to share—and what you can do to help children develop into caring, thoughtful people—it's important that we look at two things: the child's developmental readiness and the culture of the family.

Issues for Parents: A Culture of Sharing?

The culture in which a child grows up influences what that child learns about sharing, privacy, ownership, and the relationship between individual and community needs. Janis recalls: "A friend of mine from Colombia told me that two-year-olds in his country don't go through a period of 'mine' the same way children do here. He explained that Colombian children have far fewer toys and that they are taught, from a very early age, that individuals survive only when the community pulls together."

When you look at the society we live in, it's clear children are being taught a different message. Our nation is built on individualism, competition, personal worth, and ownership. We admire those who have acquired the most, who are the best, who stand out in some way. A lot of our focus is on what we have, how we can get more, and what we can do to protect what's ours. Sharing freely is not the predominant inclination in this society.

Shu Lea speculated on the impact this has on our kids: "So many of our adult possessions are off limits to kids. From the time they're very young, kids are being taught that there are certain things they can't touch or play with. We tell them, 'This thing belongs to Mommy and that thing belongs to Daddy.' And I can't help but wonder how much of that contributes to the difficulty they have learning to share. I see it as one more area in which our particular culture and our particular lifestyle make child rearing more difficult."

It's ironic, in light of this larger cultural context, that most parents place such an emphasis on the need for young children to share. To a large extent, we are asking our children to do something that runs counter to a cultural norm. We want them to practice something different from what they see around them.

How Does My Family Feel About Sharing?

Families vary widely in their values around sharing. There are families in which all of the toys in the family are considered joint property. When children have friends over, all of the children in the household are welcome to play with those friends. No one would think of closing the door and saying "You can't play here." At the other end of the continuum are families in which each child has his own separate toys and place to play and no one in the family is asked to share any belongings or friends.

Most families fall somewhere in the middle. Pilar explained: "Our boys are five years apart. At first we expected Glen, our oldest, to share everything, to gracefully relinquish every toy he outgrew. He and Andy shared a room for six years. But then Glen started having a really hard time. Every one of his toys was broken or had missing parts. So we got each boy a footlocker, complete with keys and their names on them. We told them, 'This is your private space and nobody can touch what's in your footlocker.' It seemed really important, especially for Glen, to have some privacy, some kind of boundaries."

Leah, whose birth children are three and five, came up with a similar solution. "Our foster kids get gifts from their parents that are really important to them. Those toys give them a sense of belonging that they desperately need. But we are a huge family and we have to share. We cannot buy individual toys for each child. We don't have the money or the room.

"What we finally came up with is that each person's bed is their special place. While they're in their bed, they won't be disturbed, except by invitation. No one else touches the stuff that's on their bed. They can bring their special things out into the common areas of the house, but if they don't want to share them when they're done, they need to bring them back to their bed. That gives them a sense of protection and ownership.

"This works for my kids, too. They have to share so much already with the foster kids: their parents, their house, their friends. They need a safe place where they can retreat, as well."

Where families fall on the continuum of private vs. communal rights determines what they are going to model and teach about sharing, personal rights and responsibilities, and the role the individual plays in relation to the larger family and community. And a lot of it depends on the parents' own needs for private time and space.

But even in families where sharing is modeled and emphasized, children frequently go through a stage where they're just not developmentally ready to share, even though their environment supports it.

Food for Thought: Sharing

- What did I learn in my family of origin about sharing? Are those values I want to pass on in my family now?
- Are there other values about sharing or being a member of a community I would like to teach?
- How do our family members share with each other? With the larger community?

Developmental Readiness: Issues for Toddlers

It is our belief that you can't force a child to share. By definition, sharing is something that's freely offered, freely given. Yet many parents spend a lot of time trying to *make* their children share. In large part, this is due to the fact that many parents find it hard to believe that their kids are going to be able to learn to share without being prodded or cajoled into it. It is hard to hold on to a vision of children as evolving into sharing, empathetic people while they're grabbing, hitting, and screaming at anyone who approaches their things.

Phyllis, who was in a parent group with Janis for years, explains: "Kim used to systematically go around to each of the children in our toddler group and grab whatever it was they had in their hands or push them down. I was mortified and Janis had to repeatedly reassure me that Kim was a very social person who would one day be able to express those impulses in a safer, more successful way. That was six years ago. Now Kim is eight and she's one of the most sensitive, socially perceptive people I know."

Most children, like Kim, go through a period of time in which they can't share. If, however, you understand the building blocks that enable children to share, it can help you develop the faith that kids will get there, even though their current behavior may still be far from showing the empathy, flexibility, and generosity you hope they'll eventually achieve.

Understanding the Concept of "Mine"

In order to share what's yours, you have to understand that it's yours to begin with. For most toddlers, that exploration begins sometime during the end of their first year or early in their second. Children hear Daddy saying "Don't jump on my bed." Mommy says, "Put Mommy's hammer down." Big sister says, "Give me that. That's my brush." They begin to realize that "my" and "mine" are powerful, pivotal words, yet toddlers don't know exactly how they work. So they begin to explore them.

This is the stage in which you see toddlers rushing over to the neighbor child and knocking her off the rocking horse, screaming "Mine!" The fact that your child hasn't shown interest in the rocking horse for months doesn't matter; at that moment, it's become the most important thing in the whole world.

In a child care setting, you'll see a child who is grappling to understand "mine" desperately holding on to all of the trucks or all of the dolls or all of the play-dough in the room. The child is so sure there isn't enough that he's driven to hold on to all of it, even if that means he doesn't have any hands left to play with.

At this time, children are defining themselves in terms of their possessions: "This is my *arm*. This is my *truck*. This is my *bellybutton*. Here *I* am!!"

Do Eight-Month-Old Babies Really Share?

Many of us delight in watching "sharing" between our eight-month-old babies. That glorious moment when our baby discovers how to pick up an object, reach it out to another person, and open her hand as the other person takes it is a moment of triumph for parents. "YES!! I knew my child would know how to share." But shortly after we get off the phone proclaiming our child's generosity to her grandfather, something changes. She begins to reach objects out to others, only to jerk them back and smile the moment the other person reaches for them. And we're left asking "What's happened here?!"

Children discover handing toys to others almost the same way they discovered handing toys back and forth between their own hands. Doing it with others is delightful because the other person often smiles, says "Thank you" or starts mouthing the toy immediately. At this stage babies' "sharing" is based on the delight of cause and effect, not on the

more complex principle of empathy, which develops later on.

Therefore, the next experiment in baby's study of cause and effect is to offer his cup to someone and to pull it back when she reaches for it. In doing so, he gets to find out things like "Are you still interested in it?" "What do you do if I don't let it go?" "If I hand it out again, will you still reach for it?" So, baby continues his study of cause and effect, of how social interactions work, and of how people show they are interested in something. Parents, meanwhile, wonder wistfully about where their "sharing" baby went.

By the time children become toddlers, they spend more of their time grabbing or holding on to toys than they do freely relinquishing them. Some toddlers spontaneously continue to "share"—passing a cherished item on to another child—but their sharing isn't predictable or dependable. It's not until three or four that most children begin to share more easily and consistently.

At first toddlers think that something is theirs if they are holding or touching it. They don't understand that another child can play with their toy and the toy won't disappear. In their minds, if someone else is holding their teddy bear, it no longer belongs to them and they don't know if they're ever going to get it back.

As Janis often tells parents, "Put yourself in your child's place for a minute. Can you imagine how overwhelming it would be if you looked around your home and felt like you had to defend everything that you felt was yours from people who showed up at your door with dollies and moving vans? Sometimes to toddlers, friends look like the moving company."

Developing a Concept of Time

For the first couple of years of life, children experience life only in the present. They don't know that any moment exists besides this one. So when another child is holding on to their special cup, they're unable to imagine a future moment in which they'll get it back. If this moment is all there is, their cup is gone forever.

Sometime during their second or third year, most children begin to experience time on a continuum. They start to say things like "Yesterday we went to the zoo." That yesterday may refer to an event that happened months or weeks ago, but it shows that the child is beginning to have a sense of the past. As children begin to understand "later," "tomorrow," and "after your nap, we can go to the park," they begin to understand that if they let a toy go, it could come back to them later. A sense of time that stretches beyond the immediate moment is essential to a child's ability to share.

Understanding That There's Enough

The child who's clutching all the playdough or all the sand toys or all the dolls doesn't understand the concept of "number" and, therefore, can't readily figure out if there's enough for everybody. That's why it can be helpful to put away the one fancy red fire truck when your eighteen-month-old son has a friend coming over. Having one coveted item around when you know two or more toddlers will be playing together can be a set-up for conflict.

Giving children experiences of there being enough can sometimes help them understand that there *is* enough. At the lunch table, for instance, Janis might hand a cup to one child and then hand her a second cup, saying "This cup is for Melanie." That's very tangible for kids: "I've got one that I can hold in my hand and use, and now I have one I can pass on, too." (Though, sometimes, kids will need one in *each* hand before they can pass a third one on.)

Sometimes you can initiate an experience of sharing before a child might be ready to initiate it herself. You can bake two loaves of banana bread to take over to a friend's house. You can clearly set up two baskets. You can say to your child, "Let's put the bread that we're going to keep in *this* basket. Let's put the bread we're going to take to Odelia's house in *that* basket." Tangibly, right in front of her, your daughter can see that there is bread to stay at home and bread to take to Odelia. There may be times when your daughter still won't be able to give that banana bread away once you get to Odelia's, but this kind of activity can begin to teach children that there is enough to share.

Gaining this sense of "enough," by the way, is not dependent on having a lot of toys. In

families where kids have fewer things but where people share their time and attention freely, children learn that there is enough, that they'll get what they truly need.

Experimenting with Social Interactions

In order to learn to interact in a cooperative way with other children, toddlers first have to explore a variety of other kinds of interactions. Have you ever noticed that children will pass by several, lovely, unoccupied toys to nab the one toy held by another child? And if by chance that other child gives up that toy and turns to another, the first child will suddenly want the newly picked up toy?

Children are more interested in social interactions than they are in toys. It's almost as if they're saying "That was fun! We're relating! Let's do that again." Toddlers are attempting to explore, connect with, and get to know other children. Yet because their social skills are still developing, all they can figure out to do is grab the toy. It's almost as if they're exploring the question: "How are we going to be together in the world? When I take your thing and then you come chase me, is that kind of like playing together?"

Adults often respond to this behavior by bringing more toys, separating the children, or labeling them "grabby" or "selfish." Instead, you can reflect what you see, support children in their communication, and, if need be, help them find solutions: "It looks like you want to play with Janessa." "Can you help Gaby find another truck?" Or "Could you both fill up the sand bucket?" These kinds of responses help children understand that what they really want is to play with each other and that there are other, more successful ways to make it happen.

Developing Empathy

Another element critical to sharing is the development of empathy. When you understand that your friend has feelings separate from yours, and that having the pounding bench will cause her to be happy, you can choose to give that toy to your friend because you care about her feelings.

The ability to empathize is a continuum. Even newborns will cry in response to another child's cries. But until children grow to see themselves as separate from other people, with separate feelings, they can't truly empathize.

The capacity for empathy is largely determined by age and readiness. But there are things you can do, even with babies and toddlers, to help lay the groundwork for developing responsiveness to other people's feelings.

The most critical part of developing empathy is awareness of feelings. Teaching children about their own feelings is an important first step. Children can learn about other people's feelings when parents talk about how they feel: "When you keep throwing your oatmeal on the floor, I feel mad!" Or "I love you. I'm so happy just to be with you!" And when you facilitate children's interactions, you can also identify feelings and model empathy: "Lupe's stamping on the floor and saying 'No!' It looks like she's really mad right now." "Victor's crying. It looks like he's really sad that he has to go home."

When children are taught to listen and respond to their own feelings and to the feelings of others, empathy arises naturally, and wanting to share is one of the most natural outcomes.

When sharing happens spontaneously, the moment is often a memorable one, as Reed, the father of three-year-old Chris, recalls: "I'll never forget it. After months of hoarding all the toys, Chris tentatively held one of his stuffed animals to a child standing nearby. Then he began handing out all of his stuffed animals. It was as if the tables had turned and he'd suddenly discovered the power of giving."

Preschoolers and Sharing: Have We Arrived Yet?

Three-year-olds who have had experience playing with other children will most likely be in a "got it–lost it" place with sharing. There will be times when they share easily and other times when they may still be trying to hold on to all the fire trucks. At four years old, successful sharing and negotiating will happen in comfortable relationships, but it is often punctuated by big, loud power struggles over things or the direction of the play. We can support the continued development of empathy and sharing in these children by facilitating listening, negotiation, and problem solving.

Sharing will be an issue on and off during the next years in children's development, but they will be developing more sophisticated language and negotiation skills with which to figure it out. During these years there may be stresses or other issues that impact a child's ability to share, but the earlier developmental factors of sense of time, empathy, and "sense of enough" should be established.

The Importance of Modeling

Modeling is one way parents can help children learn to share. Let's say your neighbor, Martha, and her four-year-old, Katie, come over to visit. When it's time to go, Katie doesn't want to leave. You try to help by offering her a toy that belongs to Rita, your two-year-old. Rita grabs the toy and starts screaming "No! Mine!" Now both kids are holding on and crying. You realize you probably made a mistake. What else could you have done?

You could have said to Rita "Katie's having a hard time leaving. Do you have something you can send home with her so that she could feel better?" When Rita answered, "No," you could have replied, "Well, I think I'll look in my things and see if there's something *I* have that we can send home with Katie." Then you could

What About Taking Turns?

Frequently parents who want to teach their children about sharing introduce the concept of "taking turns." When we teach children to take turns, we let them know that "sharing" is something we value. Turn-taking can also give children a structure in which they can successfully alternate the use of particular toys.

In and of itself, however, turn-taking doesn't "teach" sharing. True sharing and generosity are based on empathy. Children can master the mechanics of taking turns before they have the developmental capacity for empathy. They can learn to give up a toy because it is the other person's turn without ever learning that the other person has feelings. Although this is not true "sharing," many parents find it useful in social situations.

Turn-taking can be a useful intermediary step on they way toward learning to share. However, it is important to remember that not all children will be able to do it successfully. While some toddlers can learn the logistics of taking turns with substantial help from adults, others, who aren't cognitively, temperamentally, or developmentally ready, won't be able to do so.

Another crucial issue in turn-taking is that when it is directed by an adult, it doesn't give children a sense of solving their own problems. When turn-taking is the only solution children are taught to use, they rely less on themselves and more on adults and the "rules."

Although turn-taking can be beneficial, it's important to remember that it isn't the final goal. It's crucial that children also be helped to develop the empathy and compassion that underlie "true" sharing.

take Rita with you to find something interesting—a spool of thread or an old magazine—so she could witness the interaction and see firsthand the pleasure it brings Katie. Observing this, Rita might think "This is an exciting interaction to be involved in. I want to be part of it, too!" If we take the pressure off children, they're freer to discover the power of generosity.

When you think in terms of modeling, it's also important to remember that sharing "things" is not the only way to teach kids about generosity. It's also useful for kids to see people sharing of themselves. You can give generously of your time, your listening, your concern. When kids are around people who are generous in spirit, they learn to share more readily.

Strategies for Success

Here are some specific things you can do to minimize conflicts when children are in the developmental stage in which sharing is difficult:

• **Put special toys away.** If your child is having a hard time sharing toys, don't leave something out that's new or especially treasured when another child is coming over. Older toddlers may be able to participate in this sorting out process: "Eliazar is coming over. Are there some special things you'd like to put away in the closet before he comes?" Or "You just got your new lamby. If it's here, Eliazar might want to play with it. Is that okay with you, or shall we put it away?" Or "What toys shall we put out for Eliazar to play with?"

Despite these efforts, there may be times your child won't be able to follow through on the sharing he planned to do. He couldn't quite anticipate how it would feel for Eliazar to play with the sparkly ball. But over time, this strategy gives children a sense of choice, which ultimately makes sharing easier.

• **When a child insists on keeping something of his own, see if he can find something else for the other child to play with.** You can say "Is there something else you can give Emily to play with?" Or "Can you go get a toy for Emily?" Sometimes if you let your child hold on to what he wants, he'll have more of a sense of control and predictability, and will be more willing to find other toys for his friends.

• **Focus on neutral playthings.** Try putting all or most of the toys away and bring out those no one owns, such as the plastic containers and lids from the kitchen. Try giving each child a piece of colored chalk and going out on the sidewalk. Play that isn't focused on particular toys diffuses the ownership issue.

• **Meet in neutral territory.** Although children can learn a lot of valuable things by working through conflicts, there may be times when playing at your home isn't the best idea. If your daughter is continually struggling with other children using her things, you might want to try meeting for a month or two at the park, at another child's home, or out in nature. On the beach, there are a million grains of sand, endless pieces of seaweed, and a whole vast ocean, and no one child owns it. Opting for neutral turf sometimes can be the best solution when nothing else is working and your tolerance for conflicts has worn thin.

• **Don't force kids to give things up in the name of sharing.** Control is critical in sharing. In order to truly share, kids have to be the ones to make the decision that they want to do it. If you try to teach sharing by wrenching things out of kids' hands, the lesson will be lost.

There are times, however, when it may be necessary to physically take something away from a child. If Willa's blankey gets snatched by Connie, and she refuses to give it back, you may need to gently take the blanket away from her, explaining, "This is Willa's special

blankey and she needs to have it whenever she wants it. It's kind of like your special bunny."

In Time, It Will Happen

Learning to share is generally not a smooth or graceful process. But it does happen. The child who is grabbing or holding on to armloads of toys at two will have much longer periods of sensitivity, empathy, and social success by four or five. By giving children the gift of time and respect, by honoring their feelings and the feelings of others, by allowing them to explore socially, and by modeling cooperative, loving human behavior, you provide your children with the building blocks that will enable them to mature into the loving, compassionate people you want them to be.

25. "But Girls Can't Do That": Helping Children Move Beyond Limiting Gender Roles

"Sugar and spice and everything nice,
that's what little girls are made of.
Snips and snails and puppy dog tails,
That's what little boys are made of."
TRADITIONAL CHILDHOOD RHYME

Babies are born into the world with no awareness of gender at all. But by the time they are two or three, many boys and girls are already exhibiting stereotypical behavior. Girls are playing in the kitchen, feeding their dollies, and pretending to go shopping. Boys are playing with cars, balls, trucks, and action figures.

Many parents take this kind of play for granted, assuming that girls automatically will be one way, and boys another. They believe such behavior is biologically determined or assume that the drift toward such "norms" is inevitable.

However, narrow definitions of girls and boys are limiting and inaccurate. Many girls love to initiate rough, physical play, and lots of boys prefer quiet activities such as cuddling, reading, and dressing up. Within each gender there is much wider variation than there is between genders.

So what *does* make a girl a girl and a boy a boy? There have been lots of studies done to determine whether behavior is influenced predominantly by hormones and chromosomes or by children's experiences at home and in the larger world. While genetic factors are clearly important, it's impossible to separate out the influences of nature and nurture. And it's undeniable that there are lots of environmental factors that we, as parents, can influence.

The rules of behavior children learn in their early years affect them throughout their lives.

As parents, as families, and as a society, it's imperative that we give our children the widest range of opportunities possible so that both girls and boys are taught to know their hearts, to speak their minds, and to pursue their dreams.

In this chapter, we look at the way our expectations about gender shape our perceptions of our daughters and sons. We suggest ways parents can keep options open for children—by providing healthy role models, by carefully choosing books and toys, and by learning to mediate children's experiences in the world. We explore the pervasive role video games, television, advertising, and children's movies play in influencing gender-stereotyped play. Finally, we examine what parents can do to broaden "gun play" and "Barbie play" beyond narrow limitations.

The Evolution of Gender Identity: A Developmental Overview

Infants don't know what gender they are or that gender exists, but in the first year of life, babies begin to differentiate between men and women. Some babies use the term "Mama" to refer to all women and "Dada" to refer to all men.

Between two and three years old, children can usually "name" their gender, but most still don't know what it is that really makes them a girl or a boy. Nor do they know that gender will remain constant throughout their lives. Your two-year-old daughter may put on Dad's hat, proclaiming "*I'm* the daddy." At least momentarily, she is convinced that she can be a "daddy," that switching gender is as easy as switching hats. Likewise, three-year-old Justin might proclaim, "When I grow up my tummy is going to get big so I can have a baby and be a mommy."

Typically, as children near four, they start to embrace their gender and incorporate it as an essential part of their self-concept. However, they still are not convinced that their gender won't change.

By this age, if not before, most children start experimenting with the obvious, stereotypical objects and behaviors associated with their gender. Girls become interested in dresses, fancy shoes, hair doo-dads, and makeup. Boys embrace action figures, weapons, and sports.

This makes sense in terms of the way young children define gender. Many preschool children believe that the length of their hair, their clothes, the type of shoes they wear, or the kind of toys they play with is what makes them a girl or a boy. Four- and five-year-olds often hold fiercely to behavior stereotypically associated with their gender to ensure that their gender doesn't "change."

Children of this age often define who they are by proving who they're not, heartily defending against colors, clothing, or games associated with the "other" gender: "I'm not wearing that! That's a girl's shirt." "I'm not going to play that. That game is for boys." Four- and five-year-old boys are sometimes seen hitting dolls or throwing them around. This may indicate not just a rejection of a girl's toy but also indicate an interest in playing with a toy that is "forbidden."

The fact that preschool children can distinguish gender categories and figure out the characteristics society attributes to those categories is a testament to their emerging intelligence. Sometimes they are so insistent about those categories because they are proud that they have figured out the "rules."

Since preschoolers engage in "either-or" thinking, it can also be difficult for them to accept the information that there actually *is* a local female firefighter, because society's rules say that firefighters are supposed to be men.

The more stereotypical the gender images children have seen, the more rigid they are likely to be. But even children who've been exposed to a diversity of gender roles through their books, playthings, and the people they know are still likely to go through a period in which they embrace many of the stereotypical characteristics of their gender.

However, by the time children reach seven or eight, most of them who've been previously exposed to nonstereotypical information will be able to call up those earlier ideas. The seeds for more open-ended possibilities are planted in early childhood, and children who've been exposed to them will gradually be able to allow themselves more diversified experiences and activities.

The Making of a Girl, the Making of a Boy

When we have a new baby, the first question most people ask is "Is it a boy or a girl?" On one level, this question is a matter of social convention. On another, many of us believe we're going to know something about that baby if we know its gender.

Janis recalls, "I've been in toddler observation classes in which there were three or four boys, one of whom was really active, loud, interactive, and busy, two of whom were quite subdued and calm, staying close to their parents, and maybe one who was somewhere in the middle. What's been interesting to me is that parents will look at the active child, disregard the other three, and say to each other 'Oh, isn't he just like a boy!' "

Once we establish stereotypes, we often begin to look for examples that perpetuate those assumptions and look past examples that don't support them—in this instance, the other boys in the room.

A couple of the parents in Janis's classes have done an experiment of dressing their baby up one day as a "girl" and going to the mall, and the next day as a "boy" and going to the same mall. The "boy" babies got comments such as "He's such a little bruiser," "Looks like he's going to be quite a football player," "He's so strong," and the same baby the next day, dressed as a "girl," got comments like "She's so delicate," "She's so pretty," or "She's so quiet."

Clearly, social conditioning influences children from the very beginning of their lives. Studies have shown that from birth, parents treat girls and boys differently. Parents hold girls closer and talk to them more than they do boy babies. Research has also shown that parents carry girls facing toward their bodies and boys away from their bodies.

Pretty Little Girls?

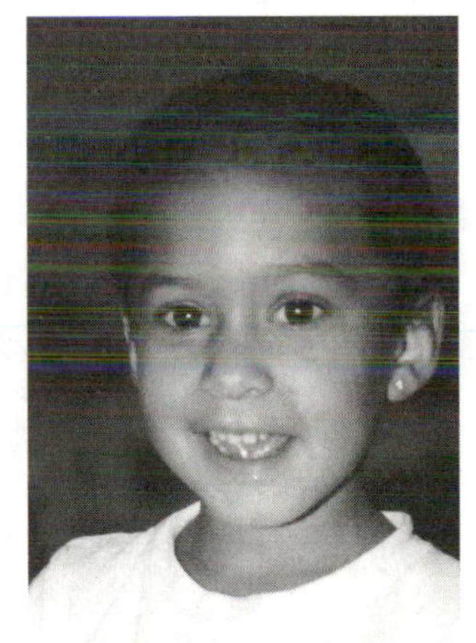

From the time they are born, girls get most of their recognition for their appearance. Appearance isn't stressed nearly as much for boys. As Janis recalls, "I've heard people say to boys 'Look at those beautiful, long eyelashes. What a waste that a boy got them!' "

Parents have felt concerned about excessive attention to their daughter's looks. Paul explains, "Our youngest daughter, Marisol, has classically beautiful features. Until she was five, we kept her hair long and flowing. The only kinds of remarks she ever got out in the world were about how beautiful she was, about how she was going to have to fight to keep all the boys away, even about how sexy she was. My wife and I were really concerned about the things she was hearing about herself, so we cut her hair in a pixie and started dressing her in pants and overalls. Overnight, the comments about Marisol's physical beauty stopped. Through a cosmetic change, we shifted the focus from her looks and created room for people to notice other things about her."

Girls are also hampered in their physical activity and prowess by many of the clothes they are expected to wear. Sue recalls, "I remember my daughter being in a dress when she was learning to crawl and she kept crawling up the inside of her dress and getting stuck. It was a totally ridiculous piece of clothing as far as mobility was concerned."

Janis remembers: "When my sons were young, a friend of mine brought her daughter over to visit. The little girl needed some shorts for an outing we planned, so I dashed into a store to get a pair on our way. Later when we started hiking to the beach, she got on her bottom to slide down the hill, and I had to stop myself from saying to her 'Be careful! You're going to get your shorts dirty,' something I'd never said to my boys. I realized I'd gone to the girls' department and bought the shorts they offered girls—white or light pink—definitely a color that said, in essence, 'Don't be active.' I'd only bought shorts in the boys department before and those had always been dark shorts. Not having had a girl yet, that was a real eye-opener."

Boys also face limitations in terms of clothes. When little boys want to experiment with clothes outside of the norm for their gender, parents often have a very strong reaction. Janis recalls: "I remember one dad, Marty, who was really challenged because his four-year-old son, Parker, wanted a tutu. Parker's best friend, Tanya, was really into tutus, so of course Parker wanted one, too, and he wanted to wear it all the time. For Marty, this brought up all kinds of assumptions about gender as well as all the confusion we have in this culture around gender and sexuality. Marty worked hard to sort all that out for himself so he could give Parker the message 'You can dress up in all sorts of different ways. Pretending doesn't threaten your maleness.' "

Obviously we don't want girls to give up opportunities to be fancy sometimes or proud of how they look, nor do we want boys to replace all of their practical clothing with fancy dress-ups. We want all children to have the opportunity to be seen as whole people, to be comfortable, active, and physical in the world, and to be acknowledged for their full complement of skills.

Children and Gender: Issues for Parents

Many of us have struggled in our own lives to redefine what it means to be a woman or a man. Yet despite changes in relationships, work, and the larger world, many of us bring expectations to our relationships with our kids based on gender stereotypes. Old misconceptions such as "Mothers take care of children in the early years, and then fathers step in," "Boys need wrestling, girls need hugging," or "I wanted a daughter so I could have someone to talk to" can interfere with building full relationships with all of our children.

The society we live in also poses challenges to those of us who want to keep children's options open. We are still surrounded by stereotypical images. Even some of the "advances" reinforce old misconceptions. Recently, National Public Radio ran a story about a new line of building toys for girls. Finally, here was an acknowledgment that girls like to play with blocks! But the girl-blocks were pink, as if that were the only color girls would play with, and prefabricated, because the manufacturer assumed that girls don't want to build, they merely want to play house in completed structures.

Most of us also experience conflicting values within our families. Chuck, father of three-year-old Raffa, had mixed feelings when Uncle Will sent Raffa a football helmet and jersey: "I appreciated Will's generosity, and I know these are just toys, but I don't want Raffa to get the message that we expect him to play football or that he has to be an athlete to make it as an African American man."

Really changing our expectations, our ways of thinking and being, is a long-term process for us, for our families, and for our society.

FOOD FOR THOUGHT: GENDER ROLES

- When I was a child, were there times I wished I was the other gender? How did I imagine that would change things for me?

- If I look around me at the images in my home (books, magazines, TV, videos) and in the larger culture, what information are children getting about what males do? About what females do?

- If I look at my child's play space, toys, and clothes, what kinds of play do they encourage? If my child was the other gender, what kinds of toys would he or she have?

Opening Up the World: What Parents of Babies Can Do

- **Create an open-ended environment for your child.** Preparing a place for your new baby is an exciting and caring thing to do. Many parents, upon hearing that they're expecting a girl, lovingly create a room full of pink ruffles, "sweetness" and bows. Upon hearing they're expecting a boy, out come the basketballs, trucks, and rough-and-tumble playthings. From the time they are born, children are influenced by our expectations. Being thoughtful about the environments we create for our children is a significant way we communicate our beliefs.

- **Choose clothing for babies that allows for freedom of movement and active, messy play.** Both boys and girls need clothing that encourages rather than inhibits mobility. Dressing all children in simple, practical clothes also leads to fewer assumptions based on gender.

• **Be aware of ways you might treat boy babies and girl babies differently.** Babies need equal opportunities for holding, cuddling, talking, and independence.

Opening Up the World: What Parents of Toddlers and Preschoolers Can Do

• **Respect the power of language.** The adjectives we use to describe girls and boys, the way we talk about men and women, the pronouns we use to describe people in various professions (Are all flight attendants "she" and all pilots, "he"?) shape children's perceptions of themselves and their gender.

• **Talk about people whose lives expand beyond traditional gender roles.** Talk about the nonstereotypical characteristics of people in your family and community (without going overboard so people wonder why you're making such a fuss): "Uncle Morris makes the best pasta salad I've ever tasted." "Mom is so good with numbers that our family's checkbook is always balanced." "Your daddy really knows how to help you feel better when you get hurt." "Our friend Luz makes the plans for bridges that go all the way across rivers and canyons."

• **Look at what you're modeling in your own life.** The people children see in their immediate environment give them clues about gender-appropriate behavior. So it's important to ask yourself: "What are the gender roles of the adults in our family?"

Even though work is the arena we most often associate with gender and power, what we do for work, and where we do it, is only one aspect of our gender identity. The way we communicate, make decisions, relate to money, divide family responsibilities, make friends, pursue hobbies, and nurture ourselves all provide opportunities to demonstrate nonstereotypical behavior to our children.

• **Counteract images from the media.** As children start getting information about gender roles from magazines, advertising, and TV, they use it to try to make sense of the world. Our job is to help them sort through these messages. How might this look at various ages?

Toddlers take in whatever they see as reality. Jessica learned this one day when she was leafing through a mail-order catalogue with two-year-old Heidi. Jessica was horrified to see page after page of girls dressed in pink playing "princess" and page after page of boys engaged in active play and building. Looking at the pictures, Heidi stated matter-of-factly, "Boys build."

Jessica's heart sank. She turned to Heidi and said, "The people who made this catalogue didn't know how much girls like to build. Let's take some pictures of you building and paste them in this catalogue." And that's what they did—a very effective response for a two-year-old.

Three- and four-year-olds often explore gender roles through imitation. Three-year-old girls might move their bottoms or shoulders in ways that mimic images they've seen on TV. How can you respond to this kind of imitation?

When your daughter says "Look at me wiggle my bottom," you can say "Sometimes you wiggle your bottom and sometimes you wiggle your knees. What else can you wiggle?" By responding this way, you deflect the idea that girls are interesting only when they move certain parts of their bodies.

By the time children are four or five, you can also respond directly to the stereotypes they're seeing. You can let them know that there is information you don't agree with: "Some of the people who publish magazines think that women are interesting only when they act like that, but there are lots of ways for girls and women to be interesting. Let's think of some. . . ."

Another stereotype kids often see on TV is male characters responding to hurt and sadness with a shrug or by lashing out in anger. It is important in these situations to talk about what is happening and to think of alternative responses: "That was a really sad thing that happened to him. I bet he feels like crying," or "Maybe he doesn't know that it's all right for men to cry. I bet he could tell his friend 'That hurts my feelings.' "

Helping Preschoolers Expand Their World Through Play

One of the primary ways children explore the parameters of their gender is through play. As we've already established, preschool children's play becomes increasingly segregated, with girls engaging in "girl's play" and boy's engaging in "boy's play."

There is nothing inherently wrong with either of these kinds of play. The healthy impulses in traditional boys' play involve learning about physical strength, coordination, and the mysteries of mortality. Play themes given to girls involve relationships, communication, feelings, and appearance. All children explore power and magic, although boys and girls explore these concepts very differently. All of these themes are fascinating and worthwhile, but when they're explored only by one gender and not the other, both boys and girls lose out.

In this society, it's important to recognize that when children "choose" their toys and their play themes, they're not really choosing freely. Millions of advertising dollars have gone into convincing your child that the toys worth having and the games worth playing are the ones he or she sees on TV.[1]

Even if they don't see the popular TV shows and movies that shape and dictate children's play, children see other kids in the neighborhood or at preschool playing those games; they see the images on kid's clothing, toys, sneakers, and lunch boxes. Those images and themes are pervasive.

Whether children ever buy the toys that are being advertised or not, they absorb the messages about "appropriate girls' play" and "appropriate boys' play." Since the societal messages are out there, and kids, no matter how sheltered, are exposed to them, it's necessary and inevitable for children to do *some* exploration of the cultural definition of their gender. Such play gives children important information about the roles and expectations that exist in our society.

Just because children are involved in stereotypical play, however, doesn't mean they can't also branch out into other kinds of play. By observing children's play and intervening in selective ways, we can help move children toward more open-ended choices:

• **Be thoughtful about the toys you provide for children.** When children are engaging in gender-stereotyped play, two issues come up—the content of the play and the props they use to engage in that play. Children are compelled as members of this culture to want, and often to beg for, the particular products that are being pushed at any given time—models of the latest Disney, superhero, or cartoon characters as well as the specific props (guns, lasers, transformers,

[1] We thank Nancy Carlsson-Paige and Diane E. Levin for their excellent analysis of these issues in their clear and thoughtful book, *Who's Calling the Shots? How to Respond Effectively to Children's Fascination with War Play and War Toys* (Philadelphia: New Society Publishers, 1990). For an insightful, in-depth analysis of war toys and war play and the role television plays in children's play, we strongly recommend their book.

Barbies, Little Ponies, makeup sets) that go along with that play.

Some parents hold the line and don't buy any of these materials, teaching their children some lessons about fads, advertising, and consumerism in the process. Others buy the toys and the sweatshirts and the lunch pails *before* the movie is released, because they want to please their children and help them fit in with their peers. Still other parents give children limited access to some of the materials in order to give them a chance to explore the cultural mandates for kids their age. This exposure may happen through playing with other kids' toys, getting gifts, or because a parent compromises and buys one or two of the more innocuous toys a child is fascinated with.

• **Help children explore popular themes using homemade props.** You can also let children explore popular play themes without buying commercial props. You can make them (or help children make them) instead. Charlene, the mother of a four-year-old who was obsessed with Superman, said, "Ray was absolutely fixated on Superman. We didn't have a TV, but he learned about Superman in preschool. When he went to the bathroom, he'd leave his belt in the shape of an S outside the door. When he pooped and the poop was in the shape of an S, he'd scream and cry if I tried to flush it away. I refused to buy him any of the Superman paraphernalia, but I did sew him a beautiful cape with an S on it. It was the basis for years of creative fantasy play." (If you don't sew, an old pillow case and a marker could do just fine.)

Other parents have helped their children make cardboard swords, wrist bands, wings, or headbands. Sometimes the process of designing and creating props together turns out to be more fun than the "play" itself and offers children another kind of creative learning experience.

• **Help children expand their play.** When children are involved in a particular play theme, you can ask them about the story line of the play and then provide props or ask questions that might help expand the play into new areas. You can say to boys involved in superhero play "It looks like one of your Skeleton Warriors got hurt. Can you take him to the hospital?" That might lead to nurturing play around bandaging, doctoring, and caring for an injury. Or you can say "The Power Rangers haven't had any lunch. They need food to help them stay strong! How about cooking some lunch for them?" Kids could make pretend food or accompany you into the kitchen to help make a real lunch.

If children haven't been doing anything in the art area, you can ask them if they'd like to make costumes to go with their play. You can ask "What do Power Rangers wear? Is there a way you could make that?" Children can be involved in choosing material, cutting it out, sewing, and gluing on decorations.

Parents can also help children develop meaningful lives for their "action figures" outside of their advertised functions. You can say to children things such as: "Tell me about this Power Ranger." "Who takes care of him when he gets hurt?" "Does he ever feel sad?" "Who's his best friend?" "What does he like to do after he's done fighting for the day?" "Does he have any brothers and sisters?" "Whom does he live with?" "Does he have a mother?"

As girls are doing their house play, you can also help them expand into areas they might not readily choose. If their play is primarily happening indoors, you can think of ways to bring the play outside. You might do this by bringing some of the blankets, dolls, or other toys outside or by making sure that girls have access to wheel toys and wagons. You could also put some dishes, wooden spoons, or play pots into the sand, dirt, or another outdoor play area. Add a tub of water or a hose to encourage messy, creative outdoor play.

• **Encourage boys and girls to play together.** This encourages children to try things they might not try if they were playing only with children of the same gender. Doreen recalls: "When my oldest son was five, he had one special friend who was a girl. Whenever she came over, he engaged in a lot of fantasy play that he never seemed to do with his friends who were boys."

• **Offer toys that are gender-neutral or that are "supposed to be" for the other gender.** If children are only asking for toys that are traditionally defined for their gender, that may be because they haven't perceived the possibility of branching out beyond those toys. Offer your children alternatives. Boys can benefit from having access to dolls, grooming toys, and kitchens as well as trucks and building blocks. Girls can enjoy tools, balls, mechanical toys, and sports equipment as well as tea sets and stuffed animals.

When children resist such toys because they're "boy's toys" or "girl's toys," gradually counter those stereotypes. You can say "Maybe the people who made those toys only think that girls are interested in cooking, but your Uncle Eduardo loves to cook." Or "I know some girls who really love to play with trucks." If your child absolutely refuses to play with toys identified with the "other" gender, you can provide open-ended toys that aren't stereotypical for either boys or girls.[2]

• **Model and encourage activism.** When you're choosing presents for friends, it is a good time to talk to children about gender-specific toys: "I wonder what Shana is getting for her birthday. Do you think anybody is going to get her a toy she can run with or build with? I wonder what we could get her that would be different?" Or "You know, the people who made these tea sets didn't put any pictures of boys on the box. I'm going to write them a letter to remind them our friend Seamus likes tea parties, too."

• **Take on the toy stores and toy companies.** Parental activism has forced toy manufacturers to make changes in toy lines. On a local level, parents have convinced individual toy merchants to change what they stock in their store as well as how prominently they display certain items. A protest over the "good" and "bad" Arab twins in the Rambo line led Coleco to remove those action figures from the market. Another toy company, in conjunction with a citizen's peace group, organized a toy trade-in in which war toys could be exchanged for teddy bears.[3]

Karyn recalls: "When Bryan was four, he got some money as a present and I took him to the local department store and said, 'Let's go in and see if we can find a toy.' I had the idea of buying him something that would support the creative play he was already doing—a pot to cook with, a boat for the waterways he was digging in the backyard, something to expand

[2] See "What Is Our Role in Children's Play and Learning?" on p. 289 for specific suggestions on these kinds of play materials.

[3] Carlsson-Paige and Levin, *Who's Calling the Shots?* p. 135.

his fantasy play. So I started to go toward the cooking toys. But they were on the 'girl's aisle.' Bryan knew it was the girl's aisle—the whole aisle was blazing with pink. He said, 'I don't want to go there. I'm a boy and I need boy toys.'

"I said, 'Okay, we can probably find something over there.' So we went over to the 'boy's aisle.' Everything there was black or dark-colored. Everything had a war theme. They were all what I called death toys—toys to kill people, maim people, hurt people. My heart just sank. It was disheartening for Bryan, too. He already knew that I wouldn't buy those kinds of toys. The only toy we could agree on was a ball, and neither of us was very satisfied with that.

"I felt like I needed to do something. I wanted Bryan to know that my conviction about war toys was really deep. So before we left the store, I talked to the salesperson. I said, 'Why do you just stock your shelves with war toys for boys? Why are you telling boys that this is what they should want to do?' She said, 'You've got it all wrong. We buy the toys kids like. This is what they want.' And I said, 'You're teaching him that because he's a boy, he needs war toys. There's no choices for my family here.' And we left the store.

"I was furious that those were the only choices available to him. Here was this beautiful little child and the only option open to him was to buy a weapon. I felt so strongly about it that I helped picket some of the stores that Christmas."

Whether your activism is refusing to buy certain toys, providing noncommercial, nonstereotypical play materials for your children, talking to your children about the realities of advertising, getting together with friends and making agreements about the toys you will support, or working with local political groups to make change, your children will perceive the strength of your convictions.

Responding to Superhero Play: Preschool Boys with Guns

Around the age of four, children broaden their knowledge of the larger world and consequently their awareness of being small in the world increases. To compensate for this new sense of vulnerability, many children begin engaging in superhero play. In doing so, they are asking such questions as "How can I have power in this world?" "How can I make things happen?" "What is magic and how will it work for me?"

Children's involvement in this play is directly proportional to their sense of vulnerability. Sometimes it's hard to see a child who's running around, doing the kicks and the motions of powerful superheroes, and to recognize that underneath, he may be feeling fearful or powerless.

The Evolution of War Play

Fighting and adversarial play in which one group is fighting another has been a staple play theme for generations. Media and culture have determined the nature of the good guys and the bad guys—whether they're cowboys and Indians, Luke Skywalker and Darth Vader, or the Power Rangers and Lord Zed. Children have played with the acceptable set of tools for their generation, be they rocks, sticks, bows and arrows, rotten apples, swords, guns, or laser swords.

The main difference between the war play we engaged in and the play children are doing today is that the toys in today's war games are tied directly into specific TV shows and superheroes. The uses of these toys are circumscribed by narrow themes presented on TV and memorized by children. Many of the toys are realistic replicas of real weapons. Often the weapons are already attached to a certain character with a narrow, inflexible persona. All of these factors limit children's creativity, create play that is ultimately less satisfying, and generate a much stronger obsession with war and war themes.

He'd Eat His Sandwich in the Shape of a Gun

Boys' interest in guns can be baffling in its intensity. Julie recalls, "When he was four, Randy was fascinated with guns. I didn't want to buy him realistic weapons or guns that made shooting noises, but I did buy him a couple of squirt guns and a pop-gun with a cork. And my husband made him a rubber-band gun."

Olga, the mother of three grown sons, says, "My boys were very interested in guns, but I never let them have 'play' guns. We used real guns for hunting in our family, and I didn't ever want them to think that a gun could be a toy. When they were old enough, my boys learned how to use real guns safely."

Maureen said it was hard to hold to her convictions. "I never let Jeffrey have any guns. I felt like I had to take a stand against the toy industry. I stuck with that even though there were times Jeffrey stood there and screamed 'I hate you!' because I wouldn't let him have a gun. Jeffrey would eat his sandwich in the shape of a gun and then walk around with his half-eaten sandwich shooting. It was an urge that was insatiable."

Helping to Expand and Broaden Gun Play

If your child is fascinated with guns, war play, and action figures and frequently plays out violent themes from TV shows, there are things you can do to help broaden that play and encourage nonviolence:

• **Work to understand what causes the play.** Children are working out important issues when they engage in war and superhero play. To begin with, they are trying to understand our society's love affair with guns. Kids are driven to figure out "What is it about guns that is so important?" "How do they work?"

Another thing that drives preschoolers toward gun play is that they are struggling to figure out death: its significance, its causes, its cures, and its permanence. Guns become tools to explore mortality themes in play. You often see this curiosity played out in games where children kill someone, take him to the hospital, fix him up again, then kill him again, then take him to the hospital, and so on.

The final thing children explore when they play with guns is the social response to that play: "Why are adults horrified when I point my finger into this shape, pretend to pull a trigger, and say 'Bang! Bang!' " "Why did Dad come rushing across the yard when I shot my friend, Asia, with my laser gun?" "Why does he then sit and watch people with guns on TV?" Children are driven to figure out adult responses to weapons, violence, and death.

• **Establish guidelines you feel comfortable with that allow children to work out some of their questions.** When children are compelled to play a certain game, and we try to prohibit it, it usually drives the game underground, giving us no access to our children's play and no chance to help them figure out the concepts they're struggling with.

Make it clear to children that any kind of play that hurts, intimidates, or scares another child is unacceptable. Then clarify the rules about guns in your house. "In our family, we don't point guns at people or other living things." "You can only shoot at this target we've put up on the wall for you." Or "We don't buy play guns from the store, but it's okay for you to make pretend guns with your fingers or out of other toys."

Some families allow gun play in specified areas. "When you play chase games with guns in the house, your little brother gets scared, so if you're going to play with guns, I want you to do it outside." This teaches kids that other people's feelings need to be considered in play.

• **Provide your child with props that have multiple uses.** When a child holds up a popsicle stick and says "Bang-bang," in the next moment that "gun" can transform into a thermometer for taking a sick person's temperature. It can become a microphone or a cane or a baton. But when children play with highly realistic guns, their props can't change with their play; their guns can only shoot and kill. Generally, the more realistic the weapon, the less flexibility and creativity the play can have.

• **Facilitate children's play.** You can help children set up rules that will make the play feel safe. You can teach them to ask each other for permission to be shot. You can tell them, "Tekkai is crying. He doesn't like being shot. You have to ask someone's permission before you play that game with them."

You can also help children who are feeling scared tell the other kids that they don't want to play: "Tekkai, you can tell Lyle not to shoot you."

• **Give children information about guns in the real world.** While making it clear that you know that their play is pretend, you can let children know that real guns are dangerous, that real guns have real bullets that can hurt and kill people, and that it's never safe to play with real guns.

• **Make your values and feelings clear.** As much as children need to push away from us and develop their own ideas, they also care deeply about our values. If you say to a child "I feel upset when I see you playing that way because someone in our family was once hurt by a gun. Seeing you play like that reminds me," or "I'm uncomfortable when you play that way. I don't like what real guns do, so I don't like seeing people pretending to use them," your children will begin to understand your thinking and the values that matter to you.

• **Interfere with the myth of "enemy."** The idea of the "bad guy" is pervasive in our world—in stories, movies, television, the way we approach problem solving. This can make it hard for children—and for us—to move beyond the myth of "enemy."

Cognitively, preschool children have trouble moving beyond either-or thinking. However, we can begin to challenge their polarized way of thinking even before they're ready to move beyond the "bad guy–good guy" dichotomy.

You can ask such questions as "What is a bad guy?" "How do you know he's a bad guy?" "Was he a bad guy when he was a baby?" "What turned him into a bad guy?" "How could he change from being a bad guy into somebody else?"

Ultimately, through such interventions, you teach kids that there are people who do unsafe or hurtful things, but that people aren't magically or forever "bad guys." As Janis recalls, "In the middle of his gun phase, Calvin did something that showed he'd really been listening to the things I'd told him while he was playing with guns. He built a gun out of Legos 'that was going to shoot the guns out of the bad guys' hands and make them peaceful.' He'd learned if he was going to talk to me about guns, he had to throw the idea of peace in there somewhere. He'd also started to get that concept that bad guys were not a fixed quantity, that they could change."

• **Stress nonviolence and connection among different groups of people.** When we help children build a sense of community with other people in the world, there's not the same need for adversarial play. Instead, we help create feelings of compassion and a growing interest in communication.[4]

• **Give children information about people working to establish nonviolence in the world.** Children sometimes play with guns because they're trying to master their fear of violence or war. If we talk about the ways people are working toward peace and nonviolence, it can help children feel safer and therefore less compelled toward gun play. Janis recalls, "My kids started asking about war and people hurting each other at about the same time that they were really interested in playing with guns. I talked to my kids about the things I did, and our friends did, to make this world a more peaceful place."

• **Give children alternatives to gun play that also reinforce competence and their sense of power.** Teaching children real-life skills such as carpentry, cooking, sewing, and construction can sometimes take energy that's being put into gun play and redirect it in a new direction. Spending time in nature is also an empowering experience for many kids. Figuring out how to balance on a log across a stream, seeing how far they can throw rocks and whether they can make them skip on water, climbing hills and trees, exploring uncharted territory, dissecting owl pellets, and finding and collecting natural treasures are all satisfying challenges for young children.

[4] See Chapter 26, "Preparing Children to Live in a Richly Diverse World," on p. 354 for ideas on how to do this.

Barbiemania: Preschool Girls with Teenage Dolls

Girls' fascination with Barbie (and similar fashion or grooming dolls) comes from their interest in pretend play, their desire to emulate their peers and older siblings, and their need to try out roles they might be playing in the future.[5] The problem is that Barbie has been associated almost entirely with activities that are stereotypical. Her main play function has been around clothes and appearance. She hasn't been marketed for her problem-solving abilities, her intelligence, her creative thinking, the significant work she does, or her physical capabilities. Barbie doesn't even have feet that allow her to move in any kind of active way; it would be very difficult to ride a bike, play basketball, or walk comfortably with those feet.

Keith is perplexed by his daughter's interest in Barbie: "Ali wants four Barbies for her fourth birthday. Her obsession with Barbie and all her outfits is a real stretch for me. In the family I grew up in, no one paid attention to what they wore; we took pride in *not* taking an interest in how we looked. Barbie is thirty-two, twenty-two, thirty-two. I subtly try to tell Ali that she doesn't have to look like that. I say things like 'Barbie could put on a little weight. It looks like she hasn't been eating enough.' "

Young girls, like Ali, are developing ideas about how value is achieved, and Barbie reinforces the idea that appearance is the most important thing in life. It's very hard for girls to

[5] Barbie is not the only toy on the market that raises the kinds of issues we deal with here. Numerous toys targeted for girls perpetuate gender stereotypes. Although many of the examples we give here focus on Barbie specifically, the ideas in this section apply equally to other toys that reinforce a narrow gender definition for girls.

escape Barbie's three-dimensional image of how they're supposed to look. Barbie sets an unrealistic standard. No matter what girls do in terms of diet or exercise, they won't end up looking like their idol. Even the Barbies that have made an attempt to be "ethnically diverse" have exactly the same body and nearly the same features; only the color of the plastic skin and the clothing have changed.

Raising Barbie's Consciousness

Whether girls play with Barbie or not, many get involved in extensive doll and house play in their preschool years. Here are some ways to help them expand and broaden that play:

• **Acknowledge what it is that children are working on when they're playing with Barbie.** You can say, "Tell me what you like about Barbie," "Looks like you like to play pretend games with Barbie," Or "It's interesting to think about how girl's bodies change when they get older."

• **Tell children how you feel about Barbie.** You could say, "I don't like Barbies, because they don't look like real mommies," "I like dolls that you could do more interesting things with," or "Sometimes girls who play with Barbie think they need to look like Barbie in order to be beautiful, but there are lots of wonderful ways for girls to be beautiful—both in how they look and in what they do."

• **Provide alternative toys which meet the same needs.** There are a lot of wonderful multiethnic dolls on the market. While many children enjoy baby dolls, as they get older they become increasingly interested in "kid" dolls. Look for dolls that are durable and waterproof.

While dressing and undressing dolls is useful to practice and fun to do, Barbie has clothes that are very difficult for young children to get on and off. Look for dolls that allow children to do the dressing themselves. Some dolls that are bigger or more manageable give children the opportunity to create some of their own doll clothes out of pieces of fabric, by wrapping, tying, taping, or pinning.

For other kinds of dramatic play, children also like little, hand-size people figures. Many companies make multiethnic, multiage sets of figures that include both males and females. Homemade or store-bought puppets also provide hours of pretend play fun.

• **Delay children's exposure to Barbie.** Because Barbie carries such stereotypical messages about "girlness," it can be useful to put off children's exposure to Barbie until they are old enough to engage in a dialogue about gender roles and expectations. A four-and-a-half-year-old is better able to think about Barbie's limitations than a two- or three-year-old.

Julie explained, "Someone gave Kira a Barbie when she was two and a half. I put it away for a couple of years. I didn't want Kira to have Barbie until she could think a little more critically about who Barbie was. When I finally gave the Barbie to her, Kira was very interested at first. Six months later, she lost interest and decapitated her."

• **Limit the number of store-bought props.** If your daughter has a Barbie, buying as few of Barbie's accessories as possible will provide your child with more opportunities for imaginative play. With the addition of creative materials and props, many children have expanded Barbie's character and gotten into elaborate dramatic play.

You can ask girls, "Does Barbie have a house? What would it take to build one for her?" You can provide construction materials such as fabric, blankets, boxes, couch cushions, old sheets, tree branches, or blocks so they can build Barbie a house, a car, an office, or furniture. With four- and five-year-olds, you could bring out nails, wood, and hammers and help them build things for Barbie. Creating Barbie's environment themselves, rather than having a prefab set, allows children to expand into play that involves construction, engineering, physics, and math.

• **Extend children's thinking.** You can ask children: "What if Barbie wanted to be a doctor? What kind of school would she need to go to? What would she need to learn?" "I bet Barbie would like to play a sport. What sport do you think she might like?"

• **Provide other examples of beautiful people.** You can say "That woman is so beautiful. Look at the lines around her eyes, she looks like she has laughed a million times in her life." "Your Aunt Marjorie has the most beautiful round body. She gives the softest hugs."

Children's Books and Bias

Language is one of the most powerful ways we transmit social information to children. What we say to children, the songs they hear, the movies they see, and the books they read give them information about the world, about social norms and values, about what boys and girls can do.

Historically, 90 percent of children's literature, including books about animals, have included a male main character. When there was a female main character, she was usually doing some kind of stereotypical activity. These are the books most of us grew up on. Little boys and little girls have gotten two very different pictures about who they are in the world from the information available to them in books.

With preschool-age and older children, this disparity can be addressed by entering into a dialogue with children. When a stereotypical portrayal comes up, you can say: "The person who wrote this book doesn't know that boys like to dress up, too! If we had written this book, what would we have done?" This kind of thoughtful discussion is an important part of sharing books with preschoolers.

But babies and toddlers don't have the capacity for critical thinking. Whatever images they see go right in. So it's much more critical that the images they see and the language they hear are diverse and inclusive.

Fortunately, there is now a wealth of high-quality children's literature available that beautifully teaches children about the diversity of the larger world and the openness of their own possibilities.

Choosing Books with an Eye Toward Diversity

When choosing books for your child, it's a good idea to look for a balance of images. No one book will have everything. Some books show men as nurturers but demonstrate little ethnic diversity. Others have wonderful depictions of cultural diversity but reinforce the idea that boys are the ones who get to have all the adventures. It can be helpful to ask: In my child's book collection, are there books that . . .

- Depict children as competent, resourceful, problem-solvers?
- Show girls and women as active, independent, full participants in life?
- Show people of differing abilities in a variety of competent roles?
- Show ethnic and cultural diversity?
- Show fathers and boys as sensitive and nurturing?
- Show different kinds of families? Show extended family members?

Non-Sexist Children's Books

To help you in your search for diverse, wonderful books for your child, we heartily recommend the following.

Books for Babies

Honey, I Love, Eloise Greenfield and Jan Spivey Gilchrist, Harper Festival.

A young African American girl talks about the things she loves in her world. Ages 1 and up.

Hi! Ann Herbert Scott, Philomel Books.

A toddler on an errand with her mother encounters the difficulty of being a small child in the world of adults. Margarita is saying "Hello" to everyone, but no one will reciprocate. After many attempts, she is finally successful. This book has many pages that show the world from a toddler's eye view. Ages 1 and up.

When Grandma Came, Jill Paton Walsh and Sophy Williams, Puffin.

Grandma comes to visit Madeline after her travels all around the world and she tells her granddaughter that no matter where she's traveled, she's never seen anything as wonderful as her Madeline. Anglo family. Ages 18 months and up.

Books for Twos

Shoes from Grandpa, Mem Fox, illustrated by Patricia Mullins, Orchard Books.

Everyone in Jessie's family has an idea about the clothing she needs, but all she really wants for her adventures is a comfy pair of jeans. There's wonderful language, repetition, and rhythm as well as lovely illustrations of Jessie's adventures. Anglo family. Ages 2 and up.

Miss Tizzy, Libba Moore Gray, illustrated by Jada Rowland, Simon & Schuster.

A diverse group of friends enjoy spending time with their African American neighbor and elder, Miss Tizzy, in all kinds of creative ways. When she gets sick, they get a chance to return some of the love she's given them. Ages 2 and up.

Guess Who? Margaret Miller, Greenwillow Books.

All of Margaret Miller's Books, *Where Does It Go? Can You Guess? Whose Hat? Whose Shoe? Who Uses This?* use photographs to pose humorous questions to children. *Guess Who?* asks "Who cleans your teeth?" and on the opposite page, the choices are "A cat?" "A shoemaker?" "A window washer?" "A rubber duckie?" to which children delight in yelling "No!" Then you turn the page and see "A dentist!" Young children love the absurdly wrong answers. But the real beauty of Miller's books is that a diverse group of women and men, girls and boys are shown in a very matter-of-fact way in all kinds of nonstereotypical roles. Ages 2 and up.

Our Granny, Margaret Wild and Julie Vivas, Ticknor and Fields.

"Some grannies live in apartments, big old houses, old people's homes, little rooms in the city, trailers, farmhouses, cottages by the ocean, nursing homes or nowhere at all." So begins this wonderfully illustrated tribute to every size, style,

- Show healthy families with a variety of income levels?
- Show families dealing with real-life situations and problems?
- Show urban and rural as well as suburban settings?
- Show diversity in a natural, matter-of-fact way? (Children need books in which diversity is an incidental part of the story, not the main focus.)

It's important to assess individual books on these levels and also to be aware of the total range of books your child has available.[6]

[6] For more on choosing children's books, see "Sharing Books with Children" on p. 300 and "Children's Books That Accurately Reflect Our World" on p. 372.

shape, type, and color of grandmother there is. Ages 2 and up.

Books for Three and Up

Mr. Nick's Knitting, Margaret Wild, illustrated by Dee Huxley, Voyager Books.

An older Anglo man and woman form a friendship around their shared love of knitting. They knit together every day on the train on the way to the city, until the woman gets sick and has to go to the hospital. Lovely, heartwarming, funny illustrations. Ages 3 and up.

Cherries and Cherry Pits, Vera B. Williams, Greenwillow Books.

Bidemmi is an African American girl who loves to draw, and she loves cherries. The two themes intertwine in the delightful stories Bidemmi draws and weaves throughout this magical book. In the end she harvests her own cherries and shares them with everyone—even people who arrive on planes from Toronto and Nairobi. Ages 3 and up.

Amazing Grace, Mary Hoffman and Caroline Binch, Dial Books.

Grace, a young girl, whose family is from Trinidad, revels in all kinds of fantasy play and sets her sights on playing Peter Pan in her school play. Some of her classmates tell her she can't play the part because Peter Pan isn't black and isn't a girl. But through the support of her family and the strength of her own creative spirit, Grace triumphs. Ages 4 and up.

William's Doll, Charlotte Zolotow and William Péne DuBois, HarperCollins.

A young Anglo boy who wants a doll is refused by his father, who instead buys him all kinds of toys that are "supposed to be for boys." Finally, Grandma gets William a doll. She wisely understands it will help him become a nurturing daddy one day. Ages 4 and up.

A Chair for My Mother, Vera B. Williams, Mulberry Books.

All of Williams's books are favorites in our households. All share beautiful illustrations, wonderful story lines, and a warm, intimate depiction of real family life. *A Chair for My Mother* describes how three generations of Latina women save coins in a jar to replace a comfortable chair that was lost in a fire. The follow-up, *Something Special for Me*, shows the girl heroine, Rosa, struggling to decide what she wants for her birthday. In *Clap Hands and Sing*, Rosa learns to play the accordion, helps take care of her ailing grandmother, and starts an all-girl band that plays at community parties. Ages 4 and up.

Nora and the Great Bear, Ute Krause, Dial Books.

Young Nora decides she wants to learn to be a bear hunter. The story of her apprenticeship to the hunters and her meeting with the Great Bear show her courage and determination. All the characters are Anglo. Ages 4 and up.

Emma, Wendy Kesselman, illustrated by Barbara Cooney, Dell Picture Yearling Books.

A lonely seventy-two-year-old Anglo woman discovers the artist within her and develops a new fulfilling life. Based on the life of Emma Stern. Ages 4 and up.

So, What About Television?

One of the most pervasive influences on the development of children's gender roles is television. Before we look specifically at how television colors boys' and girls' perceptions of gender, it's important to take a look at children's experience of television in general.

The first thing to consider is how much time young children spend watching television—a national average of four hours a day. According to Annamarie Pluhar, executive director of The Television Project, this means that children spend more time watching TV *before* they go to kindergarten than it would take to earn a college degree.[7]

When thinking about what all this TV watching does to kids, there are two important things to consider. One is the "medium," the experience children have watching television, regardless of the content. The other is the content itself.

When children watch television, there are implications for their physical development. During the four hours that most of our children sit and watch television each day, they are not engaging in the active processes necessary for their learning: crawling, pulling up, toddling, climbing, running, jumping, rolling, throwing, dancing, drawing, building, or turning the pages of books. They also are not exercising their eyes. Research has shown that extensive television watching limits the development of children's visual tracking skills—the ones that help them read a line of words across a page.

We know that young children are active, interactive learners. They learn by making things happen, by trying new strategies, by testing their ideas in the world, by receiving natural feedback from their efforts. Social interaction is critical to their learning. Television fails to meet any of these needs. Instead, it offers children an almost exclusively passive, nonsocial experience. As Nancy Carlsson-Paige and Diane Levin put it, "Children are unable to affect what happens in any way except by turning the knobs."[8]

Also, children's metabolism slows while they are watching television so that they seem to enter a trancelike state. In this state, images and ideas enter consciousness without the viewer being able to critique them. Dr. Kyle Pruett calls this television's "mind-numbing effect."[9]

Another aspect of the "medium" is the compelling quality of television images. Because of incredible advances in technology, television is able to present images that appear to be magical and larger than life. Such images and ideas hold an extraordinary significance to children and can actually become more powerful than experiences they have in real life. In her landmark book *Growing Up Free*, Lette Cottin Pogrebin cites two remarkable studies that underline the influence television has in children's lives: "Four- to six-year-old children were asked the question, 'Who do you like better, TV or Daddy? TV or Mommy?' Twenty percent preferred television to their mothers and 44 percent liked it better than their fathers. Another survey she cited found that junior high students believe television more than parents, teachers, friends, books, radio, or newspapers."[10] During the four hours that most of our children watch television each day, they are not connecting with family members in meaningful ways.

The Content of Children's TV Programming

Aside from the problems inherent in the medium of television, there are also problems associated with the content of programming for children. Most children spend more time in front of the television than they do in school, yet commercial programming is not written and produced by educators who have children's well-being and intellectual development in mind. Most of it is produced by toy companies, whose single-minded eye toward profit influences all of their programming decisions.[11]

What television producers and executives refer to as "educational programming" is not what

[7] Annamarie Pluhar, interview with Laura Davis, January 5, 1996.

[8] Carlsson-Paige and Levin, *Who's Calling the Shots?* p. 10

[9] Kyle Pruett, "TV: The Good! The Bad!" *Good Housekeeping*, September 1994, pp. 204 and 228.

[10] Lette Cottin Pogrebin, *Growing Up Free* (New York: Bantam, 1981), p. 357.

[11] Carlsson-Paige and Levin, *Who's Calling the Shots?* p. 11

most of us think of as useful curriculum for children. According to a 1990 study by the Carnegie Council, *Yogi Bear, The Mighty Morphin Power Rangers, Woody Woodpecker,* and *America's Funniest Home Videos* were deemed "educational and informational" by television stations.[12]

Television has supplanted many of the sources of traditional education for children. As George Gerbner, of the Annenberg School for Communication at the University of Pennsylvania, warns: "A child is born into a home in which television is on an average of seven hours a day. For the first time in human history, most of the stories about people, life, and values are told not by parents, schools, churches, or others in the community who have something to tell but by a group of distant conglomerates that have something to sell."[13]

Despite these facts, many parents often think, "I watched television and it didn't hurt me." Yet it's important to look at the changes in the content in children's television, not only since we were kids but also in the last few years. The number of violent acts shown on TV has tripled since the deregulation of the television industry. *TV Guide* reports that a violent incident is shown on TV an average of once every six minutes.[14] In children's weekend programming, there's an average of eighteen violent acts per hour.[15]

The most famous children's television show in the world in 1996, *The Mighty Morphin Power Rangers*, which combines live action with animation, revolves around an ongoing battle between the forces of good and evil. According to the UCLA Television Monitoring Report, "Each episode . . . conveys the same underlying message: violence is not really horrible and no one is really hurt by it. . . . The show leaves the impression that the Rangers' actions are socially acceptable and even redeeming."

The report goes on to say "Because of the live action, the show seems more realistic. . . . The characters are real people from a variety of ethnic backgrounds, and, therefore, are much more likely to become role models for the young audience than are animated heroes."

Finally, the report concludes, "When children are asked about *The Mighty Morphin Power Rangers* they do not mention teamwork or commitment to common goals, but they will excitedly talk about the fighting."[16]

Leonard Eron, chair of the American Psychiatric Association's Commission on Youth and Family Violence, writes, "There is absolutely no doubt that higher levels of viewing violence on television are correlated with increased acceptance of aggressive attitudes and increased aggressive behavior. . . . Children's exposure to violence in the mass media, particularly at young ages, can have harmful lifelong consequences."[17]

Stereotypes and Television

Violence, however, is not the only content issue in children's programming. TV is also full of gender stereotypes. Some of these stereotypical portrayals are blatant. As George Gerbner tells us, "Starting at 90 days old, when children can first focus their eyes on a TV screen, they spend four-fifths of their TV-viewing time

[12] Monte Burke, from TV-Free America, in an interview with Janis Keyser, January 5, 1996.

[13] George Gerbner, "Women and Minorities in Television: A Study in Casting and Fate," Report to the Screen Actor's Guild and the National Federation of Radio and Television Artists, June 1993.

[14] Marion Wright Edelman, "Testimony Prepared for the Joint Senate-House Hearing on Keeping Every Child Safe: Curbing the Epidemic of Violence" 103rd Congress, 1st session, March 10, 1993. As reported in "NAEYC Position Statement on Violence in the Lives of Children," *Young Children*, September 1993.

[15] From a 1996 fact sheet put out by TV-Free America.

[16] UCLA Center for Communication Policy, "The UCLA Television Monitoring Report," September 1995.

[17] Leonard Eron, "American Psychiatric Association Report on Violence and Youth," 1993.

watching prime-time programming, which continues to be filled with sex-stereotyped characterizations. The remaining 20% of the time, kids watch children's programming, which is even more stereotypical and exploitative than prime time."[18]

Other times stereotypical information comes across in more subtle ways. Commercials carry hidden messages to let children know if they are advertising "girl toys" or "boy toys." Research has shown that commercials for girls' toys contain more fades, dissolves, and background music; those for boys' toys contain more live action, frequent cuts, sound effects, and loud music.[19] Very young children have demonstrated that they have learned these cues, and parents have made similar observations. Sabrina remarked, "I can tell, when I'm in the other room, just by the sound of the commercial, whether it's aimed at girls or boys. Ads that target little girls have tinkling music and soft lights and the play is generally happening indoors. Boys' commercials have louder music and show rugged play that is usually happening outdoors."

While there has been progress in recent years to include more ethnic and cultural diversity in television programming, omissions and stereotypes are still prevalent. George Gerbner

[18] Gerbner, interview with Laura Davis, January 6, 1996. Gerbner adds, "These facts haven't changed much in twenty-five years. They are stable expressions of a resistant and troublesome value system and global marketing system."

[19] Patricia Marks Greenfield, *Mind and Media, the Effects of Television, Video Games and Computers*, Cambridge: Harvard University Press, 1984.

What About Video Games?

Video games hold a special fascination for children. Images appear on the screen, electronic sounds emanate, there are buttons and levers to operate, they are advertised on TV, and the "big" kids play them.

While the largest audience for video games is the elementary to high school set, many children five and under have, or are asking for, video games. Are these good toys for young children?

The issues for children playing with these toys are similar to the issues around watching television. Even though video games are "interactive," the player doesn't get to perform one-tenth of the action—the characters on the screen are running, kicking, climbing, flying, and the player is just moving fingers. Nor does the player get to be creative in any significant way. When he gets to choose, his choices are limited by the creativity of the creator of the game rather than by his own imagination. For the most part, electronic games are solitary, moving children away from cooperative social interaction so essential to their healthy development. Even when a game is designed for two players, the focus of the game is on the screen, not on the other person.

Children are drawn to these games for many of the same reasons they are drawn to television—the fast action and the powerful images. Children are also interested in video games because of the illusion of power.

The content of video games is also problematic. Even the simplest games promote competition rather than cooperation, and most include eating, squashing, blowing up, or otherwise obliterating an "enemy." Other games involve human characters who fight to kill, injure, and maim each other, many with graphic gore and violence that even exceeds that on television. Like television, video games often carry racist and sexist images.

The repetitive nature of video games mesmerizes young children, who often spend hours glued to the screen and the controls. Because toddlers and preschoolers need to learn through active, social pursuits, it's best to put off introducing these games to children during their earliest years. And if they are available, it's important that their use be limited and carefully monitored.

explains, "A disproportionate number of ill-fated characters come from the ranks of poor, Latino and foreign men, both young and old, African-Americans, and poor women. At the bottom of fate's 'pecking order' are characters portrayed as old women and mentally ill, perpetuating stigma of the most damaging kinds. . . . The world of television seems to be frozen in a time-warp of obsolete and damaging representations."[20]

While public television is better on many counts than commercially produced television for children, there are still incidences of stereotypes as well as the ongoing issues of the medium itself.

Managing the TV in Your Life

Given these well-proven facts about television, as well as the fact that 99 percent of households in the United States have at least one television (more than the number that have indoor plumbing and heat), figuring out how to help children develop the healthiest possible relationship with television becomes a high priority for parents. Some families, like Laura's, have taken the radical step of disconnecting the cable or giving away the TV, and have afterward reported a lessening of family squabbles, an increased feeling of connection among family members, and more hours spent reading and in other creative pursuits. But most families are striving to find the middle ground—a balanced, sane relationship to television in which they feel in control of the TV rather than vice versa.[21]

[20] Gerbner, "Women and Minorities in Television."

[21] A support for families who are keeping their TVs but wanting to help kids become media saavy is The Children's Television Resource and Education Center, 340 Townsend Street, Suite 423, San Francisco, CA 94107, (415) 243-9943. A private non-profit group, C-TREC publishes and distributes helpful educational flyers on topics such as children and commercials, music videos, surviving TV violence, helping children survive video games, and others. Individual copies are free. Call or write for more information.

For many, making the decision about the role of TV in the family is a complex process. Not only do children have their opinions about it, but parents and other adults in the family don't always agree. There are disagreements about how much and what TV the parents themselves should watch and about what each parent considers appropriate viewing for children.

After talking it over, many parents have been able to make compromises. In one household, Joanne didn't want her husband, Guy, to watch violent shows while the children were up. He decided to tape them and watch them after the children were in bed. In another family, Pat felt strongly that the children should have some time when TV wasn't available at all. His partner, Devon, didn't want the kids to be out of sync with their TV-watching friends. After much debate they finally agreed to turn off the TV one weekend a month.

And in Janis's family, there hasn't been a concrete compromise, but there has been a gradual move toward peaceful coexistence. "Television has been an area of conflict in my family. Leon and I have very different ideas about its use, and it seems that after twenty years of trying to convince him, he still doesn't understand that my way is right. So when he is with the kids, they watch just about anything, and when I am home, their viewing gets limited and editorialized. It's not easy for me to let this one go, yet I've also learned to appreciate Leon's basic opposition to censorship."

If you have a TV in your life and want to help your children learn to watch with a critical eye (and in moderation), here are some suggestions:

- **Provide attractive alternatives to television.** If there is an emphasis on reading in your household and there are other creative play possibilities available, TV will be less inviting.

• **Set up some environmental controls.** Place the TV in a less prominent place, maybe not in the main family area. Have it in a cabinet that closes or drape a cloth over it when it's not in use. It is important, though, that the TV is within adult sight or earshot, so that children aren't left to watch for hours without adult supervision.

• **Limit children's viewing.** It's important to know what your children are watching. This means watching for yourself some of the programs that are being made for the children's market. You can closely monitor the shows your children watch and limit the actual minutes they spend in front of the screen.

• **Plan ahead with children what they will watch.** Talking to children about how to choose programs and making a plan in advance with them about what they are going to watch helps children understand your values in relation to TV and also helps them develop a pattern of thoughtful, limited watching.

• **Tape children's shows and remove the commercials.** Commercials in children's TV shows are usually stereotypical, and most urge children to consume junk food and buy, buy, buy. If you have a VCR, it's possible to tape some shows for your children and edit out the commercials. (Newer VCRs are set up to do this automatically.) Also, if you tape programs, you can choose what your children see when the time for TV viewing comes around.

• **Encourage interactive viewing.** TV is a passive medium; all of the ideas, creativity, and information are put out by someone else. Fast-paced action shows or highly edited, quick-moving programs make it even harder for children to interact with what they're seeing. Shows that move at a slower, more human pace allow more room for children to pause; to respond and interact with what's happening on the screen. Also, taping a single good show and letting children watch it repeatedly (as children love to do) can encourage them to develop a more creative relationship to the images.

• **Watch with your children.** If you watch TV with your children, you'll be able to monitor what they're seeing and respond to things that might scare or misinform them. You will also be able to interact with them in ways that encourage more than just their passive involvement in the show: "Why do you think that person is hiding? What do you think is going to happen next?" "Did you like the way that ended? How else could it have ended?"

• **Help children develop critical thinking skills.** In a misguided attempt to eliminate sexism from children's television, TV executives have introduced new women superheroes who kill the bad guys right in step with the male superheroes. However, just because she is a superhero, she has not neglected her "appearance." Most often, she is scantily dressed in skin-tight clothes with plenty of cleavage exposed. This is supposed to represent progress—that "sexy" girls and women now kill right along with the boys.

These are issues you can talk to your children about: "It seems like she should be wearing pants to climb that mountain." Or "It looks more like she is dressed for swimming than for hard work." "Those superheroes are stuck with fighting all the time. I bet you could think of another way to solve that problem." It is important that both girls and boys learn to be critical viewers.

Children who've been taught critical thinking skills begin to internalize a voice that responds to stereotypes. Janis tells the story about her seven-year-old friend, Matt, who had gotten so used to her remarks about what was on TV that he started to watch commercials and say such things as "If Janis were here, she'd say, 'Why isn't a man mopping that floor?'" Through his comments, it was clear that Matt had started building his own critical voice. Even if children initially resist or seem not to hear the information we give them, talking about stereotypes plants a seed that leads them to question media images later on.

• **Help children recognize when the content of TV programming does not reflect real life (or your values).** If children are scared by something they see on TV, you can make such comments as "It sounds like that television program you watched at your friend Kiyoshi's house was scary for you. Can you tell me about the scary parts? I'm sorry that something so scary was on TV." Or "The dangerous things you see on TV aren't real, they are pretend, but it can still be upsetting and confusing to watch them." Or "Some people think that TV programs aren't interesting unless people are hurting each other or doing scary things, so the people that make TV programs use a lot of violence. I don't agree with them. Our family and lots of our friends enjoy other kinds of stories."

• **Use carefully selected videos and movies.** It's not an easy task to choose appropriate videos for children. Even movies or videos that are "made for children" are often scary and full of stereotypes. Many, which might be appropriate for older children, are inappropriate for toddlers or preschoolers.

Because of the marketing saturation that surrounds the release of particular movies, it can be difficult to make careful decisions about what is—and isn't—appropriate for your child to see. When all the other four-year-olds your child knows have already seen the newest Disney release, you may feel some pressure to let your child join her friends. It is, however, useful to see movies or videos in advance, to talk to friends who share your values *and* have seen the film, or to read reviews before allowing children to see them.

If your kids do watch videos, it's important to know that there are many alternatives to the popular commercial movies and videos for kids. There are videos available that are simple, single-subject presentations of things such as tractors, trucks, animals, or life on the farm. There are also children's music concerts. There are even some videos that are wordless, using music as a background. These encourage children to develop a story line and dialogue of their own. Generally, the simpler and less complicated the video, the more room there is for your child's creative participation.[22]

• **Postpone introducing television to children.** Some of us might feel that a child who doesn't have TV is "missing something" or that we're neglecting a part of her education if we don't provide television. Yet young children don't need TV. In fact, they become increasingly competent as learners the more chances they have for active play. If children establish independent ways to entertain themselves early on, they will be able to call on those skills even after television is introduced. If you've decided to include TV as a part of your child's life, you can start by introducing it to older toddlers and preschoolers in short periods. Young children don't need two-hour videos or even whole thirty-minute programs. They could start with ten or fifteen minutes of selected shows.

• **Turn it off.** Inspired by National Turn Off the TV Week, many families have pulled the plug on the TV one day a week, one week a month, or for

[22] For families who are using video with children, we recommend those produced and distributed by Bo Peep Productions, P.O. Box 982, Eureka, MT 59917, (406) 889-3225. Their award-winning videos for preschoolers are engaging and enjoyable without being overstimulating. They move at a child's pace and are full of men and women in nontraditional roles as well as people of all ethnicities and abilities. Write or call for information on specific titles available.

Facts About Television*

- Percentage of households that possess at least one television: 99.
- Time average American spends watching TV each day: more than 4 hours. At this rate, by age sixty-five, that person will have spent *nine years* of life watching television.
- Upon graduation from high school, the average American child will have spent more time watching TV than in school.
- Percentage of Americans who regularly watch TV while eating dinner: 66.
- Percentage of Americans who can name The Three Stooges: 59.
- Percentage that can name up to three justices of the Supreme Court: 17.
- Number of videos rented daily in the U.S.: 6 million.
- Number of public library items checked out daily: 3 million.
- Number of minutes per week that parents spend in meaningful conversation with their child: 38.5.
- Number of minutes per week that the average child watches television: 1,680.
- Percentage of children ages six to seventeen who have TVs in their bedroom: 50.
- Percentage of day care centers that use TV during a typical day: 70.
- Percentage of parents who would like to limit their children's TV watching: 73.
- Number of murders seen on TV by the time an average child finishes elementary school: 8,000.
- Number of violent acts seen on TV by age eighteen: 200,000.
- Percentage of Americans who believe TV violence helps precipitate real-life mayhem: 79.
- Number of thirty-second commercials seen in a year by the average child: 20,000.
- Percentage of best-selling toys in 1985 that were tied to TV shows: 100.
- Percentage of parents who routinely underestimate the amount of TV their children watch: 50.

* These TV facts were compiled by TV-Free America. See below for more information.

a week each year. During that time, children (and all family members) often rediscover all kinds of lost pastimes and pleasures. However, initially for some families, there are squabbles as people begin to figure out how to interact again without TV.[23]

[23] For more information about turning off your TV, contact TV-Free America, 1322 18th Street, NW #300, Washington, D.C. 20036, (202) 887-0436; Fax: (202) 887-0438; e-mail: tvfa@essential.org. This group also sponsors the annual National TV-Turnoff Week. For $5.00, they will send you an information-filled resource kit to help you organize a TV turn-off in your community.

Other helpful resources include the classic books *Four Arguments for the Elimination of Television* by Jerry Mander (New York: Morrow, 1978), *Unplugging the Plug-In Drug* by Marie Winn (New York: Penguin, 1987), and *Amusing Ourselves to Death* by Neil Postman (New York: Viking, 1985). For ideas about life without TV, try *365 TV-Free Activities You Can Do with Your Child* by Steve and Ruth Bennett (Holbrook, MA: Bob Adams, 1991).

- **Examine the benefits to you when children watch TV.** Do you use TV to get a few needed moments of quiet? To enable you to throw dinner together in peace? As a reward? Television can provide that "extra set of hands" in our busy, sometimes overwhelmed families. Clearly, using television as a baby-sitter is a decision that many of us make based on the needs of the family or our own needs, not always on the needs of our child. While doing this for very short periods isn't necessarily problematic for children, longer, more regular periods of being "parked" in front of the television can interfere with the active play and social interactions young children need.

You may need to find alternative ways to get the time you need. Perhaps there's an older, responsible child in the neighborhood who could come over while you prepare meals, care for a sibling, or do laundry. Maybe there's a family with whom you could do a regular child care exchange.

• **Monitor your own TV habits.** Although children experience pressure from peers to watch TV, they learn a tremendous amount from our own viewing habits. If the TV is a substantial part of your own life or is something you keep on continuously in the background, it's unlikely that you'll be successful limiting children's watching.

• **You can make a difference.** The work you do in your own home helping children become critical thinkers and develop a healthy, nondependent relationship to television will also be significant in your larger community. Children who have developed a thoughtful relationship to television will make a difference in their circle of friends.

If you are interested in making an even wider impact in relationship to children and television, you could become a member of an organization, such as The Television Project, which educates parents about TV and promotes alternatives and strategies for controlling television use.[24]

[24] You can write to The Television Project, 11160 Veirs Mill Road, Suite 277, Wheaton, MD 20902, or call (301) 588-4001. You can also e-mail them: 76507.1755@compuserve.com.

FOOD FOR THOUGHT: CHILDREN AND TELEVISION

• What was my relationship to television when I was a child? What is my relationship to it as an adult? Are there any changes I would like to make?

• How is television currently used in my family? Are there conflicts in my family about television?

• Do my children just watch TV that is intended for them, or do they also watch when another member of the family has it on?

• How do my children transition out of watching TV? Is it smooth? Difficult? What kind of moods are they in after watching? Do their moods change depending on the content of the programming?

• Has my family ever gone without TV for a period of time? How did they respond? How do I think life in my family would change without TV?

• Are there changes I would like to make in my family's TV viewing? What might be a first step?

26. Preparing Children to Live in a Richly Diverse World

"On my mother's side, there was a Lithuanian Jew and a Protestant who came over on the Mayflower. My dad is African American and Native American. I guess you could say I'm the all-American girl—Anglo, Black, Jewish, and Native American."

TIYA, *mother of two*

We live in a diverse society. With immigration, worldwide mobility, and new communication technologies, we are in greater contact with people from different races, cultures, and countries. Our children are meeting and becoming friends with kids who are linguistically, culturally, and physically different from themselves. There are more opportunities in our neighborhoods, stores, child care centers, schools, and churches for children to play with people whose families look different from theirs. Kids are interested in these differences, and unless they are taught otherwise, they can easily accept, bridge, and learn from them.

However, our society is full of divisions and separation. Although most of us want our children to be enriched by close ties to all kinds of people, many of us harbor fears about people who are different from us, and those fears often get passed on to our children. Krista relates, "When I'm out with my children and I hear a language that isn't English, I feel uncomfortable. I don't like not being able to understand what is being said. I feel left out, and then it's hard to be friendly."

Even when we want our children to grow up as free of stereotypes and prejudice as possible, we may not know how to make that happen. Norman shares, "Our immediate community is pretty homogeneous. I've always wanted my children to be comfortable relating to all kinds of people, but living where we live, that's pretty difficult. I can't just go up to the one Chinese family in town and say 'Hi, please tell me about your culture.'"

Other families struggle with different aspects of prejudice. Many of us who've faced discrimination in our own lives now have to help our children deal with being teased, and sometimes physically hurt, because of the color of their skin, the religion they practice, the way they look, the structure of their family, or the language they speak.

Maria remembers the day she first faced racism with her son. "He came home from day care asking me 'Mommy, is Spanish a stupid, bad language?' He was only four. He seemed so vulnerable. I wished I could protect him from all of that."

Natalie, whose son is biracial, has also had some painful experiences, "Twice I've been called a nigger when I was getting out of the car to buy groceries. Quincy is only eighteen months old. How do I explain that to him?"

Kit recalls, "When I was little, I always got teased about my hand-me-down clothes. I would have given anything for a new pair of shoes. When Missy came home from child care and said that kids were mean to her because her sneakers were ugly, I just wanted to cry."

And Gordan remembers sadly, "Mirabai has always talked about her adoption matter-of-factly, but this year in preschool some of the other girls began to taunt her, saying 'He's not your *real* daddy.' "

In order to teach children to appreciate themselves and to honor diversity, parents first have to ask themselves "How can I help my child feel proud of who she is?" "How can I help her feel good about people who are different?" and finally, "How can I overcome the barriers I feel in myself so I can experience more openness and connection to other people?"

This chapter will help you develop answers to these questions. We begin by looking at how children learn about themselves—and how they come to recognize similarities and differences in others. We explore the obstacles parents face in teaching children about diversity and present a four-part model for teaching toddlers and preschoolers about fairness, justice, and prejudice. Finally, we give specific suggestions for answering some of the difficult questions that come up as children begin to notice differences out in the world.

Learning About Me, Learning About People Who Are Different: A Developmental Overview

Children under the age of three assume that the rest of the world is just like them and their families. Appropriately, their perspective is completely self-centered. This is delightfully portrayed in the family portraits of children this age, who often draw themselves as the biggest, most central person in the family.

During the first few years of life, children begin important learning about their unique cultural identity. At first they learn about their family's culture implicitly. They "know" how close you are supposed to stand to someone when you talk to them, they "know" how to greet someone you haven't seen all day, and they "know" thousands of other cultural rules for being and interacting in the world. (At three, they don't always *follow* these rules, but they do know them.)

As children near the age of four, they begin to classify things into categories, differentiating between people with straight hair and curly hair, people with light skin and dark skin, people who are wide and people who are thin. They may start saying such things as "Isaac doesn't celebrate Christmas like we do," "Alicia has light brown skin and I have dark brown," or "Why does Dawn live with two moms?" As they start making these observations and asking these questions, children begin their explicit education about the ways people are different.

Parents' responses to these comments and questions are crucial. Simple, informative responses give children words and names for what they're noticing: "Isaac's family is Jewish. Our family is Christian." "Alicia's family is Filipino American and our family is Afro American." "Dawn's moms are lesbians. That means she has two moms. In our family, you have a mom and a stepdad." Through our description of differences, children begin to assimilate our values and beliefs about diversity.

Between the ages of five and seven, children begin to shift their perspective so that they see the world not just from their own vantage point but also from the vantage point of others; they begin to see themselves as others see them. This new ability to perceive themselves in comparison or contrast to someone else sometimes show up as competition: "My hair is longer than yo-ours!!" Or in kids wanting to be just like their friends: "I wish my skin was the same color as Shantika's." Or in fears that no one will like them: "Nobody else in my class needs braces to walk," or "People will tease me because of my glasses."

How Do Children Learn Prejudice?

Children aren't born being afraid of differences. While some may be wary of new things, given support, children become comfortable with differences. However, between birth and five years old, children are learning larger societal values. By the time they are four or five, most children "know" something about which skin color, languages, jobs, physical characteristics, and abilities are considered important—or unimportant—by the larger society. Some children learn derogatory terms for particular groups or people by hearing them on TV, in their neighborhood, or at the dinner table.

When preschool-age children begin to experiment with power and control, they sometimes use what they have learned about undervalued groups to tease and exclude other children: "Girls are stupid." "You can't play here, your hair is dumb." "You're a cuckoo, you talk funny." "You don't have a da-ad!" At this point, children are engaging in prejudiced behavior that they have learned through imitation and by reading societal cues. This doesn't mean that they are already "prejudiced." However, without active intervention, this kind of imitation can grow into real prejudice.

Teaching Children About Diversity: Issues for Parents

All of us face questions, dilemmas, embarrassments, and fears when we consider teaching our children about diversity: "I want my girls to speak Tagalog, and I also want them to feel comfortable with the English-speaking kids on our block." "I don't know what to tell my kids about what culture we belong to. I've always thought of us as just plain American." "My daughter wouldn't stop staring at an albino man who was sitting across from us on the subway. I didn't know what to do." "My son is deaf and he sounds different when he talks. I'm worried he's going to be made fun of."

As parents, we are faced with figuring out how to talk to our children about diversity and injustice when many of us are still in the process of exploring our own beliefs. None of us grows up in this society without learning stereotypes and misinformation about particular groups, and once we "learn" these ideas, we are never fully free of them. Figuring out how to acknowledge and deal with our own biases is one of our challenges as parents. And since we don't just learn stereotypes about people in "other" groups but about our own, as well, we also have to avoid passing on "internalized" prejudice about ourselves to our children.

Steve realized this one day while watching the football game with his friends and his five-year-old son, Joey. "We were joking around and somebody told a Polish joke. I began to laugh, just like I always do, when Joey turned to me and said, 'Daddy, we're Polish, aren't we?' Suddenly I realized, 'Wait a minute, what am I teaching my son about who he is?' "

Many parents feel uncertain and fearful when dealing with people who differ from them in significant ways. Not having had many opportunities to meet people who are different, they feel unsure, scared to reach out, afraid of being uncomfortable, of saying the wrong thing, or of offending people.

Other parents have to face their own rage as they try to help their children understand culture and prejudice. After a lifetime of experiencing or witnessing discrimination, many parents struggle to present a realistic yet optimistic vision to their children about living in a society that is still rife with prejudice.

Some of these same families also have to deal with the additional obstacle of their children's resistance. Children quickly read what the larger world thinks about their culture and may begin to hide the food they eat or refuse to speak their native language.

Vanita recalls, "I always cook traditional Indian food for my family. I remember the day my son came home from kindergarten and said, 'Mom, don't send chapatis and dahl in my lunch any more. All of the other kids eat sandwiches, and Darren said my lunch was gross.' "

These losses, fears, and angers pose considerable challenges for us as parents, yet they can also pose an incentive for us to work to create a world in which our children can feel good

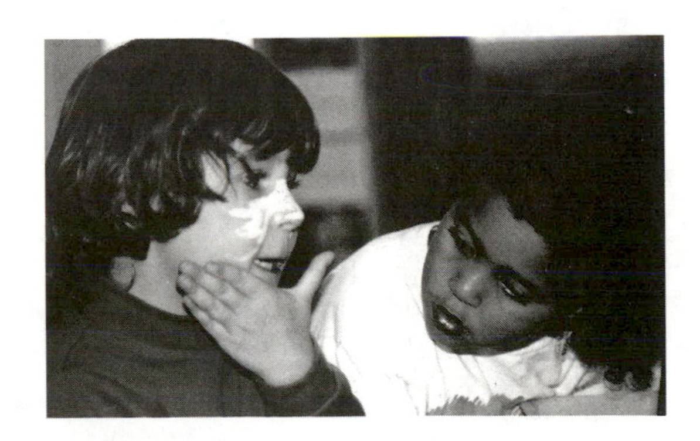

about themselves, have positive experiences of diversity, and learn to value justice.

FOOD FOR THOUGHT: CHILDHOOD LESSONS

- What are some of the stereotypes I learned as a child about groups that I belonged to? About other groups? How was I hurt by these stereotypes?

- What memories do I have about how I learned these stereotypes? Did I resist those messages in any way?

Working Against Stereotypes and Prejudice: An Anti-Bias Approach

When we think about prejudice, some of us mistakenly believe it only hurts the people it's directed toward. It's less obvious to see the toll it takes on all of us: the confusion we experience when presented with stereotypes, the energy we expend trying to sort out and understand the misinformation, the underlying feelings of fear, the friendships and human community we miss out on. We are all hurt by prejudice, and all of us need to work together to eliminate it.

There has been a great deal of research about what helps children grow up able to respect themselves and people who are different from them. Educators who have worked to create a curriculum to counter the prevailing prejudices in society have developed what they call the "anti-bias approach" to education.[1]

There are four components to anti-bias education. The first is appreciating yourself as a member of all the groups to which you belong. The second is appreciating others who are members of different groups. The third is recognizing the prejudice and societal unfairness that exists because of membership in certain groups. The fourth is figuring out how to respond to that unfairness by standing up for yourself and by becoming an ally to people in other groups.

Children's capacity to understand and benefit from all the components of anti-bias education increases through the school-age years. But even toddlers and preschool children can benefit from experiences that introduce these themes.

Helping Children Appreciate Themselves

It's important for children to know and feel good about who they are. Basic to strong self-esteem is feeling proud of who you are as a

[1] The term "anti-bias curriculum" comes from the work of the A.B.C. Task force, a group of early childhood educators from Pacific Oaks College and the Los Angeles area. They developed the anti-bias curriculum in direct response to what they observed: that when kids were allowed to have free choice and free play in an open preschool environment, they were already choosing gender-stereotyped play by preschool age. They also found that preschool children were beginning to absorb societal stereotypes about various ethnic groups and people with disabilities. They decided to work to develop a curriculum that helped to counter the stereotypes and biases the children had already assimilated. The result was the anti-bias curriculum.

In 1989, the NAEYC published the book, *Anti-Bias Curriculum: Tools for Empowering Young Children*, by Louise Derman-Sparks and the ABC Task Force (Washington, DC: National Association for the Education of Young Children, 1934 Connecticut Ave. N.W. 20009-5786). The ideas in this section are drawn largely from the work of this task force as well as from many other dedicated individuals who have done groundbreaking work on ending bias, unlearning racism, and building bridges across differences. In particular, we'd like to thank Carol Brunson Philipps, Ricky Sherover-Marcuse, Lillian Roybal Rose, Aurora Levins Morales, Louise Derman-Sparks, and Julie Olsen Edwards for their pioneering work.

unique individual and good about all of the groups that you belong to.

The groups children belong to have to do with their ethnicity, their cultural background, their language, their religion, their gender, the structure of their family, their age, their size, their physical abilities, and their socioeconomic class. You can help your child feel good about being a member of these groups in the following ways:

- **Teach children about their culture(s).** Culture is of critical importance to children. Through culture, families teach children who they are and how to be that way: "This is your name. This is who you are. This is where you came from. This is how to be in the world." Culture provides children with a crucial piece of their identity.

Yet even children who have assimilated a lot of the customs, traditions, speech, and style of their culture may not have a name for who they are. You can tell them: "We're Puerto Rican American." "We're Sephardic Jews." "You're Cajun and Italian American."

As parents, we play a crucial role in teaching our children about their cultural heritage. Maggie, the adoptive mother of three, explains the steps she's taken to help her daughter from Chile learn about her country of origin. "I want Eliana to embrace both parts of who she is. I make sure we are connected to the other Chilean families in the area. She has pictures of Chile, toys, instruments and artifacts from Chile, we eat Chilean foods, we have actively looked for caregivers who are bicultural, and we have plans to take her to Chile."

- **Use extended family as a resource.** Being around extended family is a natural way for children to learn about their culture. Yeseñia went to great lengths to ensure that her children stayed connected to their grandparents. "I remember hearing kids say, 'I hate going to Grandma's house. She speaks Spanish.' I decided, 'That isn't going to happen to me.' So when our kids were born, my husband and I spoke only Spanish to them. When they first went to school, they knew very little English. I sent them to bilingual classes, and now they're both fluent in Spanish and English. I wanted them to be able to communicate with their grandparents; I wanted them to know how much they had to offer."

- **Research and record family history.** Whether you have extended family around or not, you can pass on old family stories. Record stories from elders that are in danger of being lost. If you don't know much about the groups your family belongs to, undertake some research with your kids. Ask relatives, read books about your people's history, experiment with recipes or traditions from your family's places of origin.

What Is Our Family's Culture?

The first step in honoring diversity is acknowledging and honoring where we ourselves are coming from. All of us operate from a cultural context, most of us from more than one. Becoming aware of your family's cultural heritage is integral to preparing your child to be an active member of a culturally diverse community.

Many of us have names for our cultures or stories about our ancestors: So much is embodied in the words "We are Muslim." "You are second-generation American-born Japanese." "We are African American." "Our family is Catholic." "Serving our country has always been the greatest pride of the Blackwell family."

But names, histories, and stories are only the beginning of the way culture impacts families. Culture plays a large role in the decisions we make as parents—the number of children we have, what our children eat, how they pray, what they celebrate, how they are disciplined, the language they speak, and what we try to teach them. Culture underlies our perspective on many issues critical to family life: autonomy, obedience, dependence, independence, responsibility, work, time, and communication, among many others. Yet many of us pass on traditions and beliefs and ways of being so naturally that we're not always conscious of how much of our teachings are based on our culture.

In Janis's workshops for parents, she asks people to bring in something to share that is representative of their culture. She tells them it can be something contemporary or something with historical roots. In giving the assignment, Janis asks parents to consider the following: "How would you describe your family's culture or cultures? What represents those cultures to you? What are your family's traditions? Which do you want to pass on to your children?"

In response to Janis's assignment, people have brought in food, songs, photos, stories, dances, boots, feathers, books, cookie presses, quilts, and a variety of other family treasures.

On the designated night, Janis begins by talking about culture. "While most of us think about culture as a fixed set of traditions and customs, it's useful to remember that culture is never stagnant. Culture is dynamic, always adapting to new influences: the demands of economics, geography, and political events as well as the families and individuals who carry it on.

"Culture also varies from one person to the next. Just because someone is part of a particular culture, you can't make assumptions about what he believes, how he lives or who he is. As educator Eugene Garcia explains, 'The only way to gain authentic cultural knowledge about a child and their family is one individual at a time.' We have a wonderful opportunity here tonight for each of us to share with others our own perspective on our 'culture.' "

She then pulls out a grimy-looking, well-used notebook binder. She holds it up and begins, "One of the things that represents my family's culture is this cookbook my mother put together. She took a lot of the recipes that had gone all through the family and made notebooks for all the kids and all the cousins. The recipes hold family stories; they say things like 'served to Bill on our first date' or 'Leon's favorite apricot whip.' This cookbook is a lot like my extended family. It has recipes from my mom's and my dad's families, and from my stepdad and his family. It continues to grow as new recipes come in, as new people come into the family and bring their traditions with them. My notebook's covered with goo and has all kinds of stuff sticking out of the pages. That fits my view of culture as something that's always evolving.

"Food is a metaphor for culture in our family in other ways, too. There are certain unwritten rules about organizing big family gatherings. One is that you never ask our family to bring appetizers because we always show up late. Another tradition is that Grandma always gets cranky right before the food gets on the table because something has gone wrong—the food isn't all hot at the same time or people haven't come to sit down right when she called them. All of those little idiosyncrasies are an integral part of my family's culture."

Yeseñia holds up a picture of her large, close-knit extended family and begins her story: "My parents came from Mexico more than forty years ago. They came for a vision of a new, better life. They worked in the fields. They worked in the canneries. My mother got up early to get us ready for school and to make tortillas. They worked hard to provide for us.

"I'm the oldest of three children. When I started school, I didn't know a word of English. The school called my mother and told her not to speak Spanish to us, that she was holding us back. I remember her crying, telling my father 'What am I going to do? How can I not communicate with my children?' It was hard for us. But my parents believed in education. It's a real tribute to them that all their children went to graduate school.

"I'm married now and my husband and I have two children, a son and a daughter. My parents were very religious and they passed that on to us. And my husband and I have passed that on to our children. We pray on our way to school. We pray at dinner. We thank God for what we have. At night, it's part of our ritual. The children have a bath, they have reading time, and then we pray. Religion is our family."

Marcia, the mother of a one-year-old, holds up a beautiful hand-made pouch. "I'm one-eighth Mohawk. When my parents got divorced, I was cut off from that part of my heritage. Now I'm trying to reclaim it.

"One way I'm doing that is by making a family bundle with my son, Gene. Last year, I made him this pouch and lined it with rabbit skin. Then we went to Gene's godparents' and each of us put something in the bundle. His godfather put in a crystal he'd dug up in Arkansas. Gene's godmother put in a little person she'd cut out of sheet-metal. I put in sand from the Grand Canyon. Gene didn't put anything in because he was too young to understand what we were doing.

"Each year on Gene's birthday, we'll open the bundle, talk about everything inside of it, and add something new. When he leaves home, he'll get to take the bundle with him. He'll carry it knowing it's full of stories from his childhood and special gifts from people who love him."

Abe breaks into our thoughts: "One of the things that best represents my culture is sawdust. That comes from my early childhood in Pittsburgh when I lived at my grandmother's house with my family, my uncle's family, my grandmother, my great-uncle and my great-aunt. Down the street was my grandfather's butcher shop. There was sawdust all over the floor and chickens out front. Across the street was my uncle, the baker. It was an Orthodox Jewish neighborhood. We kept Kosher. There were a lot of different languages around—Yiddish, Russian, Hebrew, and German and Polish. For my first six years, I was immersed in a very Jewish culture."

Every one of us has a rich and valuable cultural legacy to pass on to our children. By acknowledging our culture and discovering the traditions we want to pass on, we create a growing sense of family pride. As we simultaneously teach our children to respect the uniqueness of other families, we lay the groundwork for appreciating diversity.

• **Teach children what's special about your family.** In the toddler and preschool years, parents can begin to point out their family's beliefs, customs, and values. When you explain, "In our family, we make a big to-do over birthdays," "In our family, we don't use the word 'stupid,' " or "Our family believes in Jesus," you teach your child about what makes your family special.

Children also need names and descriptions for what's unique about their family: "Families have different amounts of money. Some families have enough money to buy their kids lots and lots of toys. Our family has enough money to rent an apartment so we all have a place to sleep, to buy you a pair of new shoes when you outgrow your last pair, to always have dinner on the table, and enough love to make sure there is always a hug when you need one." Or "In our family, you and your brother came to us through adoption. You have birth parents as well as us."

Children also need words for what is special about them: "Your muscles work differently from other kids' muscles. That's because you have muscular dystrophy."

The information you give will need to be tailor-made to your circumstances. Janis remembers an early conversation with her middle child, Calvin: "When he was three, and I was pregnant with Maya, I had the following conversation with Calvin in the bathtub: I said to him, 'Your skin is brown. My skin is pink. Your skin is brown because it has something called melanin in it. My skin is lighter because it has less, except for these little spots called freckles where my skin is darker. You're brown because your daddy is brown. And you're *light* brown because I'm white. People like your dad are called African American. People like me are called Anglo American. You get to be both. What do you think that this baby growing in here is going to look like?" And he said, "It's going to look like me. Light brown."

• **Provide positive role models.** Children need to see positive images of people who look like them out in the world. They need to see other people who are similar to them in terms of skin color, gender, family structure, culture, class, and physical abilities. In some communities, this is a natural part of daily life. For other families, those that live in a community in which they are the only "Jewish family," the only "Japanese family," the only "family with two dads," it's especially important for children to meet other families that share the same circumstances.

• **Provide your child with dolls, toys, and books that positively reflect the groups they belong to.** Children not only need to know people who are like them, they also need to have pictures and playthings that reflect who they are. Toys, dolls, and puzzles are all available with images of various ethnicities, crayons come in multiethnic skin tones, and there is children's literature available that reflects a wide range of diversity.

• **Watch for bias against your child's "groups" in the media.** Children's TV, video, and films are full of stereotypical messages. You can carefully monitor and select what your child is exposed to. If your preschool child does watch something that has derogatory messages about particular groups, talk about it.

Helping Children Appreciate Others

If children begin with a foundation of feeling good about who they are, they can be readily taught to appreciate people who are different. To facilitate their appreciation of diversity, you can:

• **Help your child meet all kinds of people.** Give children direct experiences with diversity. In some communities, this happens naturally. In others, where diversity is not so readily available, you can find a play group or a preschool or a park where lots of different kinds of kids go.

Parents have done all kinds of things to broaden their children's experience. Patricia, whose son's grandparents lived far away, started volunteering as a driver for a Meals on Wheels program that served food to older people who couldn't leave their homes. She took her son, Michael, with her and, in doing so, enabled him to build friendships with elders he might not have known otherwise.

• **Provide images that reflect diversity.** Children who don't have direct access to people from other groups can still learn about these groups in a natural way. You can do this by introducing books and pictures that show all kinds of people engaged in their daily lives. It's important that these representations aren't stereotypical (disabled people who are helpless, single-parent families that are poor, people of color depicted as service workers). In terms of ethnic diversity, the images shouldn't be limited to people from other countries but should also reflect the diversity in our own country.

• **Talk about it.** Many of us erroneously believe that the best way to overcome prejudice is by overlooking differences and pretending that everyone is the same. Yet it's not the differences that cause the problems; it's the discrimination society creates based on those differences that create the problems. As parents, it's important that we help children see—and talk about—the differences as well as the similarities.

Mei explains: "I do not subscribe to the tenet that being color-blind is best. I don't want my kids growing up saying 'There's only one race—the human race. We're all the same.' We're *not* all the same. I highlight differences for them because I want them to see the beauty in all the differences."

• **Broaden your family's experiences by learning about the arts and traditions from other cultures.** The best way to do this is to make friends with people from different cultures or groups, so there's a natural exchange. You can also join in on communitywide cultural events. Take your child to hear the thunderous power of Taiko drumming, to see the beauty of Balinese dance, or to enjoy the brilliant colors in a Chinese New Year's parade. You can get books that talk about the Day of the Dead, Kwanzaa, Passover, Chanukah, Ramadan, or other celebrations. Respectfully exploring other peoples' traditions and arts can provide wonderful experiences the whole family can share.

It is important, however, that your child's experience of other cultures isn't limited to holiday celebrations or food. Culture is an intrinsic part of who people are; presenting just what people eat or what they do on particular holidays can oversimplify the complexity of any given culture.

• **Teach children that diversity applies to everyone.** Ultimately we want to help children understand that diversity doesn't just have to do with people other than themselves but that diversity applies to them, too. From another person's viewpoint, they look different, too.

• **Work on your own appreciation of diversity.** What we teach our children is inextricably tied to what we believe and how we feel about diversity. Working with our own experience can be a critical part of opening up the world for our children. That can mean building friendships across group lines or participating in churches or community groups that include a wide range of people.

• **Work on your own prejudices.** No one is entirely free from prejudice. The Museum of Tolerance in Los Angeles, an interactive museum that focuses on ending bias, has a dramatic way of getting this across. Bethany explained, "You walk up to the front of the place and there are two doors. One says 'prejudiced' and one says 'not prejudiced.' The one that says 'not prejudiced' is locked. For me, that was a very rude awakening. Having grown up in a household that honored other races, cultures, and religions, I was taken aback by not being able to go through that door. I was *forced* to go through the prejudiced door. By the time I got out the other side, I'd realized that through the media and what's around me in the society, I had, in fact, picked up some prejudice. That was a big revelation for me."[2]

Being aware of our own conditioning and biases is critical to helping our children keep their minds open. Jack explains: "I came from white, Southern, racist culture. I've worked to change that by acknowledging the profound facts of racism in our culture. I've educated myself about the nature of racism. Yet even though I feel very far from the attitudes I was raised with—it's so rooted in our culture, that you have to take it one day at a time, and struggle with it all of your life. To think that I'm somehow beyond what I came from is to not acknowledge how deep it runs."

It is important and often painful to think about the misinformation we still carry with us. Yet it's only in identifying those stereotypes that we can become conscious enough not to act on them or pass them along.

Helping Children Learn About Unfairness

When we as adults think about unfairness and prejudice in the world, we're likely to think about people being denied housing or jobs. But children's first perceptions of unfairness are more likely to arise out of their day-to-day experiences. To a child, unfairness might look like someone getting the juice

[2] The Simon Wiesenthal Center's Museum of Tolerance is a "high-tech, hands-on experiential museum that focuses on two themes through unique interactive exhibits: the dynamics of racism and prejudice in America, and the history of the Holocaust—the ultimate example of man's inhumanity to man." The museum is located at 9786 West Pico Boulevard, Los Angeles, CA 90035. For more information, you can contact the Museum of Tolerance at (310) 553-8403.

pitcher before them or someone taking a toy away from somebody else. Dealing effectively with these situations in children's lives lays a groundwork for their understanding of prejudice and societal unfairness later on. Here are some suggestions for supporting children's growing capacity to recognize unfairness:

• **Support children in resolving their own conflicts.** When dealing with conflicts, we can help children explore their own feelings about fairness: "How did you feel when Joey got the pitcher before you?" "What do you think would be fair?" "How could you make sure that Olympia gets a turn *and* you get a turn?" When children have a chance to state their own position and to listen to someone else's position, they learn the basis of fairness.[3]

• **Respond to hurtful language and name-calling.** Sometimes one child will say to another "You have stupid eyes!" "You have funny hair." "Your legs are ugly." "You talk weird." When your child says something like this, it's important to respond on a number of levels:

Set a limit: "I can't allow you to hurt other people's feelings."

Offer social information: "Name-calling hurts people's feelings."

Give accurate information about the other person: "Lani was born with legs that work differently from yours. She uses her canes to do all kinds of things."

Look at the larger context: "Does my child have access to people or images which can help her see this characteristic as a part of the norm?"

Look for the source of the comment: "Where did my child hear this? Has she been exposed to hurtful or biased messages?"

[3] For an in-depth look at helping children resolve conflict, see "Children's Friendships: Cooperation and Conflict" on p. 304 and "Sibling Rivalry?" on p. 410.

• **Don't let children exclude other children because of the groups they belong to.** Children exclude other children from play for many reasons, but sometimes the exclusion is based on a perceived difference: "You can't play with us because your moms are fags." "You can't play here because your skin is brown." "You can't play here because you have holes in your pants." You can respond to these kind of exclusions as an issue of fairness by teaching kids that they can't exclude someone or treat her poorly because of who she is.[4]

• **Mediate images children see in the larger world.** When you're reading a book to your child that doesn't reflect a lot of diversity, you can say, "The person who wrote this book was thinking only about people who live with a mom and dad. She wasn't thinking about families like ours. Maybe we should write a book about what it's like to live with a grandma, a baby brother, and a cat."

Recently Janis had an opportunity to talk to Maya about a disturbing experience they had while visiting Disneyland. "As we watched the Disneyland parade together, I noticed that all the princesses and all main characters were white and that the only people of color were the 'bad boys' in one of the stories. I said to Maya, 'This parade is making me really upset. I'm mad because they didn't include any princesses with brown skin or with dark or curly hair. They only included blond princesses, and I don't think that's fair. The people who made this parade think the only thing that people of color can do is to be the 'bad boys.' We know that that's not true."

Helping Children Take a Stand Against Prejudice

Unfortunately, kids are sometimes the targets of slurs and attacks because of their membership

[4] See " 'You Can't Play with Us': Exclusionary Play" on p. 316 for more on this idea.

in a particular group. Children may be direct targets of discrimination, or they may be witnesses or observers of it. In either case, it's important to educate and support children when they are confronted with bias.

• **Listen to the hurt.** If your child has been the target of discrimination or if your child has witnessed someone else being hurt, it is important to first acknowledge your child's pain. "It can feel horrible when someone calls you names (excludes you, teases you). I'm so sorry that happened to you." Or "It can be really upsetting to see someone get treated that way. I'm so sorry that happened."

• **Give information.** Tell your child that what happened is not acceptable: "It is not all right for people to say those things." Let children know that name-calling comes from ignorance and doesn't have anything to do with the person who's been teased: "The person who said that to you doesn't really know you. If they knew you, they would know that you are a good friend, that you love to climb and eat pepperoni pizza. What else would they know if they knew you?" This allows the child to recapture some of his lost sense of self.

You can also explain where teasing usually comes from: "Sometimes people say those things because they are afraid. They might have been told that people who look like DeLayne are scary or bad. That's not true and people who think that way are losing out. There are a lot of friends they are going to miss having." Or "Sometimes children say mean things to each other because someone has been mean to them and they are trying to make themselves feel better by being mean to someone else, but that doesn't work."

• **Offer support, action, or protection.** It is too much for children to respond to discrimination alone. It is important that young children know that adults will help and support them through these experiences: "I am going to talk to our neighbor to let her know that she can't treat you (or your friend) like that." "I'll go with you next time you walk that way and we'll talk to those kids together." "We can write a letter to the newspaper (the store owner, the child care center director, your teacher, the principal) to let them know what happened and how we feel about it."

• **Speak up when you hear slurs.** When you and your child hear someone make a prejudiced comment, don't just let it go by. If someone at a family gathering makes an offhand remark, such as "Well, you know those lazy Mexicans . . ." your response is critical. It's important for children to see you standing up for what you believe. You can chime right in and say "The Mexican people we know aren't lazy. They do a lot of different kinds of things. Mr. Lopez across the street from us runs a grocery story. His niece, Paula, is a lawyer. Her brother, Antonio, is a school teacher. And I see other Mexican people working really hard to pick the strawberries and lettuce that we eat. It's not true that Mexicans are lazy."

• **Offer a vision of social change.** You can tell children: "Did you know that there are a lot of people working to change our world so people won't hurt each other that way?" "They even have classes for teachers to help them learn how to help children." "Your uncle Teddy works with a special group called the NAACP whose whole job is to stop people from being unfair to other people." "There are even people who are writing laws to stop people from being unfair to others."

• **Invite children's initiative.** Once children know that they are not alone, you can elicit their ideas about what to do next: "Let's think about what you can do if something like that ever happens again." "What would you like to say to that person who hurt you?" "Tell me what you want to say and I'll write it down." "What do you think we could do to teach people not to hurt each other?"

This is also an important learning opportunity for children who have observed discrimination that they are not the immediate target of. Young children will often offer support to the child who is being hurt. Janis's daughter Maya tells the story of her friend who was being teased. "People were calling Aleta names. I went over and stood by her and asked her if she wanted to play."

You can also teach children how to speak up for their friends: "What could you say to the people who were calling her names? You could say 'That's not true. Those are hurtful names. I don't want you to say that to my friend.' "

• **Building community leads to optimism about the world.** Helping children respond to unfairness, whether that unfairness is directed at them or at another group, teaches them that it's everyone's job to work for greater understanding and justice. It's empowering for kids to learn "I can make a change when things are unfair. And that means if something wasn't fair for me, other people would be helping me, too." Knowing that kind of community exists is a powerful piece of optimism we can give kids.

FOOD FOR THOUGHT: PRIDE AND DIVERSITY

• What would I like to teach my children about the groups that they belong to?

• What opportunities does my family have to see and interact with people who are different from us?

• Are there ways I could imagine myself taking a stand against prejudice and injustice?

Answering Children's Questions

Young children haven't learned social rules of etiquette. They may not yet know that we don't point at someone on the bus and say "Why is that man so fat?" "Why is that woman's skin dirty?" "Why does that man have such a stupid face?" "Why is that woman lying in the doorway like that?" When they ask those inevitable questions or make remarks that make us wish we could slink away, it's important to rise above our embarrassment and use the situation as an opportunity to teach our kids about diversity and respect. Here are some guidelines for handling those embarrassing moments:

• **Acknowledge what children have noticed.** You can say "You've noticed that man's face is different from yours." "You've noticed that woman's skin looks different from yours." "You've noticed that boy is using braces to help him walk." "You noticed that woman sleeping in the doorway." Statements like these appreciate the fact that your child has seen something, even if he doesn't yet have an appropriate name for it.

• **Give your children social information.** When your child singles someone out by pointing, staring, or talking about the person, let him know that people often feel uncomfortable when people point at them or talk about them. You can move away and respond to your son's questions right away or let him know you'll talk about it later.

If you sense that the person might want to respond to your son herself, you can say "It looks like you have some questions about that woman's crutches. You could ask her if she'd like to talk to you about them." When you do this, you help your child get information on his own.

Learning About Leon: Laura's Story

This story talks about the way Laura responded to Eli's two-year-old questions about the fact that Leon has one leg and uses a wheelchair. In it, Eli learns about differences without learning stereotypes: he has a chance to ask questions and have them answered repeatedly, gets to explore the similarities and differences between himself and Leon, learns to view Leon as a strong person with many skills and capabilities, and has the opportunity to make a human connection with someone different from himself. Although this story focuses specifically on a child's questions about a person with a disability, this approach can be used with any of children's questions about people who are different from them.

Janis's husband, Leon, has diabetes. Several years ago he had to have one leg amputated, and now he uses a wheelchair. One morning on my way to take Eli to the Toddler Center, I stopped to drop something off at Janis's house. When we pulled up, Leon was sitting in his wheelchair in the middle of the street, being picked up by the Liftline, a wheelchair-accessible van that supplies transportation for disabled people. Eli watched with fascination as the ramp lowered to the ground. He saw Leon roll on to the ramp and watched the ramp lift Leon's chair up until Leon could roll himself into the van. But what fascinated Eli the most, what he couldn't stop talking about, was the fact that Leon only had one leg. Leon was wearing shorts and no prosthesis that morning, so Eli could see Leon's single leg—and his absent one—quite clearly.

All the way to day care, and far into the morning, Eli kept repeating "Leon. One leg missing. Leon, one leg missing." When I picked him up later in the day he was still talking about it: "Leon, one leg missing." That night, after dinner, we were all sitting around in the living room and Eli started in again: "Leon, one leg missing." Then he stopped and took an inventory: "Eli, two legs. Mama, two legs. Karyn, two legs. Bryan has two legs. Leon has one leg missing."

That night before bed, when we were snuggling in our big chair, Eli wanted to talk about Leon again. I told him a long story about how our family knew Janis and Leon's family. I told him that Karyn had been friends with Janis and Leon for a long time and that Janis and Leon had three kids. Eli said, "Again." And he had me repeat the story several more times. The last time I added, "Leon has diabetes, his leg got infected, and the doctors had to cut it off. But it doesn't hurt Leon," I said. Eli listened intently. "Diabetes," he said. "Diabetes, leg off. Leon, leg not there."

The next morning when I saw Janis, I told her about Eli's latest obsession. She gave me a picture of her family to show Eli, suggested we come over to visit so Eli could get a closer look, and suggested that I tell Eli that Leon has a stump, so that Eli would know he had something—not just the absence of a leg. And she suggested that I tell Eli all the things Leon could do, so that Eli could understand not only what was different about Leon but also what was the same.

That afternoon, I showed Eli the picture Janis had given me. "Leon, one leg missing," he said. I explained who everyone was in the picture and I told him that Leon had one leg and a stump. Eli was very interested, and kept repeating "Stump. Stump. Stump." I told him that Leon couldn't walk and that he used a wheelchair instead. I told him that Leon loved to cook and play with his kids and that sometimes he went to the store and bought food for his family. Eli and I made a whole list of things that Leon might buy at the grocery store. Eli contributed a lot of ideas, including all of his favorite foods: "Leon buy yogurt. Leon buy green apples. Leon buy pizza!" Then I told him that Leon loved music and that he had a lot of records. "Zippedy-do-dah," Eli interjected. A jazzy rendition of Zippedy-Do-Dah was Eli's favorite song. "Yeah," I said. "Maybe Leon has that song, too." And after all of that, Eli said, "Again," and I went through the whole story several more times.

Finally, Eli seemed satisfied and

was ready to move on to other things. But later that night, when I was singing him "Hush Little Baby" before bed, Eli urgently interrupted me with a brand-new idea: "Leon, shoes?"

"Leon only wears one shoe, Eli," I told him. "He only has one foot." After that, Eli was quiet for a long time. I asked him, "Would you like to go see Leon?" Eli didn't hesitate for a moment. "Yeah," he said. "Go see Leon right now." I smiled and smoothed down his hair. "Maybe tomorrow, Eli," I told him. "Right now it's night-night time. Leon's probably asleep right now."

The next day, we went to visit Leon. Leon was sitting in his chair by the stove eating a piece of cornbread and cooking up a pot of greens. At first Eli ran off and busied himself with a toy truck and a book about a mouse who lived in a pumpkin. Leon put on a tape of kid's music for Eli. Leon and I chatted about our older boys and college and a variety of other things. Eli asked for yogurt and played with Maya's lunch pail. But eventually Eli walked right up to Leon with his eyes open wide, staring at his leg and his stump. "Doctor cut it off," Eli said. "Dr. Berman," Leon told him. "Uh . . . uh . . . uh . . . with scissors," Eli said. "No, Eli. He didn't use scissors. He used a scalpel." Eli tried out the new word: "Scalpel. Scalpel. Scalpel." Then Eli looked at Leon some more, his mouth open with concentration, and concluded, "This leg up and this leg down." And so we talked about the fact that Leon only had one leg that reached the ground. And Eli observed that Leon only had on one shoe. And remembering our conversation from the day before, Eli said suddenly, "Leon buy yogurt." "Yes, Eli," Leon replied. "Sometimes I do buy yogurt." And that seemed to satisfy Eli. Seconds later he was completely focused on a shaker of Cajun seasonings and I told him it was almost time for us to go. I helped Eli with his raincoat, he said "Bye, bye, Leon," and we drove home.

Over the next week, Leon's story came up a few more times. We kept the photograph of Leon and Janis's family taped to Eli's mirror so he could look at their family. But basically, he seemed to have worked the whole thing through. Leon's one leg was no longer his most predominant characteristic. The fact that he liked to buy yogurt far superseded his disability.

You also let him know that the woman with crutches is someone who can speak for herself.

However, approaching someone you don't know about a physical characteristic or disability requires a high level of sensitivity. While some people might welcome an honest interchange with your child, others may be tired of being singled out because of how they look. It's important to be sensitive to what it might be like for someone to always have to deal with his or her appearance first in every interaction.

• **Choose the timing for the conversation.** Many times you'll be comfortable responding to your child's questions in the moment. But at other times, your child's comments may take you by surprise. Children's curiosity sometimes challenges us to do our own thinking, and we may not feel ready to deal with the issue our child is raising. Other times, circumstances won't allow you to talk right away.

If, for any reason, you feel you need some time before you answer your child, you can say "That's a really important question. I'd like to talk to you about that later on." If the child persists, saying, "But I want to talk about it now!" and you don't feel ready to respond, you could clarify the limit: "I know you're really curious. And I'm going to talk with you more about it when we get to the car."

• **Use descriptive words rather than evaluative ones.** When a child notices that someone is different, it's important to respond using descriptive, nonjudgmental language. When your child turns to you on the bus and says, "That person has stupid eyes," you can say to your child "That man is Chinese. Most people who are Chinese have eyes like that. He uses his eyes to see just like you do, and his eyes aren't stupid."

By correcting children and responding with a descriptive word instead, we help them broaden their thinking. We teach them that being different doesn't make someone funny, weird, or ugly.

• **Talk to your child about the diversity of the human experience.** When your child says, "Why is that man's nose flat like that?" you can say "People's noses come in a lot of different sizes and shapes. That's what makes people so interesting." When your child asks, "Why doesn't Jamie Lee have a dad?" you can say, "Jamie Lee has two moms because that's the kind of family she has. You know how in our family, Daddy and I fell in love and then decided to have you? Well, the same thing happened for Jamie Lee's moms. They fell in love and wanted to have a family." Comments such as these let children know that diversity is a normal part of the human continuum.

• **Help your child learn more after the event.** You can go to the library and find books that deal specifically with the characteristic the child has noticed or that incorporate that kind of difference incidentally, as a natural part of the story.

Sample Dialogues

The extent to which you answer a child's questions will depend on the child's age, the nature of his curiosity, and what you want to teach. It's important that your explanations be simple, clear, and appropriate to your child's level of understanding. Here are some sample responses:

. . .

Child: Why is that lady so fat? She's taking up two seats!

Parent: People's bodies come in all different sizes. Some people are big and some people are small. Some people are tall and some people are short. You're noticing that person is a big person. That's the way some people's bodies are.

. . .

Child: Why is that woman dirty?

Parent: It looks like you're noticing that she has brown skin. You know, her skin is supposed to be brown. It's not dirty.

Child: But why is her skin supposed to be brown?

Parent: Her skin is supposed to be brown because she had something special that makes it brown called melanin. Probably her mom and her dad also had brown skin. And other people in her family do, too. Children often look like their parents, and that goes for skin color, too.

Child: But will her skin always be brown?

Parent: Her skin will always be brown. After she takes a bath, her skin is still exactly that same color.

Child: Eww! But it's dirty.

Parent: She's really not dirty and it's not okay for you to call her dirty. That could really hurt her feelings. Skin comes in a lot of different colors, and that's the color of her skin. There are people who have skin that's even browner than hers and people who have skin that's lighter than yours. It's not because their skin is dirty. It's supposed to be that way.

. . .

Child: Eww! That person's face is icky!

Parent: You're noticing that that person's face looks different, but his face isn't icky. Everybody's face is different in some way. I'd like to talk to you about this later.

Parent: (After leaving the situation) You were really curious about that man's face and I wonder if you felt scared.

Child: Yeah, why does his face look that way?

Parent: I'm not really sure why. Every person has his own special face, and some people are born with faces that look like that. Sometimes people's faces get hurt and then they look different. But it doesn't look like that man's face is hurting right now.

Child: But why does his face look different?

Parent: It looks to me like that man's skin might have gotten burned. Sometimes when people get burned, their skin grows back in a different kind of way. That may be why that man's face looks kind of tight and stretched and wrinkly.

Child: Will my face ever look like that?

Parent: Probably not. Those things don't happen very often. But you know what? Even when someone's face looks different, they can still be a kind person, a friendly person, a smart person.

. . .

Child: Why is that woman sleeping in the doorway?

Parent: Maybe she is tired and she doesn't have another place to sleep right now.

Child: Where is her bed?

Parent: Some people don't have houses or beds of their own. Some people are homeless.

Child: Why is she homeless? Why doesn't she have a house?

Parent: It's sad, isn't it? Everybody should have a place to live.

Child: So why doesn't she?

Parent: There are lots of reasons people become homeless. Houses and apartments cost money, and not everybody has enough money for one.

Child: I know. I can give her my dollar I got for my birthday.

Parent: That's a wonderful idea. A place to live costs more than a dollar, but we could give your dollar to the homeless shelter. They feed homeless people and give them a place to sleep at night.

Beyond Tolerance

We have an unprecedented opportunity before us: to learn to live with joy and dignity alongside those who are different from us. As Maya Angelou once said: "It is time to teach young people early on that in diversity there is beauty and there is strength. We all should know that diversity makes for a rich tapestry, and we must understand that the threads of the tapestry are equal in value no matter their color; equal in importance no matter their texture."

For the benefit of our children and their future, we can build a world in which real openness, fairness, understanding, and cooperation, not just tolerance, are the norm. Fortunately for us, building those bridges happens one step at a time in small, daily ways that are accessible to all of us, no matter where we're starting from.

Children's Books That Accurately Reflect Our World

As we explained earlier, it's important for young children to see images that reflect the diversity of the world around them.* The following books beautifully and respectfully present a variety of cultures, physical abilities, family structures, and ethnicities:

Books for Babies

Tickle, Tickle, Helen Oxenbury, Simon and Schuster.

This is one in a series of four big, multiethnic board books for the youngest child. The others are *Clap Hands, Say Goodnight,* and *All Fall Down.* Lovely bouncy round babies, up-close illustrations and simple words make these wonderful first books. Ages 1 and up.

My Five Senses, Margaret Miller, Simon and Schuster.

A lovely photo book with simple words about our senses. Includes a delightful diversity of children. Ages: 18 months and up.

Mama Zooms, Jane Cowan-Fletcher, Scholastic Books.

A young Anglo boy has all kinds of fantasy adventures on the lap of his mother as she whizzes around in her wheelchair. Very simple text. Ages 18 months and up.

Jonathan and His Mommy, Irene Smalls, illustrated by Michael Hays, Little, Brown and Company.

Jonathan and his mommy go out for a walk and they take all kinds of steps: running steps, reggae steps, ballet steps, itsy-bitsy steps, giant steps, backward steps, and crazy criss-cross steps. This wonderful depiction of an African American mother and son is sure to inspire your child to want to make up all kinds of creative steps on your next walk around town. Age 18 months and up.

One Sun: A Book of Terse Verse, Bruce McMillan, Holiday House.

Wonderful photos of a Southeast Asian-American boy and his multi-ethnic friends playing on the beach, accompanied by two word poems that fit each illustration: Blue View, Lone Stone, Snail Trail, Sand Hand. Ages 18 months and up.

So Much, Trish Cooke and Helen Oxenbury, Candlewick Press.

A lively look at an African American extended family preparing a surprise birthday party. Every relative from Auntie Bibba to Big Cousin Ross comes in and wants to squeeze, hug, kiss, and eat the baby all up! The repetitive language patterns and the baby getting all the special attention makes this a favorite with the very young. Ages 18 months and up.

Books for Twos

Dancing Feet, Charlotte Agell, Gulliver Books.

A wonderful get-under-your-skin kind of rhyme accompanies special illustrations that show all the great things feet, hands, eyes, and mouths can do. The illustrations show cultural and ethnic diversity, various body sizes, and other kinds of differences, too. Never didactic, this book is a good example of diversity that is fully integrated. Ages 2 and up.

Something from Nothing, Phoebe Gillman, Scholastic.

A beautifully illustrated Jewish folktale full of rich images of shtetl life. Joseph's grandfather has made him a beautiful blanket. When it wears out, his grandfather snips a little here, snips a little there, and he turns the blanket into a wonderful jacket. From a jacket, it becomes a vest, a Sabbath tie, a handkerchief, and finally a button. But then Joseph loses the button, and what can his grandfather do? Ages 2 and up.

All of the Colors of the Earth, Sheila Hamanaka, William Morrow.

A beautifully illustrated, simple, warm book about the many colors of kids: "Love is amber and ivory and ginger and sweet, like caramel and chocolate and the honey of bees, dark as leopard spots, light as sand . . ." Ages 2 and up.

Bread, Bread, Bread, Ann Morris, photographs by Ken Heyman, Lothrop, Lee & Shepard Books.

* See "Children's Books and Bias" on p. 343.

This author-photographer team has worked together to create a number of wonderful thematic books about worldwide diversity, including *Hats, Hats, Hats, On the Go,* and *Loving.* Each has a very simple text that accompanies beautiful color photographs of hats, bread, vehicles, or love in different parts of the world. Ages 2 and up.

Max Found Two Sticks, Brian Pinkney, Simon & Schuster.

An inner-city African American boy with nothing to do finds a way to create drums and play music that reflects the sounds of the city. Ages 2 and up.

Who's in a Family? Robert Skutch, illustrations by Laura Nienhaus. Tricycle Press.

A beautiful book about the great diversity of families in the human and animal kingdom. Includes elephant families, dog families, chimpanzee families, single parent families, biracial families, gay and lesbian families, three-generational families, and many more. Amidst the warm illustrations of daily family life is the simple message, "Who's in a family? The people who love you the most!" The back page has room for kids to paste pictures of their own families. Ages 2 and up.

Books for Three and Up

Come a Tide, George Ella Lyon, pictures by Stephen Gammell, Orchard Books.

A poor rural Anglo family from Kentucky weathers a flood. Lovely illustrations full of beautifully weathered faces and incessant rain. Ages 3 and up.

Char Siu Bao Boy, Sandra Yamate, illustrated by Joyce M. W. Jenkin, Polychrome Books.

The story of a Chinese American boy who loves char siu bao (steamed pork buns) and brings them with him to school for lunch every day. When the other kids make fun of him, he tries to eat the foods they eat. But then he gets them to taste char siu bao instead. Ages 3 and up.

A Special Trade, Sally Wittman, HarperCollins.

Old Bartholomew has been a special friend to Nellie from the time she is a little baby. One day Bartholomew falls on his step and is taken to the hospital in an ambulance. He is sad; now the walks they've taken everyday are over. But when he comes home in his wheelchair, Nellie takes him for walks—just like he did when she was a baby in her stroller. Anglo characters. Ages 3 and up.

City Seen from A to Z, Rachel Isadora, Mulberry Books.

Twenty-six beautiful black-and-white illustrations complement this wonderful alphabet book about ethnically diverse New York City life. Words such as car wash, pigeon, window box, and jazz are featured. Ages 3 and up.

Too Many Tamales, Gary Soto and Ed Martinez, Scholastic Books.

Maria helps her mother make tamales for a big Mexican American family Christmas Eve celebration, and she is convinced she dropped her mother's diamond ring in the masa. So she and her cousins force themselves to eat all the tamales to find the missing ring. Too many tamales! Ages 3 and up.

Cleversticks, Bernard Ashley, Crown Publishers.

Ling Sung is feeling frustrated by his inability to do tasks like dressing himself, writing his name, and buttoning his own jacket. Just as his confidence is wavering, he discovers his own special talent. The preschool setting of this book is wonderful for children who may be spending time in child care. Ages 4 and up.

Palm Trees, Nancy Cote, Four Winds Press.

This story is about an African American girl and her friend on a hot summer day. It deals with a challenge to their friendship and describes how one girl comes to appreciate herself and her hair. Ages 4 and up.

Very Last First Time, Jan Andrews, illustrated by Ian Wallace. Atheneum.

Eva Padlyat, a modern-day Inuit girl, goes with her mother along the sea bed when the tide is out to search for mussels. Finally, she is old enough to venture down into the world between the ice and the sea bed alone. Gorgeous illustrations. Ages 4 and up.

Grandpa's Town, Takaaki Nomura, Kane/Miller Book Publishers.

Beautiful woodcut illustrations accompany this story about a Japanese grandfather taking his grandson to the city and the public baths. The boy, who initially thinks his grandfather is lonely, comes to realize just how full his grandfather's world actually is. Set in Japan. Bilingual in Japanese and English. Ages 4 and up.

Can You Catch Josephine? Stephane Poulin, Tundra Books, Canada.

A single dad in Canada, who couldn't find any books about single dads and kids, decided to write and illustrate his own. The fabulous result is the Josephine series. All of the books focus on Josephine, the cat, who always gets into places she shouldn't be in. In this book, Josephine sneaks into the little boy's school and havoc results. The story is simple and the illustrations tell many tales of their own. The boy and his father are Anglo; other characters vary. Ages 4 and up.

Mama Bear, Chyng Feng Sun, illustrated by Lolly Robinson, Houghton-Mifflin.

A Chinese American girl and her mother save for a special Christmas teddy bear, only to discover that they already have something warm and cuddly at home. Ages 4 and up.

Just Plain Fancy, Patricia Polacco, Dell Publishing.

A wonderful story of two Amish girls who find an abandoned egg that they care for until it hatches into a peacock. A second book, *Mrs. Katz and Tush,* outlines a wonderful friendship between a young African American boy, Larnel, and his elderly Jewish neighbor, Mrs. Katz, that springs up over an abandoned kitten, Tush. Ages 5 and up.

The Duke Who Outlawed Jellybeans and Other Stories. Johnny Valentine, illustrations by Lynette Schmidt. Alyson Wonderland.

A beautifully illustrated book of five fairy tales full of intelligent, competent children: brave girls and sensitive boys whose adventures include stopping unfairness and being kind to others. Many of the stories include gay and lesbian families as a natural part of the story. This beginning chapter book is appropriate for children 5 and up.

Mama One, Mama Two, Patricia MacLachlan, pictures by Ruth Lercher Bornstein, HarperCollins.

A sensitive, beautiful picture book for children being raised in foster families. A young girl and her foster mother tell each other the story of how the girl came from mama one to mama two. Told with great respect for everyone involved. Ages 5 and up. Note: Introducing the idea of a mother who can't care for her child could be upsetting to younger children.

• Part Six •

Family Relationships

27. Parenting with a Partner

"Democracy is a small core of common agreement, surrounded by a rich variety of differences."

JAMES BRYANT CONANT

Raising children is one of the most joyous, intimate, and challenging things two people can do together. When you parent with a partner, you share in the miracle of life and delight together in your child's antics and discoveries. You benefit immensely from having another person who is as crazy about your child as you are.

While for many the notion of parenting with a partner implies a spouse or a life partner, there are many ways to include other people in your child's life. Many single parents identify friends or members of their extended families to develop special relationships with their child. And some develop significant networks in which they share some of the responsibility of parenting.[1]

Sharing parenting can bring resources such as time, energy, new perspectives, and complementary skills to your family. Yet sharing the care of your child with another person also holds challenges. It requires articulating your life goals and aligning them with those of another person. It means being accountable, finding compromise, sharing control, balancing needs, and working through conflict.

In this chapter we begin by addressing issues for couples who are becoming parents for the first time. We then expand to talk about the issues of concern to all adults who are sharing the care of their child. We introduce the concept of "gatekeeping," discuss what to do when a child prefers one adult over another, and talk about how to handle differences between parents or other primary caregivers. Finally, we look at issues for parents who are separated or divorced and discuss ways to make shared custody work.

New Parents: Issues for Couples in the First Year

When we have children in the context of a relationship, that relationship is permanently altered. The first year of a child's life is a thrilling, stressful, and growth-producing time for couples. The focus shifts from the needs of the couple to the needs of the baby. Instead of relating to "my wife" or "my husband" or "my

[1]While much of this chapter focuses on "couple" relationships, there are other parts that also apply to sharing parenting with other important people in your child's life.

partner," new parents are learning about their spouses as "Zane's father" or "Lily's mother." And they're relating to themselves in a new way, as well.

For some couples, the birth of a child brings increased intimacy. Stuart recalls, "The first year of Caitlin's life was a joyous time for Claire and me. Our hearts were opened up by Caitlin's birth. We had a single-minded focus—this miraculous new life we'd been entrusted with. We were united in our purpose and we'd never felt so close. That first year was an exhausting, wonderful time."

Sue remembers, "There was a new softness in Sherman when Forest was born. There was that precious time the first few weeks after the birth when we would all wake up together in the middle of the night for feedings. And even now a few years later, there is a level of sharing that we experience in being parents that is different than anything we shared before we had kids."

Other couples feel less intimate during their baby's first year. Mothers who are nursing and doing most of the physical nurturing of the baby sometimes have decreased needs for physical contact, just at a time when their partners are wanting more touch and reassurance.

Juliet remembers, "I felt like I had someone on my body all the time. I loved nursing Jonathan, but I didn't want anyone else touching me. I couldn't stand anyone else making physical demands of me. And that was pretty hard for Rick to accept."

Chan, a new father, recalls, "I felt shut out. I'd been used to having Maylynn available, and suddenly she was absorbed in caring for Kian. Because they were nursing around the clock, I felt left out a lot of the time. Kian wanted her mom; she didn't want me. I felt lonely. I gained a child, but it felt like I lost my wife."

Becca laments, "I feel good about the first year of Tucker's life, but I feel sad about the loss of intimacy with Franklin. We really need to make our relationship as a couple a focus again."

Often it's near the end of the first year that parents start picking their heads up from the intensity of dealing with a newborn and infant, and begin the process of reestablishing their identity and connection as a couple.

Nurturing Your Relationship: Ideas for Parents

With new babies and with older children, as well, it's essential for partners to find ways to stay close and connected. Feeding your relationship is important for you and for the health of your family as a whole. With some forethought and creativity, you can develop new ways to keep your relationship strong:

• **Enjoy your baby together.** Many busy couples spend a lot of time "trading off" time with the baby: "Okay, it's your turn." It's important to have some family time every day in which you both enjoy the baby together—marveling as she grabs her toes or rolls over or squeals with delight.

• **Make the most of intimacy in the moment.** You don't always need extended time alone to connect with your partner. A tender hello, a kiss in the middle of the day, a hug, or a five-minute backrub at night are ways to remind yourself that you are a couple as well as a family.

• **Wait until you're ready, but take time for just the two of you.** Time away gives you the necessary space to rebuild and reenvision your relationship as a couple. However, people have different timetables in which they feel comfortable being away from their kids. Some are ready earlier; others take longer. In many couples, one person is ready before the other. It's important that you don't feel overly pressured to leave your children, but at the same time, you may need to stretch a little in order to make it happen at all. Ultimately, it is important to have some time alone with your partner, away from the constant needs of your kids.

• **Start small.** Try leaving your baby with a trusted caregiver for an hour, and gradually work up from there. Build on small successes.[2]

• **Be resourceful.** Parents who aren't blessed with willing friends or extended family members have gotten time alone by doing trades with other trusted parents—each couple taking a night or afternoon once every few weeks to watch the kids. Other parents have hired a caregiver weekly or monthly to ensure some quality time alone. Some toddlers, and many preschoolers, are ready for sleepovers with a relative or a familiar caregiver, or at a best friend's house.

• **Plan ahead.** Planning for time alone together may feel less fun to you than letting it happen spontaneously, but it can be a start. As Faye explained, "Planning is essential. You have to set up those Saturday night dates in advance or they just don't happen. It's rarely 'The kids are both at somebody else's house. What should we do?' "

• **Make it regular.** When your time alone with your partner is infrequent or unpredictable, it may be more frustrating than satisfying. Jack, who waited until Heidi was six months old before he and his wife had any time alone, explained, "It was crazy. We hadn't been alone together in over half a year, and we had one-and-a-half hours. In that hour and a half we were supposed to make love, resolve all our differences, and have fun. It was too much pressure. We had too many built-up expectations, too many unspoken needs. We ended up fighting the whole time. It was a real lesson for us. We'd set ourselves up for failure."

• **Try a morning date.** When you're thinking about taking a few hours away from your kids, don't limit yourself to the traditional "evening out." Parents are often exhausted at night and it can be hard to enjoy each other—or even stay awake—if your time to be together comes at the end of a busy, demanding day. As Janis puts it, "Don't just give each other the armpit of the day."

Try making a date in the morning. Kids often have an easier time being cared for by someone else when they are rested—not fatigued from the day. Many can handle their daytime routine being disrupted more easily than their bedtimes. As one perceptive preschool teacher remarked, "Kids are older in the morning than they are in the afternoon."

• **Make your relationship a priority.** Mei explains: "In our family, the hardest thing to do is to find time for Les and myself. Somehow everything else takes priority. I arrange the kids' activities and schedules. Then I arrange my own. Les and I are both people who have our own activities and interests, and we always seem to manage to schedule them in, but then there's no time left for the two of us. I really believe that the marriage is the centerpiece of a family. Everything should revolve around the marriage. I'm not living my words yet, but that's what we're striving for."

Mothers As Gatekeepers

Sometimes parents—particularly mothers—have trouble letting anyone else, even partners or other trusted adults, take care of their children. Because of the way motherhood is defined in this society—"Mothers are always available, always loving, always there"—letting

[2] See Chapter 13, "The Dance of Separation" on p. 116 for ideas on successfully planning for time away.

someone else take care of their kids leads some mothers to feel as if they're losing their sense of purpose or their "specialness." The myth of the perfect mother can lead to feelings of self-doubt and ambivalence: "Do I really want my child to succeed with someone else?" "If someone else can take care of my child well, where does that leave me?"

At the same time, many mothers feel overworked and complain about the fact that they have to do it all, that they're not getting enough help. Yet sometimes they play a role in creating and perpetuating that dynamic.

"Gatekeeping" is the term we use to describe the ways parents consciously or unconsciously limit or control other people's relationships with their children. Sometimes gatekeeping is overt: a mother never leaves her kids in anyone else's care. But often it's more subtle than that. Gatekeeping shows up whenever we try to orchestrate other people's interactions with our children.

Dalia, a single mom, explains: "Whoever takes care of Zach, I tell them, 'This is the way you heat the bottle. This is how you give him the bath. This is how you change his diaper.' I have a zillion and one rules. I try to temper them, but I still try to control the way everyone is with Zach. I guess I just want to be the boss."

Joe complained about being shut out of the decision making: "A couple of times when the girls were little, my wife was going out and she wanted to tell me exactly what to do while she was gone, minute by minute. And I said, 'Wait a minute! Let me be with my children. Let me do it the way I want to do it. Let me figure it out.' "

June, whose partner, Gina, is the biological mother of their daughter, explains her frustration: "Every Monday night, Gina takes a class. It's my night alone with Catherine and I really look forward to it. But right before she goes out, Gina always manages to find some way to give me instructions: 'Her blue pajamas are in the dryer.' 'She needs a diaper change.' 'Give

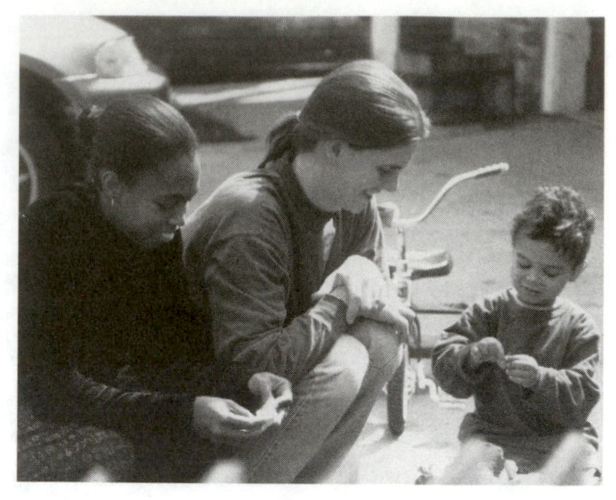

her the leftover squash in the refrigerator.' Sometimes the instructions are couched in things Gina says to Catherine: 'Maybe Mama June will take you for a walk,' or 'Maybe Mama June will give you a bath and sing you the rubber duckie song.' The whole time I know she's not really talking to Catherine; she's talking to me. And I resent it. I don't want to be told what to do. I'm not a baby-sitter. I have my own ideas about how to spend time with my daughter. Why can't Gina let go and just walk out the door?"

When we repeatedly criticize our partners or others for "mistakes" they make with our children, saying "That's too much cereal!" or "Why didn't you remember to bring a diaper with you?" or "That shirt doesn't match those pants," we undermine their relationship with our kids and often frustrate them, making it hard for them to be actively involved.

Take a moment to ask yourself: "What do I say when Dad puts the baby's shirt on with the buttons in the back instead of down the front where I think they belong?" "How do I react when Grandma puts the diaper on too loose?"

Gatekeeping and Gender

In our society, women are the ones expected to know how to be with children. So when the gate is closed on fathers, it is often readily accepted, largely because it dovetails so well with the messages men get in this culture. Because men are largely still viewed as "secondary parents" and mothers as "primary parents," it can be hard for men to step forward and take their place as significant, nurturing parents.

Eric explains, "When Lauren was real little, even before she was born, I remember feeling a lot of fear that I wouldn't be as good a parent as Susan, just because I'm a man. I wasn't sure I could trust my judgments or that Susan would trust me. I had fears of being extraneous, like a fifth wheel. As a man I don't feel as secure about my ability to connect. Even before we conceived Lauren, I remember telling Susan 'I don't want to be left out. I know you're going to be really good at this, but I want to be part of it, too.' "

In families, sex roles are sometimes reinforced in both overt and subtle ways by both men and women. As Janis explains, "In a lot of families, when Dad does take the baby out, it's still Mom who packs the diaper bag."

Brenda explains, "I think fathers are cheated out of finding out 'What am I good at? What do I like to do as a father?' If as mothers we're filling up their time with 'Do this,' and 'Cover that,' they're deprived of finding their own way with their children."

Women often say of their husbands "Oh, he helps me a lot." In other words, "It's all my responsibility and he helps me do my job." Or "Stan is baby-sitting," as if it's not a father's regular job to be with his children. Language is powerful. Saying "Stan and I work together to take care of our kids" gives a very different message than "I'm lucky. He's a good man. He helps me out a lot."

Opening the Gates: Sharing in the Caring

The most important thing for our children is a strong, nurturing connection with us. From that secure base, our children can benefit from close relationships with other significant adults.

Being thoughtful about allowing others to truly participate in the care of our children is important, but for some parents, it's also a challenge. How much gatekeeping we do has a lot to do with the models we've seen, family and cultural norms, our needs for control, and the quality and kind of support that is truly being offered.

Here are some things to consider as you think about supporting your partner and other loved ones in having close relationships with your child:

• **Pass on information in respectful ways.** The parent who is with the child more does have practical information to pass along—what the child has eaten, when she napped, when she had her last diaper change. It's important to pass information on in a way that doesn't undermine the other parent or treat him like a stand-in; that still respects his competence and enables him to make decisions.

• **Make decisions together.** To move from a gatekeeping relationship to one of shared responsibility, we need to be clear that we want not just help but equal participation. We need to move from being the person who organizes everything in her head, and then gives assignments to others, to someone who shares decision making: "How should we organize the care of the kids this week?"

When we start thinking as a team about the work that needs to be done, we truly share the tasks of nurturing.

• **Support your spouse as a parent.** Take the time to appreciate the care, thought, and love your partner and others give to your children. Feeling supported rather than criticized is crucial to feeling welcomed and valued.

• **Within safe parameters, allow your child to bond with someone else.** If someone outside of your immediate family—an extended family member or close family friend—wants to develop a stronger relationship with your child, and you feel safe and confident about that person, take steps to let that person build a significant relationship with your child.

• **Let other people participate in daily caregiving routines.** Include other people in feeding children, putting them down for naps, changing their diapers, bathing. Closeness often blooms during these routine daily interactions.

• **Step back.** When Aunt Lauren comes over, let her spend some time alone with your six-month-old. Do some chores around the house. Go in the kitchen and make lunch. Arrange for them to spend some time together at Lauren's convenience, not just when you happen to need a baby-sitter.

• **Let other people participate when your child is struggling.** Let other people spend time with him when he's cranky, or walk him around when he's yelling in a restaurant.

• **Teach your child about the specialness of his relationships.** Talk to your child about your friend Stella when she's not around. Prepare him when she's coming by. Let him know how special it is that he's going to get to see her.

• **Open up the world.** It takes a certain amount of letting go to expand your family and let other people in. But the rewards are immense. When you allow your child to love and bond to someone else, your child's world becomes larger and safer. So does yours. When you trust another person with your precious child, you have the chance to learn that the world can be safe beyond your arms, beyond your control.

• **Take this chance to learn about love.** To allow your child to love someone else, you have to believe that love is not a finite substance that gets used up or spread too thin. You have to give up the notion that loving someone else means your baby will love you less. You may be afraid that love is a limited commodity, but it's not. It's an expanding resource.

FOOD FOR THOUGHT: GATEKEEPING

• In what ways am I supportive of the people who share in the care of my child? Are there ways I could be more supportive?

• Are there ways I've criticized my partner's interactions with our child? Are there ways I've felt criticized?

• What's the difference between having standards for my child's care and controlling things too rigidly?

When Children Prefer One Parent over the Other

Children often favor one parent over the other. Sometimes it's triggered by a developmental change or need, and other times it's in response to something that's happened in the family: one parent goes back to work or has to be away for longer hours, a sibling is born, or Grandpa moves into the house. It's hard for kids to focus equally on two people at the same time. Even though kids love both their parents, there's often a leaning one way or the other.

Some children favor the person they spend more time with, or the parent with whom their time is more predictable. Others favor the parent they see less often. Children also may favor the person whose temperament or interests more closely match their own.

Sometimes children's preferences shift over time. Gil explained: "It sure hurt when Sharon was ignoring me, when all she said when she was with me was 'Mommy! Mommy! Mommy!' But then there'd come the times it was the opposite: 'Daddy! Daddy! Daddy!' "

This favoring of one parent over the other can be really hard for the less-favored person. Debbie, the mother of one-year-old Ana, explains: "When I first went back to work, Ana didn't want to be around me. She wanted Marlon to hold her. But then he'd need to go off and do something and I'd try to take her. And she'd cry for him. I remember this one night when he had to go out. Whatever I did for her, it wasn't the right thing. I tried giving her a bottle. I tried walking her. Nothing worked. She wanted her father. Finally, she cried herself to sleep."

It's a very different experience to be with a child who's crying for the other parent than it is to be the person the child wants to be with. As Ron explained to Bonnie one day when their daughter, Tammy, was still quite young, "My time with Tammy is very different from yours. Half the time she's with me, she's at the back door crying and whining for you."

When you are parenting with a partner, one, if not both, of you will eventually end up in the less preferred position. That experience, although it can feel terrible, actually gives you a unique opportunity—the chance to demonstrate unconditional love to your child. As the person who has to hang in there when your child really wants to be with the other parent, you get to say "I know you're sad. I know you want to be with your mom, but I'm still going to be with you. I'm still going to be here." Even when your son spends his whole time with you crying for his other parent, staying present and consistent with him is significant.

As adults, we know the breadth of the relationship we have with our children, but our children don't automatically know the depth and permanence of their connection with us. By gently persevering with them, we teach them about the parameters of the relationship: "I'm your dad. You can turn your head away from me for days on end and I'm still going to be your dad. I'm still going to be taking care of you and listening to your feelings, because that's how dads are."

On the other hand, if we are so shaken by our child's "rejection" that we reject him in turn, saying "Well, in that case, I won't talk to you either," our child gets the message that relationships are pretty fragile things and that love is highly conditional.

Strengthening Your Relationship with Your Child

If you're in the position of being the "less preferred" parent, there are some things you and your partner can do to strengthen your relationship with your child:

- **Spend regular time alone with your child.** If care is not being shared equally, the first and most important thing you can do is to spend regular, consistent, predictable time alone with your child. Time you all spend together as a family is wonderful, but it is not the same as time you spend alone with your child. Children need lots of opportunities to build that special sense of trust and connection with the parent they're feeling less close to.

• **Don't expect things to be equal.** It's okay for children to have different relationships with the adults in their lives, parents included. Woody, father of one-year-old Mia, explains: "It's only natural that Mia would have a different kind of bond with Leslie. But their bond doesn't diminish the one Mia and I have. I have no doubt that she needs me as a parent."

• **Set the parameters of what children can and can't control.** Children need clear limits set when they're pushing one parent away. If Sam is cuddling with Mommy and Daddy comes up, and Sam starts yelling "Daddy, go away! I don't want you here! I want to be with Mommy!" Mommy could say "Daddy's going to sit here, too. You're welcome to stay with both of us." Or Daddy could say "You know what? I want to be close to you and Mommy right now. So I'm going to sit right here. Would you like to stay with us?"

• **Develop special activities that only you share with your child.** Baking gingerbread together, walking to a certain fountain, playing the wiggle-like-a-snake game, or singing favorite songs are examples of simple ways you can establish special activities that happen only when your child is with you.

• **Pay attention to the things your child really likes to do and do them.** The "preferred" parent can help by not doing those things as much with the child.

• **Be available when your child asks to be with you.** Instead of saying "As soon as I'm done with the newspaper," drop your paper and play. If you delay, the opportunity may be lost.

• **Pay attention to what happens when both parents are with the child.** When you're all

home in the evening together, and the child needs something, who gets up? Make sure that the "nonpreferred" parent has regular evenings when it's his or her responsibility to get the child whatever she needs. (But be sure to tell your daughter what's going to happen ahead of time if it's not what she's used to. Part of children's resistance is "But you're not the person I was *expecting* to help me.") In this instance, the "preferred" parent will need to refrain from giving directions, advice, or stepping in, unless invited to do so by the other parent.

• **Be the nurturer when your child gets hurt.** When your son gets hurt, the preferred parent can be "busy" so the nonpreferred parent gets to be the nurturer. "Preferred" parents tend to swoop in whenever there's a conflict, problem, or injury. When this happens, they give children the message that the other person isn't capable of solving the problem. By holding back at times, the "preferred" parent shows confidence in the other parent and creates room for that person to create a deeper bond with the child.

• **Reassure your child that there's enough love to go around.** You can support your child's relationship with her other parent ("Boy, you really love your daddy! I really love Daddy too. He's pretty special!"), even as you work to build up your own. Your child shouldn't feel she has to give up her special relationship with her other parent in order to be with you.

• **Get support from your partner.** As well as loving and encouraging you during this difficult period, your partner can support your relationship with your child. When you are gone, the two of them can pick leaves for you, make you a drawing, cook you a special dinner, or call you at work. They can talk about you, look at pictures of you, and make plans for how to greet you when you arrive.

• **Give it time.** It's important to remember that children's loyalties can, and often do, switch. It's easy for the preferred parent of today to become the less-preferred person tomorrow. Try not to take these changes personally.

• **Persist in your relationship, even if it's hard.** Sometimes when children prefer one parent, the other parent sinks more and more into the background, yielding to the child's preference. While it's important not to "force" your affections on your child, you need to continue being a presence in your child's life. Keep spending time together, even if it's not always easy.

• **Don't give up.** Your children deserve your consistent, loving presence in their lives no matter who they're focusing their attention on in the moment.

When Partners Disagree

When you're parenting with someone else, you inevitably become aware of the fact that you don't see eye-to-eye on all things. Each of us comes to a relationship with our own unique cultural background as well as our own family and childhood experiences. As a result, we carry certain assumptions about children, relationships, and family life. Often we're not aware of these assumptions until we bump up against a different set of beliefs, and sometimes our first reaction is to feel there's something wrong with the other person: "You must be kidding! That's way too much fuss over a simple birthday." Or "Aren't holidays important to you?" Or "How can we be close if we don't eat dinner together? Don't you want our family to be close?"

Many of us feel uncomfortable with practices that are different from our own, and some of us would rather have our partner change to fit our way of doing things than try to create new ways of doing things together. However, taking the treasured parts of each parent's background to create new family's traditions is a valuable and important part of building a partnership. Along the way you may find yourself asking "What's really important about my way of doing things?" "What's really important to my partner?" "How can I be enriched by my partner's perspective?" "What differences can we live with?"

Many of the conflicts that occur in families happen because of differing values and expectations. Those conflicts often revolve around simple things—what breakfast is, who makes it, where people sit, what people wear, how the checkbook gets balanced, how things get cleaned up, and who writes the thank-you notes.

Every couple goes through a process of sorting these things out, and when we add kids into the picture, it becomes even more challenging. We're on brand-new ground with old expectations. The things we may have already worked out as a couple don't necessarily work once we have children. What seemed resolved may seem unresolved again.

Taking the opportunity to look at your differences, finding the common ground and developing new ways of doing things is an ongoing process. Here are some things that can help:

• **Aspire toward an open mind.** If you come to discussions with an open mind rather than a "set answer" you want the other person to agree to, you lay the groundwork for shared decision making. If you say to your partner "You need to give up going to the gym on Saturdays because Lori needs you to be with her at swimming lessons," he is probably going to feel resistant. If instead you say, "Lori is going to start swimming lessons on Saturdays and one of us needs to be there with her. I've got my accounting class and I know it's your time at the gym. Let's talk about how we can work this out," you're much more likely to come to a mutual solution.

• **Bring up differences privately.** Unless there's a question of safety, try not to interrupt your partner in the middle of an interaction with your child.

Mei says learning to hold back has been an ongoing process: "I remember times I didn't like the way Les was handling something with the kids. I'd butt in and he'd immediately snap back, 'Let me handle this my way.' So I'd step back. Afterward we'd talk about our different points of view. Now I try to avoid interfering, but it's hard. I still want to say to him 'Don't use those words! Say it like this!' And I know he wants to say to me 'Calm yourself! Don't lose it so quickly.' But we both really work to hold our tongues."

• **Create an atmosphere in which it's safe to disagree and hash things out.** If both partners move away from the stance "My way is right. Your way is wrong," they can develop safety within the relationship for both people to examine their values, expectations, and beliefs. Some important questions can emerge in the process of that self-examination: "What do I believe?" "How did I learn it?" "Is this really something I want to pass on?" "What do I want to teach my kids?" Taking the time to delve into such questions can be clarifying and instructive.[3]

Also, when you go back to the basics of what you believe, it's a lot easier to get to the bottom of differences than it is when you stay on the surface, fighting about the specific manifestations.

• **Look at recurring disagreements.** Many couples have ongoing differences. Some are small irritations that can even be humorous at times. However, other disagreements may be indicative of unresolved areas of conflict and resentment. When serious ongoing conflict exists in a relationship, it eventually affects the health of the whole family. It becomes difficult to be effective parents and to work cooperatively. If there is this kind of friction in your relationship, it is crucial that you get support in working toward resolution.

• **Separate the current issue from old hurts you may be carrying.** Sometimes it's hard to solve problems because the current situation reminds us of other times we've felt hurt or unacknowledged. Learning which circumstances are likely to trigger old defenses and ancient feelings can help us keep the past from interfering with communication and problem solving in the present.

• **Clarify the problem.** Sometimes we are clear before we begin a discussion about what really matters to us—our bottom line. But often we don't figure that out until we've talked

[3] For more on clarifying values, see "When Your Values Differ from the Values of Your Partner" on p. 4.

for a while. You may go into a disagreement thinking the problem is that your partner isn't spending enough time with the kids and ultimately you discover that the real problem is that you aren't getting enough breaks. While there's only one possible solution to the first problem, there are several possible solutions to the second. Your partner, a relative, a neighbor, another parent, or additional child care could all help to alleviate the load. By defining and communicating our real concerns, we set the stage for effective problem solving.

• **Communicate the relative importance of each issue.** When you're in the heat of disagreement, you may feel like your idea is the most important thing in the world to you. As you cool down and listen to your partner's ideas, you may be able to reassess what matters to you the most: "I feel very strongly about Molly getting picked up on time from day care, but I don't care as much about whether she naps at the same time every day." With this kind of honest prioritizing, it's more likely you can both get the thing that's most important to you.

• **Avoid blame.** Blaming generally makes people defensive and interferes with the problem-solving process. Statements such as "You never get Patsy to bed on time" don't allow much room for finding solutions. Statements such as "Patsy's having a lot of trouble getting up for preschool because she's tired in the morning. I'd like us to figure out how she can get more sleep" open the door to mutual problem solving.

• **Listen until your partner feels heard.** Your best tool in a disagreement is listening. Listening means giving your full attention, not interrupting, not defending yourself. If you're each feeling misunderstood or if there are a lot of strong feelings being expressed, it can be useful to restate your partner's position back to her until she feels that you've really understood her feelings and her point of view. If each of you gets a chance to do this, tension decreases and you gain important information about each other.

• **Brainstorm and choose possible solutions.** Once you've each had a chance to be listened to and you've clarified the problem together, you can begin generating possible solutions. The first step is to think of any solution that might be possible. The second step is to choose which one seems the best and to plan how you will implement it.

• **Acknowledge your partner's contributions.** Often in disagreements we focus on what we don't like or what we want to change. We sometimes forget to let our partner know what we appreciate about him. Take any opportunity you can to give this feedback: "I really love the way you use humor with the kids." "I love the way you encourage Zaida's creative play." "You always make Jake and Kelsey the best snacks."

When There Are Still Differences

There will probably be times when you and your partner still don't agree. Even after repeated discussion and negotiation, you may continue to have some basic disagreements. Common conflicts between parents have to do with appropriate discipline methods, safety, uses of television in the family, what's expected of children, and what's expected of parents.

What implications do these differences have for children? How important is consistency between parents? What does it mean for children to deal with two different beliefs or styles?

What's important for children is not that there is absolute agreement on every issue, but that there is some consistency, some basic commonality of beliefs, and a mutual respect and appreciation for the differences between their parents.

Let's take the issue of safety. In one family, Leroy thought it was okay for two-year-old Myra to play with sticks as long as she was supervised. Myra's mom, Vi, thought sticks were unsafe and wouldn't let Myra touch them. If Vi made derogatory comments about Leroy, saying "Well, you know your dad! He'll let you do anything," that would undermine Myra's confidence in her father. If, on the other hand, Vi said, "This is Mommy's idea of what's safe and this is Daddy's idea of what's safe," Myra begins to understand "My parents respect each other, even though they have different ways of doing things."

However, there will be times that you won't be able to sit back and accept what your partner is doing as a parent. Betty Sue explains: "James is a really attentive dad. But when Teri turned two he started tickling her mercilessly, until she would start hitting at him to stop. James still thought it was funny. I told him that I thought his tickling was very disrespectful to Teri and that I wanted him to stop. I said it was *very* important to me. He didn't quite understand why, but he did see how strongly I felt about it, so he stopped."

At times like these, you'll need to keep talking until you find some agreement. Leah and Kate spent months struggling over their different styles of putting their kids to bed before they found a mutual solution. Leah explains: "When I put the kids to bed, the kids talk about the best and worst parts of their day and I ask them if there's anything that stands between us that we need to talk about. The whole thing takes ten minutes. That works for me. I'm with the kids all day. I want them in bed. I want to have some adult time.

"Kate takes at least forty-five minutes to put them to bed. And after they're in bed, if they cry out 'Mama! Mama!' she goes back in there and rubs their backs or sings another song. Kate is at work all day. She's not tired of them. She *wants* to spend time with the children.

"We finally made the decision that whoever's putting the children to bed puts the children to bed, and the other parent sits down and shuts up, unless the first parent asks for help."

It's not a problem for the children in this family that their parents put them to bed differently. Kids can usually accept differences in the way people care for them. Children learn "This is what I do with Mama Leah. This is what I do with Mama Kate. This is what I do with Grandpa." It's much more significant for children that people be consistent within themselves—that one parent has a fairly predictable range of responses, even if they're different from what the other parent or Aunty does in the same situation.

However, when children encounter responses that are different from the ones they've come to expect, they may need to "test" in order to explore the new response: "Will you still react that way if I do this again?" Children also may "test" when parents are together, as if to ask, "Whose rules do we use now?" Knowing this can help us be clear in our responses: "I know that you and Daddy always play ball in the house, but I don't like you to do it when I'm home."

While we can never find absolute consistency between parents, we can work to reach common goals and to respect our partner's differences.

Fighting in Front of the Children

In Janis's groups for parents, one of the most commonly asked questions is whether parents should fight in front of their children. There are several important issues to consider.

Some of us have "learned" ways of fighting that we don't want to continue in our current relationships. Many of us come from backgrounds in which we didn't see any fighting; conflicts occurred behind closed doors, and as far as we knew, they didn't happen. We may have sensed angry, unresolved feelings, but they weren't outwardly acknowledged.

Then there are those of us who've come from families in which fighting happened all the time, but without successful resolution. Neither of these models offers much guidance for building healthy conflict resolution skills in families. In order to figure out whether (or when) it's appropriate to fight in front of your children, consider the following:

• **Look at your current style of fighting.** Do you listen to the other person's point of view? Do your arguments stick to the issues? Do you yell? Do you call the person names? Is your fighting violent or physical? Do your fights teach your child about effective conflict resolution?[4]

• **Assess the conflict you're in.** Many arguments are inappropriate with children present. Adult topics, fights about the children, loud and scary voices, hurtful language, or violence should not happen in the presence of children. Some fights are so emotionally laden that they require our full focus. When we don't have any attention left to reassure our children or respond to their fears, our kids may end up feeling confused, vulnerable, and scared.

On the other hand, less-heated arguments that allow you to stop and reassure your kids if they get uneasy can actually provide valuable lessons to kids about expressing anger and working through disagreements.

Often, going into a argument, you don't know what kind of conflict it's going to be. You may start fighting in front of the kids and partway into it realize, "Oh, this is bigger than I thought." If you determine that a fight is heated, serious, or out of control, make every effort to put it on hold until you're away from your kids. At that point you can say to your kids, "I can see we're going to need some special time to figure this out, so we're going to stop now and work on it later."

• **Develop conflict resolution skills.** Practice the basics of successful conflict resolution—focusing on the problem, active listening, using "I" messages, and brainstorming solutions, so you can model an effective problem-solving strategy.[5]

• **Observe your child's responses.** Sometimes children ask questions about what's happening directly. Other times they'll ask for help or reassurance indirectly. They'll do things to get attention—they'll be funny, try

[4] See "To Yell or Not to Yell?" on p. 222 for more on family styles of dealing with anger.

[5] These skills are defined in Chapter 19, "Moving Beyond Punishment" on p. 218.

to hug and kiss you, cover your mouth and say 'No yelling!' or start crying themselves.

Jack, who's been married for seventeen years, explained, "We fight in front of Heidi. When moods are bad, conflicts happen. Skirmishes break out. But we're working on being able to have disagreements that have a high degree of respect for one another, to acknowledge the differences of opinion, the hurt feelings, without just being abrasive toward each other.

"When we're having a bad fight where there's not much respect for each other, Heidi lets us know right away. She starts crying, she yells 'Stop it!' or she withdraws. And when we're having an argument and we're communicating well, even though strong opinions are being expressed, then Heidi seems okay. Her reaction is a real barometer for us of how fairly we're fighting."

This is not always the case. Certain children, because of their temperament, are always uneasy around conflict. Other children go through developmental stages in which they're more or less comfortable with angry feelings. Knowing your individual child will help you best assess her needs regarding family conflict.

• **Talk to kids about what is happening.** You can say "Dad and I have different ideas about this. We're both feeling pretty angry right now, but we're working to figure things out." Giving a name to the feelings they are witnessing and reminding them that a resolution will happen reassures children.

• **Talk about the outcome.** Tell children when there's been a resolution. In an age-appropriate way, share what you've worked out. You can say "Remember when Mom and I were fighting yesterday? Well, we talked more last night and we figured out that we're going to take turns helping you go to sleep at night."

Drew explains, "Sally and I have argued in front of the kids, and sometimes, it's scared them. We always go back and talk to them about it. We try to show them that we can be angry at each other, talk about it, and then make up."

• **Set aside regular time just to check in with your partner.** Even when there is not an active "fight" between you and your partner, make time to talk about how things are going, to talk about what's hard, and to prevent little problems from escalating. Setting aside time to work through conflict can free you from some of the ongoing daily squabbles that can undermine closeness.

• **It's worth it.** Working out disagreements is a natural part of having a viable, growing relationship. Making the time to resolve differences is important to the health of your family as a whole. Children who never see their parents work through a conflict lose out on an important lesson in human relationships. By allowing children to see us involved in interpersonal struggles—and by showing them that those struggles can be resolved—we model valuable problem-solving skills they'll need to use in relationships for the rest of their lives.

When Parents Separate: Making It Work for the Children

While many relationships successfully weather the inevitable conflicts that occur, some couples discover that their differences far outweigh their agreements. In some of these families, the result is separation or divorce.

Due to the dramatic increase in the divorce rate over the last forty years, there are an increasing number of families in which children are separated from one parent on either a temporary or a long-term basis. Hundreds of thousands of children in our country travel between two households—whether during vacations or on a daily, weekly, or monthly basis.

While seeing both parents is highly beneficial to most children, kids in this situation face unique challenges. Potential issues for the traveling child include not having a clear sense of "my house," missing the parent they're not with, having to cope with different values and expectations, and not having their belongings or friends when they want them.

When parents live far away, it can be hard for children to maintain a feeling of continuity between both of their homes. Kira, who's eight and has been traveling between her mom's and dad's houses since she was four, said, "It's kinda hard. I really love both my parents, but when I'm at my mom's house, I don't get to play with Eden, 'cause she lives too far away. And when I'm at my dad's, I don't get to be with my baby brother."

In circumstances where ex-spouses don't get along and values clash, a deeper level of problems emerge. Sheila, whose divorce had a lot of acrimony, explains: "My kids have spent most of their lives traveling between my house and their dad's. I've missed them terribly and I've had to give up a lot of control about the kinds of things they were exposed to. They learned a lot of things over there that I didn't feel good about. The values in the two households were so different, the kids ended up being like chameleons, able to adapt themselves to any situation, and I can't help but wonder what that's going to mean for them as adults. Will they know what they want for themselves, or will they be people pleasers?"

Many of the problems two-household families face surface because separated and divorced parents often have trouble negotiating a healthy, working relationship after a breakup, separation, or divorce. Yet many families have successfully worked out situations in which children travel between homes.

Sheryl, who shares custody of her daughter with her ex-husband, Gene, recalls: "Our arrangements about time have never been rigid. I knew if I was flexible, Gene would be flexible in return. And we were always generous about letting Carla run back and forth for things. She kept a set of clothes and toys she liked at each house. We never did much packing."

Cecily, who's shared custody of her children with her ex-husband for the last eight years, feels that the arrangement has worked well for everyone in her family: "Todd moved out when Geneen was only four months old. Toby was four. We had an amiable separation and we both wanted the divorce. From the beginning, we embraced coparenting as a special relationship. Instead of defining everything in terms of divorce, we redefined the relationship as a coparenting one and then worked to make that a good thing. We approached the situation with a positive attitude.

"We've always tried to normalize things for the kids. We created a predictable structure, something they could count on. We've always talked about the whole thing in a very matter-of-fact way: 'Is it a dad night or a mom night?' We've taught them to see the advantages: They get a fresh parent. They get to live in two places. They don't have to see us fighting anymore.

"For me, the hardest thing about what we're doing is other people's attitudes. There's a lot of projecting. People pity the kids or feel afraid for them. And there's no reason for that. Our situation has worked for all of us."

In this successful coparenting arrangement, Cecily and Todd demonstrated flexibility, respect for each other, good communication, and a shared commitment to honoring their children's needs. Although few coparents will begin with all of these things in place, working toward them and keeping the following basic principles in mind can go a long way in helping your family make a successful transition to two households.

Communication Between Parents

While effective communication may be one of the most difficult things for recently separated couples to do, it is nonetheless crucial to the success of two-household families. Since lack of constructive communication is frequently one of the factors contributing to separation, most divorced couples who want to be coparents will need to work to make it happen. First, couples need to acknowledge that effective communication is essential to the success of their child's two-household experience. Next, systems need to be created that will enable couples to communicate constructively.

Each couple will have its own specific needs, and most will need the support of a third person, at least at first: a professional mediator, a skilled mutual friend or family member, a rabbi, a pastor, or a counselor. Some couples find that face-to-face communication works well for them; for others, written communication or the phone are their best means of communication. Still others need the structure of meeting in a public place to ensure a feeling of safety. And some families discover that it's useful for stepparents to be involved.

Tom, a father who's shared joint custody for nineteen years, remarked, "Once my ex and I were both in new relationships, communication became easier. For a while all four of us met to talk every week. We used that time to make decisions and to iron out disagreements. Abby and I also spent a half hour during both of Rico's weekly transitions sharing information about baseball, school, runny noses, and the like."

Regularity of communication is another critical factor. If parents wait until a crisis before they begin to communicate, it is difficult in that moment to build the skills and trust needed to do mutual problem solving. It may also perpetuate the notion that effective communication is impossible. But instead, if you anticipate that there will regularly be decisions to be made, information to share, and difficulties to work out, you can plan a consistent time to meet. Having regular time together when things are not in a crisis allows you to practice listening and talking under slightly easier circumstances. It can also give a sense of consistency to your coparenting relationship.

Cecily says communication has really been a critical part of working things out in her family. "The first three or four years we were doing joint custody, Todd and I talked on the phone every night after the kids fell asleep. We talked about practical things. We checked in. We shared those parental moments of pride, bragging about the kids and what they were doing. Now that the kids are older, we seem to call each other at work during the day, and it's much briefer.

"We've always communicated pretty well. We have our disagreements, but we're both so familiar with our patterns that as soon as things start degenerating, one of us says 'Wait a minute. Let's try this a different way.' Usually, that's enough, but I remember one time when I felt Todd wasn't paying enough attention to what Geneen was doing with her friends at his house. I thought he was being too loose and he thought I was being judgmental. My current partner, Dana, facilitated some meetings for us, and did such a good job that we got back on track pretty quickly."

Effective communication not only gives you a chance to work together to make the best decisions for your child, it also affords your child some sense of integration of his two-household experience.

Communication with Your Child

While every coparenting couple needs to set up some formal structure for adult communication, a communication system that includes your child is also important. If a child leaves one home and moves to the next without any overlap, not only is the transition likely to be difficult, but the child becomes the only keeper of her history. While many parents may not be comfortable sitting down and sharing experiences during each transition, there are other ways communication about your child's experience can occur.

Some parents have found it useful to sit down with their child and a journal: to write, draw, or scribble about their time together before the child makes the transition to her other home. When she goes to her other home, the journal makes the move with her and she has a ready means by which to share her recent experiences with her welcoming parent. The journal helps the child integrate both parts of her life.

For some a journal may seem a daunting or an impossible task. A simple note or a bag with relics of your time together (rocks, photos, pinecones, drawings) can also stimulate sharing.

Kids often get the message, real or imagined, that they are not allowed to talk about their experiences with one parent with the other. This puts an extreme burden on the child to keep her life tightly compartmentalized. Ultimately she will have a closer, more comfortable, trusting relationship with parents who can acknowledge and appreciate how important *both* parents are to her.

Equal Time?

When planning your child's schedule, obviously parents are going to have lots of time factors that need to be considered. Yet it is imperative that the child's needs come first whenever possible. It is also critical, however difficult, to remember that "equal" time—spending exactly the same number of hours with each parent—may not be best for the child. While consistency, frequency, and predictability are extremely important, especially for young children, "equality" is not the essential ingredient for significant relationships with both parents.

The Need for Respect

A child also deserves to have both of her parents respected. It is critical for the child that parents work to find the part of the other parent that they can support and appreciate, so they can communicate that to the child, rather than the hundreds of things that they don't like. Differences can be talked about descriptively rather than judgmentally: "When you're with your dad, you eat vegetarian, when you're with me, you eat meat."

This is not to say that you have to lie to a child about difficult issues. If your son's mother is an active alcoholic, when the subject comes up you can deal with it compassionately rather than with blame: "Alcoholism is a sickness your mother is struggling with. I'm sorry that she can't always take care of you the way that we would like for her to. I know that you miss spending time with her."

Sometimes you will be faced with your child's disappointment with the other parent. Your daughter's mother has promised to pick her up and doesn't show. Your son's father doesn't acknowledge his birthday. While it would be tempting to join your child in his anger at his other parent, it will be most useful for you to listen supportively to his feelings: "You look really disappointed about not hearing from your mother. Do you want to talk about it?"

While your feelings of anger, rejection, and hurt may make it difficult to talk compassionately with your child about her other parent, it is important to remember that your child's relationship with the other parent is a part of her and that negating or belittling that relationship negates or belittles a part of your child.

Ardena explains: "My ex-husband and I have had to learn to talk respectfully about each other, to not put each other down in front of the kids. Sometimes that's been hard. There have been times I felt concerns about some of the things that my ex-husband was doing, as he did about me. But I always have to come back to the bottom line—DeShana and Raul love and need their father—and it's not my job to point out all of his shortcomings."

Small things such as acknowledging that your child misses her other parent while she is with you lets your daughter know that you value her relationships with both parents and that you appreciate all of her feelings, even the hard ones. Judith remarked, "When Megan says she misses her dad, I tell her very matter-of-factly that she can call him. And then I remind her when she's going to see him next so she'll know what to expect." Such simple acknowledgment teaches children that they can have full relationships with each parent without losing or threatening either relationship.

The Abundance of Love

One of the things children in step-, blended, or two-household families have to struggle with is the fact that parents sometimes erroneously communicate the idea that there's a finite amount of love—that if you love your mother, it means you love your father less, or that if you now love your stepmother, you love your mother less. Actually, the more permission children are given to have full and nurturing relationships, the richer each of their relationships becomes.

28.
Building Strong Sibling Relationships

if i cud ever write a
poem as beautiful as u
little 2/yr/old/brotha,
i wud laugh, jump, leap
up and touch the stars

SONIA SANCHEZ
"TO P.J."[1]

Brothers and sisters have the opportunity to develop unique and significant relationships. Siblings share your family culture and history. Siblings knew you when. Sibling relationships have time on their side: They usually start at the beginning of life and last until the end. Helping children learn how to make the most of their relationships with their siblings not only helps you get through the day, it's also an investment in your family's future.

Ironically, the word most frequently associated with sibling is "rivalry." This widespread concept assumes that there are limited resources and nurturing in a family and that as the family gets bigger, those resources are spread thinner. In this system, we expect that significant relationships will happen only between the parents and children in the family. Therefore, siblings have to compete for their parents' attention.

Instead, what if we looked at the family as a circle in which each new person brought rich relationships to every other person in the family? What if we move beyond the belief that adults are the only "givers" or "providers" in the family?

When we look at family relationships in this way, we open the door to more balanced, reciprocal relationships between all family members. This doesn't mean there won't be conflict between siblings. Conflict is a natural part of all close relationships. But the conflicts between siblings can be handled in such a way that children learn valuable lessons in communication, listening, love, forgiveness, and resolving differences.

[1] Sonia Sanchez, *It's a New Day* (1971), p. 18. Detroit: Broadside Press.

Sibling Relationships: Issues for Parents

To a large degree, our own family experiences shape our expectations about sibling relationships, and our expectations play a big part in determining the siblings relationships our children have with each other.

Hal explains: "I come from a really close-knit family. I have three brothers and all of us are still really tight. If there was one thing our parents taught us, it was 'Look out for each other!' And we always did. I've always been able to count on my brothers and they've always been able to count on me. Now I see my own kids being there for each other. They've seen how important their uncles are to me, so I guess the message sank in."

Peter remarks, "I was the older child in my family and my partner, Ryan, was the youngest in his, and that really affects how we see the relationship between our children. I find that it's often easier for me to take sides with our older son, to see how annoying his little sister is to him. Ryan, on the other hand, is especially sensitive to what he calls 'bullying' of our daughter by her big brother."

Patricia, the mother of two young boys, says her lack of experience colors her perspective: "I was an only child. I don't have a clue about sibling relationships."

Expectations about sibling relationships can vary widely within a single family, as Janis explains: "Leon and I came to our family with very different beliefs about siblings. In his family, it was unheard of that siblings would have separate or unique activities, that they would need privacy, or that they would feel the need to do things without their brothers and sisters. In my family, siblings weren't really expected to associate with each other if they didn't want to. Together, coming from those two different worlds, we had to find ways to encourage our own children to build close sibling bonds."

It's useful for parents who are in the process of enlarging their families to consider what they already "know" about the nature of sibling relationships. For instance, do you believe that siblings primarily support and love each other? That they stick together and nurture each other? Or do you believe that they mainly compete for attention and hurt each other?

Many of us have beliefs about sibling relationships that we don't want to see perpetuated—that siblings are unsupportive, belittling, or competitive, and, worst of all, predestined to be that way. For those of us who have an inkling that there must be another way but aren't quite sure what it is, talking to people who have strong relationships with their own siblings or who have children who are close can be useful. While we can't ensure that all siblings will be soulmates, holding a vision of cooperation rather than rivalry can lay the foundation for trusting sibling relationships.

FOOD FOR THOUGHT: SIBLINGS

- What kinds of relationships did I have with my siblings? What did those relationships teach me? Are there ways I would have liked those relationships to be different?

- What is the nature of the relationships between my children? Are there ways I'd like to see those relationships grow and evolve?

- What hopes do I have for my children's sibling relationships over the long haul?

Bringing Maya Home: Janis's Story

The following story demonstrates some of the challenges and pleasures involved in developing a different perspective on sibling relationships.

I remember sitting on the couch with my infant daughter and her older brother. As I began to wonder if there would be enough of my hugs and time to go around, I looked over at him holding her and realized that what was happening between them was not only nurturing her but Calvin, as well. I realized that it was as satisfying for him to hold his sister as it was for him to be held and snuggled by me. "Ah-ha!" I thought. "Now our family has even more resources rather than fewer."

But, as you may have guessed, they weren't snuggling forever. Soon afterward, Maya, the (brand-new, delicate, fragile) baby was lying on the living room floor in the sun. Her energetic brother leaped across where she was lying and kicked her with his foot. She started crying and as I started over to her, Calvin immediately came over to me and said, "I'm sorry, Mom."

I realized at that moment that this was between Calvin and his sister. So I told Calvin to talk to Maya about it. As he bent toward her, bringing his four-year-old face up close to her scrunched-up red one, touching her cheek with his play-stained fingers, she began to quiet. He said, "I'm sorry, Maya." He continued talking to her and gently touching her, and as he did so, she began to know him as a gentle and caring person. Calvin left that interaction not as a person who had kicked his sister but as an active, curious, compassionate person who had made a mistake and had helped to fix it.

Yet even though I can tell this story now, it wasn't easy for me to let them have that time and space. Several times during their interaction, I wanted to jump in, to pick up "my" crying baby and comfort her. I had an urge to yell at Calvin for being careless around his sister and to send him away. I wanted to interpret her crying for him, as if he couldn't understand it herself: "It hurts her when you kick her." (You are not only clumsy, but you can't read a simple human communication.) But part of me knew, deep down, that she wasn't "my" baby. She was her own person and a full member of our family with individual relationships with each one of us. And so I took a deep breath, trusted and watched as their relationship began to grow and deepen.

Introducing New Siblings

Sibling relationships begin when we bring a second child into our families. This can happen through birth, adoption, remarriage, or foster parenting. In the section that follows, we focus on new infants who come to families through birth or adoption, although some of the issues discussed here will also be relevant for families who are expanding through other means.

The way you introduce a new baby into your home is an important first step in building positive sibling relationships. What you do before the baby comes, how you arrange for the baby's arrival, and, most important, how you support the older children and the sibling relationship once the baby has arrived all play a role in helping older brothers and sisters make a healthy adjustment to the changes a new baby brings. What you can do most effectively in each of these areas has a lot to do with the age and developmental level of the older children.

Before the Baby Is Born: When Older Siblings Are Under Two

With babies and young toddlers, there's very little preparation you can do ahead of time. Your child's sense of time and ability to imagine the future will limit his capacity to picture what life with a new baby will be like. Since young children have a difficult time imagining how the family will change, most of the adjusting to a new baby will happen after the baby arrives. But there are some steps you can take with very young siblings-to-be before the baby's arrival:

• **Have the sibling-to-be spend time with babies.** Look for opportunities for your child to see, touch, play with, and interact with other babies.

• **Limit conversations about the new baby and keep them concrete.** Young children can get overwhelmed and confused with lots of talk about babies before the baby shows up. Talking about babies in the early expectant period should be brief and follow the child's lead. In the last weeks before the new baby is due, you can talk a little more. In the case of a pregnancy, the mother's growing belly will provide natural opportunities to talk. With adoption, your preparations can provide similar opportunities. Keep your conversation simple and concrete: "This is where the baby will sleep. New babies sleep a lot." Or "The baby will wear this little shirt. You wore a shirt just like this when you were a baby." Or "Babies cry a lot. It's how they tell us what they need."

• **Establish a strong support system for the older sibling for the time following the arrival of the new baby.** With a very young child, this is the most important preparation you can make ahead of time. Setting people and resources in place so siblings get attention, nurturing, and support in the days and weeks following the arrival is essential.

Before the Baby Is Born: When Siblings Are Two or Older

Because their sense of time is more developed, older toddlers and preschoolers can begin to anticipate a new baby's arrival. In addition to the strategies just listed, you can also:

• **Let them play with the baby's things.** Older toddlers, preschoolers, and school-age kids may be interested in exploring the baby's things. When presents come in, let the older children unwrap and play with them. It can help older siblings feel less like "all this stuff is just for the baby."

Janis recalls: "I remember coming home from a shower with a pile of gifts. The older kids were just delighted playing with the diaper pail, climbing inside the bassinet, and exploring the toys. Especially for my four-year-old, playing with the things helped him realize, 'Oh, there really is going to be a new person who's going to use these things.' "

• **Help the older child revisit her babyhood.** Looking at the older child's baby pictures or an album that describes how she entered the family can be a valuable way for her to explore the changes that are about to happen. Young

Introducing New Siblings Through Adoption

Adoptive parents are faced with unique issues and questions as they plan their families. There are questions about using private or public agencies, about adopting children from this country or outside it. There are questions about age, gender, and race; about open or closed adoptions. There is research about agencies, countries, and families. There are uncertain timetables, hopes, and disappointments. There are adoptions with a long lead time and adoptions that happen overnight.

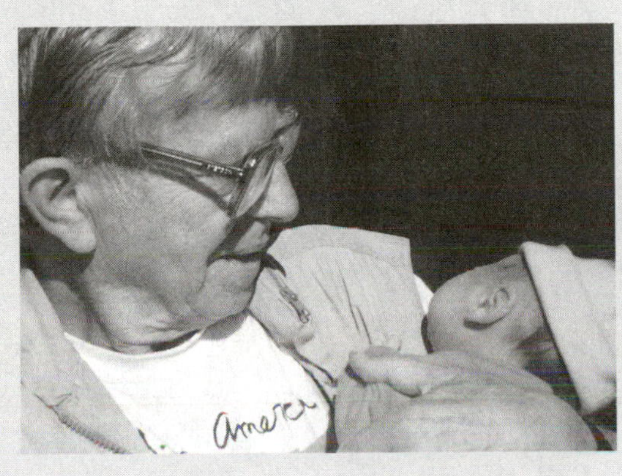

Figuring out how and when to involve siblings in the decision-making and adoption process requires careful planning and consideration. At what point should the sibling be informed that there may be a brother or sister on the way? Should the sibling spend the month in another country with his mother waiting for the new baby? Should the older sister come to the hospital to meet the birth mother and pick up her new sister? Which of the adoption meetings should the older sibling be a part of and which aren't appropriate?

As with any impending family change, a child should be told about it once it is fairly certain to happen. The timing and kind of the talking should be in line with the older sibling's ability to understand and also to wait.

It is important for adoptive parents to get support as they make these decisions. Talking to other adoptive families, joining adoption support groups, making connections with other families who have used the same organizations or have adopted children from the same countries can also be helpful.

One family, who adopted their first child seven years ago, is about to adopt a second. The mother, Carla, describes the way they've worked to prepare their son, Parker: "At first he got wind of it because the adoption agency sent us a picture. He was happy that it was a boy. He took the picture to school to show all of his friends. It was quite exciting until the realities of struggling with the bureaucracy of adoption agencies hit. I think Parker saw too much of that. One night when I had gotten some difficult news, Parker started crying and saying, 'I want to be an only child. I think this adoption is a big mistake.'

"He started walking around asking 'Do you love me, Mama?' So we slowed way down and talked to him about how we decided to adopt him and how we'd decided that we wanted another child in our family. We told him stories about his own babyhood and about the adoption agencies we dealt with when he came into our family. And we talked about the exponential quality of love. We told Parker that love wasn't like a pile of candy that gets smaller if you have to split it; that if you split a pile of love between two kids, you end up with twice as much."

Eventually, Carla and Parker spent a few months in Paraguay, meeting their baby and finalizing the adoption. There were some stressful times for the family, being in a new country, working with a different legal system and being separated from Dad, but Parker really felt a part of welcoming his new brother.

How each family chooses to include older siblings in the adoption process will vary depending on the needs of the parents, the child, and the circumstances of the adoption. Despite the uncertainty that is involved, expanding families through adoption can be exciting for the whole family.

children are egocentric; they think of everything as it relates to their own experience. Having a chance to explore, "What was being a baby like for me?" can help create a bridge between the older child's experience and the new baby who is to come.

Telling stories that start, "When you were a baby . . ." can also be a useful way of conveying information to your older child about what babies are like. Because the information is centered on them rather than on the forthcoming baby, they're more able to take it in and assimilate it. Later, after the baby comes, it can be fun to continue this dialogue: "See what Jamila is doing? When you were a baby, you used to . . ." Talking about their infancy and babyhood helps children feel included and connected; it can remind them that they had many of the same experiences the new baby is having.

• **Bring the older sibling along on prenatal visits.** When a new baby is arriving via a pregnancy, letting the older child participate in prenatal visits can help foster a sense of participation. The appropriateness of this strategy will depend on the age and temperament of the older child and the mother's needs for privacy with her midwife or doctor.

• **Allow children to help prepare for the baby.** Preschoolers can participate in such activities as washing plastic toys, folding clothes, and putting them in drawers.

• **If children want to, let them pick out something they want to give the baby.** Preschool kids might enjoy going into their old toy collection and picking out one or two things they think the baby might like to play with. (Toddlers, however, may not be ready for this kind of sharing.) The more control older kids have over choosing things to share with the baby initially, the less vulnerable they will feel about the baby moving into their territory.

• **Find or make a book about the new baby coming.** There are a number of books written specifically to help older siblings with the transition. We particularly recommend *On Mother's Lap* by Ann Herbert Scott. It's the wonderful story of a young Inuit boy who's sure there isn't room on his mother's lap for him and boat and puppy and dolly—and his baby sister. You can also make your own book using pictures of your family and a simple story line.

• **Enroll your child is a sibling preparation class.** Many family birthing centers and some hospitals offer classes to help prepare older siblings for the arrival of a new baby. If you're considering such a class for your older child, talk to the instructor or visit the class to find out what's covered and to see if it fits your child's age and needs. If you're planning to have your child attend the birth, and you feel he is old enough, it can be helpful to watch a birthing video together and to discuss it so he'll have some idea what to expect.

• **Expect some changes in the final month before the baby is born.** In the last month before the baby comes, particularly with a visible pregnancy, older children often get clingier, develop new fears, or show signs of regression. These changes can be connected to a shift in the parent's focus in preparation for the impending birth, to lowered parental energy, or to increased anticipation of the new baby arriving.

During the Birth

Planning carefully for the older child during the labor and delivery of the baby is important for the older sibling as well as for his relationship with the baby. The first decision parents face is whether to have the older child at the birth or not. While this has always been an option for mothers who give birth at home, more and more birthing centers and hospitals are also allowing siblings to participate in the birth process.

Parents have different levels of comfort with the idea of children being present at a birth. This has to do with cultural norms, the birthing woman's sense of modesty, her previous experiences with childbirth, her child's age and temperament, and her desire to have her children there. Parents also need to assess whether seeing a birth would be appropriate for the sibling in question. At certain ages and for certain children, seeing blood or hearing Mom scream or cry out could be very scary.

Parents have come up with a variety of solutions for siblings during the birth. Some have planned to have older siblings present for the entire labor and birth, to go in and out of the birthing area at will. In some of these families, older children are given specific jobs to do—cutting the cord, bringing over a warmed receiving blanket, being the one to discover and announce the baby's gender, or some other age-appropriate task. Some families plan to have siblings stay nearby so they can be brought in just when the baby is about to be born or immediately afterward. In other families, siblings stay at home or with friends and then come to meet their new sister or brother after the intensity of the birthing process has passed and Mom has had a little chance to rest.

Welcoming the Baby: When Siblings Don't Attend the Birth

Children who come to meet the new baby after she is born have several needs during the time of labor and delivery. The immediate issue the older sibling will be dealing with is separation. For some children, it may be the first time they have been away from a parent overnight.

If children go to the hospital to visit, there are a few other things to think about. For most children, hospitals are unfamiliar or strange. Children may feel uncomfortable visiting their parents there. Another challenge is that hospitals aren't really set up for kids' favorite activities, such as running, jumping, talking loudly, and crying. In order to deal with these challenges, you can:

• **Help children with the separation.** Children who are missing their parent(s) will need reassurance. Giving them information ahead of time about what to expect and having them stay with trusted people in familiar surroundings will help ease their transition. You may want to plan for your older child and his caregiver to do a special activity or outing together. Children may also want to call to talk to their parents on the phone.[2]

• **Visits to the hospital should be short and flexible.** The child should be able to leave whenever he needs to.

• **Siblings should be accompanied by a familiar adult.** The older child may have particular needs during a visit to the hospital. If he's accompanied by an adult whose only responsibility is to be with him, he has a better chance of getting them met.

• **Mom should be available to greet the older sibling, if possible.** The sibling is going to envision seeing the same old mom. If he walks in and her arms are full, he may feel concerned that she won't be able to hold *him*.

• **Help the older child bond with the baby.** Allow as much contact between the new siblings as possible. If the older child is interested, you can show him all the parts of the baby's body, inviting him to touch or get close to the

[2] For more specific ideas and strategies for dealing with unusual separations, see Chapter 13, "The Dance of Separation" on p. 116.

baby. You can "introduce" the older child to the baby, telling the baby all about her big brother.

• **Provide for the time after the hospital visit.** You may want to plan for your child's caregiver to take him on a special outing after the visit—a trip to the park, to the ice cream store, to visit a friend. It might be hard to leave Mom after finally getting to see her. Having somewhere else to go may ease the transition.

• **Think about presents.** The older child may enjoy picking flowers to bring to the hospital. She may want to make a drawing to tape on the wall that the baby can look at. She may want to choose a special blanket to bring to the baby. While the family members in the hospital don't "need" presents, bringing something can help the older sibling feel included.

Welcoming the Baby: When Siblings Attend the Birth

Witnessing the birth of a sibling can be a memorable, special experience. If you are considering having your older children present at the birth of a baby, it's important that *each* older child has a support person whose job is to focus exclusively on that child's needs. This person should be very familiar with the child and fully capable of reading the child's verbal, nonverbal, and emotional signals. He or she will be providing for your child's needs, helping the child take breaks as needed, or removing the child if necessary. The support person should not have any other duties during the birth. It's also important that the birthing mother feel comfortable with the caregiver so that she can tell that person what she wants for both herself and for her child: "Take him outside for a while." Or "I'd like you to hold him."

Children will often regulate their own participation at a birth. When Janis's youngest child was born, Lee was nine and Calvin was four. "Lee watched attentively pretty much the entire time. Calvin at one point got down on the floor and started doing some drawing. He chose to take a break and he missed the moment when Maya actually popped out. By focusing on something else, or by going in and out of the room, both children took the breaks that they needed."

Seeing a sibling being born can create powerful bonds. Bethany, the mother of two teenage girls, explains: "Isabel was four when she was at Sophia's birth. I had her stay with her uncle in the waiting room while I was in labor. He entertained her with crayons and books. When I started pushing, he brought Isabel in. She stood there and urged me on. She gave a play-by-play of everything that was happening. She was the first person to hold her sister, and I believe that really made a huge difference in their relationship."

It's important to emphasize that siblings can develop close, loving, strong bonds without participating in the birth of their younger siblings. Decisions regarding childbirth are intensely personal, and no one should feel pressured to include older siblings if it's something she's not comfortable with or if it doesn't work in her particular family or birth setting.

After the Baby Comes Home: Making the Adjustment

Once the new baby arrives home, the real adjustment begins. A new baby takes time for everyone to get used to. Just as most parents move into having a second child with some ambivalence—"What am I giving up in terms of my relationship with my first child?"—children also move into the sibling relationship with ambivalence. This ambivalence often shows up in the early weeks and months of the new baby's life through regression, testing, and what parents often interpret as "jealousy."

Understanding the impulses underlying these behaviors can help us respond to our older children appropriately and with compassion.

Shortly before or after the baby's arrival, older children often want to try out being babies again. They might refuse to use words, revert back to baby talk, or say "Waaah!" Children who've given up cribs, diapers, or bottles might want them back again. They might want to experiment with crawling and nursing. This can be unnerving for parents who are thinking, "Whoa! I can't be taking care of two babies! I need to have a big kid here!"

Our sense of our older child changes when a new child comes into the family: "All of a sudden you look so old and so big." Our expectations of our older child increase, and simultaneously, she starts regressing and acting like a baby.

Why does this happen? In part, older children may be trying to get some of the attention the baby is getting. They may also be trying to figure out what babyhood is all about, and that's something they can't figure out just by watching the baby—they have to *do* what it is the baby is doing. Older siblings also try out baby things to get a perspective on the fact that they're *not* babies anymore: "When I nurse, it feels different." "When I crawl up on your lap, it doesn't feel the same." "When I try to wrap up in my baby blanket, my body doesn't fit the way it used to. I guess I'm not really a baby anymore."

As a parent, it's useful to support your older child's need to regress without going overboard. It's normal for your older child to want to explore nursing, bottles, getting in the crib, climbing in the cradle, crawling, being fed, and using baby talk. You don't need to worry that your older child is going to get stuck back in being a baby. After some exploration of babyhood and adjustment to the new baby, their normal urges to grow and to use their more sophisticated skills and competencies will reemerge.

Sometimes children react to the arrival of a new baby with anger and testing. While many of us expect anger directed toward the baby, often it is directed toward us instead. To the child, it feels as if her parents are the ones who have changed. Your child may start pushing against limits so you will show her how you can still keep her safe, even though there is a new brother or sister in the house. This testing can be very tangible—you sit down to nurse the baby and your toddler starts pulling books out of the bookshelf or climbing up on the kitchen counter, as if to say "Can you still stop me?"[3]

Is It Really Jealousy?

Parents often say that their older child is "jealous" of her new brother or sister. But a lot of the time, the older child isn't jealous, she's just trying to figure out the new family dynamics. Suddenly the parents have a lot of attention going in another direction. So the older child may be trying to figure out, "What happened to my parents?"

Most children won't have been able to anticipate the extent of the changes that would

[3] See "From One to Five: Why Are Children Always Testing?" on p. 240 for suggestions on how to respond to this kind of testing.

occur. Seeing how much their family has changed opens up all kinds of possibilities. The child may wonder, "How does my family work now?" Or "If my family can change in all these big kinds of ways, what other big changes could take place?"

Often the things we interpret as jealousy—the older child wanting to wheel the baby back where she came from—is not so much jealousy as it is a search for familiar ground: "I want to be able to predict things the way I used to."

People often assume that young siblings are expressing feelings of jealousy when they poke, prod, or pinch their baby brothers or sisters—or push down a newly mobile baby. Sometimes the pushing *is* a way for the older child to say, "I don't want you around! I don't like you right now!" But more often, the older child is trying to learn about the baby's body: "Who are you? What makes you work? Are you real? What makes you cry? What makes you stop crying?"

Toddlers and young preschoolers don't automatically know that babies are people. After all, babies come in a different size. They don't talk. They don't walk. They don't have teeth or eat solid food. They don't do a lot of things young children have grown to expect from people. So the older sibling sets out to explore the baby for signs of life, much as he or she would explore any other object—physically. As parents, it's important to respect the older child's curiosity about the baby *and* to set clear limits about what's safe.

It's also important not to be undone by our children's negative comments or hurtful behaviors toward a new baby. They are a natural part of confusion, of wanting things back the way they were, of not wanting to share us, of worrying, "Wait a minute! Is there going to be enough space for me?" But the fact that older siblings feel mad or want to get rid of the baby one moment doesn't negate the fact that they may have fond and excited feelings for the baby the next.

Older children need permission to express their full range of feelings about their new sibling. When we allow our older children to express their difficult feelings, we demonstrate our confidence in their ability to love and care for their sibling even if they're feeling angry and hurt in the moment.

When your older child says, "I don't want that baby. I don't like Gracie" rather than saying, "Yes you do. You love your sister," you can do some active listening: "Sometimes it feels hard to have a new baby here. Sometimes it feels like you don't like her. Can you tell me what's hard?"

When you reflect children's feelings back and they feel heard, positive feelings emerge naturally. Paula explains: "My second youngest daughter was eight when her little brother was born. She was so excited about having a new baby, but when she found out what it was really like, she fell hard.

"My experience is that parents have a huge amount to do with sibling relationships. All of the kids I've raised have had close relationships with each other and I think in part, it's because I really honored the feelings they had when they got supplanted by one another. Being supplanted by a younger sibling, when you're used to being the baby, is really hard. I wanted to acknowledge and respect that. So I always made room for the older children to talk about what they hated about the baby, about how things would be better if she wasn't there. I didn't expect constant rational behavior out of older siblings. I asked them to tell me if they felt like I was favoring somebody else. Giving voice to those feelings really made a big difference for my kids. It didn't have to be a hidden pain."

In a lot of families, these kinds of "negative feelings" are repressed and considered dangerous. Yet it's only when they're fully expressed that there is room for older kids to see what could be good about their new and changed family, that a healthy sibling relationship can really start to emerge.

Supporting Older Siblings

• **Be available to the older child.** This is the most important thing you can do. Children need to feel that you're still there for them, that they'll still be loved and cared for in the family. Being close to them in familiar ways is an important way to reassure them.

Paula recalls, "I always had 'alone dates' with my older kids, starting soon after having a baby. It was hard because I didn't feel like leaving the baby, but the need of the older children was huge at that time. They needed to feel special. So every other week, I'd take each kid out alone. Maybe we'd go to dinner, maybe we'd take a walk, but always it would be something where we wouldn't get interrupted, where we'd have a chance to talk and I'd get to really listen. It was time that was really valued on both sides."

• **Encourage friends and family to pay special attention to older siblings.** Often in the excitement over a new baby, older children get overlooked. Find ways to encourage family and friends to focus on the older siblings, as well. Trudy recalls, "During my baby shower when I was having Lisa, Jeffrey was three and a half. I asked my friends to bring gifts for the big brother. I had plenty of hand-me-down baby things for the baby. It was going to be a much bigger deal for Jeffrey than for the little baby who didn't care what she got."

While gifts can help, attention is what children crave the most. Families have put notes on their front doors: "Please remember to spend some time with Tasha." Or "Quentin's needing some reassurance and attention right now. Please spend some special time with him when you come in."

• **Keep up the older child's routines.** Playing with their friends, going on familiar outings, spending time at their regular preschool can all be beneficial for siblings. It can be really exciting to be around the house when a new baby is there, but it can also be a welcome relief to have some things that don't change.

Take your child's lead in this. Some children will be eager to return to their regular routines as soon as possible; others will want to stay home to keep track of what the changes are. Be as flexible and responsive as you can about your child's wishes.

• **Go at the older child's pace.** Kids may be very interested in the new baby, or they may be disinterested and ignore the baby for a while. Let your older child's curiosity and interest determine the level of interaction he has with the new baby.

• **Help the older sibling get to know the baby.** By participating in the baby's care and by observing the baby with you, your older child can learn about his new brother or sister: "See how she throws her arms back when she hears a loud noise." "See how she's found her hand to suck on." "Do you see the way she turns her head when you walk by. It's her way to say 'hi' to you."

• **Encourage safe and gentle touching.** Help your older child find safe, gentle ways to physically interact with the new baby. Give your older child information about how the baby can be touched, held, and hugged. Even when children begin by hitting or poking, giving them a chance to interact softly rather than immediately removing them may help them feel successful and connected.

• **Let children play an important role in the new family.** Your older child can play a significant role by showing off the new baby. When someone comes to see the baby, you can ask your older child, "Nicky, would you like to

Ten Relationship Builders for Siblings

1. **Allow and encourage siblings to nurture one another.** Janis sometimes calls this one "Working yourself out of a job." There are many opportunities for care and nurturing in families that children love to participate in: comforting a crying sibling, delivering a snack or a kiss, helping with nightly backrubs, joining in family hugs. If you include siblings when you are snuggling with one of the other kids, they get reminded that there is enough to go around: "Help me kiss your brother, please, I can only reach this cheek. Would you get the other one?"

   Often siblings can offer empathy and the voice of experience to each other. When two-year-old Sara begins child care and feels unhappy about saying good-bye to Dad each morning, four-year-old Joanna might be able to tell the story of how it was for her when she started child care. When five-year-old Nop scrapes his knee skating, three-year-old Jessie might be able to show her healed elbow and deliver a Band-Aid to him.
2. **Encourage siblings to share accomplishments with each other.** When one child has accomplished something, make sure the whole family gets to see. "Wait a minute, you better go show baby Nell where you lost your first tooth!" "Save that somersault! Your brother Simon has to see it." "Wow, we're going to have to show your big sister that you just learned to roll over!" At first children may be uncomfortable with their sibling being in the spotlight. You can cuddle with the audience sibling and say, "I really wanted you to see this, we've been waiting all day for you to get home." Or when the audience sibling says, "That's nothing, I can . . ." you can respond to her need for the spotlight and also encourage her to appreciate their sibling. "Oh! Do you have something that you would like to show us, too? Great! As soon as Willy is finished, we all want to see what you can do."*
3. **Arrange for siblings to spend time together.** Our kids' lives are often full of school, child care, classes, TV, video games, and friends. It is important that siblings have regular, unstructured time in which to explore their relationship and discover how to play together.
4. **Help siblings set the stage for success.** There are times in sibling relationships when there is particular stress and conflict. During these times especially, you may be able to help children find a successful way to connect that might shift the dynamics or help them get back on track. Through observation, you may have ideas about what activities tend to be successful for your children. Some children are always successful when they take a bath together, go camping together, build forts together, or draw or dance together. They might not always remember how to get into one of their successful activities and may need a suggestion or some support from you.
5. **Make sibling books for your kids.** For Chanukah when Eli was almost a year old, Laura made Eli and his sixteen-year-old brother, Bryan, matching books that featured pictures of both boys with big captions underneath: "My Big Brother Bryan" and "My Little Brother Eli." Eli's book said things such as "I've known my Big Brother Bryan all my life." "Maybe someday he'll teach me to skateboard

* For more on appreciating children's accomplishments in a relaxed, noncompetitive way, see "The Problem with Praise" on p. 22.

and use Legos too." Bryan's book had captions such as "When Eli came home from the hospital, I held him. He was really tiny." "I'm going to know Eli my whole life." Eli "read" his book at least a hundred times and Bryan really loves his, too.**

6. **Make something with one sibling to give to the other.** A plate of peanut butter cookies? A puppet? A picture?
7. **Have one sibling plan a big surprise for the other sibling.** Have one sibling be in charge of an outing the other sibling would like—like a trip to the fire station. Ask, "Where do you think your brother would like to visit?" "What snacks should we take along?" "Where could we set up a big tent for your sister to play in when she gets home?"
8. **Set up special family time, activities, or outings to nurture close sibling bonds.** What special time looks like will vary depending on your particular family's needs. Some families like to set aside special time at home—a game-playing night, a cooking project, or a turn-off-the-TV night. Other family time might include a family walk, a trip to the museum or zoo, or delivering goodies to a neighbor.

   Morgan relates, "I make sure our family goes camping every couple of months. When we get away from the distractions of everyday life, we really get to be with each other, and the kids play differently than they do at home."
9. **Create family sharing and family appreciations times.** Making time for each person to tell a little something about their day helps develop a tradition of family and sibling sharing. Adults can help preverbal children "share."

   You can also start a family activity where people get to express their fondness for each other. "Before we eat dinner, we're going to have a special family time. Everyone will get to say something that they like about somebody else in the family." Then you can start to show the kids what it might look like: "I really liked playing catch with Lisa!" "I liked that Daddy cooked such great spaghetti yesterday." "When Miranda held the gate for me, it was easier to get my bike through. That helped me!"

   You can help children clarify their appreciations, or just wait until they figure out how to do it themselves. When one child says, "I like that Roz has a Game Boy," you could shift the focus away from an appreciation of her possessions with, "What else do you like about Roz herself?" or "Do you also like it when she gives you a turn?"

   And as children get older, you can expand the activity so that each person says something about every family member.
10. **Begin a tradition of family meetings.** Once you have established family sharing times, you can begin to extend them into family meetings. Family meetings offer members a chance to acknowledge each other, to talk about problems they are having in and outside the family, to work together to figure out solutions, and to plan special family times. In family meetings, everyone gets a chance to talk. At first, parents will need to structure the time, but as children get older, they can take turns "chairing" the meetings. Some families have meetings every week. In others, they happen more spontaneously when someone feels like calling one.***

** For more specifics on making books for your kids, see "Making Books for Your Kids" on p. 298.

*** We particularly like *Raising Kids Who Can: Using Family Meetings to Nurture Responsible, Cooperative, Caring and Happy Children* by Betty Lou Bettner and Amy Lew (New York: HarperCollins, 1992). This clear, outstanding guidebook tells you how to have successful family meetings.

show the baby to Uncle Joe or would you like me to do that?"

• **Let the older child play an important role in the new baby's life.** Families have found all kinds of ways to let older children participate actively in younger children's lives. Leon tells the story of the role he played in naming his younger brother: "They were going to name my younger brother Winston, a name I didn't like. I said, 'No, you *can't* name him Winston.' It offended my young sense of poetry. If you would have seen him, you would have agreed. He was as red as a lobster, but since I couldn't call him 'Lobster,' I called him Lionel, which is the name he still bears, Charles Lionel.

"When we told our oldest son, Lee, that we were going to have another child, he quickly asked, 'What are we going to name him?' When we asked for his opinion, he volunteered his own name and was quite insistent that we name the new child 'Lee,' just like him. We finally figured out that we could use 'Lee' for Calvin's middle name, just as I'd given my brother his middle name."

• **Expect a delayed response.** Sometimes there's a honeymoon period of a week or two in which the older sibling seems to be having a smooth, easy adjustment. During this time you might find yourself thinking, "I don't know what I was worried about. She's so sweet with the baby. Everything's fine." Then something switches and your older child realizes, "Wow! Things have really changed! It looks like they're really going to keep this baby forever!"

• **Expect changes over time.** Often, just about the time the family has reestablished its equilibrium, things change in the relationship between the siblings. The baby everybody's gotten to know starts changing into a mobile toddler. The older sibling who's been relaxed and easy with the new baby suddenly shows signs of annoyance and frustration.

What happens for the older child is this: "The baby who used to sleep and eat and nurse and cry and lie in her car seat is now beginning to pull my hair, grab my toys, or crawl across the room toward my tricycle. Every few months, I have to get to know an entirely different person than the person I'd gotten to know already." That can be stressful for the older child who has to learn a new set of responses as the baby changes.

Younger Child, Older Child: Building Responsive Relationships

Often in families, a lot of responsibility is given to the older children to take care of the younger ones. It's wonderful for older children to get to be an important part of the nurturing team, to learn how to take care of babies, to learn how to read a baby's language, a baby's signals. Yet this dynamic can become problematic for older children if their responsibility for younger siblings begins to cut into their own time to be a child. It can also become limiting to an older child if it's a one-way street, in which the older child doesn't get to experience the younger child giving back or nurturing in return.

There are many ways the younger child–older child relationship can be reciprocal. The older child can teach, model, and provide nurturing, thereby gaining a sense of personal competence and specialness: "I'm the one who can make Mackenzie smile." "I can rub Naomi's head to help her fall asleep." But there are also ways the younger child can delight, support, and interact that can be beneficial to the older child.

Janis tells the following story: "When six-year-old Calvin was old enough to be scared of the dark, his two-year-old sister Maya was wonderfully oblivious to the scary things the dark could cover up. So every time he needed to go into the dark garage, he took his little sister with him so he could feel safe."

Younger children can also provide a wonderful audience for their older siblings. Younger brothers and sisters are naturally fascinated and charmed with what older siblings can do; they love to watch and to share their excitement in their older sibling's accomplishments and abilities. They provide an in-house cheering section that can boost an older child's spirits.

Younger children can also allow older children a chance to be playful in ways that might no longer be happening with their peers. Leota remarked: "Careening down the steps in a sleeping bag with his three-year-old sister is something my eight-year-old son wouldn't do with one of his friends. There's a special kind of abandon he can explore only with his little sister."

Time Together, Time Apart

When you're thinking about siblings, it's always an interesting dilemma to figure out how to allow one person the privacy he needs without allowing him to hurt his sibling's feelings. Celia, who lives in a blended family, explained the approach she took with her birth son and his younger stepbrother: "When we first moved in together, Peter and Bobby were really close. But as Peter grew up, he was more bothered by his little brother. I said to him 'That's okay. You don't have to have Bobby with you as much, but you can't *only* exclude him. You have to come up with two things in the week you can do that include him. Then during the times you're excluding him, remind him that those times are coming: 'On Tuesday, Bobby, we're going to do such and such.' "

Janis employs a similar system of give-and-take in her family: "Our kids can have a private activity, alone time, or a friend over, but they first need to help their sibling figure out a way to make that transition—to find something to do or to arrange another time to spend together. It makes perfect sense to me that my kids would never just slam the door on their sibling and say 'No, you can't come in here! This is my room!' They care too deeply about each other to do that."

Sharing Between Siblings

Each family is going to have its own expectations about personal property, privacy, and how much is shared in the family. Early on sharing is fairly easy with new siblings, because young babies don't need toys and generally don't care what they're holding. So the older child can be in charge of the toys for a while: "If Mikey doesn't care about playing with that, it's fine for you to play with it." But if the older child is rough with his younger brother, yelling or screaming "Mine!" grabbing or pushing the baby down, you need to set clear limits and stop him. You can say, "It's okay for you to hold on to some of your toys or to trade things, but I don't want you to yell at Mikey or scare him. And I won't let you push him over."

Even before the younger child starts to voice much of a complaint about having something taken away, you can establish with the older child that part of getting what he wants is also taking care of the younger child. When Deana grabs a toy from her baby sister, you can say, "It looks like you want to play with that toy. Can you find something else that Michelle can play with?" In doing so, you teach Deana that she can't just take something without considering her sister's feelings.

At the point Michelle starts to identify what she wants and begins holding on to particular toys, the process of negotiation gets much more involved and requires a different level of parental facilitation.

Sibling Rivalry?

In the groups Janis runs for parents, one of the topics that is brought up with the greatest regularity is the fact that siblings spend so much time struggling with each other. One night, the dicussion went like this:

Denise began: "The noise in my house is incredible. The girls are always arguing over who had it first, who gets to sit where, who knocked over what."

Ross jumped in. "My three-and-a-half-year-old and my five-year-old play together for hours on end, but about twice a day they have the biggest fights you've ever seen."

Maggie added, "You know, I say they are always arguing, but when I really think about it they play beautifully about 90 percent of the time and argue about 10 percent. It's just that the arguments are so much harder to listen to."

Susie observed, "They seem to fight the most when they first get together after being apart. If we spend the whole day at home, they can play wonderfully all day long."

Kahlil recalled, "There was a six-month period when it seemed like my kids were fighting more than they were doing anything else. Sheri had just turned two and Rico had just turned four. After that, things really seemed to calm down."

In most families with siblings, there is frequent conflict. As we discussed at the beginning of this chapter, how we interpret our kids' fights is largely a matter of our perspective. If we believe siblings are destined to be rivalrous, their fighting makes sense to us in that context.

When our kids fight, we conclude, "That's how siblings are," or "I knew it! There's not enough of me to go around!"

If, on the other hand, we believe that children choose the safe relationships they have with siblings to practice and work out important issues of communication, negotiation, and control, their fighting will make sense to us in that context. And to a large degree, our perspective determines our response.

If you feel that children's fighting is always counterproductive, you're likely to take steps to try and prevent it. As Laura explains, those steps can sometimes be quite extreme: "One family I grew up with did everything they could to keep their kids from fighting. They were an upper-middle-class family with two children and a large playroom in their basement. One of the basement walls was lined with parallel shelves that held duplicates of the same toys—two Monopoly sets, two Yahtzee boards, two Magic Eight balls—so that there would be no reason for the children to fight over toys."

Families who emphasize individualism over team-building sometimes look as if they're trying to raise two or more "only" children. Parents in these families sometimes feel that it would be more ideal for each child if they didn't have a sibling to cope with. This belief is soon picked up by the children, who consequently spend lots of time wishing they didn't have siblings.

Janis explains: "I once saw two siblings get into an argument that quickly escalated into hitting and punching. Immediately their parents stepped in and separated them. Each took one child to comfort and 'reason' with. At no time did they bring the children back together to finish the interaction.

"Both children had been very hurt by their sibling. Each walked away feeling 'My sibling is an unavoidable burden I have to put up with. When inevitable fights break out and I get hurt, the best solution is to be comforted by an adult.' "

Both children left that conflict somewhat comforted yet carrying lots of resentment toward their sibling. If they'd been supported in resolving the conflict together, there could have been a very different resolution. They could have been taught "These are the kinds of conflicts that happen between people. They're based on misunderstanding. I know you two care about each other. Let's help you get together so you can get back to that place where you can feel good about each other again."

What Is the Parent's Role in Children's Conflicts?

Children's conflicts are dealt with in several places in this book. In-depth guidelines supporting children in resolving their own disputes can be found in Chapter 22, "Children's Friendships: Cooperation and Conflict," and Chapter 23, "What Enables Children to Share?"

Many of us get scared and anxious when our children fight, so we throw a solution at the problem. We jump in, take sides, and enforce a solution of our own making: "Okay, Roland gets to play with the scooter for five minutes and then Brandy gets a turn." While this may temporarily "fix" the conflict, it doesn't give children the opportunity to learn the valuable lessons that come with being taught to resolve conflicts on their own.

As parents watching a conflict between our children, it is often "obvious" to us who is at fault or who is being unreasonable. What we don't see is what happened just before we arrived on the scene or what has happened in the relationship all the times we weren't watching. There are always dynamics we have no way of figuring out.

Pearl described an incident that demonstrated this clearly: "There was a period in which my three-year-old son kept physically attacking his five-year-old sister. I was really worried about it. 'What was wrong with Sean? Why did he keep hitting Alison?' But then one day I was in the kitchen listening to them in the next room. They didn't know I was there. Alison started needling Sean, really going at him, and finally, in total frustration, he hauled off and decked her. Alison started screaming 'Mommy! Mommy! He hit me.' After that, I had a much better idea of what was going on." Yet even with this new insight, Pearl still didn't really know what preceded her daughter's need to pick at her brother.

When we arbitrate a conflict between our kids by coming down on one side or the other, we inevitably tip the scale. While it may seem like we've "solved" the problem by enforcing a solution or "getting the kids to be quiet," the fact is the problem isn't over. Any time we enter a conflict on the side of only one person, the other person gets seriously outweighed and will need, at some time in the future, to get back at the sibling (usually when we're not looking). If only one person "wins," no one really wins and the "getting even" only escalates.

This is not to say that we should "shut the door and let them battle it out," a solution that is often recommended but that is neither safe nor particularly effective. When left to their own devices, children who haven't had support in learning positive conflict resolution skills will simply try to end up on top, meaning that whoever's bigger or cleverer "wins," at least temporarily. In that scenario, one child is always the loser. Neither child comes away with any tools to bring to the next disagreement or with the sense that he can successfully work through a conflict.

It takes practice to determine when to intervene in our children's conflicts. Usually there are several little skirmishes a day that children can get through themselves. Through past experience, listening, and paying attention, we can learn to determine whether a conflict is escalating or resolving itself.

Janis recalls: "I was in the kitchen one day and I heard Lee and Calvin arguing in the other room. Pretty soon, Calvin appeared in the door, looked at me and began to complain, 'Mom, Lee . . .' Then he trailed off and returned to the other room to work it out with Lee. Just as he was about to tell me all about what his big brother had done, he remembered that it was Lee he needed to talk to and that he had the skills to do it."

When you sense that children will be able to work things out fairly on their own, it can be useful to let them do so. However, there will be numerous instances in which children need our support or guidance. When we do decide to intervene, it is important that we don't take the conflict away from our children, that we learn to intervene in a way that teaches essential problem-solving skills. If, as parents, we come into the conflict supportive of both children and help them discover their own solution, everyone's chance for learning increases.

When siblings are helped to find mutual solutions, the frustration each of them felt initially in the conflict is replaced by a growing sense of competence. Feelings of anger and alienation are replaced with feelings of connection. Their adversary becomes their ally.

Through their experience with their siblings, kids get a sense of whether they can solve conflicts in intimate relationships. If they develop an optimism about it—if they expect to be heard, if they expect to listen, and if they learn to negotiate with their siblings—they're going to come out of the conflict a lot more self-assured and also more able and willing to deal with future conflicts constructively.

But What If There's an Age and Skill Difference?

In Janis's group one night, Deborah, mother of five-year-old Jessica and two-year-old Paul, brought up a pressing concern about her kids' fighting. She asked, "What happens when you have two kids who are unequal? Jessica can outthink Paul and run circles around him. It's easy for her to outmaneuver him. She always ends up with all the toys. I feel like I have to stick up for him because he's the baby.

"But at the same time, this dynamic has been going on where Paul hits Jessica and she just sits there and takes it. Jessica calls to me and yells, 'Mom, mom, he's hitting me!' And I say to her, 'Move! Get up off the floor and move.' It scares me. I watch her sit there like that and I think, 'Is she going to be someone who sits there and lets some guy beat on her?' But at the same time, I don't want her to whomp him back. She's much bigger and stronger than Paul."

Janis responded: "One of the things you can do is tell her, 'Don't let him do that to you.' That doesn't imply 'whomp him back,' it communicates 'Keep yourself safe.' If that's your focus, you can step in, gently and firmly hold his arm so he can't hit her, and ask her, 'How are you going to keep yourself safe?' Holding his hand while you ask her gives her a breather from being hit so she can think about your question.

"Let Jessica be the one to come up with the ideas. If she says, 'I could move,' support her idea: 'Yeah, you could move.' You can also help her come up with other solutions: 'You could put your hand up. You can hold his hand or move it away. You could yell 'Stop!' " Model a loud voice for her. Let her know that she can yell *and* do something physically. Give her a clear message, 'You don't have to let him hurt you. You can stop him.' Otherwise you're colluding with early 'girl training,' teaching her to be passive, which can influence her role in other relationships, as well.[4]

"At the same time, it's important to ask Jessica, 'What is Paul trying to tell you?' To even pose that as a question helps her acknowledge that she's heard him. If she's taken his toy and he has feelings about it, he has the right to tell her about it. As long as he feels he's been done wrong to, he has the right to share his outrage, to cry in her presence. If you support Paul in expressing his feelings, and you help Jessica stay there and listen to what he has to say, it equalizes the situation. Jessica may be quicker, but if she stays to hear the full extent of Paul's feelings after she's outwitted him, he's absolutely equal to her.

"So when Jessica snatches the toy from him and runs away, you can help her come back. Once you have the two of them together, she and Paul should both get a chance to talk:

[4] See "Loud Girls" on p. 54 for more on the importance of encouraging girls to use loud voices when necessary.

'Paul has some things to tell you. Do you have anything you want to say to him?'

"Taking this approach teaches your kids to communicate directly, to stand their ground, to face conflict head on. And if you help them through this process enough times, they'll gradually learn to do it on their own."

When They Finally Bloom

Once you have created a vision about the kind of relationships you hope your children will develop, the work begins. Facilitating conflicts between siblings doesn't immediately create harmony in the family. Janis remembers watching two of her children scrapping loudly in the living room one day before reaching their resolution. "I remember thinking to myself, 'I guess a well-functioning household is not necessarily a quietly functioning household. Sometimes you are going to hear the gears turning, LOUDLY.' "

The process of helping children learn relationship skills can sometimes feel hopeless, for most siblings don't immediately demonstrate fully cooperative relationships. In fact, nurturing sibling relationships can feel like cultivating a slow-germinating seed. We plant it, water it, fertilize it, weed around it for what seems like forever before we finally see the tip of a little green sprout peeking up through the dirt.

We foster communication, respect, and problem solving, yet sometimes our children seem to be screaming and tugging at each other continuously. Every so often, we may get a tiny glimpse of an empathetic interaction, a generous gesture, a tender touch that encourages us to continue cultivating the kind of sibling relationship we want our kids to have. It's important that we continue to work toward our vision, because caring sibling relationships provide lasting connections that can sustain our children throughout their lives.

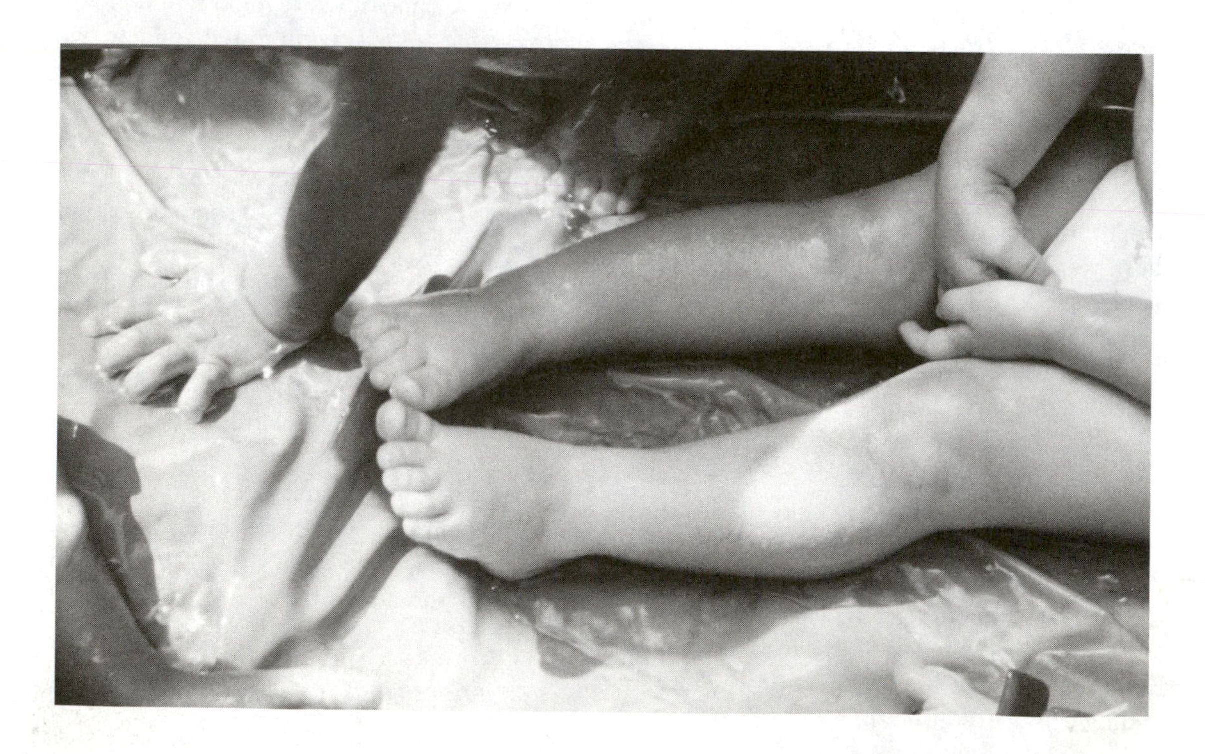

Afterword: Growing Up, Growing Together

The first five years of our children's lives are critical times for them as well as for us. As our children grow from infancy to kindergarten, we mature from being new parents to seasoned travelers on the parenting journey.

As newborns, our children learn about connection, safety, and love. We delight in their first gummy smiles, share their triumph as they roll from their backs to their bellies, and are challenged by hours of crying, disequilibrium, and sleepless nights.

As toddlers, our children establish their independence, find out who they are, and begin to learn about the world around them. We are enchanted by their first sentences, thrilled by their ability to jump and throw and run, and, at times, dumbfounded by the strength of their emotions and the power of their will.

In the preschool years, our children learn to exercise their own ideas and move out into the community. We are enthralled by their imaginations, their friendships, and their exploding abilities with language. Simultaneously, we are bewildered by their repeated challenges to our control.

At no time in life is growth as swift or as encompassing as it is in these early years. And that's as true for us as it is for our children. We begin our journey as new parents full of love, hope, and the commitment to do the very best we can. In the first five years of our children's lives, we move from uncertainty to clarity to uncertainty again. Through hard work and daily practice, we develop a vision for our family, refine what we want to teach, and continually clarify our own philosophy as parents.

In doing so, we establish a foundation for all the learning, growing, and changes that are to follow. As our children move into their middle years and the larger world, we will be faced with new joys, challenges, and frontiers. But the lessons we've learned together in these precious early years equip us with the flexibility, the resourcefulness, the humility, and the humor we need to meet the adventures that lie ahead.

Index